BEING
The Source of Power

BEING
The Source of Power

Exposition of the Being Framework™ v1.1, a radical paradigm to cause leadership through awareness, integrity and effectiveness

ASHKAN TASHVIR

First published 2021 by Engenesis Publications

Copyright © Ashkan Tashvir 2015

Ashkan Tashvir asserts the moral right to be identified as the author of *BEING* and all associated products.

ISBN 978-1-922433-00-8 Paperback
ISBN 978-1-922433-03-9 Hardback
ISBN 978-1-922433-01-5 Epub
ISBN 978-1-922433-02-2 Kindle

A catalogue record for this book is available from the National Library of Australia

publications.engenesis.com

All rights reserved. No part of this publication may be reproduced or transmitted, copied, stored in a retrieval system, distributed or otherwise made available by any person or entity (including Google, Amazon or similar organisations), in any form (electronic, digital, optical, mechanical, or otherwise), or by any means (photocopying, recording, scanning or otherwise) without prior written permission from the publisher, except in the case of brief quotations embodied in critical reviews and certain other non-commercial uses permitted by copyright law. For permission requests contact the publisher on either +61 (02) 9188 0844 or publications@engenesis.com

Edited by Phaedra Pym – awaywithwords.net.au

Book design and production by Eric & Thymen – exlibris.com.au

Disclaimer: This book is intended to give general information only. The material herein does not represent professional advice. The author expressly disclaims all liability to any person arising directly or indirectly from the use of, or for any errors or omissions in, the information in this book. The adoption and application of the information in this book is at the reader's discretion and is his or her sole responsibility.

In the name of Truth and Beauty

I dedicate this book first and foremost to my creator,
and also to my grandparents, parents, my wife, Atefeh,
and our baby girl, Diana, who is on her way
to being out there in the world soon.

Contents

Foreword	xiii
Preface	xvii
Introduction	xxvii

Part 1: Discovering Being — 1

Chapter 1: In Search of Truth, Meanings and Reality	9
Chapter 2: Existence and Being	29
Chapter 3: Discovery vs Invention	49
Chapter 4: The Ontological Model	59
Chapter 4.1: Shaping an Ontological Model	69
Chapter 4.2: Knowing Human Beings Through the Being Framework Ontological Model	77
Chapter 5: Time Matters	95
Conclusion	99

Part 2: Aspects of Being — 101

Section 1: Meta Factors — 105

Chapter 1: Awareness	107
Chapter 1.1: Access to Reality	115
Chapter 1.2: Epistemic Humility	124
Chapter 1.3: Web of Perceptions	130
Chapter 1.4: Narrative Lens	138

Chapter 1.5: Perspective Quadrant	143
Chapter 1.6: Shadow	150
Chapter 1.7: Vision	161
Chapter 2: Integrity	171
Chapter 3: Effectiveness	183
Section 2: Moods	197
Chapter 4: Care	201
Chapter 5: Fear	213
Chapter 6: Anxiety	221
Chapter 7: Vulnerability	231
Section 3: Primary Ways of Being	243
Chapter 8: Authenticity	247
Chapter 9: Responsibility	273
Chapter 10: Freedom	293
Chapter 11: Courage	303
Chapter 12: Commitment	315
Chapter 13: Gratitude	325
Chapter 14: Higher Purpose	337
Chapter 15: Empowerment	351
Chapter 16: Presence	361
Chapter 17: Peace of Mind	381
Chapter 18: Compassion	391
Chapter 19: Love	401
Chapter 20: Contribution	417
Chapter 21: Partnership	429
Chapter 22: Forgiveness	437
Chapter 23: Self-expression	447

CONTENTS xi

Section 4: Secondary Ways of Being   461

    Chapter 24: Assertiveness   469

    Chapter 25: Proactivity   485

    Chapter 26: Confidence   493

    Chapter 27: Persistence   503

    Chapter 28: Resourcefulness   513

    Chapter 29: Resilience   521

    Chapter 30: Accountability   529

    Chapter 31: Reliability   539

Part 3: Being, in Action   545

    Chapter 1: The Being Profile   551

    Chapter 2: Transformation Methodology   563

Where to from here? Resources for further action   611

References   617

Acknowledgements   635

Author Biography   639

Foreword

I first met Ashkan more than six years ago when he was CTO of an organisation that provided integrated business service offerings for small to medium-sized businesses.

I was not surprised to find Ashkan as a leader in such a workplace. Rather than delivering-cookie cutter commoditised services for their hundreds of business owner customers, Ashkan and his team would always begin by inquiring into their customer's business vision and determining whether or not the leadership team was effective and authentic to ensure their workforce could perform at their best. Importantly, the team also ensured the customer devised relevant and effective strategies and systems for the market they were in. Only then, through this powerful lens, was the service offering tailored to the business.

I found very rare qualities in Ashkan during the months we worked in close proximity within the same office space. As a consultant who has performed due diligence globally for Mergers and Acquisitions on fitness leadership teams and the organisational structure of target companies, I have always found encountering quality leaders like Ashkan to be both compelling and satisfying.

Ashkan struck me as rigorous, with a tremendous drive and capacity to discover the reality of what is happening and to organise people to accomplish intended outcomes. I later discovered that he is also scholarly, logical and possesses a broad and deep education. I found him to be driven by both a reverence for truth and an abiding curiosity to see the whole from the sum of its parts.

Having a Masters of Information Systems from Central Queensland University and currently in the process of completing a research degree in Leadership Transformation at Sydney University, Ashkan is well-credentialled to take on the complexity of human beings in a well-structured and systematic way. It requires good balance in the writing to capture the expert knowledge of the fields examined in this book in a way that a broader audience can understand.

The genesis of this work

About four years ago, Ashkan, who has built many sustainable and profitable businesses himself, founded Engenesis in Sydney, Australia, a business with a team focused on investing in and supporting innovative startups and organisations.

It is said that good ideas are plentiful and that the vast majority of startups fail. From the hundreds of startups he studied, Ashkan discovered that the attitude and behaviour of the founders, both towards their goals and their colleagues, were the causal factors in an alarming failure rate. In other words, good ideas were/are not being realised because of the way human beings are BEING. Furthermore, Ashkan saw that what he and his team were experiencing with startups applied equally and systemically in society, creating undesirable outcomes and directions in business, markets and politics. For Ashkan, this was the turning point that led to the writing of this book.

Truth and wisdom matter

Having discovered that outcomes hinge upon human BEING, Ashkan realised that the truth about ourselves is the forgotten treasure, lost in the din of the noise and outcry of modern times. You need only look at how much the news and social media compete for our attention to realise this.

Consider what human civilisation has accomplished in a few millennia of development. We can marvel at how far we have come. But where are we going? In the ever-increasing pace of technological advancement, take a moment to consider if we are headed in a direction we want to go and whether or not the world we are creating is a world worth living in.

We now possess the ability to end all life, make our planet uninhabitable through climate change, amplify suffering and produce inequity for people everywhere. Yet, when our human wisdom and understanding is fully available to us, we accomplish remarkable and marvellous things. This wisdom is not acquired easily or quickly. Rather, throughout human history, our wisdom has been built upon many brilliant contributions from the sciences, humanities, business and the arts. These include dazzling insights from great thinkers and scholars, poets and performing artists who invoked something deep inside us, and athletes who extended the boundaries of what is physically possible for us, and entrepreneurs like Steve Jobs who daringly built remarkable companies.

Some foundations of wisdom are gained through the development of understanding and insight from study, engaging with different people and organisations, travel and broad life experience. Beyond that, Aristotle points to such things as living a life of virtue and the pursuit of excellence in the context of character. I think this path needs to be followed to be considered wise. A good example of this is achieving mastery in a discipline or sport where one is challenged with physical reality. Wisdom and insight into Self comes from the development of mastery and skill over many years of pushing one's limits to deal with physical reality.

Consider elite high jumpers, rock climbers, big wave surfers, etc.; such people are poised and gracious, with nothing to prove. They are at one with themselves and can talk authentically about Being and the human condition in all the work and challenges they face in their accomplishments, which is a matter of character in the Aristotelian sense. Ashkan is an accomplished martial artist who trained and practised Karate Kyokushin and Aikido, in addition to his many other accomplishments. He has spent a lifetime gaining wisdom through various channels.

Purpose

The primary purpose of this book on Being is enlightenment and service, to enable us to design and build a future for ourselves, our organisations, our children and subsequent generations, to give them their heritage and birthright of a world worth living in.

As someone who has richly explored the breadth and depth of the most impactful contributors to fundamental truths about human beings, Ashkan wrote this book to be of service to you, your organisation and society. He wrote it as a guide, so you don't have to venture into the maze of human history yourself, or at least to provide a comprehensive foundation for those of you who are curious and inspired to learn more.

The challenge offered to you is to take the understanding you gain from this work and find the courage to apply it in ways that will make a difference for the future of a world worth living in and the greater good.

I wish Ashkan well with the publication of this important work and that those who read it go on to lead and guide others to worthwhile futures and outcomes in the things that really matter.

John Lowe,
Umina Beach, NSW
May 2021

John Lowe has had a long career in technology, financial markets and strategy. He is a complex systems thinker, designer and builder.

Most recently, John has been on the technical buy-sell call and post-acquisition strategy team as a strategist/analyst for a leading New York private equity firm for several all-cash deals of global technology firms in the $1bn – $4bn range. Locally, John is appointed by ASIC as an independent financial markets expert. In this role, he is the primary author of mandatory independent technical market readiness reports for several new exchanges that have opened in Australia, including Chi-X.

John is a five-time Australian bridge champion and was an accomplished recreational alpinist. After learning mountaineering with Alpine Guides in Mount Cook, New Zealand, he climbed 4,000-metre peaks in Switzerland while working in Zürich as a member of the team that first built the Swiss National Stock Exchange.

Preface

Many discoveries are born of fury…

I was wide awake. It was 3.35am and I was as alert as if it was midday. My mind and heart were racing, and the anger and frustration welling inside me had reached a point where I felt I would burst; I couldn't take it anymore. As I lay there in the dark, I was intensely aware of and present to the misery, dysfunction and unworkability that exists in the world and its devastating impact everywhere. That pivotal moment arose at a time when I was dealing with an enormous amount of inauthenticity and lack of integrity all around me, on every level, from the people I worked with and commercial partners to suppliers, government services, banks, etc., with obstacles on every front. On a global scale, I, like everyone else, was being bombarded from all sides with news of the gross dysfunctionality in our world, everything from wars to domestic violence, lack of preparedness in the face of natural disasters, fraud, disease, poverty and collective psychosis. I had become so concerned about this widespread and pervasive disregard for reality and the subsequent dangerous and sometimes subtle deception in the world that I couldn't shake it from my mind. Night after night, I was unable to sleep. It felt as though I was experiencing the suffering in the world within each and every cell of my Being. All the old wounds I had managed to heal in the past were rising back to the surface, bringing back memories of the unique collection of experiences I had been through that were so impactful, it was as if they had altered my DNA, the very fabric of my Being. In that moment, I had become so acutely aware that the intensity of my fury, combined with my deep care and compassion for humanity sparked a fire within me that erupted in a raging desire to take action. There was no turning back, no retreat. My path forward was crystal clear and I was suddenly calm. The urge was ignited.

I was born in Iran at the end of the war with Iraq. When my mother was pregnant with me, she and my father fled from the city a few weeks before I was born to take refuge in the country in order to protect us both from the potential impact of chemical weapons. I then spent my childhood in a country that had been through a revolution followed by a war that lasted eight years. Despite this, I have been blessed in so many ways and have lived a rich and varied life so far. Aside from being born into a nation that had endured so much, some of the other things I have been exposed to, many also not of my own conscious choosing, include being detained for the 'crime' of expressing my thoughts in poetry, compulsory military service, several failed attempts at building lasting relationships, and crashing from a life of prosperity to poverty and suffering in my youth. I have been building businesses since I was a teenager and have studied faith, a number of religions, and various disciplines of philosophy in great depth, as well as academic studies, including IT and software development and multiple disciplines of thought. I have studied and practised martial arts and have read and studied the works of many of the world's most renowned thinkers, poets and novelists. I have travelled to some of the greatest civilisations on Earth and left my homeland for a new country and culture while building multiple businesses, generating wealth for myself and others. I have climbed the heights of the ladder of virtue but have also experienced the depths of regression, self-annihilation, victimisation and self-sabotage. I learnt that with light comes a shadow that must be overcome to survive the valleys and troughs of life and rise up again. All of these experiences have given me unique exposure to human beings and the world we live in. I feel particularly blessed that many of these experiences occurred from teenagehood through my early twenties and led me to transform how I participated in the game of life from an early age.

During my life, I have observed and been associated with many smart but miserable people, both personally and professionally. Some considered themselves to be intellectuals but were living their lives in a manner that was totally incongruent with their knowledge and what they claimed they were striving to achieve. They weren't practising what they preached, far from it, many of them couldn't even take care of themselves or their families and would spend hours intellectualising how different concepts, theories, the system, the economy, politics or even their parents were to blame. I acknowledge I could easily have been lured to sink into this darkness myself. In fact, it would be fair to say I was on the verge of succumbing to the same misery. However, being the young, remarkably curious and adventurous truth seeker and observer I was, I developed what I call a 'bullshit detector', the result of having been raised in an environment where almost everyone isn't just two-faced but has multiple faces, and various schools of thinking do their best to brainwash you. I needed this bullshit detector to see through the charade and I found it served me well. So, since the departure of those illusory ideas, I made a conscious decision to commence the journey of truth seeking and dissociate myself from the group and others like them. Since then, I have found I am far more empowered to contribute to myself and others. Meanwhile, some of them have hit rock bottom and yet they continue to mock and criticise people like me while still blaming their lack of accomplishments on external factors rather than looking at themselves. This lack of responsibility and victimisation seem to be so normalised in our era that even talking about responsibility may be considered radical for many.

Both in my role as a business venture builder and as an investor, my goal was to find the 'right' teams and individuals to work with and invest in; those who displayed the kinds of qualities and attributes that matter most when it comes to extraordinary performance and results. The question was, what are the qualities and attributes of the 'right' teams and individuals? We reached out on multiple separate occasions to around 1800 self-proclaimed founders and entrepreneurs and had a series of detailed conversations with them to determine if they possessed the qualities and attributes we considered would make them worthwhile candidates for investment. Of the almost 1800 people we spoke to on each occasion, only a very small number were able to convince us that they were worthy of our time and capital. Over the next several years I studied leaders and high achievers from all walks of life and corners of the globe to discover how they managed to produce their intended results – results well beyond most people's imagination. It is worth noting that while I admired their achievements, I didn't necessarily agree with their intentions, morality or benevolence. I was studying them purely from an objective point of view to determine why and how they managed to create a life of effectiveness, prosperity and fulfilment while many others could barely put food on the table and pay the bills. Importantly, I also studied unsuccessful entrepreneurs, leaders and investors, and this gave me a unique insight into why the majority of startups fail, most venture capitalists are not profitable and why there is too much wastage of resources and time. I found it was primarily not due to lack of capital, technology or venture building techniques. It was predominantly because of who and how they were being.

One of the things that became apparent during my studies was that visionary leaders have the ability to 'see in the dark' as a result of their vivid awareness, and it is this initial high level of awareness that sets them on the path towards effectiveness. Furthermore, I learnt that their effectiveness in their endeavours led them to fulfil the objectives they had set for themselves, which in most cases led to a by-product of prosperity. I discovered that this paradigm sets them apart from others. This discovery sowed the seed for the development of the Being Framework™ and the writing of this book.

In conducting the study, my intention was to identify the common qualities we all possess but relate to or execute differently and to discover the patterns that hold true and are common amongst the highest achievers of the human race. During the course of my research, I also found that many of the high achievers I studied contributed to humanity far more than others through their inventions, service, knowledge, etc. Unlike some of the 'intellectuals' I used to associate with, the knowledge possessed by these high achievers clearly served them (and others) well. This led me to hypothesise how much better the world would be if there were more of these well-polished and effective people who could design and implement more effective systems and create a far more prosperous life of wellbeing for us all. After my research, I also came to the conclusion that while intelligence and material wealth are important, they are not enough to live a truly fulfilling life. Many celebrities and 'successful' people eventually come to a similar conclusion when they realise that despite their financial and professional success, there is still something missing; they lack satisfaction and contentment. At some point it hits them that what and who they have become is their greatest accomplishment in life. I concluded that in order to achieve true success in life that keeps us fulfilled, who and how we are BEING is the true source of our power. This was the eureka moment of clarity I had been seeking. The next step was to give my discoveries context and create a tangible framework that would help others – specifically leaders, entrepreneurs, coaches and anyone who wants to be the leader of their own life – find and be in charge of their source of power. And so the Being Framework™, Being Profile® and Transformation Methodology™ were born.

While considering human beings as having a series of absolute essential attributes may seem an archaic way of thinking, I have dared to revive this notion in the form of a framework that has a genuine, practical context, backed by research and empirical data, that is, in part, aligned with the objectivity of human nature or nature in general. More specifically, we are all instances of the class: Human Being, meaning we share a series of attributes which constitute our nature/essence that connect us and make us, in part, scientifically studiable. I learnt that the way each of us relates to these attributes is not only studiable but also measurable. In other words, we all share the same attributes, but the health of our relationship with each attribute varies from one person to the next and can change over time. This notion of truth seeking and adopting a scientific approach has been ridiculed by some post-structuralist 'philosophers' as if everything is a construct and relative and mutable. In my observations and studies, I have found that many people are indoctrinated by this post-modern view without necessarily knowing where that is coming from.

Aristotle[1], one of the early philosophers, argued that everything has a 'proper function' and that something is 'good' to the extent by which it fulfils its function and 'bad' to the extent that it doesn't. For example, the function of a plant is to flourish, grow and reproduce. Adopting the Aristotelian view, a plant is considered 'bad' at being a plant if it fails to fulfil these criteria. It could be said that this holds true in many dimensions when it comes to human beings as a species too. The key difference though is that human beings are capable of being intentionally conscious of their consciousness. In this framework, I refer to this intentional consciousness as 'awareness'. Human beings also have a relatively high level of autonomy, so we are inherently responsible. In other words, it is

---

1   Aristotle (384-322 BC) was a Greek philosopher and polymath during the Classical period in Ancient Greece.

our responsibility to **choose to surrender** to our 'proper function' and primal qualities and adhere to that nature. Furthermore, we are rational and social creatures with the ability to reason and get along with our tribe mates or pack members.

Collectively, we have the freedom and responsibility to keep learning – this is the way Existence has created us to be. The choice is which pathway to take – the pathway to growth or regression? The fact that we can choose freely is both a curse and a blessing; it comes as a non-negotiable part of the package of being a human being. This simple fact makes things significantly different for us in comparison to other species. It distinctly sets us apart. Don't get me wrong, I am **not** reducing human beings to nothing more than a set of functions. To the contrary, besides these qualities, I acknowledge that human beings are more than just the sum of a common set of qualities or attributes (Essence). We can therefore conclude that we also possess a one-of-a-kind quality deep within that is unique to each of us. I call this 'Unique Being'. Therefore, in contrast to the pure Aristotelian/Essentialist view, I assert that we possess both a Unique Being AND Essence (which I refer to as 'Being' in this book), an assertion that is backed by renowned philosophers such as Mulla Sadra[2] and Martin Heidegger[3], who greatly influenced my thinking when creating the Being Framework. This assertion is key to the entire framework, as you will discover. So, you could say a well-polished, integrous person is someone who has chosen to surrender to their primal 'proper function' while continuously daring to keep knowing, actualising and manifesting their Unique Being, expressing themselves and making their unique contribution to the world, expanding the collective reality out there and impacting other people's lives. They would know how to deliver the hard truth without breaking someone's heart and how to break bad news gently. They would offer someone constructive criticism as a means of support without crushing them. They don't let others dominate them, including those

---

[2] Mulla Sadra (1571-1640) Persian philosopher and theologian. The main part influenced by his work in this framework is the explanation of Existence and its distinction from Essence.

[3] Martin Heidegger (1889-1976) was a German philosopher and a seminal thinker in the Continental tradition of philosophy. He is best known for contributions to ontology, phenomenology, hermeneutics, and existentialism.

with aggressive tendencies. They are critical thinkers who aren't readily fooled, deceived or manipulated while also being authentic, courageous and assertive enough to know better than to attempt to fool others, and so on. This person is far more likely to be a leader who is effective or who at least could tell who to follow. We are the only species who may end up following unpolished and unstable 'leaders' and ironically be proud when they are elected!

Stories have been used throughout time to convey 'right' from 'wrong', 'good' from 'bad', and 'pure' from 'evil', commonly through heroes (protagonists) and villains (antagonists). While I am in favour of stories to bring tangibility to often complex issues – in fact, I have always loved stories and parables – the issue I have with the use of words like 'good' and 'bad' is that it implies an underlying 'virtue', or lack thereof, in every situation. If you have to figure out what virtue there is in every situation, how can you possibly ever learn to be 'virtuous'? Religions, political parties, cultures, activists, movements and even many of today's so-called 'gurus' and 'human science experts', including some psychologists, may do their best to persuade you to adopt their standards as they create a parallel reality and attempt to push their agendas. I knew the solution had to be a **non-judgemental** and **values-free** framework that equips you with tools that support you to shape conceptions of the qualities that matter when it comes to the effective exercise of leadership and leading a life of fulfilment in a practical way. Being values and judgement free, the Being Framework uses words like 'polished', 'effective', 'healthy' and 'integrous' over 'good', or 'bad'.

There is no right or wrong, good or bad in how you are being. It is what it is. How you are being will generate certain outcomes or consequences for you. There is rich literature around language and how many meanings became lost in translation over time or have simply been ignored. For example, Aristotle's reference to *Hexis* has widely been interpreted as 'virtue'. However, based on extensive studies, I have chosen to align myself with the interpretation of *Hexis* as being a 'stable disposition', or 'way of being'[4]. My intention with this research into words and meanings was to discover and uncover meanings relevant in this context

---

4 'The Dynamic of Hexis in Aristotle's Philosophy', Pierre Rodrigo: *Journal of the British Society for Phenomenology*, Vol 42, No. 1, January 2011.

and convey them in a simple, non-judgemental language that would be readily understood and not misinterpreted, ensuring we are all on the same page.

My first challenge was to find the source of knowledge, including people who are shining examples of effectiveness and integrity, discovering in the process how to recognise them with responsibility so that I could model the qualities that led to their overall success, wellbeing and fulfilment. This is why I not only studied high achievers whose accomplishments and wellbeing I found, in most part, to be the by-product of their well-polished Being, but I also tapped into various disciplines of philosophy and science to articulate them. Hence, this framework and book are founded on multidisciplinary studies, including, but not limited to, ontology, epistemology, phenomenology, anthropology, analytical thinking, various disciplines of psychology, psychoanalysis, behavioural studies and cognitive science.

You may ask, why bother? The answer is because we CARE. More specifically, it is a common human experience to care about wholeness (integrity) and the pursuit of perfection. Most of us aspire to grow and climb the ladder of effectiveness, from competency to mastery, while for some, it's even more than that – it's about being at the pinnacle of humanity and honouring the dignity of humankind. Being integrous and effective allows us to achieve a life well lived and realise and fulfil our potential. It is human nature to want to hit the targets and achieve the objectives we set for ourselves, our family and our organisations. But we cannot be fulfilled if we are not effective in our endeavours, personally and collectively. And we cannot be effective if we are not integrous human beings. Furthermore, we can't be effective if we are not aware of where and how we need to be effective in order to fulfil our objectives. Put simply, to be most effective, all the cogs in the machine – the parts that shape us into a whole and complete human being – must be working at an optimal level. You could say integrity is like **being well**, being 'well put together', or the 'wellbeing' of our Essence/Being. So, while an aware person transcends to a higher level of consciousness, this awareness may also lead them to become an integrous person whose satisfaction and happiness is not dependent on chasing any one particular thing. An aware and integrous person views the world and participates in life with sharpened sensibilities. They work and keep working on qualities of their Being so that they can see brilliance and beauty in the commonplace and derive immense joy from sights, sounds and experiences of everyday life. They are deeply present to the fact that if joy is to be found, then it is to be found in the here and now and not in something they imagine, wish or hope for in the future.

This framework is not about positive thinking or affirmation and it's not a quick-fix recipe for success. It doesn't suggest that opportunities will miraculously fall in your lap if you follow the guidelines. Instead, it will draw your attention to the extraordinary power of discovering and honing your well-polished qualities (your light side) and casting the light on and transforming your unpolished or troubled aspects (shadow). If we adopt the Aristotelian view, doing so will ensure you do 'good' things in life. However, I prefer to say it will empower you to be in charge of your life and circumstances and expand our collective reality by **being a contribution** to the whole of humanity as opposed to **being a liability** due to living a life of untapped potential or worse, allowing the dark side to consume you and becoming a malevolent force in the world. Someone who is in charge of their life and circumstances, at least for the most part and as much as they can be, has the pleasure of sinking into bed at the end of an exhausting day pursuing their career, raising a family, building their organisation, serving humanity or whatever it is that they find meaningful, with gratitude and the satisfaction of knowing and acknowledging their recent accomplishments as a result of transformation and pushing themselves to be the very best person they could be. I hope this work leads you to a life of thriving, pushing your limits, high performance and high achievement, a life of fulfilment, wellbeing and meaning for yourself and others.

Introduction

Before you read this introduction, I strongly urge you to go back and read the Preface if you have skipped or merely skimmed over it. It outlines why this book was written and provides critical foundational information that brings context to the content, thereby supporting you in your understanding of the book in its entirety.

I have invested an enormous amount of time with my team over recent years seeking relevant tools that would provide a holistic view of the fundamental qualities required to be a human being of influence, a leader. We needed to find an effective way to identify integrous leaders who are truly present in all aspects of life and contributing to and serving themselves and others without crumbling in the face of inevitable adversities in life. We tried many different personality tests, psychological assessment tools and interview techniques in an effort to gain a deeper understanding of human beings. But none shed light on the real qualities we were seeking in candidates. These tools weren't without merit, but they did not give us the accurate knowledge and insight our research and experience had taught us we needed about each individual or team. For instance, they didn't give us any meaningful insight into their level of *integrity, responsibility* and *authenticity*, amongst many other qualities we had identified as being essential in any high performing leader. As a result, we knew those tools were unlikely to predict the probability of longevity and success when contemplating investing millions of dollars and significant time in their businesses. They may be highly competent and experienced individuals in their field with brilliant ideas and exciting business concepts, but without the right qualities at both an individual and team level, we knew their businesses would never be sustainable.

To categorise people into groups, such as personality types and socio-economic classes, suggests we are fixed objects who are unable to transform. That is an absurd and destructive notion on every conceivable level. Similarly, to only focus on behaviours and seek shortcuts and quick-fix approaches without diving deeper to address the major causes of frustrations, lack of fulfilment, disappointment and dysfunctionality is equally futile, as it wouldn't lead to sustainable long-term change. While many think the major causes of business failures are associated with the technical aspects of a business, such as revenue models, technology and market demand, our studies and experience have revealed that the number one reason businesses fail to survive, let alone thrive, is **people**, or to be precise, the individual and collective **BEING** of the people involved, particularly the founders and leaders. This was one of the key and distinguishable revelations, amongst other deeply personal insights, as explained in the Preface, that led to the development of the Being Framework, the Being Profile and the Transformation Methodology as well as the writing of this book.

BEING presents a radical paradigm shift in the way we see human beings, in particular, the qualities required for leadership, performance, *effectiveness*, fulfilment and leading a well-lived, meaningful life. It explores the art, science and practical application of mastering how to be an effective human being and leader by providing you with a deeper understanding of who and how you and others are being, as opposed to just behaving on the surface, which ultimately determines how you/they participate in life, personally, professionally and as a team. Fundamentally, this book will guide you to identify and model the reality of who and how you, and others, are at the core of your/their Being in an ontological[5] manner.

Every human being has something mysterious and almost intangible within, something unique to them. I refer to this as our 'Unique Being' and, like the black box of an aircraft, our Unique Being holds the key to unlocking what lies within – our unique talents and gifts. It is necessary

---

5   Ontology is the branch of philosophy that studies concepts such as existence, being, becoming, and reality. It includes the questions of how entities are grouped into basic categories and which of these entities exist on the most fundamental level. Put simply, within the context of this book, ontology is the study of what is real versus what is not real based on the view that there is only one reality or truth.

from several perspectives – societal, economic, philosophical and psychological – for each of us to project the manifestation of our Unique Being to the world. Otherwise, why are we here? What is our purpose if not to lead a life of fulfilment and make a meaningful impact on the world? In order to achieve that objective, we must first understand how various Aspects of Being shape our behaviour, thereby enabling and empowering us to make better decisions and take more effective actions towards our ultimate purpose and objectives in life. My teams and I have found this to be the most important thing when it comes to high performance, *effectiveness* and leadership in the business world but also if you wish to be the leader of your own life.

The current dominant disciplines focus on correcting behaviour directly, but those behaviours are only the end outcome. To focus solely on those external, visible aspects is like only watering the leaves of a tree. In order to make effective and long-lasting change, you must address the deeper issues, watering the roots of the tree, which is precisely what this book and framework is all about. *BEING* is for leaders, coaches, entrepreneurs and anyone committed to growth in one or more areas of their life. So, this book is relevant to anyone who has a desire to live a fulfilled life, personally and professionally. Ultimately this book provides you with the knowledge and tools that will help you tap into your Unique Being and project it to the world, opening up amazing opportunities for you, personally and in business.

We are all living in a world that is changing at an exponential pace, and, whether or not you are aware of it, we are all changing and transforming too. This framework will enable you to lead, influence and shift those changes in your favour. This is precisely what true leaders do. There is an art and science behind every objective study, this framework being no exception. There are certain patterns that work and others that don't; it would be naive to think otherwise. This should not be confused with the notion of a simple 'recipe for success', which the Being Framework is not. However, this framework will significantly and exponentially increase the probability of hitting your targets and hence achieving fulfilment and leading a life well lived. This is in contrast to most 'self-help', or leadership books that prescribe what to do and how to act. This framework focuses on how to BE so you can DO what you need to do to HAVE what you want in life. Once you manage to get in the habit of constantly polishing and transforming your Being, you will manifest effective, healthy behaviours and make decisions that suit you, serve your objectives and possibly benefit others as well.

The benefits to be gained from this book will have a profound effect on you, your community and the people you work with and lead. It will encourage you to undergo a radical paradigm shift in relation to how you think about yourself and others, particularly in the context of leadership, performance and *effectiveness*. Those insights will flow throughout your team/organisation and into all dimensions of your life. Through this paradigm, you will see life – your life and the lives of others – with greater clarity than ever before, as though you are looking into a mirror and seeing the blind spots revealed for the first time. You will expand your knowledge and gain the tools to gauge where you are now and the techniques to take you where you want to be. It will also give you a deeper insight into the people within your organisation, helping to improve issues like recruitment and retention, and drive team productivity and organisational performance.

How to read this book

This book is structured over three parts. *Part 1: Discovering Being*, lays out a helicopter view of the paradigm[6] and its core components: the Being Framework Ontological Model, the Being Profile assessment tool and the Transformation Methodology. Part 1 also walks you through the fundamental knowledge and core concepts you need to be familiar with in order to grasp the framework as well as the research and discovery process my team and I undertook before designing and developing the framework and associated components. *Part 2: Aspects of Being*, dives deeply into the Being Framework Ontological Model, walking you through the Meta Factors, Moods and Ways of Being relevant for leadership, performance and *effectiveness*. *Part 3: Being, in Action*, introduces you to the Being Profile, the core tool associated with the Being Framework and the world's first and most comprehensive and effective ontological profiling tool by which all Meta Factors, Moods and Ways

---

6   In the context of this book, we use the term paradigm and framework interchangeably.

of Being can be measured with a high degree of accuracy. You will learn the background of why and how the assessment tool was developed and a practical explanation of how to use it. Part 3 also introduces you to the Transformation Methodology, a series of processes and principles designed to lead you on a journey of metamorphosis and show you how to gradually become effective in all Aspects of Being.

You will notice that whenever I refer to the individual Aspects of Being (Meta Factors, Moods, Primary Ways of Being and Secondary Ways of Being) they appear in italics, for example *effectiveness*, *awareness*, *vulnerability*, *resilience*, and so on. Perhaps you have already made this observation for yourself. This is to clearly identify them as Aspects of Being and differentiate them from the conventional use of the word. For instance, while *freedom* is a Primary Way of Being, the word 'freedom' is also shown at times without italics when it is not referring to *freedom* as a Way of Being, like 'freedom of choice'. There are also times when you will see the words, 'meaning' and 'reality' beginning with a capital letter (Meaning and Reality) and the reason for this is explained in Part 1.

This is not your typical self-help book. It is a reference book designed to be studied and reflected on. Don't expect to read it just once and then put it aside on a bookshelf to gather dust. I would also strongly urge you not to skip or skim over any part as every chapter and sub-chapter adds another critical layer, building on the foundation of knowledge needed for understanding and practical application. Studying the book will influence your narrative lens and your understanding of human beings and how we experience ourselves and each other in various contexts in life. While you will notice that I regularly dive into what is commonly considered 'philosophical conversations' as well as some academic discussions, I have never had any intention to discuss abstract or theoretical philosophy here or turn this into a purely academic body of work. So, as much as this is not your typical self-help business book, it is also not purely a philosophy book or academic piece of writing. My intention in referencing academic sources and philosophical schools of thinking at times is simply to put them forward as relevant and meaningful conversations designed to set the scene, create the grounding on which we are building this framework and support you to deeply understand the nature of human beings and our ability to transform.

Parts of this study, especially some of Part 1, may stretch you; some parts may even confuse you, have you questioning concepts you thought you understood, or it may have you questioning or disagreeing with some of the content. All of this is perfectly fine. Should this occur, a second or even a third reading of those parts will clarify any confusion or misconception. Once you have a clear conception of the crucial groundwork laid in Part 1, the rest of the book will flow more smoothly. Last but not least, this book is likely to challenge your current perception of matters, yourself and others as well as your worldview, beliefs and opinions, which may at times be confronting. It may even inspire you to rewrite some of the stories you have created about yourself in the past, stories that have hidden the authentic YOU. Remember, to dive into the unknown, especially something that may not make total sense to you at the start, takes *courage, commitment,* openness (*vulnerability*), *responsibility* and patience. But first, anything new begins with *awareness*. I invite you to embark on this journey of discovery, *awareness*, insight and learning with an open heart and mind.

PART 1

Discovering Being

Our world today is filled with confusion and man-made constructs. The dominant paradigm or way of thinking in academia, particularly in what is known as 'human sciences', the media, politics and popular culture, seems to be that almost everything is mutable and relative, meaning we can invent almost any construct we want to without first conducting a reality check. This dominant paradigm is commonly reflected in the self-help industry where some so-called experts or 'gurus' suggest we can change anything simply by thinking positively, practising some tips or tricks or reading a book. Then at the other end of the spectrum, we have those who think everything is fixed and rigid, including our personality types, suggesting we are somehow hardwired to be how we are, as though we don't have the ability to polish ourselves, transform and thrive. This is hardly surprising when you consider that in the business world, human beings are referred to as 'resources'. This essentially reduces each individual either to a commodity that depreciates over time and can be traded, or to nothing more than their immediate functionality while paying little to no attention to who and how they really are deep down (their Being).

When human beings are seen – even by themselves – as resources, like commodities you can buy and trade, only their surface behaviours are observed, leaving their deeper qualities hidden and therefore ignored. This commonly leads to reduced productivity levels, which naturally has dire consequences for a business. Failing to pay attention to an individual's deeper qualities can also prevent them from living a fulfilling life. Why do we need to care about the deeper, hidden qualities of those who work in our organisation? Aren't the observable behaviours all that matter? The answer is twofold. Firstly, a person's behaviour only partly reveals who they really are and secondly, it is those deeper qualities that drive their behaviour and performance. Our Aspects of Being are like the parts that make up the engine that drives the system.

Just as a person's behaviour within the workplace only partly reveals who they really are, the same is true beyond the workplace. Think about modern dating culture. We tend not to show our real self, the layers beneath the surface, when meeting someone new. This commonly leads to the establishment of a superficial and transactional relationship, and by transactional I am referring to when one or both parties expect something immediate in return for giving, without a willingness to build a deeper relationship over time. I am not making a moral judgement about modern dating; I am merely making the point that for any relationship to be fulfilling, whether it be personal or professional, all parties need to know, show and be who and how they are at a deep level at all times and let the other party make decisions based on accurate, authentic knowledge.

The above facts prompted me to work on developing a framework that would serve to fill that void and delve beneath and beyond the surface, a relatively comprehensive paradigm or framework to help us understand human beings better when it comes to leadership, performance and *effectiveness*. In conducting my research, I found there are abundant resources available to help people assess and work on individual Aspects of Being, like *responsibility*, *presence*, *confidence* and *assertiveness*, to name just a few. However, there was no overarching model or framework into which each individual Aspect of Being could slot like the pieces of a jigsaw puzzle. Nothing considered our Being holistically and, importantly, the relationships that exist between each Aspect of Being. Unless you understand both the big picture and the relationships, it would be like trying to complete a jigsaw puzzle blindfolded! The framework explored in this book delivers the big picture that was missing. It also provides the ability to zoom in on each individual Aspect of Being and shows the relationships that exist between them. While the Being Framework is not claiming to encompass all Aspects of Being relevant to human beings, it does incorporate the most significant aspects, based on our extensive research, in the context of leadership, performance and *effectiveness*.

As explained in the Introduction, my hope is that by the end of this book you will have undergone a paradigm shift in terms of the way you see yourself and others. This framework will be the beacon to guide your way, just as it has been for me, my teams and for the many people, coaches and organisations we have since introduced it to because it will enable you to see human beings in great clarity for the very first time.

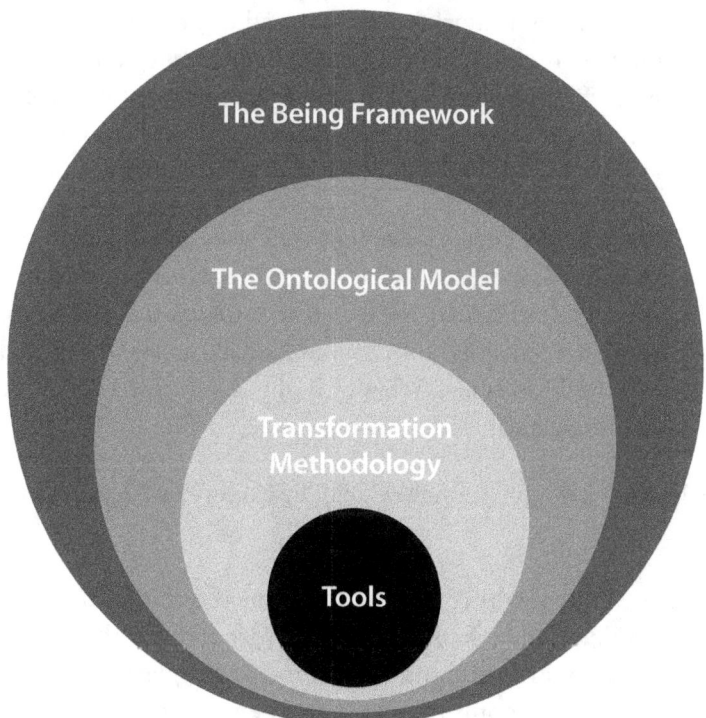

Figure 1: The Being Framework

The main objective of Part 1 of this book is to lay out a helicopter view of the paradigm, which I have called the Being Framework, as shown in *Figure 1* and its core components:

- **The Ontological Model** – A description of knowledge as a set of entities and the relationships that hold true between them. Put simply, the Ontological Model is where I mapped out the qualities of human beings that are tied to our performance, leadership and *effectiveness* in four distinct layers: Meta Factors, Moods, Primary Ways of Being and Secondary Ways of Being.

Combined, these are referred to as 'Aspects of Being'. In this way, the Ontological Model gives us the ability to see the qualities of ourselves (how we are being) and others with great clarity and depth, offering a new, more powerful lens through which to see human beings, including ourselves;

- **Transformation Methodology** – A high-level model and series of processes and principles that lead us on a transformational journey. It begins with raising our *awareness*, before culminating in a sudden and dramatic transformation, becoming effective and polished in all Aspects of Being, travelling from how we are being right now to how we want to become; and

- **Tools** – The core assessment tool associated with the Being Framework is called 'the Being Profile'. It is the world's first and most comprehensive and effective ontological profiling tool for performance, *effectiveness* and leadership by which all Meta Factors, Moods and Ways of Being, as outlined above, can be accurately measured.

These layers within the framework will be explored in detail later in the book.

Part 1 also walks you through the fundamental knowledge and core concepts you need to be familiar with in order to grasp the framework, as well as the research and discovery process I undertook to build an effective channel of communication and entice you on this journey of discovery about your own Being, the Being of individuals on your team and how this knowledge and understanding links to personal and team *effectiveness*. This can exponentially increase the probability of becoming fulfilled in all aspects of your life. More specifically, we will explore truth, meanings and reality; clarify the confusion surrounding Existence and Being; and discuss the difference between meanings and words, distinguishing between the absolutes of this world and the layers of reality we create ourselves. We will examine the crucial distinction between discovery and invention, exploring habitual ways of thinking and paradigms and gaining an appreciation of how ontology, epistemology and phenomenology helped establish the research paradigm for this framework. The Discovery vs Invention chapter will also explain the meaning of those disciplines and how they are key to answering some of life's big questions. Then we will be ready to dive deep into the shaping of the Being Framework Ontological Model layer (see *Figure 1*) to maximise the benefits you will gain from it. This will be followed by an introduction to the Meta Factors as well as Moods and Primary and Secondary Ways of Being and the part they all play in the Being Framework. Part 1 will end with Time Matters, explaining why Being is a 'now phenomenon'. Don't worry if some of these terms are unfamiliar to you right now. The aim, after reading Part 1, is that you will have a clear, high-level understanding of the entire paradigm/framework and the meaning and relevance of its associated terminology.

Let's begin with a discussion on truth, meanings and reality. Since the beginning of time, researchers and scholars have searched for and debated the meaning of Being, Human Existence, and even Existence itself. It is important that we have this discussion here as it will give you an important insight into how and why the first seeds were sown towards the development of the Being Framework and the research upon which this work is grounded. Gaining an understanding of the foundation and significance of the Being Framework, as described in this book, will also allow you to appreciate where I am coming from in terms of some of our habitual ways of thinking and paradigms. After all, a paradigm shift won't occur unless you first understand and change how you see or think about something, in this case human beings.

CHAPTER 1

In Search of Truth, Meanings and Reality

Sometimes people don't want to hear the truth because they don't want their illusions destroyed.

Friedrich Nietzsche
German philosopher, 1844–1900

The Simorgh Story[7]

The birds of the world gather to decide who is to be their sovereign, as they believe they have none. The hoopoe[8], the wisest bird of them all, suggests they should find the legendary Simorgh. They all agree in excitement. The hoopoe leads the birds, each of whom represents a human fault, which prevents humankind from attaining enlightenment. The hoopoe tells the birds they have seven valleys to cross – the Valley of Quest, the Valley of Love, the Valley of Knowledge, the Valley of Detachment, the Valley of Unity, the Valley of Wonderment and the Valley of Poverty and Annihilation – in order to reach the home of Simorgh, which lies on the summit of Ghaaf, a place no one had ever reached before.

---

7   The Simorgh Story is an ancient mystical masterpiece written around the 12th century by Persian poet Farid ud-din Attar (commonly known as Attar of Nishapur) from his book, *The Conference of the Birds*. The book was edited and translated by Sholeh Wolpé, W. W. Norton & Co, 2017.

8   The bird known as the hoopoe has been a common motif in the literature and folklore of eastern Mediterranean and Middle Eastern cultures from ancient to modern times. It is often associated with kingship, filial piety and wisdom.

Editor and translator of Attar's *The Conference of the Birds*, Sholeh Wolpé wrote, 'When the birds hear the description of the valleys they must cross, they bow their heads in fear and distress; some even die of fright right then and there. But despite their trepidations, the others begin the great journey. On the way, many perish of thirst, heat or illness, while others fall prey to wild beasts, panic and violence. Finally, only thirty birds from what began as all the birds in the world make it to the home of Simorgh. In the end, the birds learn that they themselves are Simorgh; the name 'Simorgh' in Persian means thirty (*Si*) birds (*Morgh*). They eventually come to understand that the majesty of the Beloved is like the sun that can be seen reflected in a mirror. Yet, whoever looks into that mirror will also behold his or her own image.' In other words, each bird is carrying a piece of Existence within. What they had been searching for was right there all along. The journey taught them that they had to search within to find what they were looking for, not seek it externally. They discovered this was not an easy journey to undertake and they had to overcome enormous challenges to find it. In the case of human beings, I call the piece of Existence within 'Unique Being'. This is the part of ourselves we ultimately want to tap into and project to the world. We will explore Unique Being and its relationship to the Being Framework later. Why did I begin a discussion on truth, meanings and reality with this excerpt from an ancient Persian mystical masterpiece? I used this story as a metaphor to depict the relationship between us and Existence and represent the fact that our perception of the truth does not necessarily match Reality, much like the birds' perception of the legendary Simorgh did not match the truth that they were in fact on a quest to find themselves, to discover Existence, eventually realising they are each part of it.

Meanings and words

Have you ever been in a situation where you're having a conversation with a friend or business associate and you come across a discrepancy in the common understanding and use of a word? Perhaps you found it necessary at the time, for the sake of coming to an agreement, to double check the meaning of the word in a dictionary. Thanks to the World Wide Web, this can be done in an instant. Just Google the word and up comes an array of dictionary definitions. Look closely though, and you would see that various dictionaries define the same word in different ways; in some cases, the definitions vary quite considerably. Is it any wonder that two intelligent people could understand the same word so differently?

Google the word *'courage'*, for instance, and you will find a number of definitions. The *Oxford English Dictionary* defines *courage* as 'the ability to do something that frightens one; bravery'. The *Merriam-Webster Dictionary* defines it as 'mental or moral strength to venture, persevere, and withstand danger, fear, or difficulty'. The *Cambridge Dictionary* defines it as 'the ability to control your fear in a dangerous or difficult situation'. And the *Macmillan Dictionary* defines it as 'the ability to do something that you know is right or good, even though it is dangerous, frightening, or very difficult; the ability to be brave when you are in great pain'. Can you see the dilemma? How can we effectively communicate with one another if the authors of dictionaries can't agree on the one definition? You would think these authors would exercise alignment on the meaning of words, but instead they leave it up to us to make a choice. But shouldn't we all have access to the same meanings? After all, as Martin Heidegger wrote in *Being and Time*, 'Language is the house of the truth of Being'.

What if you gave one of your team members a written instruction to perform a task and they failed to deliver the task correctly because they misunderstood one or more of the words used in the instruction? The impact of not fully understanding the meaning of an instruction can have unwanted and sometimes dire consequences. Imagine if a pharmacist misinterpreted an instruction by a doctor on a patient's script. That could possibly result in the patient overdosing. Let's not forget also that our understanding of the meaning of words comes predominantly by reference and association as we grow up, not from dictionaries, creating even more error and difference. We pick up words and meanings from early childhood and carry those throughout life. Often it is only when someone points out that we are using a word incorrectly that we have the urge to look it up in the dictionary. Without studying words, we tend to rely on our perceptions and assumptions, which aren't always correct.

Transcendent Meanings are beyond words. Without them there would be no notion of truth, Reality, Existence or Self, for example[9]. Transcendent Meanings distinguish between the absolutes of this world (like the laws of the universe) and the versions of reality we create ourselves, either individually or collectively as a group or society (things like money, taxation, social media and any other man-made invention). The reason it is important to discuss this distinction early in the book is to clarify that, as a truth seeker, my objective right from the start was to become aware of the Reality of human beings and therefore confirm that every part of the Being Framework was centred on transcendent Meanings, not meanings that have been invented. Let me explain, beginning with the layers of reality that exist in the world.

Layers of reality

The word 'reality' is overloaded. It is also ambiguous because it refers to three separate Meanings: the absolutes of the world, which I call First-layer Reality; the reality we collectively create, which I call Second-layer Reality; and your own version of reality, which I call Third-layer Reality. Why is this important? It is important because we need to treat them differently. In the context of this book, whenever I refer to First-layer Reality – also referred to as Reality with a capital R – I am alluding to what is out there in the world, the ultimate projection of Existence. So, Meaning and Reality have a lead capital letter when they refer to something that can't be denied or debated, like the laws of the universe, Meanings as defined by the Higher Order/Existence/Ultimate Reality. Otherwise, they are expressed in lower case. Similarly, Existence has a lead capital letter when it refers to the ultimate Reality in the universe but is in lower case when it refers to the conventional use of the word by most people when referring to something that exists. Third-layer Reality will be explored in the Awareness chapter.

One of the most obvious examples of First-layer Reality is gravity. We cannot deny or argue its existence. Take aeroplanes, for example. It is not scientifically valid to say aeroplanes defy the law of gravity. On the contrary, when the Wright brothers invented the aeroplane, they

---

[9] 'Transcendence constitutes selfhood', *On the Essence of Ground*, Martin Heidegger (1929).

first learnt and acknowledged the laws of physics (one being gravity) in order to ensure the plans for their invention were congruent with Reality. Any glitch in the system as a result of breaching any of those laws or Meanings would have endangered lives. These are facts, not opinions. If there is a hungry dog in the backyard, or if a particular type of mushroom is poisonous, opinion is irrelevant. It is what it is.

When I refer to Second-layer Reality however, I am referring to the constructs we invent. A construct is an idea or theory containing various conceptual elements, typically ones considered to be subjective and not based on empirical evidence[10]. An example is when someone invents a theory or concept, which a large number of people eventually agree with before doing a reality check. I am not saying constructs are bad or wrong or even that they aren't useful. To the contrary, as an entrepreneur and engineer, my job is to invent things. But I am encouraging you to differentiate between the layers of reality because each is to be treated differently. If a Meaning is transcendent and therefore sitting under First-layer Reality, you can take a positivist[11] approach towards it. Simply put, a positivist approach is using measurable ways to check the validity of a Meaning and is at the core of scientific endeavours. Therefore, you can be certain about it. For example, *fear* is not something we have made up. All animals and human beings experience *fear*. It is tied to the limbic system[12] in the brain and is measurable. We should accept it as a fact. Concepts, ideas or meanings that sit under Second-layer Reality and Third-layer Reality, on the other hand, are debatable and negotiable. Since they can be interpreted in different ways, you may take a pragmatic approach towards those meanings to determine their relevance to the current era or your circumstances. For example, whether or not it is time to refine our tax system or legislate new laws for living in a strata title apartment building are both examples of Second-layer Reality and therefore open to debate. Similarly, the story you tell yourself about 'xyz' is an example of Third-layer Reality and may be invalid. How you interpret matters in life may not necessarily be congruent with the facts.

---

10 *Oxford English Dictionary.*
11 Positivism is a philosophical theory stating that certain knowledge is based on natural phenomena and their properties and relations.
12 All the components of the limbic system work together to regulate some of the brain's most important processes.

Two or more people sharing an experience but ending up telling themselves completely different stories about it is an example of Third-layer Reality. A friend once told me that she struggled for many years in her relationship with her father because she misunderstood something he told her when she was seven years old. Her parents had divorced twelve months earlier and he wanted to introduce his new partner to her. He told his daughter that he was introducing the two of them because he loved his new partner. My friend told me she had misconstrued this to mean that he no longer loved her because he loved his new partner instead (she had only ever heard her father tell her mother – his ex-wife – and herself that he loved them). My friend carried this burden with her well into adulthood. And it all stemmed from a story she created herself. The point is, we shouldn't give Second-layer Reality and Third-layer Reality too much credit because those versions of reality are mutable, debatable and open to interpretation. First-layer Reality, on the other hand, is not mutable or open to debate or interpretation. Either we acknowledge that fact or we pay the price.

Words

Words are essentially tools. They are a means to communicate and describe both transcendent Meanings (First-layer Reality) and constructed concepts and ideas (Second-layer Reality and Third-layer Reality). Words are limited. Therefore, it is wise to search for the underlying Meaning, which may require many words, sentences or even a book to explain, rather than tackle a word at face value. Let's look at an example. The word 'star' refers, in the first instance, to a natural luminous body visible in the night sky. But in another context, the word 'star' can be used to describe a celebrity. Even though the word 'celebrity' is a construct, we can use the word 'star' instead. So, the same word can refer to different things depending on the context and, at the same time, a Meaning can be described using different words.

Meanings

Truth or Reality is such a broad phenomenon it can seem vague and therefore difficult to comprehend. In order to study truth or Reality, we must break it down into smaller, more digestible chunks. Some call these chunks 'laws'. But I call them Meanings. I am not referring to meaning here the way Aristotle described it as *Telos*, which in Ancient Greek simply means 'end goal', or 'purpose'. I am also not referring to it as the meaning or definition of a particular word. Please bear with me here, as this is difficult to describe, but very important to understand. The closest word to describe Meaning the way I use it is 'concept'. But even that is not totally accurate. I deliberately do not want to downgrade a Meaning to a concept because a concept is when a human being perceives[13] and then develops a conception[14] of a Meaning. We may all perceive or conceptualise Meanings differently, but the Meaning in question is always the same, regardless of how many interpretations there are of it. Let me elaborate. In Persian, the word *Ma'ni* is defined as the meaning or definition of a word. Then there is another word *Ma'na*, which refers to Meaning, a small chunk of the Reality. A third word derived from *Ma'na*: *Ma'navi*, commonly translates to 'spiritual' in English. However, that translation is incorrect. Some of you may be familiar with or have heard or read a quote from Rumi[15], the Persian poet and mystic. One of Rumi's books is called *Masnavi Ma'navi*. *Masnavi* is simply a form of poetry normally used for lengthy stories, but the word *Ma'navi* means looking into the world of Meanings by tapping into the transcendent Meanings of the universe or Existence, which sits within the realms of First-layer Reality.

Access to Reality leads to *awareness* and why this is important

The Greek word *Aletheia* means 'truth', or 'disclosure' in philosophy. It was used in Ancient Greek philosophy and revived in the 20th century by German philosopher, Martin Heidegger, who significantly influenced this body of work and is referred to many times in the book. The Greek translation of *Aletheia* literally means: 'the state of not being hidden; the state of being evident' and 'factuality or reality'. Heidegger brought

---

13 Perception is about *awareness*, to suddenly see (become aware of) something, like a eureka moment. We will discuss this further in *Part 3: Being, in Action*.

14 To develop a conception of something may take time. It occurs when you develop an idea of something in your own mind (usually through a process of internalisation and thought). We will discuss this further in *Part 3: Being, in Action*.

15 Jalāl ad-Dīn Muhammad Rūmī (1207-1273), also known as Mowlawī, and more popularly simply as Rumi, was a 13th-century Persian poet, faqih, Islamic scholar, theologian and Sufi mystic.

renewed attention to the meaning of *Aletheia*, by relating it to the notion of disclosure, or the way in which things appear as entities in the world. *Aletheia* is the opposite of *Lethe*, which means 'oblivion', 'forgetfulness', or 'concealment'. I would take this a step further and describe *Lethe* as 'ignorance' (to intentionally ignore something), or 'negligence' (a lack of *care* to seek and discover the truth/Reality). Now, when it comes to *awareness*, it is ignorance in its other context (lack of knowledge) that, to a large extent, gets in the way. But that is not the full story. There are also times when we are negligent and intentionally ignorant, when we are unwilling or not caring enough to pay attention and become aware. If you live your life in a state of *Lethe*, lacking the *care* to pursue the truth or intentionally ignoring it, you will suffer and cause suffering. The whole premise behind the Being Framework is the pursuit and discovery of truth/of the Reality (*Aletheia*) of how human beings perform in life, which is a fundamental prerequisite to gaining *awareness* (the start of the journey towards *integrity* and *effectiveness*). The framework breaks this Reality down into smaller, more digestible chunks (Aspects of Being), making it easier to become aware and access the truth, thereby allowing us to study ourselves and others holistically.

Some may argue that this discussion is too abstract and philosophical. But to learn about philosophical topics like truth and the distinction between the three layers of reality is like having meaningful conversations with yourself about anything in life, and this should never be optional if your intention is to be effective and fulfilled. We human beings must be aware of Meanings. The more aware we are, the more effective we are in our endeavours and the better equipped we will be in the face of adversity and challenges, which are inevitable for each and every one of us at various times in our lives. Failing to raise our *awareness* to the three layers of reality can result in unwanted or even dire consequences. Imagine if you were unaware that the mushroom you picked and are about to eat is poisonous. Or imagine trying to build a meaningful relationship with your life partner if you are unaware of how to be in a relationship, for example, how to be authentic, how to be self-expressive, how to be responsible, how to be committed, and so on. But how would you know how to be authentic and responsible, etc., if you don't know what they mean. Once I introduce you to the Being Framework Ontological Model, you will recognise these words and Meanings and appreciate that they all sit under First-layer Reality.

Let's return to the word *'courage'* for a moment, which you will recall has a number of dictionary definitions attached to it. Aside from those definitions, which have all been created by human beings, the word *'courage'* actually refers to a Meaning that is primal. *Courage* is intrinsically connected to human beings regardless of ethnic background and culture. It does not matter what language you translate the word into or even if you were to call it 'x', it still means the same thing at a primal level; it has the same Meaning at its First-layer Reality level. *Courage* is a Way of Being that conveys an aspect of humans that has been part of us since the beginning of time across all cultures on the planet. But, as we have seen previously, the authors of dictionaries don't necessarily agree on this point. So, the question is, do we invent meanings or is there a pre-existing Meaning that is there for us to discover? The answer is both. We are the creators of words but not the transcendent Meaning they refer to. There is a Meaning that already exists; we have simply given it a word and a description to define it. So, even if we use different words, as is the case when we speak in different languages for example, the Meaning is still the original Meaning. To illustrate my point, let me introduce you to the Being Framework's ontological distinction of *courage*. *Courage* is the state of being that gives rise to the ability to make decisions, move forward and take action when you are frightened, worried or concerned for your safety and/or the safety of others. *Courage* is not the absence of fear; on the contrary, courage shows up when fear is present.

In the Being Framework, I am using the word *'courage'* to refer to the transcendent Meaning of *courage* that even other beings – besides humans – possess. It is a quality a mother bear or lion would manifest when something threatens her newborn cubs. I would even hazard a guess that dinosaurs manifested this quality. The Meaning of *courage* is 'being able to step forward when *fear* is present'. It refers to a Way of Being that a leader requires in the face of adversity in order to withstand uncertainty and danger. *Courage* is what gives us the power to take risks. This is a quality required for anyone who wants to be a high achiever and effective.

Meanings and the Ontological Model of Being

By now you may be getting used to my approach of questioning things on a deeper level. So, why is it important to understand more about the

Meaning that words are actually referring to? In my development of the Ontological Model of Being in the context of leadership, performance and *effectiveness*, I had to use words that point to Aspects of Being such as *authenticity, commitment, love, freedom* and *courage*. So, I had to ensure that I described those Aspects of Being in accordance with their primal Meanings. As I pointed out earlier, my intention was to describe the Reality of Being, not something I made up.

I discovered and modelled the Ontological Model of Being based on extensive research into the literature that exists on every Aspect of Being. When you check the dictionaries on the various Aspects of Being as presented in this book – and which we chose after studying almost 300 accomplished global leaders, past and present, including Steve Jobs, Bill Gates, Nelson Mandela and Gabriel García Márquez, to name just a few – you will find the distinctions applied to them may not always be the same as you would find in other sources. This is common among philosophers who find themselves limited by words and language and may therefore be enticed to expand on certain words to convey a meaning.

So, Meanings are beyond words. Words are essentially tools; a means to communicate and describe transcendent Meanings and constructed meanings. So, rather than be obsessed by words, it is wise to search for the underlying Meaning the words are referring to, as intended by the user of the word. When we go through the various Aspects of Being in Part 2, the aim is to guide you to understand the Meaning each word is referring to. It will require an open mind, open heart and the restraint to refrain from listening to the opinion of others about what they believe *responsibility, love, commitment, authenticity,* etc., mean. Everyone will have an opinion, but not everyone will know, or want to know, the truth. Be prepared for that.

Hexis and *Eudaimonia*

There is rich literature in philosophy and theology about the qualities that make us human beings. However, as I touched on in the Preface and am elaborating on in this chapter, over time, many of those Meanings became lost in translation or were simply dismissed. Some words relating to our qualities were mistranslated to mean virtue, morality or ethics. Over centuries, those translations became accepted as the truth, until people like me started to study and question them.

Looking into the works of Aristotle was extremely helpful. The Greek philosopher used the Greek word, *Hexis*, which he received from Plato, to denote what is considered by many to mean 'moral virtue'. But the word does not merely mean passive habituation – just a series of to-dos and not to-dos, rights or wrongs, sins or virtues. Rather, *Hexis* is an active condition, the means by which you participate in life, make your decisions and behave. Now, I am unsure if what Aristotle actually meant by *Hexis* was what we consider virtue to mean today: 'goodness', 'morality', 'purity', etc. The answer to that question will never be known. All I can say with certainty is how it has been interpreted. So, while *Hexis* is a term that is commonly translated as state, stable disposition, habitus, way of being or even possession, many renowned thinkers over time confused that translation with virtue, virtue theory, ethics and morality. For the sake of clarity, I would like to be clear that I do not concur with the common translation of *Hexis* as moral virtue, which suggests that it manifests itself in an action/behaviour that counts as 'right'. Rather, I have chosen to align myself with the interpretation that Aristotle's *Hexis* is an individual's prevailing tendency to hold oneself in a 'stable disposition' as well as ways of being by which one participates in life, makes decisions and behaves. In other words, I am aligned with the view that *Hexis* is a way of being and the practical road to effective action, not what is known as 'moral virtue'.

Aristotle used *Hexis* in reference to the 'health of', or 'wellness of' something. Therefore, you will notice that when I discuss our qualities or Aspects of Being later in the book, I often refer to having a healthy or unhealthy relationship with each of them. Together, these qualities constitute your Nature, Essence or Being, or how you are. In reading the book, you will also notice that I refer to Ways of Being, Aspects of Being and states of Being to align with Aristotle's original intention with the use of the word, *Hexis*. More specifically, I understand *Hexis* to be robust character traits or a collection of qualities (Aspects of Being) that, once sufficiently developed, will lead to predictable effective behaviours that ultimately lead an individual to fulfilment and prosperity. In the Aristotelian sense, that person may be considered 'good', or 'virtuous'.

However, rather than using the words, 'good', or 'virtuous', I choose to describe an individual who is well-polished and effective in relation to their Aspects of Being as someone who manifests discernment and *integrity*. In other words, they choose powerfully to be integrous and effective in order to succeed in their endeavours, which not only leads to their fulfilment – hitting the targets they set for themselves – but also to being constructive and beneficial to others. One example of a *Hexis* or Way of Being is *courage*. An unhealthy relationship with *courage* would be cowardice, when *courage* is lacking, or recklessness, when there is an excess of *courage* or bravado. Neither is a healthy and effective Way of Being and therefore wouldn't contribute to your *integrity*, let alone lead you to fulfilment and prosperity.

Now, you may ask why? Why should we polish our Aspects of Being? Aristotle's answer was: *Eudaimonia,* a Greek word commonly translated as 'happiness', or 'welfare'. However, more accurate translations have been proposed, such as, 'human flourishing', 'prosperity' and 'blessedness'. I choose to refer to it as redeeming oneself to be free and autonomous in order to lead a well-lived and meaningful life of fulfilment. I would assert that most, if not all, human beings want to be fulfilled. It is in our nature to set goals and want to reach them. Now, I acknowledge that we may set very different goals, but we all set goals in one form or another. The pathway to fulfilment, contentment and wellbeing differs from one person to the next. For instance, what one person considers wealth may differ greatly from how another person perceives it.

Long after Aristotle, Existentialist philosophers such as Nietzsche[16] and Jean-Paul Sartre[17] challenged the idea of Essence (referring to Aristotle's Essentialism and asserting that the qualities of human beings

---

16   Friedrich Wilhelm Nietzsche (1844-1900) was a German philosopher, cultural critic, composer, poet, philologist, and Latin and Greek scholar whose work has exerted a profound influence on Western philosophy and modern intellectual history.

17   Jean-Paul Charles Aymard Sartre (1905-1980) was a French philosopher, playwright, novelist, screenwriter, political activist, biographer and literary critic. He was one of the key figures in the philosophy of existentialism and phenomenology and one of the leading figures in 20th-century French philosophy.

are not that easy to be understood categorically and to be individually studied, and that human being existence precedes their nature). I am not intending to delve into a deep philosophical discussion here, but I would like to declare that I am more aligned with Martin Heidegger and Mulla Sadra's view that human beings have **both** Existence and Essence, as opposed to just Existence or just Essence, in common. Put simply, what this means is that we all have a Unique Being and we project this uniqueness to the world through our decisions and behaviours. But unless we understand and become aware of the fundamental qualities (Being/Essence) we all share as human beings, we may never tap into and project our Unique Being and therefore may never achieve fulfilment, prosperity and wellbeing (*Eudaimonia*).

It is worth repeating here that, as autonomous beings, **we are free to choose** the path we take while simultaneously being surrendered to Reality, the fundamental rule of Existence. For example, you get to choose to be committed to a cause or not; you get to choose to be proactive or not; you get to choose to be authentic or not; you get to choose to be courageous or not. However, you cannot choose to be fearless because *fear* is a fundamental and essential quality we all possess as human beings. That is Reality or a law of Existence. Without *fear*, we cannot choose to be courageous. If you ignore that fact, you are either not aware or you are not authentic and delusional, meaning you will not be as effective as you could be if you acknowledge Reality. Another example is honouring your relatively high level of autonomy as a human being. That is also a choice, and my studies have shown that this is an essential quality required for being a leader, including the leader of your life. If you live your life from the viewpoint that you are a victim and have no say in how your life goes, you are choosing to see it that way.

Collective psychosis

As mentioned at the start of Part 1, the primary purpose of this portion of the book is to zoom out and explore the big picture, examining the background to the Being Framework and its core components as well as the studies that contributed to this body of work before zooming in to the qualities of human beings (Aspects of Being) in Part 2. So, with that in mind, let's now consider the big picture ramifications if we avoid studying the nature of human beings and their primal qualities as a collective group. What happens when there is a collective dissociation from reality and a collective lack of *awareness* and *integrity*? The consequences are dramatic, potentially terrifying and real; I assert they should be more than enough to keep us committed to avoiding any pathways that may lead us out of *integrity*. Let me share with you what a world in which collective psychosis dominates looks like.

According to Carl Jung[18], the greatest threat to civilisation lies not in external forces, the forces of nature or with any physical disease, but with our inability to deal with our own psyche. We are indeed our own worst enemies. Let's call this 'collective psychosis', which is essentially what happens when there is a dissociation with reality on a collective scale. In other words, it is the epidemic of madness that occurs when a large proportion of a society loses touch with reality and descends into delusion. When delusion, toxic thinking and a lack of *integrity* become the norm, we can be readily persuaded to follow others like sheep, including electing and following unstable, malevolent 'leaders', the ones who only act as if they are leaders as opposed to actually **being** leaders. Nobody can achieve and maintain a position of power alone. All tyrannical leaders in history were followed by 'normal citizens' en masse.

There have been many examples of collective psychosis throughout history, such as the witch hunts of the 16th and 17th centuries, the rise of Totalitarianism in the 20th century, genocides, systematic terrorism, collective discrimination and racisms. Many people were killed during some of these events and times, often in the worst possible ways, despite committing no crime. They were simply scapegoats. Similarly, the rise of dictatorships in places like the Soviet Union, Nazi Germany and North Korea were largely the result of a collective detachment from reality and subsequent descent into delusion and paranoia. Logic, reasoning and human decency don't exist within such regimes and the results have been devastating. Individuals within such infected societies are morally and spiritually defeated, unconsciously descending to become

---

18   Carl Gustav Jung (1875-1961) was a Swiss psychiatrist and psychoanalyst who founded analytical psychology. Jung's work has been influential in the fields of psychiatry, anthropology, archaeology, literature, philosophy and religious studies.

unreasonable, irresponsible, erratic, less effective and unreliable beings. In this book, I refer to these people as being unpolished, ineffective and as having unhealthy relationships with various Aspects of Being. When an entire society sinks to such a low level, crimes that one person may never consider in a million years are freely committed by the collective group as individuals become swept up in the madness. Those who are suffering collective psychosis may be unaware of what is happening and blind to their own descent into madness.

If you are reading this thinking that collective psychosis only happened in historical times and is irrelevant in our current era, you are being delusional. We are living in an era in which truth is not taken as seriously as it should be. Through the actions of many, from politicians and activists to business leaders, journalists and economists, people are losing touch with reality. This is a great threat to humanity because it leads us to become 'hypnotised sheep', as Carl Jung called those who succumb to collective psychosis. This framework focuses on the *integrity* of individuals and collective beings in a structured way, which is exactly what is needed to cause a paradigm shift because the reality is, collective psychosis is enduring, and we will always need to be aware of when a collective dissociation from reality is occurring so we can respond appropriately.

Again, psychosis occurs when there is a detachment from or loss of a healthy relationship with reality. As a result, emotions, ideas, thoughts, opinions and beliefs are overwhelmingly delusional and hence inauthentic, leading to a lack of *awareness* about verifiable reality and a disinterest in becoming aware, leading to ignorance and negligence. Put simply, when psychosis prevails, insanity rules. Imagine if someone believed you were a threat to them and decided to act on their imaginative fear. In life, this could be all it takes to trigger a range of irrational responses, from sacking the wrong person or wrongfully leaving your spouse, to murder or acts of terrorism. While in some cases such delusions and lack of proper access to reality are the result of a mental breakdown, which would require psychiatric help, they are more often than not the result of an unhealthy relationship with our Aspects of Being, particularly Moods like *fear* and *anxiety*, to the extent that it may lead to an inability to handle even the simplest daily activities. It is at this point when many are led to choosing excessive drug or alcohol use in an effort to escape reality. Not only is this type of behaviour counter-productive, but it is also likely to exacerbate their existing misery and suffering, the very thing that led them to drugs and alcohol in the first place. Once this happens, the individual is caught in a vicious cycle of victimisation, self-sabotage and blame, pointing the finger at everyone and everything but themselves. Imagine the result when this happens on a collective scale!

Not only have I studied many examples of collective psychosis throughout history, I also have firsthand experience of it. For example, in my native country, I could easily have been arrested just for walking in the street with a friend of the opposite sex or for voicing my opinion. I was even arrested and detained once for expressing myself through poetry! While I am discussing the topic of collective psychosis on a global scale, you could readily apply this conversation to the organisation you run or other organisations and entities you deal with. I have personally dealt with many corporations filled with 'hypnotised sheep'. Perhaps you can relate?

Whether your perception and narrative of what is going on is based on delusion or reality will open the door to destructive or constructive behaviour respectively. Here is where your Moods and other Aspects of Being ultimately lead your thoughts, decisions and behaviour. An unhealthy relationship with any or all of your Moods (*fear*, *anxiety*, *care* and *vulnerability*) and various other Aspects of Being creates insecurity and fragility. Scale this up to an organisation or society that is predominantly made up of weak, insecure, broken, inauthentic, powerless individuals and I'm sure I don't need to spell out how easily a descent into collective psychosis could happen and the potentially disastrous ramifications of that. However, if the society or organisation is predominantly made up of self-reliant, aware, integrous, effective and inwardly strong and powerful individuals, the gateway is open for positive and constructive outcomes to occur. Unfortunately, many leaders of organisations and societies are either oblivious to this reality or deliberately avert their gaze away from it. Why? Because it is uncomfortable to be vulnerable and authentic enough to acknowledge and face the troubled sides within and collectively. However, they eventually pay the price for their lack of *vulnerability* and *authenticity* because failing to acknowledge reality prevents them from taking positive steps towards rectifying the problems. For example, stress can bring about the best or worst in people. How people deal with stress will define the outcome and this largely boils down to their relationship with *fear* and *anxiety*. When collective psychosis prevails in an organisation, it becomes an unhealthy environment in which people only work because they have to, and they look for any opportunity to escape. This leads to presenteeism[19], lack of performance, unresolved conflicts, office politics, high employee turnover, corrupt power dynamics, etc., ultimately impacting revenue and profitability. Ultimately, businesses collapse, people lose their jobs and directors go bankrupt. There are severe consequences to turning a blind eye to collective psychosis. This is where acknowledging and then polishing and transforming these relationships is critical if you want to effect change, both at an individual and collective level. Polishing your Aspects of Being is, in part, an **antidote to suffering**. This also holds true, particularly in the scope of this book, when it comes to our ideas about human nature, human potential, and the 'proper function', *integrity* and wellbeing of individuals and society or smaller entities or groups such as organisations, teams or families. All of these, at least in part, shape our value system and create our 'moral compass', and then our deeper qualities (Aspects of Being) drive our behaviours.

Like Carl Jung, I am interested in uncovering how ideas influence individual and collective development and have taken this interest to the next level by creating the framework we are examining in this book. We passively accept ideas others create for us and that we are being bombarded with from various sources. Like the human body, our mind has an inbuilt immunity to such invasion and this immunity varies from one person to the next. This is one of the many reasons it is so important to work on our Aspects of Being. An individual who is not here to maintain an integrous, stable, mental wellbeing is far more likely to collapse in the face of inevitable adversities of life, constantly being shocked due to a lack of *awareness* all the way to being overrun by *fear* and *anxiety* and suppressing all their Moods to the point where they are utterly powerless and unfulfilled. This can lead to self-annihilation and sabotage which, in part, creates a culture of collective victimhood as opposed to wisdom, *responsibility* and *freedom*.

---

19   Presenteeism is when employees are at work, but they aren't actually working; they're physically there, but they're not productive.

Passive conformity rarely promotes individual wellbeing and prosperity. On the contrary, it disconnects us from reality and consequently weakens us, makes us prone to unhealthy relationships with *fear* and *anxiety*, drives us to excessive hate, tricks us to simply adapt to whatever environment we are living in and causes us to regress psychologically and mentally, degrading our image of human nature and our potential. History has vividly shown us that humans are very susceptible to these illusions and neither technological nor scientific advancements have immunised us against such illusory ideas. Sometimes an over-fascination with these distorted parallel realities can lead to fanatical obsession, overruling us like demons and disconnecting us from people or matters, no matter how well-meaning or reasonable they may be. Instead of uniting us, they divide us into categories, shackling and polarising us instead of promoting inclusivity.

As I mentioned in the Preface, there was a particular moment in time when I was suddenly struck by the horrors of what has been happening in the world for centuries. In our modern era, such horrors are being amplified with the use of technology, resulting in even greater delusion and detachment from reality, both on an individual and collective scale. I have studied and experienced such horrors first hand and felt the pain with every ounce of my being. I know what it is like to live in a society where collective psychosis is the norm and where freedom of speech is undermined or compromised. But I also know it doesn't have to be like that. Collective psychosis doesn't happen by chance. There are patterns that can be observed and studied through our Aspects of Being that can make or break us individually and collectively. It all starts with the very person you have the greatest responsibility for and influence over – YOU – followed by your immediate circle of influence (your family, your team, your organisation) all the way to the whole of humanity.

The difference between rational, irrational and arational matters

In the world we live in there are rational matters and there are irrational matters. Two plus two equals four, not seven. Gravity is real. Those are rational matters. There is no alternative but to accept them and any deviation or attempt to ignore those facts would come at a significant cost. For instance, to ignore that gravity exists would lead to a bridge collapsing or an aircraft crashing. We also know that a cat cannot be a giraffe, just as we know a table cannot be liquid. To believe otherwise would be irrational. History, and particularly science, has taught us the clear distinction between rational and irrational matters. However, at times the difference between rationality and irrationality is not so crystal clear. These are the times when it may be necessary to take a risk and choose sides in pursuit of what will make life, or more specifically, our experience of life, more worthwhile, leading us to work on enhancing that experience.

Since the Enlightenment era of the late 18th century, the time of German philosopher Immanuel Kant[20], whose work has since greatly influenced many, we have come to understand that we do not have direct access to the truth or Reality and that anything we come to know about anything, with knowledge being the result, is acquired through our human lens and conceptualisation. Despite this however, we were able to discover ways to check the validity of our knowledge when it comes to rational or irrational matters. Now, while we should acknowledge the fact that we understand things from our own perceptions and conceptions, this should not give us permission to say, 'Let's just come up with any low quality, untested assumptions, beliefs and opinions'. The proof of that is our technological advancement with workability being the ultimate measurement. We should always check the workability of our perceptions. However, not everything that matters in our human life sits clearly and comfortably within the categories of rational and irrational matters. This has made it necessary to consider a third category: arational matters, which the *Oxford English Dictionary* defines as 'not based on or governed by logical reasoning'. Why do we need this third category? Why is it not enough to consider only rational or irrational matters? Simply because there are matters that impact us which are beyond our human intellect.

When it comes to arational matters, we can simply and passively shrug our shoulders and plead ignorance. But the issue here is that the complexity of life requires us to make decisions and, at times, choose

---

20   Immanuel Kant (1724-1804) was a German philosopher and one of the central Enlightenment thinkers. Kant's comprehensive and systematic works in epistemology, metaphysics, ethics, and aesthetics have made him one of the most influential figures in the history of Western philosophy.

sides. Leaders are required to deal with unstructured problems all the time. Imagine if a CEO faced with an unstructured or arational problem ignored it simply because of a lack of understanding and knowledge of the issue. Saying we don't know and being content with the fact that we don't know (*Lethe*) may not work in our favour. Here is where I believe we should dare to be vulnerable and take a risk. We should take a leap of faith, make intuitive decisions or choose sides. There are times when we have no option but to take a calculated risk by leaning towards a side when there is uncertainty or we have insufficient knowledge about something. For example, one could argue that it seems rational to kill someone over resources in a time of famine or shortage, but we have collectively made the arational choice to value human life over anything else. While there is no clear line between rationality and irrationality in the case of killing someone over resources, we choose to value human life out of faith. Aside from an example like this, there are Meanings that simply sit beyond our cognitive capabilities, rational mind and intellect, Existence being the ultimate example. Our limitations as human beings don't allow us to see the totality of Existence and all about it and in it. At the end of the day, we are the fish in the tank, at least for now!

While the majority of this book and the Being Framework itself are based on objective (some would say scientific) studies and therefore focused on rational matters using the fields of ontology, epistemology and phenomenology, bear with me for now as I explore the most important arational matter of all: Existence, the Ultimate Reality. The next chapter also examines the meaning of related subjects that continue to cause confusion due to the many and varied meanings applied to them, including Possibility of Existence, Human Existence, Nature, Essence and, of course, Being: the subject of this book. This discussion and clarification lay the crucial groundwork for your understanding of the rest of this book.

CHAPTER 2

Existence and Being

There is much confusion when it comes to existence and Being, and this confusion even extends to the world's most renowned thinkers and philosophers, both today's and from history. Many different ideas or meanings around the term 'Being', for instance, are used interchangeably and the words describing it can be unnecessarily complex, overloaded and, in some cases, even bastardised. Existence, Possibility of Existence (life), Human Nature, Essence, Being, Soul, Spirit, Self, Ego, and so on are all words you may be familiar with. But what exactly do they mean? And what is the difference between them when so many appear to refer to the same thing, namely, human beings?

Take Being, for instance, which Martin Heidegger sometimes described as the totality of human experience. Heidegger did not confuse the objective Being or Essence (*Wesen*[21]) with his more subjective concept of 'being there', or 'being out there in the world' (*Dasein*[22]). He also did not confuse Being and *Dasein* with existence as an idea or concept in isolation.

Heidegger used the expression, *Dasein*, to refer to the experience of Being, which means 'being there'. This has a clear context – you being there, out in the world.

---

21 *Wesen* is a German word that, in Heideggerian terminology, refers to Essence.
22 *Dasein* is a German word that means 'being there', or 'presence', and is often translated into English with the word 'existence'. It is a fundamental concept in the existential philosophy of Martin Heidegger, particularly in his magnum opus, *Being and Time*. Heidegger uses the expression, *Dasein*, to refer to the experience of Being that is peculiar to human beings.

However, if we use the term 'Being' for the subjective experience of existence, such as, 'dogs are a manifestation of Nature, of Being or Existence, in an almost pure form', it causes much confusion because it suggests a reference to existence from an objective point of view. After all, Nature has been around for billions of years. But subjective experience has only been around for less than a billion, when creatures with nervous systems evolved. Many people follow anti-science thinkers in assuming that subjective experience can never be explained by objective methods, such as the methods adopted in the creation of the Being Framework. However, progress is being made on developing neuroscientific theories of consciousness, hence the gap between what exists (ontology) and human beings' experience of it (phenomenology) is beginning to close, which should lead to greater clarity and therefore less confusion. If you are confused at this point, fear not. That is precisely the point I am making here, that confusion exists, even amongst academics and great thinkers.

Part of this confusion stems from the fact that we use both words, 'being' and 'existence', to refer to the same Meaning. Even the *Oxford English Dictionary* defines the word 'being' as 'existence' in the first instance, followed by 'the nature or essence of a person'. And 'existence' is defined as 'the fact or state of living or having objective reality', followed by 'continued survival'. Meanwhile, Heidegger uses the German word *Sein* to refer to existence in the broader context of 'continued survival'. Therefore, in the untranslated original title of his book, *Sein und Zeit*, *Sein* should technically have been translated to 'existence', or 'to be'. So, I assert that Heidegger's renowned book title should technically have been translated to 'Existence and Time', or 'To Be and Time', but they just don't have the same ring to them as the actual translation, *Being and Time*, do they? When I say Being in the context of this book, the word is referring to the second definition of 'being' in the *Oxford English Dictionary*, which is 'the nature or essence of a person'. This is congruent with what Heidegger refers to as *Wesen*.

Now, let's consider the *Merriam-Webster's* definition of existence – 'the state or fact of having being, especially independently of human consciousness and as contrasted with nonexistence'. This is the closest definition I could find to represent the Meaning I refer to in this book when I use the word 'Existence' with a capital E, as it is in direct contrast to nonexistence or nothingness. There is factually no such thing as nothingness; there is always something, and that 'something' is Existence. We are in it; we are all its manifestations, and we are always in the presence of it. More on this shortly.

Last but not least, instead of focusing on the notion of 'to be or not to be', or existence, we, as human beings, are to be concerned with the totality of our experience of life as it is in reality. Heidegger brilliantly describes this as *In-der-Welt-sein*, which translates in English to 'being-in-the-world', and *Dasein*, which translates to 'being there'. In a broad sense, *Dasein* refers to our present experience of living in the world. In the context of this book, you can view 'the world' as your workplace, your family, etc.

Before you ask yourself, 'What have I got myself into by starting this book?', let me remind you that while we are discussing 'philosophical matters' here, this is not purely a philosophical book in the conventional sense. It is important that we discuss these matters up front as they lay the foundation for the far more tangible, concrete and practical content to follow. Without this foundation, you would likely struggle to comprehend the content in Parts 2 and 3.

In this chapter, we will explore some of those meanings in more detail, beginning with Existence, and draw clear lines between them for the purpose of clarity, so that you not only understand the foundation of the research that led to the development of the Being Framework, but that you will also begin to gain an appreciation of its benefits and applications to you and your team.

Existence, the Ultimate Reality

Let me dare to describe the indescribable and encourage you to do your best to grasp the ungraspable! Existence is Existence. Existence is the most obvious and primal truth of all; it is the Ultimate Reality. But it is perhaps so obvious that it is ingrained in our language. We say, 'I exist', 'trees exist', 'my dog exists', 'water exists'. They all have existence in common. While our existence isn't front of mind for most people, we all know we exist; even a baby knows it exists. In fact, all self-organising beings are conscious of their existence, as all beings are in the presence of and under the influence of Existence. It is very important to understand that we are not talking about the 'idea of existence' as a concept or theory, but that we are talking about Existence in its exact, objective, and practical form as the most important Meaning of all. The reason for this is that we are all in the presence of Existence all the time and everywhere. The best analogy I can use is light. We know light exists; it's there, all around us, but we don't see it. We see the objects illuminated by light, but we don't see light itself. Ironically, we are blind to light!

Existence is absolute and it demonstrates itself in all things, beings and Meanings (referring in this context to Meanings such as gravity). All beings are a reflection of its manifestation in the same way that a beam of light passing through a prism breaks into a multiplicity of colours and all truths, laws and rules of the universe sit within Existence. Existence dictates them to us. No one decided one day that gravity would exist, just as humans didn't decide that we would have two eyes, not one or three, or determine how they would function together to enable us to see. The very fact that Existence is the Ultimate Reality encourages us to know that there are truths, laws and transcending Meanings in the universe, and that Reality, as much as we can discover, can and should be studied using objective methods.

Existence is the Ultimate Reality, the supreme power. It is the lawmaker and ruler. Our opinions and perceptions are irrelevant in its presence. Existence is the coming together of all quantised parts of the universe. Everything we know is restricted to the knowledge of the parts that have appeared in ways that our limited human brain can comprehend. For the sake of the argument, let's call it God. Search the word 'God' in the dictionary and you will find a very similar definition to what I call Existence. For example, the *Merriam-Webster Dictionary* defines God as, 'the supreme or ultimate reality: such as the Being perfect in power, wisdom, and goodness who is worshipped (as in Judaism, Christianity, Islam, and Hinduism) as creator and ruler of the universe'. From this we can surmise that it's not a question of whether or not God exists. God IS Existence. This has nothing whatsoever to do with religion or anyone's belief systems.

When we are present to Existence and all in it, we can at least begin to appreciate how each being – particularly each human being, considering the scope of this book – is a world in and of itself while simultaneously being an infinitesimal part of a much greater whole, which I refer to as Existence. If you are aesthetically inclined, you can acknowledge that there is beauty and brilliance to be seen, admired and appreciated in every part of nature. So, why wouldn't every being, including every human being, be worthy of being studied and appreciated? While the main focus of this book is our Being or Essence, let's acknowledge that we are so much more than just an instance of a species corresponding in character and kind. We have a Unique Being.

If you are philosophically inclined, you may have contemplated the question of why there are beings rather than nothing. This simple question led many philosophers towards the mysterious joy and pain of truth seeking, their studies eventually leading them to a higher level of *awareness*. If you are scientifically inclined, you would dig deeper and do your best to identify and discover patterns in your findings. And if you are more practically inclined, you would know by now that it is almost impossible to become highly effective in something you are unaware of. My point is, there are multiple reasons, from various perspectives, to dare to know the Meanings within Existence and surrender to its laws.

If you are still questioning the Meaning of Existence and its connection and relevance to us, consider this: if there is no state in which there is nothing at all, then there must always be something. I'm sure you would agree that there is no debating that. Furthermore, if there has always been something, then it makes sense that this 'something' cyclically rearranges itself into an infinite number of constitutions and beings, from micro-organisms, plants and animals, to us human beings. A higher order always sets the rules, laws and Meanings; this shapes Reality. And this higher order, which we call 'Existence', continually fine-tunes itself in order to maintain its integrity. As each of us is an infinitesimal part of Existence, our Being, actions and the simple fact that we are 'being out there in the world' matter; we all have a unique impact to make, which is why I am encouraging you to be the leader of your life by being free, autonomous, aware and authentic. So, whether or not you realise it, we are all contributing to the integrity and wholeness of Existence. In other words, there is an interdependent relationship between Existence and all beings, including each and every one of us. We are integral to Existence and Existence is integral to us.

In our era, a common narrative we hear is that, as science progresses, God gradually disappears and becomes obsolete. However, I would say that not only does the existence of science testify the validity of the Ultimate Reality (Existence), but also that as knowledge and our collective *awareness* progresses – including science as a way of knowing – the inaccurate and misconstrued interpretations of God/Existence are destined to be disproved to the point where they will eventually disappear. This is good news for the truth seekers of the world but a sad fact for those enticed by the temptation to create parallel realities and obsessed with being right as opposed to being in love with and in search of truth.

There are multiple theories and narratives about how the world and human beings came to be, which obviously sit outside the scope of this book. But for those of you wondering why we are talking about Existence or God, let's return to an excerpt from the tale of Simorgh for clarification…

> *If Simorgh unveils its face to you, you will find*
> *that all the birds, be they thirty or forty or more,*
> *are but the shadows cast by that unveiling.*
>
> *What shadow is ever separated from its maker?*
>
> *Do you see?*
>
> *The shadow and its maker are one and the same,*
> *so get over surfaces and delve into mysteries.*[23]

The Simorgh story is symbolic of human beings. The moral of the story is that while we have no influence over Existence, we all carry a piece of it within us, which is our Spirit, Soul, Unique Being or Self, however you choose to articulate it. While it is not my intention to focus too much on God or Existence, nor is it my intention to debate anyone's belief system, I raised the subject because we are discussing truth and the Reality of human beings. Furthermore, it was imperative to distinguish Existence from Being and Unique Being from Aspects of Being. By expanding the lens all the way out to Existence, you will

---

23 From *The Conference of the Birds* by Attar, edited and translated by Sholeh Wolpé. NY, W. W. Norton, 2017.

appreciate where we all fit in the equation. If we do not choose to acknowledge Existence – the Ultimate Reality – it would make no sense to go through any discovery process. For example, if everyone's liver functioned differently, there would have been no point for anyone to scientifically discover a treatment for liver disease. The very fact that we acknowledge Existence justifies and amplifies the need to discover the truth, Reality, Meanings and the laws of the universe, as opposed to making up stories and constructs where there are transcending Meanings. Now, as I said in the previous chapter, I am not suggesting constructs are bad. But even for the invention of constructs like money and the banking system, we needed to discover the fundamental truths first, for example human beings' intrinsic need for exchange (money) and security (banks).

It is important not to confuse Existence with Being or Essence, the characteristics or qualities all human beings have in common. As far as comprehending the Being Framework is concerned, the key is that your Being, or Aspects of Being to be exact, are the parts of you that you can have an enormous influence over, as long as you are committed to polishing them and undergoing a process of transformation. More on this later. For now, all that matters is that we are on the same page about the fact that Existence gives rise to Being/Essence and that there is Existence beyond our Being. It is also important for you to understand that when I refer to Aspects of Being, I am referring to human qualities we all have in common that can be observed, studied, measured, polished and transformed, not to your mysterious Soul or Unique Being. These qualities are covered in depth in *Part 2: Aspects of Being*. So, like the birds in the Simorgh story, we all carry a piece of Existence within – our Unique Being – and we also have Essence or Being in common, and these qualities and characteristics can be refined, polished and transformed. This transformation will empower and enable your Unique Being to be projected to the world, making you far more influential in your endeavours in life, professionally and personally, hence increasing your *effectiveness* and the probability that you will hit your targets and live a fulfilling life.

Let's return to Existence for now. Some time ago, I was debating some of the laws of the universe and Existence with a friend of mine, a university professor and intellectual sceptic who would often question the structure of systems, government, families and many other entities. I recall a particular discussion with him when he was questioning Being and Existence. My response was to tell him the following joke.

> *There once was a horse who was looking for a job. She saw a job advertisement in a newspaper from a circus hiring new talent. She immediately picked up the phone and called them.*
>
> *'Hello, I am a horse. I was wondering if you have a job for me?'*
>
> *'Do you know how to jump through fire?' they asked.*
>
> *'No!'*
>
> *'Do you know how to flip over?'*
>
> *'No!'*
>
> *'How about walking on a rope?'*
>
> *'Unfortunately, I can't do that either.'*
>
> *'Oh, sorry. Then we don't have a job for you.'*
>
> *Just as they go to end the call, the horse cuts in and says, 'Wait! But I am a horse, and I am talking!'*

The very fact that we exist and we are talking should suffice for us to be humble enough to own the Possibility of Existence (*Dasein*) powerfully, accept it as the gift it is, show *gratitude* and do something meaningful and worthwhile with it. The horse understood this, but the circus owner clearly did not!

Possibility of Existence

Possibility of Existence is life itself. It is the state of being there, out in the world (*Dasein*). In other words, the fact that we exist is a gift, so we should make the most of every possibility. You are either there or you are not there. To be, or not to be?[24] Or, as Heidegger says, *Das Sein* as opposed to *Das Nichts*[25]. We are alive! That in itself is the Possibility

---

24 *Hamlet*, William Shakespeare (1564-1616)
25 Martin Heidegger (1889-1976)

of Existence; we are being there as opposed to not being there. This is something we all have in common, even with other beings like dogs, cats and ladybugs. It's quite common for us human beings to forget that we are actually alive. We take it for granted. Intentionally being conscious of the fact that we are alive and not letting all the mundane day-to-day activities distract us from that is a key to living a life of contentment, personally and professionally, including the building and running of thriving organisations. That is fulfilling the Possibility of Existence. Remember, we participate in life – we are being out there in the world – through our Being, or Aspects of Being to be exact. Our Moods and Ways of Being help us project the true manifestation of our Unique Being to the world.

The simple fact that we are alive, that we possess a relatively high level of autonomy and freedom and are conscious in this moment is as magical to me today as it has always been. We can talk, think, feel, wonder, explore, discover, make sense of things; we can know and experience. We can choose to be present to and truly aware of our consciousness with intention. The fact that I understand things and the fact that I am writing at this very moment; the fact that I can observe a single leaf falling from the tree outside my window and lifted into the air by a gentle breeze, turning silver and gold as it dances in the sunshine and catches the light; the fact that I am observing my dog growing each and every day; literally everything I am in the presence of; I am still astonished by it all and I simply cannot **not** be present to all this and not be left in wonder. This is the power of being there (*Dasein*). Too many people today don't take the time to be in the presence of the abundance that is all around them, which makes me wonder if their lack of *awareness* leads them to live in misery by choice. If only every human being would choose to embrace the Possibility of Existence and do something they find meaningful with it, our world would be infinitely richer for it. But to do so requires you to develop *awareness* of what's possible and polish your Aspects of Being to become more integrous, effective and fulfilled We will examine each Aspect of Being in Part 2.

Referring back to Martin Heidegger, who, as I said, was a strong influencer for this body of work, *Dasein* or 'being there in the world', is a basic constitution of our existence. To exist in the world means to be embedded in it within a complex web of relations, to be familiar with it[26], and to be open to it in a way that matters to us. As I mentioned earlier, Heidegger used the term, *Dasein* in his book, *Being and Time*[27]. He even made the meaning of Being more cognitive and tangible by giving it a narrower context – 'being there (*Da*) in the world' – which is relevant and helpful given the Being Framework's context of leadership and *effectiveness* in business, as 'there', in a narrower sense, can also be viewed as your organisation or your family.

The fact that we are being there in the world, ready to care and engage, ready to participate, gives context to our existence. Moreover, our relatively high level of autonomy (*responsibility*) ensures we can choose. For the most part, the outcomes we produce are defined by the constant small decisions we make and act upon. Firstly, we acknowledge that we are alive, that we are 'being out there in the world'. Secondly, we acknowledge that we are not alone. Thirdly, we share existence with others; we are all connected with each other in 'being out there in the world'. We choose powerfully to embrace the Possibility of Existence because we find it worthwhile, and this leads us to care enough to work for its betterment. Last but not least, we acknowledge that we are, for the most part, free. This opens up an enormous number of possibilities, some of which we can act upon now because they are visible to us, while others we must first discover and be open to learning about, like being open to change in business and seeing transformation as an exciting opportunity rather than something to hide from due to fear of the unknown and/or apathy. Our outcomes and achievements will largely be defined by how well we see reality, the extent to which we are aware, as opposed to holding delusional opinions on things that ultimately don't work. And we will make sound decisions on a daily basis and execute those decisions effectively. That is making the most of the Possibility of Existence.

---

26   Heidegger, Martin. *Being and Time*. Trans. by E. Robinson and J. Macquarrie. NY: Harper, 1962.

27   Heidegger elaborates further that the entity to which the signification, 'Being-in' belongs is *Dasein*, which has the character of and is in each case 'I myself am [*bin*]': "The expression, *bin*, is connected with *bei*, and so *ich bin* ['I am'] means in its turn 'I reside', or 'I dwell alongside' the world, as that which is familiar to me in such and such a way." (BT 80, 54).

Being a human being

There is far more to human beings than just our behaviours or what we do, hence the term human being and not human doing. We go much deeper than the behaviours we display outwardly. When the great French philosopher, mathematician and scientist, René Descartes[28] famously said during the time of the Renaissance, 'I think, therefore I am', he was essentially concluding that he only exists because he thinks, at least that is how I interpret it. 'To think' is a verb, meaning it is in the realm of doings and not being. While I acknowledge the work of Descartes, I assert that there is something missing in his famous proposition. It doesn't acknowledge that his power comes from his Being. You cannot think unless you are being there first. So, the way I see it, Descartes' proposition would make more sense if it were reversed: I am, therefore I think.

Descartes defined thought (*Cogitatio*) as, 'what happens in me such that I am immediately conscious of it, insofar as I am conscious of it'. Today this concept is studied further in computer science, cognitive science and cognitive technologies. It is a dominant way of thinking that seems to assume there is nothing more to human beings than our cognitive abilities. If this makes you wonder whether machines and technology could eventually outperform and take over human beings, I can assure you, in my capacity as a technologist and philosopher, that machines and technology will never **fully** outperform us. AI[29] driven software, for example, is nothing more than a series of algorithms created by human beings that can learn over time. To say it threatens to replace us because it could technically outperform us in part and conclude it will outperform us in totality is a logical error called 'Fallacy of Composition'[30]. That's like arguing that if my front door is bigger than your front door, then my house must be bigger than your house, or if there are two great

---

28   René Descartes (1596-1650) was a French philosopher, mathematician, and scientist. A native of the Kingdom of France. One of the most notable intellectual figures of the Dutch Golden Age, Descartes is also widely regarded as one of the founders of modern philosophy.

29   Artificial Intelligence.

30   Fallacy of Composition is a type of formal fallacy or logical error that says if it is true in parts then it must be true on the whole. Logic refers to valid reasoning, whereas a fallacy is the use of poor reasoning.

players on my soccer team then my soccer team must also be great. So, if a machine could out-perform a human being in a few abilities, that does not mean it could out-perform human beings as a whole in everything. After all, we could turn it off with a flick of a switch any time we choose.

Technology does not exist in a true sense. It is not conscious of its consciousness, as human beings are. Such cognitive abilities lead us to advance technology, a fact that impacts me as much as everyone else. However, rather than be threatened by it, I am participating in building things using technology, the Being Profile being a prime example. So, don't get me wrong, I have enormous respect for that. As a matter, of fact I am very interested in the bridge between cognitive technology and cognitive science. All I am saying is that I don't just stop there because, as human beings, we have more than just cognitive abilities. At the end of the day, AI and robots are simply tools; they operate in response to our instructions and algorithms and, while they have the capacity to learn, they will never exist in a true sense. Therefore, AI and robots will empower us rather than threaten us, as long as we are committed to being integrous and polished human beings[31]. After all, they are our creations, so congratulate yourself as a human being for the very fact that we can create such complex systems. Ultimately, we should pay our respects to Existence for making it all possible. It truly is remarkable, don't you think?

Your Unique Being

Once again, we are entering the realm of the indescribable. While we human beings have a lot in common, each of us is incredibly unique! You are the only YOU in the world; you do not have a clone or a duplicate. This uniqueness manifests itself within us from early childhood to our teenage years. For instance, we are drawn to particular fields, sports, cultural pursuits, etc.; we find certain activities more interesting than others. Some seem to be our primal gifts (talents), others may come from our experiences and upbringing. Our Unique Being is the part that is gifted to us. As so poignantly expressed in Attar's story of Simorgh, it

---

[31] Technically, AI and robots could threaten those who are unwilling to empower themselves. Those people have the potential to become addicted or slaves to them.

is that piece of Existence that keeps us alive, carries our uniqueness, our passion, our innate talents or callings. While this may all seem a bit mystical, my studies revealed that the majority of the world's great leaders rely on their callings and intuition in setting the direction of their organisations or dealing with the unstructured problems they face, so it is very relevant to anyone who has a desire to live their best life.

Your Unique Being could be referred to as the 'Soul', or 'Spirit' by some. It's WHO you are. If you work on your Aspects of Being, the qualities you have control over and can transform, you increase the probability of projecting what's inside that black box – your Unique Being – to the world. Moreover, two people's abilities may be identical, but what they do with those abilities may differ. Steve Jobs and Michael Jackson are classic examples of two human beings who successfully and powerfully projected their Unique Beings to the world. So, apart from the Being or Essence you inherit as an instance of the Class: Human Being, you also have the one and only YOU, which is the Unique Being you project to the world.

As I said at the start of this section, in discussing your Unique Being we have once again entered the realm of the indescribable. As a result, this book doesn't delve deeply into that part of you; it can't because that part of you is unique to you and therefore subjective and personal. It is the black box that carries your true Self, and as such, it holds the key to your calling, your purpose and talents as a leader, just as it holds the key to the passion, purpose and talents of each and every individual who joins your company. So, to have the knowledge and tools that allow your Unique Being to shine and be projected into the world is the ultimate outcome. That is what the Being Framework brings to the table.

You are carrying this precious gem, the unique YOU. Like a diamond, it is rare and therefore incredibly valuable. You are so scarce that there is and only ever will be one of you. So, if you fail to work on the channels and qualities that enable and empower you to project the manifestation of your Unique Being to the world by polishing and transforming your Aspects of Being, not only will you fail to fulfil your potential, but it will also negatively impact your results. Furthermore, the world will never gain from the benefits that only the real you can deliver. The Being Framework Ontological Model, together with the Being Profile and

Transformation Methodology, hold the key to unlocking that potential. Who knows, maybe you are the one who could sing the song that no one else could or discover the cure for an incurable disease that no one else could. Or perhaps you are the one who could create a business that changes the world. Imagine if people like Steve Jobs, Bill Gates, Mother Teresa, Nelson Mandela, J.K. Rowling and Beethoven had never managed to unleash their Unique Being to the world. Don't let the world miss out on the radical, beautiful, unique YOU.

Paradox of Importance

We can perceive our importance in one of two ways. On the one hand you may subscribe to the view that we come into this world, live for a period of time and turn to dust when we die. Thinking this way could make you assume that, in the grand scheme of things, we don't matter too much. This could lead you to question the point of it all. So, why not be selfish, irresponsible, hedonistic and live a life of pleasure based on the premise that life is short? On the other hand, you could perceive yourself as a node in a network of people and matters in life. This is what I call the Paradox of Importance. Even a leaf dropping from a tree has its scientific, tangible and measurable impact on the universe, so why wouldn't your decisions and actions have an impact? You can cause a ripple effect and expand reality, both for yourself and others. When you invent something innovative or compose a unique piece of music, and so on, you expand on reality (Second-layer Reality). We tend to have a limited view of our impact on the world as we only experience immediate reactions or results. But our influence goes far beyond the first response, making it a lot more important than we account for. For example, in the world of art and music, some works are most revered many years after they were created, in some cases after the death of the creator. In a coaching scenario, it is not uncommon to see no or very little change in the behaviour, performance and *effectiveness* of a person being coached for several weeks or even months. This can lead some coaches, especially those new to it, to feel disheartened, as though the lack of immediate results reflects badly on them. Growth begins with the sowing of seeds. It takes time and consistent effort before the fruits of our labour appear.

A common practice I undertake when I am building a high-performing team, whether it be for a client or in our own company, is to play a game designed to highlight each person's importance to the team. I take a strip of duct tape and attach a number of strings to it, whereby each string represents one team member. So, if there are six team members, I attach six strings to the duct tape. Then I place a ping pong ball on the duct tape and ask each team member to imagine the ball is a chunk of uranium and highly explosive if dropped. The team's mission is to carry the duct tape holding the ball across the room and gently release the ball into a bowl placed in a corner of the room. Once the team begins the exercise, they quickly work out the best strategies to fulfil the mission, the best one being for everyone to pull the duct tape with equal force to ensure the ball stays in place. If one of them fails to do what is required, the ball is likely to be dropped. This mission represents the importance of every individual member of a team and aligns with the Paradox of Importance I just talked about. When one person 'drops the ball' (underperforms) for whatever reason, it affects every member of the team. As a result, the mission may not be accomplished.

While some would consider it an intangible asset from an accounting perspective, my team and I came to the conclusion, following our research and studies, that people – the collective Unique Beings, Aspects of Being, experience, knowledge, skills, etc., of all the people in a business – are the most important asset of all. The culture within your organisation and how committed your people are to polishing their Aspects of Being as individuals will determine the kinds of strategies they come up with as a team and the decisions they make at all levels: executive, strategic, tactical and operational. This ultimately reflects on their performance, *effectiveness* and productivity, which in turn reflects on the company's profitability and bottom line and increases the level of joy, contentment and satisfaction they experience as individuals in the workplace, qualities that flow on to your clients.

Essence, Being and Aspects of Being

Martin Heidegger used the word, *Wesen* (Essence) often in his writings[32]. In fact, it was one of his key words, like *Sein* (to be), *Dasein*

---

32   *Journal of the British Society for Phenomenology*, Vol 19, No.1.

(being-there) and *Mitsein* (being-with). Mulla Sadra used the word *Maahiyat* (quiddity) to refer to almost exactly the same thing. Like their English translation, the German word, *Wesen*, and its Persian equivalent, *Maahiyat*, are so enigmatic that many (perhaps most) people don't understand what they mean. Essence (Being) is a word that is so mysterious, that, in my view, the transcendent Meaning it is referring to has become almost unintelligible. Heidegger referred to a number of other words derived from *Wesen* in his writings; some were actual words, others were constructed: words like *Wesenhaft*, *Wesentlich*, *Wesensbestimmung*, *Wesensstruktur* and many others. In fact, his fondness of crafting words created a new term: 'Heideggerian terminology'. The point I am making here is how easy it is to overcomplicate things. *Wesen* (Essence) is closely linked to *Sein* (to be) but it's not exactly the same. Your Unique Being is the part of you in which you carry a piece of Existence, like the birds in the story of Simorgh, while your Essence represents the qualities that enable you to convey your Unique Being to the world. Confused? Let me explain what Being and Unique Being are in the simplest possible way.

Unique Being is WHO you are – let's call it 'who-ness' – while Being is WHAT you are in terms of your make-up relative to others – let's call it 'what-ness'. Technically speaking, Being is 'quiddity': the inherent Nature or Essence of someone or something which constitutes its common distinctive features and qualities. The Latin root of the word quiddity is *Quid*, which literally means 'what', therefore Being is what and how you ARE in the world (your 'what-ness'). However, as we are far more than just the sum of our qualities or what we are as human beings, I more commonly use the phrase, 'how you are being' as to me this depicts a more accurate picture. It is the unique attributes and qualities that a species (e.g. human being) shares with others of its kind. To make our Being more tangible and usable in the real world, I broke down the Being or Essence of human beings into smaller, digestible, readily understood and relatable qualities which I call 'Aspects of Being' in this framework.

Each of us is an instance of the Class: Human Being, meaning we are corresponding in character and type. We are designed to be born with two legs, two arms, two eyes, one heart, and so on. We also share the same Essence, Being or Aspects of Being, most of which are primal to all human beings. When I introduce you to the Being Framework Ontological Model, you will learn that it models the Essence of human beings by breaking down the Class: Human Being into certain qualities and characteristics, most of which are not only primal to each and every one of us but also studiable, measurable and changeable. Many are also observable. You can polish your Being (Aspects of Being) and in so doing, unleash the potential within by tapping into your Unique Being, as discussed in the previous section. This means you are not hardwired to remain as you are right now. You can transform.

Like humans, roses share certain qualities and characteristics. Every rose has stamen, a pistil, style, anthers, filaments, petals, and so on. Now, you may create an artificial rose that looks identical to the real thing. But something would be missing: the part of Existence that particular flower is carrying within, making it a rose, not a daisy or a handcrafted item that resembles a rose. In the context of this book, I refer to the Unique Being as your primal inclination and gift: the mysterious uniqueness of you as an individual who carries a piece of Existence within, like the birds in the story of Simorgh. While your Being (Aspects of Being) is measurable, I did not find the Unique Being that lies within you as being measurable during my studies, which is probably because that mysterious entity is part of Existence itself. Our Aspects of Being are like the attributes of a rose. These attributes, which are as primal to human beings as the attributes of a rose are to that species, are the qualities we can work on in order to become more authentic, responsible, free, courageous, compassionate, and so on.

Once a person starts polishing or transforming their Being – or Aspects of Being to be exact – they remove the blockages that are preventing them from expressing their true Self (Unique Being) to the world. Let me make it more tangible in a business and leadership context. If you are not truly responsible as a leader and you don't honour your relatively high level of autonomy, you may not make choices aligned with who you really are and would likely only manage to get jobs done out of a sense of obligation rather than with grace. As a result, you may end up letting circumstances drive your organisation into becoming something you never intended it to be. Similarly, if you fail to act on the problems that arise in your company, carrying a sense of guilt and letting issues pile up instead; if you keep blaming the market, competitors, employees, the economy, etc., for the shortcomings in your business, it will eventually lead to its demise. If you have ever been through the liquidation process, you will know exactly what I am talking about. I have worked in and with companies that have experienced the very worst in business: collapse, bankruptcy, people losing their jobs and families being torn apart. On a bigger scale, if federal government leaders fail to exercise a high degree of *responsibility*, the suffering is felt nationally. First to feel the impact is the nation's GDP[33], then the budget deficit will rise, placing the country in even more debt. Then purchasing power is impacted, which in turn leads to the value of the currency plummeting and the job market being impacted. Can you see the domino effect here?

> *For want of a nail the shoe was lost,*
> *for want of a shoe the horse was lost,*
> *for want of a horse the knight was lost,*
> *for want of a knight the battle was lost,*
> *for want of a battle the kingdom was lost.*
> *So, a kingdom was lost – all for want of a nail.*
>
> The Nail. LA: DC Comics, 1998[34]

If you look into thriving economies, you can trace their success back to how responsible the leaders and workforce are collectively being in those economies. *Responsibility* is just one example of an Aspect of Being relating to the Class: Human Being. The same is relevant when it comes to all the other Aspects of Being that my team and I identified as those that have a huge impact on our performance and *effectiveness* in business.

In summary

We covered a great deal in this chapter. And for many of you, the material may have been unfamiliar. I acknowledged the confusion that exists around various philosophical terms and meanings, even amongst

---

33 GDP: Gross Domestic Product is a monetary measure of the market value of all the final goods and services produced in a specific time period.

34 This proverb is found in a number of forms, beginning as early as the 13th century.

the world's greatest thinkers and scholars, most notably around the concepts of Being and Existence. I hope that after reading this chapter you have gained clarity around the distinction. Let's just acknowledge and accept that we exist; we are out there in the world, or, as Martin Heidegger said, we are 'thrown into this world'[35]. So, while Existence may not have a clear and tangible context, our Being has both a very clear context and boundaries. Like any other project or game we engage in, the game of life also has a series of rules (Meanings). As a matter of fact, the rules help make the game more enjoyable and rewarding. As the rules become clearer to us in our journey of *awareness*, we can move towards a degree of *effectiveness* and ultimately mastery in the way we play the game.

Existence is the Ultimate Reality. This very fact encourages us to know there are truths, laws and transcending Meanings, and that at least parts of Reality can be studied using objective methods. We learnt that if we do not choose to acknowledge Existence as the Ultimate Reality, it doesn't make sense to go through any discovery process. Let's agree on this protocol here and now. We also learnt that Possibility of Existence refers to our experience of life, the state of 'being there'. By Possibility of Existence we are saying that your existence is a gift to yourself and all beings so that you can choose to make the most of every possibility.

When I refer to your Unique Being, I am referring to the unique YOU, who you are: your 'who-ness', your Spirit, Soul, the black box or Self, the part of you that can guide you to receive and respond to your calling. It is the piece of Existence you carry with you for life, which you can consciously choose to tap into and express to the world. However, this can only be achieved if you work on the other side of your Being: your 'what-ness', Essence or how you are being. This is you as an instance of the Class: Human Being, the qualities (Aspects of Being) you have in common with others. These are the qualities that can be polished and transformed, including *authenticity, commitment, love, empowerment, courage* and *responsibility*, to name just a few.

---

35 From the book, *Being and Time* (German: *Sein und Zeit*) which is a 1927 book written by German philosopher Martin Heidegger, in which the author seeks to analyse the concept of Being.

Later we will dive deeply into the Ontological Model layer of the Being Framework and explore those Aspects of Being in detail. But first, we will examine the subject of discovery versus invention in order to understand and appreciate the foundation of Reality on which the Being Framework is based.

CHAPTER 3

Discovery vs Invention

When the mind's eye rests on objects illuminated by truth and reality, it understands and comprehends them, and functions intelligently; but when it turns to the twilight world of change and decay, it can only form opinions, its vision is confused and its beliefs shifting, and it seems to lack intelligence.

The Republic, Plato
Greek philosopher, ca. 423–347 BC

The above excerpt from *The Republic* by Greek philosopher, Plato, highlights a simple truth. We can only function intelligently and operate as effective human beings when our conception of the world is congruent with Reality. That's why this book is founded on discovery, not invention, constructs or subjective matter that is open to interpretation. It's not about coming up with a new theory, nor is it about turning to 'the twilight world' of inventions and misleading, fabricated information. It is also not my intention to categorise people, as is the common objective of many of today's generic personality assessments and pseudo-scientific practices.

The Being Framework reflects the Reality of human beings in an ontological sense as widely understood to be a valid way of discovery by philosophers such as Martin Heidegger and Mulla Sadra and psychoanalysts such as Carl G. Jung[36]. Ontology is part of the major branch

---

36   Carl Gustav Jung (1875-1961) Swiss psychiatrist and psychoanalyst.

of philosophy known as metaphysics[37]. In simple terms, it is the philosophical study of the nature of Being, becoming, existence or Reality. An example of ontology in practice is when the attributes and qualities of existing entities are studied and discovered through objective methods that enable us to better understand and apply them in the broader world and in our own lives. Ontology and ontological modelling are explored in more detail in the next chapter.

While I don't wish to dwell on complex ideas, it is crucial to appreciate the foundation of Reality on which the Being Framework is based in order to understand the framework presented in this book. Why is philosophy relevant to us as human beings today? The answer becomes clearer when you appreciate that the origin of the word 'philosophy' comes from the Greek word, *Philosophia*, which means 'love of wisdom'. To gain wisdom and practical knowledge, philosophers are on a constant quest of learning and inquiring into the truth. Since the time of Plato, philosophers have used various methods, such as questioning and debating, in order to attain the knowledge and truth they sought. They were on a journey of discovery based on an understanding that transcendent Meanings exist.

Habitual ways of thinking and paradigms

We are born into a culture with a pre-existing language, set of values, and accepted codes of conduct, behavioural patterns and paradigms of thinking. Unless we are encouraged to question those pre-existing paradigms or develop an inner desire to do so, we tend to accept that this is just the way things are. For instance, we often use words without thinking because we know what they mean, or at least we think we do. Let me explain.

As we learnt earlier, words and definitions are the creation of human beings. They were created purely to make sense of actual Meanings and facilitate communication. It is for this reason that the early philosophers didn't take words at face value. They focused on the Meaning, which is like the deepest layer beneath or foundation of the word that attempts

---

37   Metaphysics is the branch of philosophy that examines the fundamental nature of reality, including the relationship between mind and matter, between substance and attribute, and between potentiality and actuality.

to define it. So, by their very nature, words have the potential to deviate from the Meaning, which can make communication challenging.

In this context, I want to highlight the distinction between the Meaning referred to by the word 'discovery', a fact based on truth, and 'invention', a made-up or fabricated piece of information wrongly presented as a fact with no truth behind it. This distinction is central to the Being Framework. The word 'discovery' will be used multiple times throughout this book, so it is important that it is understood in line with its philosophical and original Meaning: finding the truth of something which already existed, which is in direct contrast to the meaning of the word 'invention': to make things up. In the narrowest sense, the word 'discovery' refers to the purported eureka moment – the moment of *awareness* – when a new meaningful insight into the laws of the universe is made[38].

In our current time and culture, it seems to be quite common for people to downgrade or ignore facts and replace them with personal preferences, unvalidated perceptions or opinions. There can be many reasons for this. Some simply don't know any better. Others believe that a personal opinion is reflective of the truth or Reality and is open to debate or negotiation. And then there are those who accept a statement that is declared a fact without questioning it. This makes it difficult to distinguish an opinion from a fact.

Let's say an engineer has been engaged to build a bridge over a body of water. Their work must first and foremost be based on discoveries, in this case, the laws of physics and engineering. Without that crucial foundation, the bridge is at risk of crashing into the sea once the first vehicle attempts to cross it. Our opinion on this is irrelevant. It is a fact that must be acknowledged and accepted.

I once heard a very well-known celebrity say, during an address before a massive audience, 'Speaking your truth is the most powerful tool you have', which resulted in clapping and cheering. I would like to think that when she said, 'Speaking your truth', she was inviting each member of

---

38 'Scientific Discovery', *Stanford Encyclopedia of Philosophy*. [Online edition.] Stanford, CA: Stanford University, 2018.

the audience to be authentic, honest and vulnerable. Increasingly many speak of 'my truth', or 'that is true for me' as though truth is just a matter of opinion, preference or choice! While you can have your experience, interpretation, perspective or perception of something, your truth/reality (Third-layer Reality) is not the same as the truth/Reality (First-layer Reality). Holding this belief causes people to assume, 'If your truth is not similar to my truth, then you must be wrong', or, 'If the truth held by my group identity is not the same as the truth held by your group identity, then you must all be wrong'. This is in fact a form of narcissism and intellectual bullying.

Let's take a closer look at this. When any subject is studied, whether it be by a single person or a group, its truth is to be discovered. We can all agree on that. Every individual or the group studying the subject sees it from a different perspective with the sincere intention of discovering the truth. When everyone is open-minded enough to see the subject from all possible perspectives/angles, this well-rounded, 360-degree view is defined as truth seeking, which leads to discovery of the truth. Without a 360-degree view, individuals or groups may be tempted to focus solely on their own perspective and become obsessed with being right. This is not the way to discover the truth. To simply say whatever you like and infer that it is your truth is not only dangerous but downright wrong. My point here is that truth or Reality cannot be relative. If it were relative, then it would contradict the very notion of truth. Reality is inescapable. The same applies when people talk about logic. They will say, 'My logic is …'. In reality, they must be referring to their thought process, not logic, because logic is a systematic study and application of reasoning. It is not that hard to formally tell if someone is using logical fallacies in an argument or misusing logic and reasoning, something that many in the media and politicians are either totally ignorant about or knowingly do simply to carry out their agendas. Unfortunately, while you hear many using the term, 'It's not logical', we do not formally study logic or logical fallacies[39] and logic is not something you are born with. It would seem truth, Reality and logic are doing it tough these days!

---

39   A fallacy is reasoning that is evaluated as logically incorrect and that undermines the logical validity of the argument and permits its recognition as unsound. Regardless of their soundness, all registers and manners of speech can demonstrate fallacies.

Fear is another good example. When a person or an animal experiences fear, the brain's limbic system is stimulated and causes the body to react in certain ways. This response can be measured in the brain and in the hormone levels released into the blood. So, fear is not something that is made up. It is real. Similarly, the law of gravity cannot and should not be negotiated. So, why would it be any different with our Aspects of Being?

So, in order to determine what makes us effective in various aspects of life, or what many would call 'successful', we must base our learning on what we know to be true in accordance with Reality. It is no different to the need to follow the laws of physics and engineering when building a bridge or the law of gravity when designing an aircraft. I have therefore made every effort for the Being Framework to describe and apply what has been systematically studied and analysed according to philosophical traditions, including, but not limited to, ontological modelling.

Philosophers vs sophists

Let's delve a little deeper into the difference between discovery and invention by examining the history of two opposing schools of thought and practices that helped shape and influence the way we see/know ourselves and the world we live in today – philosophy and sophistry.

Whether or not we have studied philosophy, we have all been influenced by philosophical thinkers. For example, philosophers like Michel Foucault[40] and Jacques Derrida[41] had an enormous influence on today's popular cultural norms and ways of thinking. We may just not be aware of it.

Let's begin with the philosophers of ancient Greece during the 4th and 5th centuries BC. It was the beginning of Western philosophy, a time when two of the most revered and respected philosophers of all time,

---

40   Paul-Michel Foucault (1926-1984), also known as Michel Foucault, French philosopher, historian of ideas, social theorist and literary critic, best known for his theories of the relationship between power and knowledge, and how they are used as a form of social control through societal institutions.

41   Jacques Derrida (1930-2004) French philosopher, best known for his post-structuralism and postmodern philosophy.

Socrates[42] and Plato[43], came to the conclusion, through their work, that there are absolutes, truths or laws in life that apply to this universe and all beings in it, including human beings. Those early philosophers were on a journey of discovering these laws, truths or Meanings. Their mission was taken further by many other philosophers, scientists, thinkers and those who pursued the study of Hekmat[44]; we could call them all 'truth seekers'. Their work laid the groundwork for what we know today as knowledge and wisdom. And we have science to thank for the many incredible advances that have been made in various disciplines of study, including the field of medicine. We have studied the body and know how it works. We know that if we wish to maintain a healthy body there are certain rules we must follow. These are not guidelines or subjective perceptions; they are facts based on conclusive evidence.

On the flip side, we had the sophists. Dating back to the time of Socrates and Plato, the sophists were teachers who practised their craft in the political arena and held a belief that they could come up with their own fabricated paradigms, perceptions, ideas or hypotheses, even if they were totally incongruent with Reality. They were significant pseudo-intellectual public figures of the time with refined rhetorical skills. They used rhetoric to manipulate the truth and persuade others. Arguing that humans are the measure of all things, the sophists were sceptical about the existence of the truth and the truth of Existence and all in it. They taught a variety of subjects, including mathematics, grammar, physics, political philosophy, history, music and astronomy, and their crafty rhetoric made them come across as wise and their teachings as legitimate.

The term 'sophist' means 'wise person' and is the term from which the word 'sophisticated' is derived. The sophists in history were masterful in

---

42   Socrates (ca. 470-399 BC) Ancient Greek philosopher, founder of Western philosophy.

43   Plato (ca. 423-347 BC) Ancient Greek philosopher.

44   Mulla Sadra defined hikmah (or hekmat) as 'coming to know the essence of beings as they really are', or as 'a man's becoming an intellectual world corresponding to the objective world' – "Mulla Sadra (Sadr al-Din Muhammad al-Shirazi) (1571/2-1640)". In Craig, Edward (ed.). *Routledge Encyclopedia of Philosophy*. 6. London; New York: Routledge. pp. 595–599. via Islamic Philosophy Online.

the art of debate and persuasion. Their mission was in direct contrast to the mission of the philosophers. It was not to seek the truth, acquire true knowledge or raise *awareness*, but to win arguments. In today's application, the term 'sophistry' is generally used to refer to manipulative forms of rhetoric, a method of misusing language to prove to another whatever one wishes to demonstrate. The expression 'leading someone along the garden path' also refers to this method of persuasion.

While the philosophers, Socrates and Plato, pursued a line of intuitive and rational thought intended to discover the truth, the sophists of that time held no values other than to win a debate for their own or someone else's benefit, commonly in the name of their profession, meaning they were paid to do so! They believed the use of clever but false arguments, with the intention of deception, was an art that could legitimately be used to pursue one's own goals. The excuse of not having access to the truth has since widely been used by many thinkers, who believe there is no right or wrong; if we can't access the truth, let's fabricate a construct! They are well versed in misusing the tools of philosophy and rhetoric to fake any construct they wish to convey, as long as it suits their objective. This stands in direct conflict with the ideals of Socrates, who chose to die rather than succumb to a non-truth. He made the ultimate sacrifice, all in the name of the truth.

Today we can observe the sophist's manipulative form of communication in many areas of society, perhaps none more so than in the media and the political arena, especially around election time. This commonly leads to attempts to manufacture consent to pass a law or persuade the public to agree to something, such as when lobbying for key changes, potentially leading to a state of collective psychosis. 'Manufacturing consent'[45] is a form of rhetoric that stands in direct contrast to education, which leads to the acquisition of knowledge and wisdom. It is when some, like commercial advertisers, bankers and politicians, attempt to manipulate others and manufacture consent as opposed to educating and empowering them with true knowledge and *awareness*. I am not suggesting that all politicians are corrupt or manipulative. But we all know that the skill of a speechmaker or debater in the lead-up to

---

45   This term is derived from *The Political Economy of the Mass Media*, by Edward S. Herman and Noam Chomsky, 1988.

an election is often fundamental to winning an audience and ultimately an election. Commonly this involves an element of massaging the truth. To put all of this into context, the philosophers discovered while the sophists were masters of invention.

Imagination, invention and the laws of Existence

As human beings, we have the unique ability to use our imagination. While this is a blessing in many ways, it can also be a curse because we can easily be enticed to create our own imaginary layers of reality. We can come up with our own constructs, but they will only succeed if they are congruent with Reality, transcendent Meanings and the laws of Existence. For example, gravity is a law. However, it was not invented by renowned physicist, Isaac Newton[46]; it was discovered by him. When the Wright brothers dreamt of inventing the first aeroplane, they had to acknowledge the laws of physics and develop aeroplanes that were congruent with these laws; otherwise the machines they imagined would never have left the ground. So, while there is nothing intrinsically wrong with developing constructs, such as conventions or theories, we must not lose sight of the fact that they are inventions (Second-layer Reality), not laws of Existence that have been discovered (First-layer Reality). We should not give them too much credit. Instead, we should be open to changing our perceptions when we are presented with discoveries.

Why is it so important to understand the distinction between the discovery of truth/Reality and invention? The simple answer is that any time we attempt to ignore or bypass the laws of Existence, we pay for it. In other words, you can't twist the fabric of Reality without it flipping back in your face! For example, if you manipulate the truth with a client who is violating the law of *authenticity* in order to push a hidden agenda, there may be a short-term benefit, but in the long term it simply won't hold up. Too many businesses and corporations have gone down this track to varying degrees and the lies and manipulations that eventually surfaced have had severe implications. In today's business landscape, trust is often misused. As a result, people have become more wary around the issue of trust.

---

46 *Philosophiæ Naturalis Principia Mathematica (Mathematical Principles of Natural Philosophy)*, published in 1687 by Isaac Newton.

The Royal Commission into Misconduct in the Australian Banking, Superannuation and Financial Services Industry[47] between 2017 and 2019 was a classic example of what can happen when *commitment* and *authenticity* are not upheld. Another well-known example is the class action against US chemical giant Monsanto[48] over claims that their commonly used herbicide, Roundup, causes cancer. In 2018, a San Francisco jury issued a $289 million verdict in damages to cancer patients in the first trial against Monsanto, with thousands more currently awaiting trial. It has therefore been proven in a court of law that Monsanto misled consumers by suggesting Roundup's active ingredient doesn't pose a health risk to humans. This is a consequence of acting without *commitment*. The same holds true when it comes to our personal lives. When trust breaks down in a relationship, it can often be traced back to inauthentic behaviour and/or lack of *commitment*. So, if we want to reduce suffering or solve a problem, the first logical step is not to be part of the problem by creating more man-made constructs with the intention of covering up the truth.

The Being Framework includes qualities that are not based on any theories or hypotheses, including personality theory. We will discuss qualities that are so primal to human beings that some may consider them common sense. Ultimately, this book is founded on the Reality of what it means to be human, and particularly an effective human being, a high performer, a leader of influence. The intention of this chapter was not to walk you through the history of Western philosophy, but to give you an overall perspective of where the Being Framework is positioned in the context of discovering truth and Meanings as opposed to invention or fabrication. I encourage you to continue reading with an open and analytical mind and an open heart.

---

[47] The Royal Commission was established 14 December 2017 by the Governor-General of the Commonwealth of Australia, His Excellency General Sir Peter Cosgrove AK MC (Retd).

[48] *The Guardian* (11/08/2018), 'Monsanto ordered to pay $289m as jury rules weedkiller caused man's cancer'.

CHAPTER 4

The Ontological Model – A holistic approach to modelling the Reality of human beings

Truth is ever to be found in simplicity, and not in the multiplicity and confusion of things.

Isaac Newton
English mathematician, physicist and theologian, 1643–1727

People often ask me how I conducted my research and how I came up with the Ontological Model layer of the Being Framework. As explained in the previous chapter, my intention was to discover the Reality of human beings. So, I made a conscious decision when starting this journey to leverage ontology[49], a field of philosophy that studies the nature of Reality – what is real and what is not, what exists and what does not – in order to articulate the knowledge and model the Reality of human beings.

When I refer to the phrase, 'Reality of human beings', I do so in the context of performance, leadership and *effectiveness*. My aim was to get to the bottom of the factors underlying people's performance,

---

49   While the etymology of the word 'ontology' is Greek, the oldest existing record of the word itself, the New Latin form *Ontologia*, appeared in 1606 in the work, *Ogdoas Scholastica* by Jacob Lorhard (Lorhardus) and in 1613 in the *Lexicon Philosophicum* by Rudolf Göckel (Goclenius). The first occurrence in English of ontology, as recorded by the *Oxford English Dictionary*, online edition, 2008 appeared in *Archeologia Philosophica Nova* (*New Principles of Philosophy*), by Gideon Harvey, 1663.

effectiveness and fulfilment. And with that I mean performance in a general way, not limited to the professional world, such as the way we set KPIs[50] for staff. I am referring to the way we engage in work, participate in projects, contribute to society, participate in relationships, and so on. Furthermore, by tapping into ontology, I have endeavoured to formulate and articulate these studies in such a way that ensures they can be understood and used by almost anyone, not just philosophers or psychologists!

In discovering the Reality of human beings and our relationship with *awareness*, *integrity* and *effectiveness*, I have shaped my research accomplishments in the form of reusable and extendable knowledge, through an ontological model[51], focused on the qualities that drive performance and cause *effectiveness*. While many reading this book may be unfamiliar with ontology, let me bring it home for you using a couple of simple analogies. Believe it or not, all of us deal with ontology on a daily basis in some form. When you open the fridge to check if you have milk for your morning coffee, you are tapping into ontology. Your goal is to see if milk exists (in your fridge), or doesn't exist. The answer can only be yes or no. At a meta level, the fact that milk exists in the greater scheme of things is irrefutable. If someone were to ask you if milk exists, the answer is, yes it does. The same is true if you were asked if tomatoes or apples exist. Of course they do! They may not exist in your fridge, but they do exist in the universe. When you go for a blood test to determine if your vitamin D levels or other blood markers are at the level required for optimal health, they either are or they are not. These examples are reality checks and not based on opinions. Opinions won't get you far if you want to increase your health, or make a latte without milk for that matter! You need feedback based on Reality.

Like the examples above, the Being Framework examines the extent to which an individual has a healthy relationship with their Aspects

---

50   KPI (Key Performance Indicator) evaluates the success of an individual or an organisation or of a particular activity in which it engages.

51   An ontology (ontological model) is a formal, explicit specification of a shared conceptualisation that is characterised by high semantic expressiveness required for increased complexity (*An Analysis of Ontologies and their Success Factors for Application to Business*, Christina Feilmayr and Wolfram Wöß, January 2016).

of Being. For example, are you being responsible in the face of what happens in your life? Or are you a victim of circumstances? In other words, are you honouring your relatively high level of autonomy or are you allowing events and circumstances to dictate your path? Is a person you are hiring being authentic or do they have a hidden agenda? Obviously, identifying these Aspects of Being is not as straightforward as checking the fridge for milk or pondering the existence of the tomato. But imagine if you had a way of identifying the Reality of Aspects of Being in order to create more predictable outcomes. This is what motivated me to develop the Being Framework and guide you in your conception of the paradigm and model as you continue studying the content of this book. How this model works will be explained in more detail later. For now, I would like to lay some more of the groundwork to give you a better understanding of how the model came to be and why you should trust it.

Ontology and epistemology

While I have no intention of diving too deeply into abstract philosophical discussions, it is worthwhile walking you through some of the key philosophical questions in life; questions like, how can one arrive at the point of knowing something? And how does one determine what is real and what is not? There are various disciplines and approaches to help us address those key philosophical questions. Two of those are ontology (what is real and what is not) and epistemology (how we come to know that reality and understand that knowledge). In combination, ontology and epistemology help establish a research paradigm. This leads us to develop the paradigm/framework itself, which ultimately can result in a paradigm shift.

As discussed earlier, when it comes to ontology – what is real and what is not – we create models to represent and map the part of Reality we are discovering. This is called an ontological model. Let's now examine the definition of an ontological model and delve a little deeper into the meaning of epistemology before evaluating the high-level relationship between the two.

An ontological model is a receptacle for knowledge, much like a glass is a container into which we can pour water. Ontological models are one of the most effective ways of forming and communicating knowledge in academia and business. I chose ontological modelling because it brings all parties on the same page in terms of the format of that knowledge. They achieve that objective very effectively. We will discuss how ontological models are created in the next sub-chapter.

Epistemology[52] is the branch of philosophy that examines the nature and origin of knowledge or ways of knowing. This discipline examines the validity of the acquisition and presentation of knowledge and the scepticism surrounding various knowledge claims. Epistemology poses questions like: What is knowledge? How can knowledge be acquired? What are the essential conditions and limitations of knowledge or a way of knowing? And what structure does knowledge have? In other words, how do we come to understand something? In developing the Being Framework, the question that needed to be addressed was: how do we come to understand human beings? While these are topics the average person wouldn't typically investigate, it is important to touch on them in order to give you a high-level overview of the foundation on which the Being Framework is built, as this will allow you to gain the greatest benefit from studying this book.

Why is understanding how we come to know something so important? The answer is simple: we are studying the Reality of human beings and are here to become aware because we cannot be consciously effective in matters we are not aware of. Too many people today take information on board without investigating or understanding the origin of the information or questioning whether or not it is even grounded in Reality. They lack curiosity and don't care about the basis on which they accept or reject information. There can be many reasons for this, from complacency to simply being too busy to launch into an investigation each time they are presented with new information. Whatever the reason, when people accept or reject new information at face value, their decision comes at a cost. Let me explain why. In order to communicate knowledge, parties must agree on the 'way of knowing', just as they need to be on the same page in terms of the format of that knowledge (e.g. with an ontological model) before they can effectively communicate what

---

52 The branch of philosophy concerned with the nature and origin of knowledge. Epistemology asks the question: how do we know what we know?

they know. What is meant by 'way of knowing'? Essentially, we all tend to have a preferred way of acquiring knowledge and understanding about the world around us. Some prefer reasoning and logic, critical thinking, and/or science, while others prefer language, faith or intuition, to name just a few examples. So, while ontology examines what is real and what is not, epistemology examines how we can understand that Reality, Meaning or knowledge. In combination, ontology and epistemology helped establish my research paradigm for the Being Framework. Why am I sharing this with you? It is no different to an academic needing to make their research paradigm clear to demonstrate credibility of their study and findings. Providing you with the background to my research not only creates transparency and credibility around this study, but it will also give you a deeper understanding of the Being Framework.

Let's return to ontology for a moment. There are a number of ontological approaches or viewpoints that can be adopted. I will just touch on the three most common:

1. The viewpoint that there is only one Reality or truth.
2. The viewpoint that there are multiple realities.
3. The viewpoint that reality is constantly negotiated, debated or interpreted.

A dilemma emerges when you have three fundamentally different viewpoints. My intention is not to debate or justify one over the other. These viewpoints are so fundamental to the core that it is up to each and every individual to decide where they stand regarding the nature of each research project. As discussed in *Chapter 3: Discovery vs Invention*, I subscribe to the first viewpoint, namely that there is only one Reality or truth, at least when it comes to human beings' Nature or Essence. We will explore ontology further in the next sub-chapter, *Shaping an Ontological Model*. Again, this by no means implies that we cannot create concepts, theories, constructs or inventions; of course we can! We are imaginative, creative beings with the cognitive ability to ensure our inventions work. However, to ensure our inventions work in the most effective way possible, they must be congruent with Reality. If they are not congruent with Reality, we must at least be open to refining them.

Let's return our focus to epistemology. As discussed, epistemology is the study of how we, as individuals and collectively, come to know or understand knowledge. In other words, epistemology examines how we perceive our own thought processes and how we think others come to understand or make sense of things, ultimately leading us from subjective perception to conception and finally to wisdom. This is extremely important in terms of how we communicate with others because it sets the foundation of our understanding. If this foundation differs between two people, it makes communication difficult or even impossible.

As is the case with ontology, there are a number of approaches or viewpoints that can be adopted when it comes to epistemology. Again, I will just touch on the three most common approaches:

1. The viewpoint that knowledge can be measured using reliable frameworks and tools.
2. The viewpoint that reality must be interpreted to discover the underlying meaning.
3. The viewpoint that knowledge should be examined using whatever tools are best suited to solve a particular problem.

Combining the ontological and epistemological approaches described above results in the following three most commonly used research paradigms, particularly in the human sciences:

1. Ontology: one single Reality/truth, and epistemology: knowledge can be measured[53].
2. Ontology: multiple realities, and epistemology: knowledge must be interpreted to discover the underlying Meaning[54].
3. Ontology: reality must be constantly debated and negotiated, and epistemology: use any tools suited to solve the problem[55].

The approach I adopted for creating the Being Framework Ontological Model was the first one. Why? Because it deals with primal qualities of human beings. My intention was to come up with a means to shift human performance and *effectiveness* and produce leaders. So, I was

---

[53] Referred to as Positivism.
[54] Referred to as Constructivism.
[55] Referred to as Pragmatism.

left with no other option but to engineer it this way. If we compare this to medical research, or more specifically, to the search for a cure for a particular disease, science works under the premise that there is a Reality about the disease that can be discovered. Understanding the Reality of the disease in question will allow researchers and scientists to develop a cure based on the way the disease interacts with the human body. Now, unfortunately when it comes to human sciences, we are far more lenient, especially in the current century. This is the case with some academics too, despite the fact that their objective should always be to seek the truth, not invent fabricated constructs.

Reality and knowledge are crucial aspects of the Being Framework in the context of performance, *effectiveness* and leadership. However, as human beings, we tend to view information through the filters of personal perspective, our own narrative lens, web of perceptions and based on our experiences, our environment and what we see and hear through the media. Topics like narrative lens and web of perceptions will be explored in detail in the Awareness chapter. When we view the world through a filter, we have a tendency to make up stories, often delaying or preventing our access to Reality or what is really going on, and that comes at a cost. Sometimes our distorted interpretations and self-created, self-serving and cherry-picked stories appear so real to us that they control our Moods and emotions, often leading to decisions and actions founded on inauthentic beliefs and opinions rather than fact and Reality. This is typically a valuable entry point for coaches and other mentoring experts, who have the proficiency to guide the people they work with to discover the reality of a situation. By understanding the reality of events, we have the opportunity to influence the situation in our favour and become more effective.

Phenomenology

'Phenomenology is the study of structures of consciousness as experienced from the first-person point of view. The central structure of an experience is its intentionality, its Being directed toward something, as it is an experience of or about some object[56].'

---

56   Smith, David Woodruff, 'Phenomenology', *The Stanford Encyclopedia of Philosophy* (Summer 2018 Edition), Edward N. Zalta (ed.).

While ontology is concerned with the nature of Being or Reality and epistemology examines the nature and origin of knowledge, phenomenology is the study of experience. More specifically, it is the philosophical study of how things appear to be in the eye of the beholder, not necessarily how things actually are. In other words, no matter what is happening in Reality, individuals may experience or interpret it differently. Our interpretation influences how we define ourselves, both for our own Self and for others. We create a persona, a made-up identity, and this influences how we react to situations and, in turn, the results we produce. Some would argue that most people act in accordance with who they define themselves to be rather than who they really are the majority of the time. To do so is living an illusion.

An example of a phenomenological illusion is a mirage. Triggered by atmospheric conditions, a mirage can create the illusion of a body of water in the middle of a desert, a phenomenon caused by the refraction of light as it moves through warmer, less dense air. As light refracts downward, it causes the eye to see water-like colours below the horizon, creating the illusion of a body of water, where in reality, there is nothing but hot, dry sand. Or let's say you spot a coiled length of striped rope in the corner of your backyard. As you approach it and reach down to pick it up, you suddenly recoil in fear as you realise that what you thought was a length of rope is in fact a snake! Both examples are no different to our perception of Aspects of Being or Reality. However, phenomenology deals with more than just illusions. For example, the fact that we all collectively experience fear leads us to take fear as a phenomenon. But fear is both a phenomenon and a Reality. We study the Reality of fear in an objective manner through ontology, whereas we study our collective experience of fear as a phenomenon through phenomenology.

Similarly, we can all be deceived by our lack of *awareness* of our own Aspects of Being and how we are perceived by others. This is because the truth sits beyond other people's perception of us and the same is true for our perception of them. For example, you may be under the impression that patience is one of your great virtues, only to learn, through honest feedback from a colleague, that you aren't as patient as you thought you were. But then again, who is to say that your colleague's perception is the truth? Many people subscribe to a 'majority rules' philosophy in life.

But even if the majority of people in the world said the Earth is flat, that doesn't mean it is!

The first step in making sense of the world and becoming aware is to develop self-awareness. *Nosce te ipsum* – know thyself – is a phrase widely attributed to Socrates and echoed by Aristotle. It essentially means that the key to understanding others is to first understand yourself and who's pulling your strings. The ability to get what you want has a lot to do with how you choose to take responsibility for polishing your own Aspects of Being. You either use your mind or you are used by it. None of us came into this world with a fully polished Being or an instruction manual.

Self-understanding and self-development require you to identify the things that distract you and cause you to stray off track. In other words, what's pulling your strings in the moment? This will be discussed further in the Responsibility chapter. It's all part of what it is to be human. We all have things that distract us. Self-awareness is the key to letting go of those distractions so you can get back on track and back to business. Furthermore, as a leader of an organisation, you cannot take any of your people any deeper than you'd be willing to go yourself. Your organisation and its results, including profitability, can easily be limited by your own limitations. That, in part, is why it is so important to polish your Aspects of Being.

Having a false impression of oneself can often lead to undesirable results. Imagine the potential repercussions if an impatient manager was given the responsibility of interviewing job candidates for an important role in the company. In their impatience to get through the interviews, the manager may not take the time to sufficiently explore key aspects of each candidate's Being, or Aspects of Being, to be exact. This could lead to challenges down the track when the wrong candidate is rushed into a role for which they are not suited. Oblivious to their own impatience, the manager is left wondering why the new recruit isn't working out. It's like a blind spot when driving. Just because you can't see the truck doesn't mean it's not there!

The Being Framework will raise your *awareness* about the Reality of your Aspects of Being and extend your understanding of others. Once you begin inquiring into your Being, your *awareness* towards how it relates to the results you achieve in every aspect of your life will grow exponentially. This new *awareness* will lay a strong foundation that, once built upon with the deeper layers of the Being Framework, will ultimately put you in the driver's seat of your life.

CHAPTER 4.1

Shaping an Ontological Model

Now that you know what ontology is and have an understanding of why I chose it to shape my research paradigm for the Being Framework, let's delve a little deeper into ontological models. My aim is not to teach you how to build an ontological model, but to ensure you have a sufficient understanding of the shaping of the Being Framework Ontological Model layer to maximise the benefits you gain from it, for transparency and to give you the level of depth required to confidently have faith in the model.

You will recall that an ontological model is a description of knowledge as a set of entities – in this case, human beings, Ways of Being, Moods and Meta Factors – and the relationships that hold true between them. In line with this description, my team and I needed to create an ontological model of the human being. As you can imagine, a task of this magnitude was no easy feat. But I knew that the potential to turn something traditionally considered intangible into measurable, readily digestible chunks would create a major point of difference from other paradigms, while simultaneously ensuring the Being Framework wasn't focused on philosophy at a purely abstract level. My intention was to break down the complex and make it tangible and comprehensible to ensure business leaders, coaches and mentors could reference it as a framework to help themselves and others. It's like having access to a special type of looking glass that allows you to see through human beings, including yourself and people in your organisation, in a way that nothing else can.

Arranging data and information into structured knowledge

As useful as the various disciplines of philosophy are, ontological modelling enabled me to take things to the next level by applying an objective and scientific method to the framework. As a result, not only does the Ontological Model of human beings introduce a sharable and reusable representation of knowledge, it can also extend to the uncovered knowledge about the domain, which in this case is human beings. Many academic disciplines or research fields choose to use ontological modelling to reduce complexity and structure data into information and knowledge. Ontological models are effective tools that help us improve problem solving within that domain and enable us to answer complex questions and display relationships across the domain.

Each and every day we are all bombarded with massive volumes of data. The problem is, most people don't have the skills or the tools to process the volume and complexity of this data, known as 'big data'[57], much of which is actually about ourselves and other human beings around us, such as our partner, our children, staff, colleagues, venture partners, neighbours, clients and fans. The data we typically gather comes in various formats and is neither readily accessible nor digestible by the average person. It is unstructured and therefore confusing. The beauty of an ontological model is that it provides a means to highlight the entities in a given subject and show how those entities are related by defining a set of concepts and categories that represent the subject. Ontological models express relationships and enable us to link multiple concepts to other concepts in a variety of ways. In short, ontological modelling is a method of modelling a large volume of unstructured data into structured knowledge. My aim with the Being Framework is to give you access to a model that allows you to better understand human beings, including yourself, so that you can make more effective decisions and take more effective actions, leading to your fulfilment.

Every ontological model consists of three main components: Classes, their Attributes (the attributes or qualities of each Class) and the Relationships between the Classes. The Relationship between two Classes, where one is the Subject and another is the Object, form what is known as a 'Triple' (Class 1, Class 2 and their Relationship form a Triple).

---

57   Big data is a term derived from the IT sector and refers to the large, diverse sets of information that grow at ever-increasing rates. It encompasses the volume of information, the velocity or speed at which it is created and collected, and the variety or scope of the data points being covered. Big data has become more significant since technology has made it possible for us to accumulate large volumes of unstructured data from various applications.

SHAPING AN ONTOLOGICAL MODEL

Triples are central to ontological models. Triples that form part of an overarching ontology can be merged to provide a comprehensive view of the real world within that ontology. This approach was used by many philosophers and scientists in the past, although it may not have been called an ontological model back then. Today, this approach is used in many fields, including computer science, cognitive technologies and cognitive science, amongst others. There are even standard languages (RDF[58] and OWL[59]) to visualise and articulate ontological models.

Let's examine a relatable example that demonstrates how Triples work in an ontological model. Refer to *Figure 2: A Triple consists of Subject Class, Object Class and Relationship (Predicate)* as you read through the example.

Example: a person is employed by an organisation.

In *Figure 2* below, 'Person' equates to the Subject Class, 'Organisation' equates to the Object Class and 'Has Employer' defines the Relationship between the two Classes.

This is a way of representing and visualising how things ARE in the real world. We are simply modelling them.

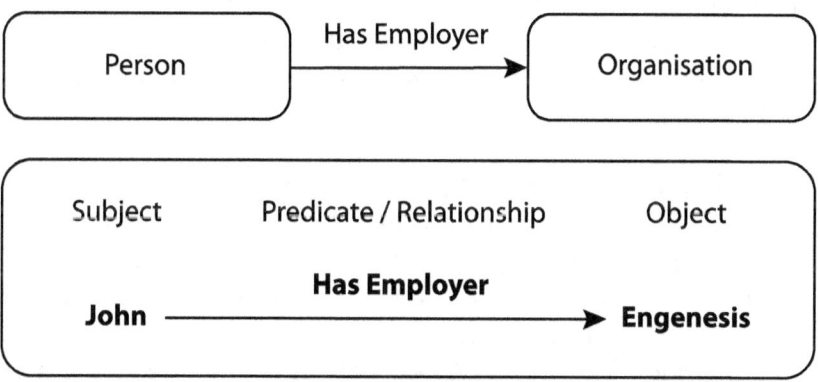

Figure 2: A Triple consists of Subject Class, Object Class and Relationship (Predicate)

---

58   RDF Resource Description Framework.
59   OWL Web Ontology Language.

Once the Triple is defined as a concept, we can create a concrete instance and can assign real values to it. In our example, the values are: 'John' (an example of the Class: Person), 'Engenesis' (an example of the Class: Organisation), and 'Has Employer' defines the relationship between them.

Let's say we had a Class name: Person in the above example. Like any Class, Person can be assigned a series of attributes/qualities, like Occupation, Date of Birth and Ethnic Background. Each attribute of an instance of that Class can then be assigned a value.

Fact vs fiction

Ontological models also have rules, where the rules must correspond with Reality. In the real world, it is valid to say 'an organisation HAS many people', but we can't say 'an Organisation IS a Person'. That is invalid; it doesn't correspond with Reality. However, we could say 'a Person works in an Organisation' because the relationship, HAS Employer, is aligned with Reality. Another example of a rule is: the colour 'purple' cannot be used as a value to define someone's gender attribute for the Class: Person. Clearly that wouldn't make sense. Similarly, the value for Date of Birth (as an attribute) cannot be a date in the future. Such information would be invalid; it doesn't correspond with Reality. As the knowledge produced via this model is congruent with Reality, it is valid and can be considered an accurate form of measurement.

Naturally, human beings have many more Moods and Ways of Being than described in this ontological model. However, in the context of the Being Framework, I predominantly focused on the domains of performance, *effectiveness* and leadership and therefore selected Aspects of Being that are aligned with those domains. Once someone has a snapshot view of their Aspects of Being, they are able to map out the areas in which they are stuck or how they are being in each of those areas. That knowledge will enlighten them on the particular areas they should work on, ideally under the guidance of a qualified coach, to shift their Aspects of Being so they correspond with their desired outcome.

For example, it is virtually impossible for a human being to be a high achiever, effective and influential if they have a low level of *responsibility* or they don't honour their relatively high level of autonomy in action. This is why so many people fail to ever achieve what they want in life. They don't own it. They allow their circumstances to lead them instead of working on their Being so that they can influence their circumstances. We see this on a daily basis working with leaders. There are so many real world examples. The Being Framework allows you to take charge of this and many other aspects of your life, as will be explained in forthcoming chapters.

Not all models are ontological and grounded in Reality. It is important to be aware of this. In fact, there have been many models constructed from fiction in the past and this practice continues. So, it is crucial to examine the validity of a model and assess the intention of its creator before accepting it as valid. Is the model grounded in Reality or not? Many man-made theories and constructs exist in the world. Darwin's Theory of Evolution is a classic example. It is a theory and yet many perceive it to be the truth. In fact, many people don't realise that the whole purpose of a theory is that it is open to being proven wrong so the truth can be discovered. Once a theory is proven to be true it becomes a law, a rock-solid truth and hence a discovered transcending Meaning and part of Reality. It is worth noting that there are also Meanings that don't require validation. For example, in geometry, we know that from point A to point B, only one straight line can be drawn. This does not need to be theorised or proven. I call Meanings like this 'axiomatic oughts'. We can only model them and surrender. Furthermore, there are various personality tests available today that are based on constructs and not on what is primal to human beings.

Shaping the Being Framework Ontological Model

Now, let's look at how the Being Framework Ontological Model was shaped. In my work, the main Classes are 'Human Being', 'Primary Ways of Being', 'Secondary Ways of Being', 'Meta Factors' and 'Moods' and we examine the relationships between those Classes. We will study this in more detail in the next sub-chapter.

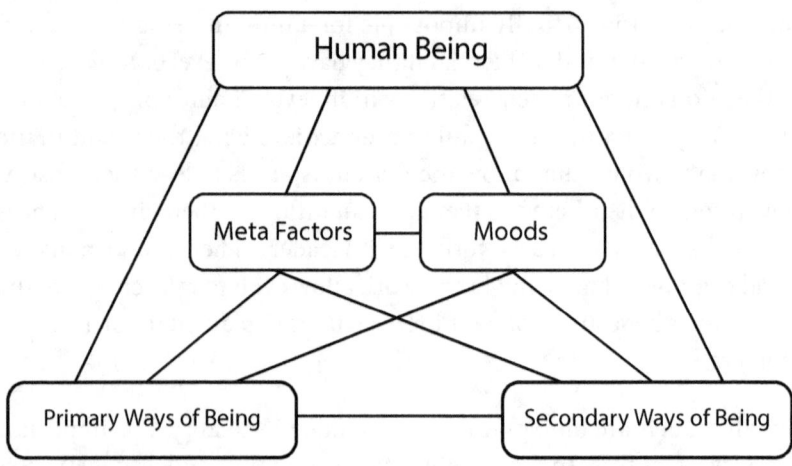

Figure 3: High-level structure of human beings' Essence (Aspects of Being)

The relationship here is one Human Being can have 'x' number of Moods (in the case of the Being Framework, which focuses on performance, *effectiveness* and leadership, there are four Moods). Each Human Being also has 'x' number of Primary and Secondary Ways of Being. Therefore, there is a one-to-many relationship between a Human Being and their Ways of Being.

Ontological models are extensible, a factor that is highly advantageous to this approach. As we gain more information through the discovery process, we can add more to the overall model and therefore expand our knowledge. For example, when my team and I first created the Being Framework, we had only twelve Primary Ways of Being and no Secondary Ways of Being. This has since been extended to sixteen and eight respectively.

The Being Framework Ontological Model is judgement-free and non-positional

It is important to be aware that the Being Framework Ontological Model is judgement-free and non-positional. There is no right or wrong, positive or negative. It is congruent with Reality; it is what it is. In developing the Being Framework Ontological Model, I was inspired by Michael Jensen and Werner Erhard's Four Ways of Being. This body of work formed part of a research paper, published at Harvard Business School[60], that focused on the foundation for being a leader, the effective exercise of leadership and how to create a high-quality personal life and an extraordinary organisation. Four of the core Aspects of Being – *authenticity, integrity, responsibility* (originally called 'being cause in the matter') and *higher purpose* (originally called 'being committed to something bigger than you') – have since been extended to sixteen Primary Ways of Being, eight Secondary Ways of Being, three Meta Factors and four Moods in my ontological model, which is non-positional in its entirety. In other words, the whole ontological model layer of the Being Framework is not at all concerned with morality – what is good and bad, right or wrong – how things should be, or fixed views from other disciplines, such as behavioural psychology, Personality Theory, specific culture and religion.

Now, while the Being Framework Ontological Model is non-judgemental, there is an element of expectation in the context of leadership, performance and *effectiveness*. For example, while the framework is non-judgemental in that it doesn't label you to be a 'bad person' if you don't have a healthy and effective relationship with *responsibility*, if you are aiming to lead an organisation, you HAVE to be responsible or there are going to be consequences. That's because the framework, as a whole, articulates the extent to which human beings follow through on who and how they really are. Moreover, it asserts that an individual's Aspects of Being, and consequently their behaviours, can be polished and ultimately transformed. This will be clarified in the coming chapters.

For all the reasons explained in this chapter and the one preceding it, I found ontology to be the right choice to model the Reality of human beings within the defined scope of performance, leadership and *effectiveness* and in the context of leading a thriving organisation and a fulfilling life. While I knew the objective studies backed my approach, the real test would be putting the model into practice. I can unreservedly say it passed with flying colours. Since its launch, the Being Framework

---

60 Erhard, Werner and Jensen, Michael C., *Four Ways of Being that Create the Foundations of A Great Personal Life, Great Leadership and A Great Organization, Harvard Business School NOM Unit Working Paper No. 13-078,* Barbados Group Working Paper No. 13-01.

has been used with great success by coaches, leaders, executives and investors, amongst others, under the guidance of my team and me. We have also taught and accredited a number of consultants and coaches, and continue to do so regularly, and they too are now achieving great success with their clients using the framework.

The rest of this book gradually unpacks every aspect of the model. By the end of it, you will be in a position to gauge your current state of Being. You will also understand how to break this down further into an assessment of each of your Meta Factors, Ways of Being (Primary and Secondary) and Moods within the scope of this framework. You can then use this knowledge as a roadmap to navigate the areas you need to work on in order to achieve the outcomes you desire in life. Once you have increased your *awareness* around your Aspects of Being and developed a deep conception of it, you will be surprised at how much more understanding you will have developed about yourself and also about others. All of a sudden, the way forward to achieving your objectives will be crystal clear.

CHAPTER 4.2

Knowing human beings through the Being Framework Ontological Model

Human beings are social creatures. We exist in society, in the community, in the workplace and as part of a family. So, nobody could argue that we are not tangible in the context of the world. Therefore, in the Being Framework Ontological Model, our Being is articulated, expressed and modelled in line with the various places and roles we find ourselves in life. That's what I mean by 'knowing human beings'. In other words, the model doesn't assess your Meta Factors, Moods and Ways of Being as though you are in a bubble, completely alone and isolated. It assesses those factors in context with your life in the real world. So, by offering you insights into how you are being in the world and engaged with others in your life, the Being Framework Ontological Model empowers you with knowledge that can be applied in all areas of your life.

Being is a unitary reality and phenomenon

Rather than contrast certain qualities, such as *love* and hate, the Being Framework Ontological Model assesses the health of your relationship with each quality. In other words, it models Being in a very precise way to determine the extent to which you have a healthy or unhealthy relationship with a particular Aspect of Being, such as *love, responsibility, integrity* or *vulnerability*. In this way, it helps you determine the extent to which you could be effective in a particular Aspect of Being if you were to polish or transform your relationship with it.

By 'healthy relationship', I mean how are you **being** with your Aspects of Being or how do you relate to them? Let's say there is a hungry dog in your backyard but you are totally oblivious to it. That is due to your unhealthy relationship with your own *awareness*, one of the Meta Factors in the model. Or perhaps you are aware that there is a hungry dog in your backyard but you are pretending there is no dog there at all. This has to do with your relationship with both *vulnerability* (one of the Moods) and *authenticity* (one of the Primary Ways of Being). Another alternative is that you see the dog, you know she is hungry but you are ignoring and neglecting her because you're too busy doing something else. In this scenario, you are aware and authentic about the presence of the dog and the fact that you know she is hungry, but by refusing to take the necessary action and feed her, you are being irresponsible, meaning you have an unhealthy relationship with *responsibility,* another Primary Way of Being.

As mentioned in the previous sub-chapter, the Being Framework Ontological Model is non-positional and judgement-free. So, how you relate to each Meta Factor, Mood and Way of Being and the consequences that brings to your life is simply how it is. There is no right or wrong. You don't need to be a certain way. If you said, 'I don't want to be responsible', then so be it. However, if you told me that your objective is to lead a company, then a high level of *responsibility* would be mandatory. It all depends on your objective. This is true for every Aspect of Being assessed through the model, whether it be *authenticity, responsibility, commitment, freedom, courage* or *vulnerability,* to name just a few. As you will see in the coming chapters, clear distinctions are applied to each Way of Being, Meta Factor and Mood because the Meaning each Aspect of Being is referring to must be quantifiable, rather than purely qualitative to be effective.

Why this framework and model?

The Being Framework is a holistic framework that has been designed to empower people, particularly business leaders, entrepreneurs and professionals. It will empower you to grow and develop by enabling you to express your Aspects of Being more fully. This will lead you to create a meaningful, fulfilling and extraordinary life and an organisation in which you not only fulfil your own goals and objectives, but also positively impact the lives of others. The Being Framework Ontological Model empowers you to achieve this objective by allowing you to assess your relationship with the full spectrum of Ways of Being, Meta Factors and Moods. In this way, it provides a lens through which you can be more effective in reading your own Being and the Being of others. For those who wish to take it further, the Being Profile measures those relationships with a high degree of accuracy and the Transformation Methodology is for those who choose to work on polishing their Aspects of Being and go through a full transformation. Both are explained in more detail later.

Let's look at two examples to compare the Being Framework Ontological Model with other models. Deloitte[61] designed and developed a system or model called 'Business Chemistry'[62] after undergoing extensive research, which highlighted that if they put four types of people – Drivers, Pioneers, Guardians and Integrators – together in a team, they would be high performers. The Deloitte research team felt that their model gave leaders and their teams a common language for discussing similarities and differences in how people experience things and prefer to work. Then there was the work of Carl Jung, who noted that within the collective unconscious, there exist a number of archetypes[63] (patterns of behaviour), such as the Mother, the Father, the Warrior and the Hero, and so on. These are just two examples of different models people refer to. In developing the Being Framework Ontological Model, I wanted to use a language that would be readily understood by everyone using predominantly primal qualities fundamental to every human being, particularly in the context of performance, *effectiveness* and leadership. This makes the Being Framework Ontological Model clear, real and relevant.

If we compare Deloitte's explanation of a Pioneer according to the Business Chemistry System with the way the Being Framework's ontological language examines and articulates the same types of qualities in a human being, we can see a clear difference. The Business Chemistry System states that, 'Pioneers value possibilities, and they spark energy and imagination on their teams. They believe risks are worth taking and

---

61   Deloitte Touche Tohmatsu Limited, commonly referred to as Deloitte, is a multinational professional services network with headquarters in the UK. It is one of the Big Four accounting organisations and the largest professional services network in the world by revenue and number of professionals.

62   Vickberg, Suzanne M. Johnson & Christfort, Kim. 2017, 'The New Science of Team Chemistry: Pioneers, Drivers, Integrators, and Guardians', *Harvard Business School Magazine*.

63   An archetype is a primitive mental image inherited from the earliest human ancestors.

that it's fine to go with your gut'. Their focus is big-picture. They're drawn to bold new ideas and creative approaches. Using the Being Framework Ontological Model to assess an individual, their level of *care, freedom, awareness, vulnerability, courage* and *higher purpose* would tell us whether or not they have the traits of a Pioneer but in a language that can't be misconstrued. This would determine to what extent they 'spark energy', see and value new possibilities and opportunities (*freedom*). It would also let us know how open they are (*vulnerability*), how willing they are to take a risk and step forward despite the presence of *fear* (*courage*) and how well they see and value the bigger picture (*higher purpose*), and so on. The same holds true in describing Jungian archetypes. We can easily describe and explain each archetype using the primal qualities within the Being Framework Ontological Model. In fact, the language used in the Being Framework Ontological Model is clearer and more fundamental than the language used in other models, such as the Deloitte and Jungian examples. Using the Being Framework, model and tool, we can articulate the breakdown of complexity to smaller more fundamental chunks and ultimately measure them accurately.

The Being Framework Ontological Model Layer

Awareness	Integrity	Effectiveness	
Vulnerability	Care	Anxiety	Fear
Authenticity	Peace of Mind	Empowerment	Compassion
Commitment	Freedom	Contribution	Forgiveness
Responsibility	Self Expression	Love	Courage
Higher Purpose	Presence	Partnership	Gratitude
Resourcefulness	Proactivity	Resilience	Assertiveness
Confidence	Reliability	Accountability	Persistence

Figure 4: The Being Framework Ontological Model Layer

Of all the complex entities in this world, human beings would have to be the most complex. As discussed in previous chapters, my approach with the creation of the Being Framework was to dismantle the big puzzle into smaller, more digestible pieces to enable you to assess how you or someone else 'are being', or participating in life within the context of performance, leadership and *effectiveness*. If you recall the framework as a whole, it consists of the Ontological Model, the Transformation Methodology and Tools. Now, let's zoom in to the Ontological Model layer of the framework. This is the model we use to read and understand a human being at a deep level, well beneath and beyond the surface, particularly in the context of performance, leadership and *effectiveness*.

Why is it necessary to go so deep beneath the surface? For the simple fact that what people say and the way they behave – the observable aspects – don't necessarily convey what drives them. To determine what drives a human being, it is necessary to look deeper to learn who and how they are being, as this is what drives their decisions, behaviours and ultimately the results they produce.

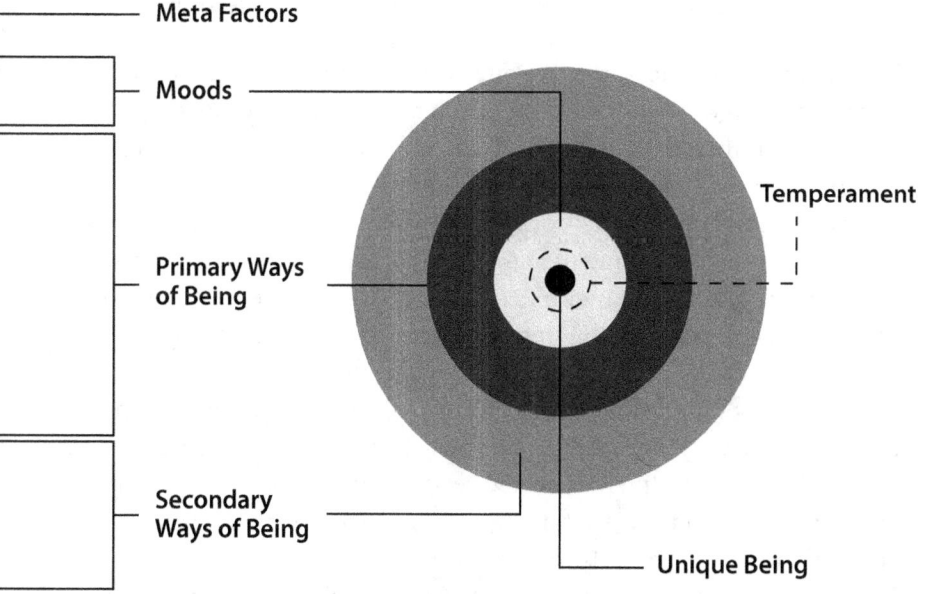

The right-hand side of the model represents a complete human being. At the centre is the Unique Being, which some people would call spirit or soul. Essentially this is the real YOU, who you are meant to be according to the talents and gifts you were born with. The next layer is Moods, which, in the context of this model, are *vulnerability, care, anxiety* and *fear*. Between Unique Being and Moods lies our Temperament, which is partly biologically based, meaning it is hard-wired from birth and relatively independent of learning, values and attitudes. But it is our Moods that we can polish and transform.

Temperament is a subject that is outside the scope of this book. However, it is important to note that the study of Temperament, including, but not limited to, the Big Five Temperament Traits: Openness, Conscientiousness, Extraversion, Agreeableness and Neuroticism (OCEAN); the four temperament types: Sanguine, Phlegmatic, Choleric and Melancholic; and Jungian Personality Types were closely studied and taken into account in the development of this model as our Temperament influences our Moods. In fact, multiple disciplines of psychology were studied in developing the Being Framework, including, but not limited to, Positive Psychology and Behavioural Psychology. However, we discovered a need for more fundamental language to describe human beings in the context of performance, *effectiveness* and leadership.

There are relationships between our Unique Being and our Moods, which establish our emotional state. These Moods drive us to have a healthy or unhealthy (strong or weak, effective or ineffective) relationship with our Primary Ways of Being. For example, if we have a healthy relationship with *fear* or *anxiety*, we may respond differently to the Primary Way of Being of *self-expression* than we would if we had an unhealthy relationship with *fear* or *anxiety*. How we relate to our Moods will either suppress or amplify certain Ways of Being. Together, our Moods and Primary Ways of Being contribute to how we relate to our Secondary Ways of Being. For example, a more courageous and authentic person is more likely to be and act confident and assertive in life. Combined, these interconnected relationships affect the decisions we make and the actions we take, which in turn affect the results we produce and our accomplishments in life. *Awareness, integrity* and *effectiveness* are Meta Factors and not Ways of Being for good reason.

For instance, *awareness* contributes in a unique way, as it refers to what we see or don't see, what we pay attention to or ignore, the perceptions we hold, or our points of view, and how congruent those perceptions are to reality. You need only think back to the example of the hungry dog in the backyard to understand what I mean here.

So, now that you have been presented with the Being Framework Ontological Model in its entirety, let's break down each layer further, beginning with the Unique Being (YOU), which we touched on earlier.

Unique Being

Even in identical twins, each has certain qualities that are unique to them. You could have identical twin girls and find one is drawn from a very young age to ballet and piano, while her sister would prefer to play soccer, despite being raised in a family of dancers and musicians. They each have their 'thing'. As we learnt earlier, our Unique Being develops from our innate calling and talents. This part of us is quite mysterious and therefore I dare not even attempt to describe it too deeply in this framework. However, it is important to acknowledge and touch on it in this book because our Unique Being is very relevant to leadership, performance and *effectiveness*, the core subject of this body of work. Why? Because besides their Aspects of Being, most of the world's greatest leaders also rely on their calling and intuition when making decisions and dealing with many of the unstructured, complex problems they face. They know and understand their Unique Being and align their lifestyle to it. This brings *integrity*, wholeness and grace to their lives by ensuring they are not consumed or enslaved by their purely rational or materialistic objectives. By acknowledging and tapping into their Unique Being, others begin to see them as unique and one-of-a-kind individuals, leading many to develop what is commonly referred to as a 'personal brand', which in turn commonly results in raving fans, followers and delighted clients. If you fail to recognise, project and fulfil your potential by knowing and projecting your Unique Being AND polishing your Aspects of Being, you – your uniqueness – will be ignored, humanity will suffer and you will miss out on the rewards and benefits. So, why would you even consider ignoring your greatest and most valuable asset of all? Like the black box in an aircraft, your Unique

Being is uniquely yours; it's the reason you have your 'thing'. It's YOU at the deepest level.

As is the case with Temperament and Moods, whereby your Temperament affects your Moods, but it is your Moods that can be polished and transformed, your Unique Being impacts your Aspects of Being, and vice versa, but only your Aspects of Being can be polished and transformed. So, polishing and transforming your Aspects of Being, which you have the power to choose to do, will help you tap into your Unique Being and project it to the world. This book doesn't delve deeply into that unique part of you, for the reasons described above. However, it is important to be aware of it because it holds the key not only to your calling, purpose and talents as a leader, but also to the calling, purpose and talents of your people, current and future.

The ultimate purpose of the Being Framework is not only to map out and become aware of one's fundamental Aspects of Being, but also to give you the tools to polish and transform aspects of your Being that will help you tap into your Unique Being. This will enable you to shine and project that uniqueness into the world. By developing *awareness* of the aspects of your Being that require your attention and are needed to achieve whatever you desire in life and then learning how to polish and transform them, as described in the coming chapters, you will remove the barriers to your innate greatness and open the door to unlimited opportunities. If you are dealing with *fear* or *anxiety* or feeling blocked in your ability to express who you are (*self-expression*), or lacking *awareness* of your innate gifts, etc., you may never fulfil your true potential. Imagine if author, J.K. Rowling had given in to *fear* the first of many times her manuscript for *Harry Potter* was rejected. She may have succumbed to that *fear* and never pursued her calling. The Being Framework Ontological Model, together with the Being Profile and Transformation Methodology, hold the key to unlocking your potential. The key to remember is this: the more polished your Aspects of Being, the higher the chance that you will discover and get in touch with your Unique Being. Furthermore, your polished Aspects of Being will enable you to project the manifestation of who you are – your Unique Being – to the world for even greater impact.

Meta Factors

Referring back to *Figure 4*, you will see that the Meta Factors: *awareness*, *integrity* and *effectiveness* sit over and above all other Aspects of Being in the model. They are the highest level factors that are tightly linked to your performance, power and ability to lead in life. *Awareness* has an impact on every Primary Way of Being and an indirect impact on every Secondary Way of Being. Every Primary Way of Being and Mood has an impact on the *integrity* of your whole Being – the extent to which your Aspects of Being are polished and the extent to which you have an effective, healthy relationship with each and every one of them. Consequently, your *integrity* and your Secondary Ways of Being constitute your *effectiveness*.

I have called *awareness*, *integrity* and *effectiveness* 'Meta Factors' from the Greek, *Meta*, which directly translates to 'after', or 'beyond' and is a prefix meaning 'more comprehensive', or 'transcending'. *Awareness* is being conscious that we are conscious. It is a quality that appears to be unique to human beings, a true gift for which we should be extremely grateful. Within the context of this body of work, I narrowed the scope to the *awareness* of human beings: ourselves and others. For example, we are not directly discussing your *awareness* of how money or banking systems work. However, my research revealed that someone who has strong *awareness* of themselves and others tends to educate themselves and become more aware of other beings, meanings, and environments too, which ultimately determines their performance and *effectiveness* and amplifies their ability to lead a fulfilling life.

The constant dance between *awareness* and *effectiveness*

No matter who you are, if you are making decisions in life based on false knowledge – in other words, misinformed decisions – you cannot be effective. Even the most intelligent and talented people can't make effective decisions with incorrect information and delusive knowledge. First, we need to know and become aware, and subsequently make our decisions, choices and actions based on our *awareness*.

Let's break this down. First, we receive and perceive (come to know) new knowledge. This is often described as a lightbulb or eureka moment. Then we start to develop a conception of our newly acquired knowledge by asking questions from the right people, reflecting and contemplating on it, and perhaps applying critical thinking to the knowledge in the form of tests and analyses to verify the information. Once satisfied, we internalise the knowledge and make it our own, slotting it into our memory bank until we find an opportunity to draw on that knowledge and apply it in a practical way. Through consistent application and practice, we eventually become competent and then proficient in applying that knowledge until it gradually becomes an inherent part of our Being. It is at this point that we can say we are effective in that endeavour. An actual transformation has occurred at a certain point during that process. I call this the constant dance between *awareness* and *effectiveness*. Becoming aware of the area we need to work on tells us exactly where our *integrity* is suffering. In other words, which part of ourselves is not working effectively.

In the context of this framework, you may lack *integrity* in any one or more of the Ways of Being or Moods identified in the model (*commitment, responsibility, authenticity, care,* etc.). It is a constant dance because, deep down, we all want to continually grow and expand our boundaries. It is our inclination as human beings to seek growth and better ourselves as we progress through life. The beautiful journey from *awareness* to *effectiveness* will be discussed further in *Part 3: Being, in Action*. We will also explore these Meta Factors in greater depth as well as the journey from one to the other as we analyse and work on our Aspects of Being. As for the other, equally critical Meta Factor – *integrity* – for someone to be integrous, all the cogs in the machine are working at an optimal level. If your relationship with a particular Aspect of Being is not as healthy or effective as it could be, you would start by becoming aware of it. Then you could have a go at guessing where the issue lies or accurately identify and measure it. Once you have *awareness*, you would work on that Aspect of Being, with or without a coach or mentor, and ultimately transform it to become a more integrous, and therefore, more effective human being. If you don't know or care whether or not your conceptions of the world are real and you neglect to establish a solid relationship with reality (through *awareness* and *authenticity*), you will fail to achieve the things you want in life. This is where your true power resides – hence Being is the source of your power – and here is where *awareness* as a Meta Factor is vital because if you are even relatively aware, you can move towards being integrous and effective.

Someone with an unhealthy relationship with *awareness* simply cannot be effective. Just as all oranges are round but not all round fruits are oranges, all effective people are aware but not all aware people are effective! For instance, you cannot be effective at building a bridge if you are unaware of the laws of physics. However, the health of your relationship with other factors or qualities within you can get in the way of your *effectiveness*, for example *fear, anxiety*, or a lack of *courage*, amongst others.

Moods

We all experience emotions. To be more accurate, not only do we experience them phenomenologically, but they are real and scientifically measurable through the release of chemicals in our bodies. Naturally there are various emotions that lead us to experience feelings of anger, sadness, contempt, joy, surprise, excitement, and so on. Once something triggers us, our emotions rise within us. When we respond to those emotions through our own interpretation and made-up stories, we call those responses 'feelings'. In this way, we make our emotions mean something. And if we reiterate these feelings, they set our Moods. Once Moods are set, they can self-perpetuate to the point where you may end up in a recursive loop that is difficult to escape, like a rat constantly running on a wheel.

While emotions are like bubbles in that they have a relatively short lifespan, Moods can last for days, months or even years. For example, let's say you lose a client, which makes you feel sad and resentful. Fuelled by your emotions, your immediate reaction is to write an email to the client. You do your best to articulate how you feel in words, However, on reading the email back, you realise that what you have written lays the blame on the client who you feel has not seen your value and is being unfair. Or perhaps you find yourself blaming poor service on one of your colleagues or staff members. By holding onto your resentment, you have made the client's decision to leave mean something that is likely a long way from reality. After all, there could be many reasons for the client leaving that have nothing to do with you or anyone else in the company. Your emotional reaction sets you up to become anxious. All of a sudden, *anxiety* is set to be your dominant Mood for a while. You dug the hole and now you are in it! As a result of this experience, you may treat other clients differently, negatively impacting your results in the future. For instance, it could make you less authentic, it could cause you to care less, be less compassionate or less communicative, and so on, setting off a negative chain of events that could impact you for weeks, months or even years. So, your Moods can influence your Ways of Being, which ultimately reflects in your behaviours.

According to Martin Heidegger, Moods are ways of disclosing our Being, or what I would call our Unique Being, to the world. They largely dictate how we participate in life and how, in part, others perceive us. People may call it 'your manner', 'personality', 'attitude', etc. It's how you introduce yourself to others and how others come to know you. The way you conduct yourself through your Moods has an enormous impact on many aspects of your life. For example, how you come across may impact an interviewee's decision to join your company or an investor's decision to invest capital in your business concept or whether or not the person you are dating chooses to commit to being in a relationship with you, and so on. While widely considered controversial, a fascinating aspect of Heidegger's analysis of Being (*Dasein*) in *Being and Time*, is the way he describes Moods. Instead of referring to a Mood as an internal state, Heidegger argues that Mood is 'a constitutive aspect of Dasein's being in the world'[64]. More specifically, Heidegger refers to Moods as 'state of mind' (*Befindlichkeit*), which is a manifestation of how we human beings automatically attune ourselves to the world around us, moment by moment. He said Moods are one of the elements that define the Nature (Essence) of the Reality of a human being. They provide context in which we engage and participate in life; they define our relationship to whatever we are up to at any given moment. For example, while arguing with your spouse, your dominant Mood may be *anxiety*

---

64 Lewis, Tyson E. (2017) 'Heidegger and Mood', in *Encyclopedia of Educational Theory and Theory*. Singapore: Springer.

over the potential consequences of your spouse leaving you. And while you may not be aware of it at the moment, you are always in a Mood. We are never free of Moods. Our existence, Being and *Dasein*, in general, become a burden if we don't master our Moods by establishing a healthy and effective relationship with them. Inspired by the work of Heidegger, I took it further, following additional research, adding *vulnerability* to Heidegger's Moods of *care, fear* and *anxiety*.

At the most immediate level of being-in-the-world, Heidegger asserts that there is always a Mood that 'assails us' in our unreflecting care and devotion to the world. A Mood, Heidegger notes, 'comes neither from 'outside' nor from 'inside', but arises out of being-in-the-world, as a way of such Being'[65]. Notice, Moods are only possible because *Dasein* is fundamentally a worldly experience of being-in-the-world. Therefore, we can conclude that Moods arise from being-in-the-world. While we may turn away from a particular Mood, we are merely shifting to another Mood; Moods are part of the Reality of being human. So, a Mood is always involved in our encounter with anything in the world as we attune ourselves to the situation, via our Moods, to ensure we are able to participate in the experience of being there, to play our part in the world. This totality of experience – of being there – is constituted by the attunement of a Mood or state of mind. Think of it as tuning yourself into the symphony of Existence and playing in harmony and time with others in it. This is the true projection of the manifestation of your Unique Being, your expression of Self and unique *contribution*.

Moods are the most immediate layer we tend to tap into when responding to both internal and external triggers. Then we channel the Mood out through our Ways of Being, after which it shows up in our behaviour or in what we say. For example, let's say your partner says something to you which immediately brings up your *anxiety* Mood. If you don't have a particularly healthy relationship with *anxiety*, this Mood may cause you to hold back what you want to say in response, as it will show itself in some of your Primary Ways of Being, like *authenticity* or *self-expression*. This could then impact some of your Secondary Ways of Being, which are more behavioural and visible, like *assertiveness*, meaning you may agree or disagree without conviction (perhaps to

---

65 *Being and Time* 176/136; cf. Heidegger 1995, p.63.

please them), or show submissive or aggressive behaviour, which would escalate the problem. And just like that, a hidden conversation is created, sowing the seeds of a troubled relationship!

To see the potential impact of Moods in a business context, let's say a client complains about a new product you have launched (external trigger). Because of your unhealthy relationship with the Mood, *care*, the situation channels into your *compassion* and/or *responsibility* and/or *commitment* (Primary Ways of Being). Your resulting behaviour is to brush off the complaint, failing to acknowledge and address it appropriately and therefore losing a loyal client who proceeds to tell their extensive network about their negative experience with your company. The trigger can also be an internal one. Let's say you are sitting in solitude, reflecting on your life, when all of a sudden, feelings of uncertainty and doubt about your future in an unsatisfying job cause the *anxiety* Mood to set in. This in turn triggers a concern that you are not good enough, followed by *fear* that your boss may fire you. As a result, you decide to 'suck it up', sacrificing your relationship with *authenticity* in the process by pushing on in a job in which you are miserable. Or let's say you are receiving some constructive criticism from one of your employees on a particular matter in which you know you could have performed better. Your reluctance to be vulnerable due to your unhealthy relationship with the *vulnerability* Mood would cause you to be defensive rather than accept the criticism and learn from it. This affects your *authenticity* because you would prefer to tell yourself and others a lie rather than be responsible for your actions.

According to Heidegger, 'Mood (*Stimmung*) is a passion of the soul or an affect, something befalls us and in which we find ourselves'[66]. By 'passion' Heidegger is referring here to the fundamental ways in which we are attuned to the world. In music, the German word, *Stimme* means tune or voice and *Stimmung* is a derivative of it. So, you could say we are attuned to the world first and foremost through our Moods. As mentioned, we know, through science, that we have emotions. We also know that the way we respond to our emotions – our feelings – sets our Mood. Our Mood at any given time drives the way we 'show up' in the world (Ways of Being). In other words, our emotional state, which is part

---

66   *Being and Time*, Part 4, Martin Heidegger.

of our physiological makeup, predisposes us to manifest certain Moods in given circumstances. This, in turn, influences our decision-making processes and determines whether or not we will take action and how we behave. So, our emotions are translated to our feelings, which affect our Moods, which in turn affect our Ways of Being, drive our decisions and then our actions. Therefore, our Moods greatly impact the results we produce and our achievements in life, as highlighted in the aforementioned examples.

A healthy relationship with your Moods indicates the extent to which you are likely to have these Moods impair or affect your ability to make decisions or take action. A less healthy relationship indicates that you are more likely to defer, delay or procrastinate when making decisions or taking actions in certain situations. For example, if you don't have a healthy relationship with *vulnerability*, you are unlikely to be open and likely to have your guard up. This will impact your *authenticity*. You will be filtering information and having hidden conversations with key people in your life, which commonly leads to mistrust. It may also impact your *self-expression*. When combined, these Ways of Being will result in your relationship with the people in question being damaged or even ruined. It may lead to divorce, a breakdown of a business partnership or the loss of important clients.

To recap, while human beings have many Moods, the four underlying Moods in the Being Framework – *vulnerability, care, fear* and *anxiety* – have been specifically selected as we found them to be the most important and fundamental Moods when it comes to one's performance in life, particularly within the scope of leadership and *effectiveness*. They provide insight into the extent by which your *vulnerability, care, fear* and *anxiety* are likely to impact your Ways of Being, the way you make decisions and take action in different situations, and how you project the manifestation of your Unique Being to the world. In other words, your Moods greatly influence your ability to fulfil your potential and live a rich, full life. When you transform your Moods and polish your Being, you increase your chances of not only creating a richer life for yourself, but you also expand the reality (Second-layer Reality) for others, even for future generations through your life's passion and work, through your inventions, the books you write, your products, and so on.

Primary Ways of Being

We participate in life in various ways. I call these 'Ways of Being'. While human beings possess and exhibit multiple Ways of Being, the research, studies and observations my team and I conducted made us realise that certain Ways of Being are vital in order for an individual to be effective and powerful in life. In the Being Framework Ontological Model there are sixteen Primary Ways of Being. They are called 'Primary' because they are primal to human beings. For example, the state of being authentic is not man-made; it is not a construct. You are either being yourself or you are putting on a 'mask', showing up through a fake persona you create every time the person you present to the world is not congruent with who you really are: the real YOU.

The sixteen Primary Ways of Being are *authenticity, responsibility, commitment, higher purpose, courage, gratitude, empowerment, presence, freedom, self-expression, love, compassion, peace of mind, contribution, partnership* and *forgiveness*. There are also eight Secondary Ways of Being, which I will introduce you to next.

Every Primary Way of Being in the model is ontologically associated with all human beings. They are qualities we all possess. However, the extent to which each Primary Way of Being is present from one human being to the next can vary considerably. In other words, how healthy a relationship one individual has with a Primary Way of Being can be very different to the next person. By 'healthy relationship', I am not suggesting 'optimal health' across the board equates to perfection. Remember, the model is free from judgement. Furthermore, full presence and a healthy relationship with all sixteen Primary Ways of Being all the time would be impossible. But while it is impossible to be perfect in each and every Primary Way of Being 100% of the time, we can work towards perfection in each Primary Way of Being to ultimately become a more integrous and polished Being.

Enhancing the health of your relationship with the Primary Ways of Being will gradually enable and empower you to make more effective decisions and take more effective actions. Ultimately, this will lead you to BE effective, which in turn will lead you to produce the results you need in order to achieve what you most desire and live a fulfilling life, professionally and personally. Your *effectiveness* also impacts the *integrity* and *effectiveness* of your team and vice versa. The more people in the world become integrous and effective Beings, the more we will start to see positive impacts across communities, societies and all of humanity. In fact, it would be fair to say that the solution to most of humanity's problems lies in leveraging the *integrity* of individuals.

The Being Framework's Primary Ways of Being distinguish the fundamental ways through which we project the true manifestation of our Unique Being to the world. These unique aspects impact our behaviour, performance and the subsequent results we produce in life. In other words, they determine the way we participate in our work, engage in projects, contribute to society or the team we play in, engage in relationships and life and also how we grow, have an impact on others and experience reality around us. We will explore each Primary Way of Being in detail later.

Secondary Ways of Being

Secondary Ways of Being emerge from underlying Primary Ways of Being. For example, we know that *resilience* is unlikely to be present without *courage*, *compassion* and *peace of mind*. In order for us to shift a Secondary Way of Being, we must first go deeper and address our Primary Ways of Being and Moods. Furthermore, Secondary Ways of Being can be reliably predicted, experienced, assessed and measured[67]. Because Secondary Ways of Being are behavioural, they are more demonstrable and visible than Primary Ways of Being. For example, if you are being proactive (*proactivity*), people can observe it through the fact that you do not wait to be told what to do next and that you seek and explore opportunities, initiating action rather than reacting to things as they happen. In other words, you are neither reactive nor inactive. *Assertiveness*, *resilience*, *confidence*, *resourcefulness*, *accountability*, *persistence* and *reliability* are also readily observable in our behaviours with clear outcomes. Together with *proactivity*, they make up the eight Secondary Ways of Being in the Being Framework Ontological Model.

---

67   Using the Being Profile assessment tool.

Behavioural psychology and its related disciplines are the dominant disciplines practised, not only in the clinical realm, but also in the corporate world. This means the main focus in corporate HR lies in correcting behaviours in the workplace as opposed to diving deep to identify the root causes of the behavioural issues. There are potentially serious ramifications in an organisation when this happens, as negative behaviour in the workplace can stem from deeper issues like presenteeism, lack of communication and even more serious matters like sexual harassment. So, while identifying behavioural patterns alone won't allow you to understand yourself or someone else well enough to cause transformation, it is worth noting that I found psychoanalysis to be more effective at identifying the major cause. As mentioned earlier in the book, I have studied the work of Carl Jung in depth, particularly his work on archetypes, where he described qualities of human beings in a symbolic way. Jung's work significantly influenced my work, but it also inspired me to use more fundamental language to describe the qualities of human beings and explain behavioural factors, such as *proactivity* and *assertiveness*, in the Being Framework's Secondary Ways of Being.

For now, it is important to know that Primary Ways of Being are primal to human beings while Secondary Ways of Being refer to qualities that are more visible and behavioural. Dig deeper however, and you soon discover that they are closely linked to more than one Primary Way of Being. This by no means makes them any less important. In fact, Secondary Ways of Being are critical because they help us bridge what lies on the surface – visible behaviours and decisions – with deeper parts of us: *awareness*, Moods and Primary Ways of Being. For example, to be free or to be courageous is primal to human beings, while being confident manifests itself in a series of far more visible behaviours relative to the context. For example, while people may see me, through my behaviour and actions, as a confident public speaker, give me a scalpel and ask me to perform surgery and I can assure you I would not be confident at all!

CHAPTER 5

Time Matters

Time is the most undefinable yet paradoxical of things; the past is gone, the future is not come, and the present becomes the past, even while we attempt to define it.

Charles Caleb Colton
English writer and cleric, 1780–1832

She constantly passes. She may in fact be the most important asset we have in life alongside our Unique Being and health. She cannot be stopped but she can be managed. It is up to us how we treat her. I am talking about time! Time matters. Every single minute that you are not using with intention and *awareness* to inch closer to your goals is a loss you will regret sooner or later. And you will never get that moment back. The fact that time passes is real. It is how it is. We can't change it; that is a rock-solid truth, a Meaning, a law of Existence. Who we are being right here, right now and how consistently we maintain how we are with *integrity* as time passes, minute by minute, determines how effectively we participate in work and, more broadly, in life in general. It determines how we handle the responsibility of leading an organisation, marriage, parenthood, business ownership, and so on. And ultimately, it determines the results we produce and the outcomes we achieve in life. Being is not only real, ontologically speaking, but also a phenomenon we experience in the moment. I am not inferring that we are changing significantly every single moment, I am merely stating a truth: that our existence and Being are in part a 'now phenomenon'. It is the way you are being in this moment, as a snapshot in time.

In reference to time, Martin Heidegger wrote in his book, *Being and Time*, 'Being and time determine each other reciprocally, but in such a manner that neither can the former – Being – be addressed as something temporal nor can the latter – time – be addressed as a being'. When I first read this book many years ago, I wondered why Heidegger called it what he did. 'Being' made sense but why *Being and Time*? What did time have to do with it? It is a book I have since read a few times and I believe I now understand where he was coming from. Consistency over time matters. Maintaining the *integrity* of our Being over time is as important as maintaining daily hygiene, nutrition and fitness. It doesn't make sense to say, 'I have eaten today so therefore I will be well-nourished today, tomorrow and next week'! Fuelling the body is not a one-off project, just as getting fit won't happen if you go to the gym once and hope that your efforts on that day will sustain you for the rest of your life! The same is true for your Being. Transforming your Being from its current state to the desired state requires a long-term *commitment*. By 'desired state', I am referring to a state that will produce the results you are seeking and deliver a higher level of fulfilment. Remember, there is no point going through a transformation if you are not prepared to polish your Being daily, moment by moment. Anything worthwhile requires maintenance.

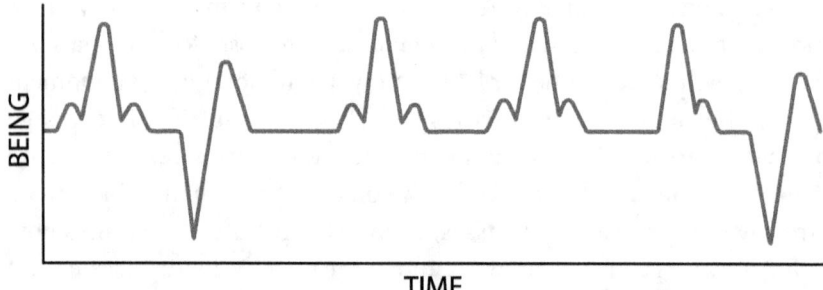

Imagine your life mapped out on a timeline. How you are being right now is one point on that timeline. As time passes, you are moving towards the future you. The peaks and troughs are normal.

In a few months you may be one of the following:

1. Less integrous and effective than you were: some of your Aspects of Being levels have declined, making you less responsible, less authentic, less calm, less free, etc., than you were a few months ago, or

2. As integrous and effective as you were: you have worked hard to maintain your Aspects of Being at the same level making you as responsible, as authentic, etc., as you were a few months ago, or

3. More integrous and effective than you were: you have focused on polishing your Ways of Being over the past few months resulting in you becoming more responsible, more authentic, etc., than you were a few months ago.

How would you compare yourself today to a month ago, a year ago and five years ago? Your Being requires maintenance over time. It is a continual process of polishing, transforming and maintaining. How seriously you polish your Being or how far you take it depends on your objective. For instance, if you are overweight and your objective is to lose ten kilograms, it takes effort and time to achieve that outcome. Once your goal weight has been reached, a maintenance program is required to ensure the weight doesn't start creeping back on. However, if your objective is to be an Olympic athlete, you would significantly up the ante on your daily physical health and wellbeing routine, training daily and working with the right team of experts, from coaches and mentors to physios and dieticians, to work on qualities like your strength, mental health, technique and diet.

Similarly, as an entrepreneur or business leader, your objective determines the level at which you will work on your Being – Aspects of Being to be exact – like your *commitment*, your *authenticity*, your *responsibility*, your *resilience*, and so on. You may choose to simply maintain the *integrity* of your Being by regularly assessing how aspects of your Being are going and working and polishing them as required. It's like having your car serviced and replacing the oil as needed, taking your dog to the vet for a regular check-up and ensuring her immunisations are up to date, checking your computer and installing software updates to keep it operating efficiently or going to the gym to maintain your physical fitness. However, if your objective is to take your business venture to the world or reach the top of your game, you would up the ante and work on transforming your Being, usually with the help of experienced coaches and mentors. We will be discussing this in detail in *Part 3: Being, in Action*. Like an athlete who wants to compete at the Olympic level, you would constantly maintain and enhance your *integrity*, working on all the aspects of your Being in order to hit your targets. Any objective of this calibre requires constant dedication, determination, focus and sacrifice. How well you polish or transform your Being and maintain its *integrity* over time, minute by minute, day by day, month by month, will determine your future. It's about ensuring each and every cog in the machine is working at an optimal level, now and into the future.

Conclusion

We covered a lot of ground in Part 1, so it is worthwhile briefly recapping before zooming in to the core of the Being Framework: Aspects of Being.

The main objective of Part 1 was to provide you with the big picture by laying out a helicopter view of the Being Framework before zooming in on the Ontological Model. We learnt that the Ontological Model is where I mapped out the qualities of human beings that are tied to our performance, leadership and *effectiveness* in four layers: Meta Factors, Moods, Primary Ways of Being and Secondary Ways of Being. Combined, these are referred to as 'Aspects of Being'. In this way, the Ontological Model gives you the ability to see the qualities of yourself (how you are being) and others with great clarity and depth.

Part 1 also walked you through the fundamental knowledge and core topics required to grasp the framework as well as the research and discovery process I undertook to shape the knowledge and build an effective channel of communication. We explored truth, meanings and reality; we clarified the confusion surrounding existence and Being; we discussed the difference between meanings and words, distinguishing between the absolutes of this world and the layers of reality we create ourselves; and we explored the crucial difference between discovery and invention to gain an appreciation of how ontology, epistemology and phenomenology helped establish the research paradigm for this framework. We then dived deeply into the shaping of the Being Framework Ontological Model and were introduced to the Meta Factors as well as Moods and Primary and Secondary Ways of Being and the part they all play in the Being Framework. Finally, we learnt about the factor of time and why our existence and Being are, in part, 'now phenomena' in Time Matters.

So, by now you should have a clear, high-level understanding of the entire framework and the meaning and relevance of its associated terminology. Now we are ready to zoom in and explore each and every Aspect of Being, as mapped out in the Being Framework Ontological Model.

PART 2

Aspects of Being

As we have learnt, the Being Framework Ontological Model is where I mapped out the qualities of human beings that are linked to our performance, *effectiveness* and leadership. Those qualities have been broken down into four layers: Meta Factors, Moods, Primary Ways of Being and Secondary Ways of Being. Combined, these are referred to as our 'Aspects of Being'. In this way, the Ontological Model enables us to see the qualities of ourselves and others in great detail. So, when I refer to 'Aspects of Being', I am referring to all the qualities that sit within the four layers of the Being Framework Ontological Model, and when I refer to 'Ways of Being', I am only referring to our Primary and Secondary Ways of Being. Simply put, our Aspects of Being shape the context that drives our behaviours.

The aim of Part 2 is to create *awareness* around the Aspects of Being relevant to leaders, entrepreneurs and those who aim to be high achievers, as mapped out in the Being Framework Ontological Model. It highlights each end of the spectrum and, to a certain extent, the outcome and the consequences of having a healthy or ineffective relationship with each Aspect of Being. It's about how you are **being with**[68] a certain Aspect of Being, how you relate to it. A comment I sometimes hear from clients is, 'Other books tell me what to do'. However, it is not my role to tell you what to do but rather to show you the possibilities of how you can BE. We will explore a high-level overview of the Transformation Methodology in Part 3. However, even that is not a step-by step guide. It is a high-level explanation of how transformation can occur and outlines the steps involved in the process of transformation.

---

68 Not to be confused with *Mitsein* (being-with), a concept developed by Martin Heidegger.

The purpose of this book, as explained in the Introduction, is to support you to go through a paradigm shift; to see differently, like top high achievers of the world do. Learning how to shift your own Aspects of Being requires expertise and dedication. While you can do your best to transform on your own, it is best done under the guidance of an experienced ontological coach. It's like engaging the services of a personal trainer to help guide you and hold you to account on your path to greater health and fitness rather than trying to do it alone, especially when you don't really know what you're doing. And if your objective is to join the elite in business, it's even more crucial to get the right support. An aspiring Olympic swimmer would never dream of training for the world's ultimate elite swimming competition without professional coaches.

By raising your *awareness* of your Aspects of Being, discovering which aspects require your attention in order to achieve your objectives in life and then learning, at a high level, how to polish and transform them (as explained in *Part 3: Being, in Action*), you will unlock your potential to project your Unique Being to the world, thereby opening the door to unlimited opportunities.

Part 2 dives deeply into our Aspects of Being. I will walk you through each layer of the Being Framework Ontological Model, as shown in *Figure 4* on pages 80 and 81, beginning with the Meta Factors, which sit at the highest level of the model, followed by Moods (our Moods influence our Ways of Being, which ultimately reflect in our behaviours), Primary Ways of Being (Ways of Being that are primal to human beings) and Secondary Ways of Being (Ways of Being that are readily observable in our behaviour). I recommend you refer to the Model whenever you would like a visual representation of where each Aspect of Being fits into the bigger picture as you read Part 2.

SECTION 1

Meta Factors

Awareness, *integrity* and *effectiveness* are the three highest level Aspects of Being in the Being Framework Ontological Model that are tightly linked to our performance, power and ability to lead and influence. *Awareness* has an impact on all Aspects of Being, *integrity* is impacted by our Primary Ways of Being and Moods, while all Aspects of Being contribute to our *effectiveness*.

It is impossible to be consciously effective at something we are not aware of. How can we intentionally produce results in an area within which we have no *awareness*? Therefore, an increase in *awareness* always precedes an increase in *effectiveness* in any area. Once *awareness* is present, we are able to see all the qualities we require in order to be effective at a holistic level. Just as a piece of hardware requires every part to be working correctly to operate effectively, we need to have all Aspects of Being working at an optimum level to be effective. Our *integrity* is a constitution of all our Moods and Primary Ways of Being, between which there are multiple complex interactions. I have broken those Aspects of Being down into clear, distinct qualities to make them more digestible, communicable and measurable. Remember, combined with our Secondary Ways of Being, these qualities shape our *effectiveness*. We will examine this further in *Chapter 2: Integrity*. But first, let's begin with *awareness*, our first Meta Factor.

CHAPTER 1

Awareness

Awareness is tightly linked to consciousness in such a way that many use both words interchangeably. The *Oxford English Dictionary* defines 'consciousness' as 'the state of being aware of and responsive to one's surroundings'. The *Cambridge Dictionary* defines it as 'the state of being awake, thinking, and knowing what is happening around you'. As you can see, consciousness is quite broad and more biologically focused than *awareness*. While animals and plants also have a level of consciousness, they are not conscious of their consciousness. *Awareness*, on the other hand, is defined by the *Oxford English Dictionary* as 'knowledge or perception of a situation or fact', or, 'knowledge that something exists' and the *Cambridge Dictionary* defines it as 'understanding of a situation or subject at the present time based on information or experience', or, 'knowledge and understanding of a particular activity, subject, etc.'. As you can see, *awareness* has a more tangible, human-related connotation. In this framework and book, *awareness* focuses on the reality of human beings in the context of performance, *effectiveness* and leadership. However, let's take the time to zoom out to study *awareness* at a high level first.

Awareness is intentional; it is always directed at something or someone with the attribute of being in the moment. *Awareness* is a necessity, not an option. We need it to fulfil our commitments, to operate effectively, to create a positive impact on ourselves, others and to enrich our experience of life. *Awareness* is about perceiving, knowing, understanding or being intentionally conscious of any matter or concept, whether it sits within the realms of First, Second or Third-layer Reality, including events, objects, thoughts, emotions, the environment, others or sensory patterns. Once we perceive something, we can start developing our own conception of it. Developing this conception is normally achieved through contemplation, reflection and questioning, which are the steps that follow perception, enabling us to embed that new knowledge into our experience in such a way that we then own it and are ready to put it into practice. So, perception takes place in the moment, but developing a conception of what we have shaped a perception of is a process that may take time. This knowledge[69] eventually becomes wisdom we own and can start putting into practice. Through practice, execution and repetition, we gradually achieve a degree of *effectiveness* in it. We transform. This will be discussed in *Part 3: Being, in Action*.

Our level of *awareness* increases from the moment we start to see the truth about ourselves, another person, human beings in general and any matter or concept, whether it sits within the realms of First, Second or Third-layer Reality. As our *awareness* expands, so too will our ability to influence an outcome. *Awareness* is a critical Aspect of Being that enables us to reach higher levels of satisfaction, build sustainable and thriving relationships and become more effective as leaders. We can't change something we are unaware of. *Awareness* is the eureka moment that begins the process of transformation towards *effectiveness*. Now that we have discussed what *awareness* is at a high level, let me share with you the Being Framework ontological distinction of *awareness*.

---

69 Knowledge is a container for facts, structured information and skills acquired through experience or education (not restricted to formal education). It serves the purpose of gathering wisdom.

The Being Framework ontological distinction of *awareness*

Awareness is the state of being intentionally conscious of your consciousness. It is how you relate to what you know and understand as well as what you don't know and don't understand. *Awareness* is always intentional and directed at something. It is to know and understand yourself, others and the world around you, in particular the impact of the world and others on you and the impact you have on the world and others. *Awareness* is your access to knowing and understanding and is required to fulfil your intentions.

A healthy relationship with *awareness* indicates that you have a clear understanding of your impact on others and on the world around you. You are not easily misled, coerced and/or manipulated. You are both self-aware and aware of how you are perceived by others. You are attentive, alert and rarely surprised or caught off guard. You can find your way forward despite uncertainty or not knowing, and are available to consider feedback, guidance and critique.

An unhealthy relationship with *awareness* indicates that you may choose to ignore or be oblivious to matters and the impact you have on others and the world around you and vice versa. You may often be confused and shocked by matters and how others respond to you and blindsided when they fail to live up to your expectations. You may deliberately choose to ignore what there is to see. Alternatively, you may freeze or find it difficult to progress in the face of uncertainty or not knowing as you are compelled to know everything before making decisions or taking action.

As you can see from the ontological distinction, those with a healthy relationship with *awareness* have a sound understanding of their impact on others and on the world around them. However, the opposite is true for those with an unhealthy relationship with *awareness*. How may this impact you? Let's consider some examples. It could cause you to be startled when employees leave your company or if an initiative you created fails to achieve the traction you expected. You would also tend to see the world either through rose-coloured glasses (overly optimistic), or dark shades (overly pessimistic), sometimes alternating between the two. The problem with viewing the world through rose-coloured glasses, for example, is that you may find it difficult to conceive how others could possibly feel dissatisfied or unhappy in your organisation. In your mind, everything is just fine. Viewing the world through dark shades is equally problematic. That could have you believe that nothing ever goes right for you, which could ultimately lead to feelings of disappointment and discontentment with your life, or jealousy towards others.

The more you enquire into how your Aspects of Being impact your performance, your environment and others, the more you will raise your *awareness*, which often leads to action. You can become aware of a transcendent Meaning that sits within the realms of a First-layer Reality, such as, if you are constantly lacking *commitment* and breaking promises, you will suffer and cause suffering to others. You can also become aware of constructs that fall under the category of a Second-layer Reality, such as money, taxation and the law. Raising your *awareness* of such matters increases the probability of hitting your targets and accomplishing the things you desire for yourself, your loved ones, your organisation and – if working towards a cause greater than yourself and your organisation – your community, society, all the way to humanity. For example, if you don't know much about money and how the taxation system works, you could make avoidable mistakes and lose money or pay more taxes than you need to. For these reasons, *awareness* is the greatest impetus for effecting change. It is the first step towards true transformation and knowing exactly how you are being now and how you plan to become.

Awareness has a broad scope. We have *awareness* of Meanings, concepts, matters, events and people. While I touch on most of those topics in this chapter, the primary focus rests on how to develop your *awareness* of human beings, including yourself (self-awareness). When I refer to 'self-awareness' in the context of this framework, I am referring to your awareness of both your Unique Being and, most importantly in the context of this book, your Being or Essence (Aspects of Being).

The ramifications when we are not aware

Now that we have discussed the state of being aware, let's see, in a tangible way, what it looks like when we are not aware and the ramifications of that. Naturally, there are times when we are genuinely unaware of something. For example, I may be genuinely unaware of the fact that some mushrooms are poisonous and assume all mushrooms are like the ones we buy from grocery stores. When we are genuinely unaware or oblivious about something, we don't have access to its reality. This lack of *awareness* can put us at risk (of being poisoned, in the case of the example). However, when I am being ignorant, I intentionally divert my gaze, for example, not wanting to know about the impacts all of us have on global climate change, because I am neither curious nor interested in becoming aware. Human trafficking is another example. We know it exists, but most people choose to look away, to ignore it, to remain intentionally unaware. It's no coincidence that the word 'ignorance' has 'ignore' in it. Furthermore, knowing about something but choosing not to look, care and address the situation is negligence, another type of unhealthy relationship with *awareness*. When we are genuinely not aware, we can put ourselves at risk. And when we are intentionally unaware – when we deliberately look away or use avoidance tactics – it leads to either ignorance or negligence, which can have far-reaching impacts. Imagine the long-term ramifications if every human being on the planet deliberately avoided and ignored the subject of global warming or if no one cared enough to generate jobs. In the context of this book, a lack of *awareness* will prevent you from being aware of the areas that are blocking you from becoming more integrous, effective and fulfilled as a leader, coach, professional or aspiring entrepreneur. When you have an unhealthy relationship with *awareness*, the probability that you will hit your targets will remain low. This is not a prophecy. I am rationally stating a truth. If you look closely, and with *vulnerability*, you will observe this within your organisation and in life in general.

Another factor that leads us away from *awareness* is a lack of exposure, and there are serious consequences when this is the case. A lack of exposure predominantly happens for two reasons. Either we don't dare to expose ourselves or others to something we think or know will cause emotional discomfort, or we live in a society or are part of a unit, such as a family, group or community, that intentionally keeps us from being exposed to the truth and reality. Let's explore this further.

In our era, there is an expectation of and even a demand for so-called 'emotional safety' despite the fact that nobody, no matter how powerful, can possibly guarantee your actual emotional safety. The renowned original thinkers like Socrates, Plato, Aristotle and many others had no such expectation. They revelled in the emotional discomfort experienced and the emotional resilience needed on the journey to learning and *awareness*. Today many teachers, parents, lecturers, coaches, etc., are reluctant or even afraid to expose their students, children or audience to anything that could potentially trigger them in some way and cause emotional discomfort. Many children are brought up this way, both at home and at school, so by the time they enter society and the workforce as young adults, they lack the *awareness* and emotional resilience required to be effective in the adult world.

Many of us are too careful these days when exploring hypotheses for fear that our views could be received the 'wrong' way, particularly on politically sensitive topics. Even many scientists and philosophers today, whose primary role is to question and challenge the status quo, remain silent for fear of being labelled 'xyz' for denying or minimising a problem perceived and propagated by the mainstream media and mass population, despite knowing they have the evidence that proves the validity of their claims. Such legitimisation and justification of misinformation can be both harmful and contribute to a collective psychosis within a society.

Having lived in societies where delusional perceptions and ideologies are often deemed to override the truth and reality, I know how unhealthy it is to grow up and live in such a deceptive environment, one that attempts to prevent its people from accessing *awareness* through a lack of exposure to the truth, indoctrination and brainwashing. In societies and cultures like this, infected logic, emotional impulses and corrupt power fuel collective psychosis and drive behaviours and decisions, causing an epidemic of madness. Everyone is afraid of being reported, offended or labelled. They are all watching each other carefully, waiting for an excuse to block, unfriend or report someone for their different views. This is a recipe for separation, deviation and misery as opposed to unity and *integrity*, the very thing humankind needs to survive and thrive. No proper seed of workability can be sown in contaminated soil, let alone flourish. I could write an entire book on the connection between emotional resilience and *awareness*, and I have no intention of delving too deeply into it here. However, for the sake of clarity in this discussion on *awareness*, I found it extremely relevant and therefore important to touch on here.

If you drop or apply pressure to a crystal glass it will break. But human beings are not made of glass, we are not that fragile. In fact, we need to fall, make mistakes and be exposed to a disproportionate level of discomfort and stress so that we can develop *awareness*, learn from it, polish ourselves, become more integrous and transform. It's like developing our immune system. If a baby is not gradually exposed to bacteria and certain foods as they develop and grow, they are more likely to develop allergies or autoimmune conditions in the future. We need to keep exposing ourselves, our children, coaching clients and employees to the 'right' (individualised) level of emotional discomfort so that we gradually develop our emotional resilience and gain access to *awareness*. When we allow our children to be gradually exposed to challenges, their capacity to handle increasingly larger challenges will build, so that by the time they reach adulthood, they are equipped to deal with virtually anything they may face. Without giving children the opportunity to face emotional discomfort, and therefore develop emotional resilience, the world would be filled with thirty, forty and fifty-year-old unpolished 'infants' who are either leading ineffective, unfulfilled lives and being cared for by the system, their parents or others, or occupying decision-making or executive positions when they can't even take proper care of themselves, their relationships or families.

At the end of the day, if we don't choose powerfully to allow ourselves to be exposed to things we may not like, agree with or that may cause discomfort, we will never build the emotional resilience we need to develop *awareness* of matters beyond the ones we want to be exposed to.

The ramifications of not being exposed to matters for fear of the pain it may cause will lead you to live life in a filter bubble. *Awareness* has nothing to do with how knowledgeable or wise you are. It's about how you are **being with** and relate to the matters and subjects you know and understand as well as the matters and subjects you don't know and don't understand. Without adequate exposure, you risk remaining ignorant and/or negligent to the truth and reality, and this comes at a huge cost.

I will now walk you through the key *awareness* topics you need to develop a conception of in order to shape a meaningful vision in business and in life, which is why vision is the final topic under the *awareness* umbrella. After all, you cannot shape a vision without a high level of *awareness*. Those topics are: Access to Reality, Epistemic Humility, Web of Perceptions, Narrative Lens, Perspective Quadrant, Shadow and Vision. You will learn how polishing your relationship with *awareness* will empower you in so many ways, from finding and retaining great people in your organisation to attracting your ideal clients and investors who can see and have a desire to connect with your vision. Ultimately, you will discover that you cannot shape a meaningful vision without *awareness* of human beings (including yourself) and the world around you.

CHAPTER 1.1

Access to Reality

We don't see things as they are. We see them as we are.

Anaïs Nin
French-Cuban novelist, 1903–1977

Awareness is how we relate to what we know, what we don't know and, most importantly, how accurately we perceive things in the present. It's what we choose to be present to or give our attention to. It begins with an intent to want to become aware: to see things as they are, not as you merely perceive or want them to be. In other words, it begins with a willingness to make your perceptions congruent with how things are in life so that you can make better and more effective decisions. If your perception of what is happening right now or of a Meaning or a concept is not congruent with Reality, it is delusional. It can only be one or the other. Lack of *awareness*, on the other hand, stems either from ignorance or negligence.

Our *awareness* gives us access to the three layers of reality, not just our interpretation of reality. While I acknowledge that we don't always have direct access to the truth/Reality; the point is to become as aware as possible about everything and everyone we are exposed to while simultaneously not allowing what we don't know or don't understand to block, freeze or suppress us. When you first become aware of something, you are accessing the truth of the matter, or at least getting closer to it. It may be something you were previously unaware of, either because you haven't studied or explored it before, or because you have shaped an inaccurate and incongruent perception of it and have not yet aligned that perception with Reality. Imagine if there is a poisonous snake on the floor of your living room and, for whatever reason, you perceive it to be a length of rope. Your perception of it is that it is a piece of rope, but in Reality, it is a snake. In this case, you could put yourself in a life-threatening situation by misreading or ignoring the facts. I'm sure you can appreciate the lesson in this analogy. As a leader, becoming aware that it is possible to become more integrous and effective if you work on certain aspects of your Being could be a game changer for you and your business. Without having access to that reality, you could live your entire life in denial or oblivion. At the end of the day, whether or not you are aware of it, you are projecting the manifestation of your Being on your organisation and family every single day. The same is true for all team members. Think about how game changing it could be for your organisation if you and your team had greater *awareness* around that.

Imagine finding yourself stuck in a situation that feels like *Groundhog Day*[70], where you are experiencing a repetitive challenge in your life, day in, day out, but you don't understand why. To remove yourself from this seemingly never-ending cycle, like being a hamster perpetually running on an exercise wheel, it would help to raise your *awareness* of all the events, decisions, patterns, Aspects of Being and perceptions that led to this experience. Initially, it may feel like you can't see the forest for the trees. But by directing your attention to the situation and setting your intention to discover more about what is really going on, you will increase your *awareness* of it, including what led to it. This relatively healthier relationship with *awareness* will enable you to take action to correct the path, change the outcome and therefore break the dysfunctional cycle.

Reality does not care if you are or are not aware of the law of gravity, for example. And yet if you ignore it, you will definitely pay for it! The same applies to work, life and business. There is a reality about how things work. An intellectual sceptic may read this and argue that human beings and the world of ideas should not be compared with physical matters such as gravity or poisonous mushrooms. This, to an extent, is a valid point. However, I am not arguing that there is an objective Reality about everything related to human beings. This framework has a well-defined scope and boundaries. We are talking about qualities that have been found, through validated scientific studies and objective

---

70   *Groundhog Day* is a 1993 American fantasy comedy film directed by Harold Ramis and written by Ramis and Danny Rubin. In the movie, the lead character, played by Bill Murray, relives the same day over and over again.

methods, to be tied with our performance and *effectiveness*, particularly for leaders and organisations. So, I would encourage all readers, including the intellectual sceptics among you – ironically, I can be one myself at times – to be open-minded in deciding if you wish to go through this paradigm shift. By directing your *awareness* to learn about these matters, you can equip yourself to shape the world around you in a way that works for you, giving your life *integrity*. Even if you want to challenge the status quo or expand the Second-layer Reality around you, acknowledging – without necessarily accepting – that reality is a good start. It enables you to see very clearly where you are now (Point A) and where you are going (Point B). This is what high achievers and leaders of the world do. They see things with greater clarity, use and share that vision to expand the Second-layer Reality around them and own their decisions powerfully through their high level of *responsibility,* one of the Primary Ways of Being.

So, *awareness* gives us powerful access to reality (First, Second and Third-layer Reality). Gaining this access is liberating and empowering. It is also necessary for us to fulfil our commitments, maximise our achievements and the impact we have on others, and optimise our experience of life. Steve Jobs, the co-founder of Apple Computers, for example, knew this only too well. His detailed *awareness* of some of the needs of human beings meant he understood our attraction to beautiful, well-designed things and our desire for software and tools that were easy to use. Therefore, he focused on designing the optimal user-friendly interfaces. Any professional with a background in User Experience (UX) design or art would appreciate this now. The knowledge of how to design the perfect or best possible user interface came as a result of Jobs' ferociously directed intention to learn everything he possibly could about users (people). Had he not been aware of the needs of human beings when it comes to technology, he could not possibly have created the vision to satisfy those needs. It always begins with *awareness*. It is *awareness* that ultimately enables you to form a vision. It would be fair to say that Jobs created a focus on the necessity of user-friendly designs within an industry that was either oblivious to that need at the time or ignored it. He developed *awareness* around the user-friendly design for computers and applications to enhance the user's experience when working on an Apple computer and improve their efficiency when completing tasks within this domain. He raised the notion that computers don't need to be bland and boring. And his work was performed with great intention and directed focus to the point where user-friendly design has since become a central focus across all platforms. It even led to the creation of a whole new industry and occupation (UX Design).

Awareness is the first step in transformation and there is no doubt that Steve Jobs transformed the world of software and hardware design through his work. He did so not only by raising *awareness* of the importance and benefits of this change for the end user and the professional community, but he followed through by building products that manifest these ideas and principles. At the time, the software engineers and designers didn't know what they didn't know. But Steve Jobs directed their *awareness* to this area. He gave them access to reality. Similarly, the consumers were also unaware. They were oblivious to what else they could possibly want because they didn't know what was possible beyond what they already had. They were either content with what was available or, if they were frustrated with what they had, accepted it because they didn't know any better. It was only when Jobs made them aware of what was possible that they realised what they could have, which transpired into a strong desire for that product. I remember a time when accountants used to write SQL[71] database queries to draw a simple financial statement. Today that is achieved in a few clicks.

Gaining access to Reality for self-awareness

Gaining access to Reality for self-awareness requires us to look inwards for the answers. If you are frustrated at work, you could ask yourself, 'Why am I frustrated?' However, this question automatically leads most people to look for external reasons for their frustration, as it is our inclination as human beings to look outwards rather than seek the answer to our issue within. Why? Because most people don't choose to be cause in the matter of their lives (being responsible). This often leads to further negative thoughts, which could leave you feeling even worse. It is no coincidence that all high achievers that I have studied have a high level

---

71 Structured Query Language (SQL) is a programming language that is typically used in relational database or data stream management systems. Simply put, it's a way to read and write to databases.

of *responsibility*. They revel in being responsible for their lives because they find it empowering. They know that by taking responsibility, they can have an influence and effect change, as opposed to being a victim of circumstances. This is something that the high achievers of this world strive for. There is great power in having a high level of *responsibility*. It enables you to influence the outcomes you desire.

Asking, 'Why did this happen to me/us?' as the immediate response to a problem is not the most effective way to inquire into a situation because it doesn't give us easy access to our unconscious thoughts, feelings and motives. A better response would be, 'Why not me?' when something undesirable happens in your life. After all, why should undesirable situations that cause pain and suffering only happen to others and never to you? More often than not, when you ask yourself why you are acting or thinking a certain way, the answer you come up with won't be accurate. It won't give you access to reality. For example, when someone receives harsh feedback from their manager, their rationale could be, 'I'm not cut out for the job', or, 'I'm not as good as the others', or, 'I can never seem to do anything right', and so on. This won't support either party in coming to an effective resolution. Furthermore, focusing on, 'Why did it happen?' in the first instance rather than, 'What can I own?' and, 'How can I fix it?' can lead to feelings of resentment and victimisation and a sense of resignation. It could also lead you to become stuck in an investigation in a reactive manner, which in turn could lead you to fail to respond to the situation in an effective and proactive way. Imagine if during a global pandemic, all leaders focused on why this was happening or who is to blame, rather than how they could adapt and what they could do to realign their operations? When you focus on yourself, rather than your environment and what you can do about a situation, you compare yourself with your internal standards and beliefs. These standards specify how you are supposed to think, feel and behave. They are values and beliefs you have adopted over time or developed as a result of previous experiences, to which you added your own interpretations or meanings. However, those interpretations do not necessarily refer to reality. They can be very debilitating, simmering in the background without you being aware of them or the impact they are having on current events.

I am not suggesting that considering why something happened is not important. On the contrary, there is great value in understanding why. But instead of asking why in the first instance, more constructive questions to ask yourself would be, 'What can I own?', or, 'Which part can I influence?' In the example of being frustrated at work, you could ask, 'What situations cause me frustration?', or, 'What is it about the way I am responding to this particular situation that is making me frustrated?' and, 'What parts can I own in this situation?' By asking questions like this, you are directing your thoughts to recognise both internal and external factors that don't align with your passions, goals and who you actually ARE (your Unique Being). It also highlights the fact that you are being responsible for your lack of *awareness* of how things are, which will lead you to make better choices in terms of how you respond. This way of thinking and asking questions will increase your *awareness* of the situation and therefore help you create a strategy to address it rather than dwelling on negative aspects, which often leads to resignation, resentment, self-victimisation and ultimately, self-sabotage. High achievers look carefully to find or create even the tiniest thread to pull and change an outcome. They are thrilled when they can manage to find a situation they can influence. Imagine how powerful it would be if you are the one responsible for changing the course of an outcome in a positive way. Remember, you have far more influence over yourself than over anyone or anything else.

There is a movie called *Undisputed II: Last Man Standing*[72], which is the story of George 'Iceman' Chambers, an American boxing champion who is in Moscow for a boxing match when he is set up by gangsters and framed for possessing drugs. He is sentenced to a Russian prison, where he realises that boxing against other inmates is the only way out. This plan was concocted to satisfy the gangsters' 'business model', which was to have prisoners engaged in illegal, full contact fights within the prison in order to make money by gambling on them. Iceman has no idea what is going on and for weeks refuses to acknowledge that he is no longer the champion, at least not in the context of being in prison. In this strange environment, he cannot be who and how he was beyond the prison gates just as he can't expect others to praise him. He is now a prisoner in a

---

72 *Undisputed II: Last Man Standing* is a 2002 American action sports film written, produced and directed by Walter Hill.

place without rules or a referee. The power dynamics here are unlike anything he has experienced before. The plan was to have Iceman fight three matches and then he would be released once the gangsters had earned the money they wanted from him. By resisting the perpetrators, Iceman was doing himself no favours. Once he became fully aware of his situation and acknowledged it to the point where he temporarily ignored who he was outside the prison, he began to make more effective decisions, which ultimately led to his freedom. I experienced something very similar. As a boy growing up in Iran, I was aware that I would have to participate in compulsory military service for at least eighteen months once I turned eighteen. Unlike many of my friends who objected and resisted compulsory service at the time – losing their right to a passport as a result – I accepted my fate by joining the military, which was not an easy task by any stretch of the imagination, and was therefore granted a passport on completion, which gave me the freedom to travel abroad. In situations like this, it makes no difference what you believe is right , or wrong, fair or unjust. Sometimes, to achieve an effective or desirable outcome, you have to be aware of and acknowledge what you have to do to achieve it and then just do it.

We all perceive things through our own narrative lens and, based on our perceptions, shape our beliefs and opinions accordingly. Most people unconsciously adapt certain perceptions based on the media and the culture, religious background and belief systems of their parents or the carers who raised them. We are so entrenched in this that it is difficult to see the reality of things, but it is not impossible. The more you enquire into how your Aspects of Being impact others and your environment, the more you will increase your *awareness* and set yourself up for fulfilment. This is where the Being Framework can guide you to identify how you are being and how you can change in order to live your life in the most effective way possible.

Let's look at an example of how we perceive things through our own narrative lens. While it's easy to assume that the success of a romantic relationship relies purely on the feelings two individuals may have for each other in the relationship, there are, in fact, some primal and fundamental rules that determine its success. One of those is *commitment*. Without *commitment*, no relationship will succeed. Before you question me on this point, let me clarify. When I refer to *commitment*, I am not necessarily referring to being faithful. Even if a couple agrees to being in a relationship in which infidelity is acceptable, that in itself is a commitment on their part. Any breach to that agreement would increase the probability of a breakdown of that relationship. So, the point is, if you are not aware of how vital it is to establish expectations and make a commitment to your partner, your relationship is unlikely to survive, let alone thrive. We will discuss *commitment*, one of the Primary Ways of Being, in detail later. We will also explore perception (web of perceptions) and narrative lens in more detail shortly.

So, what is your relationship to Reality? How do you relate to it? Do you seek it, do you want to discover it, or do you prefer to bury your head in the sand because the facts are too daunting? As human beings capable of imagination and fabricating layers of reality, it's quite tempting to create parallel realities, either individually or collectively. Fundamentally, this is neither good nor bad, positive nor negative. For example, science fiction, fantasy and many other genres leverage the ability to create parallel realities and, as readers and viewers, we find it entertaining. But, as we discussed earlier, the point I am trying to make is that it pays to discern between the truth and the layers of reality we create. For instance, sharing your home with a dog comes with a significant level of responsibility. A dog requires regular attention, food and exercise; those requirements are aligned with Reality. But imagine if you didn't know, or worse, ignored the fact that a dog can't eat certain foods, like chocolate or onion? This lack of *awareness* or ignorance of the truth (Reality) on your part could potentially cost your beloved dog her life!

As business leaders, entrepreneurs, subject matter experts or coaches, we all need to work with others to produce services and products that can be sold to customers. In essence, our work, no matter what we specialise in, is to serve others. In my professional experience, it continues to surprise me how many leaders I work with know little about human beings, despite being highly competent in specific areas of their business. From hiring inadequate staff and placing the wrong person on the board of directors to firing someone before realising their true worth, these are just a couple of examples of leadership decisions that have the potential to pull a pillar out from underneath the business and bring about failure.

Bringing an investor or a co-founder on board with the wrong intentions can cost a company millions, if not lead to bankruptcy and cause it to collapse. Every one of these examples stems from a lack of *awareness*. I have seen them all. And even after all this time it still breaks my heart. That is why I am so passionate about humankind and have invested so much time into learning all I can about human beings and applying this knowledge into my work, including the Being Framework, so that others may benefit from it. There are some key topics to learn, understand and put into practice to avoid the ramifications of having little *awareness* of human beings. They're not even difficult. But they do require the right intention and a genuine desire to develop *awareness* and transform. Any change begins with *awareness* and a willingness to access Reality. After all, we can't change what we don't know, let alone undergo a complete transformation.

CHAPTER 1.2

Epistemic Humility

The word 'epistemic' means, essentially, anything dealing with knowledge. Epistemic humility, therefore, is being humble with your assumptions and expectations about knowing and understanding. It is recognising that you may not know something or may struggle to grasp something quickly, and that this is perfectly natural and okay. I would like to take this a step further. Consider this: as human beings we are not entitled to the truth! You could argue that we are relatively capable of 'being in search of Meanings' but that does not mean we are entitled to them. You can't simply approach an organisation or a government official and claim your entitlement to knowledge. Neither Existence nor the universe owes you an explanation. Hence, knowledge is acquired, it is not a given. YOU are responsible for being in search of the truth in order to form valid and authentic beliefs and opinions.

Epistemic humility is about being open to matters you may not know or thought you knew only to discover that you actually didn't know. You may have simply misconstrued that knowledge. In other words, your perception was not congruent with reality. It takes humility to accept that you are not always right, and to listen to or read what another person has to say or write about on the matter. More than that, it's about truly acknowledging the fact that you are not entitled to know, while also being aware that not knowing or having an incongruent perception could cost you dearly.

There are times when we all show resistance to acknowledging certain truths, even if we see sufficient evidence to warrant accepting them as truths. There can be many reasons for this resistance, anything from simply not wanting to acknowledge them, all the way through to deep psychological issues. If you purchase a new car and read in the manufacturer's manual that it is a petrol-powered car, would you try to put diesel in it? If you are told by your doctor that, according to your latest test results, you risk serious health issues if you continue to consume alcohol, would you ignore the advice because you think you know better? Would you hire someone because of the impressive claims they have made in their resume about their reputation and standing in your industry, even though you know they are not the right person for the job? Would you employ a contractor to get an important job done purely based on their nationality, gender or ideological orientation without paying attention to their level of proficiency? Would you turn a blind eye to your spouse's infidelity because of the material possessions and social status they offer you? As much as epistemic humility is about being open to things you may not know or thought you knew, it is equally about developing the ability to give up on the idea that you always have to be right. As a matter of fact, most of the time we, as individuals, are NOT right. The sooner you acknowledge this fact, as the world's high achievers do, the sooner you will be open to letting others contribute to you or your organisation's growth.

We are living in an era where everything is nicely packaged. When we go to the supermarket to buy steak for dinner, it comes neatly carved, cleaned up and wrapped in plastic on a tray. Do we pay attention to how this steak got there? Do we consider in that moment that this piece of steak was a live animal on its way to the abattoir just days before? Of course not! Yet if it wasn't possible to outsource the unpleasantries to 'the others' and we had to slaughter the animal ourselves, how many people do you think would be putting steak on the weekly menu?

In today's society, we have become accustomed to everything being commoditised and packaged for consumption, not that I necessarily have a problem with that. As an entrepreneur and venture builder, commoditisation and monetisation are inherent requirements of my role. I am merely suggesting that not everything should or could be easily commoditised like that piece of steak. Take knowledge, for example. Even when we commoditise knowledge in the form of books, courses, video content, etc., our audience cannot simply expect to receive all the knowledge contained within them, no matter how well it has been articulated. That's largely because of the nature of knowledge or how that knowledge will be received. This will also depend on how practiced and proficient the audience is in the art of learning and how accustomed they are to having a dialogue with a book or a course, followed by contemplating different ideas and developing a conception of that. It is not like going to a restaurant for a steak and being disappointed when the steak is not cooked to your liking. I have read Martin Heidegger's book *Being and Time* multiple times. And each time I read it, I pick up on new knowledge contained within its pages. I didn't buy that book with an expectation that I would acquire all the knowledge Heidegger was transferring in one reading. I recognised that it was okay not to grasp it all and that it would take several readings for it to make sense. In other words, I had the epistemic humility to be in search of Meanings, not to feel entitled to them. The same is true for many other philosophical or meaningful books and content. How do you personally relate to this?

In putting this book together, I had six languages to contend with: English, German, Persian, Latin, Greek and Arabic. I went through many different thought disciplines and scoured numerous sources before I could even begin to put pen to paper. It took years to acquire sufficient background information before I was ready to start writing. Then, once I had started, I found the writing process was peppered with moments of both joy and frustration. I faced the dilemma of deciding which words to choose, made all the more challenging when certain words in one language could not be adequately translated into another. There were multiple rounds of testing and feedback. Many of these challenges apply to any significant body of intellectual work. My point is, if you are a genuine truth seeker, you should perhaps dare to jump into the unknown, one way or another, in order to gradually gain knowledge. This is an attitude many choose not to adopt because, let's face it, it's a lot of hard work. While the main aim of the Being Framework is to apply structure to the knowledge I am communicating here, and streamline it to make it easier for you to apply in practice, you cannot expect your whole world to change after just one reading. However, my promise to you is that by introducing this paradigm, it will have the potential to change your worldview, particularly around human beings.

As I said in the Introduction, this book is to be studied and used as a source of reference. The more you come back to it, the more you will discover. So, in order for you to benefit from this content you should choose to read it with a level of *vulnerability* and practise epistemic humility. However, it's not just a matter of reading this book, or any intellectual body of work for that matter. It's about building your *awareness* of the world around you and, particularly within the context of this book, increasing your *awareness* of human beings, including yourself. As mentioned, *awareness* is the first step towards becoming effective. By learning and choosing to practise epistemic humility when it comes to knowledge, you remove the barriers and empower yourself to access reality. This can lead you towards *effectiveness*, which in turn will enable you to accomplish what you desire in life. Let me elaborate on this with a classic martial arts parable that conveys my point.

> A scholar was interested in learning martial arts. He had extensive life experience and was accustomed to being praised for his many accomplishments and receiving respect from all those he came into contact with. He also had an extensive knowledge of various Eastern traditions and had trained in other forms of martial arts in the past. One day, he decided to approach an esteemed martial arts master and ask if he would consider training him. There was something about the scholar's Being that caught the master's attention, prompting him to invite the young man to his home to discuss the subject.
>
> The master began making tea and asked the scholar what he knew of martial arts. Eager to impress, the scholar started bragging about his extensive knowledge of the history of martial arts, the different styles, and his experience in meditation techniques. He went on and on, hardly stopping to take a breath. The master simply continued to prepare the tea in silence, patiently listening to the scholar's boasts about all he knew.
>
> Finally, the tea was ready, and the master began to pour it into a cup. Once the cup was full, he continued pouring. The cup began to overflow, and tea pooled over the table and ran over the edges onto the floor.
>
> 'STOP!' yelled the scholar. 'The tea is spilling everywhere! Do you not see that the cup is full?'
>
> The master stopped pouring. Looking the scholar in the eye with a smile he said, 'You see, you are like this cup, so full that you can't add anymore. If you truly desire to learn, you must empty your cup first so it can be filled again'.

To become aware, you should choose to be a good listener, be receptive to new information, have your guard down and acknowledge that others have something to say that may add value to you. This does not mean you must accept or agree with what they have to say, just acknowledge it, let the information be poured into your empty cup, take a sip and see how it tastes. Be open and ready to learn. Be vulnerable enough to let knowledge come through. Be ready to see things as they are, without filtering them through your own intellect, rationality or web of perceptions first. The real paradigm shift actually begins to occur when newly acquired knowledge makes no sense! Why? Because if it already made sense to you, it would be in the realm of what you already know. And we haven't even discussed the web of perceptions yet. Shortly, you will learn that this adds a whole new layer to the subject.

When I was a teenager, I attended a business seminar where the speaker was telling us about the benefits of always thinking like a beginner. To illustrate his point, he held up a cup and asked us to tell him what it was. Looking around the room I could see several attendees rolling their eyes and smirking before someone finally stated the seemingly obvious in a bored tone of voice: 'It's a cup'. The presenter then asked, 'What can you do with it?' A woman piped up with a sarcastic grin, 'It's to hold my coffee'. By this time people were beginning to get impatient, wondering where this discussion was going. Finally, the speaker, still holding the object said, 'Let's redefine it, shall we?' I would say this is a concave ceramic object with a handle. Now, with that new perspective in mind, let me pose the question to you once more: what can you do with it?' This time there were a number of different responses from the room, from drinking tea to using it to water a pot plant. One attendee even said in jest that it could be used to throw at your spouse during an argument. My point is, when we are open and think like a beginner, we allow ourselves to see things from other perspectives, not just as we have always seen them. It is worth noting that this is a key quality possessed by innovators, creative entrepreneurs and artists.

Gaining practical knowledge and wisdom, and becoming truly aware of matters and people in the world is not easy, but it normally brings many rewards, making the effort worthwhile. It's hard to get to the truth about things in the world and people, including ourselves. Most people instantly create their own perception – including beliefs and opinions – never realising that taking the hard road to acquire knowledge pays off way beyond their expectations. Effective people get to the bottom of things. They are thirsty for true knowledge, knowledge that is congruent with reality. They know how human beings react in various situations and have the ability to uncover their needs and pain points. This is how they are able to create ideas, products and services that fulfil a genuine need and, by putting the right structures in place, benefit from the rewards of their ideas and efforts. They educate themselves on money matters, including the taxation system, and they know how to select suitable people for their team and for every project, and appreciate the importance of enabling and empowering them to perform well and make their own decisions. It is simply impossible to be this effective without displaying the characteristics of epistemic humility and having sufficient *vulnerability* to polish their current Aspects of Being.

Earlier, I mentioned the word 'acknowledgement', which, according to the *Oxford English Dictionary*, means 'to accept or admit the existence or truth of; recognise the importance or quality of; express gratitude for or appreciation of; accept the validity or legitimacy of'. When I refer to acknowledgement, I am saying, let's acknowledge that Existence does not owe us an explanation and we are not entitled to the truths in the universe. This simple acknowledgment leads us to show epistemic humility when it comes to knowing. We first accept this on a meta level – in the face of Existence – and secondly, when we encounter others or intellectual material, such as books. For many, it comes as a shock when they find the answers they were looking for from people, books or somewhere they were least expecting to. We are in the presence of light all the time. Light shines regardless of whether or not we are in the dark (ignorant). Ultimately, we are not the generator of the light (knowledge). Meanings are always there to be discovered; it's up to us to discover them rather than fabricate our own parallel realities and fake meanings. We must acknowledge that we are not the sun that generates the light. Consider that we are like the moon, open to receiving the light from the sun and projecting it into our lives and the lives of others.

CHAPTER 1.3

Web of Perceptions

We all perceive things differently because we do not have direct access to the truth. Whenever we come across a new object, concept or idea, we form a perception of it. We read about it, we experience it, and so we perceive it in a certain way. It is worth noting that the culture, religion, ideologies, political views, parenting styles, gurus and schools of thinking we follow, or the opinion-makers we admire, have a strong influence over how these perceptions are shaped. By the time we enter adulthood, we have already shaped our own web of perceptions.

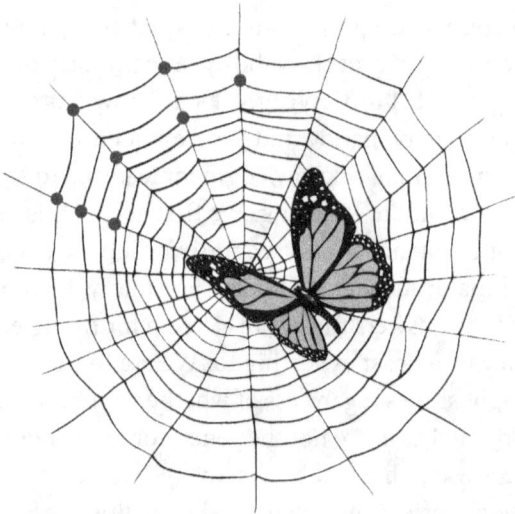

Unlike the web spun by a spider however, we are the main victim of the web we create for ourselves. But it doesn't have to be this way. We are born into this world like beautiful butterflies with the ability to fly, but instead, we either continue to crawl or create a web that traps us and threatens to keep us crawling, which prevents us from reaching the heights of our potential. Every node of the web we spin represents a single perception of something, such as: money, *confidence*, *awareness*, *authenticity*, productivity, *integrity*, *love*, marriage, employer, race, gender, honour, government, God, police, and so on. Simply put, a perception is a way we think of or get to know something. The same object or the same Meaning or concept can be interpreted and understood in different ways by different people. In other words, things can occur to each of us differently.

Our opinions and beliefs are, for the most part, shaped and influenced by our perceptions. We tend to be very protective of them, even if they are in no way congruent with reality, and despite the fact that they may not be working for us and might not have worked for anyone in the history of humankind. In other words, we humans can be delusional, at risk of living our entire lives in fantasy land! In my company, my teams and I see many enthusiastic and ambitious first-time tech entrepreneurs who come to us actively seeking an investor, despite the fact that they are a long way off being investment-ready. Just because they have come up with a potentially brilliant idea, they assume it automatically entitles them to raise a million dollars through an external investor. This perception is commonly the result of reading about the overnight success stories of tech startups on social media who claim to have raised funds simply by sending a few cold emails. So, they assume, 'If they can do it, so can I!' Unfortunately, they don't have the epistemic humility and patience to receive professional advice about how they could redirect their attention to how to be and what needs to be done to design their business in a more systematic way.

We also see many first-time investors who come from a more traditional investment background, such as property, and are seeking to diversify their portfolio as a result of being bitten by the 'high return' tech startup bug. They walk into our office full of excitement about the 'unbelievable opportunity' they wish to invest in, not realising their desire is the result of a perception that is not founded on reality. Sometimes we fail to discourage them. Despite being told it's too risky and that there are more systematic ways of evaluating the opportunity, there are times when they are not receptive, often paying the price later. The perception of the tech startup and the investors in the above scenarios were incongruent with reality. Charging ahead with their ideas, they would have found themselves wasting a lot of time, other people's work, talents and capital over many months, sometimes years. Imagine the repercussions if most founders and investors forged ahead with ideas based on perceptions that are incongruent with reality. We would eventually end up with an entire startup ecosystem residing in fantasy land! This would result in minimal job creation and an extraordinary waste of people's time, resources and money. The entire economy would suffer, as a nation's GDP is enormously influenced by how its businesses operate. For example, at the time of writing this book, the failure rate for startups in their first year is greater than 90%[73] in most developed countries. Furthermore, for every billion dollars invested in R&D within Australia, only two businesses are successfully created as a result[74]. While the figure is higher in the UK, the US and Canada, it is still unacceptable.

The high achievers of the world know the cost of holding onto inauthentic opinions, beliefs and perceptions that aren't based on reality only too well. They know because they have been burned before, and they have the scars to prove it! They've hit enough walls in their careers to know the value of conducting thorough research in order to gain genuine knowledge. So, instead of fiercely holding onto their opinions without grounds, they are open and vulnerable to learn. Of course, the wiser ones got to this point much earlier and therefore learn from the mistakes of others. Bill Gates and Warren Buffett, for instance, are renowned as being highly studious. They are also humble enough to know that they lack the time and the knowledge to uncover all the facts. Therefore, they engage people who are more competent in various fields to advise them, rather than pretending to know it all themselves. The high achievers of the world understand that getting suitable people on board and engaging the best coaches, mentors, advisors and consultants will ensure they won't waste time repeating the mistakes they've made before. Steve Jobs once famously said he always hires smarter people, not to tell them what to do, but so they can tell him what to do.

---

73 'Startup Genome Report: premature scaling v1.2' (edited March 2012). Copyright 2011.

74 Source: Australian Department of Industry, Innovation and Science (2016), National Survey of Research Commercialisation (NSRC); Reuters (2016), Top 25 Global Innovators – Government; Scimago Lab (2016), Scimago Institutions Rankings; OECD (2015), OECD Science, Technology and Industry Scoreboard 2015.

In sharing these examples, I am explicitly encouraging you to be open and vulnerable enough to let the light of truth shine on you. Let your perceptions be challenged by true knowledge. Let yourself become aware of matters in business and life in general. Failing to do so will put you in the danger zone. Athenian philosopher, Plato, described this state as 'double ignorance', a phenomenon that any leader should avoid at all costs. Plato distinguished between 'simple ignorance' – the lack of information or knowledge – and 'double ignorance' – the absence of knowledge coupled with the delusion of having genuine knowledge. We can all think of at least one person, including ourselves at times, who displays the latter! Being open and vulnerable will prevent you from falling into that danger zone. We will discuss this in greater depth in the Vulnerability chapter. For now, I'd like to share an example with you.

I was engaged to work with one of the directors of a successful, high profile food supplement company, who was struggling to acknowledge his relatively low level of *responsibility*, which led to serious issues within the company. After working with him to get to the truth of the matter, it quickly became apparent that, in his web of perceptions, *responsibility* meant thinking of a problem and carrying a sense of guilt. I challenged him to change that perception and see *responsibility* as honouring his relatively high level of autonomy. I knew that causing this shift in his perception would empower him with the knowledge that he could be – and is – in charge, rather than victimising himself because of circumstances. It was far from the outcome he had imagined. What he unconsciously expected at the time was for me to buy into his imaginary narrative that the problems within the company were not his fault. But this wasn't even important. The key was for him to shift his perception and take charge so that he could change the outcome. Without that critical shift in his perception, even the best technical solution ever created wouldn't have solved the problem because he wouldn't have been autonomous and empowered enough to execute on that. The point is, becoming aware of our perceptions is key to solving issues and moving forward.

Take a look at the image overleaf. What do you see? If you only see a rabbit, you would say, 'This is a rabbit'. Take a closer look. Once you become aware of the duality, you might say, 'Now I see it as a rabbit' and, 'Now I see it as a duck'. Or you could say, 'It's a rabbit-duck', or, 'It's a duck-rabbit'!

Austrian-born philosopher, Ludwig Wittgenstein[75], used the rabbit-duck image in his work, *Philosophical Investigations* to discuss ways of seeing. When you look at the image, you may see the duck or the rabbit. You may stop there and be satisfied with your perception, or you may investigate it further and see the duck too. In reality, the image depicts both a rabbit and a duck.

*Kaninchen und Ente (Rabbit and Duck)
from the 23 October 1892 issue of Fliegende Blätter*

But what if you had never seen a rabbit or a duck before? What if the Meaning of a rabbit and a duck were unknown to you and you had no perception or *awareness* of either animal? What do you suppose the majority of us would do if that were the case for us? We would start conducting a search query, in a similar manner to a Google search, in an attempt to find the closest stored image in our memory. This may lead us to perceive the rabbit as a mouse or cat which, of course, is factually incorrect. This example illustrates the need for all of us to embrace the higher intelligence, for example, connecting with others and tapping into their knowledge of different domains rather than limiting ourselves by staying within our own silos. This is precisely what high performers,

---

75   Ludwig Josef Johann Wittgenstein (April 26, 1889 – April 29, 1951) was an Austrian-British philosopher who worked primarily in logic, the philosophy of mathematics, the philosophy of mind, and the philosophy of language.

high achievers and effective people do. They don't just rely on what they already know or what they are competent in. They constantly educate themselves and employ others to raise their *awareness* of subjects they are currently unfamiliar with, to coach, consult or work with them. And they do so with epistemic humility.

Let's take money, as an example. In economics, money is a commodity. A commodity is something that has both 'use value' and 'exchange value'. Tomatoes can be used to make pizza and they can also be exchanged for money by the greengrocer when we buy them. However, the air we breathe is not a commodity because, while it has 'use value' (we breathe it to stay alive), it cannot be exchanged for money or any other means. In some ways, money is like tomatoes in that it can rot – through inflation. In order to save or increase the value of our money, it needs to be invested, not just sit in a bank account or safe, to ensure it doesn't lose its original value. In some of the world's financially disadvantaged nations, only less than 3% of the population invests their money. The perception that one needs to save money but not invest becomes a behavioural pattern, which leads to an inability to grow financially as individuals. Furthermore, when the vast majority of the population adopts the same mindset, it means that, collectively as a nation, money isn't being injected back into the economy. And we all know the ramifications to the national economy when that happens. I am not trying to give you a lesson in economics here. My point is that the collective perception of money, in those relatively poor countries, is incongruent with the reality of money. Therefore, their economy suffers and, consequently, almost everyone's life suffers. We pay a huge price when we hold invalid perceptions, whether individually or collectively. Effective high performers rarely pay that price; they know the value of being aligned with reality and how important it is to value *awareness*. That's why they constantly invest in true education to further their knowledge and wisdom, which ultimately reflects in the results they produce, for example, greater wealth.

Most of us don't always pay attention to what we say. Sometimes we say things without thinking or meaning to, and usually that happens because of the perceptions – particularly the beliefs and opinions – we hold. At times, we don't even know why certain words come out of our mouths.

While everything anyone says has an impact, if you are in a position of power, such as the leader of an organisation, the impact of what you say and the beliefs and opinions you share is generally magnified because of the number of people – employees and customers – it could potentially affect. If you say something is impossible, that message will spread like wildfire. Tell your team something can't happen and guess what, it's likely not going to happen! And so, in the process of transformation, it is critical that we learn to be responsible for what we say. If you want to build a business and you tell yourself it's not going to work, then it's almost guaranteed to fail. This isn't about positive thinking or being optimistic. It's about the way you relate to reality. Your level of *awareness* and *authenticity* will impact the way you deal with matters, especially if you misinterpret the reality or view it through a negative lens (more on the narrative lens later). In a similar manner, being overly positive and assuming everything will work itself out the way you want it to is also not in your best interests. The point is, you need to be real and authentic, letting your words, perceptions and actions be congruent with reality. It's about being willing to acknowledge reality and then giving it your all to bring to fruition what you see is possible.

Last but not least in our discussion on the web of perceptions, there are times when we don't even know what we are not aware of; there is a distinct lack of perception from the outset. I remember coaching the CEO of a financially successful company. Despite their success, they had a high rate of employee turnover, and the CEO couldn't figure out why. After all, his employees were on good salaries with many benefits and the company had even opened a staff bar and a cafe recently. The second issue was that they had a group of high-profile engineers who performed well individually on their day-to-day tasks, but didn't produce the desired outcomes as a team. When I started talking to the CEO about *love* and *care*, he looked at me quizzically and said, 'Come on, Ashkan, we're not here to talk about my relationship with my wife! We're here to discuss my employees and the engineering team'. In his web of perceptions, there was no place for 'soft traits', as he called them, including *love* and *care,* in the workplace. When I directed his attention to how important *love* is by highlighting examples of sports teams and how *love* can create bonds and connectedness, I managed to make him aware of how his company's lack of *love* and *care* was resulting in low connectedness amongst the team, which was one of the main reasons for the high employee turnover and lack of effective performance. These were issues he was either genuinely unaware of or deliberately chose to ignore.

Remember, we are all born into this world like butterflies. But the web of perceptions we create for ourselves threatens to trap us where we are right now, preventing us from spreading our wings and taking flight. To prevent this from happening, high achievers let their perceptions be challenged by true knowledge with epistemic humility. They allow themselves to become aware of reality and what's possible. And they don't fall into the danger zone of 'double ignorance' – the absence of knowledge coupled with the delusion of having genuine knowledge. If you are committed to being effective and a high achiever, be willing to acknowledge reality and open to learning from others. Then give it your all to bring to fruition what you see and know is possible.

CHAPTER 1.4

Narrative Lens

Everyone loves a good story. And we are all storytellers. The more time passes, the more stories we accumulate, whether they be about things we have done or events that have happened to us. Life is filled with moments of accomplishments, contentment and joy interwoven with times of adversity, catastrophe, sorrow and disappointment. The *Oxford English Dictionary* defines 'narrative' as 'storytelling, either true or imaginary'. So, we may tell stories that are not congruent with reality and therefore delusional. There is a reality about what happens in our lives, which all too often we ignore, opting instead to create our own version or interpretation of happenings, experiences and phenomena. These fabricated stories eventually become our own version of reality (Third-layer Reality) and rule our lives.

I recall a time in my childhood when my dad was upset and had locked himself in his room because he didn't want me to see him in that emotional state. When I knocked on the door, he turned me away. My immediate reaction was to make up a story about what I must have done to make my dad so angry that he did not want to see me. Obviously, at the time, I didn't think I was making up a story; I thought it was reality. The story manifested into the irrational thought that he didn't love me anymore. The reality of the situation was that he was undergoing financial pressures, which had nothing whatsoever to do with me. The story I had made up in my mind represented my version of reality (a Third-layer Reality) and that could have ruled my relationship with my dad for the rest of our lives.

We all have a customised narrative lens through which we choose to see life, our environment, people and our experiences. The stories we repeatedly tell ourselves and others as a result of this narrative lens eventually become our reality. As leaders we should pay close attention to how we shape our narrative lens and observe the extent to which it is congruent with how things really are. Why? Because that narrative lens will be handed down throughout your entire organisation. It sets the tone for your company culture and brand and will therefore become the dominant message you send to your existing customers and prospects, as well as potential new employees, to the point where your narrative lens ends up shaping your customer base and your future team.

So, what does the narrative lens have to do with *awareness*? The answer is that our narrative, in part, develops our *awareness* in the same way as being humble with our assumptions and expectations about understanding (epistemic humility) and letting our perceptions be challenged by true knowledge develop our *awareness*. More specifically, they all influence our access to the three layers of reality.

High performers usually have sound access to reality, which is why they tend to make effective decisions. Their decisions demonstrate a clear understanding of people. They also understand what people need, today and in the future, which is a significant step towards success when creating a new product or service for launch to a mass market. Henry Ford may never have created the first affordable automobile had he paid too much attention when he asked middle-class Americans (his target audience) what they wanted because, according to Ford, the overwhelming response was likely to be faster horses! His vision allowed him to see what they actually needed, and he articulated that need so brilliantly that it made his audience want it. Remember our example of why Steve Jobs was so successful with his launch of the first Apple computer? He understood that people had a need for a simple and appealing user interface, and he acted on that fact. As a business leader, having a healthy relationship with *awareness*, as Ford and Jobs did, will enable you to act on opportunities swiftly, shifting resources and talents effectively from areas of low productivity and yield to areas of higher productivity and return. This is in line with French economist and philosopher Jean-Baptiste Say's definition of the word, 'entrepreneur', which he coined around 1800: 'The entrepreneur shifts economic resources out of an area of lower and into an area of higher productivity and greater yield'. In exchange for the value you bring to your target markets, your revenue would increase and, as long as you have the right financial structure in place, you would successfully grow the company's bottom line. Fail to understand the market or articulate the perceived value of your offerings however, and you will fail to influence the customer to buy your products or services, and therefore fail to build a thriving business.

Many of the first-time entrepreneurs I work with come to me with certain perceptions of what they imagine running a business will be like. I hear things like, 'I don't want a nine to five job', 'I don't want to work for a boss anymore', and, 'I want a business that will make me a lot of money'. These perceptions are founded in the stories they have told themselves before making the decision to go for it. The reality, as many of you will attest to, is that owning a business – especially building a startup in the first few years – is 24/7, your customers, shareholders and other directors will be your 'bosses', and you won't make money if your sole focus is to accumulate money, paying little to no attention to what people need and want. One of the primary reasons so many new businesses fail is because of this narrative lens based on perceptions, manufactured news and articles on social media, not reality. It's as though they come to me wearing sunglasses, seeing everything in the dark until I encourage them to remove their shades and see things as they really are. I included these examples to highlight how being delusional, another word for not having access to reality, will not work in either your or your organisation's favour. These examples may seem obvious to those of you more experienced in business, but I used them to make the point very clear. I'm sure you can think of other examples closer to home that demonstrate what can happen when your narrative lens is distorted.

Dominant Narrative

'Let he who shouts the loudest be heard first' is a Latin saying that essentially says the stories we hear the most become the dominant narrative. The TV and news, politics, social media and popular culture are examples of the dominant forces in society that influence us through the dominant narrative because they are the ones doing most of the storytelling. When I was a teenager, I always wondered why CNN, BBC and other influential news channels put so much effort into their narration. I have since learnt that the one who narrates the loudest and

NARRATIVE LENS

the strongest is the one who rules! Therefore, the dominant narrative becomes the stories being listened to and heard the most, influencing our narrative lens, especially the narrative lens of people who are readily influenced. As they bombard us with their stories, they shape the dominant narrative to the point where many listen and follow without question. That is why we have been made to assume that certain types of people are barbaric and uncivilised, etc. It is often not until we meet and get to know these people, that we realise those stereotypes had been fabricated and planted in our minds through storytelling to favour the narrators' interests. Such fabricated stories have been used to justify racism, sexism, systematic terrorism and genocide throughout history, resulting in collective psychosis and creating separation within humanity, rather than unity and *integrity*. It is extremely important to be aware of how the dominant narrative came about and its influence on us.

High performers and effective leaders are usually very aware of this circulating dominant narrative and invest in developing the ability to distinguish truth from imaginary reality. This is yet another key pillar to their *awareness,* and hence, *effectiveness*. Leaders and high achievers of the world also tend to influence the trends, and therefore, the dominant narrative. They are powerful storytellers, opinion makers, trendsetters and style makers, as opposed to being followers influenced by imaginary reality.

I want to take a moment before I conclude this sub-chapter to point out that I am by no means suggesting that not being influenced by others is a virtue. To the contrary. From what I see, particularly of the millennial generation, everyone wants to be a leader, have a grand vision or impact the world in some profound way. So, I would say it is crucial to let yourself be influenced by the RIGHT leaders and thinkers – depending on what it is you wish to achieve – and authentic stories based on reality, especially if you are young and/or relatively inexperienced. The key point I wanted to share in this sub-chapter is that the stories we tell ourselves and others gradually form the narrative lens we see everything through, and either give us access to reality or prevent us from accessing it. This narrative lens can easily trap us. However, if you master authentic storytelling, it can help you influence others, from employees, customers and investors, to your life partner and children, in very positive, mutually beneficial ways. So, what stories are you telling yourself and others? Are they authentic and constructive? Are these stories serving you and your objectives? Or are they inauthentic and manipulative?

CHAPTER 1.5

Perspective Quadrant

Before we talk about perspective and, in particular, the Perspective Quadrant, which I will explain to you shortly, let me begin by quickly recapping some of the key terminology discussed in this chapter on *awareness*. The reason I am doing this is because some people use certain words almost interchangeably, despite there being important distinctions between them. For instance, the words 'perspective' and 'perception'. Someone may say, 'Let me tell you my perception of it', when they actually mean their perspective. I also want to show you why each of these topics is so intrinsically linked to *awareness*.

So, to briefly recap, *awareness* is your intentional consciousness directed towards a particular matter, concept or meaning, whether it sits within the realms of First, Second or Third-layer Reality. Perception is the way in which you regard, know or interpret something through the senses, including matters like love, justice, marriage, God, etc., and concepts or objects. By web of perceptions, I am referring to the nodes of the 'web' we spin, each node representing a single perception of a given meaning or concept. The nodes of the web are metaphorical for the collection of perceptions we have of meanings, because at times matters occur to us differently. Narrative lens is the lens through which you see events or situations – past or present – which leads you to tell yourself stories based on how you interpret each situation. The stories you repeatedly tell yourself and others as a result of this narrative lens eventually become your reality (Third-layer Reality). Perspective is your attitude towards something. It's where you stand on a particular matter, your point of view or how you regard something. You could say your perspective is the angle you are seeing something from. If you continually look at something from the same angle, you risk only ever seeing part of it. This is also true for a situation or an event. By consciously changing your perspective – the angle from which you see something – you will eventually see a fuller picture. It's like a 3D scanner that captures multiple images from various angles to form a more comprehensive picture that is far more congruent with reality, giving you a holistic view of whatever it is you are viewing or assessing. So, while perception refers to your interpretation or the explanation you come up with – how something occurs to you, factoring in your opinions and beliefs – when you aim to become aware of something, perspective refers to your point of view or the angle from which you see something, someone or a situation.

Let's delve a little more deeply into perspective before I explain the Perspective Quadrant to you. The word 'perspective' has a Latin root, *Perspicere*, which means 'to look through', from *Per* ('through') and *Spicere ('to look')*. So, it is a way of seeing or looking at something or someone. Perspective is how you see things, your evaluation of a particular situation or fact in terms of your point of view, which can be changed **at will**. Imagine a soup bowl that has been placed on its side on a table and two people are looking at it from either side of the table. If asked whether the object is concave or convex, one will tell you it is concave and the other will tell you it is convex. Each would have a different perspective of the same object and neither would be wrong. However, each person is seeing only part of the truth, either intentionally or unconsciously, and they can be in disagreement and argue forever. Now, let's say there is a third person who, when asked if the object is concave or convex, says that it depends on which way you look at it. That third person has opened their mind to the possibility that there is more than one way to look at something. They know that in order to have a fuller understanding of what they are looking at, they must switch perspectives. The truth is, whatever is concave is convex at the same time. Effective people see things from more than one perspective. This very fact led me to devise the Perspective Quadrant, with human beings as the subjects to be studied.

Perspective Quadrant

In any given situation, including our interactions with others, we have the choice to see things from one or more of four perspectives. I call this the Perspective Quadrant[76], as shown in *Figure 5* below.

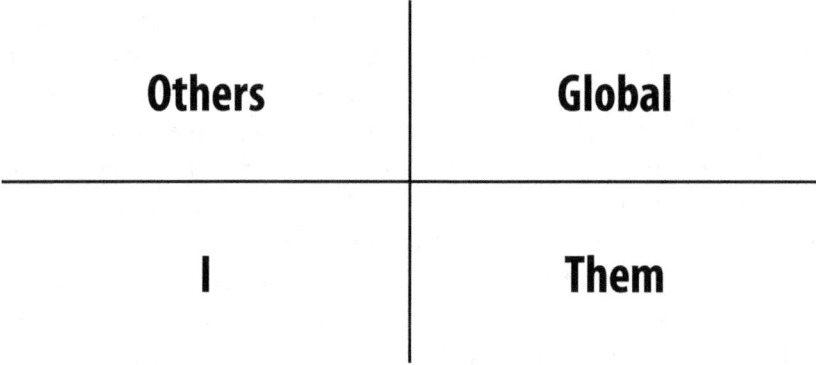

Figure 5: The Perspective Quadrant

Let me explain each of the quadrants to you.

I (first person) – refers to your perspective as an individual on a given issue or matter. It refers to the perspective you readily have immediate and direct access to. It is the angle from which you see a situation without considering any other angle. Most people stay in this quadrant, without seeing things from another person's point of view.

Them (second person) – refers to the other individual directly engaged in the matter and their perspective on it. For example, 'Them' could refer

---

76 In developing this model, I was mainly inspired by The Perceptual Positions model (and pattern) originally formulated by John Grinder and Judith DeLozier in 1987 as operational extensions of the Neuro-linguistic Programming (NLP) concept of Referential Index. By Referential Index, Grinder and DeLozier ask the question: who or what are you referring to when you say, 'that', 'they', 'it', 'him', or 'her' in a sentence? For example, if you say, 'They are the problem', the Referential Index is 'they'. Following on from Grinder and DeLozier's model, Ken Wilber, founder of Integral Theory and the Integral Institute, discovered the four Quadrants – the four integral perspectives of reality – in 1994, despite having limited knowledge of NLP. I made modifications to that model to align with the Being Framework as part of the *awareness* conversation.

to a client, an employer, an employee, your business partner, your life partner, or the opposing political party to the one you follow.

Others – refers to anyone else not directly involved in the matter at hand, although they may be impacted by it. They could be other staff or colleagues, the rest of the leadership team or board of directors, extended family members, and so on. While you (I) and another person (Them) are disagreeing over something, they (Others) are observing the matter from a different angle or perspective. Often there are blind spots not visible or obvious to two people in an argument but quite clear to others not directly involved in the matter, despite the fact that they may be impacted by it. When a husband and wife are constantly arguing to the point where they are on the brink of separation, other family members may see the matter quite differently. They may see hope where the couple thinks there is none, and suggest they seek professional mediation to help guide each party to see things from the other person's perspective. If two staff members disagree on the direction of a project, their colleagues (Others) may see the situation from a completely different angle.

Global – represents a simple, remote overview of the situation. The Global Perspective is a dispassionate, unattached view of the situation and views it as an observer, not a direct participant. It is akin to viewing an event from the other side of the world or a helicopter view.

It is only natural that, as human beings, our initial perspective of any situation is our own (I). Effective people, including the top leaders and high achievers of the world, are very aware of this fact. But while they have their own perspective of any given situation, they are also willing and able to put themselves in the shoes of others when evaluating situations or making decisions. In other words, they have the ability to see things from the perspective of others. They know it's not about being right or wrong. It's about being able to give up being right in the moment so they can capture the fuller picture. Don't get me wrong, this is not about being 'kind', or 'nice'. It's a practical way of thinking, because knowing what others think and appreciating what's in it for them enables you to influence them, whether you are selling your vision to your employees to get them on board or negotiating to win market share against your competitors. Seeing a matter from the perspective of others also enables them to be empathetic and compassionate, not just as 'soft traits', but in a practical way that raises their *awareness* to get to the bottom of matters and solve problems. This is a crucial quality to possess if you want to partner with others in business or in your personal life, attract and recruit new talent, win more clients, identify a pain point in the market, create an innovative product or service, tailor your communication so you are clearly understood by your audience, and the list goes on. I cannot emphasise strongly enough how critical this quality is.

The Leader Perspective

All four perspectives in the quadrant are valid, though none provides an all-encompassing and overarching view required for effective leadership. That's why I have included a fifth perspective called the Leader Perspective that encompasses all other perspectives in the quadrant and therefore sits above the Perspective Quadrant to provide a 360-degree view. I sometimes call this the 'Truth Seeker Perspective' because it describes an individual who seeks the reality or truth of a situation or matter from every conceivable angle, as though they are using a 3D scanner to view it. It is the most comprehensive perspective and provides the ability to see the totality of a matter or situation. The Leader Perspective is the most all-encompassing view possible. To gain this perspective requires you to see things from all four quadrants (I, Them, Others and Global). Truth seeking leaders would view matters from the Leader Perspective most of the time because they know this is the only way to access the heart of a matter, enabling them to make effective decisions and ultimately leading to optimal outcomes. They constantly zoom in and zoom out, enabling them to gain both a holistic and specific perspective when assessing and resolving any matter at hand. They may also seek the contribution of others, such as their advisors, key team members, lawyers, accountants, subject matter experts, consultants, etc., to help them shape the most comprehensive view when required to make critical decisions, highlighting their *vulnerability* (openness) and epistemic humility. We see many executives, founders and business owners who are stuck in their 'I' perspective. Because this quadrant does not take other perspectives into account, remaining there is the most sure-fire way of all not to be effective. As a leader, you must understand others in order to build trust and align them to your vision if you want them to contribute.

Let me share a true story with you. Some years ago, I was the Chief Technology Officer (CTO) of a company, meaning I was responsible for the entire IT department, which was made up of several teams. One particular team consisted of a Product Manager, a Lead UX Designer and a team of software developers. The UX Designer reported to the Product Manager and the Product Manager reported to me. The Product Manager and Lead UX Designer used to constantly disagree about various features of the product they were working on. I remember the Product Manager coming to me in despair one day, telling me he'd had enough and wanted to fire the UX Designer. I asked him to tell me the story from his perspective and listened patiently, allowing him to vent. He told me the UX Designer didn't listen to his instructions and feedback on how to design key features of the product. His words were, 'I am the Product Manager. I know what the market wants based on my data-driven evidence of our users. He (the UX Designer) is stubborn. He drives me crazy. I am the boss!' And so it went on. Again, I listened and let him vent. Once he had finished, I asked him to put himself in the UX Designer's shoes, to BE the UX Designer for the purpose of coaching and conflict resolution. During that session, I guided him to become aware of the fact that it made him quite uncomfortable playing a role, despite the fact that he knew it was for coaching purposes. Our session made him aware of the fact that he didn't want to come out of his Perspective Quadrant (I) and put himself in the second quadrant (Them) to see the perspective of the UX Designer. After some encouragement, the Product Manager eventually came to the realisation that he was totally unaware of how the UX Designer was thinking or feeling. He couldn't see things from the UX Designer's perspective because he had no idea what his perspective was; he hadn't bothered to find out. This story highlights a common phenomenon in almost any relationship and virtually any conflict, whether it be in a family, an organisation or even between politicians or the leaders of two nations.

Others (third quadrant) in this particular scenario were the software developers on the team who were constantly being distracted by the arguments between the Product Manager and the UX Designer. Their actions became so disruptive to the team, that it impacted their productivity and therefore the delivery of the software projects they were working on. This set off a chain of negative events because without successful software project completion, the strategy and marketing teams (more Others) were unable to design their marketing campaigns and plan the launch. Had the Project Manager and UX Designer put themselves in the shoes of the Others, they would have seen that it's not just about them. They would have realised that their actions stalled a software product launch, costing the organisation hundreds of thousands of dollars. 'Others' would also apply to the existing clients expecting a new version of their software by a certain date. So, as you can see, the actions of two people who fail to see beyond their own perspective can impact an enormous number of people and cost a fortune to a company. A true leader (one who puts themselves in the Leader Perspective the majority of the time) would take all matters into consideration. They know it's not just about them because they operate with a *higher purpose*, one of the Primary Ways of Being we will explore later.

We human beings can be quite apathetic about moving beyond our own perspective in order to see things from the perspective of others. However, the universe doesn't function that way and does not care much about our narrowed individual perspective. An individual who stays in their own Perspective Quadrant (I) and refuses to seek other perspectives to shape a fuller, more comprehensive picture of a given situation cannot become truly aware of anything. If you see yourself in this description, it is important to understand that you will be limited, because without seeing things from different angles, you will not be able to develop *awareness* of the reality around you. And being unaware, as we have already learnt, comes with significant consequences.

CHAPTER 1.6

Shadow

Unfortunately, there can be no doubt that man is, on the whole, less good than he imagines himself or wants to be. Everyone carries a shadow, and the less it is embodied in the individual's conscious life, the blacker and denser it is. At all counts, it forms an unconscious snag, thwarting our most well-meant intentions.

Carl Jung
Swiss psychiatrist and psychoanalyst, 1875–1961

First articulated by Carl Jung, the 'shadow' describes the troubled portions of who we are deep down, the parts of ourselves many of us are either genuinely oblivious of or choose to reject and repress. Jung referred to those aspects of us as 'our shadow self'. Although I have no intention of diving too deeply into Jungian theory on the shadow, I would like to explore shadow in the context of this framework. Furthermore, while I am borrowing Jung's term, the way the shadow is expressed in this body of work does not entirely replicate how he described it, as I am not fully aligned with its conventional usage in psychoanalysis.

So, what is the shadow in the context of leadership, performance and *effectiveness* in the Being Framework? Put simply, it is those parts of ourselves or the people within our organisation that, when we bring them to our *awareness* (intentional consciousness), we find troubling and uncomfortable. Most of us would rather hide or disguise the shadow side of ourselves – which is reflected in lower levels of, or unhealthy relationships with, our Aspects of Being, particularly *vulnerability* and *authenticity* – because they may contradict our values (priorities), or our morals. Or perhaps they violate our intentions, commitments and the expectations we have of ourselves, others or life in general. Someone who doesn't see the value in being vulnerable, for instance, would avoid being vulnerable by constantly having their guard up and refusing to be open to the ideas and opinions or feedback of others. This can cause many other issues, as you will see when we come to the Vulnerability chapter. The same is true when any other Aspect of Being is troubled, revealing the shadow side. That's because sometimes our shadow demands things of us that we are not comfortable with, like remaining loyal and committed in a relationship we are struggling with or to remove our mask (fake persona) and show our authentic Self. When people come face-to-face with their shadow, regardless of how they may describe it: the 'dark side', 'bad side', or 'troubled side', etc., they often use metaphors to describe these encounters, such as 'facing my demons', 'wrestling with the devil', or even a 'midlife crisis', or 'seven-year itch', to name just a few that you would no doubt be familiar with.

Scarcity or abundance?

The most significant shadow of all is related to the question of whether or not we are fulfilling our potential and living our best life. You may ask yourself, 'Am I living, making decisions and behaving out of scarcity or abundance?' In other words, are you living your life constantly fearful or anxious of deficiency and shortage (scarcity), or do you see countless possibilities in life, deliberately creating opportunities (abundance)? Some other questions you may ask yourself that may raise your *awareness* of the shadow include: 'How am I performing? Am I as effective and accomplished as I could be? Am I working towards fulfilment? Do I have the things I want or, more importantly, am I capable of achieving the goals I set for myself?' While we may do our best to ignore the shadow or hide it, it always sits in our peripheral vision, often arising in our *awareness*, hence its inclusion in the Awareness chapter. Sometimes this happens in our solitude, our quiet moments, when we are reflecting on our lives. Other times, external triggers may bring it up. Some may refer to this as 'rubbing salt into our wounds', but that is a misconception that comes, in part, from a lack of *vulnerability* or openness, but mostly from a tendency to self-sabotage, blame circumstances and play the victim. I know of many so-called 'gurus', or 'coaches' and authors who recommend that people become better actors rather than be authentic and face their shadow, suggesting that being a leader is akin to a stage performance. While our studies have revealed that this 'stage act' may bring about temporary results in the short-term, it very rarely leads to consistent *effectiveness* and long-term beneficial outcomes in life. Furthermore, there are many downsides to leading this double life, which can take a huge toll on our wellbeing and the wellbeing of others around us. We explore this further in the Authenticity and Vulnerability chapters.

The shadow keeps us on our toes

The word 'shadow' tends to have a negative connotation associated with it. However, anything we shine a light on will cast a shadow and our Being is no exception; that is a law of the universe. So, the shadow is actually nothing more than a reflection of ourselves. If you think you don't have a shadow side, perhaps that's because you are not casting light on it, which either points to a lack of *awareness* or, if you are covering it up, a lack of *vulnerability* and *authenticity*. No matter how hard you try to hide or run from it, the shadow is always following you; it is attached to you and won't leave you alone. So, why not acknowledge it and do your best to willingly integrate it into your *awareness* in such a way that you leverage its power? This, at least in part, may encourage you to change and grow rather than letting the shadow frighten you. The absence or shortage of *responsibility* in the face of the shadow is actually the source of malevolence in the world because cruelty and violence spring from weakness and insecurity. 'The only thing necessary for the triumph of evil is for good men to do nothing' – Edmund Burke[77].

The shadow also highlights the ideal, and that is a double-edged sword because it forces us to constantly compare ourselves to that ideal. The shadow shows us the gap between how we are now and the ideal, revealing our potential and where the opportunity for growth lies. On the destructive side, our shadow can crush us through the weight of constant judgement and shred us to pieces with criticism, leading to disappointment, discontentment and dissatisfaction. But on the positive side, the shadow, by its very nature, keeps us on our toes. It can motivate, build us up and drive us forward, which is why it is so crucial to polish and transform our Aspects of Being to shrink the darkness of the shadow and expand on the light side of ourselves.

---

77   This quote is widely attributed to Edmund Burke, including by John F. Kennedy in a speech in 1961, however there is debate around its actual origin.

While the shadow is an innate aspect of ourselves, most of us are wilfully blind, ignorant or negligent to its presence, contribution and impact. Saddest of all is the fact that we tend to hide our troubled qualities, not only from others, but also from ourselves. Hiding the shadow from ourselves and others leads to inauthenticity and a lack of *vulnerability*, causing us to constantly have our guard up and not be open to the truth, even in our own solitude. Instead of looking inward, those who hide and run from the shadow have a tendency to criticise, blame and condemn others rather than facing their own shortcomings and destructive tendencies, pretending that they are completely integrous, effective, virtuous and always right. When we lack *authenticity, vulnerability* and *responsibility* – amongst other qualities or Aspects of Being – through a refusal to acknowledge the shadow, the result is a lack of effective performance. This ultimately leads to great dissatisfaction, a lack of fulfilment in life and potential that may never be actualised. If you feel you do not resonate with this, perhaps that in itself is proof of the very point being made here, and that perhaps it would be in your best interest to question your own willingness to face your shadow.

Ignorance is NOT bliss

If you have trouble facing your shadow, it may be partly the product of your upbringing. Subjects and topics discussed and taught by those who raised you, from your parents to your teachers, may have elicited so much *fear* or *anxiety* that they may have caused you to inadvertently raise your walls so high (lack of *vulnerability*) that the shadow was not granted permission to be brought to the surface, addressed and expressed. As a result, it remained repressed within the unconscious. When the shadow is kept locked within our unconscious, it doesn't just disappear; it continues to operate independently of your intentional consciousness (*awareness*), causing the shadow to run the show rather than you controlling it. When you are hijacked by your troubled side, you feel disarmed and powerless in the face of it. The shadow could then potentially impact some, or even all, of your *Aspects of Being*, infiltrating your emotions, moods, thoughts, decisions and actions. However, while you may not have been at fault as a child – you may even have the wounds and scars to prove it – if you continue to be negligent and victimise yourself into adulthood, you will do yourself no favours at all. As an adult, you cannot remain ignorant and negligent to your shadow. From the moment you become independent, the unpleasant consequences you are dealing with are self-imposed and not purely the result of bad luck or fate. Iron is destroyed by its own rust. Likewise, our shadow can destroy us if we let it run the show. We can be our own worst enemy. So, while we all have a shadow side, some of us dare to acknowledge it, instead of averting our gaze away from it, and care enough to take charge, harness it and leverage its power to thrive rather than letting it take control and rule our lives.

Whenever I discuss anything related to our shadow, I am reminded of Jiminy Cricket from one of my all-time favourite movies, *Pinocchio*[78]. In the movie, Jiminy Cricket is the loveable character who plays the role of Pinocchio's conscience. Just as Jiminy Cricket keeps pulling Pinocchio back into line in the story, our conscience sets us back on track whenever we are deviating from the straight line, not just morally, but also in terms of our alignment and congruence with our purpose. Carl Jung said, 'Until you make the unconscious conscious, it will direct your life and you will call it fate.' This lack of *awareness* can rob you of your beautiful gift of *responsibility* (autonomy) and take you anywhere it wants to. You may call it destiny, but to a large extent you are actually paving the way yourself, hence you are responsible.

Unfortunately, too many people go with the 'ignorance is bliss' excuse. Some even turn to pseudo-scientific arguments, leveraging Personality Theory or more recent neuroscientific theories that tell us we are all 'hardwired' to be a certain way, so we should just learn to deal with it and minimise its impact. These are nothing more than hopeful delusions. Our studies of high achievers and great leaders and, more importantly, the vast experience we have working with different people and organisations, prove that transformation IS possible. Granted, it's not an easy process, but it is definitely possible and incredibly rewarding. As a matter of fact, most of the self-made high achievers we studied came from extremely troubled backgrounds. But instead of letting themselves be crushed by the darkness, they grabbed the shadow by the

---

78   *The Adventures of Pinocchio* was written by Carlo Collodi in 1883. The story was adapted for the big screen in 1940 by Walt Disney as an animated musical fantasy film called *Pinocchio*.

neck, interrogated it and transformed themselves by not only integrating the shadow into their *awareness* and experience of life but also taking charge of it rather than letting it control them. Their accomplishments, lifestyle and financial gains are the direct by-products of their willingness and ability to leverage the power of their shadow and transform. This is beyond comprehension for most people, either because they have never achieved anything like it themselves, or they haven't been exposed to, raised or trained by people with such perceptions. Thinking back to Ludwig Wittgenstein's rabbit-duck image in the Web of Perceptions sub-chapter, you will only ever see a duck if you've never seen a rabbit before. But in reality, anyone can achieve that calibre of accomplishments in their life if they are committed to undergoing the massive transformation required to become a Being who is capable of generating that calibre of results.

It is common in our societies to categorise people in economic classes, as if we are somehow hardwired to remain in a particular category for the rest of our lives. Many people also expect 'Robin Hood' to come along to distribute the wealth equally, irrespective of whether or not the recipients have a polished Being. Furthermore, there seems to be a common expectation that 'high achievers' should be penalised by being placed in a higher tax bracket, based purely on their income, assets and how much cash they have in the bank, to bring about a so-called 'equality of outcome'. It's as if people believe the wealth in our society has somehow been unfairly distributed. In reality, those who hold such opinions are so busy pointing their finger at others to make up for their own lack of *integrity*, that they fail to acknowledge that their lack of accomplishments is a direct reflection of the fact that their shadow is running the show.

I learnt, through my studies, that it is not the financial wealth inherited from parents, for example, that makes the next generation wealthy, high achievers or influential; in most part it is their parents' state of Being that helps generate that outcome. It's how parents are being, their manner and attitude, their worldview, their paradigm of thinking, how they conduct themselves and immerse their Being in the world. It's the degree to which they participate in life authentically, freely, courageously, etc., that they pass on to the next generation through education, example and opportunities. Generally speaking, our formal education systems are light years away from delivering those critical qualities to our youth. True high achievers are significantly more aware, knowledgeable and wise than the average person, which is why they outperform the majority and, in their youth, excel beyond the limitations of the formal education systems. However, most people only see the outcomes they produce, often making up stories about how they were able to achieve results far beyond those achieved by the greater majority.

Unfortunately, most people, including our politicians, create their own parallel delusional realities and act upon them. A simple glance into the systems we designed ourselves, such as our 'fair' tax systems, are testament to that. You need epistemic humility, open-mindedness, *vulnerability* and *authenticity* to pave your way towards *awareness, integrity* and *effectiveness*. Consider that even if we were to give all the money to the 'poor', they are highly likely to remain 'poor'. When I say 'poor', I am not referring to a lack of monetary wealth, I am referring to a lack of dreams and ambitions, *awareness, higher purpose*, etc. In other words, I am referring to those people being poor in the sense that they are enslaved by their shadow. They are not manifesting and attuning themselves to the world in a way that works for them, indicating a clear lack of *integrity* and *effectiveness*.

Embracing and assimilating the shadow

As mentioned, the shadow is as helpful as it is disturbing. On the disturbing side, it is ugly and scary, which is why dealing with it is so uncomfortable and confronting. No wonder we are tempted to avert our gaze away from the 'monstrous' troubled parts of ourselves and try to keep them hidden in the closet! However, the very fact that we do not want to face our shadow is precisely why we put our guard up (lack *vulnerability*) and are inauthentic. Whenever the shadow disturbs the high achievers of the world, they don't avoid it. On the contrary, they interrogate that piece of darkness, discover that unknown, and travel that unexplored realm with *courage* until they find even the tiniest thread they can grab hold of and, like the reins of a horse, use it to change course and defeat the dragon in its lair. As a leader, this is about owning whatever it is that is not serving you and your organisation well. This begins with *awareness* and then requires *vulnerability, courage, authenticity, responsibility, care, love* and many other qualities we are yet to explore deeply in this book. Some renowned thinkers consider the shadow to be far more mysterious than I describe in this framework. Daryl Sharp wrote in his book, *C. G. Jung Lexicon*[79]: 'There is no generally effective technique for assimilating the shadow. It is more like diplomacy or statesmanship and it is always an individual matter. First, one has to accept and take seriously the existence of the shadow. Second, one has to become aware of its qualities and intentions. This happens through conscientious attention to moods, fantasies and impulses. Third, a long process of negotiation is unavoidable'. Yet my team and I managed to break the shadow down into smaller chunks, rendering them far more manageable to contend with and wrestle. I am referring here to the unhealthy or lower end of the spectrum for each Aspect of Being.

If we fail to embrace and integrate the shadow side of ourselves into our *awareness*, our shadow will take control and pull our strings like a puppeteer. The level of control our shadow exerts upon us also accounts for the destructive and self-destructive behaviours so many individuals struggle with and are unable to turn around despite consciously knowing they are harmful, both to themselves and the people around them. In severe cases, this can lead to substance abuse, addiction, relationship breakdowns and even suicide. While the vast majority of us do not fall into the extreme category, we all have a level of unresolved matters going on deep within ourselves that may prevent us from living fulfilling lives.

If you think this conversation around the shadow is restricted to your personal life, think again. It is equally relevant to the workplace. After all, every organisation consists of a group of individuals, all with their own shadow selves (including your own). Just as organisations can conduct Business Process Modelling (BPM[80]) to analyse and transform the processes within the enterprise, the Being Framework – particularly the team feature of the Being Profile assessment tool – can be employed to perform a similar function to assess, direct and support their people.

---

[79] Sharp, Daryl. *C. G. Jung Lexicon: A Primer of Terms and Concepts.* Toronto: Inner City Books, 1991.

[80] Business Process Modelling (BPM) in business process management and systems engineering is the activity of representing processes of an enterprise, so that the current process may be analysed, improved, and automated.

The collective shadow of people in a team or in an organisation leads to issues like low performance, presenteeism, high employee turnover, etc. Any of these will cause confusion, wastage, and dysfunction, ultimately resulting in low revenue, low profitability and the organisation not being able to fulfil its mission. So, don't be naive and let the professional facade of your people fool you. Beneath the business attire and the fake personas, we are all human beings with our own shadow to contend with, and this is amplified when it involves an entire organisation.

Any institution that involves human beings, such as religious and government bodies, falls into the same category as organisations, but on a far bigger scale. So, when people complain of a dysfunctional government body for instance, it reflects the dysfunctionality and lack of *integrity* of the people that make up the organisation, especially its leaders, not the organisation itself. This creates a dysfunctional system, which has a negative flow-on effect on businesses and the community. People create the system – or any man-made construct, including culture – so why blame the system when we are negatively impacted? Why complain that the system needs to change when it is actually the creators/the people who need to change in order to transform the system? Our systems will only ever be as healthy and effective as the creators (our collective Beings). To transform the system, we must transform ourselves first. From a societal perspective, this is a reflection of all citizens because we are the ones who collectively elect our leaders or implicitly follow dictators. We are the ones who give them the power. I'm sure you can see the potentially far-reaching implications when the shadow is in control on such a grand scale. It is our collective shadow that results in collective psychosis.

While it is widely accepted that there is no universal method to integrate the shadow into our consciousness, in the Being Framework, we start by first raising your *awareness* around its existence and then supporting you to identify the specific areas that are impacted by your shadow through the Ontological Model. We begin by identifying and raising your *awareness* to any dysfunctions – Aspects of Being with which you do not have a healthy relationship – that are causing your performance and *effectiveness* to suffer. This allows you to see the current impacts those dysfunctionalities are having on your life with great clarity and predict the potential consequences of those troubled parts in your future endeavours. Once you are awakened to or have a perception of the shadow, you can begin to shape your conception of those troubled parts. This lays the foundation for the process of transformation, as explained later in *Part 3: Being, in Action*. While the methodology is not a step-by-step guide, it will give you the necessary groundwork to gradually develop your ability to face your shadow and take control of it rather than let it control you. This is where an ontological coach can support you to start acknowledging, and then negotiating with, your troubled parts, so you can eventually transform them one by one. The more polished your whole Being (integrous), the less power you give to your shadow side to keep dragging you down and blocking you from achieving *effectiveness* and fulfilment in all areas of your life. This is true redemption, redeeming your authentic Self, autonomy (*responsibility*) and freedom – the *integrity* of your Being in its entirety. Through my studies and experience working with people, I found there is only a very small percentage of people who are irredeemable. So, don't underestimate the power that begins with perception and conception, as that is the very source of renewal. No growth is possible until your shadow is confronted to the point where it rattles you and makes you uncomfortable – more on this in the Authenticity and Vulnerability chapters.

Whenever I talk about the assimilation of the shadow, it reminds me of Lai Zhide's *Taiji River*[81], a diagram in which the two spirals brilliantly depict the integration of the light side with the shadow.

Simplified form of Lai Zhide's Taiji River Diagram (1599)

---

81   François Louis shows a version of Lai Zhide's diagram in a 1969 representation. François Louis, 'The Genesis of an Icon: The "Taiji" Diagram's Early History', *Harvard Journal of Asiatic Studies* 63.11 (June 2003). The origin of the image shown, omitting the River Diagram superimposed on the spirals, is unknown.

As far as this framework is concerned, every Aspect of Being has a shadow side. When you have an unhealthy relationship with any of the Aspects of Being shown in the Being Framework Ontological Model, it articulates a piece of your shadow Self. You will notice that for every Aspect of Being, we have an ontological distinction – defining the quality in the context of the Being Framework. When we talk about higher levels of or a healthy relationship with each quality, we are referring to the light side, and when we refer to lower levels, we are referring to the shadow/troubled side, indicating an unhealthy relationship with that quality. The aim is to first raise your *awareness* to each dysfunctional and unpolished area, and then care enough to question it and harness its power in a constructive way, rather than hiding it from yourself and others. The ultimate aim is to transform your relationship with all Aspects of Being, moving towards wholeness (*integrity*) and *effectiveness*. In short, if you leverage its power, the shadow can encourage you to grow and gradually become a more aware, more integrous, more effective and, therefore, more fulfilled and accomplished being. This makes you capable of projecting your Unique Being to the world and, in so doing, expand the reality (Second-layer Reality) out there in a constructive way and be a *contribution* to the world. Leveraging the power of the shadow is also the gateway to honour your dignity as a human being beyond *effectiveness* and fulfilment.

CHAPTER 1.7

Vision

Where there is no vision, the people perish.

Proverbs 29:18
The New International Version (NIV) Bible

It's always hard for me to talk about vision without referencing the above quote from The Bible. In my opinion, there is no better way to describe what would be the high-level consequence of a lack of vision for human beings. We would perish. By vision, I am not referring to a goal or a dream for the future. I am referring to the more literal meaning of the word, which is to see or observe. The Hebrew word *Paw-rah* means 'to perish'. There is a biblical proverb in which a woman's long hair was let loose from her headscarf and allowed to flow freely. Unconstrained in the wind, her hair was blown in all directions, blocking her vision. The word *Paw-rah* was used in the proverb to metaphorically convey that without vision we perish.

Without vision, there is also no direction. It reminds me of a scene from *Alice in Wonderland*[82] when Alice asks the Cheshire Cat which road she should take.

> Cheshire Cat: 'Where are you going?'
>
> Alice: 'Which way should I go?'
>
> Cheshire Cat: 'That depends on where you are going.'
>
> Alice: 'I don't know. I just wanted to ask you, which way I ought to go?'

---

82   *Alice in Wonderland* is a 1951 American animated musical fantasy film produced by Walt Disney Productions and based on the Alice books by Lewis Carroll.

> Cheshire Cat: 'Well, that depends on where you want to get to.'
>
> Alice: 'It doesn't really matter, as long as …'
>
> The Cheshire Cat interrupts Alice at this point and responds with: 'Well, then it doesn't matter which way you go.'

Without vision, there is no understanding of what is going on. You simply cannot be a leader, let alone a leader worth following, if you are oblivious to your Being, polished and unpolished Aspects of Being, strengths and weaknesses and the collective Being of the people in your team. This is so critical, because without vision, nobody will be able to realise their potential, including you and every individual in your organisation. It will even impact the ability for people who join you in the future to realise their potential because it will set the direction for your recruitment strategies, more specifically, the type of people you wish to attract and recruit. You must first be aware that your vision is lacking, and this requires you to have access to reality and be willing to show epistemic humility.

Where there is no light, there is no vision; nothing can be seen. Similarly, nothing can be seen where there is no vision (when one is blind). And there is also no vision when there is too much light, such as when one is blinded by the light after looking directly into the sun. These are examples of vision in a literal sense. Metaphorically speaking, when there is too much light, it means your cup is full or you are not showing epistemic humility by being vulnerable, or you are trapped in your current web of perceptions or narrative lens. What point am I making here? Sometimes a lack of vision gets in the way of *awareness* and there are also times when our intellect gets in the way of the truth and prevents us from accessing Reality. This is precisely where epistemic humility and a willingness to be vulnerable or open is required. I have encountered and worked with many people who were blocked from reaching true *awareness* by their existing knowledge, opinions, beliefs and web of perceptions. I still do. And I am not ashamed to admit that I was one of them, and may still be in some areas of my life.

The word 'vision' is the faculty or state of being able to see, the ability to think about or plan the future with imagination or wisdom. It is derived from the Latin *Videre*, 'to see'. Someone who is visionary is forward thinking; they understand human beings – including themselves – and the environment. A visionary person challenges the status quo, is ahead of the game and is disruptive. This is partly why most leaders are not easily understood by the masses. Being visionary also comes with a level of pain, passion and suffering because it allows us to see what most can't. It gives us the *courage* to fuel our passion, respond to our calling or be so present to the suffering in the world that we use our high level of *responsibility* to do something about it. This is what I believe I have done by developing the Being Framework.

When you have vision and are so present to the suffering around you that it fuels a burning desire to effect constructive change, you can choose to articulate that vision. You can also turn your vision into a product or service and, assuming your product or service resonates with enough people, either exchange it for money as a commercial enterprise or know you have made an impact as a not-for-profit. The greater the impact you make, the more people you serve and the higher the probability that you will be wealthy and/or live a fulfilling life. As mentioned before, having vision also enables you to read human beings; to see deep within yourself and the people around you and determine your/their relationship with every Aspect of Being at any given time. This is such an important quality for a leader to possess. It is the reason I created the Ontological Model: to see each Aspect of Being within yourself and others as though you are looking through a lens. In this way, the model provides visibility and clarity on which Aspects of Being to work on for *effectiveness*.

No shortcuts to enlightenment

When our heart, eyes and ears are sealed[83], that's when we suffer the most and cause the most suffering. That's because when we are blocked to our *awareness*, we lack access to reality and are being inauthentic. It's painful and it costs us dearly. It costs us our profitability and potentially the business itself. It can cost us our marriage and our relationship with our parents or children. It can cost us our dreams and our goals. It can cost us our pride and fulfilment. Most importantly, it can cut short the

---

83   Inspired by a verse in The Quran – Al-Baqarah 2:7.

limited time we have in this world! Even the most intelligent among us cannot make good decisions and be effective in our efforts when we are misinformed. A bridge designed by the world's brightest engineer will collapse if he ignores the basic laws of physics and engineering. That's why we must keep all gateways of acquiring knowledge open. So, the very first step towards shaping a vision is to start by being willing (epistemic humility) to learn to become aware, to see more than just the surface of the matter, but to get to the bottom of it. There are simply no shortcuts to enlightenment. While this may seem easy enough to understand, many of us refuse to allow ourselves to be vulnerable and let the light of the truth override our beliefs, opinions, perceptions and the stories we continually tell ourselves and others. Sometimes this is the result of genuinely being unaware, other times it points to a lack of *vulnerability* and *authenticity*. It takes a lot of *courage* to step up to the path of truth seeking and allow ourselves to be vulnerable and authentic. But guess what? Once you take that first step, there is nothing more rewarding because it will lead you on a continual journey towards *effectiveness*, accomplishment, fulfilment and prosperity.

Shaping your vision begins with a healthy relationship with *awareness*

When you see and are fully present to the suffering that is happening around you and how it impacts you and others, and choose powerfully to address it, that is the time your commitment to the cause simply cannot be questioned. Your level of *care* – a Mood that will be explained later in the book – would be so high, that you would choose to be all in, to commit yourself to a cause or a goal with *higher purpose*, an integral part of your Being, the source of your power.

Shaping your vision begins with *awareness*. Then, if you have the *self-expression, presence, courage, authenticity* and *responsibility* to choose to act on it, you will have the *commitment* to see it through, no matter what obstacles you encounter along the way. In my experience working with many entrepreneurs, I have come to realise that one of the main reasons they feel they have failed is that they simply gave up too early. They didn't see it clearly enough to give it their all by continually refining different aspects of their business until they hit their Product/Market

Fit[84]. When I dug down to the root cause of the matter, I discovered that these entrepreneurs lacked sufficient *care* to keep working on their business idea with complete faith, persevering no matter how many times they needed to refine their idea. In the end, it wasn't that the business idea had no merit or that the entrepreneur wasn't good enough or smart enough, etc., it was a lack of vision as well as unpolished Aspects of Being that led to their failure. It is worth noting that these issues are not limited to startups or aspiring entrepreneurs. I have seen this occurring in many SMEs, mature businesses and corporations while undergoing transformation or launching new products.

With vision comes discernment

To have vision is to be so acutely aware of something that you see things beyond what others see on the surface. The depth and clarity of your vision will compel you to act and take ownership because you will see it as your calling. With vision comes discernment, which is different to judgement. Discernment, or the ability to tell the difference between one thing and another and choose accordingly, is one of the main reasons education – not necessarily of the formal variety – matters so much. Education leads to wisdom, which helps you shape a vision by discerning where to focus your efforts. Discernment will enable you to make effective decisions, and face catastrophes and adversities in life head on rather than be crushed by them.

With vision and discernment comes maturity. This in turn gives you the ability to make the right sacrifices, since no one can have it all. The power resides in your ability to discern where you focus your efforts and make sacrifices, as this will lead to the ultimate objective, which is to be effective. For instance, an athlete makes enormous sacrifices, including in other areas of their life where they may also have great potential, because they have chosen to focus on competing at the highest level. They made that decision with vision and discernment. You can do the same in your life.

---

84 Product/Market Fit, also known as Product-market Fit, is the degree to which a product satisfies a strong market demand. Product/Market Fit has been identified as a first step to building a successful venture in which the company meets early adopters, gathers feedback and gauges interest in its product.

As children, we were full of potential. The world was our oyster; we could be almost anything we wanted to be. However, as we grew up and our vision and *awareness* of who we are (Unique Being) developed, we started discerning what we wished to focus on, and this required us to make sacrifices in other areas of our life in order to be effective in our chosen endeavours. With maturity, comes the ability to predict the future consequences of the choices we make today. This is yet another benefit vision brings to the table. Shaping a vision, developing discernment and gradually moving towards maturity enables us to predict the consequences of our business and personal decisions in the future and could even lead to a self-fulfilling prophecy.

Tapping into intuition

The greatest visions are those that combine rationale and intuition. Most visionary leaders we have studied solve unstructured problems by tapping into their intuition and calling. Both intuition and calling are Meanings that are not necessarily tangible, cognitive or rational enough for the mainstream to fully comprehend. They claim to connect to a transcendent consciousness while making critical decisions. Some would call this 'risk taking', but it is more than that. In the words of Steve Jobs, 'You can't connect the dots looking forward; you can only connect them looking backwards. So, you have to trust that the dots will somehow connect in your future'. You have to learn to trust your intuition if you want to perform at the highest level. In fact, intuition is one of the most essential resources in every visionary leader's decision-making toolbox. It's about tapping into a higher consciousness than your intellect alone.

In 2013, Apple CEO, Tim Cook spoke in an interview about how intuition led him to Apple. He said he accepted the role with Apple despite having just accepted a new position with the top PC company in the world at the time and despite others telling him he was crazy to consider it, as they claimed Apple was on the verge of collapse. But he chose to ignore them and listen to his intuition. He said, 'The struggle most people have is learning to listen to it (their intuition) and figuring out how to access it. Even though I'm an engineer and an analytical person at heart, the most important decisions I've made had nothing to do with any of that. They were always based on intuition'. I have seen the same thing over and over again studying other great leaders of the world. I remember reading *The Road Ahead* [85] by Bill Gates, Nathan Myhrvold and Peter Rinearson when I was a teenager and trying to comprehend what paradigm they were living in that enabled Gates and Microsoft to be the great leader and company they were (and still are today). The title of the book alone speaks volumes. You need only pull out a few quotes, bearing in mind they were made in the mid-1990s, to see how ahead of his time Gates was.

> 'Computers are great because when you're working with them you get immediate results that let you know if your program works. It's feedback you don't get from many other things.'

> 'We'll find ourselves in a new world of friction, overhead capitalism, in which market information will be plentiful and transaction costs low. It will be a shopper's heaven.'

> 'Corporations will redesign their nervous systems to rely on the networks that reach every member of the organization and beyond into the world of suppliers, consultants and customers.'

That book inspired me to become a Microsoft Certified Trainer, a role I held for some time. Now, I am sure some of you may find this conversation on intuition hard to relate to or may struggle to grasp it, particularly as you are reading a book centred around objective studies of *effectiveness* and leadership. I completely understand, as I too was once less open than I am today to such arational matters. But I would encourage you to pay attention to the advice of some of the world's most visionary leaders and be open to your intuition, which some of you may call a 'gut feeling'. After all, as a leader, you will not always have access to accurate data to make rational data-driven decisions. While this conversation goes beyond the scope of this book, it was important to touch on within this sub-chapter as vision and intuition are intrinsically linked. They help us be discerning with our decision making.

---

85 Gates, Bill, Nathan Myhrvold and Peter Rinearson – *The Road Ahead*. NY: Viking Penguin, 1995, rev 1996. *The Road Ahead* summarised the implications of the personal computing revolution and described a future profoundly changed by the arrival of a global information superhighway.

Vision in business

Whether you are an entrepreneur or a leader of an organisation, having vision is critical. You must become aware of something REAL that the other players in your industry are oblivious to and then do your best to raise *awareness* of it with your customers. Vision is also critical in business because it raises your *awareness* of how you, and others in your organisation, are being at any given time through your/their relationship with the Aspects of Being relating to performance, *effectiveness* and leadership.

It is common for organisations to have a vision statement. A vision statement is a document that articulates the future destination of the company. It is usually intended as a roadmap to ensure the organisation is clear on where it is going and makes decisions that align with that direction. Almost every organisation has one, but not many actually manifest their vision statement through their missions. But what does an effective vision look like? And how is it created? Essentially, it begins with the founders of an organisation becoming aware of a pain point for humanity, a problem that many – or at least a segment of the market – can resonate with. They visualise how the world would look if that pain were addressed. They come up with the solution to solve the pain point and work out a way to turn that solution into a service or product that the market will see so much value in that people are willing to exchange money for it.

The greatest visions in history began by addressing pain or suffering: the pain of not being able to search for information online was addressed by the founders of Google; the pain of not being able to adequately illuminate a room was addressed by Thomas Edison; the pain of not having automated transportation was solved by Henry Ford; the pain of spending months at sea was solved when the Wright brothers invented the aeroplane; the pain of waging war in the Middle East over oil is currently indirectly being addressed by Elon Musk through a focus on sustainable energy; and the list could go on and on. In all these cases, a pain point or series of problems was identified by an individual or a team. The key point here is that, at least for the most part, the pain point was not created, but discovered.

Almost all products that serve a large portion of the population resolve a deep psychological problem for the market. In other words, at the heart of almost any successful organisation lies products or services that address a deep psychological problem within humanity. At some point, someone (or some people) became so present to the suffering and cared so much about it, that they took it upon themselves – through their high level of *responsibility* and *higher purpose* – to do something about it. Resolving the suffering of so many in this way normally brings enormous financial rewards. I am not necessarily suggesting that this applies to all businesses or that all founders view business this way. There are many business ventures that are more directly driven by financial exchanges than others. But after studying the world's top companies, founders and executives, we know that unless a business's first priority is to authentically serve and provide value to a mass market, they are not likely to survive, let alone thrive to that extraordinary level.

Our studies have found that all great leaders work with a team of coaches, mentors and advisors for guidance on various aspects of their leadership qualities as well as to help them see the opportunities and threats around them. In your own business, you could engage a coach to help raise your *awareness* and shape a vision. A common way a coach does this is by asking questions and drawing your attention to your blind spots. These sources of support alert you to some of the opportunities or risks around you that you are currently oblivious to and are therefore unable to take advantage of or mitigate. You could also work with a mentor who has been through a similar journey to show you the way. If you choose not to be guided by a team of experts, you are choosing to be limited by your own knowledge. This is yet another phenomenon that costs those who aspire to be leaders of influence. Remember, when you are a leader, it's not just about you. You are to manifest *higher purpose*. Your decisions, Ways of Being, Moods and actions impact many others. We will examine *higher purpose*, one of the Primary Ways of Being, later in the book.

So, to recap, the ultimate objective of gaining access to *awareness* is to shape a vision, be discerning and develop your *effectiveness* as a leader. Without *awareness* and vision, you cannot lead. And without vision, your business is unlikely to survive, let alone thrive. It is worth reiterating here that you simply cannot become effective in something you are not aware of. That's why *awareness* is so critical, and without *awareness*, you cannot transform.

In summary

We began this chapter by exploring *awareness* at a high level, narrowing the scope to human beings in the area of performance, *effectiveness* and leadership. We examined the three layers of reality – First, Second and Third-layer Reality – and our access to each layer. We talked about epistemic humility, which is being open to matters we may not know – or thought we knew – only to discover that we actually didn't. At times, we needed to jump into the depths of the unknown and wander into unexplored territories. We examined matters that can block our access to *awareness*, such as the web of perceptions we spin, where every node represents a single perception and threatens to trap us. The other matter that prevents us from accessing *awareness* is our narrative lens: the collection of stories we create for ourselves or are manufactured by external forces, such as culture, religion, mainstream academia and the media. We examined the Perspective Quadrant, learning that if we stay in our own Perspective Quadrant (I) and refuse to seek other perspectives (especially the Leader Perspective) to shape a fuller, more comprehensive picture of a given situation, we cannot become truly aware of anything. Last but not least, before this discussion on vision, we explored the shadow, those parts of ourselves or the people in our organisation that, when we bring them to our *awareness*, we find troubling and uncomfortable. We learnt that when we have an unhealthy relationship with any of the Aspects of Being in the Being Framework Ontological Model, it articulates a piece of our shadow Self. The aim is to become aware of these dysfunctional and unpolished areas and then care enough to question the shadow and harness its power in a constructive way. *Awareness* is the beginning of the transformation process. It's the eureka moment that begins the journey towards *effectiveness*.

CHAPTER 2

Integrity

*So, that there should be no division in the body,
but that its parts should have equal concern for each other.
If one part suffers every part suffers with it ...*

Corinthians 12:25-26
The New International Version (NIV) Bible

Besides being an entrepreneur, philosopher and technologist, I love to cook. And while I am quite skilled in food preparation, on rare occasions, the knife is faster than my fingers and I cut myself. When this happens, it is remarkable how frequently I am reminded of this little mishap the following day. Whether I am holding the steering wheel, typing on my computer or picking something up from the floor, that minor injury, which when mentioned, is almost laughable, reminds me that something is not working as well as it could. When we talk about *integrity*, we refer to it as something whole, something where everything is in its rightful place and working as it should. With reference to the cut on my finger, that small deviation from perfection and wholeness, had an impact, albeit minor, on other areas of my life. We could say the physical ability to function as intended was not integrous. It lacked *integrity*. Now, imagine if the issue was far more severe, for example kidney or heart failure or having a major accident that resulted in me being confined to a wheelchair. The impact on other areas of my life would be magnified many times over compared to the cut on my finger. As quoted from Corinthians 12:25-26 above, 'If one part suffers every part suffers with it'. The greater the deviation from *integrity* (wholeness), the greater the suffering.

Saadi[86], a renowned Persian poet and prose writer of the medieval period, took this to another level. Referring to humanity as a whole in the translated excerpt of one of his poems below, he wrote that if someone suffers or causes suffering, many others would suffer too. So, while I refer to *integrity* in the context of an individual in this book, it is worth noting that humanity has integrity too[87].

> *Human beings are members of a whole*
> *In creation of one essence and soul*
> *If one member is afflicted with pain*
> *Other members uneasy will remain*
> *If you have no empathy for human pain*
> *The name of human you cannot retain*[88]

What is *integrity*?

Ontologically speaking, *integrity* is the state of being whole, complete, sound and in perfect condition. There is nothing inherently good or bad about being whole and complete, it is just the way something is or is not. *Integrity* is required to operate at the highest level of performance and to fulfil your potential. It's about human potential. When all cogs in the machine are functioning at their optimum level, the impact will be seen in the quality of the outcome produced. If just one cog is underperforming, the outcome suffers, and it is impossible to reach our full potential. It's like when one part of the body suffers, it impacts the overall effectiveness and functionality of the entire body. You could say the body is lacking 'wholeness' because one or more parts are not operating at their peak. A system has *integrity* when it is whole and complete. Any loss of wholeness of the system, or if certain elements are

---

86   Saadi also known as Saadi of Shiraz (Sa'dī Shīrāzī; born 1210; died 1291 or 1292), was a major Persian poet and prose writer of the medieval period. He is recognised for the quality of his writings and for the depth of his social and moral thoughts.

87   This refers to common Being. Your team has an *integrity* or mutual Being, which links to the performance of the whole team. This is why we have created a team feature of the Being Profile®.

88   *Gulistan* (1258), is a landmark of Persian literature, perhaps its single most influential work of prose. Written in 1258 CE, it is one of two major works of the Persian poet Sa'di, considered one of the greatest medieval Persian poets.

missing, then the system will lose its workability. Should these losses continue, the system will eventually stop working altogether.

As *integrity* declines, workability declines, and as workability declines, the probability of the objective being reached declines. Therefore, *integrity* is required to maximise performance and *effectiveness*. Attempting to violate the law of *integrity* brings about painful consequences, just as surely as attempting to violate the law of gravity does. Put simply, high performance is not possible without *integrity*. Think of this as a heuristic[89], a technique that enables someone to discover or learn something for themselves. If you or your organisation operate in life as though this heuristic is true, performance will increase exponentially.

All Moods and Primary Ways of Being contribute to overall *integrity*. To gauge our Being – our 'what-ness', how we are being, the qualities we possess – it's always best to look internally first. But what does it actually mean to look internally, particularly when it comes to being effective in our endeavours and accomplishing what we want? And how do we gain a clear view of someone's Being (and our own), to see the deep qualities not necessarily visible externally? These were two of the fundamental questions I asked myself that inspired me to develop the Being Framework. Since looking internally is rather vague, my aim was to break down the *integrity* of one's Being into smaller, more digestible chunks, just as in medicine we break down and study different parts of the body individually so that a doctor can assess each individual symptom to determine how to address the ailment appropriately and effectively. For example, in order to diagnose what's going on, the doctor may request a blood test to determine if you are lacking in certain vitamins and minerals. If you present with back or knee pain, the doctor may request an X-ray or MRI to see what's going on. Similarly, in order to assess our *integrity*, we need to look into all subsystems of our Being. In the case of the Being Framework, which is created within the scope of performance, *effectiveness* and leadership, the constituent components

---

89   A heuristic technique, or a heuristic, is any approach to problem solving or self-discovery that employs a practical method that is not guaranteed to be optimal, perfect or rational, but which is nevertheless sufficient for reaching an immediate, short-term goal.

of *integrity* as a Meta Factor are the combination of our Moods and Primary Ways of Being.

Integrity and integration of the shadow

As discussed in the Shadow sub-chapter, when you lack a healthy and effective relationship with any of your Aspects of Being it is a reflection of your shadow. In other words, a low level in any Aspect of Being highlights the shadow side of that Aspect of Being. When that involves any of your Primary Ways of Being and Moods, your *integrity* is directly impacted. To become more integrous, the aim is to identify the troubled parts of your Being by deliberately bringing them to your consciousness and integrating the shadow into your *awareness* and totality of life experience (*Dasein*). This is how it's done. Once you are aware (perception) of a troubled part, make it a priority (start caring) to no longer be negligent and run or hide from it. The next step is to raise your *awareness* of the consequences of that piece of shadow in your life. In other words, you are now comprehending what it means in the context of your life (conception). For instance, consider the impact in your life and the lives of others around you if you were lacking in *responsibility*. Then raise your *awareness* of the ideal on the other end of the spectrum by visualising what your life would look like if that part of you was polished or transformed. Using the *responsibility* example, become aware of how things would be if you were more responsible (autonomous) and in charge of the circumstances in your life. Let the ideal judge and confront you without being crushed by it: that only leads to disappointment, powerlessness, blame, shame, victimisation and self-sabotage. Instead, let the ideal motivate you and fuel your engine to expand your boundaries, thrive and become more powerful. This is how you move towards wholeness (*integrity*), the best version of YOU.

So, while the higher ends of the spectrum of each Aspect of Being constitute your light side (*integrity*), the lower ends of the spectrum constitute your shadow, which gets in the way of your *integrity*. *Integrity* is when you are capable of effectively and consistently shifting your troubled parts (shadow) towards the higher end of the spectrum time after time as you uncover more qualities that need polishing, arranging the parts in the system in such a way that it works for you and brings workability, ease and flow. This is not a one-off project. It is a never-ending process towards true enlightenment and growth. The more you dig, the more you will find. So, it's about the ability to face the shadow with grace. That is precisely what an enlightened or wise person would do.

We all experience times in our lives when we are greatly impacted by our shadow and, as social beings, the shadow side of others. We may lose a loved one, be betrayed by someone we chose to trust, undergo a relationship breakdown, be a victim of fraud or another crime. These are all causes that can make us bitter, shred us to pieces and disorient and confound our soul to the core, making it feel like we can never recover. But as time passes, we can heal our wounds and repair our troubled parts, as long as we choose to powerfully. It's up to us to restore the *integrity* of our Being when it has been turned to dust and ashes, shattered into fragments. Even if at times it seems that all that remains of our Being is a pile of smouldering embers, it is possible to fan the virtue of the tiniest spark found in the ashes to rekindle the fire of our existence. But this is impossible without *authenticity, responsibility, vulnerability, courage, care, forgiveness, love* and *compassion*, amongst other Aspects of Being. It takes every part within us to restore our *integrity* when we are severely impacted by the shadow in one way or another, but it can be done. We can become whole again. This is true redemption. It's when we restore our *integrity* anytime we catch ourselves confused and dismantled. It's when we rise up again to become more powerful than we have ever been before.

The Being Framework ontological distinction of *integrity*

Integrity is the state of being whole, complete, unbroken, sound and in optimal condition. *Integrity* encompasses all primal Aspects of Being in the same way that the various limbs and organs are the constituent parts of your body. *Integrity* is the prerequisite to being effective and operating at the optimal level of performance and is fundamental to generating trust and workability. *Integrity* brings about ease and flow and is considered 'being well', 'well put together' or the wellness of your Being.

A healthy relationship with *integrity* indicates that you know yourself to be sufficient and mostly experience flow and workability in life. Ease, trust and consistency are present for both you and those around you. You actively address and maintain whatever may impair your *integrity*, particularly qualities that are diminished, misplaced or require refinement or transformation.

An unhealthy relationship with *integrity* indicates that you mostly experience frustration and dysfunction, with recurring problems and unresolved issues. There are many areas in your life you feel the need to fix. Others may experience an absence of workability and consistency around you, hence trust and *effectiveness* are often compromised and brought into question. Alternatively, you may be obsessed with perfection and struggle to be with shortcomings or incompletion. You may avoid pursuing matters unless success is ensured.

Why is *integrity* so important?

Integrity is critical because you can't perform at the optimum level that is required to produce the results you expect of yourself if you are not integrous, whole and complete most of the time. In other words, if you do not have a healthy relationship with your Primary Ways of Being (*authenticity, responsibility, commitment, self-expression, love*, and so on), as well as your Moods (*care, fear, anxiety* and *vulnerability*), then it is impossible to perform at the highest level and be effective in your endeavours in life. That's because your *effectiveness*, and subsequently your level of fulfilment in life, are intrinsically tied to your *integrity*. You simply cannot be effective if you are not integrous, and to be integrous, the relationship with all your Moods and Primary Ways of Being must be at an optimum level. How do you become integrous if one or more of these Aspects of Being is suboptimal or lacking? It begins with *awareness*. You cannot polish or transform any Primary Way of Being or Mood if you are not aware of it in the first instance or if your perception of it is incongruent with reality. Ultimately, you cannot be effective in something that you are not aware of. That would be like asking you to fix a problem that you don't even know exists! So, in order for you to be fulfilled – achieving your objectives – you need to be effective, and in order to be effective in your endeavours, you need to be integrous. Technically speaking, you cannot be integrous if any of your Moods or Primary Ways of Being are dysfunctional or severely lacking. And again, you can't address any of these unless, in the first instance, you are aware of them.

Integrity transcends honouring one's word and fulfilling commitments

It is important to understand that *integrity*, as defined within the scope of the Being Framework, doesn't refer to some of the behavioural aspects people commonly associate with the word 'integrity', such as the expectation that a person with integrity will honour[90] their word or fulfil their commitments. Those are only two of the outcomes associated

---

90 While keeping your word is fundamentally important in life, you will not be able to always keep your word (unless you are playing a small game in life). However, you can always honour your word.

with having *integrity*. People often say things like, 'I have integrity because I am always on time and people can rely on me to do my job properly'. Statements like this only define certain aspects of *integrity*. They refer more to fulfilling one's commitments and only go part of the way to defining *integrity*. The Being Framework goes much deeper. I am referring to *integrity* as a complex indicator of being whole and complete. As such, it has a direct relationship with all Primary Ways of Being, and Moods contribute to it. Together, our Primary Ways of Being and our Moods form an integrous human being.

People with a high level of *integrity* project that life is working out the way they want it to. When you are in the company of someone with *integrity*, such as in the workplace, you would find that things run smoothly and are more productive. *Reliability* and trust are consistently present for people with *integrity*. People with lower levels of *integrity*, on the other hand, are constantly confronted by what is missing and find that life is not producing the outcomes they desire, with frequent recurring problems and unresolved issues. When you are in the company of someone with low *integrity* in the workplace, you would experience a lack of consistency, productivity and *effectiveness*. You would question their trustworthiness and *reliability*. This is also true for the person with low *integrity*, who trusts no one and always questions other people's motives.

When clients come to me for assistance because they feel something isn't working as it should in their lives, their confusion or resistance is apparent when I begin to question their *integrity*. Their immediate reaction is to defend themselves, saying something like, 'But I always operate with integrity in everything I do'. When they say something like that, I ask them, 'But where are you out of *integrity* with yourself? For example, if you hold back on speaking up in a meeting because you think your *contribution* is not important enough, you are not being integrous'. When I raise that particular example, it usually rings a bell with them, and they immediately recognise where their feeling of unease or frustration is coming from.

So, if someone is lacking *integrity*, they normally sense that something is not quite right within themselves; they can feel it but not see it clearly. They feel frustrated and confused about why things aren't going to plan.

Because *integrity* is affected by one or more Primary Ways of Being and/or Moods, it is a matter of breaking it down to determine the constituent elements and then work on the underlying issue(s). For example, it could be a *fear* or *anxiety* issue, or it may be related to their *responsibility* or willingness to be vulnerable. When you are introduced to the Being Profile later in this book, you will see how the tool is used to map out how integrous a person is by breaking it down into the sixteen Primary Ways of Being and four Moods. *Integrity* is critical and unavoidable because it has a direct bearing on your *effectiveness*.

Integrity is a state of Being

It is important to understand that *integrity* is not something you HAVE; it is a state of BEING and as such encompasses more than just DOING things in a complete and reliable way. When I bring this conversation to business and entrepreneurship, *integrity* is one of the major players in the game. If you find that things in your business (or within you for that matter) are not working as well as they could be and that results are underwhelming, you can be certain that there is a lack of *integrity* in some parts of your business or in certain aspects of your Being. Identifying and addressing these areas will raise the level of *integrity* and subsequently transform productivity and results.

It is important to reiterate that *integrity* constitutes all your Primary Ways of Being and Moods. When all parts of our body function at an optimal level, we are integrous from both a physiological and ontological perspective. It only takes one part of that system to break down for it to affect all other parts. For instance, if our kidneys don't function properly, waste products and fluid can build up in the body. This can cause swelling of the ankles, nausea, weakness, poor sleep and shortness of breath. In a similar way, when one aspect of our Being breaks down or is lacking, other parts will suffer, and it always impacts our level of *integrity* and therefore our *effectiveness*.

If you do not have a healthy relationship with *fear*, for example, you will freeze in the face of fearful situations. If you are dealing with severe *anxiety*, if you are not being responsible and allowing yourself to be a victim of circumstance instead, or if any part of your Being is suffering or lacking, it will impact your *integrity*. In other words, these things will affect your overall Being, how you are, and therefore impact your performance, *effectiveness* and ultimately the results you produce. It is critical that you understand these relationships. If you fail to comprehend or truly value the link between Primary Ways of Being and Moods with *integrity*, you will not appreciate the remaining content being shared in this book.

The link between *integrity* and Primary Ways of Being and Moods

When I am working with a client with a low level of *integrity*, the first thing I do is examine their Primary Ways of Being and Moods in order to identify the specific areas, qualities and attributes that are contributing to their low *integrity*. Once those aspects have been clearly identified, I can provide the client with sufficient clarity and the relevant information (to raise *awareness*) and tools to begin working on those particular areas, polish their Being and transform into an integrous, effective human being who has the power to achieve the results they want in business and in life.

If you want to discover your own level of *integrity*, take a close look at various aspects of your life and ask yourself, 'Is it working for me?' For example, if you think you could be in better physical shape, the next question to ask yourself would be, 'How does my current physical fitness level impact me and which areas of my life are most affected by my lack of physical fitness?' You may find that a lack of fitness is having a detrimental impact on other areas of life besides your physical health. You may find it causes you to lose focus quickly at work; you may find that your relationships suffer because a lack of fitness may impact your *courage* or *confidence*; you may even find that your finances aren't in great shape because your lack of physical fitness affects your motivation to pursue your financial goals. When you are honest with yourself (*authenticity*), you will find that many areas of life – if not all – can be impacted by just one shortcoming. In short, if your life is not going as well as it could be, it is because *integrity* is lacking, and this requires you to dig deeper to learn why. We all experience this. This is not a finger-pointing exercise. When you take your car in for a service, it is a maintenance check to determine and repair anything that is not working at an optimal level. As we go through life, our *integrity* shifts from time to time. And the bigger the game we play, the more our *integrity* will be challenged and prone to fluctuations. That in itself is not the problem. When you observe that you are lacking *integrity*, restore it as soon as you can and move on. It is that simple, although it's not necessarily easy. There is no need to be hard on yourself about it or dance around the issue by making it look as though others are in the wrong.

If you find yourself resisting addressing a broken area in your life, ask yourself what this ineffective Aspect of Being is costing you. The answer is simple. If it is costing you loss of revenue or employees or even your health or relationship because life has become so stressful, wouldn't you want to resolve the underlying issue? Restoring *integrity* in your life is like weeding a garden. It is essential and you just get on with it without blame or shame. You wouldn't blame the garden because of its lack of weed management! An unpolished Being with low *integrity* is the greatest liability we can have. Low *integrity* and all the underlying issues that contribute to it will cost you your dreams, goals and fulfilment in life.

In summary, and before we move on to the final Meta Factor, *integrity* is a multifaceted Aspect of Being, which is why I organised it under the Meta Factors in the Being Framework Ontological Model. *Integrity* is impacted by all Primary Ways of Being as well as all Moods. It underpins the way you are in all aspects of life. Sitting between *awareness* and *effectiveness* in the Model, *integrity*, like the other two Meta Factors, is tightly linked to your overall performance, power and ability to lead. If your *integrity* is low, it means some of the cogs in the machine are damaged or severely deficient, and this lack of wholeness will ultimately lead you to be less effective in life. On the other hand, the more integrous you are, the more it will manifest itself in all of your Primary Ways of Being and Moods. In other words, you will honour every *commitment*, have *peace of mind*, be authentic, and so on.

CHAPTER 3

Effectiveness

What do you think of when you hear the word 'effectiveness'? Perhaps you relate it to your performance on a task or in a job, or how well you participate or function in life. The *Oxford English Dictionary* defines effectiveness as 'the degree to which something is successful in producing a desired result'. Ontologically, *effectiveness* is the extent to which our commitments and intentions are being fulfilled in the world. There is an important distinction here between what many would perceive to be the definition of effectiveness and what it actually means. Getting started with the right foundation will determine how effective you will be as a leader and consequently how large or valuable an organisation you will be able to build. If your goal is to build a profitable global organisation that serves a broad market and has a positive impact on many people's lives, that goal is well within reach if you strive to become effective. In this chapter, you will learn what it takes to achieve that.

In the last decade or so, my teams and I have consulted and given advice to hundreds of businesses, investors, startups and leaders on how they can be more effective in their leadership practices. In working with them to uncover the issues and roadblocks in their way, we discovered that in many cases, they had no idea what the underlying issues were. In fact, they wanted us to uncover those issues for them. Others came to us with a very specific problem that was causing them significant frustration. Examples included a clash with a board member, conflicts within the co-founding team, a lack of transparency within the team, employee retention issues, or revenue and profitability challenges, to name just a few. Whenever this happened, I would encourage them to redirect their attention away from the problem at hand and towards the major cause.

How? By asking them to search within themselves to see which part of the problem they found that they could own. Doing so allowed us to reveal the major underlying causes of that discontent, dissatisfaction and frustration. You will recall, from the previous chapter on *integrity*, that looking within and breaking down the Primary Ways of Being and Moods that are contributing to a lack of *integrity* or wholeness will raise *awareness* around those issues, thereby laying the groundwork for bringing about the change required to lead you towards *effectiveness*, personally or as a team. This is a lesson I learnt from my martial arts masters when I was just twelve years old, a lesson I later learnt had been validated and taught by many of the world's greatest thinkers, philosophers and business leaders.

The frustration our clients often experienced was the result of something missing, or not quite being in the right place. There was a distinct lack of *integrity*. Metaphorically speaking, some of the cogs in the machine weren't functioning as they should have been or some of the pieces of the puzzle were missing. These misplaced or dysfunctional pieces had led them away from *integrity*, which, as we know from the previous chapter, is key to how individuals experience themselves or others as complete and unbroken. This discovery is fundamental to becoming effective. The Managing Director of a twenty-five-year-old company came to me for coaching, extremely frustrated that company sales targets were not being met. He thought the problem lay with the sales team and kept replacing members of the team who he believed were dysfunctional. During my coaching session with him I discovered that the issue did not lie with the sales team at all. It lay with the fact that the company failed to provide adequate training for new salespeople when they joined the company. As a result, they didn't know the benefits of the core products they were expected to sell. When I raised the subject of *responsibility* (one of the Primary Ways of Being) with him, it quickly became apparent that his perception of *responsibility* was a feeling of personal guilt. In our sessions, he uncovered that there is far more to being responsible than feeling guilty and concerned. Being responsible is owning the problem and taking effective actions to resolve it. As a result, he then decided that replacing sales team members was not an effective solution in this case. The missing cog in the machine was a clear lack of *responsibility*, which came from his distorted perception of *responsibility* and his subsequent ineffective execution of being responsible.

There are times when the issues are more behavioural than primal. The Being Framework Ontological Model acknowledges and addresses this by including the Secondary Ways of Being: *proactivity, resourcefulness, assertiveness, resilience, confidence, accountability, persistence* and *reliability*. These qualities sit near the surface, closer to our behaviours and actions, and are therefore more readily observable than our other Aspects of Being. So, while it is our Moods and Primary Ways of Being (the deeper layers of ourselves) that contribute to our *integrity*, all Aspects of Being – Moods, Primary and Secondary Ways of Being – contribute to our *effectiveness*.

Let's look at an example. If someone came to me for help because they were struggling to ask their boss for a pay rise, the first thing I would do would be to look into their *integrity* by assessing the constitution of their Moods and Primary Ways of Being. This makeup would likely show me that the person's relationship with *fear* and *anxiety* is unhealthy. In other words, fear of losing their job or rejection is suppressing them. This could have an impact on their level of *authenticity*, meaning they may be filtering what they have to say. It could also impact on their *courage* and *self-expression*. These are all deeper matters impacting the person's *effectiveness* in asking for a pay rise, and therefore we would start by working on and ultimately transforming those Aspects of Being. The person in question would also be lacking in *confidence* and *assertiveness*, both Secondary Ways of Being. These qualities are more visible to others as they are more behavioural. So, after working on the deeper, more primal aspects of *fear, authenticity, courage* and *self-expression*, we would also work on techniques and ways to support this person to be more confident and assertive. This would transform their *effectiveness* in the workplace, including their success in achieving the pay rise they desire. Now, if I were to just jump straight into addressing the Secondary Ways of Being – the readily observable behaviours of *confidence* and *assertiveness* – and teach them a few quick techniques for speaking to the boss and skip the deeper Aspects of Being like *courage, authenticity* and *self-expression*, which is what the mainstream coaches and typical behavioural psychologists tend to do, it wouldn't be an effective way to address the problem because the deeper issues would remain unresolved. Yet most of the time, I still have people asking me to tell them what to do. I then have to explain to them that the solution doesn't lie in the doing alone, it's about BEING first.

Grasping at an illusion

Through my experience and observations, as well as this study, I learnt that those who at least care enough to ask for guidance from people like us typically seek a fast, simple solution for the problem at hand. They may soldier on at first, brushing the problem aside until they can no longer ignore it when it begins to cause them significant grief. Once the pain becomes unbearable, they reach out for help. However, they don't have the patience to look at the big picture and spend the time needed to find the major cause of the problem. Instead, they beg for a shortcut or a quick fix. So, instead of taking ownership for the problem and asking, 'How should I be?' they seek a series of techniques (I refer to them as 'DOings'): 'Just tell me what to do so we can fix this quickly and get back on track'.

Examples include: I don't know how to be assertive; how can I get my team to follow my instructions? People on my team keep lying to me; what can I do to stop the lies? I don't think I am confident and assertive enough; what should I do? I feel so stressed but I'm afraid to share my fears with my team because I am the CEO, and a leader should never show weakness; what can I do to get rid of my stress? How should I fire this person without hurting his feelings? I am always very responsible, and I am carrying enormous guilt for the fact that our revenue KPI is not being met; how can I let go of the guilt as it is affecting everything I do? I don't know how to report to the board; can you give me some quick tips on how to deliver a polished presentation? And the list goes on. It's like expecting a prescription for tablets from a doctor if you present with a cold. But at least those people care enough to identify that they have a problem and seek to resolve it. Whether you are a professional, a startup founder or a director of a global organisation, there are certain fundamental types of issues you will be faced with at some point in your career, in all probability multiple times. Resolving each of those issues requires more than just a quick fix.

Unfortunately, many people choose to evade the problem. Instead, they waste time investigating what their competitors or higher profile people or businesses in their field are doing to see what their own success could look like. They scour social media in an attempt to discover how a particular startup managed to secure four million dollars worth of seed funding simply by sending a few cold emails, or how a competitor is selling a lower quality version of the same product they offer yet makes more revenue, or how another competitor has managed to retain more than 40% of their staff for over a decade, and so on. Then when they interpret the data they have gathered, they only pay attention to the visible aspects of the success achieved, not all the slow, deep preparations they have made over time, such as building a decent team of high performers and effective individuals, rounds of R&D[91] and the systems and processes they have developed over time. They also fail to see the passion, *love* and close bond shared between team members, the *courage* and *persistence* they have shown, their polished decision-making processes and the collective qualities of their people and *integrity* as a team. And they ignore the opportunities those people and businesses created and took advantage of and the hard work they put into uncovering and resolving the major causes of their challenges. So, essentially, what they are doing is grasping at an illusion. Only a very small percentage of leaders get it right by being responsible and taking ownership for effectively building their business. When we pay attention to how executives deal with the people side of their organisation – also referred to as 'human capital' – and assess the reality of what's actually going on within their teams, it becomes very clear why so many businesses fail to survive, let alone thrive. It is very common to see the significance of the people side of a business being overlooked.

There are many leadership books and workshops claiming to teach people how to act as 'effective leaders', as if effective leadership can be achieved just by learning and applying a few techniques. In fact, the words 'effective' and 'leader' are juxtaposed. If you're not being effective, you are not a leader! Some of the books on leadership are more like brochures: less than twenty pages long and used as marketing bait to grab your details on their website and social media landing pages. The reality is, leadership is not just a series of techniques one can learn quickly. It comes from being aware of what is going on (vision and discernment), being integrous by continuously assessing and polishing your Aspects of Being, being visionary and leveraging your high level

---

91 Research and Development.

of *integrity* to make effective decisions and take effective actions. These are the ingredients to being a leader that others would choose to follow. Leadership is not a mantle you put on. It's a manner and a state of Being. It's how you are BEING. Therefore, building the right foundation before and while entering into a leadership role, leading a project, creating a startup or scaling your current business is the key to your *effectiveness* and, consequently, the value of the organisation you build.

The 'secret formula to success'

Many people today seek instant gratification. They want to find a shortcut or an easy way and the so-called 'secret formula to success'. However, true transformation will never be achieved quickly or by simply learning a series of techniques or DOings. Let me share the secret to success with you right now: the secret is that there is no secret! The key is to gradually become aware of the things you are not yet aware of in order to clarify your misunderstandings, develop a conception of them, put them into practice and refine them. Over time, you will become competent and then proficient in them and ultimately achieve extraordinary *effectiveness* (mastery) in what you do. This requires you to let go of the current perceptions, beliefs and opinions you are holding on to that are getting in your way and blocking you from shifting your paradigm, as discussed in the Awareness chapter. You would also recall from our discussion on *awareness* that true high achievers and leaders constantly allow their current perceptions to be replaced with authentic knowledge. As a matter of fact, they strive for it, a trait related to their *vulnerability*, the willingness to keep their guard down and be receptive to others. They embrace reality in order to develop their *awareness*. Failure to embrace reality is like ignoring the fact that the greatest proportion of an iceberg lies hidden beneath the surface. The forces that facilitate such dramatic changes lie within each and every one of us and are almost invisible, making them difficult to find. Too many of us only see the tip of the iceberg. Here is the very place and moment that we may need 'Others' – the coaches, mentors and trainers, etc. – as well as intuition and time, to influence and guide us. When combined, these resources increase the probability of producing the results we wish to achieve in life. How to achieve this will be explained in *Part 3: Being, in Action*.

Performance vs Effectiveness

Given the words 'performance' and *'effectiveness'* are used frequently in this book, it is important to ensure both are well understood, especially in terms of how they differ. Performance is relative. When we say someone is performing well, we have a comparison or a benchmark in mind. This could be the standard of performance expected within a given field that has been established by an individual or an organisation. If there is no benchmark, we cannot make a justifiable claim that someone is or isn't performing well. *Effectiveness*, on the other hand, refers to a probability of achievement or accomplishment. In fact, the word 'effective' traces back to the Latin word *Effectivus*, from *Efficere*, which means accomplish. *Effectiveness* can relate to a process or an individual. For instance, we could say a staff member is effective when they are achieving success in a particular endeavour and fulfilling their objectives, obligations and commitments. Or we could say a process is effective when it produces the required or expected results. When someone has a proven track record of being effective in various aspects of their life, the probability that they will be effective in general is high. So, it would be reasonable to describe them as effective.

Let's look at an example that illustrates the difference. A team of software engineers produce a new software program that meets very high performance standards in terms of its functionality and user interface, which incorporates numerous bells and whistles. Meanwhile, another software engineering team working for a competitor produces a similar program with everything the end user needs but without the non-essential bells and whistles. One of the key criteria for both teams was that the software had to be ready for launch on the market quickly to meet consumer demand. The second team fulfils that objective, deciding to forgo the bells and whistles for speed to market, thereby enabling the product to be launched first. The program sells like hot cakes, generating solid revenue for the company. The first team performed well on the task, but the second team was more effective because they fulfilled the objective of being first to successfully launch the program to market. To summarise, a high performer is focused on performing at a high level in accordance with a given set of standards for the tasks or functions they perform, whereas an effective person focuses on the results that need to be produced. It may be a subtle difference, but the difference is noteworthy. Therefore, you may be a high performer, but that doesn't necessarily mean you are being effective.

So, many people, especially managers and executives, use the term 'busy' with pride, wearing it like a badge of honour. It's as though they equate being busy with being effective. I used to be in the same boat. In reality, while being busy might make you appear to be effective in terms of your ability to perform multiple tasks, that does not necessarily make you effective. We describe this as the 'semblance of busyness'. Being busy and not producing results means you are not being effective, which in turn means you are wasting resources and, most importantly, time. Being busy is so ingrained into our corporate culture today that mainstream employment engagement is based on time spent and not the results produced. People get paid for spending time 'performing' and being ineffective, the direct result of the employment game we have created for ourselves. Hence many organisations deal with phenomena such as presenteeism, whereby employees are seated at their desks but not doing much in the way of meaningful work. Ironically, they may be physically present, but they are too busy to actually be present. And yet they feel entitled to earn wages as if they are doing their job effectively. Unfortunately, some employees are more interested in their pay cheque than they are in working to serve. And the managers are pushing them to be busy through micromanagement and practices such as performance reviews. What else would you expect in an environment which actively encourages busyness?

Most entrepreneurs[92] spend years trying to come up with a solution for a given problem without earning a cent for that work. They have a vision to one day monetise on their solution, only to end up disillusioned when they fail to produce the results they envisaged. This is a classic example of the distinction between *effectiveness* and performance. So, if you catch yourself constantly on the performance treadmill, it's a sure sign that you should look into your *effectiveness*. If you treat your business like a bicycle, performance is like pedalling, regardless of the

---

92   "Entrepreneur is the one who shifts resources from the areas of low productivity and yield to areas of higher productivity and return."
– Jean-Baptiste Say, French economist, 1774–1829.

direction in which you are headed. However, be aware that *effectiveness* is not something that can be worked on in isolation. While coaching someone to become more effective, a qualified coach will break *effectiveness* down into the specific and relevant Aspects of Being – Moods and Primary Ways of Being as well as the Secondary Ways of Being – to work on. Which Aspects of Being to work on will differ from one person to the next. For example, if you engage a fitness coach to help you get into shape, they will complete an assessment with you, break it down and then target the various parts of the body that you need to work on, such as your legs, abs, arms, core strength, and so on, in order to restore *integrity* to your fitness (focusing on your whole body). Similarly, the Being Framework Ontological Model, Transformation Methodology, Being Profile and other associated tools are designed to identify which specific areas are impacting your ability to be integrous and effective, such as *responsibility, presence, care,* etc., and then work on addressing each of those to restore and engender *effectiveness.*

Effectiveness is fundamental to everyone. After all, we all care about what we accomplish in life, whether it be wealth, social status, career, family, and so on. Especially in business, leaders are encouraged to care about their *effectiveness* and their team's overall *effectiveness.* To become more effective in life, the most effective way is to have a model through which we can better understand people, including ourselves. Not only would this model increase our *awareness,* but it would also provide a clear structure to support us in our decision-making when it comes to human beings. As leaders, this would make us more effective in our efforts to hire, onboard and retain staff, lead and manage our people, influence our fans and establish and maintain long-lasting relationships with our colleagues, clients and commercial partners. In business, this equates to increased revenue, higher retention and a better bottom line.

The Being Framework ontological distinction of *effectiveness*

Effectiveness is the state of being fulfilled in meeting your commitments, intentions and expectations. It is the degree to which you are powerful and accomplished in consistently producing the intended results and outcomes in your endeavours. It is the extent to which you actualise your intentions, vision and dreams.

A healthy relationship with *effectiveness* indicates that you consistently accomplish the results and outcomes you intend to with ease and flow. Your priorities are grounded in reality and you bring workability and success to your relationships and what you are up to in life. Others expect you to fulfil your commitments and consider you to be someone who pursues and produces extraordinary results.

An unhealthy relationship with *effectiveness* indicates that you are frequently challenged, stuck or thwarted in accomplishing what you most care about. You are often powerless, disarmed, overwhelmed and/or distressed. You may be frustrated by your lack of progress and workability and find it difficult to move forward in your endeavours. Others may consider you to be someone who accepts mediocrity and downgrades or minimises expectations while not completing tasks or projects as expected. Alternatively, you may have to win, regardless of the associated consequences or costs. You may be driven to the extent that you let yourself be singularly consumed by your intentions or desires despite any detriment to your health and/or relationships.

Transformation and polishing our Ways of Being

Our Ways of Being must be polished or transformed in order for us to be more effective, perform differently and achieve our objectives. There are two approaches we can adopt to facilitate that:

1. A series of slow incremental changes, working on improving one behaviour at a time (polishing), or
2. A transformational process, from raising *awareness* (perception) through to conception of each and every Aspect of Being and the application of what we have learnt until a sudden, dramatic transformation occurs. This process leads to competency, proficiency and, ultimately, mastery, which are different degrees of *effectiveness*.

The outcome of the transformational approach is undeniably powerful. However, just as the student must master the principles of martial arts, such as balance and timing, followed by the simple practices and movements before putting complex sequences together, transforming your Aspects of Being is most effective when done in a consistent, progressive manner. We need to learn to shift our Aspects of Being, one by one, before we can cause a massive transformation.

Transformation requires *commitment* and focus

If where you are in life right now is not in alignment with where you want to be, you have two choices. You can either change in order to align your Aspects of Being with where you want to go, or you can give up your ambition and stay in your comfort zone. The fact that you are reading this book suggests you are at least curious about the possibility of change. So, what do you need to do? Reading, attending conferences and courses, watching videos, participating in webinars and seeking out inspirational speakers aligned with your ambition are all possible things you can do, as they will help change your attitude and point of view. But this is only part of the story. The next steps – the conception, practice and execution – are far more challenging, but they will provide access to what you need in order to reap the rewards you seek. It takes enormous *commitment* and focus to successfully transform your Aspects of Being.

Without *commitment* and focus you can't possibly be all in. This isn't easy. Nothing worth achieving ever is. Polishing silver that has been left to tarnish takes both time and effort to reveal its true and authentic glory. Transformation takes sacrifices and invariably comes at a cost. Having a coach or mentor to guide us and hold us to account during this transformational journey is extremely valuable. We will discuss this further in *Part 3: Being, in Action*.

Any change in your fortune is the manifestation of all that deep preparation to develop proficiency and *effectiveness* over time. If you neglect to work on these internal, invisible Aspects of Being or fail to go through the *awareness* process, you are essentially ignoring the fact that not going through these fundamental changes is the major cause of dissatisfaction and frustration. Without caring enough about this and neglecting to take *responsibility* for it and act on it, you risk ending up stuck in a recurring pattern. You will reach your limit from time to time, get frustrated and look for a temporary solution to kill the pain (like paracetamol), but you will fail to cure the major cause of the pain. Can you relate to this? Being present in my own transformational journey, as well as being alongside others in theirs, has taught me that the universe has a way of keeping us where we are until we reach the point where we are ready to move to the next level. In other words, as much as you may find it hard to accept, you belong exactly where you are right now. This is what you deserve! If you want more or better, you must become your future you. The good news is, you are not a fixed object. You can transform. But first, as discussed in the Awareness chapter, you must become aware of the possibilities you can't see right now. We will unpack this further when we explore *freedom* within *Section 3: Primary Ways of Being*.

HAVE → DO → BE versus BE → DO → HAVE

The majority of people who come to us with a problem maintain a belief that they must HAVE something (more resources, more money, and so on) in order to DO something that will enable them to BE something. For instance, I need to HAVE a huge amount of capital to build my product (DO) if I am to BE successful. Or, I need to HAVE money to take a vacation in Hawaii (DO) if I am to BE happy. Or, if I

HAVE my finances sorted out, then I will give money away to charity so that I can BE generous.

The key to creating true transformation in your life, however, is to turn this paradigm on its head. BE a certain way, DO what you need to do, and you will HAVE the things you desire. This is true whether you are transforming yourself, your small business or a multinational organisation. This is precisely the thinking adopted by effective high achievers. Indeed, it is the reason they are high performers and achieve the success and wealth they desire. They work on themselves first! Solving most of the world's problems, whether it's through business, cultural work or government, relies on individuals achieving their best potential.

The **BE → DO → HAVE** principle applies equally to personal concerns as it does to starting or growing a business venture. Adopting this attitude and approach enables us to be in charge of almost any situation, whether we perceive them as positive or negative. It also encourages us to take responsibility and see what we should change in ourselves before we start blaming and pointing fingers at the economy, our team members and colleagues or criticising the very structure of existence.

While we have a tendency as human beings to focus on what we want, our desires and accomplishments, the reality is that our achievements are primarily a direct reflection of how we are being. That is why this book is called *BEING*. I encourage you all, especially investors or leaders of organisations and businesses, to make it a top priority to keep working on your Being. This may not be easy. It requires you to look inward, to focus on subtle but far more important internal changes, as these will lay the groundwork and foundation for greater and more impactful changes for you personally and for your organisation's fortune and future. Remember, 'the house built on sand will never stand the test of time'[93].

There is an enormous difference between grasping at an illusion and immersing yourself in reality. For example, being compassionate is very different from merely acting compassionately, just as being and merely acting responsible are poles apart. Once you come to realise the

---

93   Matthew 7:24-27, *The New International Version (NIV) Bible*.

important distinction between being and acting a certain way, you will not only find it incredibly liberating, but it will also represent the first step towards transformation and being true to yourself. Remember, it's impossible to become effective at something you are not aware of. At the same time, you cannot be effective at a holistic level if all the cogs in your machine are not working at their optimum level – in other words, if you lack *integrity*. This is why *awareness*, *integrity* and *effectiveness* sit at the highest level of the Being Framework Ontological Model. If you don't have *awareness* around which parts of you are not working as well as they could, you will have no idea how to become effective in those areas, which would impact your overall performance and *effectiveness*, your team's performance, and the performance of the entire organisation. As you can see, there is an enormous amount at stake when it comes to *awareness*, *integrity* and *effectiveness*.

Your work or business can be seen as a vehicle to project the true manifestation of your Unique Being to the world, as this will enable you to achieve the ultimate goal of serving others, the by-product of which is fulfilment, prosperity and wealth. And that is the key to giving your life real meaning and purpose. Remember, the true meaning of *effectiveness* is the extent to which our commitments and intentions are being fulfilled. So, ask yourself, 'How effective am I? How different would my life look if I were to increase my *effectiveness*? And what could I do to transform my *effectiveness*, not only in my own life and business, but also to manifest *higher purpose* and better serve others?'

SECTION 2

Moods

Previously, we talked about Unique Being and how we project its manifestation through our Aspects of Being. Moods are the very first layer in the process of projecting our Unique Being ('who-ness') to the world. You are constantly projecting who you are to the world through how/what you are being – how you participate in life – and Moods are the first layer in the constant ripple effect you cause. Metaphorically speaking, you are a drop of water being released into the ocean of Existence and the ripple effect is your projection. You disclose yourself first through your Moods, then through your Primary Ways of Being and Secondary Ways of Being respectively, and these disclosures lead to your thoughts, feelings, decisions and, ultimately, your behaviour. This will be discussed further in the Self-expression chapter.

We often greet each other with, 'How are you?' Technically speaking, the most accurate way to answer this question would be to declare your emotional or mental state, or what we refer to here as Moods. Martin Heidegger refers to this as *Befindlichkeit*, which translates to state of mind. For example, you can be excited, bored, sad, anxious, closed or guarded, fearful, nervous, caring, and so on. Moods are how we fundamentally attune ourselves to the world as being a part of Existence and not apart from it.

While there are many moods, I chose the four most fundamental Moods that my team and I identified, through our studies, to be profoundly tied to performance, leadership and *effectiveness*. So, while human beings have many moods, the four underlying Moods in the Being Framework are *care, fear, anxiety* and *vulnerability. Care, fear* and *anxiety* are derived from Heidegger's book, *Being and Time*, and I have added *vulnerability* to the list. *Vulnerability* was added after I realised, through my studies, that a core Mood that prevents people from being open and authentic, when there is an unhealthy relationship with that Mood, was missing. We also wanted a means of identifying the validity and *authenticity* of a person undertaking the Being Profile, and the *vulnerability* Mood serves this purpose well due to its close relationship with *authenticity*. As mentioned earlier, one of the greatest challenges in developing this framework was to break the essential qualities of human beings into smaller, more digestible chunks called Aspects of Being. However, it was even more challenging to discuss each individual Aspect of Being in isolation from the others because there are strong interrelationships between them. Moods are no exception.

In the Being Framework, Mood doesn't represent the meaning most of us associate with the word, which is a temporary state of mind or feeling. Rather, it refers to a fundamental part of human reality. Heidegger, whose writings – as you know – greatly influenced this body of work, said, 'Moods assail us'. We don't always have a say in how we are affected by the circumstances of life because at birth we were 'thrown into' a world not of our own making. Moods are primal to living beings. They give us our sense of 'being there' in the world (*Dasein*). They also give us our sense of how we are in the face of what the world offers us and how we choose to respond to that.

You could ask why Moods matter. They matter because they determine our relationship with the present and, more importantly, the future. Imagine for a moment what your future would look like to you if you were constantly experiencing *fear* or *anxiety*. Moods also matter because they impact the way we express our Ways of Being. For example, it is far more difficult to be authentic and self-expressive if you are anxious or fearful. In fact, there are numerous interrelationships between all Moods and Ways of Being in the Being Framework Ontological Model. So, if you neglect to work on your relationship with your Moods, your Unique Being would remain suppressed and the world would miss out on receiving the fullest, unleashed version of you. What a tragedy to humanity that would be! In contrast, if you have a healthy relationship with your Moods, you would unlock the first layer of your projection to the world and participation in life. Your expression of Self would be amplified, potentially leading to prosperity, genuine fame and wealth as you are being a *contribution* to humanity.

When assessing your Moods, you gain an insight into how much *care*, *fear*, *anxiety* and *vulnerability* are likely to impact your Ways of Being. In other words, how each of those Moods impacts the way you make decisions and/or take action in various situations, allowing you to fulfil your potential, help others fulfil theirs, and project your Unique Being to the world.

As you will learn in the coming chapters, Moods are critical Aspects of Being because the health of your relationship with your Moods indicates the extent to which those Moods will affect your ability to make decisions, take action and perform effectively. The health of your relationship with your Moods also determines the extent to which you either amplify or suppress the projection of your Unique Being to the world through your Ways of Being, which are predominantly expressed through your behaviours. This section explores each Mood individually, beginning with *care*.

CHAPTER 4

Care

The mystery of human existence lies not in just staying alive, but in finding something to live for.

The Brothers Karamazov, Fyodor Dostoevsky

Everything in life either grows and thrives or is gradually diminishing. When we care about something, we pay attention to it and increase our *awareness* of it; we value it, and it becomes a priority in our lives. Why would you polish your Being or set a goal if you don't care enough about life and your own development? Without sufficient *care*, you would neglect certain aspects of life and you wouldn't have the motivation to fulfil your objectives. *Care* often diminishes so gradually over time that it is hardly noticed. We may care less and less about our personal health and wellbeing, financial health, family, career, reputation, and so on. For example, you may care more about your health and body shape while dating but end up caring less once you have landed in a relationship, becoming more concerned with raising kids and other responsibilities. When *care* is lacking, it can lead to a domino effect of negative outcomes, from broken relationships, dissatisfaction and depression to extreme alcohol consumption, drugs and, tragically in some cases, the decision to dissociate oneself from life.

When you care, life becomes your priority. As a result, you find it so valuable and worthwhile that you choose powerfully to work for its betterment. This in itself inadvertently influences your choices and interactions with other beings, leading you to be grateful for everything in life. Why should we put the effort in to thrive rather than just survive? Why should we own our problems and do something about them rather than take the easier option, which is to avoid them, keep victimising or sabotaging ourselves or blame them on external factors? The simple answer is because we care. *Care* is what drives us. Heidegger referred to this Mood as *Sorge*, which is the German word for *care* or concern. A fundamental basis of our being-in-the-world is, for Heidegger, not matter or spirit, but *care*: 'Dasein's facticity is such that its Being-in-the-world has always dispersed itself or even split itself up into definite ways of Being-in. The multiplicity of these is indicated by the following examples: having to do with something, producing something, attending to something and looking after it, making use of something, giving something up and letting it go, undertaking, accomplishing, evincing, interrogating, considering, discussing, determining ...'[94]

Let's look at an example to put Heidegger's words into perspective. Just as a scientist might investigate and research in order to make a new discovery – let's say in relation to a cure for a disease – beneath the neutral, objective exterior lies the Mood of *care*, the scientist's deep concern for human beings, which fuels their desire to discover that cure. As a leader of an organisation, your products and services are the result of the *care* you have for your customers in solving their problems.

---

94 Heidegger 1962, H.56.

The Being Framework ontological distinction of *care*

Care impacts how you relate to what matters to you and influences you in such a way that you ensure the matters and people you care about are supported, protected or dealt with in the best manner possible. *Care* leads you to address whatever is necessary to nurture the person or matter and dedicate the appropriate level of time, resources and attention to them. *Care* is considered the epicentre or focal point of Being as, without *care*, nothing of importance can be achieved. When you care about something, you pay attention to it; you value it and it becomes a priority. *Care* influences how likely you are to make decisions or take action based on the level of value you ascribe to that person, relationship or matter.

A healthy relationship with *care* indicates that you have clarity around your value structure – what you value most – enabling you to prioritise matters effectively. You give those matters the requisite consideration and attention to achieve the intended outcome while avoiding damage or minimising risk. This may extend to those areas to which you choose to attach importance, influencing you to make decisions and take relevant action regardless of whether it affects you directly.

An unhealthy relationship with *care* indicates that you may often defer making decisions or avoid taking action in certain areas, particularly outside your sphere of perceived interest. You may be inclined to neglect, pass or abdicate responsibility and be apprehensive about the future. Others may consider you biased or that your judgement is clouded in areas of particular interest to you. Alternatively, you may be distracted, as everything becomes your priority. You may refuse to let go of whatever matters come your way as you are constantly fearful of missing out. Consequently, you may flit from one matter to another, leaving most of them incomplete while forsaking fulfilment.

Care is fundamental to our Being from the moment we are born. We come into this world with so much *care* that it makes us desperate to cling to this new life we have been given; it becomes the key to our survival. All self-organising beings instinctively care about their survival. This basic instinct develops as we grow to also become a desire to keep bettering ourselves. Why? Because we care. If you see life as a game, why not triumph? If life is a project, why not complete it successfully? Each of us implicitly chooses to live another day every time we set the alarm at night. We set goals and make plans for our lives. We intrinsically value ourselves and can see the reflection of this in the systems we have created that sit within the Second-layer Reality. For example, we have developed ways to own assets, we have used our relatively high level of autonomy (*responsibility*) and imagination to create insurance systems and safety rules for construction aligned with the laws of the universe to protect us. *Care* has also given us the desire to create enduring and high-performing companies and not-for-profit charities, and is the reason we embedded fire systems into buildings and invented seat belts and drink-driving laws. So, why is it then that we need police to enforce the wearing of seatbelts and alcohol consumption when driving? If we care enough to invent these laws, why do we not have sufficient *care* to constantly abide by those laws? A lack of *care* can and does have serious consequences.

Care and the shadow

Care is traditionally referred to as 'love' in various contexts. People commonly say, 'You should love what you do', but what they are actually suggesting is that you should care about what you are doing. To understand *care* better, it is worth considering what happens when it is lacking. This requires us to look into *care's* shadow. The shadow side of *care* is indifference, not just carelessness, as many assume. The word 'careless' is defined by the *Oxford English Dictionary* as 'not concerned or worried about', which links back to the *awareness-care* relationship we discussed in the Awareness chapter. We learnt that when we don't care enough to be aware of what is happening around us, we are negligent. As leaders, we MUST care, otherwise our organisations or the causes we are working toward may not survive, let alone thrive. The same applies to relationships and family.

While the subject of archetypes[95] sits outside the scope of this book, it is worth briefly referring to one of the Jungian archetypes, as described by Carl Jung, in the context of *care*: the King. For the sake of this discussion, let's imagine that the King archetype symbolises today's leader, irrespective of gender. As leader, the King is to care more than anyone else. They need to be the protector and the provider, the one who has the discernment, *effectiveness*, capability, vision and wisdom, combined with the resources to care enough to predict the consequences and take the appropriate action every time issues and adversities facing the kingdom (organisation) arise. The King must be capable of discerning and prioritising in order to determine which matter to care most about at any given time. When *care* is lacking – the shadow side of *care* – there are two consequences: the active shadow or the passive shadow prevails. On the active side, the King becomes a tyrant, a dictator who removes people's *freedom* and generates unnecessary *fear*. This pattern was common in history and mythology. For example, King Herod threatened to kill all the infants in Bethlehem in an attempt to remove baby Jesus from existence because he felt intimidated by him[96]. When the passive side of *care's* shadow is dominant, the King will no longer care about the consequences and outcomes of their actions and inactions. Adopting a 'whatever' mindset, they may no longer care about the effect on their kingdom (organisation) and people. The passive side of the King archetype is commonly referred to as a 'weakling'. When an individual is possessed by the weakling, they lack centredness, calmness and security within themselves. The defensive, inactive, numb and desensitised 'leader' may even be led to paranoia and sink into delusion.

These days it is not uncommon to see a leader who has become so disillusioned, either because they feel threatened or misunderstood by their people, or they sense a lack of *gratitude* from others and feel isolated, that they act as though they no longer care and walk away or make themselves scarce and unreachable. This impacts their *presence* and the way they communicate when they are with others. It is an Aspect of Being commonly displayed in millennials. We see this with many first-time entrepreneurs who commonly set an expectation of achieving rapid

---

95 Jungian archetypes are defined as universal, archaic symbols and images that derive from the collective unconscious, as proposed by Carl Jung.
96 Matthew 2:16, The Bible.

success. When they discover that the road to accomplishment is much tougher and longer than they had anticipated, they stop caring and give up. This translates to the high failure rate observed in the startup community all around the world. It is clear that the drive for these entrepreneurs from the get-go was not caring about solving a problem for humanity but mainly the pursuit of monetary gain. They saw it as 'a good business opportunity' rather than a chance to solve a problem they care deeply about. That's why they gave up rather than persevered when the going got tough. The question for you is, what are the main areas you care most about? Are you capable of and willing to shift where your *care* is directed during times of crisis? How is your overall relationship with *care* as a Mood? Do you care enough, or are you either indifferent or dictatorial as the 'ruler of your kingdom'?

Contentment gives us access to fulfilment

At the start of this chapter, I said that without sufficient *care*, you won't have the motivation to fulfil your objectives, which can lead to further negative outcomes if you allow *care* to gradually slip away. Let's now take a step back and talk about contentment and fulfilment, beginning with contentment. Why? Because you have to be content within yourself for no rational reason other than the fact that you are 'being there in the world', you are alive, you are free, and you have a relatively high level of autonomy. You can move towards generating the results you want because your existence matters. If you let unresolved suffering or greed (the epitome of discontentment) be the key motivation for setting a goal, you might achieve the goal, but you will not achieve fulfilment. And *care* is the key driver behind this. Let's explore why, starting with an example.

American business magnate, Warren Buffett, worked out early in his career that once he achieved a relatively modest net worth, he wouldn't need any more money to live the lifestyle he was content with. For him, that was sufficient to feel financially secure and happy. However, what fulfilled him was the art of making money. It was this passion, doing what he loved because he wanted to, not because he needed to, that made him one of the greatest investors and richest people in the world. Despite his wealth, he continued to live in the same modest home he purchased in 1953 because that was where he felt content. In a similar, way the majority of the high performers my teams and I have worked with over the years have a genuine sense of contentment with their life. Notably, our studies show that their level of contentment is not linked to their achievements. And yet they tend to outperform unhappy/discontented people, who link their happiness/contentment to their achievements and what they have. As a result, contented people are more likely to be able to do more and be more effective in what they do. That, in itself, increases the probability that they will lead a fulfilling life. Here is where I separate contentment or happiness from fulfilment, which you get from accomplishing something you consider important, something you choose to care more about. Those who are content have a higher chance of hitting their objectives (being fulfilled) than those who are constantly concerned and anxious and hungry for more and more to the point where they are consumed with thoughts of never having enough. They waste all their energy on these thoughts rather than dealing with life and business with wisdom and grace, which is how contented people lead their lives. An unhealthy obsession with the pursuit of accomplishments will not only limit the joy of the journey, but can also negatively impact the outcome.

Similar to other qualities, contentment has two distinct sides. The shadow side pulls you to constantly appease your desires and turn your back on your true calling or what you care most deeply about in the pursuit of satisfaction and instant gratification. It is elusive and insatiable. It is either settling for less than you think you deserve or an obsessive infatuation with wanting more than you have. Therefore, this side of contentment is fleeting, inauthentic and unhealthy. It is important to note that this should not be confused with being ambitious. The light side of contentment has to do with being pleased and satisfied, grateful that you are alive and fully present to the magical possibility of being. This side of contentment is the prerequisite to healthy ambition, accomplishment and fulfilment. Warren Buffett's contentment is in line with this light side of contentment and meant he would not accept mediocrity. The shadow side would have prevented him from following his passion and calling. Buffett's contentment came from a place of wisdom and peace, ensuring he didn't waste his energy and time on unnecessary matters, issues he didn't care about. In this way, his contentment acted as a powerful prerequisite to his fulfilment and that manifested itself in his obvious monetary accomplishments.

Great leaders like Warren Buffett, Richard Branson, Jeff Bezos and Bill Gates are rarely distracted by pursuing trivial matters. However, many other so-called leaders are constantly distracted and are never content, which gets in the way of their performance, *effectiveness* and ultimately, fulfilment. Because they are in positions of power, their lack of contentment leads them to make decisions and take actions that have a significant negative impact on many people. For example, they may allow themselves to be distracted by a tweet on Twitter when there are much bigger issues demanding their *care* and attention. You can see that *care* and contentment are intrinsically linked. The powerful leader has the discernment to know what to appropriately care about at any given moment.

Fulfilment results from the achievement of something desired. However, it is often fleeting because it is focused on hitting objectives and accomplishments, which are circumstantial. Fulfilment comes and goes. People tend to place the expectation of being happy on external circumstances. They commonly say, 'I'll be happy if I have x', or, 'if x happens'. If you are in the habit of thinking this way, do you realise that you're the one putting conditions on your own happiness? Contentment comes from within; it comes from *awareness* of how things are, what you can and can't control, and what you should own and influence versus what you should let go of. Being content means 'my cup runneth over'. Isn't that what life should be all about? The rest of your achievements are by-products of who and how you gradually become and what you do.

Working on our Aspects of Being allows us to be fulfilled through the achievement of our accomplishments. But sooner or later, we all get to a point where we value who and how we are becoming more than what we achieve. In other words, our greatest achievement is ultimately who and how we become and the impact that projecting our Unique Being can have on the world. That is true *self-expression*. The ultimate *contribution* we can make to the world is to be ourselves, to tap into our Unique Being and polish our Aspects of Being to facilitate and amplify that. Have you ever considered that simply being a good person is a great *contribution* to the world? You need only look at the journey of many well-known celebrities for evidence of this. After accomplishing great monetary and materialistic wealth through their work, many celebrities discovered true meaning and purpose through their philanthropic work and *contribution* to humanity. Audrey Hepburn was a notable example. After her success on the big screen, she devoted the final years of her life to humanitarian work with UNICEF. The good news is, you don't have to be rich or a celebrity to make your *contribution* to the world, and in so doing, experience this level of contentment. That is an obstacle many of us create for ourselves as an excuse to be complacent.

In our society, we have also been conditioned to settle for a false sense of contentment rather than be fulfilled and experience true contentment. Many people dread Mondays and cheer on Fridays week in, week out. They're content with a stable pay cheque, even if they hate their job. They're content in a relationship, even if they're only comfortable but not fulfilled. They've settled for a life of 'this will do', a life of mediocrity. This inauthentic form of contentment is the shadow side. Your heart and gut tell you this is not where you belong or want to be. And yet you stay, with a fake smile fixed firmly on your face, because you lack the *courage* to leave, perhaps due to societal pressures. When you are authentically content, you can't wait to jump out of bed in the morning. You regard each day as another opportunity to engage in life, in business, to **be with** your partner, to contribute, to lead and to face challenges.

Greed is a common state of Being that sabotages our potential to feel content and live a fulfilled life. Those who are motivated by greed – an infatuation and insatiable desire to get more of something – commonly fail to find true contentment because their contentment is attached to their objective. If they manage to achieve the objective, there is a moment of joy, immediately followed by the establishment of a bigger, better objective to chase. If your contentment is wholly dependent on your objectives, you will never feel content. You simply can't live a fulfilling life if you operate from greed because you will never be satisfied with what you have.

Freedom to choose and to thrive

Apart from survival, which all beings instinctively care about at the most fundamental level, the things people care about most differ from one person to the next and can change over time. But there are certain fundamental aspects of life we should ALL care about if we want to be the leaders of our lives and perform at our best. Examples include caring about the willingness and openness (*vulnerability*) to authentically become aware, honouring our autonomy (*responsibility*) and fulfilling our promises and agreements (*commitment*). The more we care, the more motivation we have to perform, to achieve and to thrive, as opposed to just survive. Ultimately, who and how we become and the achievements we accomplish in life lead to our fulfilment. There are so many possibilities for fulfilment in this world. We can build a business, we can solve problems we care deeply about, we can build a family, we can write books, we can make a movie, we can compose music. The possibilities are endless. Our relatively high level of autonomy ensures we are free to choose. We can set our own goals and engage in whatever activities we care most about. We will discuss this further in the chapter on *freedom*, one of the Primary Ways of Being. The point is, the higher your level of *care*, the more you can accomplish and the better your chances of living a life of fulfilment.

Meaning, purpose and passion

Something else we have in common as human beings is a desire to find meaning and purpose in our lives. But finding meaning and choosing our purpose[97] isn't always easy. In fact, choosing our purpose in order to lead a meaningful life can be one of the toughest decisions we will ever have to make. One of the ways we can choose something we find meaningful is to study and let ourselves be exposed to life experiences. These experiences enable us to become aware of our passion or intuitively respond to our calling.

When we are faced with tragedy, such as a family member passing away from cancer, the wound created by that tragedy often triggers us and sows the seed of a passion within us. In this case, it could be a passion to advocate for cancer research. Adults who grew up without access to proper education because they lived in poverty would be more likely to have a desire to teach or build a school in an underprivileged area than adults who received a good education. The point is, we can choose to have a purpose-driven approach towards our lives, setting a target that

---

97   As mentioned earlier, Aristotle, the Greek ancient philosopher, described it as *Telos*, which in Ancient Greek simply means 'end goal', or 'purpose'.

is linked to the things we care most about. Setting a goal that is linked to our wounds and what we are passionate about is also a healing journey; not only can we heal ourselves in this way, but we can also help others avoid the same suffering.

Interestingly, one of the original meanings of the word 'passion' is 'suffering'. The universe has had a tradition of combining pain with joy since the beginning of time. Think of the Passion of Christ[98], the story of his arrest, trial and suffering. While we are not discussing why that is the case within the scope of this book, let's acknowledge that this is the reality of how things are. While many people care deeply about raising children and make it their life's purpose, most parents would agree that parenthood can be both painful and one of the most joyful experiences in the world. Parenting is rewarding, but it's also a lot of hard work! The same is true for anything you are passionate about. If you are passionate about surfing, you know there will be days of pure bliss, when the winds are offshore, the waves are glassy, and everything is going your way. And then there will be other days when the conditions are unfavourable, making it feel more like hard work and causing great frustration. The alternative to acknowledging that whatever you are passionate and care deeply about will bring both joy and suffering, is to hold on to a hedonistic belief that the pursuit of pleasure is the most important thing in life and adopt a *hakuna-matata*[99] philosophy in life. In other words, not taking *responsibility* for the pleasant and the unpleasant, implicitly deciding to let circumstances lead your life and destiny, as opposed to taking the reins and being cause in the matter of your own life. I am not encouraging anyone to be a total control freak. It's not a matter of control. To the contrary, it's a matter of influence and leadership. Being able to choose how we respond to a given situation and influence the outcome is an opportunity we should celebrate. By design, we all have that level of autonomy, but not everyone honours it and acts upon it. It enables us to choose to influence the result or become a victim of circumstance.

---

98 The Passion of Christ is the story of Jesus Christ's arrest, trial and suffering. The word 'passion' comes from the Latin word for suffering: *passionis*.

99 Hakuna-matata is a Swahili phrase from East Africa, meaning 'no trouble', or 'no worries'. It was brought to Western prominence in the 1994 Walt Disney Animation Studios film, *The Lion King*.

When you want to accomplish a personal or professional goal in your life, it can be compared to longing for a full-blown rose when all that is visible right now is a tightly closed rosebud. The rose you imagine looks nothing like what you are looking at right now. But give it time, patience and the right amount of water, light and warmth, and it will begin to open. As the petals stretch out and open themselves to you, the rose is finally revealed in all its glory and becomes what you ultimately wanted. When you open yourself up to the opportunities that are aligned with your passion and purpose in life – things you care deeply about – those opportunities will be fulfilled in all their glory as long as you give them sufficient *care* to grow and thrive. Remember, everything in life either grows and thrives or gradually diminishes over time. We all have one chance at this thing called life. My hope for you is that you care enough to tap into fulfilment and don't settle for a life of inauthentic contentment and mediocrity.

CHAPTER 5

Fear

ear is a Mood we all experience to varying degrees. Whether the object of our *fear* is darkness, closed spaces, height, spiders, flying, being in a committed relationship, the law, aspects of our culture or religion, the truth, our parents, etc., we all have a fairly good sense of what *fear* feels like and what it does to us on a physical and emotional level. There are many stories featuring so-called 'fearless heroes' we are meant to look up to, however, empirical data and rich literature have proven that human beings do not exist in the absence of *fear*. In fact, all living beings, animals included, experience *fear* to some degree. Some would argue that *courage* is the opposite of *fear* (as explained in Part 1, some dictionaries even define *courage* as the absence of *fear*). However, *courage*, another Aspect of Being we all possess, is not the absence of *fear*, but a willingness to step forward despite the presence of *fear*. *Courage* needs *fear* to be present, otherwise we wouldn't need *courage*. Let's now examine *fear* as one of the four Moods in the Ontological Model.

In his book, *Being and Time*, Martin Heidegger describes *fear* or being fearful (*Furchtsam*) as a phenomenon. He said that the presence of *fear* is always connected to an object; being fearful of something threatening. Let's say I am fearful of cockroaches. I see a cockroach in the bath, and I am suddenly frightened. My non-cockroach-fearing partner removes the offending monster, and I am no longer fearful. *Fear* has an object, and when that object is removed, *fear* is no longer present. I would extend Heidegger's description of *fear* to being connected to something internal or external. It is our propensity or capacity to **be with** *fear*. While the immediate thought that comes to mind when we think of *fear* is to keep removing the objects associated with our *fear*, it is impossible to remove all *fear*-generating objects and situations. Therefore, the aim is to transform our relationship with *fear* so that we are not suppressed, disarmed or powerless in the face of it. Instead, by becoming courageous, we can be exposed to the triggers of our *fear* and no longer be derailed or stopped by them. When we allow *fear* to overcome us, whether it be the *fear* of something internal or external, we let danger win in our mind to the point where it shrinks our experience of life. However, when we transform our relationship with *fear*, it enables and empowers us to expand our experience of being out there in the world. This is how our relationship with *fear* works.

Fear is real

Despite the incredible advancements made in modern medicine, the brain still remains one of the most mysterious parts of the body, even to neuroscientists. While I am no expert in this domain, I did my best to study the brain, both out of interest and because of the close connection to my studies for the Being Framework. Although there is no universal agreement on the entire list of structures composing the brain system, one of the known structures – and the one relevant to this body of work – is called the limbic system. The limbic system is defined as the brain's networking system responsible for controlling emotional drives – including *fear* – and memory formation. Neural networks of the limbic system function in harmony with other brain structures to control a variety of physiological and psychological functions, including emotion, behaviour, motivation, memory formation, olfaction, sleep (dreaming), appetite, sexual drive, and so on[100]. My point here is not to focus on science, but to raise your *awareness* that *fear* is not a made-up construct or invention of humankind. It is a Meaning that sits in First-layer Reality and is so ingrained in nature that most beings experience it. A rabbit would experience *fear* while being chased by a fox and puppies may experience *fear* when exposed to an unknown sound for the first time.

Fear is neither negative nor positive

Fear, as a Mood, is impacted by your anticipation of a perceived danger or threat in different situations. It is a Mood that is often portrayed in a negative light. However, *fear* is neither positive nor negative. It is

---

[100] 'Limbic System and Behavior' by Sanchari Sinha Dutta, Ph.D.

what it is. It's a phenomenon we all experience. While we may find it unpleasant, it saves us a lot of time and can even save our life. Imagine the consequences of being stalked by a lion in the absence of *fear*!

When I was a teenager, I spent a lot of time reading poetry, especially poems written by the great Persian poet, Rumi. I remember a verse in which he wrote, 'There was a time that the evil spirit was my master'. Metaphorically, he was admitting that he was up to no good. I didn't quite get it at the time, as I used to regard Rumi as a man of virtue who could do no wrong. But since then, there have been times in my life when I have faced the dark side of myself, and the thoughts that entered my mind during those times absolutely terrified me. Those thoughts generated so much *fear* within me that I made a commitment to avoid the pathways that could lead me or others astray. Traditionally, people may have called (and may still call) this the 'fear of God', or piety. However, you may choose to look at it, I am conveying this story to highlight that if you have the *authenticity* to look yourself in the eye in a mirror and see what you are capable of, then you should not see *fear* as a negative Mood, but see it as a pathway to creating positive change and action. In Part 1, we mentioned that the Being Framework Ontological Model is not about morality or how you ought to be. It is worth mentioning that again here. By bringing personal stories into the discussion, I am not suggesting my way is the right way. It is simply a means to explain the meaning using real-world examples that I have experienced first hand.

Fear is a suppressor. Sometimes it suppresses a desire to commit a crime, and other times it suppresses us from taking a leap of faith by accepting an exciting, yet risky, business proposition. You need only look back in time to be reminded of how many in positions of power ignored *fear* and abused their power to cause corruption, leaving chaos in their wake. At the end of the day, the question you should ask yourself is, 'Do I dare to have the audacity to replace malevolence with benevolence, no matter how tempted I may be to hold on to the former?' The answer begins with your relationship with *fear* and the constant decisions you need to make about when to let *fear* suppress you and when to step forward.

The most important point to remember is that it is the health of our relationship with *fear* that counts, not whether or not we experience *fear*, because the truth is, we all do. A healthier, more effective relationship with *fear* means that generally, even though you may identify perceived threats or danger in a given situation, you are still able to move forward, make decisions and take action. A less healthy relationship with *fear*, on the other hand, means you do not have the capacity to **be with** fearful situations; you are likely to freeze, avoid taking action and defer decisions related to that particular situation. Furthermore, you would also be more likely to avoid situations in which you have experienced *fear* in the past. This in turn would suppress the expression of some of your other Aspects of Being. For example, the more fearful you are, the more it may detract from your *authenticity* and the more you may suppress the expression of the real you (your Unique Being) to the world and therefore turn your back on the gift that lies deep within you. An unhealthy relationship with *fear* may also show up in the more readily observable behavioural aspect of *assertiveness*, where you may be seen by others as someone who doesn't speak up in certain situations.

Ontologically speaking, an unhealthy relationship with Moods leads us to suppress the projection of our Unique Being to the world through our Aspects of Being, and *fear* is no exception. Therefore, *fear* – like the other three Moods – directly or indirectly impacts how we show up in the world, engage in relationships, participate in projects, contribute to our family or organisation and serve our community. Now, as mentioned, there are times when it is to our advantage to suppress the expression of certain decisions and behaviours. If you suddenly have a desire to rob a bank, you would want *fear* (or other Moods) to suppress that urge! In this way, *fear* brings a level of self-control that is highly beneficial in your life.

The Being Framework ontological distinction of *fear*

Fear impacts how you relate to perceived dangers or threats in different situations. *Fear* is always related to something particular in the world and has a distinct object or focus for its attention. It is an indication of how you ARE with *fear*, in other words, your propensity and capacity to be with *fear*. *Fear* is often associated with taking an unpleasant experience from the past and projecting it into your future or being confronted with an immediate danger.

A healthy relationship with *fear* indicates that even though you may identify perceived threats, discomfort or danger, you are still able to move forward, make appropriate decisions and take action. Instead of avoiding *fear*, you are prepared and remain powerful and courageous.

An unhealthy relationship with *fear* indicates that you are likely to defer decisions and avoid taking action when confronted or impacted by an object of your *fear*. You are also likely to avoid situations where you have experienced *fear* in the past. Others may consider you to be fearful, weak and someone who backs down, doesn't speak up or take a stand. Alternatively, you may be reckless, inappropriately putting yourself in harm's way, and may avoid managing risk.

It's your relationship with *fear* that counts

Let's return to the discussion about why it is so important to have a healthy relationship with *fear*. Referring to the more conventional explanation of *fear*, while we can remove the object creating it, the most convenient and easiest way of dealing with *fear* is not to face the object – to avoid it by being defensive and withdrawn. However, avoidance is not the best strategy to adopt, especially in the context of leadership, performance and *effectiveness*. As a leader, you simply cannot allow *fear* of public speaking, *fear* of confronting your venture partners because they aren't fulfilling their promises, or *fear* of letting go of a staff member who is letting the team down, etc., to get in the way of your *effectiveness*. This would come at a huge cost. A classic example is sales. Many people, especially first-time entrepreneurs, fear sales. They are not comfortable standing in front of a potential customer or picking up the phone to sell their vision and their new product or service. This commonly stems from a fear of rejection, which links to another Mood, *vulnerability*. It's no surprise that this has the most direct impact on the revenue of the company they are trying to build or scale. I am not suggesting you should not fear sales. *Fear is fear.* Nobody can tell you what to fear and what not to fear. The key is to acknowledge it and know that unless you develop a healthy and effective relationship with *fear*, it can have severe consequences. Imagine if most of the salespeople on your team had an unhealthy relationship with *fear* and avoided making calls to your potential customers because of it. I'm sure I don't need to spell out the consequences.

When you have an unhealthy relationship with *fear*, it impacts your *presence* and connectedness with others, which in turn may cause you to lack *authenticity* in the eyes of a potential consumer. It could affect your ability to adequately highlight the benefits of your product to the consumer and generate trust because you may appear to be hiding something. If you let *fear* win, it shows itself in your Primary and Secondary Ways of Being, which impacts the things you say and how you come across to a potential customer. This would almost always result in the customer walking away and choosing to do business elsewhere.

It is important to understand that, in the context of the Being Framework, I am not referring to the need to work on the fear of something specific, like the fear of spiders or cockroaches or heights, but to work on transforming your relationship with *fear* at a meta level. There is a clear distinction. The traditional approach taken by behavioural psychologists is to solely focus on the one thing you are fearful of. If you are fearful of more than one thing, each fear would be addressed one by one. The approach with the Being Framework is different. Adopting an ontological approach, the Being Framework encourages you to look at *fear* holistically.

Let's say you have a fear of public speaking and sales. Rather than attempting to resolve the object of your *fear*, the Being Framework's ontological approach directs your attention to how to change your relationship with *fear* itself; to ultimately BE more comfortable with *fear*, or be comfortable with the discomfort that your *fear* is causing you. That way, whenever you are confronted with any new fear-generating scenario in the future, you will be able to deal with it effectively. It's about how you are being in the face of anything that generates *fear* for you and how you are with *fear* in general. Why is this important? It's important because there may be thousands of new things that you will develop a *fear* of in the future. If you work on transforming your relationship with *fear*, you will know what to do every time *fear* strikes in the future. Those who practise martial arts spar on a regular basis with various opponents in the gym, not just to defeat that particular opponent (object of *fear*), but also to prepare themselves mentally to be confident when they compete and face any new opponent (new object of *fear*) in the ring, despite the presence of *fear*. By gradually facing tougher opponents in practice, they transform their relationship with *fear* over time. They can **be with** their *fear* and take action, regardless of its presence.

If you are fearful of something, the best way to address it, according to clinical psychoanalysis literature – one of the foundations of the Being Framework's ontological approach – is to gradually and safely expose yourself to the object or major cause of the *fear*. This method doesn't remove the object of the *fear*, but makes you braver in encountering it, much like the martial arts example. The idea is to start small and build yourself up over time. Let's say you fear public speaking. Start by presenting to a small group of five to ten people, and gradually increase the number rather than going straight for the big presentation before a gathering of a few hundred. The *fear* may always be there, but over time, your relationship with it will transform to the point where the number of people won't matter anymore. This approach will empower you to gradually expose yourself to every *fear*, face it, and make a conscious decision to embrace it.

I strongly encourage you to take the steps to shift your relationship with *fear*, rather than focus on the individual *fear*-generating situation. Just be aware, however, that you can't expect to develop a healthy relationship with *fear* overnight, and you may need assistance from an experienced ontological coach to guide you in the process. The point here is that *fear* can suppress the way you participate in life. If you want to be fulfilled (reach your objectives), be effective and be a leader of influence, it is in your best interest to transform your relationship with *fear*, rather than develop coping mechanisms to deal with the situations that cause you to experience *fear*. When you transform your relationship with *fear*, it will no longer disempower you. This is the fundamental work you must do if you want to be an authentic, high-performing leader.

CHAPTER 6

Anxiety

Anxiety is the experience of the tide going out, the seawater draining away, revealing a self stranded on the sand, as it were. Anxiety is that basic mood when the self first distinguishes itself from the world and becomes self-aware.

Simon Critchley on Heidegger
The Guardian, July 6th, 2009

No matter what story you believe about how we came to this world, whether you believe we are descendants of Adam and Eve, or you are convinced by Darwin's theory of evolution, we are here in the world. We are not debating that. As far as the context of this book is concerned, we just need to acknowledge that we exist; we are 'being there' (*Dasein*) in the world. This is a fact that we must accept, ontologically and phenomenologically. Martin Heidegger calls this phenomenon 'thrownness'[101], which refers to us 'being thrown' (*Geworfen*) into the world.

When we are born, we 'are thrown' into this world and begin our lives totally helpless. Our Moods, and particularly *anxiety*, are the first layers of our response to 'being there' in the world and all the external factors. Not long thereafter comes the realisation that we are fragile and dependent. However, with no sense of language to communicate our needs and feelings, it's understandable that we deal with what I call the 'wound of overwhelm'. This wound continues into adulthood and throughout our lives, because we know we cannot possibly know

---

101 Thrownness is a concept introduced by German philosopher, Martin Heidegger to describe humans' individual existences as 'being thrown' into the world.

everything about everything, even collectively. We are in the face of great uncertainty all the time, from wars, recessions, diseases, pandemics, natural disasters, crime and corruption, all the way to our own individual shortcomings and flaws. As if those aren't enough to create *anxiety*, we have the ultimate reason to be anxious: the knowledge that we will all die at the end of our time in this world; the only given other than being born in our lives. Such is the tragic narrative of what it means to 'be there'.

After walking you through the uncertainties, gravities and tragedies of life, you may be wondering why we're not all walking around in a constant state of *anxiety*, to the point where it makes us either freeze and suppress the expression of our Being or turn to alcohol and/or drugs to numb the pain, something too many people do. Indeed, how most human beings manage to endure the tragedies of life without breaking remains a mystery, even to the great psychologists and philosophers of the world. There's an element of magic about human beings and our ability to bounce back in the face of adversity that has filled me with wonder since I was a child. Not only do we manage to deal with the uncertainty all around us, but we do so with a smile on our face. We party, we dance, we get married – even if we have been betrayed many times in the past – and we bring new life into the world, even when the world around us appears to be ruthless, fragile and broken.

Here's the thing – *anxiety* generated by the environment in which we live circulates around us like constant noise. I call this 'existential resonance of *anxiety*'. This is more than something cognitive that can be readily studied. There are multiple aspects to it, making it more mysterious and therefore difficult to measure using traditional methods. However, we have dared to do the seemingly impossible, and ontologically assess your relationship with *anxiety* (and the other Moods) using the Being Framework, particularly the Being Profile, as explained later. It is important to mention at this point that the *anxiety* we are discussing in this chapter is of the general kind – the Mood we all deal with – and should not be confused with Anxiety Disorders[102]. If the relationship

---

102 An Anxiety Disorder is a mental health disorder characterised by feelings of worry, anxiety or fear that are strong enough to interfere with one's daily activities. Examples of Anxiety Disorders include panic attacks, obsessive-compulsive disorder and post-traumatic stress disorder.

you have with *anxiety* is extremely poor, it could possibly be classified as an Anxiety Disorder, which may require expert attention. Anxiety Disorders are beyond the scope of this book.

According to Heidegger, *anxiety* does not mean to ceaselessly fret or fitfully worry about something, which many people regard as the meaning of *anxiety*. On the contrary, he said that *anxiety* is a rare and subtle Mood, and even links it to a feeling of calm or peace. It is through our relationship with *anxiety* that the free, authentic Self first comes into existence. This notion has been beautifully captured by many of the world's great existentialist novelists[103]. It is no coincidence that *freedom*, *authenticity* and *peace of mind* are three of the Primary Ways of Being in the Being Framework Ontological Model that each have a strong link to our relationship with *anxiety*. They will each be explored separately later in the book.

---

103 It is worth noting that Martin Heidegger was very critical of existentialism.

The Being Framework ontological distinction of *anxiety*

Anxiety impacts the anticipation, uncertainty, perceived risk or lack of preparedness associated with future situations, circumstances or events. It indicates how worry, nervousness or unease about the future impairs your ability to move forward. *Anxiety* fuels the constant prediction of potential consequences of the decision you are about to make and/or the action you are about to take. *Anxiety*, as a Mood, is clearly distinct from Anxiety Disorder. *Anxiety* can be about 'nothing in particular' and is often indeterminate. It can be experienced in the face of something completely unknown to you, something you do not have a perception or conception of, hence you may be unable to articulate it. It indicates how you are with *anxiety* – your propensity and capacity to be with it.

A healthy relationship with *anxiety* indicates that although certain situations may cause you to experience *anxiety*, you are still able to make appropriate decisions and take effective action. It leads you to be attentive and prepared and considerate of any relevant risks associated with the situation, keeping you on your toes. You may leverage your *anxiety* to achieve the best possible outcome in challenging situations.

An unhealthy relationship with *anxiety* indicates that in uncertain situations, it is likely to cloud your judgement, constrain you and cause you to freeze. Others may consider you as someone who is passive, lacks discernment, procrastinates and defers making decisions. You may have a propensity to frequently anticipate the worst possible outcomes, be overly sceptical and focus on what may go wrong. Alternatively, you may be considered nonchalant and oblivious to or ignore the consequences of your actions or inaction.

The difference between *anxiety* and *fear*

In order to understand what Heidegger meant by *anxiety*, we have to distinguish it from another Mood he examined: *fear*. As we discussed in the previous chapter, Heidegger claimed that *fear* is always associated with the *fear* of something, a particular object or matter in the world. This is not the case with *anxiety*. If *fear* is being fearful of something particular and determinate, then *anxiety* is being anxious about nothing in particular and is indeterminate. In other words, if *fear* is directed towards some distinct thing in the world, such as cockroaches, spiders or flying, then *anxiety* is being anxious about simply being there in the world (existing). *Anxiety* is experienced in the face of something completely unknown. It is, Heidegger insisted, 'nothing and nowhere'. *Anxiety* is, more often than not, related to situations rather than things.

Heidegger claimed that 'being there in the world', as a whole, is revealed in Moods, including *anxiety*. As such, *anxiety* has an important methodological function in the study of human beings, which is why it is included in the Being Framework Ontological Model. The aim is to look at the Reality of *anxiety* in the truest and most practical sense, without judgement. Whether we like it or not, we all face situations and thoughts on a daily basis that can make us anxious. As is the case with *fear*, our ability to respond well to *anxiety* and **be with** *anxiety* has an enormous impact on our performance and *effectiveness* as a leader. If you simply let the darkness overcome you, you will be crushed by it and fail to hit your objectives. A person with a relatively healthy relationship with *anxiety* and adequate coping mechanisms to deal with it, on the other hand, would have a far greater chance of maintaining control rather than falling victim to the darkness. As a result, they would be far more likely to be effective, hit their objectives, live a fulfilling life and be a leader of influence. Like *fear*, we all experience *anxiety*. It's how we choose to respond to it that counts.

The *anxiety* Mood indicates how a feeling of worry, nervousness or unease about something impacts your ability to move forward, take action or make appropriate decisions. A healthy relationship with *anxiety* indicates that although certain situations may cause you to feel anxious, you are still able to **be with** the *anxiety*, take action and make decisions. A less healthy relationship with *anxiety* indicates that, in uncertain situations, this Mood is likely to cause you to hold back or defer making decisions. Others may consider you as someone who procrastinates in situations that make you anxious. It will cause you to be disarmed and frozen in the face of adversities, catastrophes or other worrying situations in life.

As much as we are thrown into a world of uncertainty, as human beings, we also find the world richly meaningful and deeply fascinating. In *Being and Time*, Heidegger described the world as 'homely', or 'cosy' (*Heimlich*). However, *anxiety* changes all of that. When *anxiety* takes over, suddenly we are overcome by a Mood that renders the world meaningless, like an inauthentic spectacle and a pointless bustle of activity. The world becomes a place that feels strange and cold (the opposite of *Heimlich*). Suddenly, we go from being a player in the game of life to an observer of a game we no longer have a desire to play because it all seems pointless. These descriptions convey opposite ends of the *anxiety* spectrum, but they paint a good picture for understanding.

Anxiety and all other Moods in the Being Framework are primal to human beings and therefore impossible to remove from our lives. To think you could get to the point where you experience no *fear* or *anxiety* is, quite frankly, delusional. I have seen some self-help gurus construct ideas that promote eliminating *fear* and *anxiety* from your life. But to expect an outcome like that is like expecting that you will grow wings and live in the clouds! That is a sure-fire recipe to set yourself up for disappointment.

Like *fear, anxiety* is neither negative nor positive

Anxiety provides access to and allows us to catch a glimpse of our authentic Self, hence the link to the Primary Way of Being of *authenticity*. Many assume *anxiety* begins in darkness, when trying to sleep, alone with one's thoughts. However, *anxiety* can appear anywhere, anytime, even in the most unassuming of situations. It could begin from an overheard conversation at work or at a party, from reading a business magazine portraying the so-called 'perfect' business leader, or from glancing through the pages of a glossy magazine filled with unrealistic, often photoshopped images of the ideal body type. Sometimes, that's all it takes to be suddenly gripped by a feeling of inadequacy and for *anxiety* to come to the fore. With this experience of *anxiety*, Martin Heidegger says, *Dasein* is individualised and becomes self-aware.

One of the primary reasons to increase our *awareness* and shape a conception of Reality is to avoid being naive in the face of adversity, or in the knowledge that there will be adversities to navigate in the future, which can cause *anxiety*. We do so on the basis of knowing that adversities constitute a major part of life. When you can **be with** your *anxiety*, when you know that danger exists and move forward despite that (by tapping into *courage*) and bring forward the appropriate responses, while simultaneously knowing your limitations, then nothing will stop you. This largely corresponds with how you ARE in the presence of *anxiety*. You may have *anxiety*, but *anxiety* will no longer have you!

The clinical psychoanalysis literature is very clear on what to do with an anxious person, and it seems most clinical specialists are in agreement on this. The literature states that it is critical to see, in great detail, what they are anxious about and to acknowledge the anxiety. They then break it down into smaller, manageable 'problems' and progressively support them to work on and solve those problems one by one. Gradually, the individual gains competency and then proficiency in managing the first problem, and once this happens, the clinical specialist guides them to solve the others on their own. Based on my own observations and our empirical data, this process is extremely effective in solving issues with *anxiety*, and also with *fear*, as discussed in the previous chapter.

Anxiety as a state of Being is quite different from *fear*. In developing a powerful relationship with *anxiety*, you may learn that the world is not as dangerous as you thought it was, based on the stories you created. These stories may be founded on statistical probability, but mathematically, the probability may be so low (for instance, 0.001% risk) that it doesn't warrant worrying about. In the case of *fear*, you may realise the danger of something is as high, or even higher, than you thought it was, and yet choose to step forward anyway. When you voluntarily choose to deal with a *fear* or *anxiety* generating situation, your body and mind use totally different psycho-physiological systems compared to the times when you are dealing with them involuntarily. The former generates positive emotions and constructive challenges, encouraging growth.

However, the latter causes withdrawal, aggression, defence and negative emotions, discouraging growth. The point to remember here is that whenever you are dealing with *fear* or *anxiety*, if you acknowledge them and tackle them head on with *courage*, it will make you stronger. Run or hide from those situations, however, and the outcome can be disastrous, especially if you make a habit of it.

As a leader, entrepreneur or professional, it is extremely important to have the *courage* to step forward in pursuit of what matters to you, your calling or objectives; to develop what some would call a 'go-getter' attitude. This doesn't come from learning a series of techniques and exercises, as typically prescribed by behavioural psychologists, but by setting yourself up to shift your state of Being, including your relationship with *anxiety*. That way you will no longer have to work on that state of Being from scratch every time you encounter an anxious situation. While a situation may be new and unfamiliar, we all know what it feels like to be anxious. This isn't about stopping that Mood because that would be unrealistic. It's about raising your *awareness* of it, so that every time you find yourself experiencing that familiar Mood, you would know how to deal with it. As is the case with *fear*, transforming your relationship with *anxiety* takes time; it's a gradual process. Over time, you will find it takes far less time to bounce back. We will talk about this more in the chapter on *resilience*, a Secondary Way of Being. That's the difference between an ontological approach and a behavioural approach to managing *anxiety*. With an ontological approach, you shift your relationship with the Mood – in this case, *anxiety* – so you know how to swiftly and powerfully intervene any time it arises.

Dealing with *anxiety* using the ontological approach described above doesn't make you anxiety-proof, however, it does give you the ability to develop *resilience*; to not let *anxiety* break you. I strongly believe this approach needs to be fostered in children from a very young age. Rather than constantly removing objects or causes of their *fear* and *anxiety*, as seems to be the norm today, I believe we should teach children to develop *resilience,* so they are better equipped to deal with *anxiety* and *fear* as these Moods arise. Instead of teaching children how to deal with bullying and developing a thicker skin, we encourage them to be naive, fragile and passive victims who melt under the slightest pressure. This often leads to Anxiety Disorders and depression later in life.

The truth is, everything in life comes with challenges. Even if you absolutely love what you do, you will still encounter hardships. There will be times when you have to perform functions and complete tasks you dislike or that take you out of your comfort zone. That's reality. However, you do have some influence over the matter. You have the power to minimise those unpleasant tasks and, most importantly, you can polish your Aspects of Being – in this case, the *anxiety* Mood – to better handle the times when an unpleasant task is unavoidable.

Stress is an inevitability in life. It occurs when opposing pressures are in conflict and become unbearable. Stress is a response to a threat in a situation while *anxiety* can be a reaction to the stress. Therefore, maintaining a healthy relationship with *anxiety* is important, especially as a leader. How are you **being with** *anxiety*? Does it freeze you for days or weeks on end, or are you able to regain control relatively quickly? It is worth noting that stress primarily arises from failure to take action over something you have control over (autonomy). So, if you find something specific is causing you stress, delve a little deeper. You may discover that it is something you have yet to take any action on, like something that's been bothering you for some time that you have placed in the 'too hard basket'. We will discuss this further in the Responsibility chapter.

As a leader, you are constantly dealing with new, unstructured problems and having to make tough important decisions on a daily basis. It's so easy to become overwhelmed and anxious when dealing with finances, the people side of the business, operations, sales, marketing, legal matters, and the list goes on. Developing a healthy relationship with *anxiety* will transform your performance and *effectiveness* in the midst of your everyday challenges. A healthy relationship with your *anxiety* Mood leads you to be in charge of your life and increase your *responsibility*, allowing you to be on top of the external circumstances that are a natural part of life. This leads to *peace of mind*, which, as you will learn later, is a Primary Way of Being that is typically quite elusive and hard to hold on to.

CHAPTER 7

Vulnerability

> *Be silent and listen. Have you recognised your madness and do you admit it? ... Let the light of your madness shine, and it will suddenly dawn on you... Be glad you can recognise it for you will thus avoid becoming its victim.*
>
> *The Red Book,* Carl Jung

To begin this topic on *vulnerability*, it is worth referring back to our conversation on words and meanings. What do I mean when I say *vulnerability* in the context of the Being Framework? By *vulnerability* I am not referring to the conventional meaning of the word, which the *Oxford English Dictionary* defines as 'the quality or state of being exposed to the possibility of being attacked or harmed, either physically or emotionally'. Through our studies, observations and working with leaders, entrepreneurs and professional leadership and performance coaches, we have come to realise that we human beings may care far more about our reputation – how we are seen by others – than we care about truth and Reality. This causes us to put our guard up in the face of the truth, and to be stubborn and reluctant to acknowledge matters in life or where we belong at this stage in our lives. We wrap ourselves up in cotton wool or – for extra protection – in bubble wrap, to keep ourselves safe, keeping our flaws, weaknesses and shadow sides hidden, to avoid being taken advantage of or ridiculed, etc. This lack of acknowledgement prevents us from growing because we don't see or seek the possibilities that are currently in our blind spots. This applies to each and every one of us to some degree. If your default Mood is set to 'avoid being vulnerable', which means you are not letting your guard down, not being receptive and not surrendering to Reality, you will suffer. Furthermore, you will most certainly cause others to suffer too. This chapter explores why and how.

What is *vulnerability*?

Many people have a problem with the word 'vulnerability' as they assume that to be vulnerable is to be weak, naive or fragile. Let me be very clear on this. Within this framework, my intention is to convey the point and depict a clear picture – at least as much as I can – of this quality that we call *vulnerability*. You could call it what you like. My obsession is with the transcendent Meaning I am referring to, not the word. Let's look into the history of the word, which may help you understand why it was chosen.

Vulnerability is ultimately derived from the Latin noun *Vulnus*, which means 'wound'. *Vulnus* led to the Latin verb *vulnerare*, which means 'to wound', which further led to the late Latin adjective *Vulnerabilis*, which became 'vulnerable' in English in the early 1600s. The word 'vulnerable' originally meant 'capable of being physically wounded', or, 'having the power to wound' (the latter is now obsolete). But since the late 1600s, it has also been used figuratively to suggest a defencelessness against non-physical attacks. In other words, someone (or something) can be vulnerable to criticism or failure as well as to literal wounding. Simply put, it means the extent to which you can receive wounds or be in a situation that can cause wounds and, despite this, have the strength to remain standing.

The Being Framework ontological distinction of *vulnerability*

Vulnerability impacts how you relate to the concerns you have with respect to how you are being perceived or thought of in different situations. It is how you are being when confronted or exposed to perceived threats, ridicule, attacks or harm (emotional or physical). *Vulnerability* is not being weak, agreeable or submissive. It is when you embrace your imperfections. It is considered the quality of being with your authentic self without obsessive concern over the impression you make.

A healthy relationship with *vulnerability* indicates that you are open as opposed to guarded or closed in receiving unfamiliar knowledge and feedback. You are willing to reveal your authentic self to others, regardless of what they may think of you or the prevailing circumstances. You may often leverage the power of being vulnerable to generate trust and build relationships. You acknowledge and embrace your imperfections to support your growth and influence. Rather than letting other people's opinions of you hold you back, you learn from them to propel you to wholeness (*integrity*) and fulfilment.

An unhealthy relationship with *vulnerability* indicates that you are likely to defer or avoid taking action or making decisions when you feel they may impair your reputation. You may also avoid or put your guard up in situations where you could expose yourself to ridicule or look foolish. You are more concerned with being seen to do the right things, looking good or impressing others than actually doing the things you know to be right. You may be inclined to sacrifice your authentic self or image to project a fake persona that you consider more acceptable and impressive to others. You tend to take criticism personally. Alternatively, you may attempt to create unrealistic boundaries to maintain a 'safe' distance, avoiding the unknown and refusing to explore new territories. You may be overly controlling of others or your environment.

Why should leaders be vulnerable?

In the context of the Being Framework, *vulnerability* is how capable and comfortable one is at being able to face their shortcomings, acknowledge the areas they need to polish and transform, and at receiving criticism and being judged. It is **being with** *vulnerability*. So, when you have a relatively high level of *vulnerability* you can accept criticism and be judged without having your guard up and freely be yourself without worrying about what others think of you. In other words, it is the capability of being vulnerable, receptive and tolerant in the face of criticism, truth and Reality, no matter the consequences. Any person in a position of power – so every leader – absolutely must possess this quality. Why? Because as a leader, you will constantly be judged, no matter what decisions you make. You may be shocked to know that even highly respected people, like Mother Teresa, have been criticised and misjudged by the public online, despite predominantly being known for their positive impact on the world. As a leader, you cannot please everyone all the time, including yourself. As Steve Jobs once said in response to a harsh verbal attack from an individual in the audience, 'You can please some people some of the time'. Therefore, it's better to choose to be vulnerable and leverage the power of that choice.

Being obsessed with your image will consume your time and energy to the point where it can hold you back from fulfilling your calling and achieving your objectives. Through the media, we observe high-profile politicians who seem to be more concerned with their public image than they are with actually making a difference on key issues. The same is quite common in an unhealthy corporate culture. Many corporate leaders are far more concerned with who will take the credit than they are with the objectives of a project and the problems it will solve for customers and/or the world. We often see this characteristic filter down throughout an entire organisation. It is far more effective to let your results speak for themselves.

I used to be involved in a company years ago where I was an employee for just over a year and a half. The company had been in operation for seventeen years when I started, but its growth was stagnant. They were attempting to innovate by building drag-and-drop complex case management software, because their chief objective as an organisation was to build a unique software product and use it to scale the business. However, every attempt failed. And yet despite this, the company survived through their service delivery. As a result of the failure to build the software, the founder finally realised that he may not have been the right person to run the company. So, he hired an experienced CEO who, in turn, began hiring very experienced people, predominantly with a corporate background, people he believed would be best for each role. I was hired to lead and manage the technical aspects of the product alongside a team of extremely talented and brilliant people. The new CEO also managed to raise a series of funds to support the growth of the company.

Just over a year later, the number of people in the company had grown to the point where they had to add another two offices to accommodate them. In addition, the software project had begun to attract much larger clients and generate cash flow which was reinvested into the product development side of the business. This was precisely the intention of the founder from the start, but it took him seventeen years to admit he couldn't do it alone. Under the leadership of the new CEO, the product development team was finally on track to develop the complex case management software they had tried and failed to build for years before he came on board. As it turned out, the founder had been sabotaging his own company by delaying projects, making rash decisions and hiring and firing unsuitable people. In so doing, he was destroying the very ship he had worked so hard to build all those years ago. To his credit though, he eventually came to the realisation that he needed to let go of his ego, step back and allow those more skilled than he was to take the helm where it mattered most. Unfortunately, it was too little too late. Realising he was no longer in full control of the ship, because the CEO was doing a better job of steering it than he was, the founder tried to take control once more, constantly intervening and interrupting all the progress being made by others. Six months later, the company went into liquidation.

How did it come to this? And what does this story have to do with *vulnerability*? The answer lies in the fact that the founder's original goal was not just for the company to grow, but for him to be the one to grow it.

In other words, he would not consider the company successful unless he was in full control and could take the full credit. It was all about him. For many years he didn't let his guard down enough to realise that others could achieve his objective more effectively than he could. He refused to trust others. He lacked *vulnerability*, and both he and every member of his team paid the price in the end. This is a very common issue in small business. In fact, based on our studies and experience, it is one of the main reasons small companies fail to grow into large enterprises. The founders don't allow their company to grow bigger than themselves! If you make it too personal (all about you), it simply won't grow. Steve Jobs once said he would always hire people who were smarter than him so they could tell him what to do. Is it any wonder that Apple grew to the size it did?

Keeping up appearances

Many people seem to care more about appearing wealthy than actually being wealthy. If you look into the statistics of the largest target market of Louis Vuitton or similar brands, they are not necessarily the rich, but the aspiring upper middle class. They are predominantly highly paid employees who want to look rich. I have many very rich friends, and I also consider myself to be rich. I know what it means to be rich with every cell of my Being. It's actually quite different from what the majority of people think. Any high achiever knows that if you empty their pockets and bank account, they can make the wealth again. It's about how they are being, and how that makes them engage in life. They know how to raise funds, come up with new ideas, influence others and build effective teams, businesses and products people genuinely need and want.

A similar misunderstanding exists when it comes to knowledge. Many in academia, particularly in the so-called 'human sciences', construct theories and do their best to prove their theories rather than seek and discover the truth. Then, through funding from those who stand to benefit from making those constructs widespread, they create campaigns or propaganda to encourage people to agree with their constructs. Eventually, those constructs become the mainstream and dominant ideas in society. I would argue that this is a form of sophistry, as discussed in *Part 1, Chapter 3: Discovery vs Invention*. It is manipulative, deceptive and fraudulent. This type of agenda sends a signal that, in order to make something real, you just have to get enough people on board with it. This is extremely dangerous because it is a betrayal of the truth. Unfortunately, it seems we are okay with normalising this in our democratic world!

Vulnerability is about acknowledging reality and being willing to be open, but in a different way from gaining *awareness*. When you genuinely lack *awareness*, it's as though you are asleep but can be awakened. However, when you lack *vulnerability*, you are aware and only pretending to be asleep, and yet it's extremely difficult to wake you up! I observe this a lot when coaching people. For example, despite having paid for a coaching session, many clients begin their session with me by bending over backwards to impress me. They will tell me they don't have any problems, they have never lied about anything in their life and that they are basically nailing it. However, the underlying truth that brought them to me for coaching is revealed once I gain an insight into what is actually going on, and how effective (or ineffective) they are in various aspects of their life. Our results speak much louder than the stories we tell, especially when we lack the *vulnerability* to speak the truth and own our unpolished or shadow sides, limitations and liabilities. Remember, a lack of *vulnerability* is when you are not willing to be open with yourself about your shadow. This is the perfect recipe for remaining stuck where you are now.

The link between *vulnerability* and *authenticity*

Many of my clients – and people in general – tell me about the things they used to have and the life they used to lead. When I was still living in Iran, almost every taxi driver I met would make excuses for their occupation, as though they felt that being a taxi driver was inferior to other occupations. They would talk about what they used to do and how circumstances drove them to becoming a taxi driver. It was as if they didn't want to be slotted into a particular category or class. There is a level of arrogance associated with not being vulnerable. You think you can have your guard up and fool others; you assume no one will catch you out. But that is not how it works. Not being vulnerable leads to a lack of *authenticity*. And those who lack *vulnerability* and *authenticity*

– the two almost always go hand in hand – do not generally make good business partners, life partners, friends, investors or employees. It is difficult to trust anyone who lacks *vulnerability* or *authenticity*. *Vulnerability* and *authenticity* both provide access to trust. Without trust, it is impossible to have effective relationships, build teams, a client base, communities, and so on. It is worth noting that we ALL have times when we are overcome by the shadow side of *vulnerability* or *authenticity*; absolutely no one is immune to this. When I say, 'those who lack *vulnerability* and *authenticity*', I am not categorising people, but merely highlighting those who often let their unhealthy relationship with these qualities be their dominant way of engaging in life.

Even if people cannot articulate it, they can usually sense a lack of *vulnerability* and *authenticity* in someone. This is why we commonly see inauthentic people with low *vulnerability* together. Have you ever met two people in a relationship who are both so obsessed with each other's image that it seems to be more important to them than who they really are? They regard their partner as an extension of themselves and therefore want them to look good. They see this as an accomplishment, which is why you will mostly observe these couples being overly polite to each other in public and putting on a fake smile to convince everyone that their relationship is second to none. But once back home and away from the public eye or family and friends, the masks come off and the truth is revealed. Once one of them is over the constant role-playing, that's when problems tend to arise. They have both created a persona and are not only acutely aware of that, but don't have any issues with it either. They see life as a stage. It's just a matter of how well they can play the role, and they would expect no less of their partner. They may even incorrectly assume that *vulnerability* is a weakness, and that not being vulnerable is a sign of their maturity and strength. If this is the case, a paradigm shift is clearly required.

Like all Moods, *vulnerability* has a direct and significant impact on every Primary Way of Being and an indirect impact on our Secondary Ways of Being. However, I want to focus on its impact on *authenticity*. Through our empirical data, we know there is a very close correlation between them. The lower your *vulnerability*, the lower your *authenticity*, and vice versa. The more you care about how you are judged by others, the more you will be motivated to filter who you really are. In an unhealthy corporate environment plagued by office politics, you may feel the need to suppress your ambitions, and therefore your *authenticity*, to avoid intimidating management. This may work in your favour if all you care about is keeping your job, but ultimately it won't work if you want to be a high achiever who can **be with** yourself and honour your dignity.

To be vulnerable is empowering

Similar to *fear* and *anxiety*, *vulnerability* is not necessarily a negative or positive phenomenon. It's just a phenomenon that is what it is. It is your ability to receive criticism, be judged and be open to acknowledging your shadow sides, the troubled, unhealthy, unpolished and ineffective parts that are not serving your *integrity* and the integrity of your life and business. It's also whether or not you can freely be yourself without worrying about what others think. Contrary to what the majority would probably believe, having a high level of *vulnerability* is extremely empowering. It means you feel free to express yourself and project the real you – your Unique Being – to the world. It means you are okay with the fact that others may see you through their own lens and therefore have a distorted opinion of you. More importantly, it means you are okay to **be with** your shadow side, with any Aspect of Being that requires polishing, transformation or maintenance. This is the gateway to growth. So, the reality of you is one thing, everyone's interpretation of you – including your own, which hinges on your *awareness* – is another. Once you acknowledge this and make peace with it, you will realise that there is no need to be obsessed with how you are seen by others. In today's world, many of us, especially in the business world, have reputation management consultants, PR experts and marketing and advertising gurus on our team, all tasked with an objective to ensure we are portrayed in the right way and seen as we wish to be seen. I assert that this would work best in the long run if you are committed to being vulnerable and authentic, so that they can portray a congruent image of who you really are. The same is true for your organisation.

Vulnerability is ingrained in nature

As we discussed in the Anxiety chapter, just the fact that we are human beings who have been thrown into this world makes us all vulnerable.

That is a simple fact. It's not personal. We all are vulnerable to disease, betrayal, lies, deception and manipulation. A global pandemic is true evidence of that. We are all in the same boat in that regard. I am not suggesting that it is as simple as that. Some of us must deal with issues that others don't have to, and vice versa. But at the highest level, as members of the Class: Human Being, we are all vulnerable. Let's just acknowledge that.

When it comes to the Being Framework, each person may not show *vulnerability* around certain Aspects of Being. Let's look at an example to explain what I mean. Let's say you were bullied when you were a kid because you didn't have the *courage* to stand up to the bullies. It's very likely that you may have become an adult who constantly feels the need to prove how courageous you are. The fact that you have the urge to be seen as courageous may stop you from working on yourself to actually BE courageous. In other words, you are more concerned with how others see you than you are with striving to actually earn that quality. There is a clear lack of *vulnerability* and *responsibility* around that. No matter what you do, others will see you through their own lens. So, it's not even worth your while to push hard for them to see you in a certain way. Just be the real you and own it powerfully. Do what you find worthwhile. Once you start doing that, once you are vulnerable and embrace where you belong instead of constantly managing the impression you want others to have of you, that's when you will let the real you unfold, and that's when others will begin to see the real you shine. And since the real you is unique, it is scarce, and therefore incredibly valuable. That is a Meaning, a law of the universe. Once you start BEING you, you become the most valuable version of you possible, which is why Being is your source of power.

People who are obsessed with their reputation are likely to exaggerate, lie or deliberately hide the truth. They are so committed to selling the persona they created that they hide behind the mask. We will discuss this further in the Authenticity chapter. I see many business owners, including first time entrepreneurs, trying to scale their business despite the fact that they don't know much about business, investment, technology, marketing and all the other elements required to build a successful business. Often, they try to sell you a persona, which in the end, costs them dearly. Those who allow themselves to be vulnerable seek help from advisors, consultants, coaches and mentors in the areas they most need assistance. For example, most angel investors don't expect their potential candidates to have much experience in business. They know it's the beginning for them, so being genuine and vulnerable enough to seek their advice and feedback around their business concept is seen in a far more positive light than if they were to exaggerate and boast in order to try and win them over. They know how to read people and build relationships founded on *authenticity* and *vulnerability*.

We can't possibly know everything, so what's the point of pretending we do and not being vulnerable and open to help from those who know more than we do in certain aspects of business and life? We discussed the importance of epistemic humility in the Awareness chapter. Remember, you cannot become effective in something that you are not aware of. And to become aware that you are lacking somewhere requires you to be vulnerable. Then, once you are aware of the area you need to work on, it takes an even higher level of *vulnerability* to take action. Furthermore, *vulnerability* is not a one-off project, something to be worked on once, nail, and live happily ever after. Like every other Aspect of Being, it requires regular maintenance. I sometimes catch myself not being vulnerable, open and transparent, and know that when this happens, it has a direct bearing on other Aspects of Being, particularly on my *authenticity* and *self-expression*. Once you know what it's like to have a healthy relationship with *vulnerability*, you won't want to take a step backwards. It's like when you have been working out for some time and become accustomed to having a fit, toned body. Slide off the bandwagon for a while, and I'm sure you wouldn't feel too good about yourself in comparison! The same is true with your Aspects of Being. Once you know what a healthy relationship with any Aspect of Being feels like, you can hold yourself to account to get your *integrity* (wholeness) back.

In short, when it comes to *vulnerability*, ask yourself, do you tend to avoid and ignore criticism, or do you allow yourself to receive feedback in good faith and follow it with conviction and *authenticity*? When you are confronted about a mistake you have made, do you bluff your way out of the situation, or own your mistake because you are authentic and in touch with Reality? Do you guard your heart against rejection at all costs, or do you have the *courage* to develop a thicker skin in the face of whatever life may bring? Are you comfortable with your weaknesses – a quality that is empowering – or do you shy away from them? Do you relish holding your cards close to your chest, usually for no good reason or benefit? Being vulnerable sets you free because it allows you to learn from the past, or your current shortcomings, and grow from it.

That concludes this section on Moods. Hopefully, by now you understand that Moods matter because they determine your relationship with the future and impact how you express your Unique Being through your Ways of Being, as you will discover in the next two sections of the book. When you gradually develop a more accurate and effective relationship with Reality through the dance between *awareness* and *effectiveness*, as well as regular maintenance of your *integrity*, polishing your Being (including your Moods) becomes an ongoing habit, not a one-off project with a series of 'tell me what to do' instructions. Constantly raising your *awareness*, polishing and maintaining your *integrity* and being effective the majority of the time in your endeavours will lead you to fulfilment in all aspects of your life – personally and professionally.

SECTION 3

Primary Ways of Being

Primary Ways of Being, such as *authenticity, responsibility, commitment* and *gratitude*, to name just a few, are the ways through which we express who we truly are to the world. They directly contribute to the results we produce in life. For example, people who are integrous across all of their Primary Ways of Being directly cause the results they experience in life. They have no need to pretend to be someone they are not because they are free to be themselves. Therefore, they communicate freely and appreciate their *responsibility* in terms of their interactions with others and the delivery of results. They are shaping their lives as they have planned, and are therefore effective and fulfilled. Remember, the merit of this framework is that when you have a polished Being, effective and healthy behaviours will unfold. In this section of the book, we are focusing on the Primary Ways of Being.

The Being Framework's sixteen Primary Ways of Being are more personal, subtle and not as easily evidenced in behaviour as the eight Secondary Ways of Being. All of these unique Aspects of Being impact our decisions, behaviour, performance and the subsequent results we produce in life. They determine the way we participate in life, our work and relationships, and also the likelihood and velocity with which we intentionally cause our personal growth.

Our individual experience of life is uniquely ours. However, sometimes this experience can be deceiving because it greatly depends on the level of *awareness* we have developed. We may have a sense of being highly authentic, while the people we interact with may perceive us to be less authentic than we think we are, and clearly see our blind spots. This creates an ideal opportunity for the Being Framework to assist in mapping out and uncovering those blind spots. It provides a powerful lens through which to raise your *awareness* of your current state of Being, providing you with the optimal starting point for change. As we mentioned, these Aspects of Being can be accurately measured using the Being Framework assessment tool, the Being Profile. You will be introduced to the Being Profile in *Part 3: Being, in Action*.

When planning an overseas holiday, most people start by determining their ideal destination, their budget and the best time of year to go. Then they would work out how much money they will need to put aside each week within a given timeframe, based on how much they currently have in their holiday fund, in order to fulfil their travel plans. Personal growth is very similar. You must first establish your starting point and what you want to achieve (your objective) so you know the areas (Aspects of Being) you need to work on, polish and transform.

Before we go into detail for each Primary Way of Being, it is important to point out that if you were to measure yourself in each area, you would have a unique combination of health scores in comparison to others. And remember, the Being Framework adopts a completely non-judgemental approach, meaning there is no right or wrong, no notion of 'you ought to be this way or that way'. It allows you to gain a snapshot of how you **are** as a reference and starting point. In this context, you are encouraged to view it as a positive phenomenon. After all, knowing how you are being as opposed to how you think you are being, or want to be, can only be positive and constructive for you. A lower level of health in any area can be viewed as a learning curve. For example, if you want to transform your relationship with *authenticity,* you must first experience what it feels like to be inauthentic, including the impact that has. After all, why would you want to change something unless you have understood and experienced the impact that **not** being a certain way is having on your life and/or the lives of others? A higher level of health in any area indicates the relatively greater health of your relationship with that particular Way of Being, acknowledging your strengths and supporting you to maintain the health of that area whilst leveraging its power in pursuit of fulfilment in life.

As a business leader, professional or entrepreneur, you will be challenged many times during your professional life, and no doubt you already have been. This could be due to a lack of *authenticity,* communication difficulties, resistance to being responsible, and so on, either on your part or on the part of others on your team, venture partners, clients, or any other stakeholders involved. Unless you understand the extent to which you (or others) are being responsible, authentic, courageous, present, empowered, free, etc., how could you possibly know where to start if you want to make a positive change?

The following chapters describe the sixteen Primary Ways of Being that were selected for the Being Framework Ontological Model. They were selected because, together, they form the most valuable building blocks to create a strong foundation for every leader and entrepreneur's personal and professional life. Mastering these Ways of Being will support you to achieve the results you desire. Based on our experience working with over two thousand clients and studying hundreds of the world's highest achievers in various disciplines, from Bill Gates and Jeff Bezos to Paul McCartney, Simone de Beauvoir, Mother Teresa and Gabriel García Márquez, to name just a few, failing to work on these critical Ways of Being can be the roadblocks to building successful businesses, being effective in your craft and projecting your Unique Being to the world.

CHAPTER 8

Authenticity

There are times when my dog interrupts me when I am working because he needs food and I pretend he is not there. I ignore his persistent attempts to get my attention because I am busy with other matters I care more about at that moment. Or perhaps I am just being lazy. I'm sure you get the drift. Essentially, at times I am just not interested in looking after my dog when I am busy with something else. Have you ever chosen to ignore that a dog who needs your attention is actually there? I can tell you from my own experience, it doesn't work! Here are my options when this happens. I could accept the truth that my dog is in need of my attention. That is being **authentic**. However, if I don't want to feed my dog and choose to ignore that he is there, I am being **inauthentic**. For instance, let's say my dog is barking because he is not getting my attention and a neighbour calls and complains. In that case, I am authentic if I own up to what is happening or what I caused with my inaction. But I am inauthentic if I tell them there is no dog. The fact is, there IS a hungry dog in my home. That is the Reality of the situation. I am inauthentic if I deliberately choose to ignore Reality. Whether or not I believe there is a dog there is irrelevant; in fact, to believe there is no dog there at all would be delusional.

A friend of mine once told me how his younger brother had refused to have regular health checks for cancer, even though their other sibling and both parents had died from the disease. He deliberately ignored knowing, opting instead to put himself and his family at greater risk. He was not even willing to have a conversation about it. In other words, he could not **be with** the possibility of having cancer, choosing not to know rather than being authentic about it and dealing with the Reality that he could potentially have the disease. Having a healthy relationship with

Moods (*care, fear, anxiety* and *vulnerability*) supports us to be authentic. In this instance, my friend's brother may have had a lack of *care* around the possibility that having cancer could create suffering for himself and others (close family, friends, colleagues and even the medical system), causing him to not prioritise the regular check-ups. Or perhaps, due to a lack of *vulnerability*, he didn't want to attract the sympathy of others. Instead, he kept his guard up because he felt that acknowledging the issue was a sign of weakness. So, he deliberately avoided the issue, telling himself things like, 'I am too healthy to get cancer', or, 'It won't happen to me'. Maybe he had an unhealthy relationship with *anxiety*, constantly wondering, 'What if it happens to me?' and worrying about what his future would look like should he be diagnosed with cancer. Or maybe *fear* of being hospitalised and/or pain caused him to bury his head in the sand. You can see from this example that *courage* is the quality we need the most in order to be authentic, and this is also where one's unhealthy relationship with Moods can get in the way of being authentic and facing Reality. Ask yourself, 'When or where am I avoiding the truth about something, because the truth is too unbearable to face?'

What is *authenticity*?

As is the case with any of the other qualities or Aspects of Being we discuss in this framework, *authenticity* has many definitions applied to it. The word is overloaded with different meanings, ranging from 'a moral virtue', or 'honesty', as denoted within religious scriptures, to the *Cambridge Dictionary* definition, 'the quality of being real or true'. A vastly different definition of *authenticity* was proposed by psychologist Erich Fromm[104] in the mid-1900s. He considered behaviour of any kind, even a behaviour wholly in accord with societal norms, to be authentic if it results from a personal understanding and approval of its drivers and origins, rather than merely from conformity to the received wisdom of society.

The primal quality we are using the word '*authenticity*' to refer to in the Being Framework is how you intentionally relate to the Reality of your true Self (both Unique Being and Aspects of Being), others and the

---

104 Erich Seligmann Fromm (1900-1980) was a social psychologist, psychoanalyst, sociologist, humanistic philosopher and democratic socialist.

world around you. You may be thinking that this description seems very similar to *awareness*, and indeed, there is a fine line between the two. One of the principal differences, however, is that *authenticity* is the **urge to want to become aware** (being completely and genuinely committed to discovery) AND being authentic about what you know. Some may argue that a better word than *authenticity* would be 'congruence'. However, congruence is simply 'corresponding in character or kind', which doesn't take into account the deeper layers of ourselves. While *authenticity* is also corresponding in character and kind, I have taken it a step further in the Being Framework by also considering the genuinity of who you really are: your Unique Being, the real YOU, the piece of Existence you carry within you from the day you are born. Before I go into more detail about *authenticity* as a Primary Way of Being, I will first present you with the ontological distinction of *authenticity*.

The Being Framework ontological distinction of *authenticity*

Authenticity is how you relate to the reality of matters in life. It is the extent to which you are accurate and rigorous in perceiving what is real and what is not. It is also how sensitive and diligent you are to the validity of the knowledge you perceive. *Authenticity* is paramount for you to carefully consider that your conception of reality – including your beliefs and opinions – is congruent with how things are. When you are being authentic, you are compelled to express your Unique Being – what is there for you to express – while being consistent with who you say you are for others and who you say you are for yourself. It is the congruence or alignment of your self-image – who you know yourself to be – and your persona – who you choose to project to others.

A healthy relationship with *authenticity* indicates that you take the time to thoughtfully consider your beliefs and opinions, as the validity and accuracy of your conception of matters is important to you. You mostly experience yourself as being true to yourself and others. Others may consider you genuine, distinct and trustworthy, and that your actions are consistent with who and how you are and what you communicate.

An unhealthy relationship with *authenticity* indicates that there may be no solid foundation for your beliefs and opinions and how you choose to examine reality, and you are often lenient and fickle with how you express your views and the truth. You may consider yourself to be fake or an imposter and often question your own abilities. Others may consider you to be someone who lacks sincerity and often acts inconsistently with who you say you are. You are frequently uncomfortable with being yourself and being with yourself. Alternatively, you may be righteous, opinionated, biased or prejudiced, considering your 'truth' to be the only truth, and may be unwilling to give up being 'right'.

The Authenticity Quadrant

Self-Image Conversations you have with yourself about yourself	**Persona** Conversations you have with the world about yourself
Beliefs Conversations you have with yourself about the world	**Opinions** Conversations you have with the world about the world

Figure 6: The Authenticity Quadrant

I created the Authenticity Quadrant to highlight the four areas we need to understand about ourselves and polish in order to be authentic: Self-Image and Beliefs on the left, which are the conversations you have with yourself, and Persona and Opinions on the right, which are the conversations you have with the world/others. In a nutshell, your relationship with your self-image, persona, beliefs and opinions defines how authentic you are. Let's examine some of these relationships more closely, beginning with self-image, the conversations you have with yourself about yourself.

Is your perception of yourself congruent with who you actually are? Are you present to your inner dialogue? Your self-image is how you perceive and conceive who you are, and what or how you are being. Is it telling you that you are superior to others, or is it telling you that you are not good enough or inferior? Both of these internal conversations are pointing to an inauthentic view of yourself. The first can lead to arrogance and the second to self-doubt and low self-esteem. Neither is being authentic. For example, just because you are more competent than someone else in certain areas doesn't necessarily mean you are more competent in all areas. This is a form of logical fallacy; it's delusional. It's like arguing that if my front door is bigger than your front door, my house must also be bigger than yours. To think this way means you do not have a healthy relationship with the Reality of yourself and/or others.

Don't get me wrong, your self-talk is valuable and can be positive and enhance joy and experiences in your life. There is nothing wrong with stating or writing affirmations like, 'I am confident', 'I have prosperous business relationships', 'I can create my dream life', or, 'I am creative and innovative', as long as you are being authentic. However, if your affirmations are not congruent with Reality, or believable to you, they are inauthentic and can lose their potency. Start by being aware of and examining your internal dialogue. More often than not, you will find it is quite negative. The first step is to observe your dialogue, identify why it is so negative, and reframe those old perceptions, including beliefs and opinions, into new and more congruent statements that reflect reality (First and Second-layer).

In the leadership space, your people allow you to lead them, at least in part, because who and how you are and what you say are aligned, meaning you are being authentic with them. However, if the conversations you have with yourself (the left side of the Quadrant) are excessively positive, you risk ending up with an overconfident self-image with beliefs that are overly optimistic. This in turn may lead you to express an arrogant persona and be inappropriately nonchalant. It may even cause you to be blindsided in the face of circumstances that happen in life. On the other hand, if the conversations you have with yourself are overly negative, you may end up being doubtful and lacking *confidence*, which may result in you projecting an overly timid and submissive persona. Your beliefs would be unduly pessimistic – worse than the reality of how things actually are – leading you to be unnecessarily fearful, anxious, defensive and defeatist. In either of the cases highlighted, your beliefs are not going to be grounded in reality as there are no solid foundations to them. Neither case is conducive to being a leader worth following.

Beliefs are only valid and effective if they are congruent with reality. As we discussed in the Awareness chapter, as a leader and high performer, you are fundamentally concerned with transforming your beliefs so that they are congruent with reality. This is not possible unless you empty your cup to allow new knowledge to flow in. The more harmonious your understanding of your self-image, the more balanced and humble, yet confident, your persona will be. Furthermore, if the conversations you have with the world/others (the right-hand side of the Quadrant) are overly positive, you risk ending up being idealistic, delusional, and unrealistic, often expressing romantic, dreamy opinions. Too negative, and you are likely to end up being cynical, sceptical and pessimistic, expressing sarcastic, cutting and acerbic opinions. The more balanced and authentic you can be with both positive and negative beliefs and opinions, the more realistic and decisive you will be, and the more congruent and accurate your beliefs and opinions will be. This links with *awareness* and establishes a healthy relationship with reality (First and Second-layer).

Another way to look at this is to consider the conversations you have about yourself with yourself (self-image) and with the world (persona). If these conversations are congruent with reality – in other words, if you are being authentic about yourself – then this will open the door to growth. Without authentic self-awareness, without the *vulnerability* and *courage* to be authentic enough to express your current self to the world/others, you will not become aware of the parts of you that are not working so that you can polish them and transform. Instead, they will get in the way of reaching your objectives. As we learnt in the Shadow chapter, when you bring your attention to your troubled parts (the shadow), they are confronting. You need to face them with *authenticity*, *courage* and *vulnerability*. This is what I mean when I say that growth can only be achieved when you have access to and acknowledge the reality of yourself. If you are aware of the shadow parts of yourself but continue to hide from them, refusing to acknowledge them, not only are you being inauthentic, but you are also blocking your access to transformation and growth.

One of the major consequences of inauthenticity is lack of self-awareness – the refusal to authentically look at yourself, particularly your troubled parts (shadow) – with no access to, or opportunity for, growth. When you are inauthentic, your energy is diverted into maintaining a fake persona, which may leave you confused or in doubt about your self-image, and struggling with incongruent and ineffective beliefs and opinions. There is little to no fulfilment in that. You struggle to **be with** and love yourself, you are stuck and, most likely, your opinions and beliefs are proving to be invalid. On the other hand, the major outcomes of being authentic are growth and the opportunity to develop each and every Aspect of Being, leading to *integrity, effectiveness*, fulfilment, satisfaction, joy and grace, whereby you release ease and flow into your life and bring workability to every area.

We habitually sell out our authentic Self for reasons such as, but not limited to, looking good, not looking bad, seeking admiration, avoiding trouble, conveying loyalty, avoiding discomfort, belonging (e.g. to a team or a group) and disappointing others. Sooner or later, we realise this costs us dearly. The actual cost is the real YOU. You may occasionally be hitting the targets you set for yourself, and perhaps you have created a persona that wins games, but deep down you know you don't really deserve all the fame, admiration, monetary gains, etc., because they are the result of the fake persona you have created and projected. While you may think achieving your goals justifies the means, once you get there, once you HAVE the things you desire, you start questioning yourself because it is now WHO and HOW you are/have become that is far more important to you than WHAT you have gained. You may end up gaining the whole world, but you would lose your Unique Being, the real YOU, your Self. As coaches, we work with many leaders who are dealing with this on a daily basis. It's a constant dilemma for leaders who want to BE successful yet not sell themselves out. The great news, according to our studies, is that not only is it possible to BE successful and BE authentic, it is the ONLY access to reaching your goals (fulfilment) and being truly dignified, content and satisfied at the same time.

When it comes to the conversations you have about the world – your beliefs and opinions – as long as these conversations are congruent with reality; in other words, as long as you are being authentic about the world, then this also gives you access to growth and success. The major outcomes of having authentic beliefs and opinions are a more accurate *awareness* of what is going on in the world and not being blindsided or shocked in the face of reality. This allows you to fine-tune and adjust your expectations, leading you to be responsible instead of victimising and sabotaging yourself. When you are being authentic about the world and others, you deal with life with grace, ease and flow. As a visionary leader, you understand and acknowledge how things are and challenge the status quo in order to effect change.

The consequences of being inauthentic about the world are significant. You are frequently going to be blindsided and delusional, constantly surprised, shocked, frustrated, angry and disappointed in your inability to change how things are. There will be limited workability and *effectiveness* in your life, since you are careless with your opinions and beliefs and they have little or no basis in reality. Even though you keep defending, reiterating and promoting them, there is no substance to them. They are only there to keep up and maintain the appearance of your fake persona. You are more concerned with impressing others than being vulnerable and dealing with reality, leading to dogmatism, considered the state of false righteousness and an unwillingness to give up being right. This provides no access to growth or the ability to build anything, including relationships, a family, organisations, teams, financial wealth, partnerships, and so on.

The word 'persona' derives from the Latin *Persōna*, which means 'mask', or 'character'. We all have personas. Our personas are the means through which we project ourselves to others. The *Oxford English Dictionary* defines persona as 'the aspect of someone's character that is presented to or perceived by others'. We choose our persona. It is the role we play. We can either adopt and gradually develop a persona, which is congruent with who we really are, leading to *authenticity*, or we can invent a fake persona for ourselves due to fear, lack of *vulnerability*, insecurities, social pressures and perceived expectations, etc., preventing us from being authentic. Once you adopt this persona you invented, you start being the worst representative of your true Self.

It is important to understand that persona is neither good nor bad. It is not as if lacking a persona makes you authentic. The key is to have a persona that is **aligned with who you are** rather than project a fake one. Your persona is intended to be an integral and inseparable part of your authentic Self. This is fundamental to what I am communicating, both within this book and the framework, hence it is part of the Authenticity Quadrant.

As we grow up, we are constantly in self-discovery mode, discovering our Unique Being and developing our persona. Combined, they give us access to actualising our full potential as a human being. I repeatedly refer to this as the true projection of the manifestation of your Unique Being to the world throughout this book. The alternative is to attempt to endure living life in the absence of a persona. According to Carl Jung,

'The man with no persona... is blind to the reality of the world, which for him has merely the value of an amusing or fantastic playground'[105]. It is like living in a dreamland. As Jung also wrote, 'the danger is that [people] become identical with their personas—the professor with his textbook, the tenor with his voice'[106]. I would add, 'the President with his office'!

As mentioned, in the Being Framework, persona is the aspect of your authentic Self that you project and is perceived by others. It prepares you (or not) for culture, society and, more specifically, the social hierarchies. It is a fundamental part of maturity and moving towards adulthood. It is the means by which you interact with the world, particularly with others. If you refuse to acknowledge, be present to and adjust your persona in the first instance, to gradually shape your unique and distinct role in the world – some may call it a career – you are likely to remain a middle-aged infant with potential that never actualises into anything. The extent to which you uncover your Unique Being, articulate it and gradually shape your conception of yourself (self-image), and the proficiency with which you gradually shape and project your persona through constant refining and polishing, also has a direct correlation with the brand (persona) of the business you are building and running.

As we discussed in the Awareness chapter, acknowledgment of reality (First, Second and Third-layer) supports us to be authentic in our understanding of how things are and how they could be. This is the first step in order to appropriately challenge and transform the current Second-layer Reality. Furthermore, being authentic also requires you to be present to the Third-layer Reality (the reality you create), by acknowledging whether your reality is genuine, and may just need refinement before introducing it into Second-layer Reality as a new discovery that fulfils a need, or if it is delusional. Bear with me, as I will shortly explain how this discussion relates to the persona conversation and *authenticity*.

As a leader, seeing (vision) and identifying/predicting the existing or potential future problems, pain and suffering of human beings (through *higher purpose* and *compassion*), allocating people and economic

---

105   Jung, *Two Essays*, p. 197.
106   C. G. Jung, *Memories, Dreams, Reflections* (London 1983), p. 416.

resources to come up with relevant solutions (*responsibility*) and delivering them to the group of people in need (market) expands the collective reality (Second-layer Reality) for everyone. This vision should be authentic and congruent with reality, otherwise you risk coming up with solutions and products for requirements that don't exist, leading to wasted time, capital and other resources. Ultimately, this would lead you to lack *effectiveness* and risk never achieving fulfilment in life. For example, Steve Jobs was acutely present to the suffering human beings endured when interacting with computers that were not user-friendly. He identified the problem (in his subjective Third-layer Reality) and validated it to be true beyond his subjective view/discovery through a process of research and communication. Once validated, Jobs and his team created and presented solutions and products which resonated with many (market/consumers). The result was that Jobs and his team gradually managed to expand and transform the Second-layer Reality (collective reality) for almost everyone, to the point where it became the new way of interacting with computers. The same is true of Facebook, Amazon, eBay, UBER, etc., as they all created new paradigms. None would have been possible without *awareness* of the layers of reality AND without being authentic.

So, how does all this relate to *authenticity* and persona? People who refuse to acknowledge the current social discipline (part of the current Second-layer Reality), or the responsibility inherent in having a role in the world remain indistinct, mediocre and with unrealised potential. In Jungian terms, this is known as 'Peter Pan Syndrome', where one does not know how to, or want to, stop being a child and embrace the reality of the world. Peter Pan never aged and never wanted to fit in. This syndrome is often glorified in the postmodern era and has greatly impacted popular culture. Being solely rebellious, anarchical, revolutionary and challenging, for example, may lead you to be nothing more than the fictional king of Peter Pan's Neverland. Remember, lack of persona, failing to align your true Self with your persona, or inventing a fake persona has a significant impact on your *authenticity*. As a professional, your persona is one of your most valuable assets. The more you refine and shape it, the more it shines. It impacts your reputation and ultimately becomes your brand, the way you and/or your organisation is perceived by others. If you are not crystal clear on your persona, fear not.

Persona is something you can choose to gain greater clarity over and develop over time.

The battle with personas has been characterised many times in the arts. One well known example is *Pinocchio*. There is a particular scene in the movie where Geppetto, the carpenter/father, encourages Pinocchio to develop his character and gain wisdom by handing him a book (symbol of wisdom) and sending him to school. On his way to school, Pinocchio is intercepted by the fox who, through his high level of *awareness*, can vividly see Pinocchio's Unique Being – his distinct talents as a one-of-a-kind, semi-autonomous puppet. The fox decides to distract and take advantage of Pinocchio for his own gain by selling him the 'dream' of being a famous actor, and suggests introducing him to Stromboli, the theatre master and antagonist in the story.

The main aim of education has always been to make our conception of reality (First and Second-layer) as accurate as possible so that we don't get crushed in the face of life's challenges, inevitable adversities, catastrophes, and malevolent forces. In the story, the fox represents an external malevolent force that is deliberately attempting to distract Pinocchio and talk him out of going to school by suggesting there is an easier way, a shortcut! He tells Pinocchio that you do not need to develop your character, polish your Being and develop skills. In other words, the fox is suggesting that it is not necessary to be authentic and do the hard work. Instead, just learn how to be an actor and treat your life as a performance, as if you are on the stage playing whatever role you wish and/or think works for you in order to feed your immediate desires and impulses. By being an actor, you can potentially ignore reality and pretend to BE whoever and however you wish to be right now, as the means to instant gratification by creating your own parallel (Third-layer) reality. And if you are a really competent and clever actor, you may fool others into believing you, at least for a while.

Pinocchio may have been an animated fiction story, but it is a true representation of how we are and what happens in the world today. Like its main character, we all come into this world semi-autonomous, and we can redeem ourselves, becoming free of both internal and external forces that get in the way of being ourselves and saying our real 'yeses' and 'noes'. There are many examples of 'foxes' in the world, from quick-fix personal development gurus and rapid behavioural change recipes to authors of books and materials, telling us how to take shortcuts to so-called 'fame and fortune'. Like the fox, they suggest there is no need to give it the time and effort required to be fulfilled when you can simply get on the stage and act to make a name for yourself in the world. Many of the entrepreneurs we work with, especially the less experienced ones, want to know how they can make it to the top quickly. They aren't necessarily happy to hear about reality! I frequently use the story of *Pinocchio* to make the point that it is quite common for people to want to be 'clever' and look for shortcuts. The simple truth is, there are no shortcuts to *awareness*, *integrity*, *effectiveness* and, ultimately, fulfilment.

The difference between persona, personality and temperament

The word 'personality' is derived from the Latin *Persona*. It is another overloaded and misunderstood word. In fact, some people confuse the two. The *Oxford English Dictionary* defines personality as 'the combination of characteristics or qualities that form an individual's distinctive character', and the *Cambridge Dictionary* defines it as 'the special combination of qualities in a person that makes that person different from others, as shown by the way the person behaves, feels, and thinks', or, 'the type of person you are, shown by the way you behave, feel, and think'. The *Merriam-Webster* defines it as 'the complex of characteristics that distinguishes an individual or a nation or group especially: the totality of an individual's behavioral and emotional characteristics'. Simply put, personality is something that is developed over time, whereas persona is the part of your personality that you choose to project to others and is perceived by them.

To avoid confusion, it is also important that we consider the difference between temperament and personality. Temperament, which we touched on in Part 1, is considered a natural part of your personality. It is the product of your genetic inheritance and a biological, instinctive part of your personality. As time passes and you grow, your personality continues to develop, and you either choose to take the lead and keep transforming and polishing it, or your personality will develop without your deliberate influence and let the temperament you were born with, the environmental forces swirling around you and your circumstances dictate the evolution of your personality. How intentional and responsible you are being impacts the shaping and projection of your persona. In other words, you may either choose to define your SELF or let your SELF be defined by the world.

Your temperament in childhood can, to some extent, predict your personality as an adult, whereas your Aspects of Being have a significant influence on how your personality turns out in the end. For example, your relationship with *awareness, care, responsibility* and *commitment* plays a major role in the extent to which you intentionally develop your personality or not. As you may recall from the Being Framework Ontological Model[107], your temperament has a direct influence on your Moods, with a subsequent impact on your Ways of Being and behaviour.

Many people tend to think that our personality is fixed, and this belief is reinforced by some renowned thinkers and psychologists. But the truth of the matter is, it's our personality (hence persona) that we gradually shape through our experiences, interactions, upbringing, contemplation and thinking. Subsequently, it is given such axiom and importance that many still believe we are hardwired to be that way. For this framework, we challenged this conventional view of how human beings are and operate in their lives and surrounding environment. Rather than seeing the world and the people in it as a set of fixed objects, we concluded, following our studies and collated evidence, that human beings are not hardwired to remain as they are being now. Instead, we discovered that the unique moment by moment choices we make define how we are for ourselves, for others, and for our relationship with all the other elements in the world around us. This fundamental shift in how we consider what it is to be human creates a whole new perspective on how we work and live, hence this can be considered a radical view. Through extensive research, we realised that this is what matters most in order to grow human potential and culture in different contexts, including communities, organisations and in our personal lives.

The downsides of creating a fake persona

Today, the World Wide Web and social media make it easy for us to create fake accounts, modify ourselves using photo editing tools and

---

107   Refer to the Model on page 80 and 81.

AUTHENTICITY

filters or convey a persona that makes us seem happier and more accomplished than we actually are. In reality, the opposite is frequently true. While all the likes, etc., that we receive as a result of creating this fake persona may deliver instant gratification, we all know that this does not get us anywhere or provide fulfilment in the long run. If you polish a fake persona like a piece of glass, it will definitely shine, but it will never become a diamond. It will not lead you to satisfaction in life because, in your solitude, you would know that what people are applauding you for is not you, it is the fake you. I learnt this through personal experience and working with others, including coaching celebrities and advising politicians who could not **be with** themselves (*love*), despite the enormous external success and following they had managed to achieve. The same applies to companies, which, through clever branding and marketing, try to exaggerate their portfolio and accomplishments. My team and I have experienced this many times when working with investors who ended up forking out considerable sums of money to fund a startup, only to learn that much of the information they were provided with was false. In the worst cases, the founder's intention from the outset was not to put in the time and effort required to build a business, but to find an easy way (like Pinocchio was enticed to do) to fund their lifestyle. This leads to a huge waste of human potential, capital, time and resources. Most importantly, it leads to their Unique Beings never being uncovered and projected to the world, ultimately resulting in a huge loss to humankind.

How often have you observed another person who is experiencing significant success or influence in life or who possesses qualities you wish you had, and secretly wished you were them? They possess something you think you don't have, and so you assume that by acquiring their talents, status or wealth, for example, you may be able to replicate their level of success, glory and satisfaction and solve all your problems. But do you really want to become a carbon copy of high achievers, like Richard Branson, Elon Musk or Oprah Winfrey, because you perceive them to be highly successful or influential? Don't forget, they each discovered their own Unique Being AND polished their Aspects of Being, which led them to unfold who they are today, and I am sure they would all acknowledge they are still a work in progress. While it is extremely important to learn from others – an openness to learning relates to *vulnerability* and epistemic humility – using your newly acquired knowledge and skills to become a carbon copy of someone else will never work in your favour in the long run, as it will backfire when your inauthenticities are revealed. The key when learning anything new is to adapt what you learn and make it your own. If you are hiding the real you from your partner, friends, business colleagues and even yourself, you are not being genuine, you are being inauthentic, and that comes at a huge cost: the real YOU.

The bottom line is, you do not need to prove yourself to anyone. I am reminded of a young guy I once worked with who wanted to build his very first startup. Rather than focusing on building a viable business, he was constantly trying to impress others. Just three months into his journey, he began to grossly exaggerate the size of the company in an attempt to impress others and gain more followers on Facebook. I remember him coming to me one day boasting that he had paid a company to sell him fake Facebook followers, which resulted in an increase of a few thousand page likes overnight. When I confronted him about the fact that he wasn't being authentic and that he was misleading people and that this was not where his focus should be at this early stage of his startup journey, he simply looked at me and said, 'You know what? I want to become someone, bro!' He was blind to the fact that he was already someone. His attitude was influenced by a low level of *vulnerability* as well as a low level of *authenticity* and lack of *awareness* around how to shape and project an authentic persona. As I mentioned earlier, through the empirical data we gathered from conducting many profiles using the Being Profile, we discovered a very close relationship between *vulnerability* and *authenticity*. In fact, these qualities generally go hand in hand. The lower an individual's *vulnerability*, the more likely *authenticity* will suffer, as we don't want to lose face, which leads us to continue to sell our inauthentic persona to the world.

When you create a fake persona, you are projecting an illusion. As an actor, your job is to deceive, to dissemble, to represent someone other than your real Self and reproduce someone else's words with 100% accuracy and conviction. Your authentic persona, on the other hand, is an integrated part of the totality of YOU. For example, if you have studied for years to become a surgeon, gradually, through knowledge and experience, that persona will become integrated as an inseparable part of you. You won't just make it up overnight. Returning to the example of the startup who purchased Facebook followers, the aim when building a social media following should be to collect real followers who are genuinely interested in your brand and offerings, not so much from a moral standpoint, but because it is the only way to create an authentic brand that achieves your objective of targeting a filtered market that is more likely to be genuine prospects for your brand and offering. This is done by building relationships through regular and consistent sharing of valuable information that generates engagement. It is a process of trial and error, tracking and learning from how real people engage with your messages and making incremental changes and tweaks to those messages in line with your findings over time. Only then will you perhaps be successful in selling your offerings to them. Generating fake followers to impress others rarely results in sales. Remember, I am not suggesting personas are unacceptable. You can only be authentic with a persona if it is integral to you. Only then will it make your interactions with others seamless. But when you are acting, and start believing that you **are** that person on the stage, it's easy to become enchanted with that persona and lose the connection to the real, authentic totality of you. We can observe this on many reality TV shows. People present a certain persona on these shows and, in doing so over a long period of time, may no longer be able to differentiate themselves from the persona they are acting out and lose touch with who they really are[108]. They may continue to lead this double 'life'. When you create a persona that is not aligned with your authentic Self, you can become so captivated with that fake, over-exaggerated persona, that you may lose interest in embracing and developing the real you. Over time, you may even forget that it was a role you were acting, to the point where you have to confront yourself and deal with the *vulnerability, fear* and *anxiety* of taking that mask off, which in itself requires extremely high levels of *care, courage* and *responsibility*. Moreover, by creating permanent fake personas, you would have yet another one to maintain, which has limited workability, as maintaining *integrity* with the real YOU is hard enough and demands a lifelong commitment.

---

108 Jung referred to this as, 'the danger of becoming identical with your persona': C. G. Jung, *Memories, Dreams, Reflections* (London 1983), p. 416.

As human beings, we excel at creating drama. But life is not a stage, even though it may appear to be at times, especially when we are dealing with the parallel realities we have created for ourselves and others. Unfortunately, we see a lot of acting and drama taking place in political and business arenas, as well as in the media. Some well-known opinion makers literally suggest that people, particularly leaders, should become better actors to pave their success. They call themselves 'pragmatists', and advise us to adjust our personas to our audience in order to push our agenda. To be victorious in the quest for success, they tell us to only reveal to our prospect, date or potential business partner what we believe they want to see. They encourage us to sell ourselves like customisable commodities or shape shifters. Even some professional coaches, mentors and advisors may guide their clients to become better actors in order to succeed in life, just as the fox encouraged Pinocchio to do.

Be authentic, at least most of the time, or suffer the consequences

Authenticity is real, it is a phenomenon. It is a quality we seek whenever we want to embark on something important, such as building a fruitful relationship. Whether we want to find a business partner or a life partner, the first thing we want to do is learn the facts about the other person, to find out whether or not we choose to trust them. The very least we expect when dealing with others is that they won't attempt to deceive us. We expect them to show us who they really are. This involves getting accurate data, so we can form educated decisions about them. No one wants to be lied to or deceived. However, no one is 100% authentic 100% of the time. We tend to deliberately choose to avoid revealing certain parts of ourselves and only communicate parts of the truth because, depending on the situation, it may not be appropriate or the right time to disclose everything. This is not the same as lying. It is keeping certain details close to our chest, at least for now. There is nothing inherently wrong with this. Let's say, for example, that you have made a minor error in a presentation to a client within a group setting. As long as it doesn't have an instant detrimental impact on the client or the business, there may be no need to point out the error immediately. You may choose to hold back and tell the client later in a private setting, when appropriate. Only a small percentage of people are vulnerable enough to acknowledge that they are not 100% authentic at all times and hold themselves to account when they know they are slipping away from being authentic. When this happens, they care so much about their *authenticity* that their inauthenticity is unbearable, and they are quick to resolve matters.

We are, by nature, intuitive beings and therefore able to sense when someone is putting on an act. We may not know exactly what is going on immediately, but we get a sense when the other party is not being authentic. If you continually put on an act with someone you are dating, imagine what would happen if you eventually became life partners? The same is true when it comes to a potential business partnership, adding a new member to your team or building a relationship with a major client. If your relationship is based on a lie or obsessively filtered information, inauthenticities and fake personas, it won't last. So, why waste your time? It is a deception to think that putting on an act and being in denial about the truth will get you anywhere. That being said, this pattern seems to be quite common in our society today, which is probably giving the impression that this is how it is done. But the truth is, it is not consistently effective and, more importantly, it does not lead to fulfilment and satisfaction. It would be much more effective to be authentic and patient enough until you meet the right person to create a long-lasting personal or business relationship with. This is why it is crucial to be authentic and establish your relationship based on reality, because there will come a time when you will have to face the consequences if you don't. The more you twist the fabric of Reality, the more distorted it becomes and the more entangled you become, losing yourself, causing great suffering and bearing the cost in the process. I have personally encountered many people who I knew were being inauthentic when working with me on a project or trying to close a deal, and I could often tell when they were about to deceive me. Even when I would catch them out and confront them over the deception, not only would they refuse to own it and apologise, but they would go a step further and accuse me of trying to catch them out, as if I had ruined the game they assumed we were playing by not conforming to the rules. It was as though they felt they were entitled to fool me by being inauthentic. We all have examples of this from both sides – where we have been inauthentic or where someone has been inauthentic with us.

Becoming authentic takes patience and practice. It begins with a conscious decision to be – or at least want to be – authentic, and to commit to discovering your Unique Being, as well as becoming aware of and transforming the current health of your Aspects of Being, which is a life-long journey. As you get to know yourself better and better, you become committed to being who you say you are and congruent with who you are discovering yourself to be. This is not something you do as a one-off project. Being authentic is the result of many choices and decisions throughout every day of your life. It requires commitment and re-commitment and ongoing *forgiveness* of yourself and others. You will be challenged many times and enticed to take the deceptively easy road of putting on your 'whatever works for now' mask (inauthentic persona) and acting out that hollow role. It is no coincidence that high achievers are in the minority and that their overall state of Being is considerably different to most people's. In fact, the reason they are high achievers is **because** of their state of Being, how they are being. They have made a conscious decision to be authentic and take ownership (*responsibility*) for polishing and transforming their Aspects of Being, not as a one-off, but continually. Like all of us, they are challenged and tested at times, but they choose powerfully not to let roadblocks get in their way of staying true to themselves and their cause (*authenticity*).

It is also important to acknowledge that, from a very young age, we are trained to adapt and suppress certain aspects of ourselves to fit in, even at the cost of losing the real us and achieving acceptable results within our schooling and corporate systems. We are also primed to hide our true selves with the intention of meeting societal expectations, and while to some degree that is advisable, we don't want to carry it so far that we stop speaking our minds or offering our points of view, just to keep a job. If it were to come to that, why stay in that job and give up your unique gift to yourself and the world? The price of that folly is far too high.

Imagine if American civil rights activist Martin Luther King Jr had delivered his famous 'I have a dream' speech calling for civil and economic rights and an end to racism in the United States as a well-rehearsed performance. Do you think it would have had the same impact? At the time, he spoke from his heart, delivering his speech with true conviction and *authenticity*, which is precisely why his speech had such a powerful and enduring impact. Imagine a tribe that is facing imminent danger from an enemy and waiting for their leader to take action and lead the tribe into battle. But what if the tribal leader had misled his people to believe that he was a strong fighter when, in actual fact, he had never participated in a single battle. In the face of real danger, acting will be just that: a performance. A leader must have *integrity* to be *effective*, otherwise he/she is not a leader. Things are bound to fail if there is a lack of authentic and capable leadership. Many businesses fail due to a lack of discerning, experienced and skilled leaders. Instead, they are led by those who have acted their way into the role.

After running multiple social media campaigns over a three-year period and reaching out to approximately 2,000 people, we found that many people called themselves 'entrepreneurs' simply because that is what they wanted to be seen as, and not who they actually ARE. In most countries, it only takes a very short time to register a company, so becoming a founder of a business is not that much of an achievement. The challenge is what you make of it. Any successful entrepreneur or business owner can confirm that building a company and achieving success is a challenging road, and not many make it to the final destination. But there is good news: you can train yourself to develop the stamina and skills needed to pull through, and being authentic about it sets a very solid foundation for success.

To be a real entrepreneur you need to **be** one. That means you need to possess a combination of certain qualities, Aspects of Being that support you in this endeavour. For example, you need to be confident when making decisions in challenging situations, you need to polish your patterns of behaviour and you need to constantly increase your *awareness* about people, business, your industry, the economy, and so on. You also need to acquire appropriate and sufficient knowledge about legal systems, accounting, technology, business strategy, processes and systems, marketing and general management, and the list goes on. Being a business owner also takes significant *commitment* and personal sacrifice. So, the Reality of becoming an entrepreneur and the fantasy of becoming one are poles apart. What does this have to do with *authenticity*? The answer is simple: you must have an authentic relationship with all of these qualities to be an effective entrepreneur. A good reality check on this statement is when you need an investor for your business startup. Investors want to see the real you and the real achievements, not what or who you pretend to be. The point is, unless you are authentic with yourself and acknowledge where you belong at this stage of your life, you simply cannot work towards becoming how you want to be and acquiring or polishing the qualities (Aspects of Being) required for being effective and fulfilled. Remember the story of George 'Iceman' Chambers, the lead character in the movie *Undisputed II: Last Man Standing*, which I referred to in the Vulnerability chapter? He had to become acutely aware of his situation and acknowledge it in order to make more effective decisions, which ultimately led him to achieving his objective, which in his case was his freedom.

Once you make a conscious decision to be authentic, the real you finally starts to be revealed. In other words, if you are leading an inauthentic life, the real you is not out there in the world for others to see and **be with**; it is suppressed, disguised and hidden away from view. You may have what Jean-Paul Sartre called 'the illusion of individuality', as opposed to the genuine individuality that results from being authentic. It is common for people to claim these days, 'I don't like to be labelled. I am an independent individual!' But do we really know what this means? Is this view authentic? It is disempowering if you are not authentic. It will cost you dearly, particularly in your relationships, not only with your loved ones, but also with the investor you may be attempting to get onboard with your new business venture or the loyal employee who is now a pillar of your business and is not so easily replaced, and so on.

Authenticity and trust

By now you won't be surprised to know that *authenticity* is one of the prerequisites to establishing trusting relationships with others. In fact, without *authenticity* it is impossible for others to trust you. Being authentic and allowing others to see the real you generates trust. There are two certainties in life: we are born, and we die. What we do in between is up to us to a large extent. If you wish to achieve a significant milestone, contribute to a greater cause or project the manifestation of your Unique Being to the world, you are not going to do it on your own. As social creatures, we must team up with others to achieve greatness.

When collaborating with a team or any individual, it is important to generate trust first.

Establishing trust requires us to be open to receiving direct and honest input from others, and that can often put us in a vulnerable situation. You need to be able to show your vulnerable side at times to generate that trust. *Vulnerability* is required to produce exceptional results with others. Remember, *vulnerability* is a fundamental quality for a leader to possess. *Authenticity* and *vulnerability are* the stepping-stones to building trust with another person. When people are authentic and vulnerable in their dealings with others, trust is seamlessly established. When organisations are built on *authenticity*, it is reflected in their brands and product offerings. Furthermore, their dealings with clients and in-house teams generate trust, and this creates the environment for collaboration. There is a direct link between the growth and success of a business and how authentic they are with their employees and clients.

To be authentic, you must reveal inauthenticities first

All of us have done things in our past that we are not necessarily proud of, and we tend to hide those things away rather than being vulnerable enough to acknowledge them. But there is real power in truth and *authenticity*, which we can only access when we acknowledge our inauthenticities.

According to Werner Erhard, an access we have to *authenticity* is through being authentic about our inauthenticity. As part of a Harvard study, he wrote:

> 'Being authentic is being willing to discover, confront, and tell the truth about your inauthenticities – where you are not being genuine or real. Specifically, being authentic is being willing to discover, confront and tell the truth about where in your life you are not being or acting consistent with who you hold yourself out to be for others, or not being or acting consistent with who you hold yourself to be for yourself.'[109]

---

109 *Four Ways of Being that Create the Foundations of A Great Personal Life, Great Leadership and A Great Organization* by Michael Jensen and Werner Erhard, November 2013. Harvard Business School.

Allowing yourself to be vulnerable enough to share the secrets you have been holding onto reveals the true you so that others can relate to this authentic you. The point is, there is no need to portray yourself as a superhuman who has everything under control and has kicked goals everywhere in life so far. On the contrary, it's powerful to acknowledge and let others know that you are one of them, which you actually are. If you depict an image of yourself that is perfect, no one will find the opportunity to support or contribute to you because they will assume you don't need their contribution. Furthermore, no one would be able to partner with you if you were projecting and protecting an 'I am perfect' persona. After all, how can anyone complement you if there are no gaps to fill? So, you would be left to do it all alone. While it may seem like there is nothing fundamentally wrong with this, in reality, it is extremely limiting. If you are working towards any major cause, you must know you will never achieve your objectives on your own. It is very important to be aware that the areas in which we are lacking provide the opportunity to create partnerships. The fact that I need you and you need me is where authentic exchange, mutual *contribution* and powerful collaboration occurs. This is why revealing the true you is vital in any meaningful relationship. Without this foundation, a successful enterprise cannot be built. *Authenticity* and *vulnerability* generate constructive friendships, partnerships and unions.

Let me bring it home with an example. A finance director in one of the companies we worked with struggled to produce useful financial reports for his CEO, resulting in a monthly dispute. The CEO was seriously concerned about the finance director's performance to the point where he began questioning his suitability for the role. We had already commenced a coaching program for the executive team and, in a coaching session with the finance director, we addressed the subject of *responsibility*. The finance director was noticeably uncomfortable and, at one point, became very quiet before slowly and hesitantly revealing, with great embarrassment, that he had never been formally trained to use Microsoft Excel, a fundamental tool in any finance role. As a result, he had been trying to do his job while hiding this shortcoming in order to avoid humiliation. During his session with us, he even revealed that he had considered resigning so that he wouldn't be found out. As you may guess, the situation was easily remedied. After a short training course, the company had a 'new finance director' who now produced effective reports for the CEO each month. By being vulnerable and revealing his inauthenticity, he became authentic and therefore effective.

Becoming clear on where you are **not** being or acting consistent with who you hold yourself to be requires *courage,* and this is commonly overlooked. If you or the brand your company is projecting are not authentic, you risk damaging your reputation or that of your company. Damaging a reputation is easy. The challenge lies in restoring it. In fact, a damaged reputation can be extremely hard to restore. I am not suggesting that you should be authentic from a moral standpoint, but more on a practical level. Be real with who and how you are in your relationships with others and be honest about your business's product or service offering. While you may experience short-term success with an exaggeration of a product or service, not being authentic and true to your product rarely works out in the long run.

I understand, from an entrepreneurial context, that the pressure and challenge to create a steady income is always there, and this pressure may entice you to bend the truth from time to time for a quick win. But it is difficult to create long-term assets if your business model is purely transaction-focused. As I said, that strategy may work in the short-term but if you want to build long-lasting relationships with your clients and develop a database of delighted customers and colleagues who trust you, being authentic will ultimately reward you. However, it won't always be easy. In fact, the journey to becoming authentic can be very uncomfortable at times, and we all have to go through that discomfort if we want to become authentic. The good news is, as we intentionally practise being authentic, our relationship with *authenticity* transforms and we become more powerful and effective.

In summary

We tend to sell out our authentic Self to avoid looking bad, to receive admiration, to avoid trouble, to maintain loyalty, to have a sense of belonging or to avoid disappointing others. However, we fail to realise how much this costs us. Being inauthentic limits us. It doesn't allow us to grow and achieve the greatness we were born to achieve. Without *authenticity,* we choose to live a double life. Being inauthentic keeps us small, obscure and ineffectual and, more importantly, not able to love ourselves and **be with** ourselves. The most tragic part about being inauthentic is that it suppresses the expression of your Unique Being so that it remains a rosebud for life, never the fully grown, glorious rose it is meant to be.

Remember, the greatest gift you are given in life is YOU, the real you (Unique Being). There is only one of you in the world. Not only is this a gift to yourself, but it is also a gift to the whole of humanity. Don't forget, as poignantly conveyed in Attar's story of Simorgh, we all carry a piece of Existence within us. If everyone truly understood the significance of this incredible gift, if they would **be with** their authentic Selves, no one would secretly wish to be someone else. There are several fake Mona Lisas in the world, but none are a substitute for the real thing. Give yourself permission to be vulnerable enough to discover and express the real you. Unless you are being authentic about your Aspects of Being, including the troubled parts (shadow), you will never be able to grow and move towards *integrity, effectiveness* and fulfilment. Last but not least, *authenticity* is a cornerstone of transformation. Unless you address your *authenticity*, it is almost impossible to transform your other Aspects of Being.

CHAPTER 9

Responsibility

Do you ever have the feeling that life is just happening to you? Life can be so complex that at times it's hard to know what's going on, let alone what's going to happen next. One morning you leap out of bed feeling excited and ready to tackle anything life may throw your way, and the very next day you wake up feeling restless, uneasy and anxious. If you subscribe to the belief that life is happening to you and there is not much you can do about it, you could end up viewing life as an ongoing threat. Constantly wondering what's around the corner, you may find yourself lost in your own stories and ideas about events that trigger you to be reactive and defensive. To make matters worse, this could be coupled with a mysterious hope that somehow your wishes and good fortune will ensure that things magically work out for the best. But do they ever just work out by themselves, without any contribution from you? Even if you try to influence situations by reacting and manoeuvring, rather than just sitting on the fence and hoping for the best, you may have experienced that this still hasn't brought you the ease and joy you so desire. The truth is, life is much more than a series of events that just happen.

Perhaps you are one of those people who has developed beyond this sense of powerlessness and evolved a new standpoint that life is happening through you, not to you. Rather than assuming the position of victim, which commonly triggers an endless game of struggle and self-sabotage, you have gained the *awareness* that you can actually influence most events in your life by choosing to respond appropriately, in such a way that it works in your favour and contributes to the *integrity* of your life. I say 'most', not 'all', because we know life can be unpredictable, much like a game of chess. You may be open enough to see the facts or truth about a situation, rather than the stories you attach to it. In so doing, you have raised your *awareness* about how things work and, equipped with that knowledge, you are far more capable of taking charge and steering life towards your desired outcomes. This realisation is usually accompanied by a great sense of personal power, replacing hope and wishes with a sense of reality and understanding of what to do. The more aware and responsible you are, the more things work out for you, not in a magical sense, but through your influence over your life and your willingness to face the facts about every situation. Furthermore, to hit greater objectives in life, not only should you start to lead and influence your own matters, but you also need to request, and be open to, the *contribution* of others. This adds another layer of complexity to the equation, as their Aspects of Being, such as *responsibility, contribution, commitment* and *presence*, not to mention their Moods, will also greatly influence the results you want to produce.

Each of us possesses a mesmerising gift, in addition to our Unique Being, by which we can greatly influence any outcome if we utilise it to its full potential. That gift is our relatively high level of autonomy. The first step is to become aware of it and acknowledge the contribution of this Primary Way of Being. I call this Way of Being, *'responsibility'*. There is a parable in The Quran where Moses momentarily feels disarmed and unequipped to fulfil his mission of guiding others and responding to his calling. In his solitude, he opens his heart with *vulnerability* and shares his concern with God. The next moment, he hears a firm whisper in his ear, 'Moses, you are the messenger of God. You have the rules in writing. Just own it powerfully'. The point of this metaphor is that, like Moses and the birds in the story of Simorgh, each one of us is a manifestation of Existence. Therefore, we are all gifted and equipped with a relatively high level of autonomy. It is up to us to choose to **own it powerfully** and with grace. This is the intrinsic value and personal dignity of every human being. This is what gives us *freedom*, the very quality (Aspect of Being) we all value dearly, no matter which culture, background or nation we come from.

What is *responsibility*?

When you hear the word 'responsibility', what first comes to mind? More often than not, people associate the word with blame or duty. Common questions around responsibility are, 'Who is responsible for this?' and, 'Who is to blame?' and they are frequently used in the same context. But each statement relates to something completely different, and it is important to know that I am **not** referring to any of those definitions in this book and the Being Framework. *Responsibility* is actually the willingness to be in charge of one's life, no matter what happens, and independent of the source of the problem. *Responsibility* also points to our commitment to own our part in any situation and do something about it, even if it doesn't result in the outcome we intended. This aligns with one of the definitions of the word 'responsible' in the *Oxford English Dictionary*, which is: 'being the primary cause of something'.

For example, let's say you lose your job because your organisation is downsizing. This is something beyond your control and you are not to blame for it. Have you directly caused it? No, but you can choose to be cause in the matter in terms of how you respond and deal with this situation. Regardless of how you respond, you are being the primary cause in the matter because it directly impacts you and there is no one else who should fix it for you. You could choose to victimise yourself, which would dishonour your autonomy or influence. You could get caught in the blame game, pointing fingers at others for the situation in which you now find yourself. Or you could take charge of the situation and make plans to find another employment opportunity or start your own business. Naturally, it's not pleasant to discover that the role you occupied within the company is no longer viable, but such is life. That decision may have been out of your hands. Regardless, it is your choice to own the problem and take the best possible actions to move on and deal with this new circumstance in your life. While it may not seem like it at first, once you make that decision to move on and make the best of it, you will discover new energy, and that is incredibly empowering. Choosing to be responsible brings the power back to you, as you are the one who is changing the course. Being responsible is the first step towards coming up with resolutions, rather than being crushed by what is happening around you.

Etymologically, the word 'responsibility' comes from an obsolete French word, *Responsible*, which is derived from the Latin *Responsabilis*, or *Respondere* (verb), meaning 'to respond'. The word did not come to imply any measure of *accountability* until the mid 1600s. For the Being

Framework Ontological Model, I have chosen the word *'responsibility'* to refer to its transcendent Meaning, which is to honour your autonomy and act on it. It is the state of choosing powerfully to be in charge and influence the circumstances, instead of letting the circumstances drive you in life. You are in charge of where you sit on the spectrum. At one end you are a **passive victim**, at the other you are an **active agent**.

The following describes the distinction of *responsibility*, as I am using it in this book and framework.

The Being Framework ontological distinction of *responsibility*

Responsibility is being the primary cause of the matters in your life, regardless of their source. It is the extent to which you choose to respond rather than react to them. *Responsibility* is distinguished by how you honour the autonomy that you have as a human being and is considered the power to influence the affairs, outcomes and consequences you are faced with. *Responsibility* is not about blaming or determining whose fault it is. Instead, it is to intentionally choose, own, cause and bring about outcomes that matter, work and produce results while also being answerable for the impact and consequences.

A healthy relationship with *responsibility* indicates that you have the power to influence the circumstances you find yourself in and/or cause. Others may consider you capable of appropriately responding to matters, which is a prerequisite to producing and bringing to fruition effective results. You fully accept ownership of both outcomes and consequences and have the capacity to make informed, uncoerced decisions. You are unquestionably the active agent in your life.

An unhealthy relationship with *responsibility* indicates that you may often be stuck, experience a loss of power, and are a victim of circumstances. You frequently experience being disarmed, as though you have no choice in influencing outcomes and there is an inevitability about your future. You may be inclined to self-sabotage and make repetitive complaints without seeking, putting forward and implementing solutions. You frequently make excuses for your lack of accomplishments while abdicating or avoiding consequences. You may be considered ineffective in consistently fulfilling the promises you make and producing intended results. You are a passive victim in your life. Alternatively, you may live life from the viewpoint of being the sole cause of matters and exert your will onto your surroundings and others or be over-responsible and attempt to control all matters all the time. You may also expect that matters should always go your way.

Autonomy – a unique, powerful and profound leadership quality

As human beings, we are gifted with a high level of autonomy, which distinguishes us from other beings. While this profound quality, or Aspect of Being, has been a field of study for many philosophers and there are conflicting ideas[110] and schools of thought around it, I am focused on the ontological and phenomenological approaches in the context of this book and the Being Framework. In other words, my focus is on the Reality and collective lived experiences of leaders and high achievers of the world with proven track records, not just pure thinkers who sat in solitude and flirted with ideas and theories.

Our high level of autonomy is unique and powerful, making it a profound leadership quality. However, unfortunately we have a tendency to undervalue its transcendent Meaning and impact because it points us to the part we play in being responsible for our own life, and sometimes we simply don't want to be responsible. But who else could be responsible for your life? When something goes well for us, we are more than happy to take the credit for it and be proud of ourselves, but when something goes pear-shaped, we prefer to pass the buck, point fingers and make excuses. Frequently, my clients come to me with ongoing problems, such as employees who are not being honest or suppliers being unreliable with agreements or promises they have made. At first glance, the issue may seem to be related to an external force and therefore beyond the influence or control of the manager or business owner. I usually start by pointing them to the common denominator in these scenarios, which is the person sitting across the table from me. I acknowledge that this is an uncomfortable situation, knowing the finger is pointing right back at them, but it is even more uncomfortable to lose revenue, clients or employees. I am vulnerable enough to openly admit that there are times when I catch myself looking externally when things aren't going the way they should. As soon as I am aware that this is happening, I choose to switch my focus internally to consider the parts of the problem I can own.

---

110   Some assert that we have free will while others, namely the determinists, think we don't. They assert that everything in life is determined by previously existing causes. I don't dwell on such abstract perspectives in the context of this book. The fact that you continuously ask yourself if you should choose this or that implies that you have a relatively high level of autonomy. That is enough to acknowledge as a leader.

Most importantly, I draw my attention to the fact that, ultimately, the responsibility rests with me as the business leader and leader of my life.

Acknowledging that you are the cause of what happens to you in life can be a bit confronting at first, but once you do, it puts you firmly in the driver's seat of your life. It leaves you with the option of managing and influencing outcomes in your favour. But for some inexplicable reason, we human beings seem to be more comfortable with the idea of maintaining our self-image, even at the expense of revenue or employees, rather than deal with the consequences and confront the idea of losing face. Which do you think is the better option in the long run?

In studying many great leaders, I discovered that, commonly, they tend to be responsible and accountable for everything that happens within and around them. Can you imagine what it would have been like to be responsible for the launch of the SpaceX Falcon 9 rocket[111] as Elon Musk was? The sheer number of people that had to be aligned through effective leadership and whose expectations and promises needed to be managed, including the risk to life and livelihoods, the multiple external forces at play, from the laws of physics to the legal matters, and all the safety checks and cross checks that had to be performed. The mind boggles at the complexity of it all! Even though Musk didn't physically have a hand in everything that needed to be done to successfully launch that rocket, he was ultimately responsible for it all. Similarly, if you are working towards a great cause, you must get used to having to deal not only with the matters you are immediately responsible for, but also to pull the strings and influence all the other matters associated with the project in ways beyond what you already know is possible. Understanding this key point will contribute to the paradigm shift I promised at the beginning of the book. The meaning and significance of having autonomy is the capability and freedom to choose how we want to **respond**. And without a doubt, with freedom of choice comes acceptance of the consequences of those choices. Developing our *awareness* supports us to predict these consequences and make well-informed decisions.

---

111 SpaceX, the company founded by entrepreneur Elon Musk in 2002, launched its first people into Earth's orbit on 31 May, 2020. At 3:22pm EST, a Falcon 9 rocket lifted off from Cape Canaveral, Florida, carrying the Crew Dragon spaceship that SpaceX designed and NASA funded.

True leaders take responsibility and solve problems, including common major problems that many would resonate with, where others either may not see solutions or refuse to own their part. They choose powerfully to **be** responsible. Don't forget, at the heart of any extremely successful business, service or product lies a deep, underlying psychological pain or problem of humankind. When you take the responsibility of solving a problem or pain point and deliver the solution to the world through your expression of Self – by projecting your Unique Being to the world – you deserve to be rewarded for your *contribution*. The larger the group of people you add value to by giving them what they value so much that they are willing to exchange money for it, the more your organisation makes in revenue and the more profit you will make if you have the right financial structures in place. The world's top companies excel at this, however, unfortunately many business owners and entrepreneurs are oblivious to it. Can you read between the lines here? Can you see that the beauty lies in the **giving**, the *contribution*, in the sense of *responsibility* for solving a problem for mankind? Therein lies the true reward. The financial rewards are simply a by-product of this.

While, as human beings, we have the highest level of autonomy of all beings on earth, that is a quality to be reclaimed and honoured, not taken for granted. Allow me to once again reference a scene from Walt Disney's *Pinocchio* movie to explain what I mean. When Geppetto first creates Pinocchio, he is nothing more than a puppet, a piece of wooden handicraft. While the puppet essentially has many elements of a human being – like arms and legs, eyes and lips – it is not autonomous like a human being is. In the scene where Geppetto looks upward to the night sky, symbolically asking the supreme power and Ultimate Reality (Existence) to transform his wooden puppet into a real boy, the angel and symbol of Mother Nature mysteriously transforms Pinocchio into a semi-autonomous being. This is where we all are in life; we are semi-autonomous beings. We must develop our *awareness* and polish our Being in order to claim and redeem our autonomy and *freedom*. It is autonomy that gives us the greatest potential to be leaders who influence circumstance, to fulfil our desires and make life better for ourselves and others. It brings us back to *integrity* (wholeness), and this is the key to becoming effective. This is true redemption and leads us to fulfilment and prosperity. If you choose not to be responsible around your *awareness*, you are likely to outsource your sanity to others, who, as both the internal and external malevolent forces, may not always have the best intentions. We will explore this conversation further in the Freedom chapter.

Victimhood

Victimhood is the state of being a victim. We all are victims at times, in one way or another. The key is to choose powerfully **not** to continuously victimise ourselves. Many talk about their rights, as if the universe owes them something. This is a cultural and political standpoint subscribed to by many all over the world. Some go beyond accepting this view; they glorify it. There have even been revolutions to create a utopian world in which nobody has to take responsibility but everyone has rights. While history has proven this ideal to be nothing more than a fairy tale, many continue to pursue it. These people talk about rights, but they seem oblivious to the fact that everyone's rights are someone else's responsibility. My intention is not to attack any particular political point of view, but merely to talk about how we **are** versus how we could **be** as human beings from an ontological perspective. The key point I am making here is that victimhood is the polar opposite of leadership and *responsibility*. You cannot be a leader (effective and of influence) and a high achiever if you choose the pathway of misery and victimhood, period! Furthermore, given what is happening culturally and politically these days, including the way our formal education, employment and taxation systems operate, to choose to **be** a leader, and not to be indoctrinated into putting on the victim mask (persona) and looking for a scapegoat, is empowering, radical and revolutionary.

The word 'scapegoat' is used to refer to a person who bears the blame for others[112]. It has an interesting history. According to the Jewish and Christian scriptures, God ordained a particular day during which the priests of Israel would atone for the sins of the entire nation using various rituals. One of those rituals involved loading a goat with all the sins of the people of each village and then chasing the goat away. It was believed that this ritual absolved the villagers of their sins, without them having to do a thing. There was no need for them to polish their Aspects of Being and behaviours, or even to become aware of their shortcomings

---

112 *Merriam-Webster Dictionary.*

and acknowledge them with *vulnerability*. The villagers were happy as long as the scapegoat (escaped goat) didn't return to the village. Perhaps the goat migrated to your home country when he was chased away!

Collectively, we continue to create or find scapegoats in life. It seems every society needs them. Let's look at a classic example. Let's say one man decides to narrate his deceitful or malevolent standpoint to a large audience and he does so with such conviction that the audience roars in approval. This further empowers the dictator and tarnishes every person in that audience with the same brush because they have chosen to follow him. Then, when things don't work out the way they want them to, the people point to the dictator, making him the scapegoat, but neglecting to consider that they are the ones who empowered him. Fascinating, isn't it? We create our own pain. We would happily feed a baby dragon until it is big enough to crush us and only then would we complain. The point I am making here is that, collectively as human beings, we are more inclined to put on the victim mask than own a problem. We want to outsource our pain, problems and shortcomings. We want daddy, the state and other external forces to take care of us. We want to be free, but we don't want to take responsibility for our *freedom*. It's easier to load the poor goat with our problems and shadows and chase him away, but deep down we all know that is delusional. We are living in an era where the dominant narrative discourages us from being responsible and leads us to believe that others should accept responsibility for our unpleasant experiences or lack of accomplishments. While victimhood may provide you with a convincing story to justify your lack of accomplishments – much like a dummy pacifies a baby for a while – it's not a sustainable solution, especially if you are a leader.

There is an important link between *responsibility*, *freedom* and gaining independence, and the glue that binds it all together is maturity. Developing maturity partly relies on our ability to predict the consequences of who we are, how we are, the decisions we make and the actions we take. It stems from our *awareness*, but it also relies on our willingness to **own** these consequences as they occur. As discussed in the Awareness chapter, the main aim of true education and *awareness* is to help us develop a more accurate conception of Reality, and gain the wisdom that enables us to know how to deal with the consequences, and not melt under pressure. So, whenever something happens in our lives, we can choose to own the consequences. It's one of the prices we pay for our freedom of choice. If you want freedom of choice, it's your responsibility to claim it. Empowering, isn't it? You can literally make a difference with your autonomy. So, whenever you find yourself asking, 'Why me?' immediately rephrase the question to, 'Why not me?' to stop victimising yourself and looking for a scapegoat. Last but not least, when it comes to developing maturity, we must also gradually develop the ability to make the right sacrifices for ourselves. You can't have your cake and eat it too. If you aspire to become an Olympic athlete or a successful startup, there are many sacrifices you must make. In fact, sacrifice is a quality that is encouraged by many religions and within certain cultures, often as a symbolic act to demonstrate the ability to give up an item of attachment. Think of something you value that you would be willing to sacrifice with *higher purpose*. It's not easy, is it? This is another quality many leaders lack. But not being willing to sacrifice something valuable with *higher purpose* can inhibit us from achieving our greatest goals and making an impact on the world. It takes maturity to realise and act upon that.

From passive victim to active agent

Unfortunately, in the context of claiming *responsibility* in life and acting as a responsible human being, our society and the rules we play by are not always empowering. These rules may be comfortable and give us a sense of entitlement, but is this actually working in our favour? Let me explain further. As I said earlier, most people believe they have certain rights, like a particular salary package or the right to find a job after completing a university degree. While this is not necessarily wrong, the context can make such expectations challenging. Entrepreneurs, for example, don't think this way. As active agents, they understand that in order for any startup to grow from the ground up, especially in the early years, its founder must be responsible beyond the norm. They have a clear vision and focus on how they can achieve the desired outcome. Thinking of salary packages, job titles and availability of work does not even cross their mind, at least not in the early years. They don't expect to be paid for the time they spend on the business they are building, but for the results they produce. They understand that the universe doesn't owe them anything. But they appreciate, with *gratitude*, that they have been gifted with their Unique Being and Possibility of Existence (life) and use their relatively high level of autonomy to embrace that. They realise that if they want business, revenue and profit, they need to focus on generating and delivering value and a life of serving others. Without entrepreneurs who subscribe to this way of thinking, there would be no jobs for entitled graduates.

Entitlement is not real; it is a delusion. A person with a deep sense of entitlement does not build a healthy relationship with reality. This attitude leads us to be passive victims, which is disempowering because it lets the circumstances drive our results, like tumbleweed, taken in whichever direction the wind is blowing. It keeps us stagnant and on the fence. It is important to acknowledge that being a victim is a part of life; as I said earlier, it happens to all of us. When people lose their jobs through no fault of their own, they are a victim of circumstance, but they don't have to maintain the victim mindset. Entrepreneurs and high achievers work out for themselves how to move out of the passive victim state to become empowering, active agents. By claiming their *responsibility*, they are also claiming their *empowerment*, and with *responsibility* and *empowerment* comes meaning. The more responsibilities you have, the more worthwhile you will find your life, and the richer the totality of your experience of being-there-in-the-world becomes. This in turn leads to a meaningful life of fulfilment and satisfaction. The irony is that every one of us feels entitled at some point in life, whether or not we want to acknowledge it. It is only when we are authentic with ourselves and take down our guard (*vulnerability*), that we can bring ourselves back to Reality and acknowledge the fact that the world doesn't owe us anything.

Choose powerfully to BE responsible

There is an expectation of leaders, whether it is in politics or running businesses and corporations, to demonstrate a way forward – a resolution – when everyone else is feeling limited or crushed by despair and disappointments. As you can imagine, this requires a high level of *freedom* in order to see the possibilities, and the *courage* to be responsible in such challenging situations, especially when all eyes are on you as the leader and expectations are high. Developing into a true leader with the stamina to be responsible during challenging times is not a Way of Being that can be stepped into on demand without training and ongoing practice.

Being responsible also translates to choosing powerfully. Just having that mindset is very empowering, even when the situation is anything but pleasant. Leaders train themselves to own the results they produce and be accountable for the results their team members produce, without falling into the blame game whenever things don't quite go the way they had intended. Leaders are okay with being uncomfortable, because they want to cause the results they desire and are driven to achieve through their calling in life. They have trained themselves to focus on the long-term benefits beyond themselves. We will discuss the notion of working for causes beyond oneself in the Higher Purpose chapter.

To be responsible in life also requires us to be vulnerable. Indeed, *vulnerability* is often the first step to becoming responsible. It's easy to blame others, circumstances or even ourselves, but it takes openness and a display of *vulnerability* to own our part in a situation. *Vulnerability* is also important because we can't fulfil our responsibilities if we are worried about what others may think of us or how our actions may affect our reputation. So, once we are vulnerable enough to own it and claim our *responsibility*, we can do something about it.

Unless you own a situation, you will remain in a phase of stagnation, and being stagnant is never comfortable. Even if you tell yourself it is acceptable to do nothing, you will find that the issue continues to nag at you in the background. Stress is common, even among the world's top leaders. I heard Jeff Bezos[113] say in an interview that inaction is one of his greatest sources of stress. True leaders are almost always ready to own things. And there is always something for a leader to own. Some could view this in a negative light, but leaders see it differently. They are extremely grateful and actually feel blessed when they discover a part of a problem, no matter how minute, that they can own. Why? Because ownership leads to influence. It allows them to pull the right strings

---

113   Jeffrey Preston Bezos is an American internet entrepreneur, industrialist, media proprietor, and investor. He is best known as the founder and Executive Chairman of the multinational technology company, Amazon.

in order to influence the matter and be part of the solution. I find it dismaying that some feel disarmed, even at the thought of owning it. No true leader subscribes to this view.

Possession and ownership

Traditionally, we use the word 'ownership' for both possession and to own or take responsibility for something. When we own (possess) something, we also take the responsibility to care for it and maintain its *integrity* (wholeness). For example, when you own a house with gardens, you must voluntarily choose to look after them if you wish to be effective at maintaining their *integrity*. If you fail to mow the lawns, weed the gardens and clean the house, you will quickly discover the ramifications of being in possession of something and not caring for it.

A friend of my dad once told me that when he was quite young, he and his friends became very attracted to Marxism and the Marxist idea of building a utopian world. A group of them were living together in a rented apartment and they were all bitten hard by the 'Marxist bug', coming to believe that ownership and possession of anything was a source of evil. So, together, they promised themselves not to individually own anything in the apartment, including their clothes, but to share everything instead. My dad's friend laughed as he explained that everything was fine until they realised that, while they each had a variety of shared clothes to use each day, the items of clothing were never washed because nobody owned them.

I remember coaching the managing director of a very young startup, who wouldn't stop complaining during one of our sessions. On and on it went, for more than forty minutes. Suddenly, it dawned on me that he was wearing the title of CEO like a badge of honour, but he hadn't yet chosen to actually BE a CEO. In other words, he had not yet powerfully chosen to be a CEO with autonomy. This is quite common, especially with first-time entrepreneurs. Most come to us with a request for what they believe they need first: capital (money and resources). However, it usually becomes apparent very quickly that capital is not the first thing they need at all. In many cases, we realise who and how they are as founders and entrepreneurs – their Beings and behaviours – have not yet been sufficiently explored. They have not yet capitalised on their own human potential and are seeking external capital to move forward, not realising they have totally missed the mark. They want funding and, more specifically, they want to outsource the funding component to investors ('the others'). Many also mention that they are planning to outsource technology development (software, apps and tools) overseas in order to reduce costs, which is another myth, but that discussion is beyond the scope of this book. The point is, they want to outsource technology and funding to others. Some even actively seek options to outsource their customer service and parts of their operations too, and my immediate reaction to such statements is to ask, 'So, what are you going to own and do in this company then?' The point I am making with these examples is that you cannot own the rewards if you do not own the burden.

Responsibility versus over-responsibility

A common misconception when it comes to *responsibility* is that it involves taking the burden of obligations and duties from others to make your own life easier or more bearable. I call this being over-responsible, as distinct from being responsible. It is inauthentic to assume you are being responsible and taking care of another when in actual fact you are depriving them of ownership of their life and taking their autonomy away from them. You are setting them on a trajectory of pain and suffering in the future. An example that many people can relate to is when a parent cleans up a child's bedroom instead of dealing with the discomfort of confrontation and holding the child to account for their lack of *responsibility*. This is very common in parenting, as parents naturally want to make matters easier for their children. Helping a child do their homework is valuable and commendable, though doing their homework or assignment on their behalf is not. To be clear, over-responsibility is inauthentic and is not considered *responsibility*. By taking responsibility away from others, you are deliberately contributing to them shaping a distorted conception of reality. This deprives them of courageously facing the inevitable challenges in life, as it leads them to set expectations that are not congruent with reality. As a result, they will frequently be shocked and surprised when they are in situations where they are required to be responsible. Being over-responsible, which points to an unhealthy **care-responsibility** relationship, only deceives yourself and prevents you from being authentic and responsible.

The same holds true for leaders. Many businesses cannot grow simply because the leader is not willing to appropriately delegate responsibilities and hold others to account. Instead, they exhaust themselves, juggling multiple tasks as the 'Chief Everything Officer', while deep down adopting the victim mindset and resenting having to do what they falsely believe is their duty. There is a distinct difference between a leader who is effective and capable of building and running a scalable enterprise and one who, despite their best intentions, ends up remaining a small business owner for life. The former is likely to be vulnerable and responsible around not trying to control everyone and everything. They know that getting involved in everything will limit their growth, energy, capability and the size of their enterprise. In the latter instance, however, the business owner is afraid to let the organisation become any bigger than they are themselves and this unhealthy relationship with *fear* and *anxiety* will limit the business's growth. This is quite common; it's what differentiates a typical small business from an effective, scalable enterprise.

Another relationship worth touching on here is **vulnerability-responsibility**, as being controlling is the opposite to being vulnerable. When our relationship with *vulnerability* is unhealthy, we are likely to keep our guard up and refuse to be vulnerable. We will also start trying to control and/or avoid being controlled by others. In any event, control is an illusion. The more we try to avoid being controlled or try to control others, the less vulnerable we can be. Eventually, we become control freaks, avoiding any area of life where we feel we are not fully in control. Control freaks are unable to **be with** *vulnerability,* for fear of losing their semblance of control. Many leaders fall into this trap, believing that controlling is managing. In actual fact, *responsibility* goes by the wayside when a leader tries to manage everything in their organisations for fear of relinquishing control. This state of Being is also common in relationships, whereby one person tries to control the behaviours and/or actions of another. Being aware of and acknowledging this inauthenticity is the first step towards redeeming yourself from it. Notice where and with whom you are trying to control a situation or avoid being controlled. Identify what this is costing you, and start taking responsibility for your life while releasing them to be responsible for theirs too. Ultimately, to even think that you can control most things in life, particularly in an organisation, is inauthentic in itself. A healthy *vulnerability-responsibility* relationship is critical as a leader.

Own it, clean up and move on

Problems don't just magically disappear. We can be in denial about them, but for how long? Is this empowering? Taking action is always more empowering than procrastinating or avoidance. Have you ever noticed how you actually drain your energy by procrastinating? Once you understand and apply the positive impact of these simple steps, as illustrated in *Figure 7: Being Responsible in Action,* you will become empowered, and that is a great place to be. And, as you can see, it really is simple, but not necessarily easy to put into practice all the time.

Figure 7: Being Responsible in Action

Referring to the diagram above, you can see that being a responsible leader when faced with any problem, whether it be in your organisation or in life, requires you to follow three simple steps.

1. **Own it**. Acknowledge that **you** are responsible, even if the source of the problem lies with others. It is extremely empowering to claim ownership of a problem because it allows you to take the reins and manage the resolution. The greater the proportion of the problem you can own, the more power you have to influence the outcome.

2. **Clean up**. Resolving the problem, including any appropriate apology (without resentment), must happen immediately after acknowledging it. Don't delay. If a glass of water has been tipped over your phone, it makes no difference who has done it, you must remove the water immediately or face the consequences.

3. **Move on**. Once the situation has been resolved, it's time to clear your mind, remove any lingering resentment, forgive yourself

or others and put it behind you, 'get complete' and move on. We will discuss this further in the Forgiveness chapter.

Let's say one of your employees promised to deliver a piece of work that was to be handed to the shareholders and they missed the deadline. You would start by owning your part in the situation. Perhaps your instructions weren't as clear as they could have been. Maybe you provided inadequate resources to complete the project in a timely manner. Perhaps, on closer analysis, you discover a need to amend your processes or procedures. It could also be that more training or coaching is required, or that you haven't invested enough in team building practices. It could even be that the staff member in question is not the right person for the role, and you have known this for some time but failed to do anything about it. Whatever the reason – and there are myriad possibilities – own your part in it. The next step would be to determine what blockages you can remove in order for your staff member to get the job done now. This is the cleaning up process. Last but not least, once the work has been completed, move on without holding a grudge, carrying resentment or labelling your staff member as unreliable.

The same principles and practices would apply to the staff member. They should own the fact that they have missed the deadline, and acknowledge it without excuses and apologies, committing to getting it done immediately, even if it means staying back late to make up for lost time. Once the work is complete, they should move on without carrying any guilt or resentment about having to work overtime. While these three steps are simple, it takes *courage* and *vulnerability* to adhere to them and they can take some time to master. In working with clients, whether as individuals or teams, my coaching staff and I normally need to closely support them in this process and ensure they keep holding each other to account. It's easy to blame external forces or 'the others' and make excuses. The point is, not being responsible will cost you dearly, particularly if you are the leader of an organisation. Being cause in the matter is a stand you take throughout your life, and in every situation, personal and professional. It's a declaration you make to yourself. Being willing to view and deal with life from this perspective is empowering and puts you in charge.

The reality of our time here on Earth is that things change. Right now, there is so much happening in the world that none of us have any direct influence over. That is Reality. There are times when the most responsible thing to do is simply listen to your gut and make intuitive decisions before taking a leap of faith. The main point of this chapter was to raise your *awareness* around the fact that, as leaders, the quality of doing your very best to influence the circumstances in any given situation is crucial in order for you to be effective. You may not be able to influence the situation 100% of the time, however, the more you do, the more you can steer the yacht on the course you desire. While you know you are not the generator of the wind, you are the captain of the ship and the master of your own destiny. Just be aware of your *vulnerability-responsibility* relationship. In other words, avoid being a control freak. Unlike the responsible captain of the ship, the control freak is the one who frantically blows hot air toward the sail against the current of the ocean. Good luck to them if they think that will get them far! The wind will always be there and out of our control. That is Reality. So, I encourage you to be aware of and acknowledge that, and also to be constantly in discovery of your Unique Being and take responsibility for honing your relatively high level of autonomy.

CHAPTER 10

Freedom

> *Some birds are not meant to be caged, that's all. Their feathers are too bright, their songs too sweet and wild. So, you let them go, or when you open the cage to feed them they somehow fly out past you. And the part of you that knows it was wrong to imprison them in the first place rejoices, but still, the place where you live is that much more drab and empty for their departure.*
>
> Rita Hayworth and Shawshank Redemption:
> A Story from Different Seasons, Stephen King[114]

I first saw the movie, *The Shawshank Redemption*[115], when I was a teenager and the above quote really resonated with me. Today, the only thing I would question is why 'some birds'? Surely no bird is meant to be caged. Just as a caged bird has an instinctive drive to free itself, we humans also have an intrinsic desire to be free and exercise our free will. When our *freedom* is violated – or we violate it ourselves – that is when we become present to the fact that this is not how it is meant to be, and that is when we realise just how significant *freedom* is to us. Many novels and movies are based on this unique phenomenon. When others exert their power over us, undermining our *freedom*, we are quick to man the barricades and even sacrifice our lives for it.

---

[114] *Rita Hayworth and Shawshank Redemption* is a novella by Stephen King from his 1982 collection *Different Seasons: Hope Springs Eternal*. It is thought to be loosely based on Leo Tolstoy's 1872 short story, *God Sees the Truth, But Waits*.

[115] *The Shawshank Redemption*, starring Tim Robbins and Morgan Freeman, is a movie adaptation of the Stephen King novella, *Rita Hayworth and Shawshank Redemption*.

What is *freedom?*

The Meaning the word *freedom* refers to has been significantly abused and misused throughout history, most notably in our current era. *Freedom* is often associated with doing something we want to do without restrictions or external constraints. However, that is not how I am referring to *freedom* in the context of this book. Well-known post-structuralist philosophers like Jacques Derrida and Michel Foucault, whose thoughts greatly influenced today's popular culture, talked about *freedom* as if it's caused by external factors, like the environment and conditioning. While many think *freedom* is a phenomenon we set out to achieve, ontologically, it is the state we **choose to be**. Imagine if we could do whatever we like without any restrictions? Is this true *freedom*? I encourage you to finish reading this chapter and come back to this question, as I expect you will have gained a different perspective on the Meaning of *freedom* by then.

By *freedom* in the context of this framework, I am not referring to the fact that, in our society, we are free to wear a bikini on the beach, exercise our religious practices and rituals, exercise our sexual liberty, voice our opinions and consume alcohol almost anywhere we want to. I am referring to the 'state of being free'. Sure, we are allowed to do any of the above, yet that doesn't free us from the habitual ways of thinking or paradigms that prevent us from going beyond who we know ourselves to be and how we are being. As a matter of fact, the examples of freedom of choice listed in this paragraph have the potential to take us hostage in the form of an addiction, so do they really liberate us?

Freedom comes with choosing and owning a decision and taking full responsibility for the consequences in any given moment. Some may argue that this statement makes no sense. I have observed many people who avoid taking responsibility for being a parent or a business owner, and their lack of *responsibility* made them slaves to this prison they have created for themselves. It wasn't due to their circumstances – although they may choose to see it that way – that they experienced a lack of *freedom*. It was, for the most part, because of the choices they made or the way they chose to respond to something life brought in their way. In the following distinction, I'm referring to a state of being free, without being limited by circumstances over time.

The Being Framework ontological distinction of *freedom*

Freedom is living life from the viewpoint that you always have options. It is your capacity to choose to be, do, say, feel and think whatever you wish without being controlled, coerced, constrained or limited by unwanted external forces while simultaneously accepting any subsequent consequences of your words or actions. You acknowledge that you have the choice to act despite constraints imposed on you while accepting that there are limitations associated with the reality of being a human being.

A healthy relationship with *freedom* indicates that you see options and possibilities available to you and can create opportunities when the need arises. When you are being free, you are not at the mercy of manipulative or distorting forces. Others may experience you as someone who chooses not to be restrained by situations or challenges imposed on them and communicates openly without constraint. You may actively consider self-discipline and self-imposed restrictions to prioritise what you most care about. When you have a healthy relationship with *freedom*, you refuse to succumb easily to the manipulation or domination of others.

An unhealthy relationship with *freedom* indicates that you often experience being held back and suppressed in the face of circumstances in your life due to a lack of options and may feel trapped or coerced. Others may experience that you withhold and are limited in what you can accomplish, contribute and communicate. You may wait for opportunities to be created and offered to you by others or miraculously land in your lap. You may often feel resigned and disarmed and frequently give in to others or external forces. You may feel imprisoned, stuck or frozen by your inner desires, shackled by dysfunctional habits. Alternatively, you may see and consider too many options, which often leads to paralysis. Avoiding self-imposed routines and disciplines may cause you to lack the momentum required to make progress.

Are you trapped in your current web of perceptions: your beliefs and opinions that don't work or aren't working for you? Are you restrained by your narrative lens? Are you easily manipulated by external malevolent forces? Have you outsourced your sanity to the mainstream media? Have you fully subscribed to a particular political party, a guru, a religion, an ideology or a school of thinking without exercising due diligence? Do you often have your guard up and resist true knowledge and *awareness*, meaning you have an unhealthy relationship with *vulnerability*? Do *fear* and *anxiety* often hold you back? Are you inauthentic the majority of the time, hiding behind the fake persona you either created for yourself or felt forced into by society or your culture? Do you lack the autonomy (*responsibility*) to pull your own strings? If you found yourself nodding in the affirmative to many of these questions, it indicates that your level of *freedom* is low. As a result, you are limiting the possibilities you create for yourself and your life. That's because when we have an unhealthy relationship with *freedom*, we are unlikely to see and create opportunities, and if we don't know an opportunity exists, how can we act on it? All of the above will limit your *freedom* and suppress your *self-expression*. As a result, your *contribution* to your life, and life in general, would be limited. You are where you are because you have allowed your dreams to be thwarted and defeated by the reality (Second-layer Reality) out there.

The state of being free is to choose powerfully in every moment. *Freedom* brings about the ability to say your authentic yeses and noes! My grandpa used to tell me there are three things that matter the most when it comes to the dignity of human beings: truth, beauty and *freedom*. He told me to never let anyone – myself included – take them away from me, and one of my Aikido masters taught me that my greatest enemy is myself. These lessons may seem clichéd, but they are important because they are true. And one should have a healthy relationship with *authenticity* to take them on. These simple, yet profound, teachings were proven to me later in life when I went through some devastating situations and adversities. If you find yourself questioning why I have included such simple teachings in a book for leaders, entrepreneurs and high achievers, I can assure you that after living quite a complex and intellectually sophisticated life so far, I have found the most fundamental answers in the simplest lessons I used to skim over or ignore in the past. This is a lot harder to discover than you may think because their simplicity blinds us to them. We tend to think complex problems should have complex solutions, which is not necessarily true. The secret is in the simplicity. Often the answers closest to our eyes are the ones we don't see.

Freedom and suffering

I would like to draw your attention to the fact that *freedom* has a natural association with suffering, and that the two go hand in hand. So, while being free is something to which we all aspire, it comes with a heavy burden. Being free means constantly making decisions (freedom of choice). It is our *responsibility* when exercising our freedom of choice to make effective decisions and there is often a measure of pain associated with that great *responsibility*. When a decision results in a positive outcome, we are happy to take credit for it. But what if things don't turn out well? The *fear* or *anxiety* alone that things may not work out is enough to suppress many of us. That's partly why we let others decide for us or why we are afraid to write our goals on a piece of paper, for *fear* that we may not achieve them. There are always consequences associated with our *freedom* and freedom of choice, including when we choose to act or not to act. Furthermore, as discussed in the previous chapter, this is associated with our maturity to predict these consequences and own up to them. We all have many options available to us to choose to **be** a certain way and **do** (or not do) certain things. It is worth noting that the active shadow side of *freedom* leads to chaos, tyranny, misuse and abuse, and to us being fickle with our perceptions, beliefs and opinions. This makes us prone to inauthenticity or breaking our commitments and promises. The passive shadow side of *freedom*, on the other hand, often results in paralysis, procrastination and inactivity, which generally leads us to constantly being in a state of dilemma, confusion and to a lack of *persistence*.

As you can see, *freedom* comes at a cost, but the cost is worth it because *freedom* is a beautiful, magical phenomenon. Not only do we exist and *care* about our existence, we are also free. Imagine how much better your life would be if you could wake up every morning and choose to be a certain way or do certain things. The truth is, you can! Even on a larger scale, imagine if everyone in society exercised a high level of *freedom*, making effective decisions when it comes to the law and the environment because of their ability to predict the consequences and harness their actions. This would allow for less interference from the state, the government and our legal system. The more oblivious that citizens are to the consequences of their actions or how they are being, the more interference is required by those in power. In other words, the less collective self-control is being manifested and exercised by individuals, the more control is required by the state, the government and the legal system. Once again, it goes back to the *integrity* of individuals.

Discipline will set you free

A very accomplished entrepreneur, who later became one of my mentors, once said to me, 'Discipline will set you free'. Those words have stuck with me over the years, and I have found them to be accurate. When I observe successful investors, business owners and entrepreneurs, they have strong work ethics and generally adhere to very strict routines and precise timelines. Some may assume this makes them prisoners of their own tight schedules and that this could cause them to experience limitations in other areas of their business, but in fact the opposite is true. In the end, they are able to achieve their objectives because they sacrifice a level of *freedom* for it when they need to. Meanwhile, most other business owners and entrepreneurs remain slaves to their so-called 'freedom' by keeping busy but not being effective or not putting in the required amount of effort to achieve their objectives. There is *freedom* in powerfully choosing to take on a great responsibility like being a business owner, a parent or a community leader. As part of the study for this framework, I realised that many of the Fortune 500 company leaders either have a military background or have also practised martial arts at some point in their lives. From firsthand experience, I can vividly see how the order and discipline instilled in me through martial arts and my military service greatly contributed to my accomplishments.

The shadow side of *freedom*

When we have an unhealthy relationship with *freedom*, we can either suppress ourselves, our thoughts, feelings and ultimately the authentic expression of our Unique Being or, alternatively, we may think *freedom* is about not having any boundaries, disciplines or values and therefore choose to respond and act on our impulses and temptations in an obsessively liberal way. The former may lead to the suppression of rage and resentment, resulting in victimisation, sabotage and destructive behaviour. The latter may cause us to relinquish all responsibilities, which may ultimately lead to lawlessness, chaos, anarchical behavioural patterns and unrest. This is where we give ourselves permission to break our promises and commitments. Examples include breaking the law, abusing the rights of others, oppressing others, removing power, bullying and manipulation. We can clearly observe this form of unhealthy relationship with *freedom* in people who are habitually unfaithful in relationships or continuously running up debts with no intention to repay them. In business, we may observe this when employees or employers abuse or misuse resources or their power and are dishonest and deceptive in their dealings. A collective unhealthy relationship with *freedom* can change the fabric of society or an organisation so significantly that it becomes unlivable and unviable.

Being obsessively free and lenient in terms of the way we deal with our web of perceptions and narrative lens – how we interpret events or stories in our lives – and choosing not to be authentic about our self-image, persona, opinions and beliefs commonly results in confusion, ignorance and negligence. When we are so liberal, yet closed-minded, that we avoid letting our conception of reality (First-layer and Second-layer) become congruent with how things actually are, we risk becoming stuck in a parallel distorted Third-layer Reality, a version of reality we created ourselves. This obsession and leniency does not allow for critical thinking. By this stage of the book, you would likely appreciate how such a misconception of *freedom* impacts one's *awareness*, *authenticity*, *integrity* and, ultimately, *effectiveness* and fulfilment in life. For example, this distorted view is common amongst startups, where the founders have a delusional expectation that they are entitled to receive funding, even though what they have is little more than a pipedream and nothing even close to a business concept, let alone a viable business. We have experienced this phenomenon first hand on many occasions. These 'dreamers' often appear shocked and react angrily when they are rejected, believing they are worthy of investment on the merit of their idea alone. It is also not uncommon to observe this in more mature businesses and corporations, whereby assumptions and hypotheses are made about a new product or product feature with little or no validation through appropriate research. In many of these cases, thousands, or even millions, in capital and man hours are invested into building things that the owners later realise are not viable and don't attract any interest from the market.

Freedom enables you to see possibilities

Freedom comes from within. It is not given to you. *Freedom* enables you to see possibilities, where others may only see constraints. Life will keep presenting you with gifts, but it's up to you to recognise them, pick them up and unwrap them. These gifts or possibilities are everywhere, and with your *awareness*, *freedom* and *responsibility*, you can choose to see and own them. This is where the relationship between *awareness* and *freedom* comes to the fore. *Freedom* is linked to *awareness*, as we need both vision and discernment to identify possibilities and move forward with them. It is likely that there are existing solutions to most of your problems. There are case studies, reference materials and experts out there to help you. Yet in working with people, I have come to realise that many are quite oblivious to this fact and either suffer by remaining stuck on a common problem they can't resolve, or they keep trying to reinvent the same wheel.

Nelson Mandela[116] is a notable example of someone who possessed a high level of *freedom*. Mandela was imprisoned for twenty-seven years, during which time he endured long periods of solitary confinement, suffered various illnesses and experienced physical and mental abuse. Despite all the external limitations and hardships imposed on him, he was able to maintain sovereignty, his vision for the anti-apartheid revolution and, most significantly, *freedom* throughout the duration of his imprisonment. How was he able to do that when he clearly was not a 'free' man? Obviously, it is difficult for an outsider like me to make assumptions about how a powerful man like Nelson Mandela managed his relationship with *freedom* while in prison, and I don't wish to take part in a guessing game, though if I were to reference the Being Framework, I would connect his *freedom* to the fact that he

---

116   Nelson Mandela (1918-2013), South African anti-apartheid revolutionary and philanthropist who served as President of South Africa from 1994 to 1999.

had a powerful relationship with *higher purpose* and that he displayed immense *courage* in his approach. Notice that *freedom*, *higher purpose* and *courage* are all Primary Ways of Being that were clearly present. Nelson Mandela also owned his choices and decisions and took responsibility for his life and circumstances. Obviously, it wasn't his choice to be imprisoned, so that was clearly an infringement of his freedom and human rights caused by external forces. Despite this, Mandela managed to maintain his influence over his state of Being and keep his sovereignty by choosing powerfully and deliberately how he was going to BE while in prison. This is how he maintained his healthy relationship with *freedom*, as the alternative would have been to remain silent, submit and fall victim to the fact that he was not a free man. Another example worthy of mention is the Russian writer, Fyodor Dostoevsky[117], who spent four years in a Siberian prison camp, followed by six years in exile, yet he managed to contribute to humanity with his unique masterpieces. There have been many other notable examples in history.

Whenever we are striving to realise our ideals, we are expressing our Unique Being, and this brings a sense of *freedom*, even under the most oppressive situations. Life imposes constant dilemmas on us, and we must deal with them as they come. It is not always how we envisioned things would happen, but such is life. We can reclaim our power in these situations by making empowered choices. This is based on our internal sense of *freedom* to choose how to respond. If you think that this level of *freedom* is optional as a leader, I would encourage you to reconsider your perception. A leader without a healthy relationship with *freedom* limits the entire organisation's performance and achievements. It is the leader who should be among the first to see possibilities where no one else is present to them. *Freedom* is a quality all forward-thinking, visionary, creative leaders possess and maintain. Remember my question from the beginning of this chapter? Imagine if we could do whatever we like without any restrictions. Is this true *freedom*? What do you think?

117　　Fyodor Mikhailovich Dostoevsky, sometimes transliterated Dostoyevsky, was a Russian novelist, philosopher, short story writer, essayist, and journalist.

CHAPTER 11

Courage

There is great misconception around the quality of *courage*. Many assume it is simply the ability to confront a dangerous situation without flinching or giving up. When an individual exhibits bravery, the perception is that they are fearless and dauntless, and that this exemplifies *courage*. And likely because of this conception, many view *courage* as a quality possessed only by heroes or heroines, but that couldn't be further from the truth. As you will discover in reading this chapter, which I consider to be one of the most significant chapters in the book, *courage* has a direct relationship with every other Way of Being[118] and is a primal quality we all have a relationship with and relate to in one way or another.

Like *freedom*, *courage* is a central theme in many novels and movies. That's because *courage* is real; we all relate to it. In the movie *Braveheart*[119], the lead character, William Wallace, a Scottish rebel, delivers a spectacular display of *courage* when he leads the Scots in the First War of Scottish Independence against King Edward I of England. In fact, *courage* as a Way of Being has been romanticised to such a degree that many assume only certain types of people possess it. Do you think William Wallace was afraid when he led the charge? Of course he was! Does that make him any less courageous? Absolutely not! Wallace, like so many other great warriors and leaders, stepped forward despite his *fear*, and that is *courage*. *Fear* and *courage* are inseparable. We cannot

---

118 Directly with Primary Ways of Being and indirectly with Secondary Ways of Being.
119 The 1995 movie *Braveheart* is an impassioned epic about William Wallace, the 13th-century Scottish leader of a popular revolt against England's tyrannical Edward I.

be courageous in the absence of *fear*. *Courage* enables and empowers us to **be with** any consequences that might occur in the face of being out there in the world, daring to BE as opposed to not be. We are courageous **despite** our *fear*. The aim is not to let *fear* tie you up and suppress you, but to have *courage* in the face of *fear*.

While there are many assumptions about *courage* and being courageous based on various definitions and interpretations, once again, let's not get caught up in the wording and go beyond that to the actual Meaning (First-layer Reality) of *courage* which is the quality of stepping forward despite *fear* being present. Now, let me make the distinction I have chosen for the quality we find in leaders clear.

The Being Framework ontological distinction of *courage*

Courage is the state of Being that gives rise to the ability to make decisions, move forward and take action when you are uncomfortable, frightened, worried or concerned for your safety and/or the safety of others. *Courage* is not the absence of *fear*; on the contrary, *courage* shows up when *fear* or discomfort is present. *Courage* enables you to continue to be of service and pursue objectives, even when circumstances appear insurmountable, unpleasant or dangerous.

A healthy relationship with *courage* indicates that you are likely to look for ways to move forward, make decisions and take action, even when you are afraid, feel threatened or are challenged. Others may consider you brave-hearted, daring and spirited, and someone who stands up for their values and in defence of others when challenged.

An unhealthy relationship with *courage* indicates you may freeze, shut down or withdraw in the face of difficult circumstances or when you are challenged or frightened. You may be inclined to avoid confrontation and be hesitant to express and assert yourself or deal powerfully with uncomfortable situations while tolerating unwanted circumstances. You may avoid confronting and looking into the reality of matters if they challenge or frighten you. Alternatively, you may be reckless in dealing with dangerous or high-risk situations and be unable to predict the consequences of your bravado. You may also underplay and diminish the impact of how you are being and your actions.

So, *courage* is clearly not just for heroes and it is not optional. Everybody relates to it in varying degrees and we need *courage* to survive and thrive. In fact, *courage* is the key to solving most of the world's critical problems and is one of the two most fundamental qualities a leader must possess. And, just as a reminder, by 'leader' I am not only referring to those in charge of people, organisations or in positions of authority, but also to any individual who wants to be in charge of their lives. The other fundamental quality all leaders must possess is *authenticity* and I will explain why shortly.

Life is full of hardships, adversities, confronting challenges and suffering. Commencing the journey of knowing, let alone being effective and powerful, demands *courage*. It is virtually impossible for a leader to take appropriate risks without *courage*. Furthermore, a leader who is in charge of an organisation couldn't possibly deal with the high level of stress associated with addressing the many unstructured problems that typically arise several times daily within any organisation without *courage*. With maturity comes the ability to predict the consequences of the risks we take in life and an *awareness* of just how courageous we must be to tackle the inevitable challenges that lie ahead, to be like David in the face of Goliath, to move forward despite feeling terrified.

Courage and *authenticity*: Dare to be YOU!

Courage and *authenticity* are the source of our relationship with Reality, the source of attuning ourselves to the world and to the very possibility of our existence. So, both qualities have unique significance in life and therefore also in the Being Framework. It's impossible to be authentic if we are not courageous. After all, it takes *courage* to **dare to be YOU**: the real, authentic, one-of-a-kind, beautiful you. In fact, it takes *courage* to dare to **be**, to be 'out there in the world'. Without *courage* you would not dare to assert yourself, making you the shy and passive one at the table of life. As a consequence, your Unique Being would not stand a chance of making an impact on the world, and what an utter tragedy that would be. Let me break it down to help you appreciate the extraordinary significance of *courage* and *authenticity* to every one of us.

It takes *courage* to limit how much you adjust who you really are, including your words and feelings. It takes *courage* to say your real yeses and noes, to assert yourself even when you're secretly shaking in your boots. It takes *courage* to be free, and to think, be and say who you really are. It takes *courage* to let go of your inauthentic perceptions, made-up self-image or personas that are incongruent with your Unique Being. It takes *courage* to break through your current narrative lens and have the epistemic humility to pursue truth and Reality, even if it comes at the risk of being offensive, confrontational and provocative. It takes *courage* to be vulnerable, to let down your guard, admit ignorance and open the door to knowledge, knowing it will lead you on the pathway to true wisdom. I take my hat off to those who dare to want to know and to step into unexplored territories. It takes *courage* to receive and accept criticism, to take it on the chin, resolve the issue and move on with your head held high. The courageous persevere in the face of great challenge and adversity while they are also the first to step forward and move out of their comfort zone.

It takes *courage* to dare to transform, to stand out, to be responsible, committed and 'all in, boots and all', despite the 'what ifs?' and pressure from others to conform. It takes *courage* to honour your calling or *higher purpose*, putting the concern of self aside and choosing the pathway of service and the road less travelled over the pathway of ease and comfort. It also takes *courage* to let others contribute to you, to accept generosity and kindness with humility and grace. To be in partnership with other human beings takes *courage*, to ignore your cold feet and trust your gut that you've made the right decision to commit to the one you love or your business partner. In any relationship, personal or business, it takes *courage* to be truly present with another and to convey *gratitude* or *love*. There is always something to be grateful for. When someone comes to you seeking comfort, it takes *courage* to be compassionate and not to take the easy option and turn a blind eye. It takes *courage* to be willing to just **be with** them, even if there is nothing you can do to ease their pain or burden. It takes *courage* to forgive and it takes *courage* to be calm in the face of all the challenges and difficulties being bombarded at you in life. By now you should see the significance of both *courage* and *authenticity* and how closely related they are to all the other Ways of Being.

Courage is primal

Courage is a primal quality – hence a Primary Way of Being – that can be observed in the animal kingdom as well as in human beings. Whether it's a parent or the leader, animals clearly display *courage* when protecting their offspring or the herd, pack or pride. Like humans, animals also experience *fear* and *courage*. They instinctively know that when a threat is present, causing *fear*, they must be courageous to protect themselves and others. To expect *courage* without *fear* would be like expecting rain in the absence of clouds. The reason I am referring to this primal Way of Being and survival mechanism is to reinforce the content explained in detail in the Discovery versus Invention chapter within Part 1 of this book. My point is that we are **discovering** the Meaning of *courage* (referring to First-layer Reality) that already exists and is transcendent, meaning it is **beyond your subjective experience**.

Being courageous describes a deeper meaning of being there in the world. Without it we would cease to exist as a race. Life can be full of hardship and it takes *courage* to face challenging circumstances and to be responsible when things seem to spiral out of control. Being authentic and speaking up for yourself requires you to be courageous and *courage* is essential for sound leadership. Leaders are often seated in the front row of an auditorium and they often travel business or first class, and they cop it from their critics for such privileges. If you liken it to the animal kingdom, the leader of the pack may get the first and best piece of meat after the hunt, but that privilege comes at a cost, the cost of being ready to manifest *courage* when the time comes. Similarly, whenever a company needs to be defended against a downturn in the economy, everyone expects the leader to act, to lead from the front and to do the right thing. The leader is the one who must make the tough decisions and manage high levels of risk. This demands great *courage*.

The relationship between *courage* and Moods

There is an inseparable relationship between every Primary Way of Being and every Mood: *care*, *vulnerability*, *fear* and *anxiety*. However, when it comes to *courage*, the relationship is particularly significant. Let me touch on these relationships here, beginning with *fear* and *anxiety*. While I have already talked about the fact that, ontologically speaking, *courage* cannot be present in the absence of *fear* or *anxiety*, it's worth delving a little more deeply into this important relationship.

It's profound and at the same time a paradoxical truth that *courage* isn't actually *courage* at all unless there's some level of *fear* or *anxiety* associated with it. Unless we experience a moment's hesitation before taking on something felt to be hazardous and threatening, being courageous has no meaning as that moment of hesitation is where we choose to be courageous or not. From a psychological perspective, some may choose to only categorise *fear* and *courage* as physical, moral, rational, etc., but I have deliberately not done that within the context of the Being Framework, opting instead to keep the conversation at a deeper fundamental level with respect to Moods.

When we think of fear in general terms, there is always an object or phenomenon associated with it (fear of something: spiders, flying, public speaking, etc.). However, *fear* as a Mood, as explained in the Fear chapter, is about how to **be with** *fear* (our relationship with *fear*). Once you work on polishing your relationship with *fear*, the fear is still there, but you would know how to **be with** it and step forward with *courage*. If you have a fear of flying, knowing how to **be with** that fear by learning certain coping mechanisms will give you the *courage* to take a flight without freaking out. Learning and practising how to **be with** *fear* (or any other Mood) is like knowing how to fish as opposed to being given a fish. The same is true for *anxiety* as, in order for you to **be with** concerns regarding what the future holds for you – an *anxiety*-generating thought – you need a healthy relationship with *courage*. *Courage* does not need to have an object, as you are either courageous in the face of *fear* or *anxiety* or you're not. As long as you are authentic, you cannot fake being courageous. You can, however, pretend to be confident, which is behavioural and context-based, but that is inauthentic and not the same as being courageous.

We have observed *courage* going beyond particular objects of *fear* many times in history. Cyrus[120], Alexander[121], Napoleon[122] and many other renowned military leaders in history willingly put themselves on the front line and risked their own lives rather than sitting in an ivory tower protected by guards and pushing others to fight the battles they waged themselves like many of today's so-called leaders do. My point is, *courage* beyond the greatest fear in life, which is the fear of losing one's life, did not stand in their way. Samurais, Vikings and many other warriors had a similar conception of *courage*. This is further proof that *courage* only arises when *fear* or *anxiety* are present. When someone is courageous enough to risk their own life for a cause greater than themselves, as firefighters, police, soldiers, medical practitioners and other frontline workers do, that is *courage*. The same is true when one is ready to face uncertainties around the future and the *anxiety* this can create. Any great leader, any person of influence who is up to a big cause, must be able to courageously **be with** a huge, ongoing level of uncertainty. It is worth noting that this also demands a healthy relationship with *awareness*. It's about being courageous enough to step forward despite your *fear* and *anxiety*, even if you don't yet fully understand the matters involved. Having this ability is indicative of a healthy relationship with *awareness, fear, anxiety* and *courage*.

Care is another Mood that has a close relationship with *courage*. In fact, *care* is a source of *courage*. We are most courageous around the matters and people we care most about. That is a phenomenological fact. The empirical data collected from studies of human beings, including our study, proves it. Let's call it the *care-courage* relationship. A mother bear cares so deeply for her cubs that she will instinctively confront any danger to protect them. Humans would do the same to protect their children. These are primal and physiological instincts. However, human

---

120 Cyrus II of Persia, commonly known as Cyrus the Great, and also called Cyrus the Elder by the Greeks, was the founder of the Achaemenid Empire, the first Persian Empire.

121 Alexander III of Macedon, commonly known as Alexander the Great, was a king of the ancient Greek kingdom of Macedon and a member of the Argead dynasty.

122 Napoleon Bonaparte, born Napoleone di Buonaparte, byname 'Le Corse', or 'Le Petit Caporal', was a French statesman and military leader who became notorious as an artillery commander during the French Revolution.

beings have evolved to strive for a relationship with *higher purpose*, beyond these primal and physiological instincts. These are the matters we choose to set above our own Self because we care so deeply about them. Some would choose to set raising children as the subject of their *higher purpose*, or a career, an organisation, their country, their religion, and so on; others would select a cause as their relationship with *higher purpose* in life, often not wanting to limit themselves to just one. Some may even set pleasure-seeking above anything else (hedonists). I am not making a judgement call here; I am making the point that whatever we choose to care deeply about can lead us to be more courageous and enable us to overcome any fear associated with it. This is partly why many well-accomplished leaders and entrepreneurs subscribe to the mantra, 'follow what you are deeply passionate about'.

No matter what path you choose, if you seek greatness and strive to be effective at that one thing, you can count on the path being rocky or even mountainous and treacherous along the way. If you don't have the passion and don't care enough to make it through, you will give up sooner or later; you won't have the *courage* to make it. Remember the Simorgh story? *Care-courage* is one of the reasons only thirty of all the birds in the world succeeded on their quest, despite the many adversities and challenges they encountered on their journey. Insufficient *care* about the cause they are striving for is one of the main reasons there is such a high rate of failure amongst startups. I personally don't consider it failure when someone gives up before going through multiple iterations, which is the case for so many. I believe the goal wasn't important enough to them from the start. They just didn't care enough to be courageous and risk the inevitable temporary failures along the way. We will discuss this further in the Persistence chapter.

Courage will only arise where there is a **perceived** risk, whereas *vulnerability* is only present where there **is** risk. Therefore, a healthy relationship with both *vulnerability* and *courage* is vital as they are intrinsically entwined. Furthermore, *courage* is not only required in the face of *fear*, but also in the face of *vulnerability*, *care* and *anxiety*, as they may arise together. Transforming your relationship with each and all of these Moods requires a healthy relationship with *courage*. We need to give ourselves permission to choose to be courageous. Remember, *courage* is not always fortitude and strength. There are times when *courage* is steadfastness – the quality of being resolutely or dutifully firm and unwavering – not necessarily to fight, but to stand your ground and not be crushed in the face of the darkness, malevolence, tyranny and even the things that may be perceived to be less significant. Even simple things like asking for the right drink when you are handed a coffee instead of the tea you ordered or confronting a person who skips the queue requires *courage*. It is worth noting that while it is impossible to be vulnerable without *courage*, *vulnerability* is not always present in the courageous. As a leader or a business owner, it is important to be aware that any time you are managing or confronting risk, which is inevitable, *courage* is required.

While I acknowledge the close association between *fear* and *courage* in situations that cause frustration, conflict and misunderstanding between two people, whether in a business or personal relationship, the principal communication challenge facing both parties has less to do with the *fear-courage* relationship and more to do with the relationship between *vulnerability* and *courage*. Specifically, this is the willingness, followed by the *courage*, to stick your neck out and say what's on your mind. It is not until this happens that we can call it authentic *presence*, whereby both parties have the *freedom* to assertively express themselves (*self-expression*). Now, let's say neither party took the responsibility to establish and manage the expectations. This would raise the level of uncertainty associated with the potential outcome and its probable incongruence with what we actually wanted, increasing our level of *anxiety*. What can come to the rescue here is our *anxiety-courage* relationship. This is the *courage* that lets us step forward despite the presence of *anxiety*. When you need to go from point A to point B over a 1000-kilometre distance on a pitch-black stretch of road in the dead of night you don't necessarily need to see the whole 1000 kilometres to have the *courage* to move forward. Just seeing the distance your headlights illuminate as you inch closer to your destination is enough for you to keep going, despite being anxious. That's because your healthy relationship with *anxiety* allows you to fly on the wings of *courage*. Let me share a secret with you when it comes to coaching high-performing leaders. I almost always begin with *awareness*, *vulnerability*, *authenticity* and *courage* because I have found these Aspects of Being to be the cornerstones for the rest of the transformation process.

Courage and hierarchy

Let's return to the animal kingdom for a moment and consider a pack animal like wolves. These canines have a distinct hierarchy in their pack, with one wolf as their leader. This hierarchy is necessary for the survival of the pack when faced with danger. There is also an expectation from the rest of the pack that the lead wolf will do whatever is needed to deal with the danger and, to do that, these animals need *courage*. Wolves and some other pack animals understand *courage* instinctively and will leverage it when in danger. Significantly, in the wild the lead wolf may often eat first. This is not because they are stronger, more intimidating or coerce the others into it. It is an instinctive act of preservation to ensure he maintains the strength to protect the entire pack and strategise future hunts and the survival of the pack. Hierarchy existed well before we humans could distort the original Meaning. Since we, as humans, have a relatively high level of autonomy, these supporting mechanisms of survival have also been abused by some for self-serving purposes. As a result, many have developed a cynicism and dislike for these hierarchical structures. At the end of the day, as leaders, whether or not we believe in hierarchy, we still need the *courage* to put ourselves forward in a crisis or when faced with a challenge, not unlike the leader of the wolf pack.

It is important to note that being courageous does not equate to being aggressive. Famous world leaders, such as civil rights movement leaders Martin Luther King Jr and Mahatma Gandhi, employed non-violent resistance to lead their successful campaigns. They did not necessarily exert or support aggression, but instead they were courageous and, for the most part, authentic, which inspired many to also speak up for themselves and join movements in non-violent ways. I am not in favour of the pacifist approach they adopted simply to avoid conflict at all cost. We will discuss this further in the Assertiveness chapter.

The good news is, our empirical data reveals that when someone is courageous and authentic, they tend to be that way for life across multiple dimensions because that is who they are being. For example, someone who is courageous in their career is very likely to also be courageous in their intimate relationships. If there are inconsistencies in terms of where someone is being courageous and where they're not, I would explore their relationship with *authenticity*.

Being courageous requires us to speak up, to learn to step out of our conditioning to be overly compliant or politically correct and to make ourselves heard. Today, many seem to be obsessed with wanting to align themselves with anti-aggressive sentiments. While this may be regarded as a positive evolution, could it have gone too far? Have we lost the ability to speak up for ourselves? Have we become timid, placid and overly submissive? Have we become pacifists, fearing confrontation and confusing the difference in meaning between being aggressive and being courageous? *Courage* is a primal Way of Being and is needed to stand up for oneself in the face of adversity. At the end of the day, in order to release yourself from the manipulative, malevolent and tyrannical forces in the world, you need to deal with the darkness and that is not easy in the absence of *courage*. Without *courage* (and *authenticity*) you will never achieve the *freedom* to express your Unique Being to the world, respond to your calling and, ultimately, take actions that can lead you to accomplish what you most desire in life. Your fulfilment in life is tightly related to your *courage*. Last but not least, being courageous is dignified and tied to your self-esteem and self-worth. For those of you who don't wish to stop at the *effectiveness* and fulfilment conversation and are aiming to be at the pinnacle of humanity and honour your dignity, *courage* is one of the key qualities to develop.

CHAPTER 12

Commitment

Have you ever observed how you react internally after making a significant commitment? Perhaps you experienced a sense of excitement, urgency and anticipation. You may have also noticed feelings of doubt, *fear, anxiety* or concern that you may not be doing the right thing or that you may not meet expectations or complete a project on time. These experiences are quite common when committing to something we care deeply about as there may be great consequences if things don't go to plan, such as starting a business or getting married. A commitment is a promise, choice or decision that triggers an action to undertake something that is important and significant. However, **being** committed goes beyond that. *Commitment*, as a Way of Being, is our relationship with our promises and agreements. Some people are happy to step forward and make a commitment, but will just as readily break it when the going gets tough or a better option comes along. This is an indication of an unhealthy relationship with *commitment*. A healthy relationship with *commitment* would be evident by your willingness and intention to fulfil any commitment you undertake, no matter what gets in your way. Having a healthy relationship with *commitment* will propel you forward regardless of circumstances.

As human beings, we are social creatures by nature. Teaming up with others is par for the course for most of us. Whether we are working towards a significant cause, raising a family, building a business, sitting on a board of directors, part of a team, creating a joint venture or commercial partnership with others, and so on, none of these would stand firm without *commitment*, without the establishment and fulfilment of promises and expectations. Without a means to hold each other to account (*accountability*) anarchy would prevail. Without *commitment*

– as an individual and collectively – high performance, *effectiveness* and fulfilment cannot be expected. You may argue that we human beings have been ineffective throughout history when it comes to *commitment*, though we have clearly been committed enough to stand the test of time and, to a certain degree, thrive as a species. We have been committed to many causes because, collectively, we have cared deeply enough about them to deliver on promises that impact the common good. Our collective *commitment* to various causes has allowed us to achieve greatness and progress as a species, from eradicating common diseases, enforcing law and order and refining our political and economic systems, to raising future generations. So, clearly a level of *commitment* is a must in all aspects of life. Therefore, understanding your relationship with *commitment* and polishing this Primary Way of Being will make an enormous difference to your life and the lives of those around you, including the people you work with.

What is *commitment*?

The *Oxford English Dictionary* defines commitment in a couple of different ways. Firstly, it states that *commitment* is 'the state or quality of being dedicated to a cause, activity, etc.'. I would add 'someone' to this definition, including oneself. Secondly, it defines *commitment* as, 'an engagement or obligation that restricts freedom of action'. This second meaning is closely aligned with my study into *commitment* as it pertains to leadership, performance and *effectiveness*, the focus of this book. Why? Because when you are genuinely committed to a cause, such as your organisation's mission statement, your *commitment* will restrict your *freedom* to a certain degree. An Olympic athlete is truly committed to their sport. In order to be that dedicated, they must strictly monitor how they spend their time, the foods they eat, and the other causes and activities they must sacrifice in favour of the sport they are committed to. This contradicts the mainstream way of thinking, such as the 'have it all now' philosophy many subscribe to. You may have observed at this point that the word 'commitment' is italicised at times and not at others. This is intentional. It is italicised when it refers to *commitment* as a Way of Being and not italicised when it refers to commitment in the conventional sense, such as to make a commitment.

The Being Framework ontological distinction of *commitment*

Commitment is being dedicated to someone, something, a particular promise or cause that you care more about than anything that may stand in the way. When you are committed, you care wholeheartedly, are considered willing, dependable, trustworthy and loyal. You fulfil and honour the promises you make and appropriately demand the same of others.

A healthy relationship with *commitment* indicates that when you put your mind to something, you are all in and stay engaged until the expected outcome is fulfilled. You prioritise, working consistently and diligently towards the fulfilment of the outcome without giving up. Others may consider you dependable and focused on the things you give your word to.

An unhealthy relationship with *commitment* indicates that you may often struggle to fully invest in and maintain relationships or fulfil your agreements. You frequently procrastinate and may avoid making promises or taking on projects or ventures, even those you consider to be beneficial for you. You may avoid any discomfort associated with fulfilling your promises. Others may be hesitant to count on you or give you significant responsibility, which may be detrimental to your relationships and career. You may often refuse to provide specific and timebound promises, lack clarity and be lenient with your responses, or resort to excuses. Alternatively, you may commit to whatever comes your way, regardless of the workability, and may make unrealistic promises without due consideration.

The state of being committed is an empowering Way of Being. No intention is ever fully actualised without *commitment*. It is a quality that, by virtue of its presence alone, creates the space in which keeping your word is supported. When you are genuinely committed to a cause, not only are you contributing to that cause (*contribution* is another Primary Way of Being), but people around you know you can be counted on because whenever you have said you would do something in the past, you were true to your word. *Commitment* is when you are all in, no matter what gets in your way. One of the most important outcomes is *reliability*, a Secondary Way of Being, and therefore you would develop a reputation as someone who is being reliable. It's worth noting that it is possible to contribute without full *commitment* but it's not possible to be fully committed without also contributing to the cause. We will explore this relationship further in the Contribution chapter.

Some would refer to *commitment* as honouring your words, whereby what you say and what you do are congruent. Others say external factors dictate one's level of *commitment*. However, I would argue that how you are **being with** *commitment* – your relationship with this Way of Being – plays the major role. A high level of *commitment* will lead to conviction, which in turn will lead you to persevere. I have seen many extremely smart but miserable people in my career, and what I have observed in each case was a distinct lack of *commitment, persistence* and *reliability*. Whenever *commitment* and *persistence* are lacking, it predominantly has its roots in an individual's relationship with *care, courage, authenticity* and *responsibility*. It is also important to bear in mind that *commitment* is much more than making a token gesture of *contribution*.

The interplay between *commitment* and other Ways of Being and Moods

As is the case with the other Ways of Being, our relationship with *commitment* can be impacted by any or all of the other Ways of Being and Moods and vice versa. Let's look at a few examples. Undeniably, your level of *care* around matters will determine how important they are to you and therefore your level of *commitment*. While you may be responsible, that doesn't necessarily mean you care enough to be fully committed to the cause. Without *commitment*, you won't allow yourself to engage fully and **be all in**. For example, you may understand that it's your responsibility to take your dog for a walk every day, but you may lack sufficient *care* to be committed enough to ensure it takes priority over other things, so you grant yourself permission to skip it now and then. How many times have you committed to regular daily exercise and healthy eating only to find excuses? 'It's raining, so I'll just skip my run today', or, 'I've got too much work to do. I'll go to the gym tomorrow', or, 'I'll just have one slice of cake and get back on the diet tomorrow'. We've all been there. We begin full of enthusiasm and determination, but over time, *commitment* fades and complacency sets in. That's when the excuses come and, eventually, we give up altogether and mediocrity ensues. Notice that there is a strong relationship between *care* and *commitment*.

Fear and *anxiety* can also impact your level of *commitment*. For example, *fear* of committing to a long-term relationship is quite common in our society. A lack of *courage* or *higher purpose* – when someone is so selfish that they are unwilling to commit their time and energy to others – will most certainly undermine their level of *commitment*. In terms of your relationship with another human being, your relationship with *partnership*, *love*, *compassion* and *contribution* may get in your way of being all in. This is true in both personal and professional relationships. Not being authentic, coupled with a lack of *self-expression*, *freedom* and *presence*, can also get in the way of being committed. As you can see, these interconnected relationships can be quite complex. When you gradually increase your *awareness* and find your hot spots (where you are most lacking) you will become better equipped to effectively and accurately discover the links between Moods and Ways of Being and relate those back to what is actually happening in your life at any given time. Understanding the Being Framework ontological model will help you contemplate this for yourself. However, due to the complex nature of those relationships, working with a qualified ontological coach is most effective and will make a huge difference in understanding and working through what is missing or not working in your life.

The four facets of *commitment*

There are four key facets of *commitment*: Declaration, Expectations, Execution and Grace. It can easily be argued that without all four facets, there is no *commitment*. There may well be intention and/or action, but neither or both constitute a commitment or qualify anyone as a committed individual. Let's briefly examine each facet.

Declaration: The first facet of being committed to something or someone is to make an authentic, sincere and responsible public statement or declaration of intention. The declaration should be made verbally or in writing, rather than in your head. It is a promise that declares what you have 'signed up' for and what you fully intend to do and how you intend to be in action. This is why traditionally, many people choose to write down their commitments or create a vision board to articulate and visualise them as this supports them to be accountable. Both can be effective practices. Even more effective is announcing a *commitment* publicly, like taking an oath – as you do when you marry – because it exposes you and invites others to hold you to account.

Expectations: Setting the expectations and establishing the boundaries makes the commitment tangible and gives it a defined timeline. Explicitly indicate a certain date and time to start honouring your commitment. By timeline, I don't mean a specific due date, although this would apply for most commitments. It can also refer to a lifelong commitment, such as a marriage, which has no defined end date. Establishing the expectations also includes a commitment to periodically communicate progress and to recommit with full ownership if ever you find yourself off track. Let's say you assign a simple project to a junior member of your team and ask them to prepare a draft project plan. If they fail to include a clearly defined start and end date on their assignment, there is no commitment, even if the action plan has been well articulated. Without clearly defined expectations, you cannot track your team member's progress or hold them to account because there is nothing to hold them accountable to. As a result, you would run the very real risk of the assignment not being delivered on time, which could hold up other teams and have severe ramifications on the organisation's reputation and bottom line.

Imagine if you booked an electrician to come to your home at a specific time and he turned up an hour later without calling beforehand to explain the delay, blaming traffic for his tardiness when he eventually showed up. Even if he completed the job satisfactorily in the end, he failed to honour his commitment because he hadn't met the agreed expectation. If, on the other hand, he calls fifteen minutes beforehand to advise that he has been unavoidably delayed and will be there an hour later, as long as he arrives as promised and satisfactorily completes the job, he has honoured his commitment, which would make you more inclined to hire him in future.

Execution: Execution is getting it done, as expected and on time. It's when you fulfil what you 'signed up' for and get it done on time as promised, no matter what gets in the way. In the event that you don't honour your agreement, regardless of the circumstances, you should own it, clean up and move on, as discussed in the Responsibility chapter.

Grace: Grace is a facet of *commitment* that is closely related to the conventional usage of the word 'integrity'. Have you ever noticed that some people make a commitment, fulfil it, but then resent it afterwards or during execution? You could say they delivered on their commitment or promise. However, if resentment was the main state of Being while fulfilling the commitment, they were not being as integrous as they thought they were. In other words, they were not fulfilling the commitment with *integrity*. It's like a parent changing their child's nappy, knowing it is their responsibility and a commitment they have chosen to fulfil but carrying resentment every time they do it. Can you think of someone at work who fulfils their commitments, but often with an air of resentment? When was the last time you were resentful over fulfilling a commitment? It happens to all of us from time to time. Next time you observe this state of Being within yourself, see if you can identify the reason for your resentment. If your resentment relates to another person, perhaps honest and open communication is needed. Or perhaps time has passed, and you have come to the realisation that there is more work involved than you had anticipated, or find the work boring and something you actually don't want to do. There could be many reasons for your resentment. If you catch yourself being resentful when honouring commitments, it would be beneficial to consider the health of your relationship with *authenticity* and *freedom* as well as *assertiveness*, a Secondary Way of Being that will be discussed later.

When resentment is present, you have two choices: you could choose to hang onto your resentment or you could acknowledge it, own it, drop the resentment and complete the task with grace. Ask yourself which of the two options is more empowering. I am confident that you will agree with me that being resentful is not empowering. By choosing the second option, you will honour your commitment fully and be empowered and experience peace of mind as a result. Isn't that worth dropping the resentment? So, when making commitments or being committed to an outcome, be mindful of any pretence or feelings of resentment creeping in.

The four facets of *commitment* discussed here are simple ways to support you to navigate your way through life. All people lie sometimes, whereas declarations and intentions, defined timelines and subsequent actions don't. Anyone who has a healthy relationship with *commitment* is a wonderful treasure worth knowing and valuing and, with full confidence, I can testify that everyone has the potential to have a healthy relationship with *commitment*.

Commitment as a Way of Being

Commitment as a Way of Being is beyond just making 'a commitment'. It's about how we relate to *commitment* in various aspects of life. When someone is committed there is no hesitancy or wavering. Have you noticed how a committed team member can pull a whole team forward in the direction of the objective or goal in the same way an uncommitted individual will hold the team back? When businesses need to introduce major changes, a good starting point is identifying the likely early adopters and inspiring them to become committed to the cause. They will automatically pull the rest of the team along until the whole team is aligned and committed.

When one has a healthy relationship with *commitment,* they consistently honour their commitments to be or do what they signed up for, no matter what stands in their way. Remember the earlier example about the junior staff member who failed to deliver on the expectations of the project? From a Being perspective, it is more important that an individual has a healthy relationship with *commitment* when they join an organisation than any individual commitment they may make, which is likely to be behavioural and more readily addressed through appropriate leadership. When you have a healthy relationship with *commitment* as a Way of Being, you fulfil and live up to your promises and you can be relied upon. For example, a person with an unhealthy relationship with *commitment* may rashly accept a role while having a back door option, knowing they intend to leave when something better comes along. The same analogy applies to any relationship. The consequence of this misconceived and unhealthy relationship with *commitment* is *fear*, *anxiety* and untold suffering, with breakups in families, organisations and communities an all-too-common outcome. With *commitment*, there are no back doors! To be clear, this is relevant both ways. It is just as important for an employer to be committed when employing someone as it is for the new team member to be committed to their new role. Unless all parties in a relationship are clear of each other's relationship with *commitment* (how they relate to *commitment*), then you are already planning for disasters to arise. It is worth remembering that the most important commitments are to the object of your *higher purpose* and yourself. One of the most common sources of regret, sorrow and distress is giving up on what you were so committed to.

The same can apply collectively, at an organisational level. There's nothing better than the joy, ease and workability experienced in an environment in which *commitment* is a core value and the only acceptable way to be. In my experience working with many high-performing and effective teams, a key quality that I found these teams shared is that they take *commitment* extremely seriously. Once the mission and tasks have been set, every team member knows exactly what they are required to produce and by when. And they get it done, even if it means working longer hours than originally anticipated to get it done on time, working those extra hours without any hint of resentment. In other words, they honour their commitments. The following quote, which Steve Jobs made during an interview, is a case in point. It highlights that one of the keys to Apple's success is *commitment*. Each team leader and their people are so committed to the company cause and committed to their role and what they choose to be responsible for individually, that they get the work done, whatever it takes and without micromanagement, as though they are all part owners of the company, just like a startup.

> 'One of the keys to Apple is Apple is an incredibly collaborative company. You know how many committees we have at Apple? Zero. We have no committees. We are organized like a start-up. One person's in charge of iPhone

> OS software, one person's in charge of Mac hardware, one person's in charge of iPhone hardware engineering, another person's in charge of worldwide marketing, another person's in charge of operations. We are organized like a start-up. We are the biggest start-up on the planet.'

The role of the team leader would be to remove any blockages and obstacles getting in the way and manage the promises, expectations and resources, as opposed to managing the people. In my experience, all high-performing teams are extremely effective at this. Their collective attitude towards commitment generates trust and demonstrates *reliability*, leading the organisation/brand to be subsequently known as a trustworthy, reliable entity. This ultimately results in winning desirable, better projects, developing new products, generating more revenue and profitability, creating opportunities for growth, and so on. Essentially the opportunities are endless when *commitment* is a core value at both an individual and collective level. What a blessing for all concerned! If only *commitment* was more prevalent, as we can all relate to how frustrating it can be when this powerful Way of Being is lacking. People voice this frustration to me all the time. They tell me how hard it is to find genuinely committed people, both in business and in life in general. Committed people find committed people! Our Being Profile empirical data backs this up. You need only look into the statistics on marriage to see how a staggering proportion of the population values *commitment* in personal relationships so lightly.

Commitment is one of the Ways of Being that is more readily understood than some of the others, such as *love* and *forgiveness* (which will be covered in upcoming chapters). That's because it is a Way of Being we all relate to. We all know people who have broken their promises to us, and we have all broken promises ourselves. We are all prone to breaking commitments. Let's be honest and acknowledge this here and now, but moving forward, let's commit to not being part of the problem any longer. Gradually shaping your relationship with *commitment* as a Way of Being will bring enormous value into every aspect of your life and to the people and communities around you.

CHAPTER 13

Gratitude

The value that *gratitude* as a Way of Being can add to our lives is easily overlooked. In the business arena, *gratitude* is often regarded as a soft trait and not taken too seriously. If you subscribe to this view, and therefore believe that *gratitude* is less important than other human qualities in the context of leadership, performance and *effectiveness*, then I hope this chapter will bring about a paradigm shift for you by helping you understand just how important *gratitude* as a Way of Being is and the enormous benefits it can bring to your life and the lives of those around you.

Gratitude is primarily outwardly focused. It elicits a sense of appreciation towards the gift of life we have collectively been given as well as the relatively high level of autonomy we have as human beings and our differences as individuals. For example, we can be collectively grateful as human beings for the gift of sight and the fact that we have two arms and two legs while also being grateful at an individual level to have been gifted with a high IQ. *Gratitude* encourages us to look for the positive aspects in any situation. It greatly forms our interpretation of life and how we experience Reality. When it comes to *gratitude*, we all have two choices. We can choose to view life events through the lens of *gratitude*, being grateful for the experiences life has offered us, or we can choose to view life events through a narrative lens that perpetuates the state of being a victim, choosing to focus on the experiences life has not yet offered us. Neither option is incorrect. It simply boils down to the choices we make. How we choose to use our *freedom* and high level of autonomy (*responsibility*) ultimately defines our accomplishments and overall experience of life. High achievers mostly choose the first option but may take the second option into consideration from time to time and manage the associated risks.

It is worth reiterating that the Being Framework adopts a moral-free, purely objective ontological approach to all Aspects of Being, and *gratitude* is no exception. Rather than treating *gratitude* as a virtue, the Being Framework explores the Reality of this quality in the world. How you choose to conceptualise it for yourself and whether or not you wish to make judgements is completely up to you. It is important to stress this here because *gratitude* (or a lack thereof) is a quality that is readily judged. It is a Way of Being that has an impact on our emotional state and is strongly linked to contentment and satisfaction. *Gratitude* is a Way of Being for people to turn their focus outward (away from themselves) and connect to a greater cause, be it to other people, nature, or a higher power. In this book and the Being Framework I refer to this as *higher purpose*, which is the subject of the next chapter.

The Being Framework ontological distinction of *gratitude*

Gratitude is being aware of, present to, thankful for and appreciative of what you have or are given and your experience of life and those around you. *Gratitude* is primarily oriented towards what you consider important or valuable. It moves you beyond circumstances, self-focus, worry and suffering. It's about acknowledging and respecting all the contributions and gifts provided to you while not taking them for granted.

A healthy relationship with *gratitude* indicates that you clearly see and appreciate the blessings in life, even when circumstances may suggest otherwise. Others may consider you generous, optimistic and someone who consistently participates in life from a perspective of abundance.

An unhealthy relationship with *gratitude* indicates that you may lose sight of blessings in life and the contribution of others. You may be easily discouraged and disheartened by challenging circumstances. You may also operate from scarcity and struggle to maintain enthusiasm and motivation. You may frequently compare yourself with others, wonder why situations don't go your way or focus on what you don't have, leading to jealousy and envy. Others may consider you ungrateful, entitled, lacking in generosity and someone who frequently complains. You may also be regarded as undermining, negative and as someone who often sees problems before solutions. Alternatively, you may be overly content with whatever life throws at you and lack the ambition to stretch or challenge yourself or others to grow.

Gratitude and sacrifice go hand in hand

The study of *gratitude* is steeped in history. This powerful state of Being has been discovered and studied by many renowned scholars over time going back to the *Old Testament*, and probably even further. While few people deeply study the *Old Testament* anymore, many of us recall some of its stories from our youth. The story of Cain and Abel from the Book of Genesis is known to many and, figuratively speaking, is a prime example of how *gratitude* can be expressed (or not). I would like to use that story here to explain the ontological distinction of *gratitude* from a purely metaphorical perspective. Cain and Abel were the first sons to be born to Adam and Eve. They had the entire world at their disposal, giving them access to such abundance that they could have anything their hearts desired. They could have split the Earth in two and each chosen a half to rule had they so desired. Jehovah (God) asked them each to make a sacrifice to convey their appreciation for the gift of life. Abel was a shepherd, so he offered one of his best sheep, which was accepted by Jehovah as a suitable sacrifice because it was clearly something Abel valued and therefore worthy of sacrifice. However, Cain, a farmer, offered the worst crops he had as his sacrifice, an offer that was, unsurprisingly, rejected.

If we look at the story from Abel's perspective, he acknowledged and came from a position of *awareness* that he did not singlehandedly raise the sheep. Consider that in the back of his mind he may have been thinking, 'I am not the one who blows the wind, I am not the one who moves the clouds and causes the rain to fall, I am not the one who creates the grass seeds, I am not the one who shines sunlight upon the earth and triggers the process of photosynthesis'. Abel was aware that, as the shepherd who shifted these resources from the area of low productivity to higher productivity[123], he was merely a contributor in a chain of events. He was happy and willing to sacrifice some of his achievements because he was aware of the fact that it was not just about him and his efforts alone. This signifies Abel's healthy relationship with *gratitude* and that it was aligned with Reality. You may also recognise

---

123 Jean-Baptiste Say, a French economist who first coined the word entrepreneur in about 1800, said: 'The entrepreneur shifts economic resources out of an area of lower and into an area of higher productivity and greater yield.'

from this story that it takes *courage* to be grateful. Replace 'shepherd' with 'entrepreneur' and I'm sure you will appreciate the metaphorical significance to performance, *effectiveness* and leadership.

I can confidently say Cain did not share his brother's healthy relationship with *gratitude*. While Abel wanted to ensure his sacrifice meant something and therefore offered Jehovah one of his best sheep, Cain thought his brother was foolish to sacrifice something so valuable and, instead, chose something he could easily spare. His lack of *awareness* made him ignorant to the fact that he was not 100% responsible for the crops he grew. While Cain focused on himself, there were actually many other contributory factors. Like Abel, he was just one part of a bigger picture and process. In other words, Cain's selfishness did not allow him to go beyond himself; he lacked a *higher purpose* and the vision to see Reality. His decision to act upon a narrative lens that was incongruent with Reality caused him to suffer through resentment, envy and hatred. He refused to acknowledge and accept that he was the source of the problem and the reason his sacrifice wasn't favoured by God. Instead of owning it, he blamed an external source (Abel). Ultimately, this led him to consciously dissociate his own brother from existence (life), immediately regretting that decision afterwards. Hopefully you can see the parallels and significance to modern day life in this story and therefore appreciate why I chose it as a metaphor to describe *gratitude*.

Cain's unhealthy relationship with *gratitude* is symbolic of the ignorance, negligence and arrogance that is prevalent in the postmodern era. For example, today's farmers have a different appreciation of water as a valuable resource from most city dwellers and are therefore far more careful with their water consumption, for which they are heavily reliant on rain, and extremely grateful when they are blessed with a decent amount. We experienced one of the worst bushfire seasons on record here in Australia during the second half of 2019 and early 2020, following a prolonged period of drought. The air was so saturated with smoke and other particles from the fires that it made breathing a challenge and brought to our attention the fact that even the air we breathe is not something we should take for granted. It is not our entitlement; we are privileged to have it! Indeed, there are so many blessings and possibilities to be grateful for that we often fail to acknowledge or appreciate them until they are taken away from us. For instance, when our heart works at an optimum level, most of us take it for granted that it will keep us alive by pumping blood through the body automatically, not paying any attention to it until something goes wrong.

How many people take their own parents for granted, only to regret their lack of appreciation and *gratitude* once they are gone? Whether we are caring for our health, spending time with loved ones, appreciating our employees and colleagues or whatever it may be, worthy sacrifices must be made – giving up certain things to attain something else – in order to demonstrate that we don't take anything or anyone for granted. It shows we are grateful for our existence and for the presence of others in our lives. You see, making sacrifices is directly linked to *gratitude*. If you want to maintain a relationship, whether it be a personal or professional relationship, you will come to a point where sacrifices must be made on both sides, and that is the lesson from the story of Cain and Abel. A sacrifice is a totally selfless act of appreciation and *gratitude*, nothing more, nothing less. However, don't be fooled into thinking that the more sacrifices you make, the more you are entitled to receive in return.

The offering of sacrifices is such a common practice in many religions that it is often taken out of context. However, the primary aim of this practice has always been to simply encourage worshippers to give up something they are deeply attached to. In the past it may have been a sheep, a goat or crops, as they would have been the highly valued assets of the time. Today it may be money, attention or time. Sacrifice is a quality every leader should possess as we all find ourselves in a state of loss in business at some point, usually multiple times, from loss of turnover and profit to losing highly valued staff members and major clients to our competitors. At the end of the day, the game of life entails many losses. That is part of Reality. Preparing for those times of loss by practising making sacrifices leads us to convey *gratitude* for what they may teach us.

Let's consider a business example to further clarify the point I am making on sacrifice and its relationship to *gratitude*. A new graduate enters the job market. The market is filled with entrepreneurs who took a rocky and high-risk pathway to building their businesses. It all started when a founder took a calculated risk to launch their business idea. They developed new products and services, marketed their brand and offering and established and nurtured relationships with their target markets. Anyone who has been on that journey will attest to how hard it is. As the business grew, the owner was able to employ staff who, in a synergistic way, contributed to the efforts of the team so that the company could now afford to take on the new graduate. In other words, it took the efforts of many – the founder, the team members and the market that supported them – to make the company what it is today. When the graduate joins the company, she benefits by being able to contribute to a greater cause and the company benefits from the years of education that prepared her to be ready for the workforce. The point is, both the graduate and the company have reasons to be grateful. Ultimately, the company's clients also have reasons to be grateful that this company has the foresight to employ well-qualified staff to look after them. Imagine if we all practised *gratitude* by being of service to one another. The by-product could be money. I could keep going, but I believe I have made my point clear. The state of being grateful is when you are present to and aware of what is out there in the world (*freedom*); it's when you are truly present to the unlimited possibilities the universe has provided that enable you to survive and thrive.

Gratitude and suffering

While I said earlier that *gratitude* is a primarily outwardly focused Way of Being, that may not be the whole story. Some philosophers refer to the fact that being alive and being here in the world is a gift in itself. Surely that is something worthy of being grateful for. They even take it a step further by saying that suffering (passion) is an aspect of *gratitude*, because even when we are suffering, we are still alive and here. I admit this view may take some getting used to, let alone be appreciated, but it is not a foreign Meaning, as it has been expressed many times in history by poets, mystics and philosophers. An example is the following poem from *The Gulistan*, a collection of stories and poems written by the great medieval Persian poet, Saadi of Shiraz[124].

---

124   Saadi of Shiraz is considered one of the greatest medieval Persian poets of all time. *The Gulistan* (Rose Garden) *of Sa'di* is a landmark of Persian literature, perhaps its single most influential work of prose. Written in 1258 CE, it is one of two major works of Saadi of Shiraz (also known as Sa'di).

Laudation to the God of majesty and glory!

Obedience to him is a cause of approach and
Gratitude in increase of benefits.
Every inhalation of the breath prolongs life and
every expiration of it gladdens our nature;
wherefore every breath confers two benefits and
for every benefit gratitude is due.

Whose hand and tongue is capable
to fulfil the obligations of thanks to him?
It is best to a worshipper for his transgressions
to offer apologies at the throne of God,
Although what is worthy of his dignity
No one is able to accomplish it.

The showers of his boundless mercy
have penetrated to every spot, and
the banquet of his unstinted liberality
is spread out everywhere.
He tears not the veil of reputation of his worshippers
even for grievous sins,
and does not withhold their daily allowance of bread
for great crimes.

O bountiful One, who from thy invisible treasury
Suppliest the Guebre and the non-believers with food,
How couldst thou disappoint thy friends,
Whilst having regard for thy enemies?

Cloud and wind, moon and sun move in the sky
That thou mayest gain bread, and not eat it unconcerned.
For thee all are revolving and obedient.
It is against the requirements of justice if thou obeyest not.

Consider that it is possible to find a blessing in everything. Some of you may struggle with this statement, especially those who have experienced great loss and suffering. However, the Reality of life is that we are all victims, both collectively and individually. For example, collectively as human beings, we will all die one day, and no one knows exactly what will happen afterwards. And it is painful not to know! Individually, we are each faced with our own challenges. Some of us have a disability or ailment over which we have no control; others grew up without parents or in troubled households or in a war-torn country. The point is, we are all victims. While we could dissociate ourselves from existence in a fraction of second if we choose to, when we dare to choose to live, we must embrace life for all it is, including the pain and suffering. So, while we are all victims, we have the power to choose to stop victimising and sabotaging ourselves. Phenomenologically speaking, our studies found that most top leaders understand this, or at least that is how they choose to view each event because it gives them the power, *persistence* and conviction to move forward.

Someone who has just been told their job has been made redundant may struggle to find something about that news to be grateful for. I am not denying that it is a challenging situation that may push someone out of their comfort zone, but life throws us many curve balls. How we respond is up to us. We can focus on either the discomfort, or the lessons and adventure that result from an unfavourable event. In the past, I have had to let employees go because they were not the right fit for the job. Telling someone they have lost their job is not a pleasant or easy task and I wondered at the time how they would take it. However, I have since discovered that it resulted in exciting new opportunities for some of them, who ended up stepping into a new career that suited them better. And they were a lot happier for it. Some changed their perception from the initial frustration and anger to *gratitude* for the push that had them looking for and landing a job they felt was better suited to them. Now, I am not suggesting that you should see the positive in everything in life. To the contrary, I am simply saying that we are all under the influence of Existence and Existence does not owe us a thing, including our livelihoods, the roof over our heads, the air we breathe or even our lives and the lives of our children. The key is to become aware of this and make peace with Reality through *gratitude*. By collectively acknowledging the fact that Existence doesn't owe us a thing and making peace with Reality, we realised it was up to us to help ourselves. So, we used our *freedom* and *responsibility* to tap into the power of the brain gifted to us by Existence and created incredible technological and medical advancements and inventions. And in so doing, we have managed to achieve extraordinary advancements. For instance, we have managed to decrease the rate of children dying from diseases in the world and gradually increase our lifespan over time.

There is a German movie called *Wings of Desire*[125], in which the angels glide above the streets of Berlin to protect the people below and provide rays of hope to those in distress, without interaction. The movie is in black and white when it is being narrated from the perspective of the angels but transitions to full colour when shown from the human perspective. One of the angels wants to become a human being, despite knowing this would make her mortal, and her wish is granted. As she drops down to Earth as a human being, she injures herself. The sensation of pain and the sight of blood are foreign to her, but rather than being resentful and upset, she expresses *gratitude* for it as the sensation of pain is such a unique experience for her. The fact that we are capable of being present to the pains of humankind and are simultaneously capable of *love* and *compassion* is a phenomenon in itself. That is definitely something we can be grateful for.

> *'Throughout history and around the world, religious leaders and philosophers have extolled the virtue of gratitude. Some have even described gratitude as 'social glue' that fortifies relationships – between friends, family, and romantic partners – and serves as the backbone of human society …'*[126]

According to Summer Allen of Berkeley UC, in the above quote, *gratitude* is considered the 'social glue' that fortifies relationships. It is quite common in most, if not all, cultures that when someone acts politely or makes our lives easier in any way that we are expected to say 'thank you'. While that behaviour is so normalised that it may have lost its significance, people now expressing thanks as a habit or out of courtesy, it is nonetheless a powerful language construct to convey the Meaning of *gratitude*. The same is true when it comes to praying as part of religious or spiritual rituals, whereby we thank the universe,

---

125   *Wings of Desire* (German: *Der Himmel über Berlin*, lit. 'The Heaven/Sky over Berlin') is a 1987 romantic fantasy film and a modern fairy tale about the nature of being alive.

126   *The Science of Gratitude* by Summer Allen, Ph.D, May 2018. Summer Allen is a Research/Writing Fellow with the Greater Good Science Centre. A graduate of Carleton College and Brown University, Summer now writes for a variety of publications including weekly blog posts for the *American Association for the Advancement of Science*.

Existence, God, the ultimate power, etc., for all there is, including the very fact that we are alive or for our relatively high level of autonomy.

Research on *gratitude*

Studies have found that people who are grateful for those in their lives, from business partners, associates and staff to their intimate partner, friends and family members, are more readily able to build relationships that stand the test of time. This is valuable information if you want to build a long-lasting business. If you actively practise being grateful for your employees, you will find an improvement in workplace morale and staff turnover because your staff will feel valued and therefore develop a greater sense of loyalty. According to Dr Martin E. P. Seligman[127], a psychologist at the University of Pennsylvania, managers who regularly thank their team members may find that those employees feel more motivated to work. The research shows mounting evidence that being in a state of *gratitude* has positive effects on the general mood, relationships and capacity to learn within an organisation.

Other studies[128] have analysed the impact of *gratitude* on personal relationships. For example, a research project involving couples found that individuals who took the time to express *gratitude* to their partner developed more positive feelings towards the other person and felt more comfortable expressing concerns about the relationship. While studies such as this one cannot prove cause and effect, they can support an association between *gratitude* and an individual's wellbeing. Similarly, a research study undertaken at George Fox University[129] concluded that the experience of *gratitude* helps people feel more positive emotions, appreciate positive experiences, improve their health, handle adversity more effectively and build strong relationships. One of their analyses was conducted with teachers working in the public and private school

---

127   *In Praise of Gratitude*, Harvard Health Publishing, Harvard Medical School mentioning Dr Martin E. P. Seligman.

128   *The Science of Gratitude* by Summer Allen, Ph.D., May 2018; white paper for the John Templeton Foundation by the Greater Good Science Center at UC Berkeley.

129   *The Power, Structure and Practice of Gratitude in Education: A Demonstration of Epistemology and Empirical Research Working Together* by Jane Wilson and Rob Foster, George Fox University.

sectors. The process consisted of an introductory presentation with a three-week practice period during which the teachers were asked to complete three specific exercises before a final follow-up survey was conducted. The survey questionnaire addressed how they practised *gratitude* and what impact they could observe from that in their life. Almost all teachers who responded to the survey expressed that they were using more language that included references of *gratitude* during the day after completing the recommended exercises. The results of engaging in *gratitude* practices on a consistent basis as part of this study included the following benefits: 84% reported experiencing enhanced wellbeing, 72% reported feeling calmer in stressful situations, 55% reported noticing stronger relationships with students and/or colleagues, 50% reported experiencing a more collaborative spirit, and almost 20% reported heightened cognitive skills.

When you transform your relationship with *gratitude*, you will experience a light-heartedness and sense of happiness and contentment in life that is hard to describe. You will hardly ever complain or take things for granted and you won't have a sense of entitlement or unrealistic expectations of the universe and others because you won't live your life from the standpoint that everyone owes you something. This powerful Aspect of Being enhances your relationship with the hardships that are an unavoidable part of life and enables you to build more effective relationships with others. The same can be said for your team. Having grateful people in your organisation makes a huge difference to workplace morale, employee retention and productivity, which flows on to the organisation's bottom line. That's because grateful people are happy to be of service. Therefore, *gratitude* is definitely a worthwhile Aspect of Being to keep in mind when recruiting new people into your organisation. There will always be those who assume that just because they live and breathe, the universe owes them. Some hide their lack of *gratitude* behind populistic interpretations of justice, equality and human rights. If history can teach us anything it is that a lack of *gratitude* leaves a trail of destruction, death and misery behind. Tapping into *gratitude* will allow you to focus on the *integrity* of individuals. It facilitates better relationships and organisational cultures that stand the test of time and is fundamental to building *resilience* (a Secondary Way of Being).

CHAPTER 14

Higher Purpose

It is our inclination as human beings to have a 'what's in it for me?' attitude in dealing with most things in life. From both an ontological (Reality) and phenomenological (experiential) perspective, we are predominantly self-interested beings. Let's not argue that this is positive or negative, right or wrong. Let's just acknowledge that this is our Reality in terms of how we collectively experience ourselves and one another. However, a healthy level of self-interest can easily slide into an unhealthy obsession with ourselves – to be selfish and put ourselves at the centre of the universe on the assumption that others should serve us and receive nothing or very little in return. It's so easy to want everything for ourselves, while forsaking all others. It is also very easy to fall into the trap of only being present to our own immediate pains and problems, interests, wants and needs while neglecting to look towards the future and longer-term rewards or be present to the pains, problems, interests, wants and needs of others. When we are in this state of Being, we tend to view the world through our own narrative lens and perspective, remaining in the comfort and security of the 'I' quadrant[130]. I freely admit that this Way of Being was the most challenging of all the Primary Ways of Being to name. The best expression I could come up with to adequately describe it was *higher purpose*. However, I urge you not to get stuck in the language and be willing to open your mind and your heart with epistemic humility to see and appreciate *higher purpose* as you read this chapter.

A self-focused state of Being, wanting nothing for others and everything for oneself, has virtually become the norm, particularly in the business world. The 'I win, you lose' attitude may serve you well at a transactional

---

130   Refers to the Perspective Quadrant, as explained in the Awareness chapter.

level, say when closing a single deal, but are you in business to close the occasional deal or are you in the business of building long-term relationships with a view to closing many deals over time and earning the right to be recommended to others? Any experienced salesperson knows that there are costs associated with winning customers (Customer Acquisition Cost or CAC) and maintaining them (account management). They also know that upselling to existing customers whose trust they have earned is much easier than winning new customers. To turn a one-off customer into a long-term client takes patience. It also takes a willingness to let go of short-sightedness, knowing this approach won't work in your favour. So many businesses lose a fortune in revenue and profitability due to a short-sighted focus on the immediate reward. If you care about turning customers into clients and advocates, this self-focused, short-sighted state of Being (low *higher purpose*), with an emphasis on immediate gain, needs to shift into a focus on relationship building and the bigger picture.

Imagine if you commute to work by train and each morning you call into the cafe near the train station to purchase your morning coffee. Despite the fact that you are there every morning, the owner never addresses you by name and doesn't remember that your coffee of choice is a latte with one sugar. That's because the cafe owner is simply focused on selling 'x' number of coffees a day and therefore each customer is regarded as nothing more than a transaction. Now imagine you arrive one Monday morning to find the cafe has been taken over by a new owner. You are greeted warmly, asked for your name and the owner makes a note of the type of coffee you order. Every morning that week, you are welcomed with a smile and a 'Latte with one sugar for you today, John?' confirmation. Over time, the owner introduces new products to the cafe, including a signature blend of roasted coffee and a fresh, healthy breakfast menu. You even start arriving early some days to have breakfast at the cafe because her newly introduced menu options and service are outstanding, and you observe others doing the same. As the business grows, the owner employs staff who clearly share her values and you notice how well the owner treats them. It's clear the new owner sees her customers and staff – collectively and individually – as assets, not transactions and resources. She is intent on building relationships with them over time, and if that means she sells less coffees for the first few months in business than the previous owner did, then so be it. She is there for the long-term and the joy, *love, care, compassion, responsibility* and *commitment,* etc., are indicative of her healthy relationship with *higher purpose*. My point is, how you relate to people – how you choose to **be with** them – both internally (staff) and externally (customers), plays a major role in your accomplishments. When you are working towards a great cause or grand vision, you have to align yourself with others and build relationships if you want to fulfil your objective, whether it be with your staff, customers, venture partners or, more commonly, with all stakeholders to varying degrees.

What is meant by *higher purpose?*

Higher purpose is **not** necessarily linked to a specific objective, goal or dream you may aspire to achieve, although it may be. It is also not necessarily about pursuing the path of altruism and benevolence. *Higher purpose* is about being willing to go beyond your immediate or selfish needs and wants, not just in the moment, but also in the longer-term. *Higher purpose* is about being visionary, being willing and capable of moving forward with *awareness, freedom* and the maturity to predict the future, particularly the consequences of who you are, how you are being, the decisions you make and, ultimately, the actions you take. It is the quality of going beyond oneself and/or going beyond the present time and one's desire for immediate gratification. It is also about being generous and participating in life with an **abundance**, as opposed to a **scarcity**, mindset. For example, wars have erupted over the so-called 'scarcity' of resources, notably water or oil, time and time again in history. If this 'scarcity' was approached with a healthy relationship to *higher purpose*, we would look for more sustainable solutions that would serve all of humanity. Compare the wars over oil resources in parts of the world with the pursuit to generate sustainable energy, such as Elon Musk's approach around electric cars and solar power, and it is clear that the latter is an example of an abundance mindset.

Don't get me wrong, *higher purpose* is not about dropping self-interest altogether. Indeed, as mentioned at the start of this chapter, it is in our nature to be self-interested. Furthermore, the Being Framework approach towards this quality is not to regard it purely as a virtue, as is the case with all Aspects of Being. Remember that the Being Framework standpoint is completely non-judgemental.

There is a relationship between *higher purpose* and gratification, in particular delayed gratification. Many of you may be familiar with the marshmallow experiment, a study on delayed gratification led by Walter Mischel, a psychologist and professor at Stanford University, in 1972. In the experiment, a child was left alone in a room under observation and offered the choice between an immediate small treat (a single marshmallow), or a more substantial treat if they were prepared to leave the marshmallow untouched in anticipation of the larger reward. In follow-up studies, researchers found that children who had the patience and foresight to wait for the more desirable reward and ignored their desire for instant gratification by succumbing to the temptation to eat the marshmallow sitting before them, tended to have better life outcomes based on various measures, from educational to lifestyle and health outcomes. If we consider this in a business context, it's about realising that the benefits of leaving the profits of your year-old company in the bank at the end of the financial year and reinvesting that to grow the company outweigh the benefits of removing the profit from the business as dividends for instant gratification. Instead, it is about looking ahead and realising that by using your profits to grow the team, market your brand, align yourself with the right mentors and coaches to unlock your untapped potential, or whatever it may be for you, the rewards will be exponentially greater down the track.

So, the Meaning that *higher purpose* refers to is twofold. Firstly, it is about being visionary. It's about having the vision to see what lies ahead, to predict the future, making it strongly linked to *awareness* and *freedom*. Secondly, it's about having the willingness, patience, *courage* and foresight to delay rewards or gratification and take the associated risk, to go beyond your immediate interests, needs, wants and temptations for the purpose of achieving something more worthwhile and meaningful that brings far greater and broader-reaching rewards. As you can see, *higher purpose* is a quality that is closely associated with how you relate to patience. Furthermore, because *higher purpose* is a Way of Being that is directed beyond oneself, it can move you to counter the shadow aspect of other Ways of Being.

The Being Framework ontological distinction of *higher purpose*

Higher purpose is being drawn and compelled towards a future vision or cause greater than your personal concerns and beyond your immediate interests and/or comfort in such a way that it sets your priorities and worldview. It's going beyond yourself and your time without expecting immediate gratification to identify resolutions that will drive you towards that future vision. *Higher purpose* is considered the source of the inspiration and charisma required to effectively influence, inspire and develop others as leaders.

A healthy relationship with *higher purpose* indicates that you draw yourself forward to fulfilling challenges you wouldn't normally take on. You are resolute, willing to delay gratification and have the fortitude to go beyond your own discomfort and self-concern to fulfil your future vision. Others may consider you a charismatic leader who is visionary and committed to something meaningful and worthwhile.

An unhealthy relationship with *higher purpose* indicates that you may be shortsighted, narrow-minded, self-centric or selfish. You are mostly driven to fulfil immediate personal concerns and ambitions. You may be limited and constrained by your personal goals and desire for instant gratification while being oblivious to or ignoring the needs and wants of others. Others may frequently challenge and question your motives as a leader and may not experience inspirational leadership from you. Unable to zoom out and see the bigger picture, you may often get stuck in the present with a fragmented narration of the past and future. Alternatively, you may detach yourself and zoom out too much, being so captivated by and engrossed in your long-term vision that smaller, short-term progression seems insignificant to you. This may lead you to lose sight of and fail to appropriately address more immediate obstacles and barriers.

Discovering *higher purpose*

As much as we are self-interested beings by nature, we also have a fundamental desire and primal need to be part of something greater and beyond ourselves. It is the reason many people are attracted to religion, spirituality, philanthropy, medicine, science or a movement, to name just a few. For example, *higher purpose* is the dominant state of Being that drove mankind to discover treatments for once-fatal diseases. However, for most people, finding or identifying the object of their *higher purpose* – a cause greater than themselves – in life may not be so obvious or easy to do. When you have a healthy relationship with *higher purpose* as a Way of Being, it leads you to tap into your calling, something you are passionate about, and you would feel drawn like a magnet to aligning yourself with that cause.

When an authoritative and influential figure within a movement, church, school of thinking, etc., communicates a message in a way that resonates deeply with you, it may persuade you to choose to ignore your immediate desires and dedicate a portion of your time and attention to that cause. Those who have a healthy relationship with the *higher purpose* Way of Being, would either identify with or subscribe to a cause greater than themselves. They may even initiate a cause themselves and persuade others to align with them. Again, I am not here to argue that this is good or bad. History tells us of the dangers in aligning oneself with an inauthentic movement like a cult that manipulates others for malevolent purposes. As is the case with all Aspects of Being, there is a shadow side to *higher purpose* to be aware of too.

Higher purpose can start small. Have you ever noticed the glow in a child's eyes when they are taking care of a pet? Just by nurturing an animal or a plant as a child, knowing that the survival of that being depends on them, teaches the child *responsibility* and sows the seeds for *higher purpose*. It's about something bigger than they are and that requires them to care and be committed. It provides a source for passion and inspiration later in life. Subscribing to *higher purpose* also acknowledges that we are not alone in life. We are social creatures and are part of a whole; for any big cause we need others, and we need to rely on other people's resources. We need to become aligned and work together as a team, where being a contribution leads to a state of Being committed to a cause that is greater than oneself.

Zooming out to see the big picture

In the midst of all the confusion of the postmodern era, it's easy to become stuck in our 'filter bubbles'. For instance, when we conduct an online search, the search engine generates personalised content based on our previous online habits and digital profiles to entice us to click on certain content. Furthermore, the fact that most of us pay attention to the mainstream media in our country leads us to be fed the common dominant narrative and to form biased opinions because we are ignorant to the other sides of the story. It's also why most of us follow dominant trends in fashion, societal and political views, art, entertainment, relationships, and so on.

The business world is no exception. We can easily get bogged down by everyday issues, unable to see the forest for the trees. I observe this sometimes with my software development teams. When a piece of software enters the testing phase, it signals the start of a lengthy process of troubleshooting, problem resolution and functionality refinements for the team. This process can go on for weeks. During this time, the team can lose sight of the bigger picture, causing them to become frustrated about the tedious nature of the tasks they must perform during this important phase. They forget the fact that it is not just about the technology itself and that they are only a small part of the big picture. There are a series of events that must be carefully executed, from marketing campaigns to rollout plans and managing existing user expectations. This is the time when, as leaders, we should step in and remind our team of the amazing results they have achieved so far and the incredible opportunities the product will provide for the client. It can help them to push the pause button and zoom out to see and reiterate the big picture, so they know where and how their contribution fits into that picture. To be engaged and truly committed, your team members need to understand their contribution to something that is greater than themselves, a *higher purpose* that will revive their inspiration and passion for their jobs. When working on a project with *higher purpose*, individuals appreciate that the project is bigger than each one of them alone and are therefore able to put their personal needs and views aside and not take anything personally.

Being able to see the big picture is critical, particularly for individuals and teams that are contributing to a major cause. They must have the ability to zoom out from time to time and gain a simple helicopter view from the Global Perspective[131], or view it more deeply from the Leader Perspective to see matters holistically. This is only possible when there is a healthy relationship with the *higher purpose* Way of Being. Sometimes shifting your own attention to bigger problems when you are dealing with a smaller one can put the problem at hand, no matter how challenging, into the appropriate perspective and prevent you from becoming overwhelmed. Gaining *awareness* around the fact that whatever is happening is not the worst thing that could possibly happen can really help. If you find that you or your staff are overly focused on the details, never taking the time to zoom out to view matters from a higher perspective, you will likely discover that problems occur more frequently and take longer to resolve.

My father is a chef, so I have witnessed first hand how hectic things can get in a commercial kitchen. Imagine if you spend a day in the shoes of a professional head chef and are tasked with managing the preparation and plating of meals for the restaurant's paying guests. However, you decide to take on the job of preparing the steaks yourself, cooked to order and perfection, because you are happiest in the kitchen when you can focus on your passion rather than leading the team. So, you delegate the preparation of sauces and vegetables to other chefs on your team. Now imagine if one of the chefs ruins the restaurant's signature and most popular sauce. It may cause you so much stress and angst that you lose focus and overcook some of the steaks. While a specialist or technician should be laser-focused most of the time, that is generally an undesirable approach to adopt as a leader. This is where *higher purpose* comes to the rescue. It would have been far more effective, as head chef, to put aside your immediate desire to be involved in the cooking and oversee and guide the team instead, delegating the various cooking

---

[131] In the Awareness chapter, we discussed the Perspective Quadrant. The Global Perspective quadrant represents a simple helicopter view of a situation, while the Leader Perspective is the most comprehensive, holistic view of a situation.

tasks to your team members. Hopefully, you can see that this example demonstrates the fact that I am not approaching *higher purpose* as purely a virtue. The approach in the Being Framework to this Way of Being (and others) is practical and intrinsically tied to human Reality and experience in line with an ontological and phenomenological approach. To reiterate, I am not dealing with Aspects of Being as nothing more than intellectual concepts. I am portraying them with both objectivity and exactness, such as they are in living life.

So, if you find yourself struggling with a problem, a way of overcoming this is to find a bigger problem to solve. I know that may sound illogical, but it's what true leaders do. They continually choose bigger problems to solve. If you have kids, you have probably asked yourself many times, 'What did I do with my time before I had kids?' When you take on the role of business leader, you may ask yourself a similar question. All of a sudden, you need to deal with a whole new set of challenges, and it's easy to become bogged down in each one. However, once a bigger matter or priority demands your attention, you will find ways and resources to deal with the other issue that was previously taking all your focus.

As an entrepreneur and a business leader, it no longer works to focus wholly and solely on your favourite aspect of the business. While marketing may be your thing, you cannot ignore your legal obligations, the people side of the business, the finances and the supply chain, and so on. While you may not be an expert in all those functions – and let's be honest, it would be virtually impossible to master them all – you would nonetheless be required to make important decisions relating to all those matters. You're also not always going to have the time to analyse matters with full precision and make carefully considered, data-driven decisions. Tapping into your intuition and zooming out to view the big picture in order to make decisions and take appropriate action are par for the course when you are a leader or entrepreneur. There are times when losing time over making precise, accurate decisions would create more damage than taking a risk and responding quickly. I have found that this is where many SMEs or startup leaders get stuck. They spend so much time and effort working **in** their business rather than **on** their business that they aren't building and developing it. By focusing on the quality of *higher purpose*, which they are struggling with, we support them to shift from being an employee or technician within their own company to being a leader who can create clarity around projects, delegate effectively and hold others to account. Obviously, it is far beyond the scope of this book to go through the whole process, but the point here is to depict a clear picture of why the quality of *higher purpose* is so crucial in the business world.

The paradoxical relationship between stubbornness, surrender and *persistence*

A combination of *awareness, courage, freedom* and, particularly, *higher purpose*, will steer a leader away from being obsessed with immediate results. You may read this and question it because being results-oriented is broadly considered a virtue in the business world. However, when you choose your path with conviction, *higher purpose* and *persistence*, being overly obsessed with immediate results will distract you from freely letting your passion, talents and creativity flow. Obsession can ruin, or at least limit, the joy of entrepreneurship. If you observe the patterns of many high achievers, you will discover that they surrender from the start to the fact that success is not an inevitability and that they may not always end up where they wanted to. They understand that fulfilment is beyond a single iteration, hence they refuse to give up in the face of their first obstacle, failure or breakdown. In other words, they surrender to the fact that they may fail. This accurate and congruent conception of Reality leads them to have a healthy relationship with *persistence* as a Way of Being that gives them the tenacity to go beyond the norm and produce extraordinary results. They took an enormous risk and went all in, thinking, 'Either I will make it or I won't and I am happy to have tried and to keep trying', even if it doesn't lead to the intended result. That is why an entrepreneur is often happy to work on a product or service offering for years without getting paid or seeing immediate results.

As mentioned earlier in the book, most people want to be paid for their time. In the past, people used to have a more congruent conception of this Reality. Farmers knew it would take time for their crops to grow and flourish after preparing the soil and sowing the seeds. They were also aware of the fact that they would be faced with periods of dry conditions and that drought, flood, vermin, etc., could threaten their livelihood at any time. And yet they took a leap of faith and stepped forward. No one expected success 100% of the time in those days. According to Amazon founder and CEO Jeff Bezos, the vast majority of people choose the pathway of ease and comfort over adventure, challenge and service. However, true entrepreneurs choose the less comfortable path. Why am I raising this point? Because having a healthy relationship with *higher purpose* is key here as there is a significant difference between giving up and surrender. Warlords in historic times would literally risk their lives to lead their armies and were surrendered to the fact that they could die in the course of the battle. Where did this *courage* come from? It was the result of making their peace with the Reality that they could die, and this was due to their relationship with both *courage* and *higher purpose*. They surrendered to that fact and stepped forward.

Many people think stubbornness and insistence are key to success. We hear some so-called 'business gurus' espousing the benefits of never giving up. The truth is, if you keep doing the same thing over and over again and it doesn't serve you well, then it makes no difference how determined you are, it most likely isn't going to work. We work with many entrepreneurs who spend years insisting with dogged determination that they should push on with their idea without changing anything, even when it clearly isn't effective in its current form. They continue to go through the same patterns over and over again, like a recursive loop without any change in the outcome. Stubbornly holding on to something is different from being persistent while being open (*vulnerability*) to learning and refining your business concept until it hits the mark. We will discuss this further in the Persistence chapter within *Section 4: Secondary Ways of Being*. This vision and discernment around when to continue or when to stop is partly the result of a healthy relationship with *higher purpose*. It supports you to zoom out and not get stuck in the granularity of the matter at hand, while maintaining clarity of the bigger picture in pursuit of your major objective.

If you want to be wealthy, choose the pathway of serving others

Whenever I ask first time entrepreneurs and business owners why they chose to be business owners, many (not all) tell me they want to make more money than they could as an employee and that their number one objective is to accumulate wealth. Those who respond in this way are so obsessed with their desire for monetary wealth that they forget that the most effective way of making money is not to focus on making money! If this doesn't make sense in your current paradigm, bear with me, as this is precisely why so many fail and there are so few thriving businesses and extremely wealthy people in the world. You see, the key is to focus on **giving**. This totally contradicts the mainstream view of rich people, which is that they are arrogant, selfish, uncaring and greedy. Choose the pathway of serving others through your unique offering so that it is so appealing to a large group of other human beings – let's call it the market – that they willingly choose to exchange their hard-earned money for your offering. That is how you will become wealthy. How do you think the *Fortune* 500 companies created their wealth? Companies like Amazon, AWS, Microsoft, Apple, etc., all offer products, commodities and services that large groups of consumers value so much that they are willing to exchange money for them. Obviously, it's not as simple as that, but I'm sure you get my point. *Higher purpose* (specifically, a lack thereof) is one of the Ways of Being that we found gets in the way of people achieving what they want in life, especially business leaders. I cannot emphasise strongly enough how important it is to make the shift from focusing on the **getting** to the **giving**.

Let's zoom out and away from business for a moment to consider another example we can all relate to – the pursuit of love. Most people actively seek what is commonly referred to as 'love' in life. But when you dig deeper, you realise that, in their quest for love, many are focusing on the wrong things. They are focusing on what the other person can give them for their own personal benefit. In other words, they are looking for a lover, not the deeper quality of *love*. Ironically, that selfishness will never bring them the very quality they so desire. To experience *love* requires us to shift our relationship with – yes, you guessed it – *higher purpose*. To experience *love* demands that we let go of being caught up in ourselves and focus on the other person instead. Aside from our studies, I learnt this lesson from personal experience and, let me tell you, I was miserable at that time in my life due to my unhealthy relationship with *higher purpose*, as I was pursuing something that wasn't leading to my fulfilment. We will explore this further in the Love chapter, which has far more to do with leadership and *effectiveness* than you may think.

Many people feel pressured to have a 'perfect' life and show the world how well they are doing, instead of pursuing their deep-felt values and passions. The magic lies in the fact that when you choose to give up on your obsession and go beyond yourself, you will be more likely to achieve what you want in life. This is a rule of Existence. It is the polar opposite of the notion that it's all about you and your efforts, as some so-called 'rich' individuals would have us believe on their social media feeds. You will never see true leaders sell 'success' in this way. In a similar manner, if you don't care about your partner, business associate or friend and don't give the relationship time, effort and dedication, that relationship will perish like a garden of roses that isn't watered and fed. When we are up to something bigger than ourselves, we need to develop the ability to give up on what we immediately want in order for us to hit our bigger objectives down the track. Once you stop getting bogged down in the small tasks and problems and stop being lured by your immediate selfish desires, you will free your mind to think outside the box, to be creative and come up with new ways to tackle problems that are an inevitable part of owning a business. You will rejoice in your ability to vividly predict the consequences of **how you are being** and your actions, and this will lead you to be more proactive and less reactive. This will be discussed in the Proactivity chapter within *Section 4: Secondary Ways of Being*.

To sum up this chapter, most of us search for meaning in life, but *higher purpose* is not necessarily a goal, desire or a benevolent and altruistic cause you subscribe to in life to feel good. In this framework, *higher purpose* refers to a quality viewed in the context of seeing oneself as a part of a common being, a unity of all there is. It is a Way of Being that goes beyond personal concerns, objectives and immediate gratification in that it focuses on the sacrifices and effort needed to achieve long-term rewards as a contribution towards a greater purpose, where the individual is not at the centre. While *higher purpose* can also provide meaning, it is not first and foremost about creating meaning in your life. When you train yourself to transform and maintain the *higher purpose* Way of Being, you will find it will serve you faithfully and well in every aspect of your life.

CHAPTER 15

Empowerment

'I can't' is a phrase I hear often from clients in coaching and consulting sessions or when interacting with people in general. It's as though they see the possibilities, but choose not to pursue them because they are not empowered to do so. For example, one may say, 'I know it is possible to build a business and follow my passion, but I do not believe I **can**, so I am going to keep doing the job I dislike'. Life is full of challenges. We have to keep overcoming them as much as we can if we are up to any great cause, including our own survival. I acknowledge that our level of intelligence, upbringing, personal experiences, education, circumstances, etc., influence our *awareness*, knowledge, narrative lens, web of perceptions and current competencies, and this flows on to the extent that we may think we can or cannot do something. However, the universe doesn't discriminate. It doesn't care how well you were raised or if you aren't as intellectually gifted as the next person. When it comes to becoming 'x', or doing 'y', *empowerment* reflects your ability to act powerfully to fulfil your intentions, regardless. You are about to discover that the words 'I can' are vital to *empowerment* as a Way of Being.

Empowerment is a Way of Being we often refer to in my organisation and associated branding. It is no coincidence that the word 'power' (in relation to *empowerment*) forms part of the subtitle of this book: *BEING: The Source of Power*. However, the word 'power' sometimes has a negative connotation associated with it, morphing into a meaning of control or manipulation and commonly referred to in terms of those who hold, exert – and sometimes abuse – authority. However, that is not the Meaning of power being conveyed here in the context of the Being Framework. I am using the word in its literal form, as defined in the *Oxford English Dictionary* as 'the ability or capacity to do something or act in a particular way' and 'the capacity or ability to direct or influence the behaviour of others or the course of events'. In fact, the origin of the word 'power' is derived from an alteration of the Latin word *Posse*, which means 'to be able'. We all know power can be misused. The abuse of power is not foreign to most of us, whether we experience or observe it close to home or from a global perspective. But power in its original Meaning is neither good nor bad and is as essential to us as the air we breathe. It is what we do with it that counts, as we all have the choice, given our relatively high level of autonomy (*responsibility*), to use power in a constructive or destructive way.

What is *empowerment?*

Like other Aspects of Being, *empowerment* is defined quite differently depending on where you look. For example, in the *Oxford English Dictionary*, the word 'empowerment' is defined as 'giving (someone) the authority or power to do something', whereas the *Cambridge Dictionary* defines it as 'the process of gaining freedom and power (ability) to do what you want or to control what happens to you'. In the BEING Framework, *empowerment* is the opposite of oppression, being stuck or disarmed, a situation in which power is taken away. A world filled with totally disempowered people would be a sad, oppressive and dangerous world in which to live. You may think this seems like an exaggeration, but without a sense of *empowerment*, we would not be able to do anything, even the things we take for granted and do without thinking twice. We wouldn't be able to get out of bed or drive a car. We would not be able to negotiate a contract, execute marketing campaigns or mentor and lead others, without a sense that we can do it. According to the author of *Adolescents at Risk*[132], '*empowerment* may be seen as a process where individuals learn to see a closer correspondence between their goals and a sense of how to achieve them, as well as a relationship between their efforts and life outcomes'. Everything we do or don't do relates back to how powerful we perceive ourselves to be in life. *Empowerment* is real. It is a force that can be unstoppable when unleashed. For example, we will only put our hand up for a new opportunity or start a new venture if we feel empowered enough to do so, even if there are seeds of doubt in our mind.

---

132   D. Mechanic: *Adolescents at Risk*: New directions paper presented at Cornell University Medical College in 1999.

In order to be effective in your endeavours, you need to be empowered to achieve your objectives and/or those of the organisation. Indeed, *empowerment* is at the core of *effectiveness*. Sounds simple enough, but what exactly is *empowerment*? And how do we achieve this? In his scholarly paper, *Terms of Empowerment/Exemplars of Prevention: Toward a Theory for Community Psychology*[133], Julian Rappaport claims that *empowerment* is easier to define by its absence than its presence. He describes its absence as 'real or perceived helplessness, loss of feeling control over one's life'. When we are not empowered, we experience a strong sense of being stuck and unable to set things in motion in areas we want to progress. When you develop a healthy relationship with *empowerment*, you can lift yourself from the quagmire of helplessness, and this is where you can take action towards fulfilling your intentions.

---

[133] Julian Rappaport: 'Terms of Empowerment/Exemplars of Prevention: Toward a Theory for Community Psychology' published in the *American Journal of Community Psychology*, 15, 121-148 - 1987.

The Being Framework ontological distinction of *empowerment*

Empowerment is living life from the viewpoint of being able to fulfil your intentions while enabling and inspiring others to fulfil theirs. *Empowerment* is how you relate to your power, capabilities and real or perceived limitations.

A healthy relationship with *empowerment* indicates that you mostly experience being able to take powerful actions towards fulfilling your intentions, purpose and goals while encouraging and inspiring others to fulfil theirs. Others may experience you as someone who takes actions that produce meaningful results in many areas of life and you may inspire them to follow you as your actions also make a significant difference to them.

An unhealthy relationship with *empowerment* indicates that you mostly experience being ineffective or stuck. You may often be unable to act towards fulfilling what matters to you or look beyond the immediate obstacles. You may feel frustration, apathy, resignation or despair. Others may experience you as inconsistent, ineffective, lacking drive or energy and hard work. Alternatively, you may often overestimate your capabilities while acting superior, oblivious to the limitations at hand.

Empowerment and its relationship to other Ways of Being

Empowerment is closely linked to many other Ways of Being, so let me share a story with you to explain this relationship. A friend of mine was once robbed while walking to his car after an evening out with friends. He felt disempowered at the time to prevent the theft from happening. Thinking about it afterwards and admitting he was a victim at the hands of the thieves, my friend realised he needed to learn to protect himself in case he was ever threatened again. This *awareness* led him to choose powerfully as an active agent – with authority and autonomy (*responsibility*) – to exercise his *freedom* to enrol in a martial arts course in order to build his competency and *confidence* and learn how to protect himself. The more he practised martial arts, the more he knew that if he were ever confronted again, he would have the *courage* to step forward despite his *fear*. His initial *awareness* led to a journey of transformation which ultimately gave him a sense of *empowerment*.

If you are not empowered, it is as though your feet are stuck to the ground, causing you to be unable to act. This is where your relationship with *empowerment* comes into play and influences your actions, hence the results you produce. While being powerful is the state in which you are effective in your endeavours, in the context of this framework, being **empowered** is a part of the whole process, which is why it is considered to be a Primary Way of Being. To be fulfilled we need to be powerful and effective, and to be effective we need to be integrous. Here is the key: *empowerment* contributes to our *integrity* because it is here where we start to question whether or not we can be, do or achieve something. As with any other Aspect of Being, it is our relationship with *empowerment* that counts more than its presence or absence.

Empowerment is commonly manifested in some of our Secondary Ways of Being, such as *confidence*. If we are empowered (stepping forward because we feel we **can** do something), we typically come across as being confident. Think about the first time you drove a car or secured your first job. These experiences can often be preceded by a sense of doubt or insecurity. Once overcome, those insecurities are replaced with a sense of *empowerment* which shows up as *confidence* on the surface. A critical point to note here is that *empowerment* is a prerequisite to *confidence*.

Unless we are empowered, we won't dare to execute. With practice comes competency, which in turn leads to *confidence*.

Empowerment is double-sided

When you have a healthy relationship with *empowerment*, not only is it important to you to empower yourself and others, but just as importantly, you are also willing to let others empower you. Many leaders are empowered within themselves and also competent in empowering others. But when it comes to letting others empower them, they have their guard up, indicating an unhealthy *vulnerability-empowerment* relationship. This is partly because they think letting others empower them is a sign of weakness and could damage their 'leader persona'. Ironically, that in itself disempowers them, as they may not be able to appropriately leverage the power of others in pursuit of their or their organisation's objectives. This lack of *vulnerability* is one of the reasons many people in a position of power refuse to have consultants, mentors or coaches guide, advise, coach and empower them. Remember, we are social creatures and, as a leader, if you are working towards a big cause, you cannot effectively do it alone. Nobody is perfect, not even the world's top leaders. We can all benefit from aligning ourselves with others who possess skills and qualities in areas we don't, or in which we are lacking, and allow ourselves to be empowered by them. However, too many leaders won't let their guard down long enough to admit they need support, and they try to do everything themselves. In my experience, this is the case for the majority of SME and startup CEOs, who I often light-heartedly refer to as 'Chief Everything Officers'. Pull them out of the game, even for a short period, and the business suffers immensely, sometimes to the point of collapse because they have made themselves indispensable.

It is a myth that a leader must be a master of everything. This approach is completely unsustainable, and I can say this with complete confidence, having studied a considerable number of the world's *Fortune 500* companies for this framework. I can assure you that I have not seen a single top performing company in the world that operates under the leadership of a CEO with this mindset. As leaders, they know how vital it is to be empowered so that they may empower others and that in turn, by empowering others, they will subsequently fulfil their vision. In fact, building a sustainable business is only achieved through developing and empowering people, yourself included, because when we develop and empower our people, then – and only then – will our people build the business. I am a huge advocate of leaders who have the vision and foresight to not only hire the right coaches to empower them, but who also learn to gradually become coaches themselves. The rewards gained through the transformation of the Aspects of Being of their people, themselves and subsequently their business are beyond amazing. This was a major driver for me to focus on empowering others, hence the reason I have devoted so much time and energy on developing frameworks, programs, tools and writing books.

Empowerment can also be nurtured and amplified by putting yourself in the right environment and in association with other empowered people. For example, if you are working for a company that advocates and delivers excessive pressure and negative criticism, over time exposure to this behaviour will chip away at your sense of *empowerment* and could manifest itself as a lack of *confidence*. It is important to surround yourself with, or have access to, people who have an uplifting, empowering effect on you, both in professional and social environments. As a leader, you are responsible for creating and maintaining this network of support, as we will discuss further in the Contribution chapter.

The ramifications of being disempowered

People typically come across as inauthentic when they are disempowered – and not fully competent – in terms of their role in society or the organisation they work for or lead. Imagine knowing you are an incompetent engineer, but you are desperate to be seen by others as competent. This may lead you to be inauthentic, pretend to be competent, filter information, lie and potentially pose a risk to others. An empowered person is vulnerable enough to acknowledge their inauthenticity and seek support when they are less than competent in any area. Effective individuals understand it is their *responsibility* to do their utmost, with conviction, *persistence, commitment, courage* and *freedom* to become authentically competent, proficient and empowered. When someone is disempowered, however, they may be crushed by any of the shadow parts of *vulnerability, fear, care* and *anxiety,* causing them to become stuck, frozen or jammed. This may lead to their *integrity* being so significantly impacted that they not only lose their ease and flow as the cogs in the machine are jammed, but they may also be led to shy away from others, suppress or sabotage themselves. Their disempowerment may even lead to self-destructive behaviour.

An unhealthy relationship with *empowerment* as a Way of Being is also a root cause of some of the malevolent forces in the world. An unhealthy relationship with all or any of the four Moods: *fear, anxiety, vulnerability* and *care,* ultimately leaves many with a sense of insecurity, desperation and disempowerment, causing them to slip away from *integrity* or wholeness, as highlighted in the previous paragraph. If someone truly believes they will never earn enough money to purchase an item they feel they can't live without, they may choose to take it unlawfully. When someone feels so disempowered that they see no possibility to change or influence their painful circumstances, they feel stuck and, in extreme cases, they may dissociate or remove themselves from existence altogether. A completely disempowered person can see no hope and is therefore a liability and a danger to themselves and others.

If someone has an unhealthy relationship with *empowerment* and, more specifically, the self-esteem and *freedom* to say, 'I can', they may resort to manipulation or control. For example, an individual who has an extremely unhealthy relationship with *empowerment* to the point where they are desperate, may say or do anything in order to get or keep a job. They may hide their intentions, exaggerate their level of competency or lie about previous experience (lack of *authenticity*). Imagine the damage that employing someone like this would have on your business and team. Furthermore, it doesn't resolve their disempowerment.

Lack of *empowerment* may lead to thoughts of: 'If I have enough money, then I will be able to do certain things', or, 'If I am associated with an influential person, then I will have more power to pursue my goals'. But neither of these examples leads to *empowerment*. They lead to dependencies and, in the long run, cause suffering, which ironically is the polar opposite of being empowered.

In summary, true *empowerment* comes from within. It stems from maintaining a healthy relationship with your Moods, self-image, persona and the conviction that you have the *freedom* and autonomy *(responsibility)* to choose to do something, leading to the appropriate action(s). *Empowerment* is considered a Way of Being required for developing mastery and influence over the outcomes in your life. Therefore, it is a Way of Being required by any leader, person of influence, high achiever and high performing team/organisation to fulfil their vision.

CHAPTER 16

Presence

Early one cold morning in January 2007, a man, dressed casually in jeans and a baseball cap, rocked up to a Metro station in Washington DC and began to busk on his violin. He played for a full forty-five minutes, expertly performing six exquisitely beautiful classical masterpieces, including one of the most intricate pieces ever written. Being rush hour, the station was packed with commuters. Yet very few stopped long enough to appreciate the music. In fact, of the 1,097 commuters who walked past the busker that morning, only twenty placed money in his violin case and seven took the time to stay and actually listen. The busker earned a grand total of $32 that morning, $20 of which came from one person. When he finished playing, there was no applause, only silence. Not a soul recognised the violinist. On the flipside, the story went viral, drawing attention to people's attitudes towards buskers and how they're often ignored. Why did this story gain so much attention? Because the busker was Grammy Award-winning violinist, Joshua Bell[134], a musician many would pay a fortune to see in concert and who can command a huge sum of money for each concert performance on the greatest concert stages in the world. His busking that morning was part of a *Washington Post* social experiment on how much (or little) people pay attention. When we are not present or connected to what is happening around us it costs us dearly. Your future life partner could literally pass you by and you would be oblivious to their presence. An incredible business opportunity could land in your inbox and you would neglect to read it. Your unwillingness to be fully and intentionally in communication and connected, which is what is meant by *presence* in this context, would blind you to so many possibilities in life.

---

134 Joshua David Bell is an American violinist and conductor. He plays the Gibson Stradivarius.

From the Bell example, you would appreciate that *presence* is more than simply your ability to listen and converse with others verbally and in writing, which is what comes to most people's minds when they think of this word. *Presence* is about consciously **being with** or being intentionally and fully present to yourself, others and your surroundings. While the Reality of being human means it is technically impossible to be present to everything all the time, the universe does not care about this fact. It will make you pay every time you aren't aware and present, whether or not it is intentional or unavoidable. How well you leverage your *responsibility* to direct your attention to the matters that are most important and relevant to you and your objectives is what counts, and that's entirely up to you. You own that *responsibility*. It may seem like a cliché, but we are all connected, and there is good reason for that, after all, the branches of a tree are of the same root. Drawing your *awareness* and being present to this fact will make a huge difference in your life. While the *awareness* Meta Factor is quite broad and applies to our intentional consciousness (*awareness*) towards people (including ourselves) and matters happening within and all around us, the *presence* Way of Being has a narrower and more tangible scope. It is focused on being present to and connected with others, including ourselves.

A Reality check on *presence*

When you read a book, are you willing to allow yourself to be open enough to connect with the author in order to tap into what they are really saying? Or do you skim the pages and make assumptions on what the author means based on your preconceived ideas and beliefs? If you have a healthy relationship with *presence* as a Way of Being, the former would be true. However, if you are stuck in your current perceptions, opting not to zoom out with *higher purpose* and be present to other perspectives and narratives, or if you constantly judge while hearing people speak, rather than intentionally listening to them, it may cloud your *awareness* as to what they are actually saying. One of this book's primary objectives is to encourage you to zoom in and become aware of the Reality of human beings, including yourself. That isn't possible unless you are present and engaged. Often the place to start is to clear your mind of all the distracting clutter in order to provide space for new information to filter through. This is often referred to by ontological coaches as 'clearing' and as 'garbage collection'[135] in computer programming (more on this in the Peace of Mind chapter).

In *Being and Time*, Heidegger addresses a seemingly simple question: what does it mean to be? As well as talking about *Dasein* (being-there), as discussed earlier in the book, he also explained the term, *Mitsein*, which literally means 'being-with'. Being-with refers to an ontological characteristic of human beings, that we are always **being with** others of our kind. From a phenomenological perspective, Heidegger said this characteristic is essential to being human.[136] *Mitsein* is closely linked to *authenticity*. For example, we are inauthentic when we fail to recognise how much and in what ways our social surroundings (how we are **being with** other beings) influence what we think of ourselves and how we habitually behave. But we are authentic when we pay attention to that influence and decide for ourselves whether or not to go along with it and respond to it appropriately (*responsibility*) in such a way that it contributes to the integrity of our lives. Living entirely without such influence is not an option as we are all part of Existence (known as 'Common Being'). Common Being – also referred to as the 'unity of beings' – as metaphorically depicted in the Simorgh story in Part 1, refers to all human beings. **Being with**, in the context of this book, is the state of willingly being aware, present to and connected with others. If you are a leader and working towards big causes, it is virtually impossible to do so on your own. You need to align all relevant parties – family, your community, teams, business partners, movements, organisations, and so on – with your vision and objectives if you wish to be effective in your endeavours and lead a fulfilling life, and this requires you to have a healthy relationship with *presence*.

For the Being Framework, I have adopted Heidegger's view and interpretation of communication as 'giving information and sharing experiences with another person' and '**being with** another person', that is a co-state of Being (German: *Mitbefindlichkeit*) and co-understanding (German:

---

135 In computer science, garbage collection is a form of automatic memory management. The garbage collector, or just collector, attempts to reclaim garbage, or memory occupied by objects that are no longer in use by the program.

136 Heidegger 1962, p. 156, H.125.

Mitverstehen). I refer to this as *presence*. For example, true intimacy is only possible when we have a healthy relationship with *presence* and are fully present and connected to another person, with nothing hidden or in the way. As soon as you find yourself withholding *presence*, as in resisting **being with** someone, ask yourself why? Specifically, why and what are you resisting?

The Being Framework ontological distinction of *presence*

Presence is being so intentionally related to matters and others that you give them your undivided attention and care. It is the authentic relatedness that occurs when all parties experience being fully heard and understood. There is no distance or barrier between you and mutual understanding is fully available.

A healthy relationship with *presence* indicates that you mostly experience being connected, related to, understood and appreciated by others. Others may experience you as open and available to interact and collaborate. You remain in full communication with others with little or no distractions. You may often discern the emotions of others, regardless of what they articulate, and may clearly and accurately sense and interpret their moods. You can also bring your attention and care towards any particular matter you choose to direct your focus to.

An unhealthy relationship with *presence* indicates that you mostly experience being closed, distant and disconnected from others. Others may experience you as quiet, removed or shy and may not understand you well. They may also experience you as hurried, disinterested, distracted and unavailable for interaction and collaboration. You may often experience being misunderstood or not heard while also misinterpreting others' emotions or moods. Alternatively, you may be infatuated or besotted with others and lack discretion or discernment around them.

Working with a broad range of people over the years, from business owners to employees, I have found that an unhealthy relationship with *presence* is a common denominator when it comes to their levels of frustration. However, the perception most of my clients have of *presence* and what it really means in relation to communication is not always aligned. When my clients refer to 'communication', they are usually referring to speaking and listening skills. The truth is, you could be an extremely articulate person, yet not be fully present to the person or people you are communicating with. That's because many people have a tendency to predominantly deal with the conversation going on in their own heads rather than focusing on (being present to) what the other person is saying, a behavioural pattern that stems from their relationship with *presence* as a Way of Being. This behavioural pattern is quite common amongst human beings. When I refer to *presence* and being in communication, I am not referring to those kinds of communication skills as they are behavioural aspects of *presence* as opposed to a Way of Being. I am referring to the state of **being present** and **in communication with** another person with the intention of fully understanding what they have to communicate, being truly connected with them. This is also supported by the etymological source of the word 'communication', as it comes from the Latin *Communicat*, which means 'shared'. True communication is a far more compassionate, humane, genuine and caring approach because it means you are literally choosing to be in communion with someone, to **be with** them (*Mitsein*). It is also worthwhile to know that the word presence comes from the Latin *Praesentia*, which translates to 'being at hand', or in other words, 'being available'. As human beings, we are all capable, at least to a degree, of being present/in communication from the moment we are born. However, being capable is one thing, realising and fulfilling our potential is another. It is a quality to be developed from early childhood, at first with our parents, and continued throughout our lives if we are to master it.

The ramifications of not being present and withholding communication

There are significant ramifications associated with not being present/in communication with someone as a means to manipulate results. For example, if you are dealing with clients and desire a particular outcome, such as a sale or – tapping into *higher purpose* – a longer-term relationship for many more sales in the future, you will need to understand them. You need to learn about their challenges, priorities and needs, what they value and how they prefer to be heard and communicated with. If you don't take the time and effort to build rapport with your clients by connecting openly and honestly with them and taking steps to learn more about them, you will find it difficult to gain their attention, let alone influence them to buy your offerings. This not only applies if your business is service oriented, but also if you operate a product-based business. Before building any new product, you should create an avatar of your target market in order to deeply understand them as a group through market research, user experience and other disciplines. This is one of the most effective ways to create a product that will resonate with them and therefore encourage them to be more inclined to exchange money for it. As you can see, *presence* as a Way of Being is extremely important in business, just as it is in all aspects of life when dealing with others.

Many self-proclaimed entrepreneurs come to us with a new product they have built. On the one hand, they claim that it's the best thing since sliced bread, but on the other hand, they tell us they are struggling to win their first customer and want our help to solve that dilemma. They believe the solution to their problem is to raise funds for marketing. But they have already missed the boat by developing a product they love without getting the end users involved from the get-go to ensure they build a product the market will love too. There is a high level of arrogance and ignorance associated with this approach.

When someone builds a product without involvement from the end user, they run the very real risk that no one will be as excited as they are about their offering. Then, when it becomes clear that the market is not responding to their offering, they realise that most of their thinking was based on their own assumptions and hypotheses. It's fine to make assumptions and hypotheses at the start, but the next step is to validate and refine them in an iterative approach by getting end users involved in the development process. Unfortunately, many entrepreneurs and business owners who come to us for advice before developing their product also end up ignoring it when we explain the importance of getting end users involved from the start, and the result is the same old story. Looking at the bigger picture, imagine how much time, talent and capital is wasted in the world. This is partly why most startups and new products developed by established businesses fail. If you are on a mission to raise capital for a product or business idea, the way you communicate your pitch is directly linked to the outcome. My team and I have developed an entire framework on this topic alone and if you are interested in delving deeper into this, it is extrapolated in great detail in the Genesis Framework^{TM} [137], a business building framework for startups, entrepreneurs and organisations. My point here is to give you a very tangible example of what can happen when you are not connected and present to your potential customer or target markets and demonstrate just how important your relationship with *presence* is.

The same applies when you are communicating your value proposition through branding exercises. Next time you produce a marketing video to convey the value of a new product, for example, think carefully about the message you are putting out there. Have you managed to effectively influence the perceived benefits and value of your offering? Ideally your perceived value would be congruent with the actual value of the offering. That would suggest you have executed your communication well. It means you must have built the product and its branding, messages and sales materials with involvement from the end user from the start. If your declared value is more than the perceived value, it suggests you are exaggerating and therefore not being authentic. If, on the other hand, your declared value is less than the perceived value, then your business will almost certainly forego potential revenue in the long run.

For those of you who may still not be convinced to find *presence* tangible and valuable enough to focus on in your organisation, let me draw your attention to some other ramifications of overlooking this Way of Being in a business context. A lack of complete *presence* in business results in many issues. For example, it can lead to instructions not being precisely

---

137   The Genesis Framework^{TM} is a comprehensive series of principles, processes, procedures and tools that determine how a raw business idea turns into a commercially viable, successful and sustainable business. Based on direct experience working with over 500 businesses and interviewing and studying hundreds more, the Genesis Framework provides a breakdown of the key components every venture requires to commercially thrive.

followed, causing additional workload, a waste of precious time and money, and poor customer service. This results in the loss of customers, damage to your brand reputation and revenue loss. A lack of *presence* also commonly leads to excessive time spent in meetings without producing effective outcomes, simple tasks taking more time than they should and presenteeism, which is where employees are sitting at their desks but aren't actually working. All of these ramifications will literally cost your business dearly.

Presence begins with you

To develop a healthy relationship with *presence*, you should start with yourself. How well are you present to YOU? How well do you connect to yourself? If you are not present to yourself, you can't be true to your calling, your *authenticity*. There is no way the great composers like Beethoven, Bach and Mozart could have composed such beautiful masterpieces had they not been present to themselves, listened to their intuition and responded to their calling. If you are not present to yourself, you would also find it difficult to be present with another person. This is directly related to the Authenticity Quadrant, as discussed in the Authenticity chapter. It's about the four types of conversations you have: Self-image (the conversations you have with yourself about yourself), Persona (the conversations you have with the world about yourself), Beliefs (the conversations you have with yourself about the world) and Opinions (the conversations you have with the world about the world). If you are not honest and authentic with yourself, how can you possibly engage in authentic, straightshooting and open communication with another person, whether it be in business, with an audience or in your personal life? So, if you find that your messages are not being received by others the way you intended and you don't know how others perceive you, then you may as well be speaking in a foreign language to the other person. They won't understand what you are trying to convey to them. If you are experiencing this often, how can you expect to have a meaningful exchange with any other person, including a client? On a side note, whenever I refer to examples, I relate them to myself as well as to others. We are all in the same boat; this paradigm applies to all of us. As long as we are aware of it and notice when we slip up and why, we can respond to it appropriately and change the direction.

As you learn to become more present to yourself and then to others (*presence*), you will begin to open up to others (*vulnerability*) and, in turn, a whole new world will open up for you. All of a sudden, you will meet interesting people everywhere you go because you are **interested** in them. Businesspeople often attend networking events in the hope of making connections with people they can somehow engage in a business transaction, but their interest is solely focused on what they can get out of it. A far more effective way would be to go with the intention of meeting people for the sake of connecting with them and genuinely learning what they are interested in. I have met and connected with people on the street, while walking my dogs at the local dog park and standing in a queue, and all I did was listen, letting them speak first. People like to share their experiences, but we are all too keen to jump in and talk about ourselves. How about listening to the other person first? You may say, 'Oh, but people often talk about their problems and that's not what I want to hear', but if you are in business, that's exactly what you should be listening to! If the same problems are mentioned by a number of people, then that reveals a potential market opportunity. You could be the one to find a solution to that recurring problem and bring it to the market. You can bet that if you don't, someone else most likely will, someone who is present, open, willing to listen and sees the opportunity. A few of the people I met at the dog park have since become valued clients, just because I took the time to listen and be fully present to them.

Presence and open communication generate trust

Being present with another person is critical for *effectiveness* in our endeavours. My teams and I are sometimes approached by business owners/entrepreneurs seeking investors, but all too often, when we introduce them to suitable investors, they completely brush them off and don't take them as seriously as they should. They don't take the appropriate time to fully understand the needs, perspective and interest of each investor. Instead, they focus on themselves, assuming that to raise the required funds, they need to impress the investor by being super confident and having all the answers, without admitting to having faced any challenges, taken risks or made mistakes. They neglect to see things from the investor's perspective, and they resist being vulnerable.

The truth is, most of the successful fund raises we have witnessed occurred when the founders were being authentic and vulnerable. They made it clear that they genuinely wanted to meet and learn from the investor rather than receiving money from an anonymous or random stranger. They expressed their desire to build a relationship and partnership with the investor, highlighting that the exercise was regarded as much more valuable than just a money-making venture. When a founder is transparent, enthusiastic, open and present with a potential investor, trust is generated, and the investor feels comfortable and confident enough to consider backing them. My point is, if you fail to be present and instead come in with an overly elaborate agenda that is all about you, it won't achieve your desired outcome. It is a myth that you need to be full of confidence, puffing out your chest and singing your own praises. Any experienced and professional investor would know that a startup founder in the early stages of their business journey is unlikely to have a high level of clarity about where they are going. Even if the founder has a well-defined predictive three to five-year plan in place, the potential investor knows that the plan will most definitely change, usually many times over. Investors quickly sense any pretence and overconfidence, and when they feel they are not being taken seriously, the startup founder can kiss the funding goodbye. Direct, authentic and open communication will always achieve a better outcome. As you may notice, *presence* is closely connected with *authenticity* and *vulnerability*. At the end of the day, it shows great strength of character to admit weaknesses or challenges that have not been fully understood and worked through, and that is empowering. Most investors understand this and, with the help of the right people, can assist in overcoming those risks.

Presence and synchronicity

Every human being experiences the world differently based on their Aspects of Being, web of perceptions, perspectives and narrative lens as well as external factors, like the environment in which they live. This shapes their Third-layer Reality (the reality we construct ourselves), which is unique to each and every person. It's why two people may go through the same situation together but come out with two completely different experiences and narratives. When this happens, we do not fully understand each other's world. Instead, we're continuously pulled to see the world from our personal point of view. In closer relationships, as the number of discrepancies between the two narratives increases, the parties in question are no longer as connected as they once were because they find it increasingly difficult to relate to one another. There is little synchronicity, and this is commonly the source of conflicts and unconstructive arguments, which can eventually lead to relationship breakdowns and, ultimately, a lack of *effectiveness* in their collective endeavours and a lack of fulfilment in life. This lack of *presence* and synchronicity gets in the way of teams and organisations being as productive and reliable as they could be and therefore is a clear source of liability.

When we take a moment not to be distracted by our own Third-layer Reality and become present to what is going on for another human being, we start to see the world through their eyes. This allows us to understand their web of perceptions, perspectives and narrative lens and, by being fully present to and in constant effective communication with them, we can also appreciate their different viewpoints and build a more detailed picture of how the world looks to them. I am not implying that you should agree or disagree with them at this point. I'm talking about the stage before that. After all, how can you decide on your position without first listening to and understanding their point of view. Only then can you choose to agree, disagree or simply be neutral. When two or more people are in consistent alignment while experiencing many different things together, we can describe them as **being in sync** or **having synchronicity**. This is more than simply obtaining an understanding of someone else's point of view. It is an act of generosity because you are being present and giving your presence to another. Synchronicity is essential for anyone who is committed to **being with** others in relationships, partnerships and collaborations, hence it is crucial for anyone in a leadership role.

The connection between *presence* and other Aspects of Being

Being present requires a level of emotional intelligence. It also requires *care* – discovering that **being with** and connecting to the other person is important – *vulnerability* – resisting the temptation to interrupt and impress them – and *freedom* – to be unleashed and treat them as an individual rather than be constrained by your immediate judgement or attempt to categorise them. *Presence* also requires *courage* – to overcome the *fear* and *anxiety* associated with meeting a stranger and not be obsessed with the outcome – *commitment* – to be fully in and of service – and *gratitude* – to be grateful for their contribution, that they were generous enough to spend their time with you. It requires a sincere and deliberate desire to choose to understand what the other person has to say rather than jumping in to add your own perspective.

Effective communication happens when both parties are present to one another and authentic, when you are both willing to remove the mask and reveal who you really are in order to build a true connection. It also requires a willingness to fully comprehend what the other party has to say. Often when we are triggered by what someone else says, we may prematurely form an opinion, stop listening and react without ensuring that we have collected all the information. This trait is commonly observed in politics and the media, especially when people debate a topic and want to get their own opinion across, just as the sophists used to do (as discussed in *Part 1, Chapter 3: Discovery vs Invention*). Their entire focus is on winning the argument and is often accompanied by judgement and personal opinion as opposed to a desire to understand the other person's point of view and learn more about the topic together. That's because they are more obsessed with being right than being in search of truth and Reality. Not having a healthy relationship with *presence* comes at a significant cost. It puts a lot of extra strain on relationships and causes resistance between people, whether in business or personal relationships, and this has a tendency to continue in a vicious cycle.

Being present, direct and open with the other person, facilitates communication and supports conflict resolution. I admit it isn't always easy to be authentic and assertive with another person and it may require a good dose of *courage*. You can probably see why employers put communication skills at the top of their list of requirements when hiring new staff. While the employers focus on the skills, they really want people who are open and can therefore communicate effectively, and that takes a bit more than just the skill of being well-articulated. While high level communication skills are highly desirable, we are aiming higher in this context by considering the deeper layers of communication *(presence)*. A hearing-impaired individual who is also unable to speak could potentially have a healthier relationship with the *presence* Way of Being than an experienced public speaker simply by being more present and connected with others. Authentic and effective communication through *presence* gives people the ability to produce extraordinary results in their life by staying engaged and maintaining a high level of energy and focus. Suppressed communication through a lack of *presence*, or maintaining hidden agendas, requires a lot of energy and can be debilitating and very draining.

Taking offence – the relationship between *presence* and *vulnerability*

People these days are so often easily offended. The problem is, when we allow ourselves to be offended, we block – or at least significantly limit – our communication. That's because when we are offended, we are no longer present, as coming to terms with the insult or accusation or preparing our defence takes a higher priority than the matter in question. While this shift in priority may not be too much of an issue for some people – as long as they don't dwell on it for too long – that is not the case for a leader. As a leader, it is far more effective not to take offence at all, or at least not to let it get to you, so it doesn't pull you away from the matter at hand, from being present. It is only personal if we choose to make it personal and we only get offended when we choose to make it about us.

Most of us were not taught and trained as children how not to take offence. Instead, we were told that if someone offended us, we should attack, or at the very least, expect an apology. The same happens in schools today and also in the business world. Rather than brushing off an insult or an accusation, we have been conditioned to victimise ourselves because that is the dominant paradigm in our education systems, in the media, in business and, most notably, in politics. A more recent trend is the insistence for political correctness to protect us all from the possibility that something may offend us. Many attempts are made to create trigger-free zones in universities, corporations and society in general. While addressing this in detail is beyond the scope of this body of work, the main point I wish to make is that, as a leader, rather than making things personal and taking offence, it is much more effective to work on your relationship with *vulnerability* to develop a thicker skin when faced with challenges and unpleasant situations, as your ability to let matters go, like water off a duck's back, will allow you to remain present, aware and connected when communicating with others. This would also empower you to handle the problem at hand far more effectively than if you were to dwell on how offended you feel.

Let's take a look at an example of a leader who had a highly effective relationship with the *presence-vulnerability* Way of Being. It's 1997, and Steve Jobs has just returned to the company he was fired from twelve years earlier, despite the fact that he was a founder. On stage at Apple's World Wide Developers Conference (WWDC), Jobs was holding a rare Q&A with developers when one audience member stood up and lobbed an insult at him.

'Mr Jobs, you're a bright and influential man,' he starts out with a flat tone. The audience laughs in the pause.

'Here it comes,' Jobs responds with a smile.

'It's sad and clear that on several counts you've discussed, you don't know what you're talking about. [Audience laughter] I would like, for example, for you to express in clear terms how, say, Java and any of its incarnations addresses the ideas embodied in OpenDoc. And when you're finished with that, perhaps you can tell us what you personally have been doing for the last seven years,' he says.

At this point, the audience falls quiet, and someone is heard saying, 'Ouch!' Remember, Jobs had not been at Apple for well over seven years.

Jobs took his time to think before responding. Over the course of the next five minutes, he managed to gracefully respond to the insult as well as deliver an impromptu speech on vision.

'You know, you can please some of the people some of the time, but…' Jobs paused before continuing, 'One of the hardest things when you're trying to effect change is that people like this gentleman are right in some areas.'

He goes on to acknowledge that there are certain things OpenDoc does that he's not even familiar with, but that doesn't stop him from planning Apple's future.

'The hardest thing is: how does that fit into a cohesive, larger vision, that's going to allow you to sell eight billion dollars, ten billion dollars of product a year? And, one of the things I've always found is that you've got to start with the customer experience and work backwards from the technology. You can't start with the technology and try to figure out where you're going to try to sell it. And I made this mistake probably more than anybody else in this room. And I got the scar tissue to prove it.'

Jobs then apologises for killing off some of the software, but passionately stands by his employees who were working hard to get Apple's reputation back on track. Think about what Apple is today: the very company many of us are delighted to support by using their products!

At the end of the day, as a leader, when everyone in the organisation feels disarmed in the face of a catastrophe, all eyes will turn to you to lead the way to a resolution. This will demand your full attention. It will require all your energy, *awareness* and focus on the actual matter at hand, viewing things from the global perspective. For example, let's say your organisation is wrongfully blamed for something. You have two choices: you could react defensively and angrily about being blamed for something that was not your fault, or you could choose powerfully not to take the bait and react, as this would distract you from focusing on the facts and dealing with the situation in a calm, controlled manner. So, while being wrongfully blamed could be considered offensive, you can choose powerfully not to be offended, in other words, to not be the victim. The latter is empowering. Being both authentic and vulnerable will allow you to remain humble, not take your self-image and persona too seriously and let it be. Let others say what they will but remember not to take it personally. This practice may sound simple, but it isn't easy, especially for those who don't have the healthiest relationship with *vulnerability* and *presence*.

Let me bring this important point home with another relatable example. Let's say a manager within your organisation has been challenging you lately by agreeing to do something a certain way but doing it their own way behind your back, not realising the implications of their actions because they aren't aware of the big picture. You could handle this in one of two ways. You could choose to take offence that the manager has been ignoring your instructions, become angry, rant and rave and threaten them with job termination if it happens one more time. Or you could choose not to be offended and see it from their perspective with *compassion*. Choosing the first way could cause the manager in question, and other staff if they witness your tantrum, to see you as an incompetent leader. Alternatively, assessing the situation more deeply, you may discover that your manager's perception is that their way is superior to yours, but they haven't had the *courage* or *assertiveness* to discuss it with you, hoping instead to impress you with the results they achieve by ignoring your instructions and doing it their way. Allowing yourself to be vulnerable will support you to let go of your ego and persona attached to being the CEO and be open and present so you can communicate with them and understand the why behind their actions. This does not mean you have to condone their actions. Being present will allow you to understand their perspective and draw out their hidden conversations and inauthenticities, not to humiliate them, but to create an authentic space that generates trust and facilitates open and direct/assertive communication. This is not necessarily a soft action; you may need to confront them around their inauthenticities, but first you need to be present in order to properly listen to and understand their response. Adopting this approach will give the manager space to communicate freely without *fear* or *anxiety* about the consequences or repercussions. It would assure them that their *assertiveness* will earn your respect. Furthermore, you would gain their respect too, simply for the fact that you are showing that you are humble enough to listen and that you respect that you may not always have all the answers and you may not always be right. At the same time, you are making it clear that you are not a leader who acts spontaneously or is inconsistent and that you can't be fooled or walked over.

Not being offended and creating the space for open, effective communication in your organisation will ensure your employees don't feel oppressed and disempowered, feeling that they need to be submissive. Instead, you will create an environment of trust, an environment in which open, direct and assertive communication is encouraged and supported. Your *presence* will let them know that they are genuinely being listened to because you value what they have to say and acknowledge that their ideas may even benefit the organisation. In this way, you are also demonstrating effective communication, *presence*, *authenticity* and *assertiveness* to set an example for your employees and highlight what is expected of them. Not only does this command respect, but it also contributes to the gradual building of a high performance, effective culture within your organisation. None of this would happen if you are immediately offended and get your back up whenever something doesn't go your way. When you choose not to be offended, you will open up great opportunities. The same is true in a personal relationship. When you choose not to be offended during an argument with your life partner, you can dive deeper and identify the root cause of the conflict. It is much more effective when we learn to be present and communicate this way.

Being available for authentic communication

To communicate effectively you must be available for authentic communication. When communicating with someone, ask yourself, are you listening to the other person and really paying attention? In other words, are you being present? Or have you tuned out, pretending to listen, but in reality, you are off with your own thoughts? Pretending to listen and be involved in the communication is inauthentic. When we are truly **being with** another person (*Mitsein*), *presence* manifests other Ways of Being and emotions that resonate with others and evokes the same responses from the other person.

Communication can take four directions as shown in *Figure 8* opposite.

- Me to Me is a monologue with myself. It is when I am both a speaker and a listener.
- Me to Other Person is when I am the speaker.
- Other Person to Me is when I am the listener.
- I am also a listener when it is Other Person to Different Other Person.

If this brings to mind the Authenticity Quadrant and the Perspective Quadrant – such as considering matters from the leader/global perspective as opposed to remaining in the I quadrant – as discussed in the Awareness chapter, that's because there are direct links here to both. I encourage you to refer back to those diagrams to refresh your memory as there are significant relationships between those quadrants and communication (*presence*).

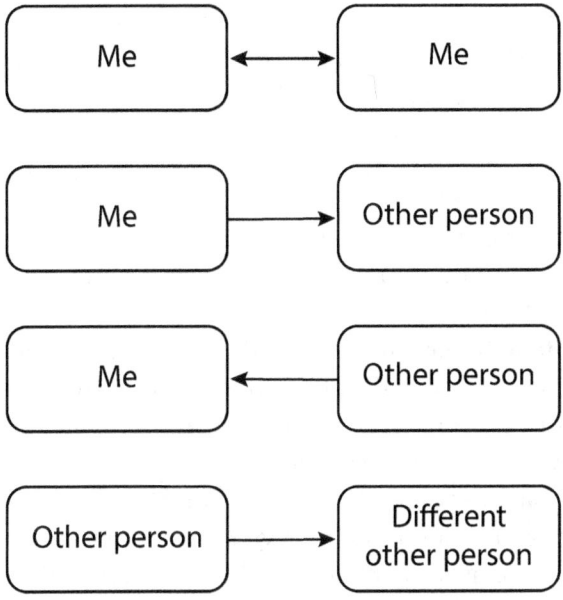

Figure 8: Directions of Communication

In summary

As *presence* is a Way of Being that is commonly misunderstood, it is worth reiterating the ontological distinction here in the summary. *Presence* is being fully and intentionally connected and in communication with others. It is the authentic communication that occurs when all parties experience being fully related to and understood. There is no distance or barrier between you, and mutual understanding is fully available. So, if you are too busy dealing with your own immediate problems and are continually allowing the hidden conversations in the back of your head to dominate, you are not connected and you are not present. *Authenticity* and *freedom* play a vitally important role here. If those Ways of Being are not being continually polished, it would be very challenging to be connected, present and aware. As a result, it would be impossible to have a healthy relationship with the *presence* Way of Being. Now, here is the interesting part. In working with various businesses and studying others, we realised that a leader's relationship with their Aspects of Being influences the relationship others in their organisation have with their own Aspects of Being. So, as a leader, if you don't establish a healthy relationship with *presence*, for instance, if you are easily offended and lacking the *vulnerability* to put your ego aside and be present to what is actually going on, it will filter through the entire organisation and the bottom line will suffer.

Failing to be present will negatively impact everything from your success in achieving sales and raising capital to your effectiveness in delegating tasks, building commercial partnerships and being present to the direction in which the market and your industry are going. It will also blind you to the many innovations that are happening all around you, where you stand in the landscape all the way to reiterating your vision and mission to your team. Ultimately this will have a detrimental impact on the performance of your organisation and therefore the results you produce. If you get into the habit of being truly present, you will see that there are possibilities everywhere, possibilities that can become genuine business opportunities. Imagine if you could come up with solutions and serve people instead of ignoring them or, worse, joining in on the conversation by making useless complaints yourself. Thanks to social media and cyberspace in general, we have access to people all over the world. Imagine the global problems you could solve if you listened and paid attention to what they were communicating rather than simply scrolling aimlessly through your newsfeed. That's the power of *presence*.

CHAPTER 17

Peace of Mind

Who can ever compose exquisite prose, and fine poetry
Captive in the cage of sorrow and rage, and mind not free?
My point is now made, to you to agree, or to disagree.

Hafez, 1325–1389

What do you want most in life? If your response is fulfilment and *peace of mind*, you are not alone. That would have to be one of the most common responses to that question. Many different disciplines, schools of thinking, religions and independent philosophers and mystics believe *peace of mind*, calmness or inner peace is a quality that can be cultivated and increased with practice, adopting various techniques, including meditation, which has always been at the centre of most traditional martial arts and yoga. As martial arts and yoga are practised far and wide throughout the world, this in itself shows the growing demand and desire for *peace of mind* across cultures. Indeed, having *peace of mind* seems to be the mantra in today's stressful times. The advancement of technology, complexity of modern life and vast amounts of information we all need to process on a daily basis in the postmodern era have made us seek *peace of mind* more than ever. But so few of us ever achieve it, and when we do, it tends to be fleeting. However, it is definitely possible to attain, maintain and nurture this Primary Way of Being, as you are about to discover.

Human beings are biologically wired to react to threats. Our response to threat is automatically triggered in the amygdala, the part of the brain's limbic system responsible for emotions, survival instincts and memory. This wiring helps us take the appropriate actions when our life is in danger. As most of us aren't regularly faced with life-threatening experiences these days, you would expect that this response mechanism wouldn't be overly active on a daily basis. However, most of us can trigger this fight or flight response simply by being stuck in traffic or having a challenging dispute with someone, and we can all trigger a similar response when alone with our thoughts. These so-called 'false alarms' are sent to the amygdala, prompting a response to a situation as if our life were in danger. To avoid these inappropriate or over-the-top responses from our brain and body's survival mechanisms, we need to learn to manage our emotions in a more appropriate manner. This is where transforming and polishing our relationship with the *peace of mind* Way of Being comes to the fore. However, *peace of mind* is not a quality that stands alone. It is not something you can have and hold onto, and it is more subtle and closely linked to other Aspects of Being. Understanding these relationships is the key to cultivating and allowing your relationship with your *peace of mind* to grow and flourish.

What is peace of *mind*?

Peace of mind is not easily defined. Perhaps the best place to start is to consider what it feels like when you don't have *peace of mind*. Think back to a time when you may have been preparing to go for your dream job. It's the morning of the interview and you know you have done everything you could to prepare. You have informed yourself about the new company's history, vision and mission, you have roleplayed the interview questions and have read anything relevant about the company you could find in your research. You feel confident and ready for whatever questions may be fired at you. Feeling positive, you suddenly notice a voicemail from the company's office to inform you that the CEO of the company, who was scheduled to be overseas, is now available and will be attending the interview. This is unexpected news, and you feel nervous. You begin to question your preparation. This leads to some doubt and questions in your mind like, 'Did I do enough? Could I have missed some critical information that the CEO will want to discuss? What if the CEO's presence makes me anxious during the interview and I lose my train of thought?' How important do you think it would be to regain your *peace of mind* before attending the interview? I'm sure you could think of many examples like this where a lack of *peace of mind* would make things extra challenging and could lead to a less than desirable outcome.

PEACE OF MIND

Peace of mind is not a term you can simply look up in the dictionary. The closest word describing it would be 'calmness', which the *Oxford English Dictionary* defines as 'the state or quality of being free from agitation or strong emotion' and the *Cambridge Dictionary* defines as 'the quality of being peaceful, quiet, and without worry'. However, I would say the state of *peace of mind* is being free from agitation, excitement, or disturbance.

The Being Framework ontological distinction of *peace of mind*

Peace of mind is the quality that supports you to remain calm, focused and think clearly, regardless of your situation, circumstances and any feelings of worry, nervousness or unease. It is an inner fortitude that withstands the turmoil around you and supports you in discerning and deciding before taking action.

A healthy relationship with *peace of mind* indicates that you mostly experience that things are handled and you are able to deal with life and circumstances around you, particularly when things may appear chaotic. You clearly distinguish appropriate priorities and remain focused under pressure. Others may experience you as calm, sensible and clear-headed in dealing with life's challenges.

An unhealthy relationship with *peace of mind* indicates that you often experience worry, have troubled thoughts and are distressed when things are not working out as well as you would like them to. Others may see you as frequently distracted, confused, stressed, overwhelmed, stuck or struggling to deal with life's challenges. You may often be consumed by internal dialogue or mental traffic and overwhelmed to the point where you cannot effectively deal with matters at hand. Alternatively, you may choose to be too relaxed while lacking concern for important matters. You may remove yourself from the matters of life, deliberately disassociating yourself from reality and the world around you, often resorting to a fabricated peaceful state. You may rely on substances, practices or techniques to distance or numb yourself from discomfort rather than tackle it head on.

Peace of mind and its relationship with *awareness*

Peace of mind is elusive by nature. This makes *awareness* of this even more critical than it is with other less elusive Ways of Being. Without being acutely aware, you will fail to recognise what is pulling you away from or disturbing your *peace of mind*. *Awareness* supports you to establish your expectations, ensuring few surprises or upsets along the way. Let's say, for whatever reason, you didn't align with the discussion about Existence in Part 1 of this book, specifically, that we are all under the influence of Existence. Even if you don't wish to adopt that view, there are rules and laws that apply to the world we live in and therefore impact us all. You may choose not to align your views with Reality, remaining caught in your own web of perceptions and viewing the world through your narrative lens, but this may leave you in a constant state of surprise, wondering why life is not playing out the way you had hoped it would. Then, when others who do align their views with Reality make decisions or take actions that directly or indirectly influence you and your life, you may point the finger and accuse those people or external factors of being distractions to your *peace of mind* as opposed to raising your *awareness* about the role you are playing in sabotaging your own *peace of mind*.

If you fail to acknowledge the differences and preferences of others, if you expect yourself to be perfect and never make mistakes, if you lack *awareness* in general, if you are inauthentic and neglect to establish a solid relationship with Reality, you will suffer and cause suffering. As a result, you may find yourself regularly being caught up in painful situations. This is a recipe for ruining, or at least limiting, *peace of mind* instead of cultivating it. People in this situation commonly ask, 'Why me?' If this is you, the best thing you could do is rephrase the question to, 'Why not me?' After all, you are not the only person in the world to suffer like this. Remember, I am not passing judgement here; I am encouraging you to create a link between your level of *awareness* (of the world and human beings) and *peace of mind*. As you know, the principal aim of this body of work is to educate and encourage a paradigm shift by supporting you to gradually develop a more accurate conception of reality (First and Second-layer Reality), so that you become more powerful and effective in the face of dealing with and handling life's inevitable challenges and adversities.

Now that we have established what *peace of mind* is and how elusive it can be, let me explain why setting realistic expectations of life is so important, particularly if you wish to establish a healthy relationship with this. Let me to be straight with you here. If you expect to be in a constant state of calmness, you are entertaining a delusion, as that's like living with your head in the clouds. I have a broad network of friends and business associates: from yogis, philosophers and religious leaders of various faiths to scientists, psychologists and psychoanalysts, including some extremely successful and wealthy people, and I can assure you none of them, not one, experience constant *peace of mind*. This is true no matter how well they may have mastered their state of Being, knowledge, principles, practices or how much wealth and abundance they have. So, next time you find yourself complaining about something that is causing you to lose *peace of mind*, I would like to encourage you to remember that you're not alone. It's how you react and respond that really counts, and this goes back to the health of your relationship with *peace of mind*. So, while we are all in this together, how we deal with distractions and disturbances on an individual level varies from one person to the next.

We all have the ability to transform our relationship with *peace of mind*. At the very least we can learn to cultivate it and allow it to grow. The main point I am making here is how important your *awareness* is in terms of how you perceive your life to be and how this directly impacts your *peace of mind*. In a similar manner, the way you relate to your other Aspects of Being, including – but not limited to – *fear, anxiety, care, vulnerability, courage, freedom, forgiveness* and, most importantly, *responsibility*, can also impact your *peace of mind*. For example, if you subscribe to the worldview that we are all passive victims to our circumstances, that life simply happens to us and we have no control of our own destiny, you would very likely find it challenging to maintain a healthy relationship with *peace of mind*. If, on the other hand, you are empowered, responsible and committed to maintaining your *peace of mind*, regardless of the circumstances, then there is a far higher probability that you will take charge of that aspect of your life. *Awareness,* as the starting point, is the key here: *awareness* of the world, knowing who you are and how human beings operate.

For *peace of mind*, flip the switch

It is a common misconception that we need to be lying on the beach in Hawaii, cocktail in hand, to experience *peace of mind*. If your *peace of mind* is attached to external factors, what do you think will happen once you are back in your normal environment? Naturally, all your worries and stresses are likely to return and wreak havoc with your *peace of mind*. Tourism advertising is one example that plays on the popular myth that we need to HAVE something (like a holiday or wealth) to DO something to BE something, but the key part of the paradigm shift we promised here is to demonstrate that the opposite is true. In terms of *peace of mind*, you should BE calm to effectively DO something – such as run your business with grace, *integrity* and joy – in order to HAVE something (such as wealth through revenue and profit, and so on).

The world doesn't stay still and give us the chance to have a perpetually healthy relationship with *peace of mind*. According to Heidegger, 'We are continuously thrown into life with all its scenarios and challenges'[138], and this is precisely why *peace of mind* is so elusive. After all, there are always going to be circumstances that we would prefer not to have to deal with. So, the greatest challenge is to develop a healthy relationship with *peace of mind* in unwanted circumstances. The truth is, we will never achieve a healthy relationship with *peace of mind* as long as we are of the mindset that there is something wrong. Consider that there is never actually anything wrong; there are only things that are missing. Instead, it's about flipping our perspective of the situation. Think about a challenge encountered in your business or in life in general and notice that if you focus on the adversity, it is easy to be overcome by worry and fear about the future, losing sight of what is happening in the here and now. Therefore, to have a healthy relationship with *peace of mind*, we must focus on reality rather than worrying about what could happen in the future.

Can *peace of mind* be practised and maintained?

As mentioned earlier, *peace of mind* is not something we can have and hold onto permanently, however, it is definitely something we

---

138 'Dasein's existence is characterized phenomenologically by thrown projection' – *Being and Time*, Martin Heidegger.

can learn to cultivate and allow to grow. So, the answer is, yes, we can choose to practise and maintain a healthy relationship with *peace of mind*. As we also discussed, it is not a quality that stands alone; it is closely connected to other Aspects of Being and it takes *awareness* to recognise what is happening with our Being and how every change affects our *peace of mind*. A technique that is useful to be aware of, particularly when it comes to *peace of mind*, is what we previously referred to as 'garbage collection', a term often used in the world of software development.

When you run software on your computer, a number of variables need to be created in order for the software application to function. In the past, computer programmers would allocate values (numbers) to each variable and would then have to deallocate those values afterwards. In other words, they would have to empty them to ensure they don't continue to occupy space in the memory or create a memory shortage known as a 'stack overflow'. Today, modern programming technologies take care of this error-prone task (garbage collection).

As human beings, we can all face stack overflow. We call it overwhelm. Think of it as your work desk. The bigger the desk you have, the more stuff you can load it up with. While I am not focusing on techniques in this book, the point is that, like computers, we should become aware of our current capacity and learn to shoulder and expand it as required. For instance, when someone tells me they have too much on their plate, I tell them to get a bigger plate. This is what leaders do; they get bigger plates. If you want to generate more products, expand your company, develop your career, build a family or any serious matter in life, you should develop the capacity to shoulder bigger burdens and take greater responsibilities. Think of it as increasing the capacity of your computer's RAM (random-access memory) by activating your garbage collection functionality to constantly prioritise stuff on your desktop and clean it up so you don't face stack overflow and risk losing your *peace of mind* and focus as a result.

Peace of mind and innovation

Of all the Aspects of Being, *peace of mind* is one of the most important prerequisites for being creative. It allows you to unleash the potential of your mind and talents to conceive new ideas and introduce change into a relatively stable system, such as your organisation. Revered by companies globally, creativity is a quality required to innovate and come up with new ideas for products and services designed to solve the problems of humanity and commercialise those solutions. As a leader, if you fail to focus on achieving and maintaining a healthy relationship with *peace of mind* collectively with your people, as well as independently, the level of creativity in your organisation will be minimal. We observed this when working with a number of organisational product and strategy teams and startups. Discovering reality and raising *awareness* requires *peace of mind* so that, as Martin Heidegger said, there is space for the light to shine and cause knowledge acquisition (known as 'clearing', or *Lichtung* in German[139]). This is not just about *awareness* on an abstract or conceptual level; it is literally about being open to receiving inspiration and/or letting your creativity shine to come up with new ideas. From *awareness* comes clearing, followed by *peace of mind*. Only then can you be effective in the area of innovation, using various techniques of ideation and brainstorming.

As leaders, coaches and professionals, you need to work with others all day, every day, so it is important to clear your mind regularly. One of the best ways to do this is to talk about whatever is on your mind, and to get whatever is bothering you off your chest. Only then can you be fully present and have the *awareness* and *peace of mind* to stay focused, regardless of distractions. If we are not in control of our thoughts, we can diminish our relationship with *peace of mind* in an instant. Remember, none of us can expect life to be easy and comfortable all the time. There will always be distractions that limit or threaten our *peace of mind*. It is up to each and every one of us to be responsible and care about increasing our knowledge and *awareness* so that we may stand with *courage, resilience* and *freedom,* despite the presence of *fear* and *anxiety*. Only then can we move comfortably back into having a healthy relationship with *peace of mind* when distractions threaten to pull us

---

139 In German, the word *Lichtung* means a clearing, as in, for example, a clearing in the woods. Since its root is the German word for light (*Licht*), it is sometimes also translated as 'lighting'. In Heidegger's work, it refers to the necessity of a clearing in which anything at all can appear, the clearing in which some thing or idea can show itself, or be unconcealed.

away from it. So, while *peace of mind* is elusive, it is a quality we can all cultivate and allow to grow through *awareness*, regular practice and maintenance. When we choose powerfully and voluntarily to surrender to reality, we are rewarded with *peace of mind*.

CHAPTER 18

Compassion

When we are being authentic, we acknowledge that, as human beings, we are social creatures by nature. We are being inauthentic if we refuse to recognise this fact and acknowledge how this influences our experience of life. Therefore, the way we habitually make decisions and take actions is significantly influenced by our social surroundings and the way we **are with** each other (referring to Martin Heidegger's *Mitsein* or being-with). Phenomenologically speaking, suffering is an undeniable and inevitable part of life. The key to minimising suffering and not being crushed by matters beyond our control is to do our best to polish our Aspects of Being (for *integrity* or wholeness) and to be aware and as effective as possible in our endeavours. This ensures we get stuck in life less often (through *awareness* and exposure) and increases our capacity to handle and respond to the suffering with grace. Fortunately, as social creatures we are – at least for the most part – not alone in our suffering. If you beg to differ, I encourage you to be vulnerable and open to raising your *awareness* and *authenticity* about this fact. As so poignantly and symbolically depicted in the story of Simorgh, we are all in this together. This isn't just a cliché, it is Reality. The reason I have chosen to start this chapter by reiterating the point that we are social creatures and that, as individuals, we are not alone in our suffering will soon become clear. Bear with me for now, as *compassion* is a quality that is commonly misunderstood.

It seems everyone these days wants and claims to be 'independent', as though it's a virtue. While I appreciate where people are coming from when making this claim, the reality is that we are all dependent on others in one way or another. We go to the doctors when we have health issues, we fulfil our needs by purchasing products and services from others and we express ourselves with family and friends. Some of us also seek assistance from coaches, mentors and advisors to minimise common mistakes in our professional lives and accelerate our growth. In today's modern world, our welfare systems, insurances, medical care and various social services take care of us when we need support. Even in developing nations, there have always been basic community support systems in place. While our support systems may be far from perfect, as social beings, we have at least invented and put systems in place to support ourselves collectively, to ensure that when we suffer, we don't suffer totally alone. If we were all truly independent of one another, we would not survive. Furthermore, the very fact that we have collectively attempted to create any of our support systems, no matter how effective or ineffective they are, clearly demonstrates that we are at least capable of putting ourselves in the shoes of those in need. Imagine a world totally devoid of *care*, *love*, sympathy, empathy and *compassion*. We could easily collapse as a species!

Why *compassion*?

While there is a connection between *care* and every Primary Way of Being, there are three self-evident Ways of Being through which we predominantly channel *care* as a Mood: *love*, *forgiveness* and *compassion*. As I said in the introduction to this chapter, *compassion* is a quality that is greatly misunderstood. Some misinterpret *compassion* for sympathy. Others regard it as a soft trait and wonder why it is included in a framework focused on leadership, performance and *effectiveness* and a few have asked me why empathy was not included in place of *compassion*. These are familiar qualities that can easily be – and often are – confused with *compassion*, but on their own, they do not necessarily lead to our expression of *compassion* (being *compassionate*). For instance, *compassion* is **not** the resonance of sympathy or pity; it's not feeling guilty, bad or sad about another's predicament, as that does not mean we are motivated to do anything for them. *Compassion* is **not** necessarily the resonance of kindness, tenderness or altruism. *Compassion* is also **not** just the resonance of empathy – understanding how someone else feels and appreciating what it must feel like to be in their predicament, which may not even be related to suffering. Sometimes 'tough love' is the only way that works to move someone out of their suffering, such as shaking someone out of the inauthentic persona they are trying to project to the world, which is causing suffering to themselves and others. Importantly, *compassion* is **not** about fixing a person or situation as improving someone's circumstances on their behalf is not necessarily supporting that person. In some cases, this may be regarded by some as controlling, demeaning or even cruel, in others it is like giving someone a fish rather than teaching them to fish. So, while many people think of *compassion* as a soft trait, it is far from it.

To explain my reasoning on the inclusion of *compassion* in the Being Framework and its ontological distinction further, it is worth taking a step back to remind you of the importance of using words that refer to their transcendent Meaning gracefully, so they serve us well within this context. Let's start with suffering, which originates from the Greek word *Pathos* ('suffering, feeling, emotion', literally, 'what befalls one') and is related to *Paskhein* ('to suffer') and *Penthos* ('grief'). Suffering is defined by the *Oxford English Dictionary* as 'a quality that evokes pity or sadness'. The word 'sympathy' is constructed from the Greek *Sym*, which means 'together', and *Pathos*. It is a word used to describe when one person shares the same feelings of another, such as when someone is experiencing grief or loss. In the modern world, there is commonly a negative connotation associated with the word sympathy, which I do not believe was the original intention. Many today associate sympathy with pity or sorrow for someone perceived to be less fortunate than oneself, such as a homeless person or someone with a physical disability. When we put ourselves in the shoes of that person however, we immediately realise that the last thing they want is pity or sorrow. No one likes to be felt sorry for, it may be seen as condescending. The point is, while some may use the words sympathy and *compassion* interchangeably, there is a clear distinction between the two, and the Way of Being we are discussing in this chapter is **not** the Meaning referred to by sympathy.

So, what about empathy? The word 'empathy' is derived from the Greek *Empatheia*, which in turn comes from *Em* ('in') + *Pathos* ('suffering, feeling, emotion'). According to the *Oxford English Dictionary*, empathy means 'the ability to understand and share the feelings of another'. Greater emotional distance is implied with empathy than with suffering. With empathy you can imagine, appreciate or understand how someone might feel, without necessarily having those feelings yourself or having a desire or willingness to voluntarily take action. Empathy is therefore more about your exposure to and *awareness* of how the suffering must feel for the other person/people. While the quality of empathy is necessary for a leader to possess because it puts us in the shoes of others and therefore pushes us out of the 'I' quadrant[140] to see the perspective of others, it isn't enough on its own. Not only is it necessary for leaders to feel empathy, but they should also have the capacity and willingness to **be with** others in their suffering as this generates a **strong desire to take action** and **do something** about the issue. *Compassion* is to be moved. This is precisely where the transcendent Meaning of *compassion* comes into play. It is the quality that would have you take action to alleviate the suffering of another instead of watching it happen from a distance.

The word 'compassion' is constructed from 'com', a prefix meaning 'with, together, in association' and 'passion' from the Latin *Passio* or *Pati*, which means 'to suffer'. As you can see, there is no footprint of sorrow, grief or pity in the word compassion. Rather, the transcendent Meaning of compassion is a combination of 'to be in suffering with someone' and passion, 'an extreme interest in or desire to do something'[141]. The latter is backed by the *Cambridge Dictionary* and the *Merriam-Webster Dictionary*, which both include a reference to having a conscious desire to help in their definitions of compassion, '… and a desire to help' and, '… with a desire to alleviate it', respectively. Note the emphasis on a desire to help or alleviate the suffering of others in addition to **being with** them in their suffering. That is *compassion*. It is a Way of Being that is necessary in business to build strong and lasting relationships with staff, clients, partners and all stakeholders.

Interestingly, in my studies I discovered that a more profound and accurate footprint of *compassion*, when compared with the intellectual and academic literature I studied, was to be found within the texts representing various faiths. For instance, the Dalai Lama (1995) defines compassion in comparable terms as 'an openness to the suffering of

---

140   Perspective Quadrant – *Part 2: Aspects of Being, Chapter 1: Awareness.*
141   *Cambridge Dictionary.*

others with a commitment to relieve it'[142]. However, within Buddhism, compassion is seen not only as an emotional response, but also as a response founded on reason and wisdom which is embedded in an ethical framework concerned with the selfless intention of freeing others from suffering. Referring to another example, all 114 chapters of The Quran commence with a description of God as compassionate and merciful. As for Jesus, he was so renowned for his *compassion* that it doesn't even warrant discussion in this book, let alone require my endorsement. Each of these descriptions and definitions align with our ontological distinction.

142　Strauss, C., Lever Taylor, B., Gu, J., Kuyken, W., Baer, R., Jones, F., & Cavanagh, K. (2016). 'What is compassion and how can we measure it? A review of definitions and measures.' *Clinical Psychology Review*, 47, 15–27.

The Being Framework ontological distinction of *compassion*

Compassion is the quality that compels you to intervene when someone is in pain or suffering and is a clear manifestation and demonstration of your care for others and humanity. It is the capacity to be with the suffering of another. *Compassion* is not sympathy or pity and is also beyond a feeling of empathy for another who is suffering as it moves and motivates you to support them, irrespective of your own discomfort or concerns.

A healthy relationship with *compassion* indicates that you mostly experience yourself as someone who will take appropriate action beyond words or platitudes and intervene when you are present to another's suffering, misery or misfortune. Others may consider you to be someone who is prepared to share and be with the discomfort or pain experienced by another.

An unhealthy relationship with *compassion* indicates that you are often unperturbed, numb or anaesthetised when others are suffering and frequently avoid being in their presence or fully contemplating their circumstances. Others may consider you cold, overly stoic or unfeeling and may not confide in you when challenged or experiencing difficulty in their lives. You may deliberately avert your attention, remove yourself from or avoid situations that bring you into close proximity or contact with someone who is suffering. Alternatively, you may impose your support on others without permission and wish to be seen as the rescuer. You may also become so embroiled in another's misfortune that you create other dramas and draw attention to yourself.

Compassion begins with a focus on you

So far, we have talked about *compassion* in relation to being present to the sufferings of others and doing what we can to support them. But what about our own suffering? The most effective way to polish your relationship with *compassion* is to start being compassionate with yourself. What does it mean to be compassionate with yourself? In the first instance, this requires you to become aware of your own wounds and shadow, bringing your shadow to the surface with continuous intention. Be present to them, and seek and practise ways to resolve your wounds, heal and deal with your shadow. When you deliver *care*, *love* and *compassion* towards yourself first, with *responsibility* and *commitment*, and forgive yourself and others for what has happened to you, then – and only then – can you expand your horizon, touch the lives of others and have the capacity to be of service to them (be compassionate with others). So, the very first person you need to be compassionate with is yourself. It is important to acknowledge that this entire framework, and the corresponding paradigm shift promised to you, starts from a point of *care* and *compassion* towards yourself, followed by *compassion* for others. Why does it begin with *care* and *compassion*? Because *care* and, in a more tangible sense, *compassion*, drive us to face our shadow and to polish and transform our Aspects of Being.

It is not uncommon to hear the phrase, 'I am just trying to be a good person', in reference to showing *compassion*. It's as though some try to play it down. I would like to encourage you not to downgrade or diminish the notion of being a good person by adding the word 'just'. By **being** a good person, you are doing yourself and others an enormous service. *Compassion* – as a key aspect of *care*, given the fact that we largely channel our *care* through *compassion* – is a source for transformation and thriving in life. While conveying and receiving *compassion* can be tough and uncomfortable, both are necessary because it takes *vulnerability* to be willing and open to receiving *compassion* from others, just as it takes *courage* to be compassionate with others.

Why leaders need *compassion*

As mentioned, when I talk about *compassion* as a Way of Being, I don't mean feeling pity or sympathy for someone. I am talking about being present to what the other person is going through and being able to share that experience with them, at least momentarily, as this enables us to start doing something about it. It is an extremely empowering act and a great service we can offer another person. It creates trust, encourages respect, increases *care* and builds a strong bond, making us more influential and empowering as leaders. When we truly manifest these qualities, we become leaders worth following – and who people want to follow – as long as it comes from a place of *authenticity*. It's the difference between acting with/showing *compassion* and **being** compassionate, the latter being our focus in the Being Framework. The difference lies in the *authenticity*. I know this is challenging and there are human limitations around *compassion*. After all, we can't care about everything all the time; it's just not feasible. But we can be aware enough around *care* to prioritise to whom or what we will choose (with *responsibility*) to direct our *care* and *compassion*. The point is, when you choose to deal with someone or something, your dedication, *presence* and willingness to be compassionate, so that the feeling for that person or matter at hand can immediately and effectively turn to action and results, is what *compassion* is all about. While being compassionate towards everyone and everything may seem like the right thing to do, unless there is tangible action taken towards the object of your *compassion*, you may as well not be compassionate at all. In other words, *compassion* is only true *compassion* when it has a well-defined context. Look at each object of your *compassion* as a project you take on and action with grace.

Recently, I started working with a new client who has been trying to launch an innovative tech business for the last twelve years. I was impressed with his grit and perseverance, but I also felt for him and his team. *Compassion* was necessary. Once I felt the pain he went through as an entrepreneur and the implications of his decisions over the last twelve years while working on his invention and commercialising it, I had the urge and passion to work with him, as I strongly believed my team and I could support him. So, I powerfully chose him as a client. Fortunately, he had sufficient faith in me and our frameworks to agree to work with us, giving my company and me the great privilege of serving him.

The ramifications when *compassion* is lacking

Like many Ways of Being, *compassion* is a unitary phenomenon. For example, the opposite of *love* as a Primary Way of Being is not necessarily hate; it is simply the absence of *love*. In other words, you can't measure it on a linear scale from hate at one end to *love* at the other. *Love* is one thing, hate is another. Similarly, a lack of *compassion* is not cruelty, it is to intentionally choose indifference – when you are numb to the pain of others or your own pain. This reminds me of a verse of poetry by Robert Frost: 'Some say the world will end in fire, some say in ice'[143]. The way I perceive this verse is that there are times when war (fire) and unresolved conflicts, tyranny, malevolence, hatred, violence and aggression lead to destruction and other times when a lack of *care* (ice), *compassion*, benevolence, altruism and *love* lead to pain and despair. This is relevant to personal and professional relationships, both with others and with ourselves.

Most first-time entrepreneurs we work with have abundant experience as technicians or in managerial roles, but not in entrepreneurship. Their talents, qualifications and expertise worked to their advantage as employees, but to become an entrepreneur, that experience alone doesn't cut it. Studying and working closely with many startups in my business building career has gifted me with great *awareness* of the consequences of not following frameworks, methodologies and patterns that work. That would be akin to gambling with their livelihoods and the lives of their loved ones and everyone else associated with their business. This *awareness* led to a healthier relationship with *compassion*, which led me to build and develop the Genesis Framework, a comprehensive business building paradigm. Any attempt to build such frameworks would have been impossible had I not directed my attention to the pain that existed and if I had not been compassionate enough to take action. This, in turn, was how our organisation attracted greater attention from our target markets, which has since resulted in consistent and sustainable revenue. It's a similar story with the Being Framework. My awareness of and willingness to be present to the misery, pain and causes of the suffering of

---

143   *Fire and Ice* is a poem by Robert Frost originally published in 1920. It discusses the end of the world, likening the elemental force of fire with the emotion of desire, and ice with hate.

human beings led to a profound relationship with *compassion* and *care*, which in turn empowered me to choose to be committed and responsible enough to do something about it. The resulting action – remembering that *compassion* results in action – became the Being Framework and its associated tools and programs. When you deeply understand the burning pain someone, or a group of people, are dealing with and deliver your product or service to solve their pain with *compassion*, your efforts and actions will be well rewarded. The very fact that you have purchased this book and are now reading it is a case in point.

Most people have a desire to serve based on what they care about and/or what they are effective at, however so very few succeed. Most top achievers are different. They do what they care about and also what they are effective at, or have become effective at over time. As a result, these top achievers execute their ideas so well that an exponential number of people benefit from it, making them financially wealthy in the process. I hope by now the relationship between passion and *compassion* and the rewards and consequences of being compassionate versus being indifferent or lacking *compassion* are clear to you.

CHAPTER 19

Love

ove has to be the most hijacked, misused, overloaded and abused word on the planet. Many attempt to describe what *love* means or sell us what they believe it should mean. Marketing departments and businesses all around the world have jumped on that bandwagon too. The concept of *love* sells. However, *love,* as a primal Way of Being, is not the quality that comes to mind for most people when they think about love. Ontologically and phenomenologically speaking, *love* symbolises one of the transcendent Meanings of Existence. Without *love*, we wouldn't be here; we would have perished as a species. This is a law of the universe and therefore cannot be questioned. So, how does *love* manifest itself in the business arena and what role does it play there? I can virtually hear some of you thinking aloud, 'Not another happy-clappy soft trait!', or, 'What's *love* got to do with business?' The answer is, *love* is not a soft trait, it's not only reserved for romantics, and it is essential for every leader and organisation.

Leaders all over the world are only just waking up to the huge cost to their business when *love* is misrepresented or absent. Despite this, most CEOs we work with struggle to recognise its importance or lose interest when we first talk about *love* as a Way of Being. Their eyes often literally glaze over and, in an attempt to divert the conversation, some even ask us to focus on what they perceive to be more important or tangible Aspects of Being such as *responsibility* or *reliability,* as though qualities like *love* and *compassion* are irrelevant to their business. The truth is, *love* is relevant to each and every one of us and to all organisations, commercial or otherwise. A global pandemic is a classic example of the need for *love* in an organisation, as it is in challenging and unprecedented times when your people and customers are at their most fragile and therefore in most need of your *care, compassion* and *love.*

If you want your people to work together in harmony and sync like players in a sports team rather than operate as a group of individuals; if you want them to have such a close bond that they have each other's back; if you want your people to care deeply about the organisation, your clients, their teammates, themselves and the projects they are working on, you must care about *love*. It is one of the most important ingredients if you want your organisation to produce extraordinary results. By the end of this chapter, I hope you will experience a shift and start to appreciate that *love* is not the soft trait many assume it to be and that, like *compassion*, *love* is a tangible aspect of *care*, making both of these Ways of Being absolutely critical for success in business.

Like *compassion*, *love* is a quality that is commonly misunderstood – probably even more so – especially when it comes to leadership, performance and *effectiveness*. In the previous chapter, we learnt that *compassion* is the capacity and willingness to **be with** others in their suffering, as this generates a strong desire to be stirred to action. *Love* is the aspect of caring for others and yourself. It is the highest possible level of **being with** another being or oneself. *Compassion* does not necessarily require a focused *love* in order to exist but is often thought of as *love* for humankind as a whole. *Love*, as Primary Way of Being, on the other hand, is intensely focused. So, while *compassion* is the expression of *care* in the context of dealing with a specific pain or suffering, *love* can manifest itself without the presence of pain or suffering. In a world that is too fast for many people to take a moment to *care* for another person or themselves, we need this human sustenance now more than ever.

Discovering the transcendent Meaning of *love*

Some may confuse *love* with passion, which is defined as 'an extreme interest in or desire to do something'. In fact, it would be fair to say that passion is another grossly overused and misunderstood word. Every second article on leadership and entrepreneurship seems to talk about passion and being passionate in business. But when it comes to *love*, passion is only part of the story. To understand *love* as a transcendent Meaning, it is worth studying its origin. The multiple meanings applied to the word 'love' since ancient times will explain why it is so easily misunderstood today. Let's start with the ancient Greeks, who used a total of seven words to define the different states of love: *Eros*: sexual and erotic desire (in a positive or negative context), *Philia*: the love you have for friends, *Storge*: the natural affection you share with your family, *Agape*: unconditional or divine love, *Ludus*: playful love (like childish love or flirting), *Pragma*: long-standing love, the love in a married couple, and *Philautia*: the love of oneself (in a positive or negative context). My intention here is not to categorise types of love, but to say how challenging it can be to use just one word to refer to multiple Meanings. In contrast to the Greek language, the English language almost simplifies it too much. For example, the *Oxford English Dictionary* defines love simply as 'an intense feeling of deep affection', while the *Cambridge Dictionary* defines it as 'the feeling of liking another adult very much and being romantically and sexually attracted to them', and 'strong feelings of liking a friend or person in your family'. Meanwhile, the *Merriam-Webster Dictionary* defines love as 'strong affection for another arising out of kinship or personal ties', 'warm attachment, enthusiasm, or devotion', and, 'unselfish, loyal and benevolent'.

In addition to the many definitions of love to be found – and these represent just the tip of the iceberg – the thousands of Persian poems I have read in my life also refer to love, but not necessarily in a romantic sense. In Persian literature, love is the central theme. All the great poets and thinkers have written about love, and the more I explored to gain an understanding of what love is, the deeper the hole became, almost as though I would never be able to reach the bottom of it. But all that changed when I looked deeper into the works of Rumi, Hafez and Saadi, three of the greatest Persian poets and thinkers of all time. They considered love to be the most mysterious secret of Existence of all. In search of the transcendent Meaning of love, I came to the conclusion that love cannot necessarily be studied and experienced as purely a rational matter. However, that does not mean it is an intangible phenomenon that can't be measured. I would like to be so bold as to place this enigmatic, yet primal and tangible, Way of Being in the category of arational matters, as we discussed in Part 1.

Bear with me now as I dare to describe the indescribable. *Love* is without a doubt one of the most challenging of all the Aspects of Being in the

Being Framework for me to articulate. As a result, you may find some of the knowledge shared in this chapter takes a little longer to comprehend. Please be patient; take your time to digest it and allow yourself to be open to what you may discover as it requires you to be vulnerable and see things from a totally different perspective to what you may be used to. Whatever your vision of *love* is at this moment in time, I encourage you to let go of current perceptions and labels you may be familiar with that *love* is nothing more than romantic feelings for another person and/or just being kind and altruistic. *Love* is far more than that. In fact, you are about to discover that you don't need another being (human or otherwise) to experience *love*, and that this quality can be experienced anywhere and at any time.

As part of some of the workshops we run, participants are asked to break into small groups to discuss each Aspect of Being after learning about it. Normally they return to the main group full of ideas and thoughts. When it comes to *love*, however, most return perplexed and quiet, as if they have no clear picture in their minds. It reminds me of Ludwig Wittgenstein's rabbit-duck image, which we talked about in the Awareness chapter in reference to our web of perceptions. If you have a distorted view of something (in this case, *love*) it is always going to be confusing and perhaps even confronting when the truth is revealed. In most cases, as I said earlier, it requires the ability and openness (*vulnerability*) to let yourself see things from a different perspective. Let's now look more closely at this enigmatic Way of Being to highlight exactly what we mean by *love*, including its relevance in the context of performance, *effectiveness* and leadership.

You will recall that Martin Heidegger's being-with (*Mitsein*) highlights how you are **being with** something, someone or yourself. It is more than just how you relate to it. It is how you ARE with it. *Love* takes this to the highest possible level; it's difficult to describe in words. The best way I can describe it is when you give something, someone or yourself your full and undivided attention for a given period of time. This takes choosing to be intentionally present to *love* rather than just passively waiting for *love* to show up in your life. *Love* is when you are so intensely and intentionally **connected** and **present** to a matter or being (human or otherwise) that it is beyond logical reasoning. It's the quality of being all in (*commitment*) out of respect for Existence and all its manifestations and the Possibility of Existence (life) without expecting anything in return. It is acknowledging and being grateful for the fact that there is Existence, and that you are part of it, instead of resigned to nothingness. That in itself is the most powerful reason of all to love. It's easy to become so accustomed to the mesmerising beauty all around us and even to the fact that we exist that we take it all for granted. Some even go so far as to criticise and question the structure of Existence, and this can lead to self-sabotage and victimisation. *Love* prevents us from succumbing to the darkness. Being acutely present and connected to the world around us and to the wonder of Existence and life is the key to manifesting *love*. I am a philosopher out of *love* and *care*. *Love* and *care* are also why I have chosen to dedicate my professional life to working with leaders, entrepreneurs and coaches. You could also say this book is a 'labour of *love*' for me. My endeavours in life facilitate my ability to contribute to humanity, which I do because I care about assisting people to embrace the Possibility of Existence, our relatively high level of autonomy (*responsibility*) and *freedom* and live a rich and vibrant life, as opposed to a life dominated by anger, resentment, arrogance, envy, lies and deceit.

So, *love* is not attachment, possession or dependency. It is also not just about romanticism, as mentioned. We tend to confuse many Meanings with *love*, but at the end of the day, *love* is not as mysterious as it sounds. *Love* is the quality that enables you to **be with** yourself and others **as closely and deeply as possible**. If I were to create a new term that most closely refers to the transcendent Meaning of *love* as a primal Way of Being, '**being with ness**' is the closest term I could come up with. It is the deepest connectedness, *presence* and *partnership* possible and the polar opposite of separation. *Love* unifies.

The Being Framework ontological distinction of *love*

Love is living life from the viewpoint of being closely and/or intimately connected and is the highest possible level of being with another person and/or oneself. *Love* is the ultimate manifestation of *care* and is not an abstract concept or something you know about or only understand from a distance. *Love* has a quality of *care* that transcends personal interests. It is a quality that may not always be considered kindness, as affectionate concern may also be expressed in a firm, stern or uncomfortable manner, particularly to nurture in a way that is both supportive and preserves the dignity of the other person over time.

A healthy relationship with *love* indicates that you mostly experience both caring and being cared for by others, a true sense of connectedness. Others experience your *care*, warmth and genuine affection towards them. You are free to convey affection and *care* without fear of judgement or concern over the need to comply. You are courageous and can endure prejudice, judgement, rejection and the discomfort of being disliked by those you love.

An unhealthy relationship with *love* indicates that you mostly experience an absence of *care*, warmth and affection in your life. You may feel numb, apathetic or anaesthetised to the *love* and *care* of others. *Love* may be experienced as relational or only with certain individuals, and your relationships are often transactional. You may not experience loving others or being loved by them and may feel lonely, isolated or disconnected and resigned about relationships. Alternatively, you may be transactional in your relationships and use affection to leverage or win favour. Or you may see others from an overly optimistic, dreamy and romantic perspective, seeing their intentions, motives and behaviours through rose-tinted glasses while being excessively protective of them.

Let's have a look at an example to paint a clearer picture of how *love* is not a soft trait and why it is extremely relevant in business. Say you hire someone on a contractual basis and agree to pay them $300 a day for their services. Do you believe this dollar amount reflects their true worth? Are you following the logic of paying someone what you believe they are worth? The Reality is that their worth is far more than that. What you pay them is merely an agreement, a contribution. You cannot buy people; people are not commodities. It is their contribution (work) that can be partly commoditised. Someone with the genuine freedom to make their own choices would choose to work in an organisation for the sake of *love*, not money, because they care deeply about what the organisation stands for and the causes it is working towards. Working for the organisation gives them confidence that it will enable them to be a vehicle for change, not only to be of service to the organisation, but also to its customers and the wider community because they know that whatever they are working on serves a genuine need. Therefore, working for this organisation facilitates their ability to project the true manifestation of their Unique Being, including their knowledge, experience and skills, to the organisation and its markets. That's the power of *love*. Naturally, paying people is important, but the notion that everyone only works for money and that anything else exists only in fairy tales or utopia is completely untrue. You need only research how the team behind the Apple iPhone worked in the beginning – and even how they work now – or how Disney cartoons are created to understand this. As a matter of fact, both Walt Disney and Steve Jobs started out genuinely loving what they were working towards and, while neither is with us anymore, their legacies – and the love of their work and vision – live on and will stand the test of time as a result. I acknowledge that this concept may be foreign to you as this is not the experience within most organisations. And yes, many people may think they have no choice but to go to work so they can pay their bills. But don't forget that we are talking about high-performing and effective team cultures here. Most teams are not as effective as they could be because they are not operating with complete *integrity*, including *love*, hence it is no surprise if this comes across as a foreign notion.

In the previous chapter, I gave the example of an entrepreneur who, together with his team, had been trying to launch a tech business for the past twelve years before he came to me for assistance. Do you think he and his team would have persevered for as long as they did had they not absolutely loved what they were doing, had they not been so present to the value they were bringing to serve the needs of a market that they were willing to work without drawing a wage? Of course not. Consider that to choose to be an entrepreneur may be an illogical choice, and while *love* may seem illogical at times, it is a very prudent quality to integrate into your life and amplify to others around you. In fact, *love* is an extremely important quality for anyone who intends to contribute powerfully to the world. To understand why this is the case at a deeper level, it is worth gaining a clear picture of what happens when *love* is lacking. To do so, we need to consider the shadow – the troubled or dark side of us, as discussed in the Awareness chapter – specifically the shadow's relevance to our relationship with *love*.

Love and the shadow

As human beings we all have a shadow side to us, however many of us struggle to acknowledge it. We hide this aspect of ourselves at times as we all have things we don't want others to know, even those closest to us, such as the stories we are ashamed of or not necessarily proud of. We all lie to ourselves at times, though we can learn, through *awareness*, to be highly integrous beings by continually tapping into our relatively high level of autonomy (*responsibility*) to polish and transform. Individuals and organisations often do their best to manage their reputations, highlighting their strengths and hiding any weaknesses. The key point I am making here is that unless we are vulnerable enough to acknowledge and distinguish the shadow (through *awareness*), we can't work on our betterment, let alone transform. So, how and where do we start this enquiry? What gives us the *courage* to face the shadow and the *responsibility* to do whatever it takes to come out of the darkness and return to the light? The answer is *care* and its primary manifestations of *compassion* and, in particular, *love*. Without *love* there is no access for you to care enough about the troubling parts of yourself, your company, your life partner, and so on, to step forward and commit to change. *Love* is the answer and is the Way of Being that draws you closer to the heart of the matter than anything else can. It enables you to embrace the complete you and others, warts and all, and this acknowledgement and respect will guide you on the journey to action and change.

We can apply the same double-edged-sword logic about the shadow to organisations and businesses. If you run a business or lead an organisation, there are no doubt aspects about your business or organisation that concern or trouble you. This leads to either avoidance of those issues and/or a desire to invent a fake persona for the company brand in order to protect how you want your brand to be perceived, rather than showcasing your company's true colours. Such strategies may deliver some immediate short-term benefits, but my studies and experience in this area have revealed that the possibility of achieving long-term redemption (see explanation below), extraordinary accomplishment and fortune is extremely low. You may be able to deceive a small group of people – or even a large group – for a period of time, but when your business or organisation is up to big causes, as is the case for the world's leading organisations, you are so exposed to public scrutiny, that managing and maintaining a fake persona becomes unsustainable. In short, building and maintaining an inauthentic brand (fake persona) will not get you anywhere in the world in the long run. And it's worth remembering that when it comes to any big causes in the world, it's going to be a long race.

Redemption is a central theme in Pinocchio, a story which is relevant to us all. Let me explain. We all come into this world as pure, semi-autonomous beings, full of potential and promise. Whether or not we live up to our potential and promise depends firstly on those who raise and educate us when we are dependent. But ultimately, we are each responsible for our own lives. We are gifted from birth to be autonomous beings, capable of taking life by the reins and charting our own course. So, we can either choose to take the pathway of truth, benevolence, *integrity*, growth and *contribution* or, alternatively, we can choose the pathway of falsehood and malevolence, which always leads to decay and downfall[144]. Here is where redemption comes into play. Just as Pinocchio is redeemed by his love for his father and for embracing his higher level of autonomy – to BE in the true sense of Existence, not as a puppet whose strings are being pulled at various times by a force, ideology or trend – we can redeem ourselves too. How? By consciously and intentionally choosing to grab hold of *love* with both hands, firstly by loving ourselves (caring about the quality of our own life, family and business) and then expanding our horizon to contribute to others and the world with *love*.

---

144   Inspired by The Quran, Surah Al-Baqarah 2:256.

For those of you who think redemption and *love* have no place in the business world, I challenge you once again to be vulnerable and open. Think back to the consequences of a time when *love* was lacking in your business, either within yourself, your business partners, your customers or your staff. I know this may be extremely hard to grasp and even acknowledge, but I urge you not to avert your gaze from the facts. *Love* can be extremely confronting. It may even move you to tears and, if so, then let it be, as it is simply your Being's response to what matters. Consider how the following excerpt from Viktor E. Frankl's book, *Man's Search for Meaning*[145] on the subject of *love* is relevant to any leader. If you work with others and want them to realise their full potential so they can contribute effectively to the vision and greater cause you are all working towards, *love* is mandatory.

> '*Love is the only way to grasp another human being in the innermost core of his personality. No one can become fully aware of the very essence of another human being unless he loves him. By his love he is enabled to see the essential traits and features in the beloved person; and even more, he sees that which is potential in him, which is not yet actualized but yet ought to be actualized. Furthermore, by his love, the loving person enables the beloved person to actualize these potentialities. By making him aware of what he can be and of what he should become, he makes these potentialities come true.*'

As I mentioned earlier, at the heart of any successful organisation's offering lies a deep psychological pain of human beings. It is *care, compassion and love* that drives the founders and their teams to develop a product or service that addresses this pain, and this creates the opportunity to eventually make a profit from it. So, the cliché, 'do what you love', should actually be, 'focus on what you have *love* and *compassion* for'. That is your 'why', the motive at the heart of what you do and why you do it. If you let your why be suppressed and limited by the darkness (shadow), none of this would eventuate. It is up to you to choose powerfully to convey *care, compassion* and *love*. In other words, you can either let *care, love* and *compassion* drive you or let a lack of these qualities

---

145   *Man's Search for Meaning* by Viktor E. Frankl, first published 1946.

(their shadow sides) suppress you. Remember, *care* is a Mood and Moods either suppress us or amplify our impact and *effectiveness*.

Phenomenologically speaking, most people want to live their lives in good faith; they want to be good people. Whether or not we are consciously aware of it, this desire is intrinsically linked to our Unique Being, the part of us that is connected to Existence itself. This has nothing to do with our morals. And it's also not about trying to measure up to someone else's expectations. It's about being true and committed to your Unique Being, soul, spirit, inner self or however you understand the term and no matter what – if any – religion you subscribe to. Just as Jacob wrestled with God, as told in the Book of Genesis, we all struggle to varying degrees with our inner-selves and with Existence itself. This manifests itself in our self-sabotaging patterns and unreasonable behaviours, causing pain and suffering. Unless you accept and acknowledge the shadow and make change a priority (through *care*) with full intention, *compassion* and *love*, how could you possibly have the passion and grit to do whatever it takes (beyond rationality) to step forward when you are facing uncertainties? This is why I called *love* an arational matter as it's not always possible to analyse everything rationally. Sometimes you have to listen to what your conscience is telling you and take a leap of faith. There are many examples of this in life, such as bringing a child into the world or starting a new business when the world is facing a global pandemic and economic uncertainty, marrying despite the high percentage of couples who divorce or when someone marries a terminally ill partner, knowing that their time with them will be short. The quality that prompts us to step forward with unwavering *commitment* and be all in, even when the odds are against us, is undeniably *love*.

Now, I am not suggesting everyone deals with such matters in life with the same level of *integrity*. The key points I am making are that you cannot powerfully move forward without *love* and *love* is **not** just associated with romance, kindness, superficial affection or altruism. *Love* is not all roses and joy either. It's often tough, and if you have ever loved and been rejected, you will know how it feels to be wounded and suffering but still be in *love*. *Love* can be harsh; it challenges you to the core and requires you to make sacrifices. You need to nurture your relationship with love daily, just as you would a rose garden. A rose garden must first be established with the right soil to give it the best foundation for growth. Then it needs the right amount of warmth, moisture and sunlight, and let's not forget the seasons. It's not always going to be spring when flowers bloom. There will definitely be times when all you see are branches, stems and thorns, but no matter what the season, you must persevere with your nurturing efforts. It's no different to building and growing a business. In my entire career working with and studying businesses, I have never seen a company thrive without a sufficient level of *love* and *care* from the founders and within the executive and core teams of the organisation. They are prepared to persevere and nurture the rose garden, no matter what gets in the way.

It's easy to say we want to change and move in a certain direction, but execution is another matter. When we fail to execute, it generates stress and worry. In the context of this book, the shadow is the part of you that constantly judges and disturbs you, preventing you from moving forward and taking action. As discussed in the Care chapter, phenomenologically, most of us have a desire to thrive or at least to become better than who we are right now (however 'thriving', or 'being better' looks to the individual). Without *care*, we would not strive to build a career, achieve a promotion or grow a business, and so on. This desire manifests itself in all layers of our lives, however, it can also take us off track if *love* is missing. To come to terms with your shadow, which many find intimidating, demands the presence of *love*. This reminds me of the classic fairy tale, *Beauty and the Beast*. The monster will always look ugly and scary, but spend time getting to know it, nurture it and polish it and the monster can turn out to be the hero. Keep gauging your performance and relationship with *love* so it softens the edgy, unpolished you, enabling you to transform and thrive. No matter how strong you are, you cannot remain untouched by the darkness or malevolent forces, including the parts of you (shadow) that tempt or encourage you to stray from *love*.

Love is a necessity

While it is easier not to care or love, if your heart and mind are not ignited by the flame of *love*, it is virtually impossible to convey it to others or to coach or lead with *love*. Again, I cannot emphasise enough that no team is capable of generating consistent, sustainable performance without *care*, *love* and a genuine bond amongst the team (the maximum level of **being with** each other). This always starts with the leader. While high-performing individuals can produce brilliant results, those results are generally ad hoc or one-off. If you are up to a big cause, you need a team of committed people (as opposed to a group of high-performing individuals) who share a strong bond and the discipline to work together towards a common goal for the duration. We have estimated that it takes seven years on average for a startup to become a self-sustaining profitable business, so it is vital that the core team sticks together during this time.

One of the major consequences, from a business perspective, when *love* is lacking is that any professional relationship ends up being purely transactional. It will be a case of: I (employer) pay you (employee) to do this work for me according to how I want it and then I will sell it to whoever (customer) is willing to pay the right money for it. Human Existence does not work that way. You can't treat people as though you are solving a mathematical equation or moving a pawn in a game of chess. And this is just the tip of the iceberg, especially when it comes to the world's fortune companies, where the consequences of a lack of *love* are well beyond this example, particularly within their core teams. If you are running a business, dealing with hardships is par for the course. It requires you to go beyond your familiar, previously explored territories. For example, there will be times when you struggle to pay your staff on time, when unexpected matters crop up and your cash flow suffers. Therefore, you need people on your team who care and love what the team is collectively working towards enough to protect you and the company vision. It's important to think carefully about this before you hire people, actively seeking people who love the vision **before** they start. The same is true when it comes to attracting your ideal customer. Loyal, long-term, delighted customers are a true asset to your business. It is far easier and less expensive to upsell and cross-sell to a loyal fan than it is to a brand new customer. If *love* is lacking, good luck with the potentially huge cost of new customer acquisition time after time.

In our organisation, no one is given a job description when they start working with us. They are supported for the first three months to create their own job description. We call this the 'Creating Opportunity Letter'. On completion, the staff member is asked to take some time to create their role and then claim it as their own. So, technically speaking, we don't offer a job to anyone. They create it, claim it and then make it their own. It gives them a sense of pride and ownership and, in so doing, establishes the foundation for *love*. The benefit for the executive team is the assurance of having our people in positions in which they can contribute the most. This should come from a place of *authenticity, care* and *love*. Thinking back to the definition of an entrepreneur, entrepreneurial leaders are those who can arrange economic resources, including people's work/*contribution* in such a way that it causes workability and value and supports people to live meaningful lives. I have found this to be the most effective way to build sustainable businesses that serve their customers brilliantly, but not at the expense of their people. As for our clients, we are deliberate in choosing who becomes a client and who is a customer, someone we assist from time to time rather than develop a long-term relationship with. In choosing our clients, we deliberately seek people we would **love** to work and partner with and who, in turn, we know will love working and partnering with us.

At the end of the day, your experience of life (you being there) is primarily what you bring to the table. As long as you keep striving to be the best version of yourself by polishing your Aspects of Being; as long as you are responsible, leveraging your autonomy as an active agent to pull yourself out of misery and reduce your pain and suffering and the pain and suffering of others; as long as you fulfil your promises and commitments, no matter how insignificant it all may seem, you are contributing to life in a positive way. *Love* (for yourself and others) is the prerequisite to all of this. Without *love*, you could not even relate to Existence and all in it, yourself included. In other words, *love* is the key to open the door to relate to the world and all beings in it (including yourself). The important link here is *care*, *love* being the most brilliant and effective channel through which to convey your *care* to the world and all in it.

Most meaningful relationships and experiences in life are challenging, but they can also be incredibly rewarding at the same time. Raising children, caring for a dog, building a company that stands the test of time or pursuing a career you are passionate about, developing a life-long relationship with your partner, regaining the trust of a friend when that trust has been broken, it's all challenging. But if *love* and *care* are present, the rewards make the hardships worthwhile. If you have an unhealthy relationship with *love*, if *love* is absent or your perception of *love* is incongruent with Reality, then you will be inclined to give up when the path becomes rocky. As a result, the very objective you set for yourself in the beginning will not be fulfilled. It sounds like another cliché, but it is the truth and in fact, *love* is one of life's most significant transcendent Meanings because without *love* you wouldn't be here. You wouldn't have survived long enough to get to where you are now as without the *love* of those who raised you, no matter who cared for you or how imperfect your upbringing may have been, you could not have even made it this far. At some point someone loved you enough to carry you for nine months, despite having never laid eyes on you. Without *love* when we were completely helpless as a baby, we would not have survived, let alone thrived. This is a law of the universe and therefore not open to debate, despite the argument that some babies are born into less than desirable and challenging situations, which I acknowledge. But even in those instances, there had to be some *love* present or the child would have perished. This law applies to all beings.

Let's look at *love* pragmatically and once again consider its absence from our lives. If we are not **being with** *love*, what's the alternative? Well, you could be numb and indifferent, staying in a constant holding pattern through inaction. Worse still, you could let hate be the dominant force in your life. Before too long you would realise that something is not serving you in your life, that something must change. That's because these alternatives to *love* are the result of failing to proactively face, **be with** and hence deal with matters in life, particularly with the troubled parts (shadow) of yourself and others. So, if you believe there is an alternative to **being with** *love*, you need to get real (*authenticity*) and have some tough conversations with yourself. For example, ask yourself, 'Why have I felt the need to create a fake persona?' The answer is a lack of *love* for yourself and the mission you are up to in life. Without *love* for yourself and the mission you are up to in life, you would constantly feel the need to reimagine this fragile, adapted sense of self, selling it to yourself and others in order to maintain your confused double life. This may give you a temporary false sense of power, but it is not coming from your Unique Being and authentic connection with Existence; it is also not coming from a place of *love*, *care* and respect for yourself and the Possibility of Existence that has given you life. Rather, it is the result of being distracted and captivated by the shadow, the parts of yourself that keep tempting you not to be yourself for various reasons, such as the perception that you need to 'fake it till you make it', or turn yourself into the person you think others want you to be or succumb to the temptation of constantly having your mask on and guard up so you don't lose face. *Love* is the key to creating the willingness to want to change that life of deceit and imprisonment, to escape the double life you are leading which is generating so much suffering for yourself, and no doubt also for others, even if you are not aware of it. You have the power to choose to let *love* come to the rescue.

Love is the heart and soul of the Being Framework Ontological Model. Without *love* this framework wouldn't exist. This powerful Way of Being is the vehicle for my gratification and the motivation for my *contribution* and being of service to others. By now it shouldn't surprise you when I say that being of service to those whose pain and suffering you resonate with and have chosen to solve with your offerings and passion is central to the survival and growth of any business. This is the authentic way of building any business, no matter how large or small, and the rewards are plentiful. It allows you to generate revenue, generate jobs, contribute to the lives of employees and customers, contribute to the wider community (through taxes and your offerings) and, last but not least, turn a profit. That's the power of *love*!

CHAPTER 20

Contribution

Are there times in your life when you feel like a victim, when you sabotage your own thoughts and feelings, sinking into an ocean of sorrow and despair as you tell yourself you're all alone and no one understands you? In most cases, those feelings are not real. When you feel this way, it usually means you are not paying attention to all the wonderful things that Existence and other beings are contributing to your life and how they are serving you. In other words, you may be taking them for granted. As we discussed in the Gratitude chapter, even if you are oblivious or ignorant to this fact, you are constantly being served, directly or indirectly by others: from your parents, extended family and friends, to your employees, governments, other taxpayers, the bank, the waiter at the restaurant you visited last night and everyone who has contributed in some way to your life and the lives of others. This includes all the inventors, prophets, teachers and great leaders who contributed their wisdom and ideas to the world so that we may all benefit. Imagine if Al-Khwarizmi[146] had never discovered algebra and algorithms. Without his knowledge and *contribution*, Edison would not have invented the incandescent lightbulb, solar and clean energy would not exist, and we wouldn't have computers.

The story of Simorgh taught us that we are all connected; we are each a node in the network of humanity. We explored this further when discussing the Paradox of Importance, namely our presence, existence, everything we do, everything we create and even the things we don't

---

[146] Muḥammad ibn Mūsā al-Khwārizmī (780AD-850AD), Arabised as al-Khwarizmi and formerly Latinised as *Algorithmi*, was a Persian polymath (also known as the Father of Algebra) who produced vastly influential works in mathematics, astronomy, and geography.

do, it all matters. It's easy for us to take it all for granted. So, whether or not you are aware of it, you are constantly being contributed to and you are also contributing, in one way or another, through your interactions with others, and this *contribution* is amplified when you project the true manifestation of your Unique Being to the world.

Imagine if the majority of the world's population thought we were all put on this earth to live off the generosity of others and society. *Contribution* would be largely one-sided, leading to a world dominated by selfishness, negligence, idleness and greed. Thankfully, our level of autonomy (*responsibility*) encourages us to choose powerfully to live a life of service (*contribution*), as opposed to ease and comfort. The truth is, we are all here to serve and to have others serve us, regardless of personal opinions, status or lifestyle. Even members of royalty, with a large team of people dedicated to serving them, are here to serve their kingdom. Parents serve their children, especially when they are fully dependent, gradually adjusting the level of service as their children develop, learn new skills and mature. In turn, children serve their parents by bringing them joy, hope and purpose. Later in life, the tables often turn when children serve their elderly parents, caring for them if they lose their full independence. Businesses, or more accurately, people in businesses, serve their customers and their employers, while employers serve their employees by generating the job opportunities. Furthermore, customers serve the business by paying for products and services, which, in part, is used to pay employee wages. We all contribute, and we are all being contributed to every day.

For most of us, contributing to or serving others occurs quite naturally, as the quality of *contribution* or service is a primal and natural phenomenon. The question in this context is: how open are you to being contributed to by others? This is often where the buck stops. In fact, people can be quite startled by that question. You see, *contribution* goes both ways. If you think you can develop a business on your own without the *contribution* of others, you might find yourself struggling to get to the next level and never fulfil your objectives. Nobody achieves success on their own.

The Being Framework ontological distinction of *contribution*

Contribution is when you are available to support and compelled to be of service to others to achieve what they are committed to and are also willingly available for others to support and serve you. It is an outward manifestation and expression of your care for others and humanity.

A healthy relationship with *contribution* indicates that you mostly experience being compelled to make a difference to other people and are open, receptive and comfortable in allowing others to make a difference to you. You experience satisfaction and fulfilment from being a contribution as well as being contributed to. Others may experience you as being intentionally supportive of them and what they are committed to.

An unhealthy relationship with *contribution* indicates that you mainly deal with challenges and breakdowns on your own. Others may experience you as unreceptive, disinterested or unavailable for support. You may lack the willingness to participate and add value to others, particularly if you know there is no immediate benefit for you. Your sphere of influence and impact on the world often occurs as narrow and limited. You may experience being unappreciated or consider that what you have to offer is of little value. You may also be resigned and cynical towards other people and question their motives. Alternatively, you may interfere instead of influence and give advice when it is neither asked for nor required. You may also pester others for help without due consideration of the impact on them.

How do you want to serve and leave your mark?

Polishing your relationship with *contribution* begins with *awareness*: to see this Way of Being vividly and as part of the Reality and beauty of life. With *awareness*, the next step is to choose how you wish to contribute to others. For instance, you could become a local politician who suggests new policies that will benefit your local community, or an entrepreneur who invents a product that improves the lives of others, or a medical researcher who comes up with a treatment for a disease, or a good Samaritan who volunteers at the homeless shelter, and so on. The alternative is to hold the view that work, for example, is purely to make a living to fund a lifestyle. People with this view have an out of balance relationship with *contribution* because they focus on themselves instead of focusing on how they can contribute to/serve others. They are quite happy being contributed to, for instance, receiving a weekly wage from their employer, but that's where their relationship with *contribution* ends. The same applies to the business owner whose sole focus is on making as much profit as possible with little regard for their *contribution* to their customers or employees. As a result, their sphere of influence and impact on the world would be limited. In the Higher Purpose chapter, we discussed how going beyond yourself to contribute actually increases the probability of fulfilment and extraordinary success. When you transform and polish your Aspects of Being, including *contribution,* you have the power to expand reality (Second-layer) by creating constructs and inventions aimed at tackling the problems of humanity.

We contribute because we care. In fact, *contribution* has a strong relationship with *care* and also with *love* and *compassion*, as those Primary Ways of Being are the two most apparent manifestations of the Mood, *care*. Without *care, love* and *compassion* we are not available to be a contribution. Let's consider an example. Many organisations, including some of our clients, struggle with presenteeism. As mentioned earlier in the book, this is when staff members are present at their desk because they know they will be paid for the time spent at work, but they aren't actually contributing to the organisation. Unfortunately, to a certain extent, our employment laws protect this pattern of behaviour. Staff that behave in this way lack the *care* factor required to contribute. They are only interested in their ultimate goal of securing a wage. People who choose a career or to build a business that serves a need they genuinely care about achieve the greatest fulfilment and success in life. It's what we commonly refer to as 'passion'. When a business leader is passionate about the *contribution* their organisation makes to its customers and/or society in general, their passion usually filters through the entire organisation and to the people they serve. In fact, because of its close connection to *care*, *love* and *compassion*, *contribution* is seen as the most noble way to make a living and accumulate wealth across cultures.

Let me share a story with you about passion and its close connection to *contribution*. Passion is one of those words that can seem like an overused cliché. Ironically, its simplicity deceives many and therefore the importance of passion is commonly overlooked. When people who want to build a business approach us for assistance and/or funding, we begin by initially assessing them in ten key areas. Topping the list is PASSION. Our aim is to ensure that they are deeply passionate about their *contribution* in terms of the business they wish to build and its core offering. We also want to ensure that this *contribution* solves a burning pain/problem in the world and that the founders care enough to work towards solving it. We learnt the significant ramifications of ignoring passion some years ago. Two co-founders approached us with a business concept that we felt had great potential. They were so competent and effective with their fundraising and customer engagement efforts that we made an exception and partnered with them, taking a stake in their business without assessing their level of passion. After eighteen months, two funding rounds and with almost 3000 active users on board, the co-founders sent us an email, right on the verge of success and scalability, stating that they were withdrawing their interest because they had lost their passion for that business. This loss of passion was the end of that company, which we believed had an exponential potential to scale globally. That lesson reminded us of the importance of passion in business and we have never neglected it since.

Many tech entrepreneurs became wealthier – at least on paper – during the early stages of the global pandemic in 2020, while others struggled financially during the economic crisis caused by the pandemic. Some may argue that it is immoral to prosper in a crisis while others suffer. However, these tech entrepreneurs looked for and found an opportunity to contribute: to create an offering that served humanity during a time of crisis. Their high level of *awareness* (of the needs of their markets) and *responsibility* ensured they proactively sought appropriate solutions to contribute to and support others (*care*) who had to stay at home or work from home. By adapting to serve people in a time of crisis, many of these entrepreneurs thrived through *contribution*.

As you know, I have studied many high achievers of the world, including forward-thinking tech entrepreneurs like those mentioned above. It was no surprise to learn that they arranged their resources and people in such a way that they produced value (products and services) they knew would be so desirable to their target market that those consumers would voluntarily exchange money for it. That's precisely why some tech companies have experienced such dramatic increases in revenue, despite great economic uncertainty in the world. I find it shocking that some people choose to sabotage or protest against the efforts of forward thinkers like those tech entrepreneurs rather than being grateful (*gratitude*) that they are contributing to our economy and generating jobs through their offerings and leadership. Due to lack of *awareness* and *authenticity*, some resentful people turn to cyberbullying or protesting. For example, we have witnessed angry demonstrators setting up a guillotine outside the family home of a highly successful, well-known entrepreneur in recent times[147]!

You don't need to be a tech savvy entrepreneur to find an opportunity to serve others. Anyone anywhere can create opportunities to serve others any time. In so doing, we ultimately serve and reward ourselves too, emotionally and financially, provided the right structures are in place. This is precisely the whole point of this framework: your Being and the extent to which you are polished will enable you to amplify (or suppress) the expression of your Unique Being to the world. Your Being shapes your *contribution* and participation in life and how you perform and expand reality. I don't know of anything more empowering. Instead of protesting because you don't like the opportunities someone else has created or your job is no longer working out for you, you can choose to be a *contribution* and create greater opportunities for yourself. Some may

---

147 A large group of demonstrators constructed a guillotine outside Jeff Bezos' Washington, DC, mansion in August 2020 to protest Amazon workers' wages the day after Bezos' net worth surpassed $US200 billion, making him the richest person in history, according to Forbes.

find this suggestion provocative or even offensive, but I am extremely clear with my intention here, which is not to judge or point the finger, but to draw attention to the blind spots. This isn't about what's fair or unfair. Life is not fair! Fairness is a myth which has been propagated for eons. Life is about choice and *responsibility*, including how you respond to undesirable or unexpected events. After all, others also have a level of autonomy and theirs may impact the choices you make. If you no longer like your job or you feel you are worth more than you are being paid, then make the choice to find another job, educate yourself, start your own business, learn new skills that are in higher demand, do whatever it takes to do something you genuinely care about and be paid according to the value you bring to the table. This is totally the opposite of having a sense of being entitled. Life is about being contributed to by others and contributing to others. The extent and type of *contribution* you choose largely defines your decisions and behaviours, which ultimately define your accomplishments and fulfilment in life. That passion can translate into a mission. However, it is worth noting that the shadow side of passion can enslave an individual in such a way that they risk losing sight of everything else happening around them. All leaders need to be mindful of this danger. When passion is directed appropriately, it fuels their mission. If not, it consumes them.

There is, of course, another side to this story. These tech giants could not have achieved what they did without the *contribution* of the people they led. After all, it was their **people** who built the offerings and delivered them to the consumers. So, the leaders developed the people, which in turn enabled and encouraged the people to build the business. Similarly, the organisation — including every individual making up the organisation — contributed to its customers and those customers contributed to the organisation and its employees by purchasing their offerings, and this is how the organisation could afford to pay its employees and generate a profit. The key point is we simply could not exist without *contribution*. Your relationship with this Aspect of Being is extremely important because it significantly impacts both your performance, the performance of your people and the results you collectively produce. The question is, how would you shift your relationship with *contribution*, to serve/contribute and to allow others to contribute to you? Both are equally important.

The Contribution Quadrant

Care about *and* Effective at	Don't care about *but* Effective at
Care about *but* Not effective at (yet)	Don't care about *and* Not effective at

Figure 9: The Contribution Quadrant

There are four ways we can choose to contribute or be contributed to, as shown in the Contribution Quadrant above. This quadrant essentially defines the way we participate in life through *contribution*, whether it be in business, in our personal lives, on a project or in almost any context. Beginning with the left side of the quadrant, we all have things we **care about** and are **effective at**. These are the things we care so much about that we have invested a good portion of our life gaining a level of *effectiveness* in them. Some may call this their passion. Generally speaking, these are the areas in which we tend to produce the greatest results, as long as we maintain an authentic persona that is congruent with those areas. There are also things we **care about** but are **not effective at**, at least not yet. In other words, we value them deeply but still need to invest the time and effort required to gradually become competent, proficient and effective in them, with the ultimate goal of mastery (extraordinary *effectiveness*). Those building a career or a new business may identify where they fit in the Contribution Quadrant. They may have a passion for their craft, product or service and know that to become effective and ultimately succeed and generate extraordinary results (mastery), they will need to take risks and make many sacrifices. People who project the true manifestation of their Unique Being to the world and expand the collective reality (Second-layer) out there have developed this healthy relationship with *contribution*.

Turning your attention to the right-hand side of the Contribution Quadrant, there are also things you do not necessarily **care about** but are **effective at**. For example, you may be highly proficient in sales but would prefer to focus on product development. Despite your lack of interest in sales, others benefit from the value and *contribution* you bring because you're **proficient** at it. However, your lack of interest means you may be unfulfilled, disgruntled and struggle to **be with** yourself (*love*) when performing that role (projecting your professional persona). You could say *effectiveness* without caring is 'hard work'. It is not uncommon to hear of people who are so passionate about something, music for example, but are afraid of pursuing it as a career for various reasons. So, they compromise, sacrificing the one thing they care most about for a degree in IT, for example, purely on the assumption that a career in IT would pay more than a career in music. With hard work and *persistence*, they may become proficient in IT, but they are unlikely to ever be fulfilled in that role. Normally when people choose to contribute this way (without a high level of *care*) it is very unlikely that they would ever become a high performer and achieve extraordinary *effectiveness* (mastery) in that field, as they would always be competing with people who are not only effective but also care passionately about IT, which would drive them to work harder and give it their all (*commitment*).

Last but not least, we all have things in our lives that we **neither care about nor are effective at** (or willing to become effective at). This is sometimes described as apathy. Some people undertake roles they detest and aren't particularly adept at making a living from. For example, someone may hate working in a commercial kitchen but accept a role as a kitchen hand just to pay the bills. Many would refer to this as having a 'job' as opposed to a career. This is very different from someone who is passionate about cooking and happily accepts a job as a kitchen hand to learn everything they can about the operation of a commercial kitchen, to observe the chefs in action and as the first stepping-stone towards fulfilling their dream of becoming a master chef one day.

A world in which we have unfulfilled people participating in inappropriate roles is a very dull and barren world to live in. Collectively, it is in our best interests for us all to be engaged in roles that we both **care about** AND **are effective at** (or working towards *effectiveness*). If you own a business, the most powerful way to choose to contribute is to shape your business and offering around the areas you care most about and do your best to employ people who also care about your offering and the needs your business addresses. Even if they are not yet skilled in what you need them to do, when there is *care* and *love*, the skills will be readily learnt. When it comes to *contribution*, caring makes the world of difference.

Are you vulnerable enough to let others contribute to you?

As social creatures, our main power lies in the fact that we are united as a species. As I mentioned earlier, if you are up to any great cause, you cannot do it alone. If you think you can, I suggest looking into your willingness to be vulnerable. This is why *vulnerability* is such an important driver of our behaviour. When we lack *vulnerability*, we have our guard up. Now, if you have your guard up most of the time, the likelihood that someone on your team can support you is low, as you are unavailable for their *contribution*. While you may think you are a substantial contributor to society, it may very well be that this assumption is not aligned with reality. If you want to develop a healthy relationship with *contribution*, you must also be willing to let others help you, and this will require you to let your guard down, to allow yourself to be vulnerable. It becomes quite obvious in romantic relationships that *contribution* goes both ways. If one partner resists being contributed to, the other partner will find it quite challenging. Imagine if you want to do something special for your partner, but they won't let you. Then imagine if this happens time and time again. How would it make you feel? It is highly likely that, after a few rejections, you would no longer offer *contribution*. In the business world, someone who has a healthy relationship with *contribution* is often known as a team player. These days, companies and businesses understand the value a staff member brings to their projects when they are a team player. That's why questions relating to teamwork are common during the interview process.

Many business owners, particularly small business owners or sole traders, think no one can do their job better than they can. In some cases, they are right, at least within the context of their own business. But this perception commonly prevents them from scaling their business, which, ironically, is the goal most are working so hard to achieve. Their unwillingness to be vulnerable enough to trust, mentor, delegate and lead others so they may contribute to the business is the very thing that is holding them back. As mentioned, top achievers know how to leverage other people's talents. This is an issue we encounter frequently when working with clients. It's as though the thought of needing others to help them hurts their ego or damages their pride, as if letting others contribute to them is a sign of weakness. However, the opposite is true. It is not weak but wise and generous to let others contribute to you and your organisation, just as it is wise and generous to contribute to others. The better our relationship with *contribution*, individually and collectively, the better the world will be. What do you care about that leads you to contribute to your family, your community, society or your organisation and your clients?

CHAPTER 21

Partnership

So far in this book we have talked many times about the notion that we are all connected as human beings. This connection is often referred to as 'common being', or 'unity of existence' by thinkers such as Martin Heidegger, Ibn Rushd (Averroes), Mulla Sadra and Ibn Arabi, to name just a few. We learnt that we are each a node in an interconnected network of human beings. We have also talked about the fact that if you are involved in any great cause, you need to align yourself with others because you will never achieve your objectives on your own. In addition to common being, Heidegger also referred to the term 'Being-with' (*Mitsein*), which he said is essential to being human, as discussed earlier. To acknowledge and be aware of this is critical if we want to build any relationship, especially a partnership, as it is the closest type of relationship. There is true synergistic power in *partnership*. While mathematically, one plus one equals two, a partnership between one human and another human may generate far more than two units. *Partnership* centres on how human beings are related to each other. It's when two or more people empower each other by choice, irrespective of circumstances.

The perceived threat of 'the others'

In our childhood, most of us were taught not to trust strangers. Ironically though, and unbeknown to us at the time, most of our success and accomplishments later in life would be as a result of dealing with people we don't know, strangers. This could include people we do business with, the new person who is about to be recruited into the organisation, the potential life partner we are about to date, the new neighbour about to move next door, they are all strangers right now. Those strangers will soon become familiar to us as being a stranger is constrained by time, *care* and *presence*. Who knows what magic could be created between those who were once strangers! As the saying goes, 'strangers are just friends waiting to happen'.[148]

In fairy tales and mythology, monsters, antagonists and other malevolent forces represent people or groups ('the others'). Because 'the others' are unfamiliar to us, we assume they are different and must therefore have goals and intentions that are not aligned with our own. But how do we know this? Could it be that our ignorance leads us to perceive them as a threat or danger simply because we don't know them yet? This leads us to make up stories and assume that they ('the others') may threaten and endanger our survival or the survival of our ideas and way of living. In Persian, the word *Deev*, which literally translates to 'ghoul', is something to fear and fight. Mythologically, *Deevs* represent 'the others' and are potentially a threat to our survival and growth. Interestingly, the word for 'wall' in Persian, *Deevar*, contains the word *Deev*. This is representative of the fact that the wall is what stands between you and the *Deevs* ('the others') as a means of division and protection.

Why am I talking about monsters, *Deevs* and other malevolent forces? Because this analogy highlights the fact that we perceive those who aren't like us or don't think like we do as a threat. This common misconception prevents us from mingling and ultimately partnering with others who may complement us well. Our fear of difference causes us to hang out with familiar people and this causes us to get stuck on the same old treadmill. Zooming out, fear of difference has led to bigger societal issues in the world, such as racism, sexism, and intolerance and discrimination within multicultural societies. Throughout history, differences have also led us to war. While such issues are beyond the scope of this book, they serve to highlight how important it is for each of us to show *care* and *compassion* and be willing to form relationships with people we don't know or are different to us. Eventually those strangers become familiar. The alternative is to collectively pay the price. Being open to expanding your horizon when it comes to partnering with others will serve you well because you may discover that in difference lies complementary skills and talents that will result in a far more powerful collaboration than if you were to stay within your comfort zone.

---

148   American poet, Rodney Marvin McKuen (1933-2015).

What is meant by *partnership*?

Partnership is the quality that makes you available, ready, capable and willing to figuratively merge a part of yourself with another, to connect and see yourselves as inseparable. When you form a partnership with another person, you generate a 'mutual being'. Establishing the right foundation is crucial. But it doesn't end there. It is critical to keep working on the relationship in order to maintain its integrity. Let me explain further. Each party is an entity, and the partnership formed when each entity comes together is a new entity that develops its own characteristics over time. It's not dissimilar to creating a hybrid fruit tree. When grown correctly, with *care* and the right nurturing, the hybrid tree generates a new type of fruit, while the original trees continue to grow and prosper as well. In a business or personal partnership, the newly generated and maintained entity has the potential to be bigger and more impactful than each individual entity could ever hope to be on their own. This requires deep *commitment* and *higher purpose*. When forming a partnership, it is also important to be authentic, in other words, not to let fake personas get in the way.

The Being Framework ontological distinction of *partnership*

Partnership is living from the viewpoint of being in union with other human beings, an entity, team or organisation in the pursuit and fulfilment of a common purpose. It is when you are available to join with others who may share the same values, goals or commitments to create a disproportionate outcome in comparison to what each of you could possibly achieve alone. *Partnership* is the state of confluence where you embrace others and are available to influence each other. It is when you choose to powerfully collaborate and empower each other, irrespective of circumstances.

A healthy relationship with *partnership* indicates that you mostly experience being together, where common purpose, vision, intentions and goals are fulfilled. Others may experience you as being on the same journey with them. You appreciate the company of others and experience being connected, belonging and moving towards the same mutually fulfilling outcomes. You are steadfast in your relationships and will appropriately challenge and support others to bring out their best.

An unhealthy relationship with *partnership* indicates that you mostly experience being isolated and on your own. You may consider yourself independent, although you may also experience frustration and resentment around what is possible to achieve alone. Others may consider you unavailable, overly independent or a loner, and you may experience a sense of not belonging or disconnection. You may tend to initiate transactional relationships based on a trade-off (quid pro quo). You may sacrifice true intimacy and are often oblivious to the value of the contribution of others and the synergy that can be generated of a greater value than you could ever cause alone. Alternatively, you may initiate superficial relationships in the hope of instant gratification rather than investing, building, nurturing and developing long-term relationships.

The key ingredients for a healthy relationship with *partnership*

While partnering with others is critical if we are working towards a big cause, it seems many of us neglect to take it that seriously. Either we don't care enough to build strong *partnerships*, or we want to but don't know how. As is the case with anything rewarding and meaningful in life, establishing partnerships is difficult. It requires at least two willing, relatively polished participants who are aware, committed and have a healthy relationship with their Moods. They must be vulnerable enough not to have their guard up, they must care about the contribution the partnership will be making – and that they themselves will make to the partnership – and they should have a healthy and effective relationship with *fear* and *anxiety*. An effective *partnership* also requires each party to be a self-expressive, courageous and authentic human being who takes *presence*, *contribution*, *forgiveness*, etc., quite seriously. In other words, if you are not sufficiently polished yourself, it's going to be a nightmare trying to build partnerships with others. Don't get me wrong; I am not suggesting that you have to be perfect before you can build a partnership. What I am suggesting is that you would want at least two reasonably polished individuals who are willing to grow and thrive on board, yourself included, before even contemplating forming a partnership. In most cases, each person will bring their own strengths and weaknesses – in terms of their relationship with their Aspects of Being – to the table.

The most important prerequisites for a successful *partnership* are *vulnerability*, *authenticity* and a genuine desire and willingness to work on building the relationship. These qualities are essential for building any relationship, though when it comes to a partnership, it is such a powerful and intentional collaboration that it is like merging parts of your **being with** the other person, a true union that is so strong it's as though invisible glue bonds each partner to the other. On the upside, as long as the prerequisites are there, you can shape the role of each partner in an iterative manner, constantly assessing and adjusting based on what is working, what isn't working, and what's missing. This is a process that takes time, and in receiving and giving authentic and direct feedback – as opposed to unconstructive criticism and judgement – with *vulnerability* and epistemic humility, you will gradually build a solid foundation for an effective partnership.

Let's have a look at an example of an effective start to a partnership. Person A establishes the expectations for the partnership in an authentic and assertive manner with Person B. Person A then asks Person B to make a commitment to take the risk of uniting with them with *courage*, which they agree to do. As the one who established the idea of the partnership, Person A holds Person B to account and lets them know any time they are not fulfilling their commitment. If they stray from their commitment, Person B is vulnerable enough to own it and immediately rectify the situation (clean up). Person A forgives Person B, and they both move on with autonomy (*responsibility*) – Own it, Clean Up, Move On – as we discussed in the Responsibility chapter. Adopting this pattern of execution, Partner A and Partner B are both participating and contributing to the development of the partnership, tracking, learning and refining as they go. This is how an effective, trusting partnership is established and built over time. As you can see, it's simple, and it's definitely not easy! In other words, do not let the apparent simplicity of this process fool you. It is both incredibly powerful and much more challenging to execute than you may think. That's why assisting top company executives and boards of directors to address their partnership issues is one of the most frequent requests we receive in my organisation. So, while it is a simple process, most people struggle to execute it. If the establishment and development of a partnership was easy to execute, we wouldn't see so many divorces and business partnership breakdowns, including the suffering caused by unhealed wounds on both sides as a result. This is where polishing the Aspects of Being and *integrity* of individuals – the foundation of this framework – comes to the rescue.

There's more to *partnership* than *contribution* and co-existence

In my business, I quite frequently observe two or more people coming together, full of excitement and anticipation, to create a business partnership only to discover soon thereafter that a mutual lack of trust and resentment is preventing them from moving forward. They come to us to help them solve their problems, without necessarily being aware of the underlying root causes. Furthermore, they are often unwilling to make sacrifices and take responsibility in order to make the partnership work, waiting for the other party to change instead of looking in the mirror themselves. *Partnership* is much more than a co-existence and *contribution* between two or more individuals. Establishing a culture where resentment is acknowledged and regularly and ruthlessly addressed creates a foundation for success. Furthermore, there is a give and take (*contribution*) that needs to happen by all parties concerned for a partnership to flourish.

Establishing, growing and nurturing a partnership, whether it be in business or a personal relationship, is one of life's most challenging endeavours because, as we said earlier, it is essentially when two individuals merge to become one entity. We have enough problems dealing with our own unpolished Aspects of Being, let alone adding another person, with all their issues and complexities, to the equation. These days, an individual's personal choice, needs and freedom of action are highly valued and tightly held. Again, I am not here to pass judgement. But developing a partnership requires both individuals to make certain sacrifices. Therefore, a partnership may impinge on some of that *freedom* and choice, and demand less focus on one's personal needs. While as social beings, we struggle with the idea of being completely alone, making sacrifices in order to be in *partnership* with another person is, paradoxically, something many of us also struggle with. This is precisely what prevents many from building strong partnerships, in business and personally, that stand the test of time.

Partnership as a Way of Being

Access to the *partnership* Way of Being starts with another Primary Way of Being: *presence*. From the start, you need to be willing to communicate, to listen, be present with, and get to know the perspective of the other person/people involved so everyone's cards are on the table (for full transparency and *awareness*). However, that simple action is challenging for many, especially those who still struggle with *vulnerability* and *authenticity*. Those people seem to lack the patience and emotional stamina to listen to everything another person needs to get off their chest before jumping in with their own needs, issues and perspective. Some even seem to wonder if it's worth their time and effort. Well, let me assure you it is more than worth it; it is critical if you want the partnership to endure long enough to see the rewards down the track. I devote a great deal of time and effort into building and developing relationships, both in business and in my private life, because I know the benefits will serve all parties well, especially when disagreements and misunderstandings occur later on. In addition to supporting others to establish and nurture partnerships, I know the enormous value in a solid partnership through my own experience with my partners in the various businesses I am involved in. Notable high profile examples of highly effective partnerships (whereby *partnership* as a Way of Being has been mastered) include Larry Page and Sergie Brin, co-founders of Google, Mike Cannon-Brookes and Scott Farquhar, co-founders and co-CEOs of Atlassian, and Bill and Melinda Gates, partners in life until 2021 and co-founders of the Bill & Melinda Gates Foundation, reported to be the largest privately owned charitable organisation in the world and one dedicated to improving the quality of life for individuals across the globe.

Establishing the right foundation for any partnership is vital. It's a matter of nurturing it, as an entity unto itself, and maintaining its *integrity* so that it may flourish over time. Remember, before partnering with another person, you only had your own *integrity* to maintain. Now you have this new entity to polish as well as yourself. A partnership built on a strong foundation of trust and understanding, in which the partners share common objectives, is worth all the effort and time you put into it. However, fail to build a strong foundation – as I observe in many businesses and relationships – and the process may become a destructive, never-ending cycle. In the same way that recruiting and training new staff can be time consuming and costly, so too is establishing business partnerships over and over again. A partnership that is focused on empowering the other person(s) to fulfil their dreams is empowering and energising for both parties. In partnerships where purpose and intention are aligned, exponential growth is a real and likely possibility.

CHAPTER 22

Forgiveness

Resentment is an emotion we are all familiar with. There are many common reasons people feel resentment towards another person, a group of people, an organisation, government, or an entire system. Examples include resentment towards a partner for breaking their commitment through infidelity, resentment towards parents for a less than ideal upbringing, resentment from a father towards his child's homosexuality, resentment from the child towards his father for his lack of support, resentment to the world for being unfair, and so on. On a bigger scale, one may feel resentment towards the judicial system for failing to deliver a harsher sentence to the perpetrator of a crime committed against a loved one, or for being found guilty of a crime when innocent, and the list goes on. *Forgiveness* is the opposite of resentment. Despite the extensive research done in this area, much of which I have personally studied, it seems that no one, including masters of various spiritual disciplines and eastern philosophies, has yet found a silver bullet that helps people forgive in an instant. There are of course exceptions in terms of people who successfully demonstrated the beauty and *effectiveness* of *forgiveness* in action. Nelson Mandela, Archbishop Desmond Tutu and Gandhi are three notable examples. But collectively, we have yet to find the magic formula. *Forgiveness* offers significant and powerful learning lessons for us in life. However, it is a Way of Being that is often misunderstood and greatly undervalued.

Phenomenologically speaking, *forgiveness* requires intention, willingness, *awareness, responsibility, care* (and *care's* two key qualities of *love* and *compassion*) as well as patience, time and reason. But what exactly do we mean by *forgiveness*? The *Oxford English Dictionary* defines the verb 'forgive' as 'to stop feeling angry or resentful towards (someone, something or oneself) for an offence, flaw, or mistake'. In his book, *Grief is a Journey*, Kenneth Doka describes *forgiveness* as 'the intentional and voluntary process by which a victim undergoes a change in feelings and attitude regarding an offence, and overcomes negative emotions such as resentment and vengeance'[149]. The distinction of *forgiveness* can differ depending on the context. For example, Everett L. Worthington Jr[150] and his colleagues, Michael McCullough and Kenneth Rachal, have defined *forgiveness* in close relationships to include more than merely getting rid of the negative emotions. They say, 'the forgiving person becomes less motivated to retaliate against someone who offended him or her and also less motivated to remain estranged from that person'[151]. When we human beings hope to forgive another person with whom we no longer want to continue a relationship, we usually define *forgiveness* as 'reducing or eliminating resentment and motivations toward revenge'. While most people probably feel they know the transcendental Meaning the word *forgiveness* refers to, researchers differ about what actually constitutes *forgiveness*. However, to keep the conversation more general so that it serves the purpose of this book and framework, the simplest way to describe *forgiveness*, based on our extensive studies, is **giving up the right to be a victim** and stop continually victimising yourself as that is not going to serve you.

---

149   Doka, K. J. (2016). *Grief is a Journey: Finding Your Path Through Loss.*

150   Everett L. Worthington Jr, Ph.D., is Commonwealth Professor Emeritus at Virginia Commonwealth University. He studies forgiveness, humility, and other character strengths and virtues within positive psychology.

151   *The New Science of Forgiveness* white paper by Everett L. Worthington Jr, September 2004.

The Being Framework ontological distinction of *forgiveness*

Forgiveness is the quality of being able to let go and move on. It provides access to restoring *integrity* to how it used to be before the act or event you are forgiving. When you forgive, you completely discard any resentment, anger or hurt towards a person (including yourself) in relation to the act in question. *Forgiveness* is not about condoning another's behaviour or actions; it is freeing and releasing oneself from the past while embracing the lesson learned. *Forgiveness* brings about ease and flow.

A healthy relationship with *forgiveness* indicates that you mostly experience freedom from resentment and choose to discard resentment, anger or hurt towards yourself and others quickly and completely. Others may experience you as someone who can move on from negative experiences or issues with ease. You look to actively resolve issues and restore relationships.

An unhealthy relationship with *forgiveness* indicates that you often dwell on and repeatedly bring up past events and have difficulty letting go of blame or shame. Others may consider you vengeful, bitter, or someone who can maintain a grudge for a long time. You may have a tendency to blame circumstances, past events or others for the outcomes you experience in life. You may also consider yourself forgiving of others but hesitate or decline to forgive yourself. Alternatively, you may frequently try to move on too quickly without learning the lessons, resolving any issues and bringing about closure. You may be considered naive and unable to discern the motives of others and often accept excuses to preserve the peace. You may let others take your *forgiveness* for granted and are susceptible to being taken advantage of.

Forgiveness and *vulnerability*

As human beings, we often find it easier to stigmatise or denigrate our enemies – 'the others', or *Deevs* – the ones threatening our survival, *peace of mind* or matters we find important like our dignity, pride, ego, the persona we project to the world and our beliefs and opinions, rather than forgive or empathise with them. In a society as competitive as ours, we may also hesitate to forgive for fear of relinquishing the upper hand or control in a relationship. For example, let's say I have made a mistake and am afraid to own it, forgive myself and apologise because I believe this would appear as though I am acknowledging my weakness. My unwillingness to be vulnerable causes me to have my guard up and hide my mistake for *fear* that owning it would disempower or disadvantage me by highlighting me as the person at fault. To consider this from a different perspective, let's say you have discovered my mistake and have two choices: forgive me, or withhold your *forgiveness* as an excuse not to let me be the preferred candidate for the leadership role you and I are both vying for, giving you the upper hand. You choose the latter, taking it as your trump card. While some may falsely believe accepting *responsibility* for mistakes is disempowering, holding on to the mistakes of others instead of forgiving them is far more problematic. I would suggest that in the example, neither of us would be worthy of the leadership role. Instead, it would be far more effective to be given to someone more willing to own their own mistakes, show *vulnerability* and who is also more comfortable with forgiving others for their mistakes.

Forgiveness and its relationship to health and wellbeing

Forgiveness is not a one-off event; it is likely that we will have to forgive again and again. *Forgiveness* isn't something that is only practised by saints or martyrs, and it doesn't only benefit its recipients. In fact, studies have found connections between *forgiveness* and physical, mental, and spiritual health, as well as evidence that it plays a key role in the health of relationships, families, communities and nations. It is extremely important to note that, like any other Aspect of Being in the context of this framework, my intention was never to see *forgiveness* purely as a virtue or from a moral standpoint. Instead, my intention was to explore and discover it ontologically and phenomenologically to reveal its exactness, essence and objectivity and, with this in mind, explore its connection to human performance and *effectiveness* from a practical point of view. So, I am not suggesting that we should forgive for the sake of *forgiveness*. The key point here is that it's not so much about forgiving the other person to be kind or as a favour, it's more about doing yourself a huge service by freeing yourself from the resentment, anger, *fear* and *anxiety* you are harbouring so you can **be with** yourself and others again. Once you forgive, it will feel like a massive weight has been lifted off your shoulders, and that's the true gift of *forgiveness*. Many may find this confusing. Here's the thing: if you keep carrying a wound, no matter who inflicted it – yourself included – you are doing yourself a massive disservice if you fail to forgive. Why? Because it will continue to impact your wellbeing and the wellbeing of those around you. Furthermore, it will impact your ability to contribute and participate in life, to express your Unique Being and project a fuller version of yourself to the world. So, there is no better case for you to develop a healthy and robust relationship with *forgiveness*. But that does not mean you should always forget, as I will explain shortly.

Scientists, physicians and psychologists who have researched the relationship between stress and illness have concluded that the ability (or inability) to forgive affects the outcome of serious illness. People who are more forgiving actually increase their chances of recovery. *Forgiveness* is not necessarily a logical process[152] and it often makes no sense to the reasoning mind, especially when we are in the heat of the event or situation. It probably isn't just hostility and stress that link a lack of *forgiveness* with poor health. According to a recent review of the literature on *forgiveness* and health, a lack of *forgiveness* might compromise the immune system at many levels. For example, the review suggests that a lack of *forgiveness* may alter the production of hormones and disrupt our ability to fight off infections and bacteria.

As a leader, you are inevitably dealing with issues that demand your *forgiveness* and generosity, as you frequently find yourself in situations where you need to forgive yourself and others for the mistakes, ineffective decisions or actions you and others may have made along the way.

---

152   Caroline Myss PhD, Medical Intuitive, international speaker and author of *The Second Mystical Law: Forgiveness is Essential.*

Being forgiving adds momentum to your organisation because it keeps it moving. Your ability to let go and **move on**, no matter how right you may think you are, will encourage people to try new things/solutions without constantly being anxious or in fear of retribution. Encouraging people to step out of their comfort zone and try new things brings ease and flow, like adding oil to an engine. Remember, righteousness always gets in the way of *forgiveness*. Do you want to **be right** or do what it takes to bring about the **right** outcome?

Studies were conducted in the lab of Everett L. Worthington to determine if people's stress levels are related to their ability to forgive a romantic partner. They measured levels of cortisol (a stress hormone) in the saliva of thirty-nine participants who were asked to rate their relationship with their partner as terrific or terrible. Those who rated their relationship as terrible tended to have higher baseline levels of cortisol. Interestingly, they also scored worse on a test that measured their overall willingness to forgive. Their cortisol level rose sharply when they were asked to think about their partners, and it was found that those sharp rises in stress were closely correlated with their unwillingness to forgive their partner. The cortisol levels for participants who rated their relationship as terrific, on the other hand, were in the normal range. They also scored better on the test that measured their willingness to forgive their partner's faults, demonstrating the benefits of *forgiveness* on their wellbeing.

Forgiving and forgetting

In suggesting *forgiveness* for your personal benefit, I am not implying that you should also always forget, as that is an entirely different matter. The strategy adopted by high achievers and top performers when someone – themselves included[153] – causes them suffering, is to forgive as soon as possible, but that does not mean they always forget. Here is the key: when you forgive, you resolve to let go of being a victim. And by no longer being the victim, you stop harbouring the negative thoughts and feelings associated with the wound so you can keep moving forward with the great cause you are up to. This will change the dynamics of your Moods, which in turn will flow through to your Ways of Being,

---

153   We are our own worst enemy, as most wounds are inflicted upon ourselves.

decisions and actions in an exponential manner, like a ripple effect. It will free you up to deal with all aspects associated with whatever is going on in your life without distraction, for example, if you are going through a separation, if you are in the process of suing someone, if you have to let go of an employee or if you are terminating a partnership agreement because it isn't working out, and so on. You may find that by no longer being a victim, you are able to forgive the other person and take the relationship to another level.

The reason we should not always forget when we forgive is to use it as a valuable learning experience. The lessons learnt from your suffering and subsequent *forgiveness* then form part of your life experience and will make you stronger. They will also give you a more accurate conception of reality (*awareness*), which in turn will lead to maturity, knowledge and wisdom as you become more exposed to and aware of new matters in life. I am by no means belittling the wounds suffered in life. I understand how hard it can be to forgive as quickly as possible, but without forgetting so that you learn from the experience. There is no question that this can be extremely challenging. But anything truly rewarding in life is hard. All high achievers and top performers gradually learnt to deal with their wounds, and each time they were wounded – figuratively speaking – they handled the situation more effectively. Can you imagine how many lies, betrayals, attacks, scandals, fake news, bullying, insults and misjudgements top leaders experience on a daily basis, let alone how often they don't receive gratitude for their efforts? They have two choices: resent and stew over these scenarios, allowing themselves to be crushed by the darkness, negativity and unfairness, or forgive, learn from the experience and move on. If you think you should forgive and forget, you may wish to check the *authenticity* of this belief. After all, can anyone really forget or pretend something never happened?

An unhealthy relationship with *forgiveness*, by contrast, is a negative emotional state where an offended person maintains feelings of anger and resentment towards the person who offended them, including themselves. Given hostility is always present when *forgiveness* is lacking, this emotional state, which is commonly held onto for extended periods of time – hence the term 'holding a grudge' – will eventually set your dominant Mood, impact the health of your relationship with your

Moods and ultimately result in suppression of your expression of Self (your Unique Being) to the world. This leads to poor performance, ineffectiveness and an inability to lead a fulfilled and accomplished life. Such are the consequences when *forgiveness* is absent.

Forgiveness is more about you than them

Forgiveness is the capacity to transcend events that may have shattered you and let them go. Regardless of whether you or someone else are to blame for an event, *forgiveness* is about letting go of the grip that grudges and anger have on **you**, so that you can move on with your life. I have worked with clients who have been through tremendous hardships in life. While some made the decision to hold onto the injustices in their life and kept suffering, others made the powerful decision – after polishing their relationship with *forgiveness* under my guidance through this framework – not to have their quality of life determined by the will and imposition of others. They learnt to keep letting go of the blame, shame, anger and suffering, in most cases coming away much stronger in the process. Many even expressed *gratitude* that this trauma had happened to them because it gave them new and valuable insights in life, new skills and empowered them to tackle more significant and challenging projects. Believe me, it is often hard to comprehend, as an outsider, how people who have experienced severe trauma can develop such a positive outlook in their life. I have also coached executives and business owners who were suppressed in their business endeavours because they could not forgive another person and/or themselves. Once we were able to release the blockage – which mostly centred on forgiving themselves – they were able to move on. As a result, they found a new sense of *empowerment* and the *courage* to become more successful in their business endeavours moving forward.

In summary, *forgiveness* is not just the act of releasing the aggressor or telling someone their action is unacceptable, although this state of being is often interpreted that way. *Forgiveness* is letting go of any form of emotional and psychological attachment to the event and not being the victim. This is easier said than done because the ego wants to hold someone, including you, responsible for why certain events happened the way they did. Resentful people want to see justice or revenge applied and want to be right. But even if you are right, that is not going to change the outcome. We like to erase traumatic experiences from our memory and 'fix' things so life returns to the way it was before the traumatic event, but this simply isn't possible. In fact, this view is delusional and therefore inauthentic. The truth is, if you are holding on to grudges, resentment and anger, you are hurting yourself because those emotions are poison to the body and mind. Once you have forgiven yourself and others, all those emotional attachments are released and gone forever. It is a healing and empowering process that gives you back your *freedom* and autonomy because you have given up the right to be a victim, and this is how you empower yourself. While this may seem simple, it is not necessarily easy. It's about choosing powerfully to restore the matter, if possible, or let it go and move on.

CHAPTER 23

Self-expression

How self-expressed are you in your life? What does being self-expressed look like for you? What gets in the way? We all get bogged down with what we can do or say or how to act. We are all constrained to varying degrees by our Moods: fear of judgement, anxiety about the future, the things or people we care about, and being vulnerable around others. While *freedom* may be the first quality that comes to mind here, *freedom* is necessary but not enough on its own. Until you polish all your Aspects of Being and radiate like the sun that cannot be quenched, these constraints will continue to inhibit your *self-expression*. *Freedom* is an undeniable prerequisite for *self-expression*, as indeed are many other Ways of Being, such as *authenticity* and *responsibility*. However, being self-expressed is far more than just being free to express yourself verbally or physically. *Self-expression* is the state of being **unleashed** and **unrestrained** so that you consistently, naturally and unreservedly project the manifestation of your Unique Being (the real YOU) to the world.

What is *self-expression*?

While *freedom*, as a Way of Being, can be subtle and internal, the state of being fully self-expressed is vividly visible and clearly evidenced in how you live. Hence the term 'freedom of expression' is the notion of having the power to project the manifestation of your Unique Being in various forms, whereas *self-expression* as a Way of Being is visibly living out that *freedom* in your life. It's about the quality of your *presence*, how you connect with another person, how you share yourself with others, how you experience yourself, how you influence the way others experience you and, ultimately, how you show up in the world. In this way, *self-expression* is the gateway to how you will be perceived and understood by others.

In Part 1, we explored Unique Being, the piece of Existence we all carry within, our 'who-ness'. We also discussed our Being (Essence, Nature), our 'what-ness', or, as we have defined in this framework, our Aspects of Being. When we have a healthy relationship with *self-expression*, it enables us to project the manifestation of both who we are (who-ness/ Unique Being) and what we are (what-ness/Being) to the world, expanding the reality (Second-layer) around us. *Freedom* provides access to being self-expressed. *Self-expression* is the ultimate form of communication (*presence*, connectedness and synchronicity) because it enables you to leave your mark on the universe by intentionally and effectively expanding reality to such an extent that you radiate an inextinguishable and irrepressible YOU. *Self-expression* is your full and active participation in every aspect of life through the projection of your **authentic Self**. This is how you engage in and contribute to the world. A visible by-product of this may be considered fame. Whether others like or dislike you, agree or disagree with you is irrelevant as your presence in the world is an undeniable reality. You express yourself, therefore you are present.

It is not possible to fully convey the Meaning we use '*self-expression*' to refer to using conventional means of communication, such as words, which are open to different interpretations. Take artists, for instance. Conventional use of language and verbal clues are insufficient to express the thoughts, feelings and ideas they wish to convey through their art. So, artists invent creative new ways that go beyond conventional means of communication. That's why the link between *authenticity* and *self-expression* is crucial. The *Merriam-Webster Dictionary* defines self-expression as 'the expression of one's own personality: assertion of one's individual traits'. And the *Oxford English Dictionary* defines it as 'the expression of one's feelings, thoughts or ideas, especially in writing, art, music or dance'. In the context of the Being Framework, *self-expression* is much more than manifesting your traits and quirks. It goes far deeper. It is the full and vivid projection of your Unique Being, which in turn becomes your *contribution* and service to the world.

The Being Framework ontological distinction of *self-expression*

Self-expression is when you intentionally and authentically communicate who you are and how you are, including (but not limited to) your points of view, beliefs, values, feelings, emotions, moods and experiences. You may express yourself freely and creatively in many ways: through your work, speech, body language, facial expressions, music and other creative arts or ways. It is the state of being uninhibited and resonating with life and everything in it and may evolve to become your unique contribution to humanity.

A healthy relationship with *self-expression* indicates that you mostly experience being free to project yourself in various ways with others, regardless of circumstances, leading to satisfaction, joy and fulfilment. You are self-expressed when you unleash your qualities to be seen, heard and appreciated.

An unhealthy relationship with *self-expression* indicates that you may frequently experience being suppressed, restricted and constrained in how you interact with others, commonly leading to a lack of both fulfilment and satisfaction. Others may experience you as inhibited, quiet, reserved or shy in different circumstances or to have hidden or rarely seen talents and qualities. You may hide your passions or interests from others for fear of judgement or ridicule. Alternatively, you may have few filters and be considered blunt or overbearing. You may disproportionately value your contribution and feel the need to outshine others. You may also be uncomfortable with silence or not being the centre of attention.

Why does *self-expression* matter?

Self-expression is natural to all creatures. A flower expresses itself through beauty and scent, the sun expresses itself by generating warmth and light and the expression of the moon is the reflection of the sun's light. Existence manifests itself through all beings including us human beings. The design of the universe is such that every being relies on the *self-expression* of other beings. Imagine if the sun decided not to shine for a day or the bees chose not to express themselves. There would be serious consequences for every other being on Earth! While other beings have no choice but to thrive and fully express themselves (they are surrendered to expression), as human beings, our relatively high level of autonomy (*responsibility*) means it is up to us to surrender and choose powerfully to be self-expressed. Why should we care? Because there is such diversity of colour on show when we are all fully self-expressed. It allows us to collectively create a beautiful tapestry that we can all enjoy and benefit from. To not be self-expressed has potentially dire consequences. This reminds me of the Simorgh story, where all beings are either tuning their instruments to the symphony of life through *self-expression* or failing to express themselves authentically and contribute to the *integrity* and unity of all beings. The latter results in them becoming liabilities that leave nothing but a dull, lifeless graveyard in their wake.

In the context of family or business, a lack of *self-expression* leads to consequences for yourself and others. Everyone is expressing themselves and relying on each other within those complex networks of interconnected relationships. As human beings, our full *self-expression* is our own personal choice. Can you imagine a world in which the likes of Beethoven, Mozart, al-Khwarizmi (who created algorithms, which led to computer technology), Thomas Edison, Tim Berners-Lee (the Internet), Alexander Fleming (antibiotics), Steve Jobs, Nikola Tesla, Dennis Ritchie (C programming), etc., had never chosen to be fully self-expressed? It is magical that we get the chance to not only exist, have autonomy (*responsibility*) and have the *freedom* to choose, but that we also have the opportunity to experience Beethoven's symphonies or use social media as a powerful means of communication. All this beauty and innovation results from the *self-expression* of us human beings collaborating, devising, inventing and conveying meaning and beauty through thought and art. This *awareness* leaves me in awe and deeply grateful. To be present to all these characteristics of Existence (First-layer Reality) and what we have collectively created (Second-layer Reality) is so valuable, humbling and beautiful despite any suffering or hardship that comes with it. Remember, every rose has thorns too.

As we have discussed throughout this book so far, the Being Framework is ultimately about the projection and manifestation of your Unique Being to the world. That's the ultimate objective of the entire paradigm. To achieve this objective requires you to polish, transform and maintain the *integrity* of your Being (Aspects of Being) so you can consistently BE as effective, self-expressed and fulfilled as you possibly can be through the revealing of a fuller version of your Self. This causes a ripple effect, as shown in *Figure 10* below. Your decisions, actions and hence your accomplishments flow from how effectively you express and project your Unique Being to the world. Of all the Primary Ways of Being in the framework, *self-expression* is the quality that ultimately enables the projection of all other Primary Ways of Being into the world, which is why I left it till last. It is the culmination of all your hard work and consistent efforts in polishing and transforming all Aspects of Being and being fully present to the fact that it is up to you to be understood and to choose powerfully to be true to who you were born to be, the real, authentic YOU.

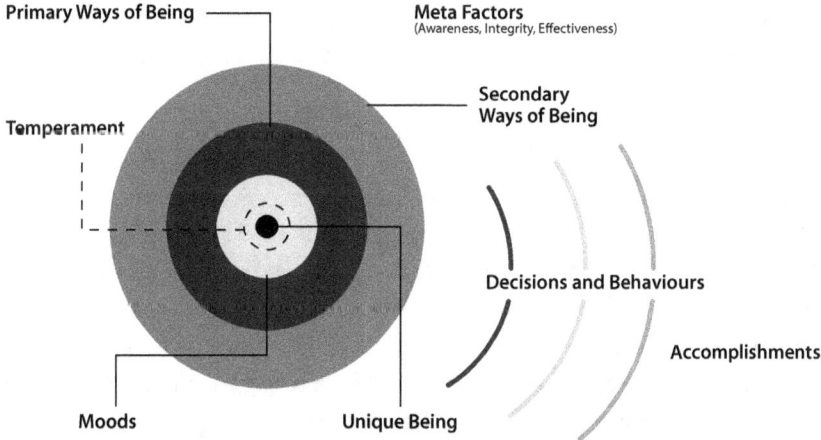

Figure 10: The ripple effect when projecting the manifestation of one's Unique Being

Do you need to be an extravert to be fully self-expressed?

When it comes to projecting one's authentic Unique Being to the world, there is a misguided belief that one needs to be an extravert to do so effectively. This isn't a new concept. Under one heading or another, theories of extraversion versus introversion have been widely discussed and debated in psychological literature for over a century. Many theories incorporate a person's degree of extraversion/introversion as a key factor underpinning their personality/temperament. I do not blame researchers for this misconception. As human beings, we have a tendency to categorise things in order to make them easier to understand because unstructured data is difficult to digest. However, if poorly done, categorisations such as these can raise more problems than they solve.

In contrast, the Being Framework ontological model uses primal and fundamental language to articulate what has been described as extraversion, introversion and ambiversion. We go deeper, looking into one's **relationships** with Moods – *fear, anxiety, care* and *vulnerability* – as well as Ways of Being such as *freedom, self-expression, courage, confidence, assertiveness* and *proactivity,* etc., from a divergent context. By breaking down the qualities of human beings into readily digestible chunks, the Being Framework encourages individuals and teams to embark on a process of transformation because each Aspect of Being can be shifted. To simply categorise people as extraverts, introverts or the latest category and buzzword, 'ambiverts', does little to help an individual, a team or humanity as they suggest that human beings are hardwired to remain as they are for the rest of their lives.

While there are those who have fixed views around the Extraversion Spectrum, namely that we all sit somewhere on the continuum, our studies to shape the Being Framework led us to assert that we are **not** fixed objects. While we can be a certain way at any given time, we are **not** destined to stay that way for the rest of our lives. We can and do transform, as I said earlier. This requires us to step outside our comfort zone, which isn't easy. If you are striving for a radically different outcome in your life and are aware of the significant benefits of *self-expression* as a Way of Being, you may feel compelled to take on this challenge. The point here is that people should not be categorised and labelled as extraverts, introverts or ambiverts for life. We all have the potential to transform. Importantly, we don't need to be extraverts to be fully and deeply self-expressed.

Self-expression and its link to *contribution, presence* and *authenticity*

We all express ourselves in a variety of ways, such as through our words, body language, the clothes we wear, our actions, art, the businesses we run, the products we produce, the career we choose, and so on. Together, these ultimately manifest as our unique contribution in the world. If a person has a healthy and effective relationship with *self-expression*, it is very likely that their expression of self will show up in the form of their contribution to the world. Furthermore, phenomenologically speaking, people find purpose and meaning through *contribution*, hence its significance in our lives. As mentioned at the start of this chapter, *self-expression* as a Way of Being is linked to all other Aspects of Being, in that any gap in your *integrity* not only impacts your *effectiveness* but also your ability to be fully self-expressed. It's like the ripple effect we spoke of earlier. The more you polish and transform your Aspects of Being, the more of your true Self you will project to the world. For example, if you do not have a healthy relationship with *responsibility*, and are lacking in *care* and/or *awareness*, this may reduce your ability to be fully self-expressed.

Over time, we human beings have developed unique, sophisticated and delicate ways, as a species, to communicate to the world around us about what is going on in our thoughts and emotions. *Self-expression* goes far beyond communication. Let me explain using a business context. All leaders want to be heard and understood. We all want others to know our point of view. So, guess who is responsible for that? You are. Most leaders believe they are not heard and understood, and our studies align with this view. As a leader and forward thinker, it goes with the territory that most people won't 'get' you unless you become aware of the fact that it is your *responsibility* to not only shape the vision but also to communicate it effectively and consistently and reiterate it over time to ensure people remain aligned. In this way, you will influence others to contribute and help you fulfil that vision. This is where *self-expression* comes to the fore because communicating the vision, plans and your point of view is not just restricted to verbal or written communication, as mentioned previously. *Self-expression* is conveyed through your *presence* and actions, tone of voice, facial expressions, body language, energy, what you stand for, the projects you take on, your priorities, the matters you care about, the way you ARE. It's how you radiate your *presence* to those around you and how you choose to impact the reality out there by being YOU, your genuine authentic Self. This is predominantly expressed through the choices and decisions you make as well as the actions you subsequently take, so it is critical that those decisions and actions are congruent with who you are and the vision you have communicated to the world.

In today's society, a lot of attention is spent on *self-expression* in order to stand out in the commercial world. Individuals and marketing departments paint a branding image that may look interesting and unique, but the question is: how authentic is it? Social media and other marketing channels are full of people trying to win us over by trying to stand out and show a unique and creative side of themselves, their products and services. But again, how authentic is this? I am not posing this question from a moral standpoint; it is a rhetorical question because the inauthenticity will ensure these messages won't stand up in the long run. In an attempt to build a business and survive in this competitive and ever-changing environment, it's easy to feel as though things are out of our control. Our guard goes up (lack of *vulnerability*), *fear* and *anxiety* start to run the show and we begin resorting to unhealthy competitive behaviour. This is not the most effective way to achieve our goals. When we are focused on our competitors, our ability to bring out our uniqueness and successfully connect it to a product or service is diminished.

We may not have a lot of influence over the external environment, but we do have complete influence over how we want to express ourselves. Because *self-expression* is how we project our Unique Being to the world, it becomes our contribution to society, projects, partnerships and more. But if our Aspects of Being are not sufficiently polished; if, for example, we are not authentic, we will fail to be truly self-expressed. I frequently observe this with my clients and, more often than not, they are unaware of the impact this has on their business, career and relationships. When our *self-expression* arises out of the need to compete and get the most followers, it rarely comes from a place of *authenticity*. Instead, it is focused on impressing others and manipulating our fake persona. But when we are expressing a true and authentic side of ourselves and our products and services, the need to compete with others is eradicated, growth occurs organically, and we gain loyal followers through trusting relationships.

When you effectively and consistently express your authentic Self, you embrace the possibility of your existence and intentionally immerse yourself in the world that you are a part of. You will be united/as one with Existence itself and surrender to the fact that you are a part of the world, not apart from it. Whether or not you are aware of it, you are a part of Existence, we all are, with all our differences, idiosyncrasies and quirks. Once you acknowledge that fact, you can own it powerfully. We need this diversity in the world and in our organisations. By diversity I am not referring to things like race, religion, ability or sexual orientation; I am referring (in this context) to a group of people who bring different qualities, Aspects of Being, talents and skills to the table, just as the ocean and forests need diverse ecosystems to thrive. Under the right leadership and guidance, and given the right environment, this diverse group of people will be free to contribute through *self-expression*, which will set your organisation on the right path – by being an authentic brand – towards sustainable success and fortune. I realise this is not necessarily the typical approach and perspective adopted in the business arena and there are many watered down or exaggerated versions of *self-expression* as it pertains to leaders and teams in the workplace. But what I am conveying here is real and it works. All top *Fortune* companies we studied adopt this approach. Whether or not they are aware of it, they display their understanding of the importance of *self-expression* in their decisions and actions. And their results speak for themselves. There is no reason why your organisation couldn't be amongst this elite group one day.

While there are behavioural and more visible ways in which we communicate, *self-expression* as a Way of Being is more concerned with a deeper quality that manifests itself through our behaviours. How much depends on the extent to which you have the urge and willingness to be connected and of service. Your reality (Third-layer Reality), your narrative, your perspective, your beliefs and opinions, your self-image (who you know yourself to be right now), your persona, your emotions, feelings and moods, all should be expressed through your Being so you can embrace your calling, execute it and make your contribution, to live your life and project the manifestation of your Unique Being to the world. Like any other Aspect of Being, some have a more effective relationship with *self-expression* than others do or are yet to have. There is glory and pride associated with our ability to gain clarity around our calling, unlock our potential and express it to the world. It's what the world's greatest artists, composers, poets, inventors, scientists and leaders, etc., have done. They were true to themselves (*authenticity*) and it was conveyed in their actions and shone through their entire Being.

What is the alternative to *self-expression*?

If you are not expressing your Unique Being to the world, why are you here? What are you doing with your life? What is your alternative? Become a copycat, create an inauthentic persona, suppress the desire to live out your calling and let circumstances, including other people and malevolent forces, pull your strings? If you don't express yourself, either you are letting life unfold as a passive being, manifesting laziness and procrastination, or you are living your life feeling like nobody understands you and you are not being heard. This can lead to isolation, loneliness or even bitterness and the decision to make victimisation and self-sabotage your dominant pattern. Rather than letting your Unique Being shine, you would be captivated by *fear* and *anxiety* and consumed by a lack of *care* and *vulnerability*.

In our organisation, we place a lot of emphasis on helping our clients identify their Unique Being and learn to incorporate this into everything they do. *Self-expression* is the path to a fuller, richer life and it also opens pathways for others to experience who you are. And isn't this what we all want? Don't we all want to feel free to project our Unique Being to the world and contribute in a way that aligns with that? Think of all the famous artists, poets, inventors, entrepreneurs and others who made a lasting impression on us because they shared their unique gift with us. People who are truly self-expressed leave a lasting legacy. It doesn't matter what your story is. Live it and show it to the world.

At the heart of many arguments is a desire and a need to self-express and be heard. Indeed, a lack of *self-expression* is one of the primary causes of relationship breakdowns, both personal and business relationships. Who do you think should own the continuous process of *self-expression*? Who is responsible? The answer is **you**. Expressing yourself is one of the greatest battles you need to win, not just every now and then but continuously. If you suppress the expression of your Unique Being, that would be a liability for humankind because the world would be left with a void that **only you could fill**. No matter how insignificant you may think you are, we are all a node in a network of people and matters in life (Paradox of Importance). Remember, your influence goes far beyond your initial response because it generates a powerful ripple effect.

I would like to encourage you not to view *self-expression* in a self-centred way. As much as it may seem like a selfish pursuit, it's definitely not just about you. Rather, I encourage you to view it with a sense of *higher purpose*. Think of it as the law of nature. Diversity, as I said, is key to its (and our) survival. As much as bees may seem insignificant in the greater scheme of things, the very survival and growth of our ecosystem is dependent on the *self-expression* of the humble bee! We need diversity in the world because a world in which people are not striving to polish themselves, be self-expressed and make their unique contribution would be tragic and single dimensional. You need only look at places in the world under tyrannical rule to see the devastating effects of a system that radically limits *freedom* and *self-expression*.

Every organisation needs a diverse ecosystem to maximise its human potential and leverage its enormous power. This is what many of the great organisations do. For example, if you were to divide their revenue by the number of people in the organisation as a simple calculation you would see they are successfully capitalising on and leveraging their human power. The same cannot be said for many SMEs. What they generate in revenue barely covers their employee costs, signalling their inability to effectively leverage the potential of their people. All organisations need a mix of people, from salespeople, operations personnel, engineers and technicians to administrators and experts in various fields. Moreover, each individual staff member would bring a different contribution in terms of their Aspects of Being to the table. For example, you would want a project manager to be conscientious, responsible, empowered, committed and reliable, whereas you would seek salespeople who are free and self-expressive. Then, on the leadership team, you would look for people with high levels of *awareness*, *integrity* and *effectiveness* meaning they are polished and well-rounded in all Aspects of Being. Having a team of well-polished individuals who are free to express themselves and their talents and creativity is an asset to any forward-thinking organisation. In other words, having the right mix of people with a broad spectrum of qualities and healthy relationships with their Aspects of Being is essential for any successful and innovative enterprise.

All beings are the outcome of the expression of Existence itself, for which no language, brushstroke or musical note could ever hope to convey in its totality. Existence does not speak in the languages we human beings have created; it sends us signals. Like the citizens of Babylon[154], we have caused great confusion for ourselves by being bound by the limitations of the languages we created. Because Existence has its own language, it is up to each and every one of us to attune ourselves to that language. All beings express themselves in some way; they are surrendered to the ultimate Reality. The sun is expressing itself the way the sun is meant to and the same is true for the moon, cats, dogs, bees, etc., The moon doesn't complain that she is not the generator of light, just as a cat doesn't argue that she should have the right to bark like a dog; they don't pursue the right to be identical or equal. Those beings naturally project their Unique Being out into the world. They are **surrendered** to it. It's only us humans, with our relatively high level of autonomy, that seem to struggle with *self-expression*. We all have a responsibility to become aware of our Unique Being and then express it through our decisions and actions. Failing to express ourselves can lead us to great suffering. There is no sustainable alternative but to express who you are deep down, the Being you were born to be.

---

154   In the Book of Genesis, chapter 11, Babylon is featured in the story of The Tower of Babel. The Hebrew people claimed the city was named for the confusion which ensued after God caused the people to begin speaking in different languages so they would not be able to complete their great tower to the heavens (the Hebrew word Babel means 'confusion').

Self-expression starts at the top

Selling is often seen in a negative light. But in essence, we need to 'sell' our ideas, visions, products and services to others all the time. If you are unable to express yourself effectively, it can impact your marketing, branding and promotional work. For example, it will inhibit your ability to effectively express your value proposition. You may respond by hiring an expert for these services, but how will they be able to identify and convey your true value if you don't know how to express it yourself? As a leader or founder of a business, you will hand this lack of *self-expression* down to your team, and it will filter through the entire organisation, from the board of directors to the receptionists, who are your first point of call to customers. Consider some of the world's most iconic and successful brands and their founders: Apple and Steve Jobs, Microsoft and Bill Gates, Amazon and Jeff Bezos, Facebook and Mark Zuckerberg. They all have unique products because the founders were able to express their Unique Being. In other words, the founders all have/had an excellent relationship with the *self-expression* Way of Being. And their *self-expression* filtered through to every team member and lives on, even if the founder is no longer there. Their *self-expression* is also reflected in their brand, which caused the world to sit up and take notice from the outset.

Paving the pathway towards *self-expression* requires you to continually work on and polish every other Aspect of Being. As mentioned, you definitely need to be authentic to be self-expressed, otherwise you may be expressive but not necessarily expressing your true Self. You may also need a good dose of *courage* and it would definitely help if you are clear on your *higher purpose*. If your purpose is to express yourself as a great leader, *self-expression* will enable you to empower your team to express themselves, and in so doing, enhance their individual talents and gifts. Your people need to be nurtured and developed because they are key to the company's ability to produce brilliant and innovative products and services. Too often, leaders are under the illusion that by selling themselves out or short in certain aspects, including their *self-expression*, they can compensate by making a win in another area. Let me assure you, this does not work. When we sell ourselves short, we are not authentic and, while there may be a short-term goal that can be achieved by doing this, we lose out in the long run. As a leader, it is so important to create an environment that fosters *self-expression*. Just be aware that it takes *courage* and *vulnerability* to do so because it requires you to empower your team to be part of the decision-making process and to align their strengths and skills with a career path so they have the freedom to strive for a goal and contribute powerfully. It also calls for systems to be in place that support a high-performing team culture. It is not something that just happens by itself.

Self-expression is the key to effectively and gracefully participate in the party of life. We serve ourselves and others through *contribution* and *self-expression*. Doing so ultimately gives meaning to our lives, so it is extremely important to take these Ways of Being seriously. As you can see, *self-expression* is definitely worthy of our attention and *care*. Without *self-expression*, your Unique Being will remain a rosebud for the rest of your life rather than the rose in full bloom it was always destined to be.

SECTION 4

Secondary Ways of Being

As discussed in Part 1, Secondary Ways of Being emerge from the constitution of the underlying Primary Ways of Being. They can be reliably observed, as we tend to project them through our decisions and behaviours, body language and even the most subtle facial expressions. When it comes to projecting our Unique Being to the world, Secondary Ways of Being are like 'the final frontier' because they are closer to the surface than our other qualities. So, when projecting our Unique Being to the world, like a drop of water, it flows through our Moods and then our Primary Ways of Being before being channelled through our Secondary Ways of Being and finally reflected in the decisions we make and the actions we take. Our decisions and actions then go on to shape our behaviours and, ultimately, the results we produce. There is a distinct ripple effect. You could also say our Secondary Ways of Being are the bridge between the deeper layers of ourselves – our Moods and Primary Ways of Being – and our actual behaviours. But as you are about to discover, Secondary Ways of Being are intrinsically linked to our Primary Ways of Being and Moods and should therefore never be assessed in isolation.

Eight Secondary Ways of Being have been identified in the Being Framework, all with a focus on leadership, *effectiveness* and performance: *assertiveness, proactivity, confidence, persistence, resourcefulness, resilience, accountability* and *reliability*. Furthermore, in modelling the reality of the Secondary Ways of Being in the Ontological Model, I have separated them into two categories: multidimensional and linear. The first four Secondary Ways of Being (*assertiveness, proactivity, confidence* and *persistence*) are multidimensional in nature while the remaining four (*resourcefulness, resilience, accountability* and *reliability*) are linear in nature. Linear means you are either one way or the other way on a linear spectrum, for example, you are either reliable or unreliable. Multidimensional means you can be one of three ways relating to that Secondary Way of Being. Take *proactivity*, for example. When you are not **proactive** you can either be **inactive** or **reactive**.

For each of the multidimensional Secondary Ways of Being, I have created a pendulum diagram to provide visual clarity around the opposing behavioural factors that can be present when one does not have a healthy relationship with that Secondary Way of Being. I found a pendulum to be an effective way to represent multidimensional Secondary Ways of Being as they cannot be represented in a linear fashion at either end of a spectrum. The difference between linear and multidimensional Ways of Being will become clearer as I walk you through each Secondary Way of Being over the coming chapters, beginning with the four multidimensional Secondary Ways of Being.

While Secondary Ways of Being are readily observable, they can also be misleading because we human beings are very capable of putting on a facade, which happens whenever we are being inauthentic and lacking *vulnerability*. Primary Ways of Being are **primal** to human beings while Secondary Ways of Being refer to constructed, non-primal qualities that are more visible and behavioural. This by no means makes them any less important. In fact, Secondary Ways of Being are critical because, as mentioned earlier in the book, they help us bridge what lies on the surface – visible behaviours and decisions – with the deeper parts of us: our Moods and Primary Ways of Being. Furthermore, if you dig deeper, you will discover that every Secondary Way of Being is closely linked to more than one Primary Way of Being.

To BE versus to act

There is an enormous volume of content available, from academic journal articles, etc. to self-help books, online videos and courses, that offer tips on how to behave in order to **come across** as more confident or assertive, to name just two examples. However, for the most part, this information will only help you to **act** confident or assertive, as though you are performing on a stage. But it will do nothing to help you to actually BE confident or assertive. You may ask, 'Isn't it enough to act a certain way? Doesn't the action matter most?' Let me answer this with an example. Behavioural studies suggest that you should always be seated with a strong, upright posture and never slouch in a meeting as this will make it appear as though you are occupying more space and manifest as confidence. But if you are truly confident, you will naturally carry yourself with a strong posture and your confidence will also shine through in many other aspects of your Being and actions. It won't be an act. It will come naturally from within, as a result of your *integrity*, and will be congruent and consistent with other behaviours you manifest. So, *confidence* is not about sitting up straight and tall and occupying more space in the room. When you are BEING confident, those attributes come naturally. The former is merely an act that may deceive some people, while the latter is authentic. Therefore, wouldn't it be more effective to work on being confident rather than merely acting confident?

It is important to understand that Secondary Ways of Being are **not** behaviours; they are **behavioural factors**, meaning they more **directly** impact your decisions, actions and behaviours than the other Aspects of Being. So, while they are behavioural, in our framework we approach them as Ways of BEING, hence the term Secondary Ways of Being. You are to BE (not act) assertive, confident, proactive, and so on, if your aim is to BE an effective person. If you ARE assertive and confident, etc., then it will manifest in your actions. Your actions will become **congruent** with how you are being. Don't be surprised if being authentic and vulnerable in this way reveals your shadow, initially to yourself and then also to others. Rather than seeing this in a negative light, it actually presents you with an opportunity to confront those shadow parts of yourself and polish or transform them. This is the ONLY access to growth. The alternative is to keep hiding those shadow sides, but this will only keep you where you are now, at best, or send you in a downward spiral.

Even if you are so good at acting confident or assertive that you fool others into perceiving you to be the most confident or assertive person they know, when you come from a place of inauthenticity, it is actually a sign of insecurity and weakness. People with a higher level of *awareness* and experience, such as some startup investors and high calibre leaders, will pick up on this quite quickly. Furthermore, you won't be able to maintain the facade for too long. Rumi wrote that our Being is constantly like 'the smell of the last raw onion we ate'. In other words, you can't hide your Being, just as you can't disguise raw onion on your breath no matter how hard you try. Even if you are an extremely good actor, maintaining a fake persona is at least as challenging (if not more) as working on and maintaining the *integrity* of your own true Being. Ironic, isn't it? So, if you can put the time and effort into transforming, polishing and maintaining the real authentic you, why waste time being a copycat? This is literally like building a house on sand; it will never stand the test of time.

Let me bring it home with a business example. Let's say your business partner asks you to do something important, however, you're not completely on board with it. To avoid confrontation and appease your business partner, you nod your head half-heartedly and reply, 'Sure', even though you fully intend to ignore the request. Meanwhile your business partner assumes that your affirmative response means you have made a promise to meet the expectation they have set, and they are now relying on you to play your part to deliver a promise they made to one of the company's most important clients. Days later, when nothing has been done, your business partner realises you have failed to deliver on your promise and their expectation has not been met. In dismissing the request with a perfunctory, 'Sure', in the hope that the issue would go away so you wouldn't have to face your business partner with your reservations about the request, you have not been *assertive* in your actions. This lack of *assertiveness* backfires when your business partner comes back with questions, their *anxiety* levels clearly heightened as they explain the predicted consequences to the company because you have not fulfilled your promise to the important client in question.

Suddenly you realise that the company could lose the client, as a similar incident in the past resulted in the loss of clients, which was on your head too. Your business partner still blames you for that and, to this day, has not forgiven you. Furthermore, you have never owned it and cleaned up, so it's been impossible for the two of you to move on from that. Your business partner may react in one of two ways: they may vent their frustration and disappointment towards you in an aggressive manner, or they may be submissive and suck it up, filter their true thoughts – putting on a facade and not being *authentic* – and tell you, 'It's fine', failing to communicate what is really on their mind. This leads them to hold resentment towards you and have their guard up (lack of *vulnerability*) while constantly having internal conversations in the back of their mind, depicting a lack of *presence*, *responsibility* and *commitment*. This can lead them to keep victimising and sabotaging themselves rather than being open (vulnerable) to having a discussion with you in order to try and find the root cause of the issues at hand, which resulted in a lack of *assertiveness* on both sides. At this point it is clear the business partnership will not survive. You cannot imagine how many businesses we have observed, studied or worked with that have undergone a very similar scenario. As you can see from this example, the underlying Moods and Primary Ways of Being manifested in Secondary Ways of Being, such as *assertiveness*, which is precisely why they should never be viewed in isolation. While many think the major causes of business failures have to do with revenue models, technology, and market demand (the technical aspects of a business), we discovered, through our studies and experience, that the number one reason is actually the collective Being of the people involved, particularly the founders and/or leaders. You could easily replace the business scenario with a personal one, as the same holds true for life partners.

As I mentioned, we are all capable of pretending to be what we are not, and most of us do it often. This is far more readily observable in our Secondary Ways of Being – our behavioural qualities – than in our other Aspects of Being, the deeper layers of ourselves. There are many traditional cognitive techniques and tools that measure these factors. Many organisations' Human Resources personnel are trained to pick up on these traits in staff. So, we are familiar with assessing and measuring people's behavioural performance because we can observe them. We know assertive behaviour, for example, because we can clearly see when it is present and when it is not. So, while there are many tools that articulate and measure certain behavioural factors or actual behaviours in isolation, they miss the big picture and also lack the link to the deeper qualities of human beings that drive our behaviours. Behaviours are like the leaves of a tree. There are so many that it is virtually impossible to assess, polish and alter each and every of them in isolation. It is far more effective to address them from the root of the tree and prune the branches from time to time if you want it to start bearing fruit. The beauty and significance of the Being Framework, including its associated tools, is that it looks at the big picture and the underlying deeper qualities and links. So, when assessing Secondary Ways of Being, the framework allows us to dig deeper to identify the threads between the behavioural aspects and the Primary Ways of Being, Moods and Meta Factors – particularly *awareness* – ultimately linking it all to your Unique Being, the real YOU. On a larger scale, it does this with a team of people and organisations too.

Behaviours are not normally displayed just once or twice. They are usually repeated. If someone is being inauthentic, there is normally an underlying pattern facilitating that. It could be the result of a low level of *vulnerability*, whereby the individual is so protective of the persona they have created that they are unwilling to let their guard down enough to let it go. Or it could be linked to *fear* or *anxiety*, or a lack of *freedom* or *courage*, and so on. Looking into the Secondary Ways of Being can lead to the discovery that something on the surface is not working. For coaches and leaders reading this, it may be tempting to jump onto a particular behaviour observed in a client or staff member and try to focus on that specific behaviour in an effort to fix it. However, that is not the most effective way to address the issue. Jumping onto a specific ineffective behaviour is so ingrained in society today. For example, there is a tendency for parents and teachers to correct individual behaviours in children as opposed to supporting them to perceive, conceive and realise so they have the ability to constantly and effectively apply wisdom appropriately, depending on the given situation. Even employment regulations state that we should put an employee on official notice if they have done something wrong or are underperforming, giving them 'x' number of days to pick up their act, usually with little to no support, or lose their job. This is like telling an employee to fake it (be inauthentic), or be fired! It is an extremely ineffective practice and more like wishful thinking that any transformation could occur on the fly. Even if you manage to communicate the issue with the individual in question, they may find a way to make you happy – by **acting** the way you want them to – but shifting Moods and Primary Ways of Being is what is actually required, and this demands the expertise of a coach trained in ontology.

If you only water the visible parts of an unhealthy tree and neglect the roots, you won't improve the health of the whole tree. So, to more effectively address any issue on the surface, we must assess the individual at a holistic level to determine the root cause. This is done by looking into the *integrity* (wholeness) of all their Aspects of Being, leading to the identification of the underlying behavioural patterns. Alternatively, we may observe the Secondary Ways of Being and behavioural patterns and then dive deeper to reveal the root causes of those patterns, bringing *awareness* to the reasons behind the behaviours an individual is displaying. Remember, our Secondary Ways of Being (behavioural factors) are linked to our Primary Ways of Being (primal qualities). While it may be tempting to jump in and polish or transform a Secondary Way of Being in isolation, it is far more effective to identify, polish and transform the deeper qualities (Primary Ways of Being and Moods) linked to it first. To neglect the deeper qualities would be like only watering the leaves of the tree.

At this point you may be wondering why Secondary Ways of Being are not considered to be a direct part of one's *integrity*. This is because, technically speaking, each Secondary Way of Being is a constituent of, and connected to, our Primary Ways of Being; they are not primal and independent. However, when it comes to projecting our more primal qualities, to be effective in our endeavours, our Secondary Ways of Being can either repress or facilitate them in action. In other words, they are closest to the application of who we are and how we are being. This is how they ultimately **indirectly** impact our overall *integrity*.

I would like to reiterate that working directly on a Secondary Way of Being is not the most effective way to address an issue with it. It is crucial to uncover, map out and address the qualities that are getting in the way of your *integrity*, *effectiveness* and hence fulfilment. There is always a hidden pattern that you can discover by peeling back the layers, starting with *awareness*, then Moods, Primary Ways of Being, Secondary Ways of Being and, last but not least, the behavioural patterns and actual behaviours themselves. The truth seekers of the world seek until they find. This requires dedication, but the rewards are immense because once the pattern is revealed, you can transform. We will explore this further in *Part 3: Being, in Action*. The key point to keep front of mind as you read this section is that, contrary to what many believe, Secondary Ways of Being, like *confidence, resilience, accountability, assertiveness*, and so on, are **not** behaviours but behavioural factors. And our Aspects of Being – *awareness*, Moods, Primary Ways of Being and Secondary Ways of Being – shape the context that drive our behaviours. Remember, Secondary Ways of Being are the bridge between our deeper qualities and the actual behaviours on the surface.

CHAPTER 24

Assertiveness

Like all other Secondary Ways of Being, *assertiveness* is a precursor to behaviour, not a behaviour in itself. This differs from the dominant view found in most psychological and psychotherapy literature that *assertiveness* is seen as a type of behaviour or skill. I deliberately decided not to use a dictionary to define *assertiveness* because this word has become so abused, overloaded and even bastardised over time. The definitions in every dictionary I turned to were so far off the Meaning we are referring to here that they weren't worth including as it would have only added to the confusion. And yet *assertiveness* was the most appropriate word we could choose for this Way of Being. In defining the word 'assertiveness', dictionaries use statements such as 'bold and forceful', or directly relate it to 'acting confident or making a confident statement', or, 'not frightened to say what you want or believe'. However, the root of the word assertiveness, 'assert', is worth acknowledging. It comes from the Latin word *Asserere*, which means 'to claim or affirm'. Of all the Ways of Being in the Being Framework, *assertiveness* would have to be the most misunderstood. It is also one of the qualities most requested by people to be coached on, despite not having a clear understanding of what *assertiveness* actually means or how profoundly linked it is to the deeper qualities such as *awareness, vulnerability, authenticity, courage, responsibility, commitment, presence, self-expression* and *freedom*. To explain all of these relationships would fill another book. So, I will touch on just a few in this chapter in order to clarify the transcendent Meaning that the word *assertiveness* refers to, especially in the context of performance, *effectiveness* and leadership.

Ontologically speaking, a*ssertiveness*, as a Way of Being, is the state of BEING assertive (as opposed to just acting assertively). It is the quality of being direct, firm, straight, undisguised and frank without being aggressive, forceful, manipulative or submissive. In other words, being assertive, as a Way of Being, leads us to project behaviours that are typically considered assertive without being either blunt and aggressive or passively accepting whatever is being thrown at us. To be assertive demands a constructive, healthy and functional degree of firmness and steadfastness. More specifically, *assertiveness* has to do with the extent to which you are willing and capable of saying no when the situation demands it, and this applies to all aspects of your life. Being assertive is also about being decisive in your decisions, upfront, clear and protective (but not defensive) of your unambiguous boundaries. It's about standing your ground – but not for the sake of being right – when tested by others, such as business partners, colleagues, family, peers or even total strangers. When an individual is being assertive, they are able to get their point across without the intention of hurting others or becoming upset themselves. It is the dispassionate state of **being with** others without being distracted, derailed or letting irrelevant matters and emotions get in the way.

The Being Framework ontological distinction of *assertiveness*

Assertiveness is when you express yourself effectively and stand up for your point of view while also being respectful of others. It is the willingness to express your thoughts and feelings and communicate your needs and expectations firmly and directly while being considerate of others and aware of any subsequent consequences of being assertive. *Assertiveness* is being resolute, straight, firm and effective.

A healthy relationship with *assertiveness* indicates that you are predominately straight and unambiguous in your communication with others. You rarely resort to threats or attempt to manipulate outcomes and are transparent with your motives. You are bold in communicating your and others' needs and expectations in terms of the outcomes required or expected. You are comfortable letting others know how you feel and express yourself without emotional outbursts.

An unhealthy relationship with *assertiveness* indicates that you may be unreasonably submissive, agreeable or aggressive, or that you predominantly rely on manipulation and domination to get your way, express yourself and communicate with others. You may frequently go along with what others decide to avoid conflict. You may also use inappropriate humour, sarcasm, teasing or underhanded comments to manipulate, bully, control or put others down. Alternatively, you may frequently threaten or use the tone of your voice to dominate or exert your will on others. As a result, they may consider you manipulative or dominating, even though that is not always your intention. Your conversations may quickly spiral or escalate emotionally while issues remain unresolved.

Almost everyone can recall circumstances and experiences when they have been outspoken, calmly clarified their expectations and set unambiguous boundaries. At the same time, we can probably also remember times when we did the opposite. Perhaps we were being overly compliant, being a pacifist and found it difficult to say no or were afraid to speak up in a meeting, perhaps regretting it later. Needless to say, those times left us feeling disempowered. *Assertiveness* is often viewed in the context of either being aggressive, inconsiderate and self-centred or even hostile. A lack of *assertiveness*, on the other hand, is commonly regarded as weak, passive and compliant behaviour. So, what exactly is *assertiveness* as a Way of Being? We can easily spot behaviour that is non-assertive: when someone is either being aggressive, manipulative or overly submissive (too nice). But what are the signs that someone is being assertive? Being assertive is an attractive quality; we are naturally drawn to assertive people. When people are being assertive, they are clear, straightforward and powerful. *Assertiveness* allows us to express a complaint or disagreement without unnecessary justifications, excuses, criticism, judgement or blame. This Secondary Way of Being may also encourage us to communicate authentic, positive emotions and thoughts, such as joy and pride, without coming from a place of egotism. Many people downplay their accomplishments to avoid being seen as big-headed or make others uncomfortable, and in doing so, they are not being assertive. Instead, they are being affable, amiable or agreeable, which means they are not being authentic to their true selves. When you are being assertive you can speak of your accomplishments with a balance of pride and humility and without guilt or conceitedness.

The potential ramifications when *assertiveness* is lacking

Our empirical data[155] shows that the majority of people are **not** assertive most of the time, even those who think they are. I believe this is largely because we are not encouraged to be assertive across cultures, particularly in our youth. Think back to when you were growing up, wherever that may have been in the world. Did your parents, teachers and other influential adults in your life tell you to be assertive? Or did they tell you to be nice, be kind, be quiet and be polite, and so on. The problem

---

155   Based on our research, studies and the work we do with clients at Engenesis, including the assessment of individuals using the Being Profile tool.

with this way of raising children is that when they grow up and enter the adult world, with all its complex hierarchies of accomplishments and fierce competition, they eventually discover – usually the hard way – that being nice doesn't serve them well, because it commonly leads to being taken advantage of, usually by aggressive, non-assertive people. This may lead to them becoming bitter, resentful and acrimonious, which in turn contributes to a sense of being victimised in multiple aspects of life. When we constantly feel victimised and/or victimise ourselves, it leads to an even greater sense of disempowerment. We feel anxious and even depressed at times, which ultimately leads us to self-sabotage and the development of self-destructive habits and behavioural patterns, like excessive alcohol consumption or gambling. This is where the link between *responsibility* and *assertiveness* is particularly apparent. When you are not being assertive, you are not choosing powerfully to be in charge of your own life, to be the active agent who pulls their own strings. Instead, you are letting yourself be a pushover, shying away from asking for what you want, as though you are expecting a third party (like the government) to come to the rescue and grant you your fair share of things.

Another relationship worth highlighting when it comes to *assertiveness* is its close link to *awareness*. How could you possibly be assertive in a negotiation when you don't know your desired outcome or debate a topic you know nothing about? A lack of *assertiveness* coupled with a lack of *awareness* (particularly self-awareness) is quite common. There are many examples, ranging from minor ones to those with potentially serious ramifications. Perhaps you lack the *assertiveness* to choose from the menu of a fine dining restaurant because the menu choices are unfamiliar. Or maybe you're settling for an unhealthy and abusive relationship due to a lack of *assertiveness* in challenging the other party or changing the circumstances coupled with a lack of self-awareness to understand that YOU are the one who can bring about change. Be aware that you're setting yourself up for disappointment and resentment through your unhealthy relationship with *assertiveness* and *awareness*. To be frank, you cannot be assertive around matters you haven't put the effort into understanding, have no clue about or when the objective is unclear to you.

Due to the nature of our business, people often approach us to raise seed capital for their startup/new product venture. I remember a conversation I once had with a founder who was determined to raise funds for her venture. When I asked her how much she wanted to raise, she had no idea. She hadn't even put in the minimal effort required to estimate or understand what it would take to get her venture off the ground. After thinking for a few seconds, she simply shrugged her shoulders and said, 'Maybe $1.5 million?' When I said this was quite high for the stage she was at with her business concept, she immediately responded with, 'How about $750K then?' I tried explaining that this is not how it works, but she interrupted and asked, 'At least $150K then?' representing a mere 10% of her original request. This is a clear (and not unusual) example of how a lack of *awareness* impacts *assertiveness*, particularly with regard to negotiations. In this instance, the budding entrepreneur clearly hadn't put any effort into understanding the outcome and what was required to raise funds. She also hadn't considered the scenario from the perspective of the investor, choosing instead to remain in the I quadrant[156]. Needless to say, she walked away empty-handed.

When *assertiveness* is lacking, it can lead to various forms of destructive or dysfunctional behavioural patterns such as aggression, passive-aggression, manipulation or passivity. The internal conflict created by passive behaviour can lead to stress, resentment, seething anger, feelings of victimisation, sabotage and even thoughts of revenge and retribution. Someone who is seen as aggressive may come across as a bully who disregards the needs, influence, authority, feelings and opinions of others. They can seem self-righteous, overbearing, superior, condescending or intimidating to others. In extreme cases, an aggressive individual may even become physically threatening or violent if they think it will result in them getting their own way. When *assertiveness* is lacking, this Way of Being drives behaviours that **always** come at a cost. Others may resent and avoid aggressive people and undermine them in their absence.

Being passive-aggressive also has damaging consequences on relationships. People with passive-aggressive tendencies can be sarcastic and complain about others behind their backs, while remaining tight-lipped in their presence. Since they feel uncomfortable about being direct – usually driven by a lack of *authenticity* and *courage* at a deeper level –

---

156   Perspective Quadrant, p145.

they find other hidden and manipulative ways to communicate their point of view and force an outcome. Over time, this is a very destructive way to BE and behave. While it may deliver some temporary wins, it is not at all **consistent** in producing effective results. I would like to reiterate that when you are being assertive, you will communicate from your authentic Self.

There is a fine line between *assertiveness* and aggression, which is often hard to discern. So, when you are being assertive, it may be interpreted as aggression in the eye of beholder. In some cultures, being genuinely assertive is perceived as aggression or being rude and disrespectful. This is quite predominant and apparent in our era, as the threshold of accepting *assertiveness* is so low that, on the surface, it can land as aggression, hence creating a decent level of confusion.

When I switched from Karate Kyokushin to Aikido, I was obviously far more familiar with the former, which I had practised for years. In Kyokushin, I would typically use strikes and blows, usually in the form of punches and kicks, to hurt my opponent. The ultimate goal in a fight was to dismantle the opponent, called *Ippon* in Japanese, which is a special form of Knock Out (K.O.). When I was first introduced to Aikido, I was forbidden from throwing punches and kicks as I was told it is purely a defensive form of martial arts. However, not long after I started, I witnessed several attempts to throw strikes and blows in the Dojo! When I confronted the instructor about this, he responded using Japanese terminology to refer to what I thought was a punch, 'This is not a *Tsuki* but an *Atemi*'. I was confused by his response because, at the time, I thought both words meant the same thing. So, I immediately judged him as someone who plays with words, and I remember being bitterly disappointed, as I desperately wanted to look up to him. I didn't realise at the time that, while *Tzuki* and *Atemi* may seem alike, they are in fact fundamentally different in nature and the intention behind them. *Tzuki* is to hurt the opponent, but *Atemi* is to distract them to give you the chance to apply certain techniques that prevent them from harming you. My initial reaction was to judge Aikido as being impractical and pacifist. Later, I had a very different conception and appreciation of this form of martial arts. So, while there are times when it may seem as though you are applying force and being aggressive when being assertive and standing your ground, it is far from aggression.

To give this a business context, let's assume you need to give a final warning to an employee who has been behaving in an unacceptable manner in the workplace. While your *assertiveness* may come across as a threat and aggressive because you are telling them in no uncertain terms that they will lose their job if they fail to pick up their act, you're not the one hurting them. They are hurting themselves by behaving the way they are.

Tall Poppy Syndrome[157]

It may come as no surprise to you to learn that the high achievers of the world deal with situations where they are subject to being attacked, harshly criticised or taken advantage of more often than lower achievers. Why? Remember our discussion around the King archetype to describe leaders? Well, when you're the King (leader) ruling your kingdom (organisation), and the buck stops with you, you are not even safe in your own bed! Almost everyone wants a piece of you and will try to bring you down. For example, if you are a high income earning individual and/or are well-known in the public arena, some may think that your success grants others permission to ask more of you, as if you arrived at your position of power and good fortune purely by chance and luck. This is mainly due to the collective inauthentic and unhealthy relationship that many people in our societies have with *responsibility*. Most people don't know that, for the most part, their different choices and overall *integrity* and *effectiveness* led to what is being seen as their 'success' by external observers. A classic example of this is seen in many of our taxation systems. In most cases, the more you earn, the higher the tax rate. This supports the widely distorted view that higher income individuals should pay a greater percentage of their income in tax. It is a viewpoint that is so ingrained in many cultures, it's as though people feel entitled to a share of the wealth made by these high achievers. I am not here to debate taxation systems. I am merely using it as an example to make a point.

If you are currently a high achiever or strive to be, get used to the fact that many will be envious of your accomplishments and try to cut you

---

157   'Tall Poppy Syndrome' is a phrase commonly used in Australia and New Zealand that describes the cultural phenomenon of mocking people who think highly of themselves (metaphorically cutting down the 'tall poppy' standing amongst a sea of other poppies of a similar size).

down to their level, even friends or people close to you. It's a worldwide phenomenon that is commonly referred to in Australia and New Zealand as the 'Tall Poppy Syndrome'. In many cultures, we value equality. While we can all agree that this is a virtue, there is an ingrained, unhealthy and unrealistic relationship with 'fairness' whereby we try to shackle or constrain higher achievers in order to close the gap with those who are not performing as well or have made different choices. This puts a cap on **human potential**. A more effective way is to empower, educate and support those striving to rise up, and this is where I strongly believe the Being Framework contributes in such a powerful way. As you become a high achiever, you are likely to become the target of bullies and/or attacks and you will have to come to terms with the fact that many may love nothing more than to see you fail.

These days, many people feel (unrealistically) that they should not be offended or triggered by anyone talking about them behind their backs or insulting them publicly. The high achievers of the world have no choice but to develop a thicker skin against the media, fake news, activists, and the list goes on. Be prepared, as you will be challenged by all and sundry, and this is precisely where *courage* and, more specifically, *assertiveness* are required. Rather than being sucked in by emotions or acting in an aggressive or submissive way, being assertive will ensure you conduct yourself dispassionately, with firmness and resoluteness. If you are setting yourself up to be a leader of influence, a high achiever and an effective person, *assertiveness* is one of the most important qualities with which you should transform your relationship. This is different from simply seeking techniques, tips and advice on how to **act** more assertively or, as many modern psychologists would say, training yourself to **show** more assertive behaviour. As I said earlier, acting assertive is one thing, BEING assertive is another. When we act assertive without being assertive, it comes from a place of inauthenticity. It's putting on a false persona. However, when you are being assertive, assertive behaviour unfolds with ease and flow. Through our studies, we have learnt that when it comes to Secondary Ways of Being, it is more effective to identify the qualities (*awareness*, Moods and Primary Ways of Being) that shape the context which drives the behaviour, than it is to work directly on a Secondary Way of Being in isolation, including *assertiveness*. It's about digging deeper to discover the more primal qualities that are getting in the way of you BEING assertive.

The Assertiveness Pendulum

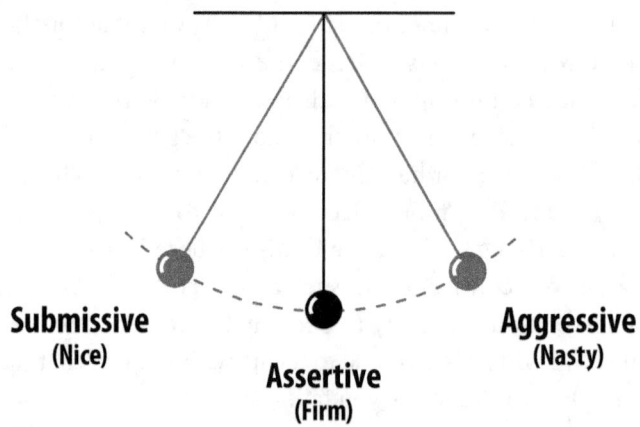

Submissive
(Nice)

Assertive
(Firm)

Aggressive
(Nasty)

Assertiveness is a multidimensional Secondary Way of Being. It is not simply a matter of being assertive or not being assertive. The Assertiveness Pendulum conveys this well because, particularly if we are not assertive, it shows how we can easily swing – like a pendulum – from one end to the next, sometimes without warning. When we are not being assertive, we are either being aggressive (disagreeable/nasty), or submissive (agreeable/nice), as shown in the Assertiveness Pendulum diagram. When we are assertive, we are grounded, which is a position of stability and consistency. It means we are balanced and not prone to sudden instability. But when we are either aggressive or submissive (at the 45-degree position), we are unbalanced and far more prone to swinging, sometimes without warning, from one state of Being to another. Phenomenologically speaking, it is a challenge to be assertive all the time. We are all capable of fluctuating from being submissive (nice) to being aggressive (nasty) but, as a leader, it is important to be conscious of your *assertiveness* at all times and, when the pendulum starts to swing one way or the other, switch your focus back to being assertive. This pendulum effect is brilliantly depicted in some examples of literature and screenplays. One example that immediately springs to mind, albeit an extreme one, is season one of the popular television series, *Fargo*[158]. The main character in the series is a quiet, unassuming,

---

[158] *Fargo* is an American black comedy crime drama television series created and primarily written by Noah Hawley. The show is inspired by the 1996 film, which was written and directed by the Coen brothers.

passive and submissive man who, for a long time, has not managed to stand his ground or command respect from others. He generally has not been assertive in terms of what he wants out of life and particularly his interaction with others, including his wife, who treats him disrespectfully. At one point in the series, the main character suddenly snaps, taking the viewers by surprise. The pendulum swings and he becomes so aggressive that he murders his wife after she insults him over his submissiveness, and he ends up becoming a serial killer.

In team building sessions, I always include a topic on *assertiveness*, which I introduce in a subtle way. I start by telling participants that aggression/nastiness is not welcome, as it significantly impacts the *integrity, effectiveness* and flow of the team, which is counterproductive to team building, the purpose of the session. I immediately back this instruction up with a question: 'So, given we won't accept aggression, what do you think we welcome here then?' And most of them respond with, 'Being nice', to which I say, 'Well, being nice is actually no better than being aggressive', which always leaves them looking somewhat perplexed. I then elaborate and say that it is **'nice' behaviour** that isn't tolerated. You can imagine the looks on their faces when they hear that! It's as though, collectively, we don't have a clear conception of what it means to be assertive. At this point, I explain why a nice or submissive teammate is no better or worse than an aggressive or nasty one by walking them through the Assertiveness Pendulum.

Imagine if one of your team members consistently arrives late to meetings, despite the fact that you have made the importance of punctuality in meetings very clear on numerous occasions and they have agreed to take that into consideration. If you were on the aggressive side of the Assertiveness Pendulum, you may humiliate them at the next meeting in front of their peers and threaten them with the loss of their job. In other words, you are implying that if they don't do what you tell them to, the consequence will be that you will hurt them (in this case by firing them). Now, let's imagine you swing to the submissive side and, instead of threatening the team member, you either ask them to arrive on time again in an overly polite and apologetic manner or hold back your anger and say nothing, despite seething with anger on the inside. Either way, your submissiveness would lead you to feel an underlying resentment towards your team member that will eventually bubble to the surface. This is a trait frequently observed in young children: 'Daddy, can you please buy me an ice-cream, please, please, please, can we go to the shop for an ice-cream?' When the answer is no, the child commonly responds with, 'I don't like you anymore', a frown planted firmly on their face in an act of defiance that signifies a threat to withhold their love.

Returning to the example of the team member who is always showing up late for meetings, a more effective way to handle the situation would be to be assertive, for example by taking the conversation offline and telling them it is imperative to arrive at meetings on time as the company does not tolerate lack of punctuality, especially in meetings. Rather than the consequence being, 'I will hurt you', by firing you, or 'I don't like you', by ignoring you or being outwardly nice but resenting you beneath the surface, it is an appropriate, proportionate and dispassionate request for compliance to company policy on punctuality. In this way, it puts the ball in the team member's court. If they continue to show up late, then they are choosing the consequences of their own accord. A critical point to note here is that when you are being assertive, you are not threatening the other person. However, they may feel threatened nonetheless. Being assertive is about being resolute AND unwavering when making your dispassionate request, without getting sucked in by emotions from the other party and/or from within, or feeling the need to resort to euphemisms to soften the impact.

The link between *assertiveness* and other Aspects of Being

Being assertive is at the heart of communication and interactions with others. It supports you to build trust and will help you express yourself effectively and stand up for your point of view, while also respecting the agreed rights and beliefs of others. It's hardly surprising that no one trusts an individual whose state of Being keeps swinging, especially on the Assertiveness Pendulum, from being submissive to being aggressive. This is a source of significant dysfunction within organisations and families. In fact, so many relationships are torn apart over this constant swing. Domestic violence is an example of the consequences when one or both parties in a relationship constantly swings to the aggressive side. Simply put, it's about being capable and willing to say your authentic yeses and noes, conveying a close connection between *assertiveness* and the deeper qualities of *authenticity, freedom, courage* and *self-expression*. If the way you communicate is passive, and you routinely say things like, 'I'll just go with whatever the team decides', you tend to avoid conflict by being vague, amiable and uncertain. This is typically conveyed in the way you express yourself, often using words like 'I may', 'I should' and 'perhaps'. In the long run, not only is this unhealthy, as you will not be able to influence the outcome to suit yourself, but it will also create problems for the team because you are not expressing your points of view, meaning others may miss out on your *contribution*. It may also cause you frustration and resentment with regard to the decisions that were taken by the team, that ultimately you did not support but failed to vote against at the time. By being assertive, not only will you be free to express your true feelings, beliefs and opinions, but you will also act upon them. Most importantly, you will communicate as your authentic Self and project a persona that is congruent with who you are deep down (your Unique Being) with ease and flow, being as authentic as it is possible for you to be.

Let's say your business partner tries to talk you into taking on another major project, even though you know your team is currently working at full capacity. You know that taking on this additional project could compromise other client work and create disgruntlement among team members due to the extra hours they will need to work. If you agree to take on the new project just to keep the peace, it may cause you internal conflict and frustration. You could also start fostering resentment and place yourself in a vicious cycle of disempowering thoughts and emotions that you could potentially carry for weeks. You may agree to your partner's request, but it would not be an authentic 'yes' response. Furthermore, since you are carrying this resentment – towards yourself, your business partner or both – you would not be able to embrace the new project with joy, grace and excitement. We see this often. In fact, many entrepreneurs and business leaders let a lack of *assertiveness* ruin, or at least limit, the joy of entrepreneurship. Some are even proud of this 'suffering', thinking it's part of the hardships of being an entrepreneur. In this case, having an open and assertive conversation with your business partner would support you in identifying a different and more effective solution for yourself, your team members, your clients and the company. But in order to address the situation fully, you would need to look into the deeper qualities (*awareness*, Moods and Primary Ways of Being) that are ultimately driving your decisions and behaviours, as discussed earlier. It is naive to think that acting assertively on just one occasion will transform your relationship with *assertiveness* forever.

Assertiveness is also fundamental and crucial when it comes to *love* and *presence* because it is based on mutual respect and *awareness*. It demonstrates that you are willing to stand up for yourself and express your thoughts and feelings regardless of the circumstances, commanding respect as a result. It also indicates that you are willing to be vulnerable and are able to handle going beyond *fear* and *anxiety*, while caring enough to work on resolving conflicts on an ongoing basis with *persistence*. It depends less on how articulate you are, and more on **how you are being** when you deliver the message. *Assertiveness* generates and is a means to access trust. While others may not appreciate your *assertiveness* if it opposes their immediate interest, they would perceive you as a person who means what they say, a trustworthy person, someone who is resolute and reliable. They know that when you say 'yes' and when you say 'no' you genuinely mean it. *Assertiveness* is a quality that commands respect, the very quality – phenomenologically speaking – that we all strive for. And yet our empirical data shows that only a very small percentage of people have a relatively healthy relationship with *assertiveness*. It also inadvertently empowers those you associate with to set healthy boundaries with others. This will ultimately minimise your suffering and reduce the suffering you may cause others, so it's a win-win for all concerned.

Assertiveness has a strong link to *authenticity*, *presence* and *courage*. The more authentic you are and the healthier your relationship with reality (First and Second-layer), the more you will feel the need to have the *courage* to BE direct, firm and assertive in your communication and not hold back. Being assertive also requires the ability and willingness to listen to others and show them respect, an important factor in effective communication. For example, negotiation without listening and being present to the other party in order to deeply understand what they are negotiating for (including their potential best and worst outcomes), without being open and vulnerable and without being willing to put yourself in the other person's shoes, is not being assertive. If you are to stand up for yourself and communicate freely in a discussion, you will require an adequate level of *courage* to remain assertive and not fall into the trap of either becoming aggressive when faced with rejection or submissively sucking it up, which leads to resentment.

Assertiveness also has links to many other Aspects of Being. For example, in order to be assertive, you must first be aware of what you want; let's call it your objective. Then you need to be committed to your objective and own it powerfully (*responsibility*), which will come naturally if you care enough about it. Furthermore, you need to be vulnerable enough not to be too concerned about any potential damage to your reputation (how you are perceived by others) and maintain a healthy relationship with *fear* and *anxiety* to support you to be courageous enough to take the leap. You must be present in your conversations (*presence*) and have the *freedom* and *self-expression* to authentically communicate your real yeses and powerful noes, which is what being assertive is all about.

CHAPTER 25

Proactivity

*There are three kinds of people:
those who make things happen,
those who watch what happens,
and those who wonder what happened.*

George Bernard Shaw
Irish playwright and political activist, 1856–950

Do you make conscious decisions and act upon them with *responsibility* and autonomy, or do you predominantly find yourself reacting to whatever life throws at you or get stuck in the thinking phase, leading you to halt, freeze and procrastinate? We all need to be proactive in the fulfilment of the requirements we choose to accomplish (or are required of us) if we want to achieve competency, proficiency and mastery (*effectiveness*) in our endeavours. *Proactivity* is a major topic in organisational psychology and very relevant to corporations, workplaces and particularly SMEs and startups, as they do not have access to as many resources as the larger players. So, to an extent, it's important for SMEs and startups to make up for their lack of resources by being proactive and resourceful. In fact, it's not uncommon to see much smaller companies gain the upper hand over the big guys when competing for business to sell a similar product or service. Look at ZOOM video conferencing as a prime example. One of the keys to this success is *proactivity*. When an organisation is smaller and its people are proactive, they can be flexible and adjust nimbly and quickly. *Proactivity* makes them far more agile and responsive in the game.

According to Professor Sharon K. Parker[159], a leading researcher on the subject of *proactivity*, being proactive is increasingly important in today's work environment. Professor Parker identified at least three major reasons for the trend in fostering *proactivity*. The first reason she identified was that the increasingly complex and uncertain workplace and constantly changing market needs set new demands on employees. This means it is no longer enough to rely solely on a pre-specified set of tasks or duties, such as you would find in a traditional job description. Instead, employees are required to utilise their own initiative to identify and address business needs rather than follow prescribed actions or wait for advice and instructions from their superior. The time of micromanagement is over. The second reason for the trend in fostering *proactivity*, identified by Professor Parker, was increased pressure for innovation. This means employees must be willing to bring about change themselves and try out new ways of doing things, particularly if they work for leading innovative organisations that, as pioneers, constantly deal with unprecedented and unstructured matters and problems. The third reason she identified was that the traditional notion of a 'job for life' has long come to an end, meaning every employee needs to be responsible for their own career. Employees who are proactive have an advantage and do well in these scenarios, leading them to grow in their careers.

What is *proactivity*?

Simply put, you are proactive when, through your decisions and actions, you actively aim to address matters that require your attention. It is what many refer to as having a 'can-do attitude' when that transpires into action. Like all other Ways of Being, *proactivity* is a key to high performance and, when combined with high levels in other Aspects of Being, leads to *effectiveness*. As mentioned in the introduction to this section, every Secondary Way of Being is linked to various Primary Ways of Being and all Moods, however, some are more clearly linked than others. For instance, there is a clear link between *proactivity* and *awareness*. When you have *awareness*, you can see and predict the consequences of your actions vividly, including the outcomes and

---

159   From the blog *Importance of Proactivity* by Professor Sharon K. Parker, ARC Laureate Fellow, Director of the Centre for Transformative Work Design and Professor of Management and Organisations at Curtin Business School.

consequences should you choose to be inactive and/or silent. Connected to the *proactivity-awareness* link is the relationship between *proactivity* and *care*. When you are aware of the consequences of being proactive versus being inactive or silent, you need to care or value the outcome enough to make it a priority to take action immediately. Your high level of *care* and *proactivity* will then drive you to own it (*responsibility*) and be committed to the cause and make things happen, which ultimately leads to *effectiveness* and fulfilment. Furthermore, a healthy relationship with *fear* and *anxiety* will also support you to be proactive and take action, That's because it involves taking the initiative to bring about a different future, for yourself, for your team and/or for the organisation as a whole.

The *Oxford English Dictionary* defines the adjectival form of proactivity, proactive, as creating or controlling a situation rather than just responding to it after it has happened. Jennifer B. Farrell and Karoline Strauss summarise three key features of proactivity in a jointly written publication[160]: anticipatory (acting in advance of a future situation), change-oriented (taking control and causing something to happen, rather than just adapting to a situation or waiting for something to happen) and self-initiated (not needing to be asked to act or requiring detailed instructions). Let's now take a look at the ontological distinction of *proactivity* in the Being Framework.

---

160 *The People Make the Place, and They Make Things Happen: Proactive Behavior and Relationships at Work* by Jennifer B. Farrell, DCU Business School, Dublin City University and Karoline Strauss, Warwick Business School, University of Warwick.

The Being Framework ontological distinction of *proactivity*

Proactivity is the quality of actively influencing, creating and contributing to a situation rather than reacting to it after it has happened. Being proactive moves you to think, plan and act in advance of an impending situation, making decisions and taking appropriate actions beforehand rather than procrastinating or waiting for the outcome. When you are being proactive, you make things happen and take the initiative to bring about a different future for yourself, your team or the organisation as a whole. Proactive individuals are willing to challenge, make suggestions and try new ways of doing things to bring about relevant change.

A healthy relationship with *proactivity* indicates that you tend to take the initiative to move things forward and bring about change. You are solution-oriented and actively seek opportunities to advance in any situation. Others may experience you as someone who is considered, frequently contributes, asks questions, takes action and will step up without hesitation. You may often anticipate what is needed in advance, respond rather than react to matters, and are prepared and willing to do what is required.

An unhealthy relationship with *proactivity* indicates that you may be unreasonably inactive or reactive. You may rely on waiting to be told what to do and procrastinate until you have everything at hand. You may only take prescribed actions and rarely plan effectively. You may often be indecisive and inactive, ignoring what you know needs to be done, leaving yourself exposed to potential breakdowns. Alternatively, you may only address matters when there is a breakdown and then react to the subsequent undesirable outcome. You may frequently be on the back foot, avoid change and defer making decisions. Others may express frustration at your apparent disinterest, lack of engagement, inaction, reactivity or your need to be fully convinced before you move forward.

Proactivity is a multidimensional Secondary Way of Being

We indicated in the introduction to this section that I separated the Secondary Ways of Being into two categories within the Ontological Model: multidimensional and linear. *Proactivity* is one of four multi-dimensional Secondary Ways of Being in the Being Framework. Ontologically speaking, *proactivity* is not simply measured on a linear spectrum. It is not like *resilience*, for instance, which is linear: we are either being resilient or not being resilient. When we are **not** proactive, we are either being **inactive** or **reactive**. Both of these behavioural factors are a reflection of having an unhealthy relationship with *proactivity* but displayed in two very different ways, as explained below.

The Proactivity Pendulum

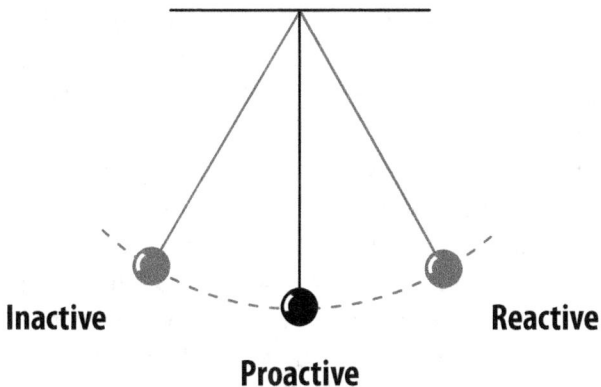

Inactive: those who are inactive tend to be suppressed, think too much and avoid acting and making decisions. They are often silent, idle and apathetic. People who struggle with *proactivity*, in the sense of being inactive, tend to be disengaged. In a team project, their presence is neither here nor there because the other members of the team are contributing while the inactive member is not. If one fails to act, there is a clear absence of *contribution* and *self-expression*. Rather than being dynamic and responsive, the inactive individual is static, disengaged and allows inertia to hold them back. They often find themselves in situations they believe life throws at them and, although they are being impacted, they make no attempt to try and influence the outcome. In their eyes, whatever happens in life is out of their control. There are various reasons for inactivity, including, but not limited to, an unhealthy relationship with any of the Moods. It could be *fear* or *anxiety* holding them back, or it may be that a lack of *care* causes indifference, leading to inactivity on the behavioural side. Or perhaps they are worried that their shortcomings will be exposed and they will get the blame if things don't go to plan, highlighting a lack of *vulnerability*, which causes them to choose inactivity to avoid making mistakes. It could also be due to a lack of *courage* or troubled relationships around *self-expression*, *freedom* and *empowerment*.

Reactive: those who are reactive, on the other hand, tend to wait for matters to happen and react to them instead of predicting the consequences and outcomes. They come up with random, impulsive decisions that have not been well thought through and this is reflected in their behaviour and actions. Reactivity is also a phenomenon whereby someone may temporarily alter their behaviour on the surface to impress because they have become aware that they are being observed. A reactive individual often allows a problem to fester and grow by failing to address it while it is still relatively minor. Once it is beyond the point of no return, they may display aggressive behaviour, make unreasonable demands and point the finger, rather than owning the matter (*responsibility*), or being accountable. So, at the time of reacting, a variety of complex emotions and behaviours may show up, including anger and aggression, if they know deep down that they are responsible for the problem but continue to point the finger and blame the world or others. They may also find it difficult to forgive themselves for the mistakes they made, further fuelling their anger. No matter the cause, being reactive is not the most effective and sustainable way of dealing with matters, particularly in the business world, including altering one's decisions and behaviour purely to conform to the expectations of the observer.

Proactivity starts at the top

There is far greater ease and flow for a business and its leaders when they have proactive team members. But like so much in life, it is a two-way street. Encouraging *proactivity* starts at the top. You can't expect to have proactive employees if you don't foster a supportive environment and culture that enables and encourages people to be proactive. While there are relationships between *proactivity* and many Primary Ways of Being and all Moods, as mentioned earlier, the four most critical links that exist with Primary Ways of Being in this context are with *authenticity, responsibility, courage* and *presence*. To enable proactive behaviour and produce beneficial outcomes, a healthy level of *authenticity* in the team member in question is required, otherwise it could lead to cynical or dismissive behavioural patterns. Furthermore, both leaders and their people must be willing to be responsible for the consequences and outcomes of their *proactivity*. For leaders, this means acknowledging the contribution of their team members and being vulnerable enough not to feel threatened by their suggestions for improvements and innovative contributions. Last but not least, effective communication underpins *proactivity* to set and manage expectations from the get-go. Employees need to understand when initiative is required and be appreciated by the business for being proactive.

Being proactive is not without risk in the current environment. 'Do it right, and you're rewarded. Do it wrong, and you're punished', seems to be today's dominant way of thinking. This once again highlights the importance of culture, which leaders of an organisation are responsible for designing and developing. Leaders are also responsible for nurturing and maintaining the *integrity* of the culture within the organisation. Critically, it starts with their **own Being** first. If you, as a leader, have qualities that are either getting in your way of being proactive or preventing others from being proactive, you must raise your *awareness* of that fact and address it with a **sense of urgency** or you will pay the price. Remember, when you are not being proactive, you will fail to perform, let alone be effective in your performance. The same is true for every person in your organisation.

CHAPTER 26

Confidence

By now you would no doubt be aware of my general lack of confidence in dictionaries, especially when it comes to the gap between their definition of a word and its actual ontological distinction. Ironically though, I am confident in – and therefore can trust – some dictionary definitions of the word 'confidence'! For example, the *Cambridge Dictionary* defines confidence as 'the quality of being certain of your abilities or of having trust in people, plans, or the future', and, 'the quality of being certain of your own ability to do things well'. The *Merriam-Webster* defines it as 'a feeling or consciousness of one's powers or of reliance on one's circumstances', and, 'the quality or state of being certain', which is my preferred definition as it is simple, meaningful and, most importantly, well aligned with the ontological distinction of *confidence*. Interestingly, when we look into the root of the word 'confidence' we discover it is derived from the Latin *Confidere*, which means 'to have full trust', with *Fidere* meaning 'to trust'. As you can see, when it comes to *confidence*, there is a strong focus on trust, so, having self-confidence is having trust in oneself. *Confidence* is the state of being clear-headed and certain, either that an assumption, hypothesis or prediction will turn out to be valid or that a particular chosen course of action or solution turns out to be the best or most effective. To be certain requires trust.

Our empirical data, combined with my own experience and the experience of several members from within our community of accredited ontological coaches, also suggests that many people have a good sense of what *confidence* means and looks like. Yet there are some misperceptions about it. Furthermore, *confidence* is up there with *assertiveness* as a quality people seek to transform. Almost everyone wants to be confident and considers *confidence* an attractive and necessary quality to possess. Yet our studies have revealed that most people struggle to acquire an optimal level of *confidence* in action. Like all other Ways of Being, while there are techniques that you can learn to make it appear as though you are more confident than you actually are, being confident goes far deeper than just a series of behaviours and your attitude towards dealing with the world around you.

In part, *confidence* comes from *awareness* of your competencies, proficiency and *effectiveness*: the extent to which you are effective at something. The same is true when it comes to your *confidence* in others and things. It leads you to be more certain and have faith that they can be relied upon. Therefore, by nature, *confidence*, as a Secondary Way of Being, is more relative in comparison to Primary Ways of Being, which is precisely why it is a Secondary Way of Being. It is important to understand that the Being Profile assesses how one **relates** to *confidence*. For example, if you have a relatively healthy relationship with *confidence*, you would be certain and own your own competencies; you would not downplay or doubt them. But you would also know when not to be confident. Let's say you are a software developer or project manager and confident in your ability to perform your role. Now imagine you are asked to perform open heart surgery without any medical training. Naturally you would not be confident to perform that role. Both examples indicate a healthy relationship with *confidence* as a Way of Being. *Confidence* stems from a combination of attitudes that, if present, result in confident behaviour on the surface, which is noticed by others.

The Being Framework ontological distinction of *confidence*

Confidence is how you relate to certainties, uncertainties, doubts and hesitation. It is the belief or understanding that you can rely on or have faith in someone or something, including your own abilities and qualities. Being confident supports you in gaining credibility and making good first impressions while dealing with pressure and meeting life head on.

A healthy relationship with *confidence* indicates you are predominantly able to forego your doubts and uncertainties and don't allow them to stop your progress. Others may experience you as self-assured or at ease, even in challenging situations. You leverage and effectively utilise available resources to move forward despite your hesitations. You are aware of and trust your strengths and abilities and back yourself fully. You can move forward in difficult circumstances, even though you know your limitations and the risks involved and are not reckless. This may encourage others to trust you when you say you can do something, and they expect you to follow through.

An unhealthy relationship with *confidence* indicates that you may be overconfident, inappropriately confident or unreasonably hesitant. You may ruminate, get stuck or be weighed down by your doubts. You may question your abilities and doubt yourself or others, even in familiar circumstances or situations. You can frequently waver in challenging situations and may experience last-minute doubts or panic you are unable to overcome. Alternatively, you may be reckless, dogmatic, display bravado or undertake excessively risky behaviour with little or no regard for the impact or outcome. Others may feel the need to check if you are okay and may have concerns about your ability to see a task through. You may often worry that you or others will disappoint, let people down or not live up to expectations. You may defer making decisions or taking action unless all uncertainties are resolved.

Allow me to draw your attention to your relationship with *confidence*; notice how you are **being with** this quality. In other words, how aware, authentic and vulnerable are you in terms of how you are, your state of Being and, particularly, your abilities?

The Confidence Pendulum

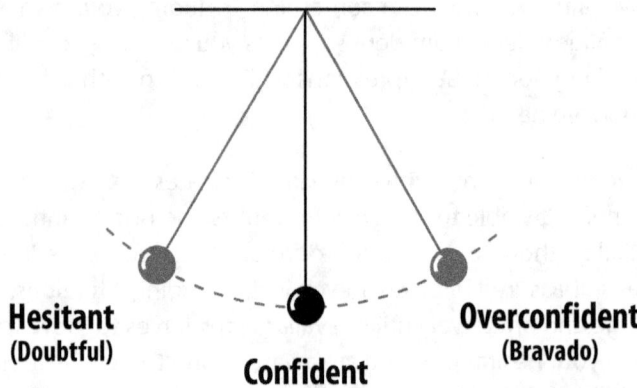

Hesitant
(Doubtful)

Confident

Overconfident
(Bravado)

As *confidence* is one of the multidimensional Secondary Ways of Being in the Being Framework, it's not a matter of being confident or not being confident. An individual who has an unhealthy relationship with *confidence* can be one of two ways, as shown in the Confidence Pendulum above: either they are hesitant or doubtful, or they are overconfident and full of bravado around matters or their own abilities. So, when you are not being confident, you are either shy, timid, uncertain, hesitant, doubtful and unsure, or you are overconfident and arrogant, which can lead you to be reckless, careless, heedless, hubristic (a self-proclaimed genius) and cocky. This can easily lead you to overestimate your abilities and the abilities of others. Someone who has an unhealthy relationship with *confidence* on the overconfident side of the pendulum is often sceptical and constantly seeks evidence from others in order to be convinced while pretending to be certain about their own abilities and state of Being in general. So, rather than taking the responsibility to convince themselves if they are unsure – through logic, critical thinking, research or other epistemological methods – they outsource the convincing and responsibility to others. A hesitant person, on the other hand, constantly seeks reassurance, primarily due to a lack of *awareness*. This is commonly the result of either not having been exposed to enough people and situations to be confident and courageous, or having an unhealthy relationship with one or more of their Moods.

Overconfidence can be due to a lack of *vulnerability*, not being able to deal with one's own insecurities. Overconfident people also tend to exaggerate the significance of their contribution towards things due to their lack of *awareness*, which causes misperceptions and misconceptions. They do their best to hide behind a fake and incongruent persona, so they maintain the facade but are insecure and fragile when the mask comes off in their solitude. Over time, this may generate a sense of entitlement, as if life and others owe them something. They may think their employer (or employees), parents, etc., are indebted to them because they feel their contribution went over and above the original agreement. This may lead them to manifest narcissistic comments or behaviours. The primary antagonist in *Alice in Wonderland*, the Red Queen, is a classic example of someone who is overconfident but insecure on the inside. In fact, most villains would fall into this category. They hide behind their bravado and exaggerated, inauthentic personas, or cast a shadow much larger than they are in order to look more dangerous, 'monstrous' and intimidating than they really are, and they use that to take control by generating fear, when they are really nothing more than a 'scarecrow'. This is deceitful and manipulative. Alternatively, they may do their best to shrink their shadow by adopting a bloated and exaggerated persona (inauthenticity) to convey an illusion of having full control of everything in their lives, so they appear more confident than they actually are. But once enough light shines on them, the inauthentic persona they have created and the bravado suddenly disappear and you see them for who they really are. The reason they become the villain in the first place is usually because they have lost all hope of accomplishing what they desire (care about) in legitimate ways. Overconfidence is also extremely common in general, particularly in the business world. Think of the type of leader who spends most of the time locked away in their 'ivory tower' ordering others to source information for them that makes them look good.

Let's take a closer look at what happens when we are not confident, beginning with overconfidence (bravado), as we commonly observe this in our work with business leaders and entrepreneurs. Naturally, my aim here is not to judge, but purely to point out our observations for the sake of *awareness*. Many business leaders and entrepreneurs we work with are quite oblivious to their limitations. This is a tricky and delicate conversation to have as, on the one hand, you need a level of irrationality, arationality and even craziness to push the boundaries and challenge the status quo as an entrepreneur, innovator and inventor. If you look into my career, you can see that I fall into that category, so I resonate with this conversation on a personal level. But on the other hand, you also need epistemic humility and *vulnerability* to avoid the common pitfalls. Perhaps you are a forward-thinking, visionary leader who sees things most struggle to see. However, your greatest challenge is to communicate the vision. This challenge is one of the main causes of the high failure rate in startups and it stems largely from overconfidence as a result of a lack of *vulnerability, responsibility* and *awareness*. The point is, being overconfident is not going to serve you well in business in the long run. In fact, it will serve you even less than a lack of *confidence* (being doubtful and hesitant).

Now, let me draw your attention to the other extreme when confidence is lacking. Being hesitant and doubtful won't do you any favours either. If you are setting yourself up to be an exceptional leader, *confidence* is critical. It has a particularly strong link to *courage*. Let me explain why. To be a leader, you are required to make decisions on a daily basis. Your *effectiveness* in that role will largely be determined by the decisions you make, no matter how significant or seemingly insignificant. While there will be times when you will be making decisions on matters you are highly proficient in and you will have access to expertise on your team to make data-driven decisions, you will also be required to make decisions about unstructured problems, especially if your value proposition is unique and your organisation is a pioneer in your industry. If this is the case – and this happens frequently today – there may not be any precedents to refer to when making decisions. Ironically, a lack of information actually justifies your endeavours to come up with new, innovative solutions and products. So, without precedents or sufficient data and information, how could you possibly be confident, certain and trust your decisions and the direction you are moving in? How can you be confident that the whole organisation, including your employees, investors and loyal clients, will follow? Here is where your *awareness*, *higher purpose*, *responsibility* and, especially, *courage* come into play. These Aspects of Being will help give you the *confidence* to take the leap of faith required to move forward.

When I refer to 'being certain', I am not referring to being certain in a scientific sense. Your decision may still be 'wrong', or ineffective or not the best possible, but phenomenologically speaking, matters in life can't all be solved like mathematical equations. By 'certain', I mean being able to firmly rely on and be both responsible and accountable for the decisions you make, including accepting their consequences and outcomes in advance. As a leader, there will be many times when you can't possibly be scientifically certain about every possibility. However, *confidence* is required for decisions to be made and actions to be taken. While some may want everything to be 'pixel perfect' and may be too conservative to take the necessary next steps until all the i's are dotted and the t's are crossed, a confident leader is the one who can **be with** a level of uncertainty and still move forward. The confident leader can also **be with** the potential blame and criticism that follows.

Confidence can be trained and developed

As is the case with so many Ways of Being, especially the Secondary Ways of Being, it may seem that some people are born with it. It may appear that some have received more of the '*confidence*-gene', but this is not true. *Confidence*, like all the other Secondary Ways of Being, can be trained and developed, your relationship with it can be transformed. It also depends to a great extent on what you tell yourself. Not having enough *confidence* can keep people from taking risks and seizing opportunities. As we have learnt, our Primary Ways of Being influence our Secondary Ways of Being. So, when people identify an unhealthy relationship with *confidence*, I start by examining their *awareness*, followed by their Moods, before digging deeper to look into their Primary Ways of Being to discover the Aspects of Being that may be influencing their level of *confidence*. It's like peeling back the layers of an onion. *Courage* is the predominant source for *confidence* but, as we have learnt in this chapter, other Aspects of Being come into play here too. Of all the Secondary Ways of Being, *confidence* is the one of the most apparent behavioural qualities that springs from *courage*; it is the one that comes to the rescue when we find ourselves in a complicated or compromising situation or relationship.

A friend of mine, who is a dog breeder, once told me that when puppies are about six weeks old, they start testing their limits and may start bullying their siblings in the litter to show who is the boss. As a responsible breeder, he observes this behaviour and deliberately separates overconfident puppies from the rest of the litter for certain periods of time and introduces them to a group of older or larger puppies so that the overconfident puppies learn to be confident and no longer overconfident. They are humbled when they realise there are stronger puppies in the world while also developing a sense of *compassion* when they learn what it means to be overpowered by another. In contrast, whenever he observes a shy, timid, doubtful and hesitant puppy, he introduces it to a group of calmer, more balanced, placid or even docile dogs to help lift its *confidence*. This practice, which is common amongst dog breeders, indicates that *confidence* is, in part, relative to the environment. Remember, when we are authentic, we acknowledge that we are social creatures. Therefore, at least to a certain degree, we measure our own capabilities and qualities against others. This is quite apparent when it comes to *confidence*. However, when comparing yourself to others, just be aware that acting confident is one thing, while **being** confident is another. More specifically, it's about how you are **being with** *confidence*.

When you find the *courage* to face your capability to succeed, your *confidence* level is more accurately calibrated. This opens up the possibility of being responsible for your *confidence* by taking measures to increase your capability to succeed. This chain of events is only effective if you tell yourself the truth about your capabilities. So, why are some people dishonest to themselves about that? Because they choose not to be responsible and counted on for their *effectiveness*. In other words, if they are honest, they can't hide anymore and play it safe. Not only does a higher capability to succeed give you more *confidence*, being authentic also adjusts your relationship with *confidence*. In other words, say, for example, you are not yet competent in an area you care about. Your authentic acknowledgement of this fact– via gauging your *confidence* in that particular context – is the most effective way to start building your *confidence* in that area. However, if there is no acknowledgement, you will remain unconfident in your capabilities and therefore also incompetent in the area you care so much about. Looking at another example, if *confidence* arises without a healthy relationship with *authenticity*, it can lead to overconfidence or bravado to cover up a lack of *confidence* to face reality about one's capabilities. This is typical of someone who is only concerned about looking confident versus being confident. People who lack both *confidence* and *authenticity* can appear timid on the surface while being manipulative and deceitful. Even though they may be perfectly capable, they could hide this fact by not taking *responsibility* for the capabilities they possess.

If you have a healthy relationship with *confidence*, you won't necessarily need all the evidence to be certain. There is no such thing as absolute certainty, especially in today's rapidly changing world. This is when you need to use your high level of *responsibility* to choose powerfully to trust, because trust is **always** a choice. As Steve Jobs said, 'You can't connect the dots looking forward; you can only connect them looking backwards. So, you have to trust that the dots will somehow connect in your future'. With this statement, Jobs was implying that, as an entrepreneur and a leader, you have to balance the matters you can be aware of with the matters you can't be aware of because they have no precedence. Your role as a leader is to powerfully make the call, where no one else is confident and courageous enough to do so, and choose to be responsible and accountable around the consequences and outcomes. Most don't have the healthy relationship with *confidence* to do that. They outsource matters and, if they don't achieve their desired outcome, commonly find a scapegoat to blame. A true leader would never be this way.

CHAPTER 27

Persistence

Persistence – also known as perseverance – is the final multi-dimensional Secondary Way of Being of the four in the Being Framework. It signifies the quality or state of pushing on or enduring despite difficulty or opposition. When I think of the word *persistence*, entrepreneurs, athletes and the warriors, knights and heroes of ancient times automatically come to mind. They signify a Way of Being that exudes tenacity and perseverance over a long period of time, usually well before they achieve their goals or fulfil their mission, and they resist the temptation to give up. If it wasn't for their *persistence*, they would not achieve their objectives. Some aspirations demand significant effort over an undefined period of time. It's like running a marathon with no specified finish line. Being persistent is one of the qualities that will get you there. It is one of the essential ingredients to enduring and being effective in any endeavour that feels like a tough, gruelling and seemingly never-ending event. *Persistence* is the state of continually being resolute or obstinate in a course of action despite difficulty or opposition. It is the quality of being steadfast when working on something despite difficulties or delays being encountered. Therefore, *persistence* demands a solid dose of patience, generosity (starting with yourself), strength and tenacity.

The word 'persistence' is derived from the Latin *Persistere* – *Per* ('through, steadfastly') and *Sistere* ('to stand'). It means continued effort and determination. If you look at the Latin derivation, you could say it is to steadfastly remain standing no matter what gets in your way. The word 'perseverance' is derived from the Latin root *Perseveres*, where *Severus* means 'strict'. A connotation of perseverance is to persist in a methodical manner despite obstacles and to persevere means 'to persistently repeat something'. So, we need to be persistent in order to persevere. This makes sense, because if you keep working on something in spite of all the difficulties you encounter, you are being strict on yourself, which will help you chip away at an endeavour, like a new product that requires a lengthy period of time to develop, including several rounds of refinements. Whether you're building a business, a long-term relationship or raising a family, it's not a sprint but a marathon. It requires consistent effort to persevere. The same is true for many other things in life, such as learning a new language or working on an invention that seems impossible, to name just a few. *Persistence* and daily effort will eventually reward you with accomplishment. Dr Lynn Margolies, a psychologist and former Harvard Medical School faculty and fellow, describes persevering as staying on course and not giving up despite difficulties and setbacks[161]. It is an important part of what it takes to be successful in many areas of life. Intelligence or talent alone aren't enough if you cannot persevere and weather frustration and challenges. Perseverance (or *persistence*) leads to accomplishment and can give great fulfilment and satisfaction when meeting significant challenges.

---

161   *When Perseverance Costs You Success*, by Lynn Margolies, PhD, PsychCentral.

The Being Framework ontological distinction of *persistence*

Being persistent is living life from the viewpoint that you are to persevere, stay the course and not give up despite difficulties, challenges and setbacks. *Persistence* is a quality that determines your success in many areas of life, as intelligence and skill alone are insufficient to overcome the obstacles and challenges you face. *Persistence* leads to accomplishment and is the access to greater fulfilment and satisfaction in overcoming life's challenges.

A healthy relationship with *persistence* indicates that you are tenacious and refuse to give up easily, especially in challenging situations. You stay on task, even when facing formidable or daunting circumstances. Others may know you to be determined, resolute, and someone who will follow through and remain focused on achieving outcomes you are committed to.

An unhealthy relationship with *persistence* indicates that you may be unreasonably inconsistent or insistent. You may be easily distracted, wavering, unsteady and discouraged by setbacks and may question your original decisions and lose heart. You may have many unfinished tasks and projects that you are unlikely to complete and justify yourself with excuses. Alternatively, you may be overly insistent – stubborn and dogged to the point of belligerence. You may rise to face the same obstacle time and again while refusing to consider alternatives. Others are less likely to believe that you will stay the course, and you may frequently procrastinate, become despondent, give up or change direction.

Persistence and patience

As mentioned, one of the prerequisites to being persistent is a healthy relationship with patience. The root of the word 'patience' comes from the Latin *Patientia* – patient ('suffering'). *Persistence* demands patience and is when you can **be with** suffering for the duration. This should not be confused with being oppressed or under unnecessary and avoidable pressure. It's also not about passively waiting for a miracle to happen. In fact, it's the opposite. *Persistence* is when you have the stamina, determination, *freedom*, *courage*, willingness, capability and capacity to not give up during the journey while repeating or trying alternative ways to finally resolve a matter. Even when you fail, *persistence* is about returning to the drawing board and trying again. A persistent individual lives life from the viewpoint that failure is only a temporary state and an inevitable part of achieving any goal. Therefore, they are confident that by going through several iterations of application, execution, exercise, practice or rounds of refinements, the objective will finally be reached. Their conception of acquiring things or reaching goals is that they will eventually get there, as long as they go for it and don't give up. Let's say you are a computer programmer and are tasked with implementing a new algorithm. You try the first option that comes to mind but it doesn't work, so you try a second option, but that too is unsuccessful. It is not uncommon to have to make several attempts before you finally succeed. It's an iterative process that involves going through a cycle of: **Execute → Track → Learn → Refine → Execute** again. This is a simple yet crucial process that is not limited to computer programmers. It is also required by engineers, inventors, athletes, martial artists, students, entrepreneurs and leaders. We will examine this process in *Part 3: Being, in Action, Chapter 2: Transformation Methodology*.

When you are persistent, you don't give up in the face of the first challenge life throws at you or you cause yourself. It means persevering even when faced with multiple challenges and failures during the several attempts you make towards achieving your objective. *Persistence* is a quality that is critical for anyone wanting to build their career over time (as opposed to just getting a job), raise a family, build and scale a business, study to be a medical doctor, train to run a marathon and the list goes on. In other words, everyone needs it. If you are not being persistent and keep jumping from pillar to post in life, you are not going to be effective and therefore you are unlikely to ever be fulfilled. This is a very common pattern that prevents people from becoming high achievers. I once had a mentor who told me, 'The best fertiliser for the farmer's farm is the farmer's feet'. It is a piece of advice that resonated with me and speaks to the absolutely critical need to persevere through the hardships on the road to accomplishment. When you read the biographies of some of the world's most revered high achievers, you discover that they have all persisted through significant hardships on their journey to success, the kinds of hardships that the average person wouldn't be able to endure without developing the same relationship with *persistence*.

It is also valuable to distinguish the difference between pressure and stress at this point. Pressure is important, natural and is required to move anything forward in life, whereas stress is when two opposing pressures meet. For example, when you have a dinner appointment with your spouse and your boss asks you to work late or you have to address an important business issue, two opposing pressures cause you to experience stress. *Persistence*, on the other hand, comes into play when we refuse to succumb to the stress. It is the quality that leads us to seek appropriate solutions in stressful situations.

A question I am asked from time to time is, 'What's the difference between *resilience* and *persistence* and why do we need both?' *Resilience* is a Way of Being that describes the ability to bounce back, like elastic, even when enormously stretched. It's the quality that enables us to restore our *integrity*, or the *integrity* of our life, whenever an unexpected event or matter comes through like a wrecking ball and threatens to derail us. *Persistence*, on the other hand, is **being all in**, as opposed to **being in and out**. It's about being willing to make sure you do not abandon your goal purely because you may think you're not strong enough to give it what it takes. *Persistence* is continuing with an approach or course of action in spite of difficulty or opposition, while *resilience* is the quality which enables you to withstand, absorb, recover, heal and adapt effectively to adversity, difficulty or sudden changes in conditions. The two go hand in hand and therefore both are key qualities for *effectiveness* when working towards the achievement of any objective. *Resilience* is a linear Secondary Way of Being and is explored in detail in chapter 29.

The Persistence Pendulum

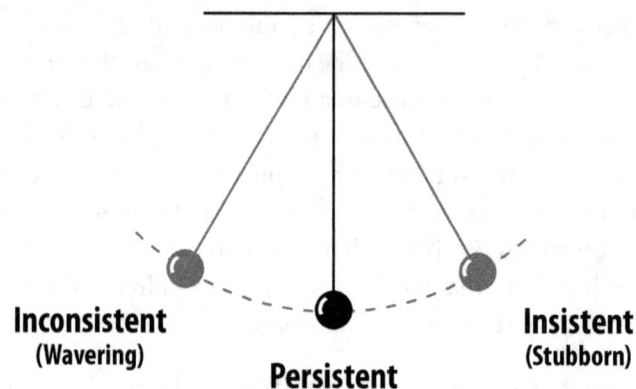

As a multidimensional Secondary Way of Being, *persistence* doesn't necessarily mean we should keep pushing on no matter what. That would be stubbornness or insistence, when the pendulum swings to the far right. When the pendulum swings to the far left, we are being inconsistent, wavering or unsteady, which is equally unfavourable. This refers to dealing with matters, from allocated tasks and projects to goals and objectives, intermittently and inconsistently or at irregular intervals rather than in a continuous, steady manner, which is how we deal with matters when we are persistent. When we are driven to prove ourselves right, are unable to commit to failure and loss, or – at the other extreme – are too accommodating with the wishes of others, *persistence* – like *confidence*, *proactivity* or *assertiveness* – can be taken to an unhealthy level. As a multidimensional Secondary Way of Being, *persistence* can show up as two equally unhealthy states of Being. Let's examine each – being insistent or stubborn versus being inconsistent, wavering or unsteady – separately to gain a clearer picture, beginning with being insistent or stubborn.

It is important to acknowledge when you know things are not going to work, no matter how hard you try or how long you work at it. To a great extent, this comes from having a healthy relationship with *awareness*, *vulnerability* and *authenticity*. It is when you have the discernment to know that the most effective way forward is to put a stop to the project, gracefully give up and redirect your attention and energy to the next journey, towards a different goal and commitment. There is such a thing as 'over-persevering', much like it is possible to be overconfident. Being insistent is when we persevere despite knowing it would be more beneficial to count our losses and move on. When we insistently and stubbornly push on, *persistence* can lead to suffering, boredom, dissatisfaction and resentment. When we are insistent, we are totally irrational, rigid, dogmatic, closed and often not mindful of the will of the other party/parties involved. A common example in business or personal relationships is when one person no longer wants to be in the relationship, following several fruitless attempts to resolve the issues between them, but the other person stubbornly insists on pushing through. While one person just wants to forgive and move on, the insistent one often makes an already difficult situation even worse. Being insistent is when we are unwilling to give up the fight despite it being the right time and the right conditions to stop and move on. It is not uncommon for entrepreneurs to adopt this mentality because they believe they need to keep going and never give up, no matter the cost. But to keep repeating the same thing and making the same mistakes time after time is not going to magically change the outcome. For example, insisting on pushing through with the sale of a product the market does not need or is not ready to buy is irrational, no matter how brilliant you may think it is. At the end of the day, you don't have control over everything, hence a healthy relationship with *responsibility* is also required here. As Einstein famously said, 'Insanity is doing the same thing over and over again and expecting different results'. Having an unhealthy relationship with *persistence* could stem from a genuine lack of *awareness* or it could be due to a lack of *vulnerability* or *responsibility,* amongst other Aspects of Being. As always, the key is to dig deeper to uncover the reasons.

When the pendulum swings to the insistent or stubborn side of the Persistence Pendulum due to an unhealthy relationship with *vulnerability,* it is like the individual knows they are being ineffective but aren't prepared to give up in case it makes them look weak and ruins their reputation. Ironically, the opposite is true. Others will see through their facade, especially when the wheels start falling off. The point is, not giving up isn't always a virtue! I will acknowledge, however, that it can be extremely difficult to discern when to give up versus when to persevere. This is when the assistance of a coach, mentor or adviser can be extremely beneficial to provide an independent perspective. When you persevere in what I call a 'wisely persistent manner', you will know when to stop and move on to the next chapter. In other words, when you have a healthy relationship with *persistence*, you learn to recognise the right time to give up and change gears. This is achieved through *awareness*, *authenticity* and a healthy relationship with *vulnerability*. After all, you have to lower your guard to admit when it is time to let go.

Now, let's examine the other possible extreme when we have an unhealthy relationship with *persistence*, which I refer to as being inconsistent, wavering or unsteady. It's when we are **being in and out** as opposed to **being all in**. This is quite common. Let me share an example that highlights what it looks like to be inconsistent as opposed to being persistent and some of the underlying reasons it may happen. I was coaching one of the coaches in our community who was procrastinating with her online programs. She had been in and out (inconsistent) for several months, indicating that being in front of the camera was something she wasn't comfortable with. Through our coaching sessions, she identified that the core reason for her lack of *persistence* in pursuing the need to get the online programs up and running was a lack of *vulnerability*. I used to tell her many times that her unhealthy relationship with *persistence* was 'costing her' and she always nodded her head in confirmation, but it was clear she wasn't totally comprehending what I meant. I believe she had a perception of what I meant but lacked the conception, meaning she was unable to relate the perception back to the context of her own life.

During a gathering with her coaching network, my client suddenly developed a clear conception of how a lack of *persistence* was affecting her. Listening to the other coaches in her network, it was a watershed moment when she learnt how much money they were making and, even more importantly, how many people they had the privilege to support and serve by running online programs, despite many being far less competent, proficient and experienced than she was. At our next session, she told me, 'I used to take your words of caution – this is costing you – metaphorically, but now I know that my procrastination and lack of *persistence* have literally cost me thousands of dollars over the last six months and many new clients'. This realisation enabled her to resonate with my point on a much deeper, more tangible level and this led her to become aware of the fact that she lacked the *vulnerability* to face the camera for *fear* of what others may think of her. While this example is relevant to our Being in general and not necessarily just to an unhealthy relationship with *persistence* and *vulnerability*, my point is, any unhealthy relationship will cost you, figuratively and literally. In the grand scheme of things, even $100K is nothing. In many cases, a lack of *persistence* (amongst other linked Aspects of Being) costs people their marriage, the business they have been trying to build for the last decade, their property, etc., and, most importantly, time, a chunk of their life they can never buy back or redeem.

Not being persistent coupled with not being *proactive* (being inactive), in terms of putting in the effort required to hit your targets, will cost you the things you desire most in your life. Unless you make your objective a priority, you won't be as persistent as that objective demands. The high achievers of the world give their objectives their all; they are willing to put in whatever it takes, while others won't. That's what makes them high achievers and why there are so few in the world. Furthermore, it's not just personal. Your *persistence*, or lack thereof, deeply affects others too. If you fail to project the true manifestation of your Unique Being to the world due to a lack of *persistence*, humanity will miss out on your unique *contribution*. While I am fundamentally reluctant to water *persistence* down to just 'hard work', let me use it here as a way of describing the effort required to give it your all. However, the ease and comfort with which a lack of *persistence* may be conquered will depend entirely on the intensity of your desire to put in the hard work, in other words, whether or not there is a deep sense of *care* and urgency around the project or cause you are working on.

Like all other Secondary Ways of Being, *persistence* goes far deeper than the superficial layer. For instance, you may look into your *awareness* to see if you are crystal clear on the consequences and tangible costs of your lack of *persistence*. How much is it costing you your fulfilment and satisfaction in life? To vividly paint this picture, *awareness* is crucial. The other area to look into is your relationship with your Moods – *care*, *vulnerability*, *fear* and *anxiety* – as most of the time, procrastination and being lame and lazy in the face of what we actually care deeply about has its roots in our relationship with our Moods. When you find yourself being inconsistent, wavering or unsteady, ask yourself, 'Do I fear failure or am I anxious about the what ifs? Am I concerned or do I care about how others will perceive me if things don't work out (pointing to a lack of *vulnerability*)? Am I free in the sense that I am present to the possibilities available to me? Or do I feel trapped or constrained, either by the distorted reality I have created for myself (Third-layer Reality), or by the collective reality created by human beings in general, how things already ARE out there (Second-layer Reality)?' If you allow such current constraints to hold you back from being persistent, you will literally let the future, more effective version of YOU be defeated by the reality you created for yourself or the reality which is already out there. This defeatist attitude can manifest itself as a lack of *persistence* on the inconsistent, wavering or unsteady side. Remember, the ultimate aim of projecting the manifestation of your Unique Being to the world through your unique *contribution* is to impact and expand the reality out there (Second-layer). This requires you to be influential beyond personal matters (*higher purpose*).

I have worked with many highly talented and intelligent people (most notably, corporates) who, despite all they have going for them, experience a lack of fulfilment in multiple aspects of their lives. I found that *persistence* and *commitment* to the virtue of faith beyond logic, reasoning and rationality are the two qualities they lack the most. By 'faith' I mean an intuitive, arational way of knowing, at a personal level, alongside language, logic, reason, emotion, intuition, inspiration, etc. Epistemologically, faith is one way of knowing, but it is more personal, like a gut feel. Faith is needed to persist when we are unable to gather sufficient data and evidence to make data-driven decisions. That's why I commonly refer to the need to take a leap of faith when it comes to persevering on arational matters, and this is precisely what high performers, pioneers and leaders do, especially when delving into uncharted waters.

CHAPTER 28

Resourcefulness

When working towards a goal, do you see nothing but the obstacles in your way and the resources immediately at hand? Do you struggle to see beyond the immediate challenges you are faced with? As the proverb goes, 'If all you have is a hammer, everything looks like a nail'. So, how can you create something that doesn't look possible at the time with the resources available? And how can you become resourceful if you feel stuck and simply don't see any other options? *Resourcefulness* is the first of our linear Secondary Ways of Being to be explored. It is the willingness and capability of finding or creating solutions to overcome challenges and the quality that leads you to pave your own way, despite the number of resources you have at your disposal. This Way of Being is extremely crucial, particularly in situations in which you feel trapped or stuck. By being resourceful, you can take steps towards achieving a goal that seems unattainable.

Being resourceful is the quality of being willing and capable of leveraging the maximum power of potential from whatever resources you already have, directly or indirectly, for example, through your network and relationships with others (tapping into their resources). When you are resourceful, you are aware of the possibilities available to you and free to tap into them. Resourceful individuals are creative, responsible (autonomous) and committed to something bigger than themselves (*higher purpose*). They operate from an abundance mentality as opposed to a scarcity mentality. It is worth noting that when looking at the etymology of the word 'resource' it comes from the Old French *Resoudre* which means to 'rise again, recover', based on the Latin *Surgere*, 'to rise'.

There is a common misunderstanding that we need resources more than anything else, particularly from an economic perspective. Working with many first-time entrepreneurs alongside more experienced ones, we have learnt that the vast majority consider everything to be resources, including human beings, and are constantly seeking more resources, both human and capital, to solve the problems they face. The notion of people as resources is so broadly accepted in society that we still refer to people and culture in business as 'Human Resources'. However, it is not authentic to consider human beings as resources. It is the work being done by human beings that may be viewed as resources.

When most startups first approach us, they tell us they lack capital and are looking for investors to inject seed funding into their business. However, in almost all cases, there are other areas of their business that require attention first and this is more critical than raising funds at this stage. In other words, they are not yet investment ready. While the myth of lacking capital continues to circulate because it is an easy way to justify a lack of progress, the high achievers of the world don't focus too much on the need to HAVE resources. Instead, they primarily focus on BEING resourceful. When Steve Jobs spoke at the D8 Conference in 2010, he explained how Apple chose the technologies to include in their products, highlighting their profound *resourcefulness*. Here is an excerpt of what he said during his address:

> 'Apple is a company that doesn't have the most resources of everybody in the world, and the way we've succeeded is by choosing what horses to ride really carefully – technically. We try to look for these technical vectors that have a future, and that are headed up, and, you know, different pieces of technology kind of go in cycles. They have their springs and summers, and autumns, and then they, you know, go to the graveyard of technology. And, so we try to pick the things that are in their springs. And, if you choose wisely, you can save yourself an enormous amount of work vs. trying to do everything. And you can really put energy into making those new emerging technologies be great on your platform, rather than just okay because you're spreading yourself too thin. Sometimes you just have to pick the things that look like they're going to be the right horses to ride going forward …'

Another classic example of *resourcefulness* is the fact that, traditionally, we fought over so-called limited resources. That's because we used to be hunters, relying on whatever resources Mother Nature made available. Once we realised there wasn't enough game in the world to feed us, hence the hunting model became unsustainable, we began farming. This generated a relatively higher sustainability rate. Today, we are collectively challenging our farming methods to be even more sustainable and ethical. A tangible example of the perceived resources shortage is the wars being waged in the oil producing areas of the world because certain leaders hold the perception that oil is a limited resource, resulting in the loss of many lives, including the soldiers that are sent there and the civilians living in those regions. Those so-called leaders are operating with a scarcity mindset. On the other hand, a forward-thinking leader like Elon Musk came along and questioned the need for fossil fuels when there are more sustainable ways of generating and using energy available to us, such as solar energy and electric vehicles. This solution would result in no more fighting over so-called limited resources, no more loss of life and potentially less pollution. In coming up with these solutions, Musk was adopting an abundance mindset. My point is not to debate these topics. I am merely talking about *resourcefulness* and the fact that, like any other Aspect of Being, it starts with *awareness*, knowing and understanding what's available out there and how you can arrange existing resources in such a way that you can leverage the synergistic power that results from this arrangement towards the achievement of your objectives.

At this point, I would like to reiterate the definition of 'entrepreneur', as coined by French economist and philosopher, Jean-Baptiste Say: 'The entrepreneur shifts economic resources out of an area of lower and into an area of higher productivity and greater yield'. With this definition in mind, let's consider a startup's co-founding team (aka the 'human capital'). Now, let's break this down into the collective Beings, qualities, experiences, knowledge, creativity, etc., coupled with the networks and relationships you have built over time, the founding customers you have managed to get on board, as well as the piece of tech or product you are building and any monetary capital that has been injected into your new venture. These are going to be your resources. Let's say, for the sake of this example, there are ten resources in total. The key difference between **having** resources and **being** resourceful is that when you are being resourceful, your ten resources, or whatever number it may be, have the potential to multiply ten- or even a hundredfold. By arranging your resources through leadership and effective processes, you generate **synergy**[162]. That is the result of interaction, collaboration and cooperation giving rise to a whole that is greater than the simple sum of its parts. In the example of the startup, the unity of the 'human resources' – the work being done by them – transformed a group of individuals into a team. It's about creating integrity and flow, whereby all the elements work cohesively together at an optimum level.

Geese fly in a V-shaped formation. This serves two important purposes: energy conservation and visual assurance. This is particularly important when they are migrating and travelling vast distances. The lead birds take turns being in the front, where most energy is required, allowing the others to follow with ease, expending less energy. When they tire, the lead birds fall back to the rear, allowing others to step up and take the load. In this way, geese can fly for a long time before they must stop to rest. To keep track of every bird in the group, flying in formation may assist with communication and coordination. Fighter pilots often use this formation for the same reason. So, by flying in formation, geese are clearly being resourceful. Birds that fly alone, on the other hand, beat their wings more frequently and have higher heart rates than those that fly in formation, wasting precious energy and therefore not being as resourceful as they could be. Simply put, *resourcefulness* is being as effective as possible in leveraging all available resources.

---

[162] The word 'synergy' comes from the Attic Greek (the Greek dialect of the ancient city-state of Athens) word *Synergia* (συνέργεια) from *Synergos* (συνεργός) meaning 'working together'.

The Being Framework ontological distinction of *resourcefulness*

Resourcefulness is living life from the viewpoint of abundance and being effective at finding or creating new ways of doing things and solving problems. When you are being resourceful, you will often look beyond pre-existing knowledge, tools, conventional systems and traditional methods to find solutions. You are profoundly related to reality and have the passion and curiosity to discover more. You often see things others miss, love to try out new ideas and willingly drop any preconceived notions or perspectives. You acknowledge that you always have options and can pave a way forward.

A healthy relationship with *resourcefulness* indicates that you rarely stop searching for new options and will primarily look for a way to find solutions, even when there is no obvious way forward. You thrive on challenges, are imaginative and rarely allow existing resources or circumstances to determine when or how you will take action. You utilise and leverage available resources to maximise *effectiveness*, producing disproportionately greater results than others may with the same resources. Others will come to you for ideas when they are stuck and appreciate you as someone creative, with a different perspective and who thinks 'outside the box'.

An unhealthy relationship with *resourcefulness* indicates that you may become quickly disillusioned or discouraged when there is a perceived lack of resources. You may often operate from scarcity and repeatedly perceive a shortage of resources to fulfil your intentions. You may also frequently find it challenging to see and utilise resources beyond those immediately in front of or given to you. Others may consider you to be someone who often fails to complete a task unless all resources are ready and available. Alternatively, you may be frivolous and use resources as though they are limitless with little or no consideration for their value.

As you can see from the ontological distinction, *resourcefulness* is a Way of Being that springs from our intention to first grapple with reality (both First and Second-layer) and then find or create a way to do something and solve a problem. In contrast, waiting and hoping for more resources or a miracle to occur is very unlikely to produce success. But with a resourceful approach, we are driven to find and/or create a way. Contrary to what many people think, *resourcefulness* is not just a chain of skill sets that relies on learning a series of techniques. It is a Way of Being. When you are resourceful, you don't allow circumstances, particularly a lack of resources, to determine when or how you take action. *Resourcefulness* puts you in the driver's seat and that is empowering. Being resourceful also inspires innovative thinking and creativity, the generation of new ideas, and the ability to visualise various ways to fulfil your objectives. It helps you to stay positive and in the flow, rather than feeling stifled and stuck. *Resourcefulness* is partly reliant on knowing what to look for and the questions to ask. It's also about leveraging the resources you have at your disposal and the power of your network. When you are resourceful, you will not shy away from putting requests to others or even being appropriately demanding and assertive. Once you transform your relationship with *resourcefulness*, you will suddenly realise how rich you have been all along (not necessarily in a monetary sense) and how blind you were to that fact because your conception of reality was skewed. You will be amazed at the value of the resources that have always been at your disposal, but that you failed to realise and utilise, and surprised by how many people are willing to contribute to you and your objectives when you are resourceful.

Phenomenologically speaking, it is in our nature to be of service to others, which is why *contribution* is a Primary Way of Being. It is also in our nature to be compassionate (hence, *compassion* is another Primary Way of Being). We are here to **be with** others. For many years I have worked with software product development teams who use a number of relatively effective methodologies and disciplines, such as SDLC, Agile and DevOps. But while all these disciplines, processes and frameworks can be very practical, I have always found that the qualities of individuals on the team were getting in the way of adequately implementing them. This goes back to the *integrity* of our Beings. In the case of the software product development teams, I would say a lack of *resourcefulness*, in particular, was getting in the way. Making progress when working on any new idea requires a healthy balance between failure or invalidation of your hypotheses and success. Without failure, you won't make progress because the only questions you will be asking are the ones you already know the answers to. As a consequence, you won't discover anything new. Experience too much failure, however, and you and your team will become disheartened. The key is to be resourceful by continually coming up with new solutions, being proactive and persistent in the process.

It is worth highlighting the strong relationship between *awareness* and *resourcefulness* because we need to develop an accurate conception of reality (First and Second-layer) in order to be resourceful. We need to know how things (resources) ARE. Ontologically speaking, *resourcefulness* is a visible and practical Way of Being. It is a quality that makes things happen. Workability is key. If we are not aware and willing to become more aware of how things ARE in the world and how human beings operate in terms of our work and *effectiveness* (which spring from our Aspects of Being), we are setting ourselves up for disappointment because, without *awareness*, we cannot be resourceful. Therefore, knowing and understanding human beings through the Being Framework is so important. Indeed, supporting people to know and understand how human beings ARE is precisely what the Being Framework is designed for.

We must also understand 'resources' and how they can be combined to be practical, hence the necessity to tap into the knowledge of others to understand how they work with those resources in terms of the patterns and processes that work and the ones that don't. This is where asking the right questions of the right people is extremely crucial, as resourceful people learn where and how to invest their future efforts – and the efforts of their teams – in coming up with solutions. By being resourceful, they continue to probe and scrutinise by asking more questions that may not have been asked before in places where no one may have looked. They do this until a new answer or solution emerges. In an article for *Scientific American*[163] John Horgan wrote the following in reference to philosopher Karl Popper: 'Resourceful people have a quality to go beyond the pre-existing knowledge and data, beyond formal systems and methods'.

---

163   'The Paradox of Karl Popper' by John Horgan, *Scientific American*, August 2018.

A resourceful individual is profoundly connected to reality, and they have the passion, curiosity and epistemic humility to uncover more about it and how things (resources) are. They acknowledge that in order for their invention to work, it must have its roots in Reality, respecting the laws of the universe and be based on discovery, not invention. Otherwise, it would be like building a magnificent house on a foundation of sand. I would like to reiterate at this point that people's work and the outputs they produce are resources, NOT the people themselves. Therefore, as a leader, it is extremely vital to know human beings and how we operate, particularly within the scope of performance and *effectiveness*, and that is exactly what the Being Framework can give you access to. Once you know and understand human beings, you can leverage their work as opposed to letting their work be wasted. That is what a true leader does. Being resourceful leverages the most out of the resources available and generates more value to serve. In the context of business, the by-product of this *contribution, resourcefulness* and service can be monetary gain and profit. Resourceful leaders see things others don't because this is where they put both their **intention** and **attention**. They expect to see the unexpected and are also prepared to discover the unwanted truth. Being resourceful requires *authenticity*, because without being authentic about discovering the truth, we are **covering up reality** rather than **discovering** and **uncovering** the reality and the answers we seek. And unless we know and understand how things work, we cannot be resourceful.

CHAPTER 29

Resilience

esilience is the degree of elasticity required to restore to our original shape, particularly when we are being enormously stretched. The circumstances of life, adversities and catastrophes, demands of others and, from time to time, even our own thoughts and emotions, can drag us away from our Unique Being, such as our calling, or simply the direction we set for ourselves as well as the *integrity* of our Being. If you have ever been through a life-changing traumatic event such as business liquidation, bankruptcy, the death of a loved one, serious illness or a relationship breakdown, *resilience* is one of the Ways of Being that will come to rescue. In fact, we need this quality most of all in times of crisis because it supports us to bounce back. However, *resilience* is also key to transformation. Just as we need to maintain our cars regularly to keep them performing at an optimal level, we must also regularly and consistently polish and maintain the *integrity* of our Being and this is where we need *resilience* to stay on track, especially when the path becomes rocky.

By now you will be familiar with the discrepancies that are apparent when we turn to dictionaries and other sources for the definition of an Aspect of Being. *Resilience* is no exception. The *Oxford English Dictionary* defines resilience as 'the capacity to recover quickly from difficulties', or, 'the ability of a substance or object to spring back into shape'. The *Macmillan Dictionary* defines it as 'able to quickly become healthy, happy, or strong again after an illness, disappointment, or other problem' and the *Cambridge Dictionary* also defines it as 'the ability to be happy and successful after something difficult or bad has happened'. In modern psychological literature, resilience is often seen as the process of adapting and adjusting well in the face of adversity, catastrophe, trauma, tragedy, threats, or significant sources of stress, which we all know are inevitable no matter how well trained, strong, wealthy and knowledgeable we are. Etymologically, the word resilience was derived from *Resiliens*, the present participle of the Latin word *Resilire*, which means 'to recoil or rebound'. However, there is another meaning which is more congruent with the quality we are referring to in the Being Framework, namely, the ability of a substance to return to its original shape after being bent, stretched or pressed. So, metaphorically speaking, when you are being pressed, pressured, stressed or stretched by either internal or external forces, *resilience* is being able to restore the *integrity* of your original shape, which is the state of being whole, complete, unbroken, sound and in perfect condition.

The Being Framework ontological distinction of *resilience*

Resilience is a quality that enables you to bounce back to your original form or even stronger when circumstances in life knock you down. You consistently leverage setbacks to adjust and learn while finding a way to rise up and continue forward rather than letting difficulties or failure overcome you and drain your resolve.

A healthy relationship with *resilience* indicates that you can consistently face difficult circumstances with elasticity, without breaking as you might if you were rigid. You trust your ability to endure hardship. Others may consider you to have the patience, strength of character and capacity to manage pain, discomfort, difficulties and challenging emotions and impulses. People may feel encouraged by you and your presence when things are tough.

An unhealthy relationship with *resilience* indicates that you may often be defeated, distressed, disarmed and broken by life-changing circumstances or events. You tend to avoid uncertainty, change or challenging life experiences. Others may describe you as weak or a victim. Alternatively, you may become entrenched, rigid or fixed to one spot, making you susceptible to fragility. You may take unnecessary punishment while numbing yourself to your pain, potentially causing you to remain in unhealthy situations or relationships.

One of the verses in a poem by the great Persian poet Rumi deeply resonated with me as being powerfully connected to the way I see *resilience* in this framework. I have done my best to translate it:

> *Whoever finds himself far away from his origin (true Self)*
> *is ever longing for the day he shall return and restore.*

This verse reminds me of a trigonometry circle chart. By the time you go from zero to 180 degrees, you are at the polar opposite end of the chart from your original position. However, if you keep going until you reach 360 degrees, you will end up right back where you started. If you have ever deeply contemplated and/or undertaken any massive change in your life journey to date, I know you would resonate with this.

The more you care, the more responsible you are. And the more committed you are to your calling and true authentic original form (the manifestation of your Unique Being), the more important it is to be resilient. When you are resilient, it's as though you are made of rubber. No matter how hard or how frequently you are knocked down by life's challenges, you have the ability to bounce back to your original shape and get going again. Rather than being let down by difficulties, resilient people overcome challenges and find a way to pull through. Life is always throwing curve balls our way and sometimes we can become victims to unpredictable and uncontrollable events that can cause pain, trauma and suffering. Other times, we can make decisions or mistakes that put us in dire situations. When we are resilient in these situations, we bounce back faster and are therefore able to continue on with our lives.

Now, at this point you may be wondering why, on the one hand, I am saying we are not fixed objects, hence we can transform, but on the other hand, I am also saying we can return to our original form. Let me remind you that your Unique Being is the part of Existence you carry within, the Unity of Being. That mysterious enigma is there to be discovered; this is your quest in life: to dig, discover and extract that unique gem and bring it to the surface. Then, through your Aspects of Being, you manifest your Unique Being by contributing and being of service. So, when it comes to your Unique Being, it's up to you to redeem it as the true opportunity and gift it is, a gift that was bestowed upon you, not something you were entitled to. It is a privilege simply to BE, let alone the fact that you have the autonomy (*responsibility*) to choose how you want to be and what you want to do with your life. Therefore, it is up to you to pull the right strings to redeem yourself. The transformation starts with the conversation around your Aspects of Being (Essence), the part of you that went unnoticed, neglected and turned to rust; that is the part of you that needs polishing and transforming. When Rumi talked about finding oneself away from one's origin (true Self) and longing for the opportunity to return and restore, he was talking about redemption. Remember, it is our Aspects of Being that we polish and transform. *Resilience* supports us to bounce back and restore our original form whenever we stray away from our quest to discover and project our Unique Being, which we are gifted with at birth, to the world.

Resilience is not toughness

Many people think being resilient is being tough, which is no surprise given the *Oxford English Dictionary* uses the word 'toughness' to define resilience. From an ontological perspective, I strongly disagree with this definition. Delve into this more deeply and you discover that the *Oxford English Dictionary* defines toughness as 'the demonstration of a strict and uncompromising approach; the quality of being strong and prone to violence'. This definition is more closely aligned with rigidity than *resilience*, which, ironically, is far away from its ontological distinction. If you are being rigid, you are not being flexible, which is absolutely critical if you are to be resilient. I first learnt this lesson from my Aikido Master. I used to practise Kyokushin Karate, known as the toughest form of karate, from childhood through to my teenage years. In this form of karate, the ultimate power is conceived as being tough and strong. Where defence is a strong focus in most martial arts, Kyokushin requires participants to demonstrate toughness by receiving and tolerating attacks. We used to receive quite heavy punches and kicks, even as young children, and to become an 'iron man', as portrayed in the matches we watched on video, was the goal. At the age of sixteen, I was introduced to Aikido and learnt a totally different philosophy. In fact, the philosophy behind Aikido was so different to what I had learnt when practising Kyokushin, that it took me quite some time to become accustomed to the new paradigm and practices. Eventually, it resonated with me in a way that Kyokushin Karate had not. In Aikido, the goal is not to withstand adverse conditions and forces, through toughness, but to receive them gently and redirect offending and violent energy coming at you through punches and kicks or even weapons from the opponent. Let me bring this home with a business example.

Imagine you are a startup. You've spent months undergoing rigorous R&D and market research and have invested a large sum of your own money and time into building an innovative piece of software, which requires a series of sophisticated algorithms, months of research, analysis, design and development and a range of talents with various skill sets. Now imagine that, just as you were on the verge of launching your new product, you realised the software does not work as intended. You begin to panic as you consider the promises you have made and realise your reputation and the livelihood of your team members are at stake. How would you be in this situation? What would you do? I have personally experienced similar scenarios. I remember being five days out from launching a product that thousands of dollars of marketing budget had gone into when my head developer was diagnosed with a brain tumour and had to be hospitalised immediately, potentially delaying the launch. We ended up reshaping the team, as he ended up being unable to work for two months while recuperating. On another occasion, my key solutions architect had to leave on the eve of our launch because his father had been admitted to intensive care in hospital. Both situations were unavoidable. I could come up with many examples of this nature. It is our ability to receive such adversities gently (not with toughness) and redirect the energy with clarity and calmness, that enables us to manage unavoidable situations like this by being resilient. These are situations we all face in life, especially as startups, leaders and entrepreneurs.

Resilience and its link to other Aspects of Being

Like other Aspects of Being, building *resilience* doesn't happen overnight. But it is also not necessarily reliant on incremental improvements. Anyone who is willing and committed can learn and develop the ability to transform their relationship with *resilience*. The possibility of becoming resilient is one reason my studies have shown that *resilience* is ordinary, not extraordinary. This is evidenced through our empirical data[164] that shows many have a relatively higher *resilience* level in comparison with some other Aspects of Being. Once you develop your conception of this Secondary Way of Being, it is crucial to work on its underlying, deeper Aspects of Being, including (but not limited to) *care, fear, anxiety, higher purpose, responsibility, commitment, courage, forgiveness* and *empowerment*, to hasten the process. Remember, this is not a one-off process. On a larger scale, we need collective *resilience*, as communities and as a society, to deal with unavoidable events like natural disasters and global pandemics, or in the face of man-made destructive plans such as terrorist attacks, wars being waged and imposed on a nation by an arrogant totalitarian nation or war crimes. *Resilience* is paramount during and after tragedy, both on a collective and individual level, to rebuild cities, towns, lives and livelihoods and restore their *integrity*.

William Shakespeare wrote in his comedic play, *As you like it*, 'Sweet are the uses of adversity which, like the toad, ugly and venomous, wears yet a precious jewel in his head'. This quote reminds me of the well-worn cliché, 'Whatever doesn't kill you will make you stronger', which sums up resilient individuals and teams well. They use *resilience* to overcome difficulties with a sense of urgency. As mentioned earlier in this book, my research into the high achievers of the world highlighted that the vast majority came from very troubled and dark backgrounds. It was *resilience*, amongst other Aspects of Being, that led them forward. *Resilience* empowered them to not be fragile and melt under the pressure of life. Adverse events can be extremely painful and difficult in the heat of the moment, but they don't have to determine the overall outcome of your life. While they may be out of your control, there are many aspects of your life you can greatly influence. That's one of the key roles of *resilience*. Becoming more resilient not only helps you get through difficult circumstances, but it also empowers you to grow and transform when polished in conjunction with other Aspects of Being.

To take effective action towards building your *resilience*, you need to start with a foundation of Reality based on the facts, not the language constructs human beings have created over time, such as the attribution of 'toughness' as a meaning of the word resilience, or the notion

---

164   Using the Being Profile assessment tool.

of 'fearlessness', for example, which is totally inauthentic and not even aligned with Reality. Transforming and polishing your relationship with *resilience* as a Way of Being means you need to first tell the truth to yourself about the traumatic events that may have happened in your life, your failures, your reactions and feelings, your capabilities and the role of others in those events. This requires *awareness, authenticity, vulnerability* and *courage*. Only then can you effectively deal with the reality of the situation and take the next step to become more resilient. Remember, we will never be effective in achieving something we are not aware of. So, our conception of *resilience* matters. A relationship that builds on an unwavering truth of *awareness* to strip the story and meaning away from the actual facts of an event paves the way for *resilience*. As long as we argue and blame others and events for the challenges in our lives, we will stifle our capacity to become resilient.

CHAPTER 30

Accountability

Accountability is distinctively different from *responsibility* as a Way of Being. Conventionally speaking, the word 'responsibility' is often regarded as choosing and accepting control over a matter, a task or someone and is commonly considered a burden or an obligation that defines our duties. However, the ontological distinction of *responsibility* that I adopted for this body of work is honouring our relatively high level of autonomy and being cause in the matter. If you are wondering why I am beginning this chapter on *accountability* with a discussion on the conventional use of the word responsibility, bear with me as it will shortly become clear.

The word 'responsible' is defined by the *Oxford English Dictionary* as 'being the primary cause of something …', which closely aligns with the ontological distinction of *responsibility* as a Way of Being. For example, every individual in an organisation, a team, a committee, a board of directors, a family, etc., may voluntarily choose to **be responsible** for a given task, a project, a department or, in the case of the managing director, the entire organisation. That is essential in order to move things forward. *Accountability*, on the other hand, is how you are **being with** your responsibilities, including during and after any unexpected situation that may have occurred which caused the promised responsibilities not to be fulfilled.

Responsibility and *accountability* – what's the difference?

Accountability and *responsibility* are Aspects of Being that are closely intertwined, commonly confused and often referred to interchangeably. This is why I felt it was so important to clarify the distinction up-front.

Accountability is how you powerfully choose to BE when responding and taking ownership of the results and promises for which you are directly or indirectly responsible. For the purpose of clarity as you read on, when responsibility is **not** italicised, I am referring to its conventional usage as opposed to *responsibility* as a Primary Way of Being.

The root of the word 'account' in accountability goes back to 'count' from Middle English, in the sense of 'counting' and 'to count'. This is derived from the Old French *Acont* (noun) and *Aconter* (verb), based on *Conter* ('to count'), which is derived from the Latin *Comes, Comit* ('companion, **overseer**, attendant'). I have intentionally highlighted the word 'overseer' because it has great relevance to the ontological distinction of *accountability* in this framework. It also strikes me that **being accountable** is similar to **being counted on** by others.

The Being Framework ontological distinction of *accountability*

Accountability is living from the viewpoint that you assume full ownership for promises and agreements made by you or on your behalf, including those inferred or otherwise. *Accountability* is fulfilling, completing and being held accountable for whatever you or your team have agreed to, regardless of the circumstances. When you are being accountable, your word can be counted on fully, without question and in every relationship or situation.

A healthy relationship with *accountability* indicates that you will complete what you or your team have agreed to do when you give your word. You choose to deliver as promised or clean up when or where you don't, without resentment. You expect to keep your promises while treating the promises of others as though they are your own. Others know you to be someone whose word has value, rigour and is powerful. You are also available and willing for others to hold you to account.

An unhealthy relationship with *accountability* indicates that you avoid making explicit promises or committing to projects and deadlines. You frequently push back and make excuses when others ask for your commitment or hold you to account. You may collude with or blame others when deadlines or promises are not met. You may abdicate to others in the hope that the agreement is fulfilled. Others may avoid asking you to commit to tasks and projects or take responsibility for managing others. You may be uncomfortable and resist challenging or confronting others when they miss deadlines or fail to fulfil their promises. Alternatively, you may use inappropriate force or your position to threaten others to complete tasks and may be considered overbearing or domineering.

Let's look further at the distinction between responsibility, *responsibility* (as a Way of Being) and *accountability* as well as the close relationship between them. This may also provide you with some valuable insights into how the distinction for *accountability* was created. *Responsibility*, as a Way of Being, refers to our innate/primal autonomy to respond to an event or matter. It is a gift that comes with the complete package of being a human being. This autonomy enables us to choose how we wish to respond to matters. In this respect, *responsibility* is a Way of Being that is somewhat bound by time. It is when we have the option to cause results or, alternatively, fall victim to events, without the willingness to respond in an empowered way (the two ends of the spectrum). Moreover, as mentioned in the ontological distinction of *responsibility* earlier in the book, it is not about blaming or being blamed for something that is not in our control but to choose to respond in an autonomous manner.

Some people associate being accountable in a negative way, as though they equate it with having no option but to do something and being blamed if they don't. This is a misguided interpretation. *Accountability* is choosing powerfully to stand up for what you, your team or your organisation has promised and/or delivered AND owning it and cleaning up, if you, your team or your organisation failed to deliver on those promises or if the deliverables didn't meet the brief. That doesn't mean the individual in charge has to clean up on their own; it means they choose to ensure the right actions are taken. Then, if any shortcomings cannot be restored based on the original agreement, they choose to apologise, ask for *forgiveness* and forgive all those involved, including themselves. Then they let it go and move on without blame or shame or being flippant about it. Standing up for an undesired outcome with *authenticity* is empowering and has the potential to restore any trust that may have been lost. If a person is accountable, as described in this framework, they are also likely to have a healthy relationship with both *freedom* and *empowerment*. The alternative is not owning up to the outcome, consequences or suffering you or your team or organisation have produced or caused through your actions or inactions, and putting up your guard. This points to an unhealthy relationship with *vulnerability*, and an attempt to downplay the severity of the matter, which is quite common in the world of politics.

Accountability is how you are **being with** your choice to respond to something you were directly or indirectly responsible for, even though you may have failed to deliver as promised and regardless of whether you delivered it late or not in line with the original brief. An example would be if, as managing director of a business, one of your project managers failed to deliver a project on time and on budget as you (the organisation) had promised and you take the rap for it as leader of the business. This is challenging for many leaders to comprehend. Referring to the Perspective Quadrant, leaders who limit themselves to viewing matters from the 'I perspective' may wipe their hands of the situation and blame the project manager. But as a leader, the buck clearly stops with you, so there is no avoiding the fact that you ARE accountable even if you weren't personally responsible. Therefore, you can choose to be responsive by openly and assertively owning the situation with *accountability* and ensuring it is addressed. This requires a high degree of *awareness*, *vulnerability* and *care*, along with a healthy relationship with *fear* and *anxiety*, *authenticity*, *responsibility*, *commitment*, *higher purpose*, *courage*, *compassion*, *presence* and *forgiveness*.

It takes great *awareness* and the willingness and ability to be truly present to know and understand exactly what is happening and be able to consider the situation from all angles/perspectives (Them, Others, Global, as well as I). And let's not forget the importance of the Leader Perspective to ensure you have the full 360-degree view of the situation. It's also critical that you choose not to take it personally. Instead, you should be vulnerable enough to avoid the temptation of being more concerned about losing face and being right than acknowledging the damage that's been done – to the other party and to your brand – and accepting any consequences with grace. Your reputation is more likely to remain intact if you own it and clean things up quickly and gracefully than if you shirk *accountability* and point the finger at others, telling the project manager he made you and the organisation look bad. The point is, it's not about you or how you may look. It's about being compassionate and putting yourself in the shoes of the other party, the one your organisation let down, and to be deeply present to the suffering you directly or indirectly caused and care enough to address it.

A healthy relationship with *fear* and *anxiety* will support you to have the *courage* to face the consequences rather than hide from them. It's equally important to be able to forgive yourself for allowing the situation to unfold the way it has and forgive the person directly responsible – in this case, the project manager. Now, this doesn't mean you will immediately move on and forget about it. The responsible person (project manager) is still required to own it and clean up the matter, and this will require *courage, vulnerability, responsibility, resourcefulness* and *resilience,* both on your part and theirs, to be empowered and confident that you are equipped and ready to solve the matter at hand. It is only when the matter has been satisfactorily addressed that you can choose to powerfully move on, but without neglecting to personally and collectively learn from the experience to ensure it is not repeated. This entire chain of events would not be possible unless you are authentic – choosing *authenticity* over honesty over deception or ignorance – and committed to your cause and the values you care most deeply about. It is also worth noting that had you been proactive, assertive, responsible and aware from the beginning, you could have avoided being in the situation where you were not being accountable for failing to deliver in the first place.

As you can clearly see from the example above, when it comes to a Secondary Way of Being such as *accountability*, many complex ontological and phenomenological relationships exist, and they all contribute in some way. That is why it takes a lot for a person to BE accountable. This is not congruent with the dominant approach adopted in societies today which is to seek so-called quick fixes or 'Rapid Behavioural Changes'. To not be accountable is neither acceptable nor effective. For example, to threaten or publicly shame a staff member with a performance review if they don't fix a problem caused by the organisation won't solve anything. To the contrary, blame will always create more harm than good.

Accountability and teamwork

One of the most important aspects of leading or working for an organisation is teamwork. As a leader, establishing and managing expectations around teamwork is critical. Running team-building workshops is one of my company's core focuses, and the emphasis in these workshops is to transform a group of individuals into a cohesive, high functioning team, like geese that show great *resourcefulness* by flying in formation. Let's run through a brief example of what happens in a cohesive team and the role that *accountability* plays in that. Obviously, it is outside the scope of this book to go through the step-by-step practice of team building. I am merely using the example to make the point that setting and managing expectations as a leader, which includes shaping a collective healthy relationship with *accountability* within the team, is extremely important in turning a group of individuals into an effective team.

Let's say Person A is the team leader and Person B is one of the team members. Person A sets an expectation within the team and allocates well-defined and specific responsibilities to each team member. She does this responsibly and authentically, conveying a healthy relationship with *presence* and *freedom*. She also does it in an assertive manner. She explicitly asks Person B if he will commit to fulfilling his responsibility. Person B commits assertively, promising to deliver by a certain time. Note that as team leader, it is critical to be very specific, both about the task and the deadline. This commitment grants Person A permission to follow up Person B and hold him to account. Now, let's say the commitment was to deliver the task by 5pm. The deadline comes and goes with the task remaining undelivered. Person B has neither delivered on their promise nor provided any explanation as to why he failed to fulfil his commitment. Furthermore, neither was fully present to the other once they realised there would be a delay, to provide the other person with an update on progress, so there is little to no synchronicity. Person A assertively holds Person B to account while also acknowledging any responsibility they may have had in their collective failure to meet the commitment. This scenario happens over and over again, not only with Person B but also with other team members.

A far more effective way is for the leader to gradually instil *accountability* into all team members in a way that it becomes ingrained in the culture for all team members to hold each other to account so it is not solely left up to the leader. In this culture of *accountability*, team members wouldn't accept anything below the standard. The collective group wouldn't accept individual members who are not conforming and keeping pace with the others and therefore letting the team down. This is what I call a self-sustaining, highly collaborative and effective team: a team where people are being powerfully led and don't need to be constantly managed (excluding exceptional circumstances). While this may seem utopian to many of you, particularly those of you with experience in leadership roles, and you may accuse me of seeing things through rose-coloured glasses, I can assure you that a self-sustaining team culture is not only possible to achieve, but very much within reach – as long as other Aspects of Being are also addressed to ensure *integrity* within the team – and highly effective in practice. I have worked with many corporations, SMEs and startups in helping them create effective teams in this way, both personally and through our coaching and consulting community, and the results speak for themselves.

Being held to account and being accountable

We can further define *accountability* in the context of promises being made, being willing to be accountable and as an act of participation from the work that American author and lecturer Werner Erhard has contributed to this topic. He maintained that 'being held to account' and 'being accountable' reside inside the promises that each person willingly gives to the other to participate. To be accountable is referring to promises that have real power. I found the following words by Werner Erhard, someone I admire in the ontological realm, very powerful and significant to this discussion on *accountability*:

> 'A promise made from the stand that who you are is your word, engages you as a participant. You cease to be a spectator, and your words become actions that actually impact the world. With a promise you create a condition that supports your commitment rather than your moods.
>
> When motivational dialog comes up about your preference versus your commitments, and you disregard the dialog in favor of doing what you said you would do solely because you said so, you distinguish yourself from your psychology. In that moment you are your word as an action, rather than only as an idea you have.

In that moment the promise becomes who you are rather than something you said; and your relationship to the world shifts. You find yourself producing results that seem discontinuous and unpredictable from the point of view of the spectator.'

Erhard further maintained that *accountability* is best exercised from a stand of being willing or ready to be accountable. This is a starting point, a neutral place to operate from and creates *freedom* to be accountable. It is a quality that brings about *empowerment*. He said that *accountability* is an act of participation because it is not an individual activity.

It is when we are being willing:

- To be a part of, AND
- To be responsible for the whole, AND
- For other persons to be a part of, AND
- For other persons to be responsible for the whole.

So, in a nutshell, a leader may not be directly responsible for all the tasks to which individual team members have been assigned, however, when it comes to the overall results produced as part of a client agreement, it is the leader who is accountable for the performance of the team and the organisation as a whole without any attachment of blame or shame.

Accountability is central to producing results in the face of challenge for individuals, couples, business partners, teams, and organisations. Without *accountability*, little is accomplished. Many people avoid *accountability* in organisations because it seems daunting and there is always a risk of being blamed. *Accountability* refers to a promise, commitment, an obligation or willingness to accept responsibility for how you are BEING and your actions. When individuals are accountable, they appreciate, acknowledge and accept the **consequences** and **outcomes** of how they are BEING and their decisions and actions for the matters in which they assume responsibility.

CHAPTER 31

Reliability

As social creatures, we need and depend on each other in various ways at different stages of our lives. We must be able to rely on each other, which means relying on the *integrity* of each other's Aspects of Being. For example, a foetus relies on the mother to take care of them throughout their development, the baby later relying on their parents to be fed, nurtured and protected. We rely on the legal system and police to keep us safe, we rely on medical practitioners to support us and our loved ones when we are unwell, we rely on our partner to keep their promises and commitments, we rely on firefighters when there is a bushfire or our home is ablaze, and we rely on businesses and individuals to pay their taxes. Employers rely on employees to contribute and serve clients and employees rely on their wages and on leadership from their employers, and customers rely on both employers and their employees to serve them in exchange for the money they pay the business for goods or services, and the list goes on and on. A world in which no one can rely on anyone else would not be a world in which we could survive, let alone thrive. In particular, if you are a leader of an organisation and committed to a great cause, being able to rely on others is critical, as we learnt in the Contribution chapter. Furthermore, *reliability* is one of the principal reasons people regard you as a leader worth following and why you were elected leader in the first place. Similarly, employees and service providers are remunerated for their *reliability*. They may have all the talents, capabilities, competencies, qualifications and proficiencies under the sun, but if they are unreliable, none of those qualities matter as they could not be put to good use. Whether you lead an organisation or you wish to be the leader of your life, if you are not bringing *reliability* to the table, you end up being a **liability**.

The root of the word 'reliability' – 'rely' – stems from the Latin *Religare*, from *Re* (expressing intensive force) and *Ligare* (bind). The original meaning was 'gather together', later becoming 'turn to, associate with', before culminating in the current dominant definition, 'depend upon with full trust or confidence' (confidence meaning 'to be able to be certain of and trust'). The *Oxford English Dictionary* defines reliability as 'the quality of being trustworthy or of performing consistently well', while the *Cambridge Dictionary* defines it as 'the quality of being able to be trusted or believed because of working or behaving well' and 'how accurate or able to be trusted someone or something is considered to be'. And in research, the term 'reliability' generally means 'repeatability', or 'consistency'. A measure is considered reliable if it would give us the same result over and over again, assuming what we are measuring isn't changing. Let's now look at the way I have described this linear Secondary Way of Being in the Being Framework.

The Being Framework ontological distinction of *reliability*

Reliability is consistently performing as intended while completing what is expected of you or agreed to fully and on time. When you are being reliable, you produce consistent results in line with promises and expectations. You can be depended on to be available, ready, fully present and show up when needed.

A healthy relationship with *reliability* indicates that you are acknowledged as someone who can be counted on to fulfil your promises. Others know that when you agree to something, it will happen as and when you said it would. You expect – and others expect you – to complete all tasks and projects you undertake as promised and on time.

An unhealthy relationship with *reliability* indicates that you often have difficulty completing tasks or seeing projects through to completion. You may be someone others choose not to count on. You may underestimate timeframes and push back deadlines. You may be frequently late for meetings and complain that you have too much to do or are running behind. You may be considered someone who lets others down, over-promises and rarely delivers as agreed. You may be unpredictable, overly spontaneous or frequently change course without considering the consequences. Alternatively, you may excessively go beyond what is required of you or necessary for the project.

Reliability is powerful and significant in any domain, leadership being no exception. When you hire an employee, you mainly engage and pay them, not for their skills, qualifications and knowledge, but for how reliable they are in applying their knowledge, experience and skills in the context of your business and also for how consistent they are in keeping the promises they make. If you are not able to rely on an employee to fulfil their promises and commitments, there is really no point hiring them in the first place, let alone paying them for their unreliability, as an employee who isn't reliable will end up making the organisation liable for any problems caused as a result of their unreliability. Your clients and end users are also paying you to be consistent and reliable. They want you and your organisation to be reliable in fulfilling their needs with full trust and certainty. They want to have complete *confidence* and trust that they can depend upon your services and products, your *effectiveness* to fulfil the promises you made and committed to deliver, which they have agreed to pay you for.

Imagine you are a solicitor representing a client who is involved in a legal battle. How would it look if you were unreliable, for example, if you failed to show up to court on time or neglected to do all the necessary due diligence to prepare your client's case for trial? Or imagine if you were depending on the right surgeon to take your loved one through a major, life-saving operation. Your choice of surgeon in this scenario would revolve primarily around their *reliability*, such as their track record of performing similar surgeries, as opposed to revolving around their age, gender, nationality or the colour of their skin. We can all recall a situation when we were in need of help during a time of crisis and called a friend, mentally scanning our list of friends first to separate the reliable friends from those who have a track record of being unreliable. These are just some of the many examples that sum up the value and necessity of being reliable.

Reliability is a quality we all desire for ourselves, the people around us and the systems we depend upon. There is a phenomenological attraction and inclination towards achieving *reliability* in most aspects of life. It is a Way of Being that, in part, led us to work towards economic and technological advancement. And yet, as a species, we are notorious for our inconsistencies. We are easily distracted, and we readily tire of performing repetitive tasks. We often daydream, frequently misinterpret, are too quick to judge and have an increasingly shorter attention span. We allow ourselves to be sucked into man-made constructs that are often incongruent with Reality and even our true nature/Unique Being.

It is worth noting that *reliability* and sustainability, while considerably different, go hand in hand. For example, for a process to become reliable, it must also be sustainable. The *Oxford English Dictionary* defines 'sustainable' as 'able to be maintained at a certain rate or level'. If a process is unsustainable, it cannot be confidently relied upon. If you lead an organisation, you know who you can trust to perform consistently well with sustainability and *reliability*. They are your **reliable** team members, the ones you know you can count on and turn to time after time when you need something done well and on time. They will give you peace of mind knowing they will always complete assigned tasks in a consistent and reliable manner. To be frank, this should be the case with all of your team members. Timeliness, or timekeeping, are highly visible and accurate indicators of an individual's relationship with *reliability*. If someone is unreliable in the small things, they are also unlikely to be reliable in the more important things in life.

Awareness, all Moods and all Primary Ways of Being play significant roles in our ability to BE reliable. For example, it is impossible to be consistently reliable if you haven't established a healthy relationship with most, if not all, Primary Ways of Being. Hiding a lack of *reliability* is futile. In fact, *reliability* is one of the most important and visible outcomes of polishing your Being, which is why it takes a more sophisticated algorithm to measure it in comparison to the algorithms used to measure other Aspects of Being in the Being Profile. *Reliability* is one of those qualities that most people pay little attention to and is the quality most overlooked by leaders, which is ironic given its significance, ontologically speaking, especially when it comes to performance, *effectiveness* and leadership. It plays an undeniable and critical role in our *effectiveness* as leaders.

The impact of being unreliable on one's psyche is far greater than we often assume. According to the author of *The Psychology of Being Reliable*, Stephen Guise[165], people know if they are unreliable to them-

---

165 Guise, S. *The Psychology of Being Reliable*. Retrieved February 27, 2018, from https://stephenguise.com/the-psychology-of-being-reliable/

selves (when they can't rely on themselves to commit to a goal, for example), or others, and they feel the impact of this deeply. While you can't control the feeling, you can control your decisions and actions. Remember that *reliability* starts with the little things, your habits: if you can't be on time to a weekly meeting, how are you ever going to get in shape, direct movies, run a high performing organisation or be a great parent, friend, or spouse? Being unreliable also destroys the trust others have in you, or you have in yourself. Not being reliable is a great source of suffering for yourself and others. When *reliability* is lacking, it ultimately crushes success and prevents the achievement of fulfilment in one's life.

PART 3

Being, in Action

If you were to choose any organisation at random and closely observe their people on a day-to-day basis, you may notice how each individual's web of perceptions, narrative lens and unhealthy relationship with certain Aspects of Being are creating so much confusion, chaos and drama that it is eating away at their individual and collective *effectiveness*, performance and wellbeing. You may also observe that the leaders of these organisations have moments where they feel helpless and disarmed, bewildered by the challenge of effectively leading their organisation. At the beginning of this book, we talked about how we are not here to be content with viewing human beings based on behaviours alone, but that we would go deeper into what drives our behaviours. We also spoke about how there is much noise and confusion in the world, resulting in part from many nonsensical, unvalidated man-made constructs. While some of the content in Parts 1 and 2 may have challenged you, my intention from the start was to simplify the complex by breaking down the deeper qualities of human beings into smaller, readily digestible chunks through the Being Framework. I did so in the hope that it would make a tangible difference to the individual and collective performance, *effectiveness* and leadership in the world. Before we delve into the practical component of this book, let's briefly recap what we have covered so far.

In Part 1, we discussed the foundation on which this entire framework is constructed and introduced you to the Ontological Model. Then in Part 2, we explored all Aspects of Being in the model, examining them one by one in forensic detail to support you to form a more accurate web of perceptions around their ontological distinctions. By now you would be familiar with the Aspects of Being that bring about the effective exercise of leadership and enable people, or teams, to be fulfilled by supporting them to achieve their objectives.

We are now on the same page about the Meaning that each of the Aspects of Being in the framework are referring to. For example, *responsibility*, as a Primary Way of Being, refers to how you relate to the degree of autonomy you have in life, not having an obligation or duty to deal with something. You would realise that we all sit somewhere on the spectrum and that our position can fluctuate throughout life, from being a passive victim who allows circumstances to take us anywhere to being an active agent who, for the most part, is in charge of the circumstances in our life. So, we are in synchronicity on the **distinctions**, at least as far as your perception of them goes. You may have even gone a step further and gradually formed a conception of one or more of these distinctions by relating them to the context of your own life.

As we approach the conclusion of this book, it is highly likely that you have begun to imagine the practical implications of using the Being Framework as a leader in your organisation and/or personally to lift your own performance and *effectiveness*. But where to begin? Explained over two chapters – The Being Profile and Transformation Methodology – Part 3 is focused on how to implement the Being Framework into your life. It explains how you start with *awareness*, possibly using the Being Profile assessment tool, and increase your level of *effectiveness* by undergoing a process of transformation (Transformation Methodology).

You may ask, why bother? The answer is simple. If you aren't regularly polishing your Being to an optimum level in the context of your life and what you care about, your experience of being there in the world will become a burden. As a leader, not only would your shadow become a burden but equally, the collective shadow of your people would also become a burden to the organisation you have worked so hard to build. Still not convinced? Let me bring it home for you. If you have team members on board who are not being authentic, responsible, committed, assertive, etc., it will reflect on the decisions they make, the actions they take and their behaviour. As a consequence, they will become liabilities to your organisation, creating more for you to fix, make up for, clean up, forgive, apologise for, etc. All of this has serious business and personal ramifications, from monetary costs and reputation damage to energy wastage and physical and mental depletion. So, whether you like it or not, you MUST care about the Being and behaviour of your people. This is where the Being Profile and Transformation Methodology are so powerful. Let's begin with the Being Profile assessment tool, explaining why and how it came to be, as well as how to use it effectively and clearly understand the benefits that can be achieved.

CHAPTER 1

The Being Profile

My observations and studies have shown that most high achieving leaders are either intuitively or rationally addressing and polishing Aspects of Being for themselves and the teams around them, even before they have been exposed to the Being Framework and its associated terminology and distinctions. However, they may struggle to articulate how they are being and what they are doing when they deal with their own shadow, going head-to-head with their troubled parts as well as the shadow of every individual in their core team. In leading and managing their people, they may also struggle to create a common language that enables the team to address their individual and collective imperfections (shadow). Distinguishing and measuring these qualities in order to clearly identify these gaps or imperfections has traditionally been a complex and difficult task. This challenge sowed the seed that gradually evolved into the ontological assessment tool called the Being Profile, which, since its launch, has been used by leaders and organisations all over the world. Let's look more closely at why and how the Being Profile came to be.

The Being Framework's Ontological Model is a valuable tool that supports leaders to gain visibility around and articulate what is happening within themselves, their people and their organisation, specifically in terms of performance, *effectiveness* and leadership. It provides leaders with a means of access to see the relationship between each Aspect of Being and their own *effectiveness* and performance, as well as the collective *effectiveness* and performance of their teams with far greater clarity. However, being practical and business-minded, I knew that implementing the Being Framework was at risk of not being adopted if it was cost-inhibitive, inconvenient, drawn out or impractical, especially for larger teams. Furthermore, I knew that to address matters in today's constantly changing environment, we also needed more concrete and tangible tools and solutions that could be leveraged and applied with accuracy and velocity.

Prior to creating the Being Profile, the process of clearly gauging where people were at with their Aspects of Being was somewhat cumbersome and, in many cases, unreliable. There was also a level of inconsistency and subjectivity in the process because the outcome was primarily dependent on the person assessing the individual and their perception and understanding of both the Being Framework distinction of each and every Aspect of Being and the health of that individual's relationship with each Aspect of Being. We also tried using some of the countless personality tests, behavioural psychometric tests and similar tools available. However, we found none to be suitable for the ontological approach upon which the Being Framework is founded as most were superficial and would often measure behaviours or categorise people into predefined personality types. Many even resort to comparing an individual's qualities and personality traits against others, which is ineffective and/or inappropriate for transformation and coaching. In short, none of these tools gave us any degree of accuracy in distinguishing the level of health of the fundamental qualities that matter most in human beings, hence our desire to create a more accurate and effective tool.

So, with the Being Framework in mind, and adopting the 'what gets measured gets understood and hence accomplished' principle, my team and I undertook further research and development to engineer a way to measure each Aspect of Being in a methodical way. The result was the Being Profile[166], the world's first and most comprehensive ontological assessment tool by which all Meta Factors, Moods and Ways of Being, as outlined in the Being Framework Ontological Model, are accurately measured. By 'Profile', I am referring to the description of all the constituent parts (Aspects of Being) that make up an individual's Being, particularly within the scope of performance, *effectiveness* and leadership. Every individual's Being Profile is uniquely different and personal. So, rather than categorising individuals as personality types by tapping into Personality Theory or only assessing their behavioural

---

166   BeingProfile.com

traits, the Being Framework Ontological Model supports individuals to study themselves and others as the **unique individuals** they are.

By measuring your Aspects of Being using the Being Profile, you become aware of how you are BEING in terms of your current default essence or what-ness (your Being). From a transformational perspective, we describe this as your 'as-is model'. Rather than comparing you to others, the Being Profile uses a raw scoring method based on the responses you provide that measure each Aspect of Being against the optimal level. The next step is to use this newfound *awareness* to move towards the **future you** – your 'to-be model' – by directly polishing and transforming your relationship with each Aspect of Being to accomplish the desired results, as you will discover when we discuss the Transformation Methodology in the next chapter. This is a process that is required for sustainable and ongoing transformation, preferably guided by an accredited and experienced Ontological Coach to support you in the transformation process. An Ontological Coach will support you to look into yourself and other people through the lens of real human qualities as opposed to man-made constructs. Remember, qualities like *care, courage, authenticity, vulnerability, responsibility*, etc., are not man-made constructs, however, personality types, amongst other popular choices, are. Importantly, an Ontological Coach will also hold you to account throughout the process.

The Being Profile has to date been used around the world within private companies and not-for-profit organisations, as well as by individuals who are interested in their own *effectiveness* and effective execution of leadership and the wellbeing and *effectiveness* of their people. As more and more people came to us and approached our network of Accredited Practitioners to complete their Being Profile, we were able to build a richer understanding of how a person's Aspects of Being play a role in their life based on empirical data.

How does the Being Profile work?

The Being Profile presents you with a series of over 200 probing questions that are used to measure each of your Aspects of Being. The questionnaire adopts a complex, multi-layered approach to factor in the numerous interrelationships that exist between the four layers of our

Being: Meta Factors, Moods, Primary Ways of Being and Secondary Ways of Being. Each question is specifically formulated to provide multiple points of information to ascertain your individual and unique profile. Because of this complex set of interrelationships, the Being Profile took years of refinement, adjusting both the questions and measurement algorithms, before my team and I were able to effectively measure an individual's Aspects of Being. It is a tool that is continually being refined and enhanced to more effectively support people to understand their Aspects of Being and the roles they are playing in their lives.

When you choose to complete your first Being Profile, an Accredited Practitioner will provide you with access to the questionnaire via the Being Profile platform on which you will create a secure personal account. It is recommended that you complete all questions as authentically as possible. If you choose not to be authentic in your responses, your decision will impair your *authenticity* and *vulnerability* scores. Once you have completed your questionnaire, a report containing a series of scores, one for each Aspect of Being, is created. This is your Being Profile. Each score represents the **health of your relationship with** that particular Aspect of Being, or more precisely, how you relate to that particular Aspect of Being. A high score in any particular Aspect of Being demonstrates a healthy relationship with that Aspect of Being and a low score would indicate a less healthy relationship. For example, if you have a high health score for *anxiety*, that doesn't mean you are an anxious person. On the contrary, it means you are relatively effective in the face of situations that cause you *anxiety* meaning you would be unlikely to collapse or freeze in situations where you experience anxiety.

As is the case with this entire paradigm, the Being Profile is entirely non-judgemental. Each time you complete the questionnaire, your scores, from zero to ten, identify the variations and challenges that arise as a result of you growing and developing, which has you excel in some areas and not in others. A score of zero or ten in any Aspect of Being, whilst not impossible, is highly unlikely. In fact, it is extremely rare to achieve either the highest (nine, ten), or the lowest (zero, one) scores for any of the Aspects of Being it measures. This aligns with reality in that very few people sit at the edge of the spectrum. While the results in your Being Profile are self-explanatory when you refer to the accompanying detailed report, the Debrief Session with a Being Profile Accredited Practitioner, someone who is professionally trained to support you to interpret your results in a practical sense, will allow you to gain a deeper understanding of the results and help you relate your Being Profile to the context of your life. They will guide you to clearly distinguish the links between the various scores and the results you are currently producing in your life and support you to contextualise the scores, the relationship between them, how you are being and behavioural patterns that are holding you back from achieving your objectives. The Accredited Practitioner will also provide valuable insight into how your Moods impact your relationship with various Ways of Being and guide you towards the next steps you could potentially undertake to polish and transform those relationships, ideally with the support of an Ontological Coach trained in the Being Framework, including the Being Profile and Transformation Methodology. Over time, the coach will get to know you quite intimately and the Being Profile gives them the opportunity to dig beneath the surface to reveal any deeply buried wounds, troubled parts (shadow) and blockages, supporting you to address these without being derailed by your deflections or defensiveness.

The Being Profile for team performance and *effectiveness*

In addition to being an effective tool to measure an individual's Aspects of Being, the Being Profile can do the same with a team. By calculating the median of every individual's Aspects of Being on a team, the Being Profile is able to deliver a snapshot of the collective Being of the group. My team and I use this feature prior to team building programs in organisations. This feature, along with the support of an Ontological Coach working with the group, can significantly amplify the *effectiveness* of the team as it facilitates the group's collective transformation. In many cases, the HR or People and Culture department heads may choose to become Being Profile Accredited Practitioners or coaches themselves and incorporate the Being Framework into their processes and routine, from hiring all the way through to training, coaching and developing their existing people.

Our enterprise and growing community of Accredited Practitioners and coaches have worked with a large number of organisations that have integrated the Being Profile across their entire operations. This means every member of the organisation has completed a Being Profile and their teams actively raise Aspects of Being in their discussions about performance, *effectiveness* and leadership. Furthermore, the organisation's recruitment process involves shortlisted candidates undertaking the Being Profile as part of the final selection process. Many also utilise the ability to conduct a Team Being Profile, which looks at a single score for each Aspect of Being for the team as a whole. This creates *awareness* around the qualities the team has a healthy relationship with as a collective, and sheds light on the team's collective shadow. This information serves to explain why the team is or is not producing results in certain areas and what works and what doesn't. By identifying a team's collective shadow, any troubled aspects within the team that are getting in the way of productivity, *effectiveness*, performance and the mental wellbeing, mood and spirit of the team as a whole are revealed. The gap between how the team is now, in terms of its current collective Being, and the ideal is what I call the team's 'collective human potential'. Herein lie the opportunities and possibilities. With this newfound *awareness*, the team has the ability to unlock that potential through the process of transformation, ideally guided by a coach with experience in the Being Framework, to facilitate transformation in the deeper qualities that are holding the team back from realising and actualising its potential. The ultimate outcome is a team in which individuals assertively and proactively hold each other to account to sustainably produce results with *commitment*, grace, ease and flow.

Being Profile case studies

One of the most common points of feedback we receive from our community of experienced Being Profile Accredited Practitioners is not only the Being Profile's remarkable precision, but also the speed at which it stimulates a conversation that becomes the catalyst for critical points of transformation, sometimes within the first session. The point here is not to encourage you to seek rapid results, but rather to bring your attention to the fact that when you identify a challenging relationship with any Aspect of Being, by uncovering the shadow side, you can choose powerfully to commence the transformation process immediately because you will know and understand (*awareness*) exactly what part(s) need to be transformed in order to move towards *integrity* and *effectiveness*. It can be likened to finding the ideal pressure point to massage in order to release a muscle or discovering the parts you need to build more muscle around. To make things more tangible, let me share some practical examples of real people and teams we have worked with and what it looked like for them.

A CEO who was working with an Accredited Practitioner had been sitting on a goal to raise investment funds for his business for a significant length of time. For some reason, he kept procrastinating, and his failure to act was severely impacting his business. After completing his Being Profile, the CEO sat down with the Accredited Practitioner. Together, they identified that while his low score for *confidence* – a Secondary Way of Being – was playing a role in his inability to raise funds, the underlying issues that were preventing him from generating trust when conversing with investors were the deeper qualities of *self-expression, authenticity and vulnerability*. When the CEO walked through the results with his coach to gain a clear conception of what this meant and what he had to do, he suddenly realised there was no need to depict a fake perfect picture of his company to raise the funds he needed. He discovered that being authentic and vulnerable, while also expressing his passion for the cause with conviction and *confidence,* were the keys to generating the trust of an investor. After working on transforming his relationship with these Aspects of Being, with the support of his coach, over the next three months, the CEO managed to successfully raise the $4.2 million he was seeking.

A global company operating in the agricultural sector adopted a people first philosophy. Despite facing a period of significant economic pressure, they made the decision to stay true to their people-focused philosophy and train one of their directors to become the Head of People and Performance by putting him through the Being Profile Accredited Practitioner training course. After building his understanding of the links between the Aspects of Being of each of the individuals throughout the organisation, their day-to-day behaviours and the results each of them was producing, the newly appointed Head of People and Performance began to see an interesting pattern. He observed that the managers who scored lower for *vulnerability* and *authenticity* were producing unworkable project plans for their departments. With this newfound *awareness*, the Head of People and Performance guided the managers to gradually be more open in their conversations with the people in their departments rather than constantly filtering themselves where there were genuine issues to be addressed. This gradually created an environment in which team members felt safe to share their thoughts and feelings and address them with transparency rather than hiding them away. In this new, more open and authentic environment, holding each other to account became the new norm that ultimately resulted in greater ease and flow across the team, a stronger workplace culture and increased profitability for the organisation.

A logistics company that had been operating for more than twenty-five years and was turning over in excess of $12 million a year approached us for support. The Managing Director we met with had reached his tipping point. He was exhausted and had lost enthusiasm for his business. A number of his team members weren't pulling their weight and, as a leader, he didn't know how to deal with it. He had so much on his plate that he often found himself working fifteen or sixteen-hour days, while he would observe many of his staff scrolling through Facebook for much of the day rather than attending to their work. According to the Managing Director, they no longer bothered to hide the fact that they were disinterested and were not working. The collective shadow of the people in the organisation had become his burden, causing him to suffer and resent coming to work.

We invited the Managing Director and his leadership team to complete the Being Profile assessment, and on completion, we sat together to discuss their results. As one would expect of the leadership team of a sizeable, long-established enterprise, they collectively scored highly for *higher purpose*. However, their scores for *responsibility* were relatively low and, surprisingly, their scores for both *proactivity* and *assertiveness* were substantially lower than they had expected. We took some time to walk them through the relationships between the gaps in these two Secondary Ways of Being and their behavioural patterns, linking them to the problems they were experiencing with the people in their organisation. It didn't take long for them to see multiple actions that they were undertaking daily that stemmed from this unhealthy relationship with *proactivity* and *assertiveness* as well as *responsibility*. We agreed to commence coaching with the members of the team. The resulting shift and transformation of the team's performance has been dramatic and has translated into significant growth of revenue and profit in only their first year of coaching. More importantly, a tired business has been reinvigorated with new life and a vibrant culture with highly engaged, productive people who love coming to work.

It is important to note that no single Aspect of Being maps to any one single behaviour. Rather, each Aspect of Being maps to a whole series of behaviours that show up in various ways for an individual. In the example above, we supported the Managing Director and his team to turn their goals and objectives into actionable items that they could commit to. For example, they were coached and learnt how to BE assertive with their teams and communicate that it was no longer acceptable for them to spend time on social media while at work instead of meeting their work commitments. The Managing Director's Being Profile results also gave him visual clarity around the times when he was being reactive rather than proactive and he began to find more opportunities to plan things in advance with the directors. Soon thereafter, he encouraged his employees to complete their Being Profile too. We worked with them as a united team, gradually highlighting one to two Aspects of Being at a time, raising their *awareness* of how this was playing a role in their own performance and *effectiveness*, as well as the performance, wellbeing and *effectiveness* of the organisation as a whole, and creating *accountability* as they polished their Aspects of Being one by one. Over time, this has resulted in the directors re-invigorating their team and completely rebranding the company with a newfound mission and vision.

Within nine months, their collective Being Profile scores had increased markedly. Having a healthier relationship with certain Aspects of Being opened up more time for each of the directors, releasing them to focus on developing their teams while supporting them to work with greater ease and flow, reducing stress and saving them time and money. However, by far the greatest achievement for each of the directors personally is that their teams have taken ownership and responsibility for the ongoing success of the business. There is newfound excitement for the future of the business and it no longer feels like 'hard work'. They now have time to focus on further expanding their business while coming to work each day with energy, vigour and excitement. Through coaching, the leadership team members became aware of the importance of addressing their own Aspects of Being and investing in the development of their people instead of just complaining. As a result, their people are now building their business, which is generating greater profitability in a sustainable way for an organisation that will endure.

It is so common in business to see leaders who have become lost, focusing on the complaints, inaction and dysfunction of their people instead of addressing their own Aspects of Being. This is another reason I believe so strongly in working with the right coaches because it is when we are lost that we most need someone else to shine the light on our Being, revealing our shadow so we can face it, work on it and, ultimately, transform. The case studies I have highlighted represent a few real-life examples of how introducing the Being Profile and ontological coaching can transform individuals, teams and organisations and subsequently bring about significant shifts in their results. Consider the possibilities for your organisation. What would transformation mean for you and your team?

In conclusion

It is worth noting that you do not necessarily need to use the Being Profile assessment tool to benefit from the Being Framework Ontological Model. However, using it will save considerable time and allow you to leverage it to its full advantage because it is far more accurate and less error-prone than merely guesstimating the health of your or someone else's relationship with each and every Aspect of Being. I have had the privilege to support many coaches and leaders, either directly or through our community of Being Profile Accredited Practitioners and coaches. After introducing them to the Being Framework and the Being Profile assessment tool and witnessing the subsequent results, which were profound in many cases – particularly for those who committed to the process of transformation – I am confident that the Being Profile will provide you with a new level of clarity to see what is happening in your team and within yourself. The results will then allow you to predict the behaviours and outcomes you are likely to see across your organisation, based on the relationships with each Aspect of Being, and commence a process of transformation, ideally guided by a qualified Ontological Coach, to maximise those outcomes. This applies to everything from hiring new team members all the way through to supporting them and your existing team members to thrive in your organisation.

CHAPTER 2

Transformation Methodology

As we have discussed, human beings are not static. We can transform. We are not destined to remain the way we are now forever. The Transformation Methodology is a series of processes and principles that lead you on a journey of metamorphosis. The transformation process begins with raising your *awareness*, best achieved by completing the Being Profile, and developing a perception and conception of what the results mean, ideally with the support of an Accredited Practitioner. The next step in the process is a desire to change and become effective and polished in all Aspects of Being, transforming from how you are being right now to how you want to become. Before I walk you through the methodology itself, I'd like to share with you why and how it was created. This will establish the foundation, provide the context and explain the Meaning I am referring to with the word 'transformation'.

When I was a teenager, I wanted to be like one of my martial arts masters. I considered him to be brave, and I remember asking him how I could become as brave as he was. Do you know what he told me? He said the answer was too simple for someone like me to accept. He knew me well. I had a very curious and logical mind that constantly needed to be convinced. I promised him I would consider his response carefully, no matter how simple. He leaned down and whispered in my ear, 'Just be brave'. Obviously, that was not the answer I wanted to hear, however, I let it sit with me for a while, to consider as I promised. It was only later that I realised my master's simple response was exactly what I **needed** to hear. However, it still left me wondering. What exactly does 'be brave' mean? Rather than articulate that for me, my master guided me to be more courageous through a series of stages that changed my relationship with *courage* and various other related Aspects of Being. This guided process literally transformed me physically, mentally and emotionally, enabling me to reach my objective, which ultimately created fulfilment in that part of my life.

The Research

The transformative process I underwent with my martial arts master was one of the key experiences in my life that set me on the path of discovery, beginning with a commitment to learn everything I could about the world's great martial arts masters. I would spend hours researching the greats, including Morihei Ueshiba, Kenji Tomiki, Kanō Jigorō, Gozo Shioda, Masutatsu Ōyama, Gichin Funakoshi and many others. I had a burning desire to know how they managed to coach and support their students to transform aspects of themselves so powerfully that they seemed to transform their entire Being, not just as a student of martial arts, but as individuals, from the way they carried themselves to the results they produced. The more I researched, the more I realised that in the various disciplines of martial arts, students are able to be effectively transformed, not only physically and through their technical skills, but in their entire Being. They become acutely aware and mindful, they obtain *peace of mind*, they transform their relationship with *fear*, *confidence* and *anxiety*, enabling them to face confrontation with extraordinary *courage*. It takes a powerful relationship with *vulnerability* and *authenticity* to be willing to go through such an extraordinary transformation. They must persevere every time they want to give up, they must be resilient, committed, forgiving, patient, etc. To become a true martial artist, the student must gradually shape their Aspects of Being in a practical, methodical manner. The alternative would be to risk injury or even death when fighting an opponent, so dedicated students of martial arts have a deep understanding and respect for the power of transformation and take it very seriously.

Interestingly, a large number of high achievers I have interviewed or studied have a background in martial arts. I believe the practice instilled a strong foundation of discipline within them – as it did for me personally – to continually persevere in their quest to polish their Aspects of Being, albeit without using the same language to describe it. As mentioned earlier, one of the most common reasons so many startups fail is not failure itself in most cases, it is a lack of *persistence*. The founders simply gave up. In the discipline of martial arts (note that it is referred to as a 'discipline') students learn, in a very practical way, not to give up, even in the most physically, mentally and emotionally challenging circumstances. Entrepreneurs and leaders can learn to do the same.

When I began to research practical ways to cause transformation in life and particularly in the commercial landscape, I discovered there was very little academic literature on the subject and the philosophical texts were far too focused on ideas and abstract theories to apply in a practical way. I was curious to know what people were doing when they wanted to change and what existing solutions were available to them. I invested considerable time and money into studying and experiencing the available tools, solutions, practices and products first-hand. I began with clinical psychology, trying various disciplines, including traditional psychoanalysis, with an objective to transform. I went in with an open mind, putting aside my scepticism at the use of the words 'therapy' and 'treatment', which imply that there is a disorder or ailment that needs to be treated or fixed.

In most of the clinical psychology sessions I attended, the psychologist categorised me as a particular 'personality type'. They then attempted to convince me that I needed to learn my personality type and temperament in order to facilitate my ability to 'cope with it'. In other words, the psychologist was insinuating that I am hardwired to be who and how I am, so I should just do my best to 'develop self-awareness around my personality type and personality traits and not let my flaws get in my way'. I found this to be quite a typical response among the common clinical practices. They defined me in a way that gave little hope that those 'personality traits' could ever be transformed. I also found the behavioural psychology approaches to be not particularly helpful from a transformational perspective. To correct every behaviour or behavioural pattern I displayed, which is what they suggested I do, would be like individually watering each leaf of a tree as opposed to watering the roots of the tree for the benefit of the whole tree. These approaches also begged the question: by what measures do these practitioners expect us to correct our behaviour? What is the norm or ideal they are comparing us to? History has proven that the norms of society keep changing. They are, for the most part, mutable, debatable and negotiable because they are predominantly social constructs we have collectively created ourselves.

From a psychoanalytic perspective, when we look at a person's life and read their behavioural patterns, we discover that there is logic to it, that most behaviours are not random. In terms of the patterns and symptoms of our behaviours, more recent behavioural psychology suggests we should either get rid of the symptoms altogether and correct behaviours directly or change our environment and the people with whom we associate as our interactions with those people may be driving our behaviour. However, in light of the fact that most behaviours are not random and are coming from within us – our deeper qualities – when we are transforming, our studies have shown that it is most effective to transform those deeper qualities (the Primary Ways of Being and Moods) as opposed to just focusing on the behaviours. So, we dig much deeper in our ontological approach to see where the behavioural patterns lead us and find the clues in our language and decision-making patterns. This is when we start gaining *awareness* around how we (and others) are BEING. The Being Framework Ontological Model supports you to map this out in terms of the Aspects of Being it examines, particularly those associated with performance, *effectiveness* and leadership. In this way, you address the roots of the tree, as opposed to just the leaves.

Now, I am not suggesting that attending the clinical psychology sessions was a waste of time. Not only were they critical for my research into transformation, but I also found certain aspects both interesting and educational. I learnt something from every session. For instance, delving into my past during my psychoanalysis sessions helped me discover more about myself and gain a deeper insight into why I had formed certain behavioural patterns. However, it still left a distinct gap between knowing about them (*awareness*) and transforming them so that I could ultimately become more effective in what were considered to be my 'flaws' by these practitioners. While undergoing psychoanalysis, I also studied many self-help books, starting with Napoleon Hill[167] and working my way through to the most recent and popular authors of positive psychological literature and the philosophy of success. While I enjoyed reading these books and learnt something from each of them, none shed any light on the process of transformation in a practical sense.

In recent years, I travelled to India to experience various disciplines of mindfulness and meditation and to China to study how Buddhist monks live. I was particularly interested in how the yogis and sadhus of India and the monks of China transformed their Being in line with what their disciplines define as 'the ideal'. Over the years, I have also studied faith – more specifically Abrahamic faith[168] – and, having been born, raised and lived in Iran for much of my adult life, I have had abundant opportunities to be a student of various other disciplines of faith, as well as mysticism, Sufism and Islamic philosophy.

As a committed researcher, my studies went far beyond my subjective experiences. I began learning more about other people through interviews and listening to their stories of transformation and failure, including the stories from within my own network, which includes a number of highly accomplished, financially successful and influential people. Some had managed to totally transform their body shape, a few had transformed from shy 'introverts' to vibrant speakers, inspiring millions around the world, some had even been homeless and destitute and are now residing in multi-million dollar homes and running thriving businesses that serve humanity. In fact, the vast majority of self-made millionaires/billionaires have come from humble beginnings. I found numerous examples like this, not only within my own circle, but also anecdotally through my global community of practitioners, coaches and business clients. Thanks to social media, such stories of transformation are available to us all on a daily basis. Hearing stories like this and seeing the reality of the situation for myself left me in no doubt that transformation is possible. If a heavy substance abuser can

---

167 Oliver Napoleon Hill (1883-1970) was an American self-help author. He is known best for his book, *Think and Grow Rich* which is among the ten best selling self-help books of all time.

168 Abrahamic faith is the way of knowing God and the universe through theology and the study of the prophets.

become clean, if a homeless person can become a multi-millionaire through their own efforts, if someone who is too shy to speak to a stranger at a party can become a globally successful speaker, to name just a few examples, then transformation is not only possible, but achievable by anyone. When I observed that you can have two people come from similar situations and one manages to transform while the other does not, I realised I had two clear choices. I could come up with an irresponsible, inauthentic and lame explanation that the ability to transform boils down to either luck or how a person's personality type or innate temperament lets them undergo transformation. Alternatively, I could adopt a scientific, objective approach and investigate the qualities and processes that enable someone to transform. As a truth seeking engineer, I chose the latter. Combined, all these experiences and thought processes contributed to the shaping of my thoughts to theorise and put into practice the process of transformation, which resulted in the Transformation Methodology.

Why transform?

You may ask, why not just accept your personality type and make your critical life decisions accordingly? My question to you is, why would you adopt such a defeatist attitude when you have the power to **choose** your objectives first and then work on the Aspects of Being that will enable you to transform and achieve those objectives? Why would you turn your back on the beautiful gift you have been given of a relatively high level of autonomy (*responsibility*)? Besides being alive, having the opportunity to be there in the world, your autonomy is the greatest gift handed down from Existence. Why would you not tap into that? Think back to the BE versus HAVE discussion in the Effectiveness chapter. While many focus on the achievement first (**HAVE → DO → BE**), the world's highest achievers adopt the opposite approach (**BE → DO → HAVE**). They focus on BEING integrous so they can DO whatever it takes to HAVE what they desire in life.

While you may expect that transformation in practice requires a highly sophisticated system, it is in fact quite simple. But that does not mean it is easy. Becoming aware of and acknowledging the shadow side of any Aspect of Being is never easy. But that is what you must do before commencing a process of transformation. It requires you to acknowledge the shadow with grace and *vulnerability* and give it context by relating it directly back to your life. Once you have determined the context, you will be ready to commence the process of transformation, taking an iterative approach and holding yourself to account until the beautiful moment – like the metamorphosis of a caterpillar into a butterfly – when the actual transformation occurs. This is not a signal to stop. On the contrary, you must keep applying yourself to increase the degree of your *effectiveness* over time. This process is more effective and happens far more quickly with the support of an experienced ontological coach, and I will explain the reasons for this in more detail shortly. But first, let's examine more closely what I mean by 'transformation' and how it differs from improvement.

Transformation versus improvement

There is much confusion surrounding the differences between transformation and improvement, which is hardly surprising given the lack of information on the subject of transformation, as I discovered in my research. So, what exactly do we mean by 'transformation'? Transformation is commonly defined in dictionaries as the act of changing in form, appearance, nature or character, to change a state. It is far more than just improving skills, increasing your knowledge or becoming a better version of your current self, for example, becoming a higher paid employee or increasing your earning capacity as a sole trader, coach or consultant. While there is nothing wrong with those objectives, making the transition from employee to effective business owner/entrepreneur requires transformation; it demands changes in multiple layers of your Being to the point where you achieve a fundamental shift in your entire state of Being, how you ARE – your Essence/Aspects of Being – and who you know yourself to BE in terms of your perception of your Unique Being. A good example is when you become a parent for the first time, which is when a radical shift occurs in who you know yourself to be. Most of your priorities change and there is no way to return to who you knew yourself to be before having a child. Even if you experience the tragedy of losing a child, you are still a parent and always will be. The transformation of BEING a parent occurs in a single moment despite there being a gradual progression toward that moment. The same occurs in any transformation, whether it be personal or business; the actual transformation is achieved in the moment, however, there are many discoveries, preparations and exercises to be undertaken in the lead up to that moment (the process of transformation). There are many examples of this. My teams and I have seen clients transform from employee to successful entrepreneur and small family businesses transform into scalable global enterprises solving problems of humanity and impacting the lives of many. While the process of transformation – the lead up and preparation to these achievements – may have varied in duration and complexity, the actual transformation in all cases occurred instantaneously and there was no going back to who they knew themselves to be before. If this seems implausible or mysterious, bear with me for now as I explain further.

Transformation requires authentic acknowledgement and declaration, both with yourself and the world (Authenticity Quadrant), about how you are being now, and this acknowledgement and declaration impacts your self-image and persona. This is about communicating to the world the new standard you have chosen for yourself. If your objective is to transform, you set the benchmark high. It's like having an objective to become an Olympic athlete versus simply becoming fitter. Often, people who have a goal to improve their fitness may stick to their training regimen for a while before slipping back into old habits. The only way forward is to keep reaching higher, as the Olympic athlete does when aiming to shift their own personal best and break world records.

When you improve your behaviour, you're upgrading, but when you transform, you fundamentally change your relationship with your Aspects of Being in order to achieve a desired outcome. When you transform, you're shaking your current web of perceptions, changing your narrative lens, shifting your paradigm, revamping processes – how you ARE and how you deal with matters in life – and at the same time rethinking and altering how you operate, contribute and participate in life. In other words, transformation is a far more **radical** step than improvement, as improvement is often a response to external influences, where altering day-to-day actions achieves desired results. Transformation, on the other hand, is when you alter core **beliefs** and **opinions** to be as authentic as possible, as we learnt when discussing the Authenticity

Quadrant in the Authenticity chapter. More specifically, transformation of your deeper qualities (Moods and Primary Ways of Being) will not only alter a behaviour but, most importantly, it will manifest itself in long-term changes to your Secondary Ways of Being and subsequently your behavioural patterns – sometimes in profound ways – to achieve YOUR desired results as opposed to conforming to someone else's (or societal) expectations.

Let's return to the example of making the leap from employee to business owner/entrepreneur as it is a good example to convey what it takes to make that transition and dispel the common misconceptions. Whether or not you realise it, if you made that transition yourself, you underwent a process of transformation. Some realise they must transform to make the switch but don't have faith in themselves to believe they could ever do it, while others think it's just like changing outfits. A typical employee assumes they are entitled to their monthly salary regardless of the impact their decisions and actions are having on the business's bottom line. They don't think about whether or not their contribution directly results in revenue for the company. However, an entrepreneur understands that there can be no such assumption when you own a business. As a business owner, being paid for time spent is out of the question. You are paid for the results you achieve and the profitability those results deliver. It could take a considerable amount of time before any profits are made at all, which is often the case. If you want to transition from employee to business owner, your mindset must change from an 'I work, I get paid' mindset to a mindset of 'I will only get paid if the work I do delivers a product or service others are willing to exchange money for and I realise this may take some time to achieve'. In reality, making the switch from employee to business owner requires you to transform your relationship with all Aspects of Being. For example, you should do your best to be more responsible and in charge as a leader and company director, responding swiftly and appropriately to the unexpected matters that impact your business to the point where it could collapse if you did nothing. You should be proactive and be prepared in the face of financial crisis and other adversities, and the list goes on. If you run a thriving business today, that is precisely what you must have done, albeit without necessarily being present to that fact. Failing to recognise the transformation required is a source of disappointment for many who attempt to become a business owner on a 'get rich quick' assumption. It is not uncommon for new business owners to give up (lack of *persistence*) and return to their old job, even if that job made them feel miserable. My teams and I see this all the time.

While improvement is predominantly a linear and single-layered process with a defined scope, transformation is multifaceted and all-encompassing. Transformation changes the warp and weft[169] of the fabric of your Being. Imagine your Being is a tapestry that you have woven throughout your life so far. Transformation requires you to undo what you have previously woven and use the unravelled threads to rebuild yourself. It may even require you to introduce new threads or discard old ones to create a totally new tapestry, the **future you**. So, improvement ultimately impacts a **part** of you and is limited in scope, but transformation impacts the **whole** of your Being (your *integrity*) as it involves much more radical and fundamental changes in the broader scope. While making multiple incremental improvements over time may also eventually bring about transformation, the clear distinction between improvement and transformation is the extent and impact of the changes brought about.

Transformation requires you to address multiple layers of your Being. For example, it's the difference between having an employee mindset and an entrepreneurial mindset. Many business owners maintain an employee mindset while attempting to build a business and it is the primary reason for their eventual downfall. An entrepreneur would focus on who and how they are BEING in order to be of service to humanity by DOING valuable work that serves a genuine need – or at least a group of people in need, the 'market' – which in turn enables them to HAVE what they most desire in life (remembering that fulfilment is not always related to money). The multi-layered changes I am referring to relate to matters you cannot bring into existence by just being how you currently are or doing more of what you are already doing. To make such dramatic changes requires you to alter your perception of matters, how you think

---

169   Warp and weft are the two basic components used in weaving to turn thread or yarn into fabric. The lengthwise or longitudinal warp yarns are held stationary in tension on a frame or loom while the transverse weft (sometimes woof) is drawn through and inserted over-and-under the warp.

about the problem and, most importantly, how you are being in the face of difficulties. When you change the web of perceptions you have held onto for a long time, it takes *care, vulnerability, courage* and *persistence*, amongst other Aspects of Being, to clear all the cobwebs that have built up over time. Those kinds of goals demand transformation.

Examples of transformational goals could be losing a significant amount of weight, running a marathon, becoming a millionaire/billionaire, becoming an Olympic athlete, quitting an addiction, no longer procrastinating, to name just a few. The following example may make the difference between improvement and transformation more tangible for you. Imagine you currently write an article for publication every quarter and have set yourself a goal to write one every month to ramp up your content marketing. If the only thing you change is the frequency of your output but nothing else about the way you write the articles, this would be regarded as an improvement, perhaps only requiring incremental changes if you wish to gradually improve your writing over time. However, if your objective is to not only increase the frequency of your articles, but also become a better writer to the point where you will be regarded as a prolific and influential thought leader within your industry, then this requires a transformation. You can't just write faster or more frequently to achieve this goal. You will need to rethink who you are writing for, what they want to know, how you come up with ideas and how you will achieve a professionally written piece that meets all objectives within the required timeframe. This may require you to create a team, hire editors, learn how to delegate effectively, shift your relationship with *accountability*, raise your *awareness* about what is going on in the world, and so on. Far deeper preparation and changes will be required to achieve this objective. Now imagine you have achieved your article publication objective and your next goal is to produce vlogs and position yourself as an active YouTuber in addition to being an influential writer. This would require another round of transformation as that goal in itself would demand more radical changes.

As you can see from the writing example, there is a clear distinction between incremental improvement and actual transformation. For starters, the intention is different when you aim to gradually become better at what you do, and while there is nothing wrong with that, when it comes to transformation, the expectations you set for yourself from the get-go are very different. Let's consider another example. Imagine you are heavily overweight, and you have just received a call from your cardiologist telling you that your current weight has put you at a very high risk of suffering a major heart attack. What would you do? Would you commit to removing certain unhealthy food choices from your diet and walking for thirty minutes three times a week? While there is nothing fundamentally wrong with this approach, the slow steady path will not be effective in achieving the necessary outcome of losing sufficient weight to take you out of the high-risk bracket for heart attack. This is literally a life or death situation that requires transformation, not slow, incremental changes/improvements.

Transformation begins with setting the expectation that you need to transform and shifting your relationship with various Aspects of your Being. In the case of losing weight for serious health reasons, this objective would likely require you to change your relationship with *commitment*, *proactivity*, *anxiety* and *freedom*, in addition to altering your dietary and exercise patterns. It would also require you to develop *persistence* (not giving up) and the ability to avoid the temptation of sleeping in rather than getting up to exercise daily and the unhealthy food choices you desire. From the Being Framework perspective, it's shifting from an unhealthy and ineffective relationship with any Aspect of Being (the shadow side) to the healthy and effective side of that Aspect of Being. This begins with *awareness*, by casting light on your Being to reveal the shadow, your troubled parts that are getting in the way of achieving your objectives. When you choose to be empowered in this way, the next step is to grab the shadow's neck and interrogate it, willing it to transform. This is the first step towards your enlightenment and transformation.

So, the process of transformation involves a series of discoveries, preparations, exercises and practices intended to ultimately lead you to transform. This is the precise moment you realise that who you know yourself to be now is completely different from who you knew yourself to be prior to undergoing the process of transformation. Referring to the example above, once transformed, you may no longer relate to the person you knew yourself to be when you were overweight, unfit and unhealthy.

Anyone who meets you from this moment on will only know you as the fit, strong, healthy person you are today. The best analogy I can think of to explain transformation is the metamorphosis of a caterpillar into a butterfly. The caterpillar goes through a series of gradual processes and preparations (the transformation process) before emerging from the cocoon transformed into a beautiful butterfly. Where she could only inch her way along surfaces as a caterpillar, she now has wings that enable her to fly. Nothing about her now resembles her former self, and there is no going back. There is nothing mysterious or magical about this. Transformation is a scientific phenomenon that can be applied in a practical way as you will see when I reveal and unpack the stages of the Transformation Methodology shortly.

Transformation is a choice

One of the keys to beginning the process of transformation with the right mindset is reaching a point in your life where you are willing to undertake, and are prepared for, a self-examination that will illuminate every corner of your Being with the truth. This will require you to confront, reconcile and absolve yourself of your current way of being in the world and your mode of conduct in honouring the space that you occupy. It will require you to carefully assess, with clarity, which decisions and actions didn't work for you and were neither integral to your Being nor congruent with your Unique Being. Let me elaborate. When you choose to transform, it's important to take all three layers of reality into consideration. For example, a fit, healthy person could technically transform into a person who is obese. Many people who were once in charge of their life have since transformed into miserable people who have allowed life to take control of them for whatever reason. That is a very real possibility for any of us if we do not maintain the *integrity* of our Being over the course of time. Some try to build a romantic relationship with a partner, full of optimism and hope for the future, only to transform into someone with an unhealthy relationship with *vulnerability* who no longer trusts anyone after a series of betrayals from different partners. While they may think this is a positive transformation and tell themselves, 'I don't need anyone in my life to be happy', in reality they took a backward leap and deprived themselves of ever finding and establishing true love and fulfilment. So, transformation in itself is neither positive nor a virtue. It is **what you are transforming into** that is the key. An individual who has sufficient *care* to value *awareness* and who is vulnerable, responsible and committed to establishing an authentic relationship with all layers of reality, would understand that there are patterns that work and others that don't. While there is no compulsion to surrender to Reality, as it is literally up to each and every one of us to choose powerfully with vision and discernment to do so, there are two clear pathways we can choose – the pathway that leads to growth and enables us to thrive, or the pathway that leads to regression and suffering. However, you are the primary cause, the active agent, you have autonomy, so you and only you are responsible to choose.

As a by-product of a positive transformation, you may inspire a ripple effect in others. Time is of the essence. It would be a shame to underestimate your potential to forever alter the course of someone else's life as a result of your newfound *awareness* and *compassion*. Remember, we are all a node in a network of people and matters in life (Paradox of Importance); the ripple effect runs far and wide. Phenomenologically speaking, most of us have a desire to serve others (*contribution* and *higher purpose*); we want to help, support, make a difference and leave a positive legacy. When it comes to *contribution*, you will recall that it is equally important to allow yourself to be contributed to, which is why allowing yourself to be coached is so powerful, not only for your own transformation, but for the ongoing ripple effect your transformation creates for the benefit of others.

Transformation and the domino effect

Transformation can be modelled by observing that nature doesn't move forward in singular linear movements. Many things happen simultaneously and symbiotically. In fact, nature takes quantum leaps all the time, and when it does, old ingredients aren't simply recombined. Something new appears in creation for the first time, an emergent quality. Hydrogen and oxygen are both light, gaseous, invisible and dry substances. It took a transformation for those two elements to combine and create water, and when that happened, an entirely new set of possibilities emerged, the most important being life itself. The wetness of water is a perfect example of an emergent property/quality. In a universe without water, wetness can't be derived by shuffling around properties that already exist. Shuffling only produces change; it isn't sufficient for transformation. Wetness had to emerge as something completely new in creation. Once you look closely enough, it turns out that every chemical bond produces an emergent quality. For example, when you combine sodium and chlorine, two highly toxic substances on their own, they produce salt, another basic element of life.

As I mentioned earlier, when you undergo a series of transformations, you alter the warp and weft of the fabric of your Being. By changing the pattern or composition of the threads and adding or removing threads, you will end up with a different fabric (emergent quality) than you originally started with. This is a metaphorical way of explaining how you transform your Being. When you add new ingredients or 'threads' to the mix, they dramatically transform your relationship with other Aspects of Being, which is ultimately reflected in your behaviours, like a domino effect, altering the course of your future. This is amplified when you transform your relationship with a combination of Aspects of Being. Suddenly, new qualities emerge in your life, like prosperity, health, happiness, satisfaction, ease and flow and peace of mind. The decisions and choices you make on a daily basis, no matter how big or small they are to you, will define your destiny and how fulfilled you will be.

The same principle applies in relationships, collaborations, partnerships and teams. No matter which context you choose, whether it be your romantic relationship, building a family, building your career or an organisation, a synergistic energy is created when two or more people transform their relationship with *partnership* as a Way of Being. When this happens, each party complements and influences the other(s) so powerfully that their newly created unity is far greater and more powerful than each of them individually. We commonly refer to this as 'community' (common unity) and this often provides a sense of purpose and meaning to people's lives. When you consider two individuals, each has a one-of-a-kind Unique Being and a relatively unique combination of relationships with their Aspects of Being. Support them through a process of transformation, however, and the unity of their Being is infinitely more powerful than they could ever hope to be as individuals. Every partnership, whether it be in business or in your personal life, requires 'common unity' to thrive. A partnership needs the intentional assembly and collaboration of two or more people to become something much greater than each individual could ever become. If you are up to any major cause and working with a strong sense of *higher purpose*, transforming your relationship with *partnership*, individually and collectively, is critical.

Steve Jobs once shared a story in an interview about an important team building lesson he learnt from an elderly gentleman who lived in his street when he was a child. Jobs recalls how the old man asked him to help him collect rocks from the garden one day. Once they had collected a handful of ordinary rocks, the old man placed them in a rock tumbler, a can containing liquid and some abrasive grit. He then closed the tumbler, turned it on and told Jobs to come back the next day. When he returned the next morning, eager to see what had happened, he was amazed to find that the rough, oddly shaped, dirty rocks had been transformed into beautifully polished smooth stones. In the interview, Jobs described the rock experiment as 'a metaphor for a team that is working really hard on something they're passionate about'. He said, 'It's that through the team, through that group of incredibly talented people bumping up against each other, having arguments, having fights sometimes, making some noise, and working together they polish each other and they polish the ideas, and what comes out are these beautiful stones'.

Transformation often comes with a level of associated pain. However, in truth, we all deal with pain anyway. For example, you either choose to wake up early every morning to go to the gym and accept the discomfort that may come with that, such as dealing with the physical pain of lifting weights, or deal with the emotional, physical and psychological pain later in life of being heavily overweight and unfit. So, the question is, which pain would you powerfully choose to undergo with your autonomy (*responsibility*)? Your decision requires a high level of *awareness* and *freedom* to see the possibilities and also the consequences of the alternative. It also requires *commitment* to be all in and go for it, accepting the pain as par for the course. In the words of Viktor Frankl[170], 'What is to give light must endure burning'. In other words, if you choose to be

---

170   Viktor Emil Frankl (1905-1997) was an Austrian neurologist, psychiatrist, philosopher, author, and Holocaust survivor.

enlightened by casting light on the shadow parts of yourself, you must endure the pain that goes with it.

The power of coaching when undergoing a process of transformation

Just as an athlete would never dream of qualifying for the Olympics without a coach by their side, having an experienced coach trained in our ontological framework will significantly amplify the *effectiveness* of your experience throughout the process of transformation and its outcome. You will find that most of the world's high achievers have a team of coaches, mentors and advisors because they know that limiting themselves to their own levels of *awareness* and capabilities will keep them small. While they know, through experience, the most effective ways to flourish and thrive, they also realise they have blind spots; essentially, they have sufficient *awareness* to realise that they don't know what they don't know. They need others to show them what's possible, either because they can't yet see what's possible for themselves or they lack the *empowerment* to realise and act upon what they are capable of. It largely depends on the end goal, willingness and level of *care* around the desired outcomes. Engaging the right people to support you requires a high level of *authenticity, awareness, vulnerability* and *courage* to let others contribute to you and help make your Being your ultimate source of power so that you can contribute powerfully to yourself, to others and to humanity. That's the point of this entire book and framework.

Our modern use of the word 'coach' is actually a metaphor. The word 'coach' was first applied in education, not in sport. In 18th century England, the term was used as a verb by students of tutors preparing them for exams. The slang reference for tutors became 'coach' because tutors quickly and comfortably carried students to their goal of passing their exams. Many coaches attempt to coach for compliance, whether it be to comply in an organisational setting or with society. They do their best to shift the person to comply with the ideals established by the organisation or societal norms, essentially seeing the individual as a cog in a machine or someone who needs to fit in rather than actually supporting them as a unique individual with unique objectives to identify, face and transform the qualities that are not serving them well (their shadow). Coaching for compliance is, phenomenologically speaking, an oppressive experience despite the coach's best intentions. It is the polar opposite of the coaching recommended as part of the Transformation Methodology, which empowers rather than oppresses and coaches you as an individual rather than trying to make you comply with an expectation or fit in, whether it be in a relationship, in an organisation, in a group, class, community, culture or a society.

For the sake of clarity and synchronicity and to ensure we are on the same page, let me define exactly what I mean by coaching in relation to the Being Framework, particularly the Transformation Methodology layer.

Coaching is an ongoing intentional conversation that raises *awareness*, and empowers and contributes to the *integrity* and *effectiveness* of a person or team to fully live out their potential for their own fulfilment and the benefit of others.

In practice, coaching for the purpose of transformation conducted by a professionally trained ontological coach:

- Focuses on the needs of the person being coached,
- Uses powerful intentional and uncovering questions to generate new levels of *awareness*,
- Clearly distinguishes the relationship between BEING, DOING and HAVING,
- Encourages application,
- Engenders *accountability*,
- Supports transformation/change, and
- Facilitates personal growth and goal achievement through the attainment of a high degree of *effectiveness*.

Now that we have established the foundation for the development of the Transformation Methodology and understand the Meaning I am referring to with the word transformation and how it differs from improvement, let's move on to the Transformation Methodology itself.

The Transformation Methodology

In the context of the Being Framework, transformation occurs the moment you travel from a degree of *awareness* to a degree of *effectiveness*. *Awareness* is **always** the starting point as you cannot intentionally become effective in something you are not aware of or have misconceptions about. As shown in *Figure 11*, the Transformation Methodology is a methodical process that begins with three distinct stages of *awareness* and leads to three distinct levels of *effectiveness* by going through an iterative Application phase. Let's begin with a helicopter overview before exploring each phase separately.

In the Transformation Methodology, *awareness* is a three-stage process: **Reception → Perception → Conception**. Reception is when you receive information or a message and become present to it; it's when your attention is drawn to something you were previously oblivious to or ignoring. It could be seen as a lightbulb moment, a warning, calling or awakening. Reception happens when you allow yourself to be open enough (*vulnerability*) to recognise that an internal or external trigger is drawing your attention to something – often a shadow part of yourself – and you choose to stop **ignoring** it, **denying** it and start caring enough to pay attention to it.

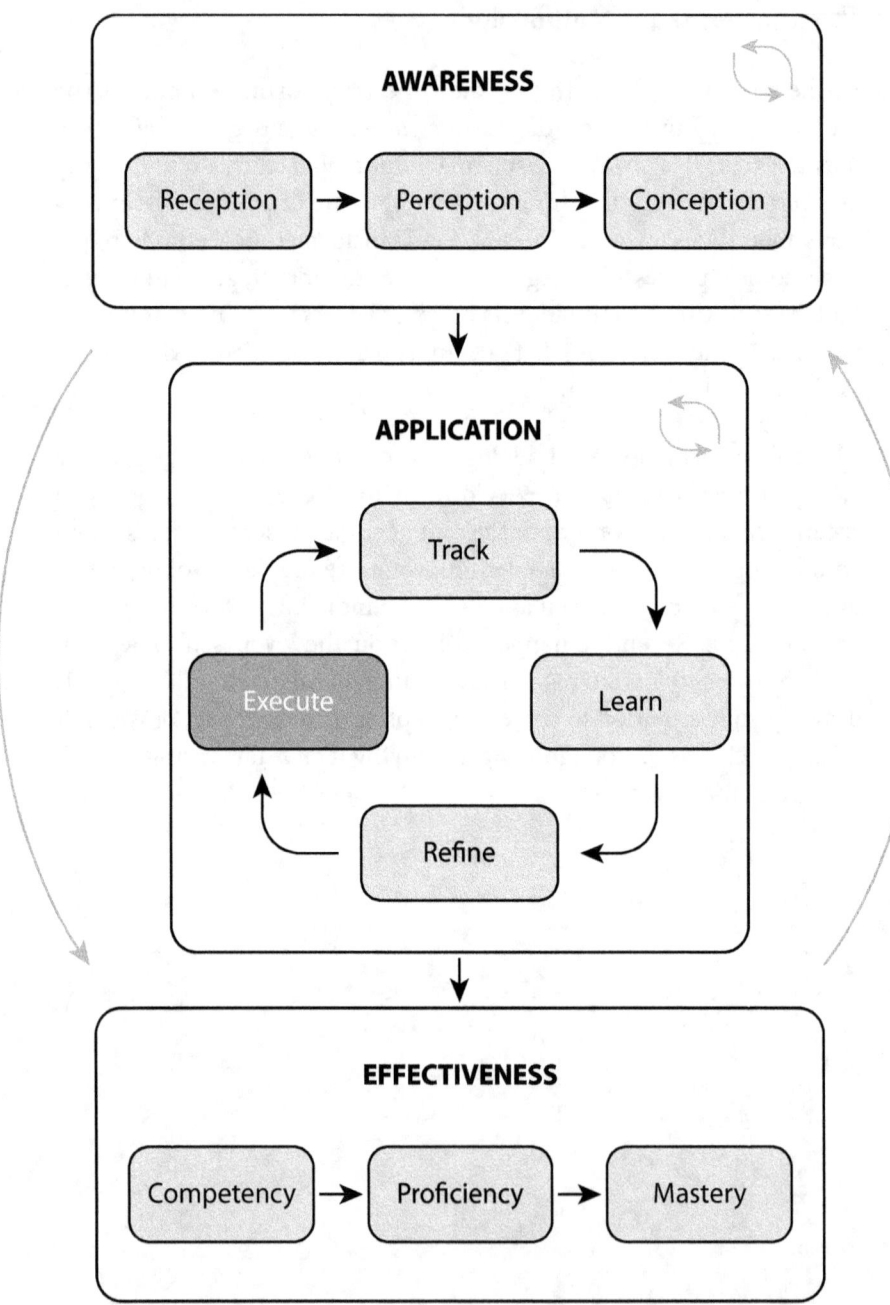

Figure 11: The Transformation Methodology

The next stage of the Awareness phase is Perception, which is where you gain knowledge of what you have received, investigate it and get to know what it means. You start learning all you can about the matter to ensure your understanding of it is congruent with Reality. Perception is the acquisition of knowledge and how you subsequently perceive something. The final stage of *awareness* is Conception, which is where you turn your newfound knowledge and understanding of the matter into practical, methodical knowledge (wisdom) that relates to the context of your life and deeply resonates with you. Your level of *care* matures during the Conception stage to the point where you are moved to start doing something about it. This newfound wisdom (conception) will support and ease your way into the Application phase.

Epistemologically, your experience with all three stages of *awareness* centres on information (Reception), knowledge (Perception) and wisdom (Conception) in that order. It is critical to undergo this three-stage process of *awareness* first because my studies have shown that in almost all cases, those who leapt straight into the Application phase before shaping a solid and authentic conception of what they were trying to achieve either ended in failure or only enjoyed superficial, temporary, unsustainable success and *effectiveness*. If you do not have a deep conception of your why and what's in it for you, you will be unlikely to persevere through the discomfort and challenges of conception, let alone the iterative stages of the Application phase.

The Application phase is where you put what you now understand into practice; it's where you exercise it and execute on it. This continuous iterative process of **Execute → Track → Learn → Refine → Execute** will dramatically and exponentially increase the probability of achieving a degree of *effectiveness* in your endeavours and ultimately becoming fulfilled (reaching your objectives).

Last but not least is the Effectiveness phase, which is three distinct degrees of *effectiveness*: Competency, followed by Proficiency, before ultimately achieving Mastery – or 'Extraordinary Effectiveness', as I call it – through the continued application of this iterative process (Application phase).

The three stages of *awareness*

In Part 2, we dived deeply into *awareness* as the first of our three Meta Factors. We discussed how *awareness* gives us access to layers of reality, how we need epistemic humility to be open enough to want to know and learn, how we all have our own web of perceptions and narrative lens that have helped shape who we are and how we view the world. We explored the Perspective Quadrant – the perspectives we choose to see matters from, including our own Aspects of Being – we introduced you to the shadow – the troubled parts of ourselves – and explained that the ultimate objective of gaining access to *awareness* is to shape a vision, be discerning and develop your *integrity* and *effectiveness* as a leader. Now, we will zoom into *awareness* further, in such a way that it can facilitate actual transformation. In other words, we are now focused on *awareness* in the context of transformation, which, as you just learnt in the overview, is broken down into three distinct stages: **Reception → Perception → Conception**.

Reception

Everything in life carries messages. But we don't always pay attention to them. It is up to you to use your relatively high level of autonomy (*responsibility*) to be open and available (*vulnerability*) to receiving them. It is only when you are connected and in sync (*presence*) with Existence and all its manifestations that you will be open to receiving the messages around you all the time and establishing a constant dialogue with the world and everything in it: the beauty of a flower, the joy of a dog running on the grass, the sound of your child laughing or crying, the physical or emotional pain you endure, the misdemeanours and betrayals of others, natural disasters, incurable diseases, low revenue or profitability in your business, relationship breakdowns, the resignation of an employee you were highly dependent on, the low rate of employee retention in your organisation, your addictions and other bad habits, your Being Profile results, the advice of your coach, and the list goes on. They are all carrying messages you can either ignore or pay attention to and receive.

When you set yourself up to **be receptive**, reception occurs. That's when your attention will be drawn to certain matters, Meanings and messages. For the most part, you are in charge of this; you can choose to be receptive by **being open** to those messages. When a message is received, some people call it a gut feeling, intuition or an aha, lightbulb or eureka moment. Others refer to it as a revelation, faith, purpose or calling. No matter what you choose to call these messages, they are phenomenologically real. In other words, they are in essence part of the common human experience. Reception is a fundamental part of us being out there in the world (*Dasein*).

This discussion reminds me of an excerpt from one of Rumi's poems, which I have translated as follows:

> *Set off to join the caravan (of all those who have realised*
> *they are to be surrendered to Existence and its laws)*
> *Human beings are like sailing ships*
> *receptive to the wind being blown by Existence.*

What I take from this excerpt is that while we all have a relatively high degree of autonomy and can make our own choices in life – we can build the ship, dare to enter the ocean and steer the ship on the course we desire – we are not the generator of the wind. We must therefore be in sync, present to and in communication with Existence and Reality, which is why *awareness*, and particularly the starting point of reception, matters so much. The opposite of reception is **ignorance** or **deception,** to refuse to receive or to deny layers of reality, most importantly, First-layer Reality. Deception is to deliberately deceive yourself and then others. When you ignore or deny the truth, the conversations you have with yourself and others (referring to the Authenticity Quadrant) are both delusional and deceptive. This causes ineffectiveness, as there is little to no workability associated with those conversations, which subsequently leads to suffering, unnecessary pain, distress and hardship.

Reception is where you start receiving a message, commonly relating to a shadow part of yourself. Perhaps something has triggered a deep, old wound, rubbing salt into that unhealed wound to the point where you can no longer ignore it. The moment you acknowledge it and are vulnerable enough to receive it is the moment of reception. It may have been triggered by a sudden revelation in your solitude, the result of reflection, contemplation, a dream or self-criticism. Alternatively, it may have come from an external trigger, such as advice from someone, criticism from your audience, client or even a total stranger, a photograph, a verse of a song or poem, a chapter of a book you are reading, a podcast you are listening to, etc. It can also be the result of being present to the suffering of others, particularly those who are now dealing with the consequences you may be unconsciously creating for yourself. For example, the twenty-year-old you may be observing others in their thirties and forties who are paying the price for wasted time in their youth, giving you a glimpse into your potential future if you make the same mistakes they did. It's a clear wake-up call to start caring more and reprioritise your life. Whether your reception is triggered internally or externally, it's a wake-up call and the moment you open your eyes, **start to care** and stop being negligent, ignorant or deceptive. As you will learn, *care* is a critical part of *awareness* in terms of transformation. Your level of *care* in relation to the matter you have received deepens in the Perception stage and matures at Conception.

Once you willingly start to care and pay special attention to a neglected part of yourself, something you have been ignoring, whether intentionally or unintentionally, it will suddenly become a priority in your life. It is empowering to identify, acknowledge and receive a breakdown in your *integrity* with *vulnerability* and *authenticity* instead of hiding behind your mask of inauthenticity as you may have always done. Finally, you are coming face-to-face with a part of your shadow (one of the Aspects of Being you are struggling with) and able to see where you are out of *integrity*. A healthy relationship with *fear* and *anxiety*, coupled with the *vulnerability* to acknowledge the gap between where you are now and how you want to be, will make you care far more than you otherwise would about your shadow so you can face it and HAVE the things you don't have now (fulfilment). Being vulnerable as opposed to keeping your walls up will shine the light on what's missing and will lead you to go after solutions that support you to acknowledge what is happening rather than delude yourself into thinking something is working when it actually isn't. Most people become fixated on ineffective solutions because they lack the *vulnerability* to receive things as they actually are. As you can see, a healthy relationship with your Moods matters greatly in the Reception phase. It is here where the process of transformation begins.

Until you reach a point, through the Reception phase, where something genuinely becomes a priority for you because you **start caring** about it, it is very unlikely that you will move towards shaping a perception of that matter, let alone discovering how it relates to the context of your life (conception). As a consequence, it is highly unlikely that you would be led to transforming that aspect of your life. Why? Because you cannot become effective in something you haven't chosen to embrace and receive; that is the bare minimum level of *awareness*. Something needs to grab your attention and focus for you to care enough to make it a priority in your life before you can come to know and perceive it, which is the next stage in the Awareness phase.

Perception

Today's generations are the most informed in the history of humankind thanks to the Internet and the vast access to information it gives us through the World Wide Web. And it seems the flow of information will only be further enhanced considering AI (Artificial Intelligence) and IoT (the Internet of Things) are on the rise. However, just because we have information at our fingertips around the clock doesn't mean we should be aiming to absorb, receive and perceive everything that comes our way or is being thrown at us. The key is to be selective and choose information that is relevant to YOU. Lacking the ability to filter information you receive and perceive can easily lead to cognitive overload. Taking in more than you can or even need to handle or process only leads to **confusion**, overwhelm, frustration, paralysis and compromised decision-making. It is inauthentic to believe our ability as human beings to absorb information is limitless. The triggers that catch your attention in the Reception stage lead you to powerfully choose the areas in which you want or need to gain knowledge in order to shape an accurate and precise perception of their meanings, whether they be laws of the universe (Meanings), or man-made constructs (meanings). Prioritising based on relevance to you and/or your organisation is critical here.

Perception is the second stage of *awareness*. It's about 'knowing', or coming to know something through a process of learning, for example, your perception of *love*, marriage, God, career, business, money, sales, *responsibility, care, commitment*, and so on. It is knowledge to be transferred. Naturally, for learning to be effective, it is critical to ensure the information you are studying is derived from reliable, validated sources. This requires you to have concern (*care*), epistemic humility and *vulnerability* around the notion of shaping a perception that is as congruent as possible with reality, using various ways of knowing, such as epistemology, logic and reasoning, science and critical thinking, to name just a few.

Perception is defined in the *Oxford English Dictionary* as 'the ability to see, hear, or become aware of something through the senses'. It is derived from the Latin root *Percipere*, which means 'to receive, understand', from the prefix *Per* ('thoroughly') and *Capere* ('to seize, take'). Metaphorically speaking, if your gateways of knowing are sealed, you will suffer and cause suffering in life. By 'gateways of knowing', I mean your pathways to receive (eye, ears, mind and heart). If your eyes are sealed, you lack vision, if your ears are sealed, you are not listening and being present to the laws and messages of Existence. If your mind is sealed, you are unable to process rational matters, and if your heart is sealed, you are not open and vulnerable to conveying *love*, *compassion* or *forgiveness*. So, clearing those 'gateways of knowing', resulting in authentic *awareness* (reception, perception, and later, conception), is critical for anyone who chooses the pathway of growth and fulfilment to thrive as opposed to the pathway of regression. Once again, this demands a healthy relationship with both *care* and *vulnerability*.

Once those pathways of knowing are open to learning and perceiving, you will be ready to willingly get to know both the shadow sides of yourself – the parts detracting from your *integrity* – and the Aspects of Being you have a healthy relationship with – the ones contributing to your *integrity*. This information will enable you to shape your perception and get to know exactly what is getting in your way of achieving what you deeply want to accomplish. The Being Framework's ontological distinctions will support you to develop those perceptions. However, don't be surprised if the distinctions also challenge your current perceptions of each Aspect of Being, such as *responsibility* or *vulnerability*, and to what extent your understanding of each of them is congruent with the actual Meanings they are referring to. I am not suggesting that your understanding is incorrect if it differs from the distinction. It's not a matter of being right or wrong. Each ontological distinction refers to the Meaning that, through this study, was found to be essential for the effective exercise of leadership. And that is precisely what is being assessed through the ontological model and measured via the Being Profile. Importantly, it is a case of being aware (intentionally conscious) and authentic in establishing a valid relationship with all layers of reality. In other words, it's about ensuring you are shaping beliefs and opinions (two specific forms of perception[171]) that are congruent with reality. This is also a matter of synchronicity to facilitate effective communication with your coach, if you choose to work with one, and to ensure we are on the same page in this body of work.

Here's an example of why shaping a perception that is congruent with reality is so critical. We would never dream of removing a fish from a tank to hug it as we would our dog or cat because our perception of fish as aquatic creatures means we know the fish would suffer and die if removed from its natural habitat. Similarly, if you wish to set up an aquarium at home, you need to be responsible around your perceptions of what different types of fish need to survive and thrive. Attempting to place tropical, ocean and freshwater fish in the same tank would never work because each species has very specific needs, from water temperature to pH levels and multiple other factors. Indeed, there are many things you need to shape an authentic perception about if your intention is to set up an aquarium. If you believe, based on your reality (Third-layer), that you can just buy a tank and put any fish you like in it, you are being delusional, hence your desire to have an aquarium will never be fulfilled. This simple analogy could be replaced with an objective to do anything in life, from establishing a partnership on the right foundation to scaling a business. Any misperception, no matter how small or seemingly insignificant, will impact the *integrity* of the whole ecosystem, causing it to break.

Our perceptions are also influenced by our perspective. An individual who is open (*vulnerability*) and who cares about gaining authentic knowledge and establishing a healthy relationship with all layers of reality would adopt the Leader's Perspective[172] when establishing a perception about something to ensure they view the matter from

---

171   Authenticity Quadrant.
172   Perspective Quadrant.

multiple perspectives rather than just their own immediate perspective ('I' quadrant). Our studies have found that most high achievers adopt the Leader's Perspective. They leverage other people's resources, talents and, more importantly, perspectives and perception of things, as this enables them to collect as many pieces of the puzzle as they can to help shape their own perception of a matter and ensure they have a fuller understanding/perception of it. This is very different from the method adopted by a typical thinker, who immediately forms opinions and beliefs as soon as an idea forms in their mind and they always pay the price for their misperceptions as a result of only viewing things from limited perspectives. Authentic philosophers and truth seekers, on the other hand, are concerned with discovery and ensuring their perceptions (opinions, beliefs, self-image, persona, etc.) are as congruent as possible with how things actually are in the world. While relativism may seek to keep the peace by asserting that facts in a given domain are relative to the perspectives of an observer, it doesn't lead to truth seeking, which is why I am an advocate for pluralism because it asserts that there are multiple means of approaching truths about the world. Your web of perceptions shapes your mindset, a significant part of your current default paradigm, and this paradigm sets people apart in the way they deal with life. Your default paradigm is what leads you to be categorised as a certain 'personality type', or belonging to a certain so-called 'economic class', or social status. That's why establishing your perceptions in an authentic manner that is congruent with how things actually are is extremely important and worthy of your *care* and attention.

Conception

German philosopher Immanuel Kant wrote, 'Concepts without percepts are empty; percepts without concepts are blind'. In other words, perception and conception are mutually dependent. Unless you shape a perception of a matter, you will never be able to discover how it relates in the context of your life, which is what conception is all about. And without relating a matter to your life, your perception, no matter how well studied, lacks relevance, so it remains nothing more than knowledge without purpose and application. As a consequence, it would be highly unlikely that you would ever be led to transforming that aspect of your life.

Conception is defined in the *Cambridge Dictionary* as 'an idea or a particular way you understand or think about something, or a basic understanding of a situation or principle, for example conception of time'. This relates to making your perception of something relevant to you or relevant to something you care about. The fact that the sun rises in the east is an objective truth. However, conception is more subjective. It is how YOU understand something and why it matters to you. So, while your perception of a matter would match mine if we were both truth seekers, our conception of the same thing may be totally different.

The Conception stage is all about asking questions like, 'How does this relate to me and my life or something I care about? What's in it for me? Why should I care or bother?' Let's authentically acknowledge, here and now, that we are essentially all self-interested beings. It is primarily for this reason that *care* as a Mood matures in the Conception stage. However, as social creatures, we also rely on others, so being self-interested is one thing, being selfish is another, and the latter is not what this is all about. That being said, conception is personal and relative, as mentioned earlier. If you have just perceived that the sun rises in the east, that information may be meaningless to you unless you determine the consequences or outcomes of that for you. This may differ from one person to the next. If you are building a house, the aspect of your land in relation to the sun will factor into your building design. A farmer relies on the position of the sun for planting crops, etc. In terms of your Aspects of Being, conception is about **why you should care** about that shadow part of you or how your healthy relationship with *higher purpose*, *compassion* and *contribution*, for example, could be transformed to accomplish a mission you care about deeply. It's about conceptualising how becoming more integrous will benefit you, your organisation, your marriage, your family and your life in general.

Conception is about understanding something, comprehending it in such a way that you can successfully relate what you know back to the context of your life or what is getting in your way. When you develop a conception of something, it is no longer just a piece of knowledge gained in the Perception stage. Your conception equips you to start putting that knowledge into practice in the context of your life. Let's call it 'practical knowledge', or, more specifically, 'wisdom'. So, where reception results in information and perception results in knowledge, conception results in wisdom. It's the ability to use your knowledge and experience to make sound decisions relevant to you in the context of your life. The ultimate goal of all three stages of *awareness* is to shape your vision, which brings about discernment when making decisions.

Whenever I run workshops, seminars and coaching sessions, it is not uncommon for attendees to claim they know all about something I have raised, telling me they have read a book on the subject, watched a video or heard a podcast on it, etc. I understand that they **know** about it, but often it quickly becomes obvious that they actually don't **understand** the subject, let alone have the ability to apply it in the context of their life. Knowing something is very different to understanding or comprehending it. While knowing something and understanding or comprehending it are symbiotically dependent, they are also significantly different. Failing to recognise this at a meta level will make your life extremely challenging. Why? Because your knowing (perception) and understanding (conception) of perception and conception themselves are the very means by which you will perceive and conceive other Meanings, concepts, constructs and matters in life. Therefore, it is crucial to have an authentic and congruent perception and conception of the Meanings referred to by the words 'perception' and 'conception' in order to understand their distinction as different, yet closely connected, stages of the process of *awareness*.

Being receptive and open (reception) is like being fertile and having the right environment in which to conceive. It's about allowing and enabling your mind to be open to being fertilised by what you receive, allowing the knowing (perception) to develop and grow through nurture and care (conception). Here is where your mind conceives what is to become your 'newborn' wisdom. As you develop *care* around the matter and willingly relate the perception you shaped back to your life and what you care deeply about (your values and priorities), you are paving the way for transformation to occur. Indeed, reception, perception and conception are prerequisites for transformation. It's when you become aware of what you are aiming to become effective in.

Earlier we talked about how conception is all about what's in it for you and your life or how it is relevant to something you care about. Let's take this a step further. There will come a time when you are so accustomed to the process of going through the three stages of *awareness* that you will find yourself receiving relevant messages and developing your perception and conception of them on a regular basis. It will become so ingrained within you that you will eventually develop the ability to make a matter relevant to the context of your life with *higher purpose,* making it relevant in a much broader context, such as with your family, your team, your organisation, your community, society or even humanity as a whole. There may even come a time when you become so enlightened that you are able to conceive and conceptualise a major problem like hunger in the world without having it directly impact you and your family, so that you can contribute with *care, compassion* and *love* to the whole of humanity. This may lead to authentic philanthropy, where you become a messenger of Existence, an interpreter of relevant Meanings and matters to human beings, our pain and suffering, our common wounds. It is at this point that you will discover how to articulate those messages in ways that will resonate with many. Who knows, your genuine *care* may evolve into your unique *contribution* to humankind. It may even extend beyond humankind to encompass all beings and nature.

Many Meanings and concepts are actually more tangible than some would have us believe. They may have simply been lost in translation. So, not only is it important for you to shape conceptions of what you have perceived and turn it to wisdom so that you can start putting it into practice and benefit from it in the pursuit of your own fulfilment, you can also expand your horizon and enhance your **scope of impact**, potentially impacting the whole of humanity when applied with *higher purpose*. Whether you see yourself as a thinker with a goal of sharing these messages or you are more business-minded and want to productise and commercialise your *contribution* as a result of your *awareness* is totally up to you; you have the autonomy (*responsibility*) to choose.

Care (intentional willingness) is the key to ensuring the steel is hot enough to hammer and forge. Without *care* around your objective, you will never be able to forge the steel, no matter how hard you hammer it. It is during the Conception stage that our aim is for *care* toward the matter at hand to mature. Here's how to develop that. When you start caring about something you were ignoring, neglecting and averting your gaze from in the Reception stage, the first step is to declare your intention, verbally or in writing. This is even more powerful if you have an accountability buddy or coach, someone who can hold you to account constantly and remind you of your intention, promise and *commitment*.

When I was a student at the Aikido dojo, all the students, myself included, would get very excited whenever we observed or heard about a new technique we had not yet been exposed to and we would hound the Aikido Master to teach us the new technique. This was despite the fact that many of us weren't even competent in the technique we had just been taught. In other words, we had not yet shaped a proper conception of the first technique, let alone mastered it, and yet we wanted to leap into learning about a new technique. Luckily for us, our Aikido Master knew better than to teach us something new before we had achieved a degree of *effectiveness* in the current technique. To put this example into context with this paradigm, this would be like becoming receptive to the fact that you need to transform your relationship with *authenticity* and developing a sound perception of this Primary Way of Being, but then only getting halfway through the Conception stage before diving into studying another Aspect of Being that is causing issues in your life. This is where a coach would support you to stay focused on the matter at hand.

The point with these examples is that if you haven't managed to create a clear conception of how your perception of something relates to you and your life, attempting to apply it in practice won't work. By the time you have developed a clear conception of a matter at hand, you could say you have sound *awareness* of it and are ready for the Application phase to commence. You can now predict the consequences and outcomes of your actions and you have acquired vision, the ability to see with discernment. Once you have managed to successfully develop your conception of any Aspect of Being, you will have the ability to discern between the consequences of your unhealthy relationship with that Aspect of Being and how your life will be once you have transformed that relationship into a healthy one. Your conception and newfound discernment engender *care*, which will urge you to make it a **priority** in your life. Your conception may also make you vulnerable and realise the need to seek assistance, perhaps from a coach or others. A healthy relationship with *anxiety* also supports you here because it will awaken you to the potential ramifications of not transforming the health of your relationship with the Aspect of Being in question, which in turn will further contribute to engendering the *care* required to make it a priority. Ultimately, your newfound conception means you are now fully aware about the matter at hand. This *awareness*, with the support of your Moods, will ease your way into the Application phase of the Transformation Methodology.

Application

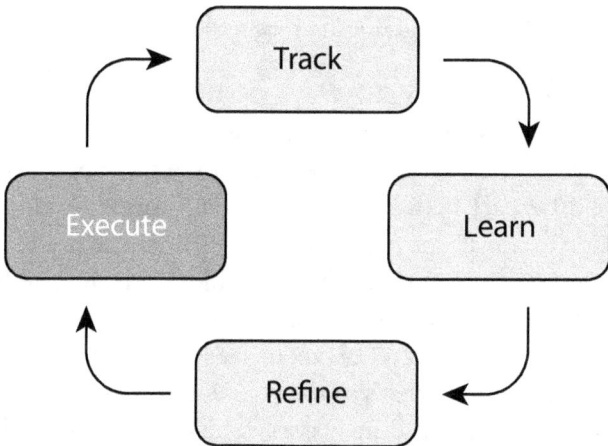

Figure 12: The Application Phase of the Transformation Methodology

If we zoom into the Application phase, we can see that the process begins with Execute, then Track, Learn, Refine and back to Execute again in a cyclical iterative process, repeating, tweaking and making progress with each cycle. Shortly, I will walk you through what happens and what to expect within each stage of the Application Phase in a step-by-step manner.

During the Application phase of the Transformation Methodology, your conception matures to an even deeper level. Once you have intentionally established your goals and objectives in such a way that they are clear and measurable, the execution begins immediately. You may start by aiming relatively low, low enough to take a quantum leap. Alternatively, you may adopt a more progressive approach. No matter how small at the beginning, no matter how insignificant it may look at first glance – to you or to others – the key is to focus on what YOU want to achieve. I would like to emphasise at this point that you shouldn't let what you or others may find insignificant deceive you. The critical matter is to begin the process of execution, no matter how insignificant step one may seem. Let me explain using a simple analogy. Imagine your goal is to light a fire in your wood stove. At first, you may use small particles of thin wood or paper to ignite the flame. Then you would move to slightly harder wood as kindling to get the fire burning. It is not until the fire is well alight that you would add your hardwood logs that can burn for a long time. A mistake many make is to begin with the hardwood, only to find it frustrating when it doesn't create the fire they so desire and set out to achieve.

You can either choose to tackle your goal purely out of **curiosity** or with **sincerity**. While there is nothing wrong with either approach, there is a dramatic difference between the two when it comes to your objective and intention to transform. Let me explain with a metaphorical example. Imagine a mysterious closed box on a table. Consider the following scenario. Jan has lost her reading glasses and desperately wants to find them, so she is keen to open the box to see if they are inside it. John is merely curious to know what's in the box. Both get close to the box and open it to discover Jan's reading glasses. John's mission is accomplished. He was curious, so just knowing what is in the box has fulfilled his curiosity. However, Jan not only discovered what was in the box, she also found the pair of glasses she was missing. Finally, she can read again, her vision is restored! Finding her glasses has made a significant change in the context of her life. Jan's objective was clearly founded on sincerity. There is a huge difference between the two approaches.

When most people read self-help books, listen to speakers, get coaching, etc., they are simply curious to discover what the other person has to say. We all know people who are constantly signing up for this program and that program. They seem to entertain themselves with the idea of discovering new and potentially exciting content, taking copious notes and nodding their heads throughout a presentation. However, unless they are coming from a place of sincerity, they wouldn't conceive the new-found knowledge. As a consequence, the newly acquired perception, no matter how accurate and congruent with reality, would fail to have any meaningful impact on their lives. Perhaps you can relate on a personal level. I know many 'intellectuals' who are quite concerned and curious about the universe's most complex matters, yet are ineffective in the most simple dealings with life, with them being out there in the context of life (*Dasein*). I found that the simple reason for this was that they lack sincerity and are merely curious. However, someone who is committed to transformation, to shifting the results in their life, would be compelled to learn because they care so deeply about the subject being discussed. It's like someone who can't sleep because they are thirsty. They would be urged into action, to get out of bed for a glass of water, because they are tackling their goal out of sincerity, not curiosity. If your intention to transform is merely founded on curiosity and not sincere intention, you should revisit and reconsider your conception of the matter and why it is important to you because it is critical that you begin the Application phase with a sincere intention to transform.

Transformation is not like a typical project for which you create a predictive plan and identify every step from the beginning. When you undergo a process of transformation, you are embarking, to a certain degree, on the unknown. You are about to step into unexplored territory, like the birds did when they began their voyage to find Simorgh. You need to begin with an open mind, choose powerfully to undergo the process of transformation and prepare yourself to be surprised and perhaps even shocked at times. It requires you to embark on the process like an innovator, as the problems to be solved are unstructured, making it impossible to measure everything accurately at the start. You will have to accept a degree of uncertainty, and most people struggle to **be with** the discomfort of uncertainty. However, needing to accept a degree of uncertainty is congruent with how you were thrown into the world, as we all were, like a drop of water falling into the ocean of Existence and all the vulnerabilities, fears and anxieties that come with it. The more you were exposed to Meanings, matters, objects and other beings, the more you adjusted your relationship with *awareness*. As you learn how to **be with** uncertainty and entering unknown territories, you may gradually train yourself to enjoy the surprises and perceive and conceive your **nervousness** as **excitement**.

Any new project typically begins with a planning stage. When it comes to transformation, however, you begin with Execution. After all, how can you possibly plan with precision when you are diving into the unknown? I am not dismissing planning, far from it. In the Transformation Methodology, planning is **part of** the Execution stage. Indeed, its integration is extremely important and makes a massive difference to the outcome. The simple fact that you are telling your mind that the process of transformation has begun makes it a clear declaration that the process has started, and you are already **in the game**. It's like when the whistle blows at a football match declaring kick-off. So, in declaring that the process has begun, there is no room for turning back or procrastinating. However, step one in the Execution stage may well involve an element of planning. This is vastly different to planning BEFORE commencing a process or project. It requires a different mindset when you are already in the game. The difference lies in the *commitment*. Let's say you have made *authenticity* relevant to the context of your life and where you are stuck right now through the Conception stage. You are now present to how your unhealthy relationship with *authenticity* (a shadow part of you) is getting in your way of fulfilment. So, you begin by declaring your intention to make positive changes around this Way of Being, starting right now. And then you may do some planning as part of the execution.

Let me share the following exercise with you, which links the Conception stage with the Application phase and supports you in following through the Application phase. However, before I do, let me give you a heads-up. You may be tempted to ignore or overlook this process as you may find it overly simple. But don't let its simplicity fool you. Our mind is programmed to think complex problems require complex solutions, which is false. As you work through the exercise, you will quickly realise how challenging and confronting a simple process like this can be. The first action to take in the exercise is to draw four columns on a sheet of paper. In the first column, write down all the occasions you can remember over the past five years when you were not being authentic. For example, a time when you were pretending to be interested in someone or something when you actually weren't, or when you shaped an opinion or belief without due diligence, or the time you projected a fake persona which was clearly exaggerated with a potential client, or when you lied to your spouse or partner. Be vulnerable and be specific.

In the second column, write down the consequences, the cost or impact of you choosing not to be authentic on each of those occasions. In the third column, articulate how differently you could have been BEING on each occasion and what you could have done differently. Finally, in the fourth column, write down what the alternative outcome could have been had you chosen to be authentic on each occasion.

After completing this exercise based on a reflection of the last five years, it's time to bring this same scenario into the present. You do this by allocating a specific time each evening (or a given time each day, depending on your usual routine) to reflect on what happened throughout the day in relation to what you are working on, in this case, *authenticity*. Reflect on and review the entire day while it is fresh in your mind, which is why you must be disciplined to do this daily, determining when and where you aren't being authentic. Write them down in a journal, applying the same four columns and questions you did for the five-year exercise but now in the present time. It's important to be as vulnerable and honest as you can with yourself when undertaking this exercise. Remember, the assumption is that you are coming into this exercise with a relatively accurate perception of *authenticity* and that you have shaped a clear conception of it – at least clear enough for now because it may shift and deepen as you make new discoveries during the Learn and Refine stages of this iterative process, as you will see.

Once you have repeated this daily reflection and journalling over a number of days or weeks (however long is necessary), the next step is to change the timing again, making it even more present, right down to a specific moment in time. Now you are in a position where you can catch yourself out on the spot, right when the matter you are working on is letting you down, in the case of our example, when you are about to be inauthentic, say in a meeting at work or in a conversation with your spouse. Instead of letting it happen, you intercept your imminent inauthenticity and choose to be authentic and act upon it (Execute). You continue to observe when and where you are being inauthentic and whether or not you are choosing to interrupt it and why. This is self-monitoring (Track) based on your perception and conception of how not being authentic is holding you back from achieving your goals and fulfilment. As you have been completing the reflection exercise for some time by this stage and you are committed to transforming and becoming more authentic, you become adept at identifying when your relationship with this Aspect of Being is letting you down (Learn). You determine what works, so you can do more of the same in future, and what doesn't work, so you know what to avoid. You also identify anything missing or redundant, so you can add or remove them as required. This is all part of the Learn stage. You then change the way you respond (Refine). Eventually you will start catching yourself in the moment and choosing to interrupt your authenticity at will before it happens (Execute). Let's look at an example to make this more tangible.

Imagine you are in a meeting and there is an important matter being addressed which requires you to be authentic, for example, ensuring you are providing accurate information so that the decision makers/stakeholders/participants can rely on you telling it how it is and not hiding or exaggerating the truth. Let's assume your current default is not to be authentic, and by now you are well aware of what this looks like. After having consistently completed your four columns multiple times so far, you now have the ability to catch yourself on the spot and turn yourself around there and then. If you don't succeed in interrupting your inauthenticity in that meeting, you step back and reflect on what happened and what you could have done differently, etc. It is rare for someone to succeed on their first attempt. In fact, the more ingrained your shadow, the longer it may take to transform it. So, you need to persevere and refuse to give up (*persistence*). That's precisely why this iterative process is necessary.

After several iterations, you may reach a point where you can shift the timing even further because you have developed the ability to predict, with vision and discernment, what will happen in the future. This is the optimal goal as a leader. Why? Because knowing what leads you to choose **not** to be authentic will enable you to prepare for upcoming events, meetings, projects, etc., in a proactive manner. When you can catch yourself just as you are about to be inauthentic, manifested as inauthentic behaviour, like telling a lie or exaggerating an achievement, you can address the matter in real time before it happens. This is how a well-polished leader would be. I call this ability '**ontological responsiveness**', or '**ontological volition**'. I am **not** referring to morality or a virtue here. Yet again, I struggle to find the perfect word to convey the Meaning I am referring to, which is essentially to avoid succumbing to the prompting of our shadow, the temptation of old habits or the easy or perhaps more appealing option for short-term gratification or satisfaction. Instead, it is consciously choosing to be authentic. I am assuming that by this stage of the book you would be clear on how the shadow impacts your *integrity*, *effectiveness* and hence what you desire to earn or gain. So, this ontological responsiveness or volition, is a very practical way to avoid letting unnecessary barriers or temptations get in your way. Eventually, you will reach a stage where you can interrupt yourself mid-sentence and choose to be authentic on the spot.

Last but not least, the scope of this self-prophecy, or predicting what will happen in the future, and nipping it in the bud before it happens, can extend beyond yourself. As a visionary and forward-thinking leader, you would expand the scope to include your team, family, organisation, community, etc., all the way to the whole of humanity. This is how a truly authentic visionary leader would be; they would then predict the future for their people and use this knowledge to shape the future of an organisation, family, a nation or, in some cases, the whole of humanity.

To recap, after you have made your declaration to transform, you commence the Execution stage (Execute), beginning with a reflection of the past five years. Then you put it into practice, tracking it daily before moving to real-time tracking once you become more advanced (Track). Each time you track yourself in real time, you learn from the experience (Learn) so that you can go back, refine it (Refine) and execute again, returning to daily reflection followed by another round of real-time execution (Execute). You may need to undergo a number of rounds of this iterative process before you're able to successfully and consistently catch yourself out, transform your Aspects of Being, focusing on your growth potential (the gap between an optimal level and your current relatively unhealthy relationships) and change your subsequent behaviours on the spot, resulting in different behavioural patterns and decision-making processes. All the discoveries you have made and the *awareness* you have attained combined with this iterative Application phase will lead you toward the very moment that you suddenly find yourself being transformed and, in the case of our example, becoming authentic. It is at that point that you will no longer know yourself to be the person you were before. You are transformed. Now, I am not suggesting that you will be perfect and have necessarily mastered your relationship with *authenticity*. But you will have achieved a **degree** of *effectiveness*, beginning with the bare minimum (competency). Then every time you undergo further rounds of the Application phase you increase the probability of shifting up a gear to the next degree of *effectiveness*. This leads us to the next and final phase of the Transformation Methodology, the Effectiveness phase.

The three degrees of *effectiveness*

As we learnt in the introduction to the Transformation Methodology, there are three degrees of *effectiveness*: competency, then proficiency and, ultimately, mastery. Your degree of *effectiveness* is directly dependent on the health of your relationship with all Aspects of Being. Athletes, artists, martial artists, musicians, etc., commonly refer to these degrees of *effectiveness* as they progress up the ladder towards their goal of mastery. There is significant literature and history around how one transforms from amateur to professional/advanced or master in any discipline. Now, when we refer to *effectiveness* as a Meta Factor in the Being Framework Ontological Model, we are referring to *effectiveness* in terms of living your life, the extent to which you can successfully fulfil your objectives and produce a desired outcome through projecting the authentic manifestation of your Unique Being and dealing with being out there in the world (*Dasein*) with grace, ease and flow. When you have a degree of *effectiveness* in your endeavours in life, it is the result of being integrous and is ultimately the key to fulfilment.

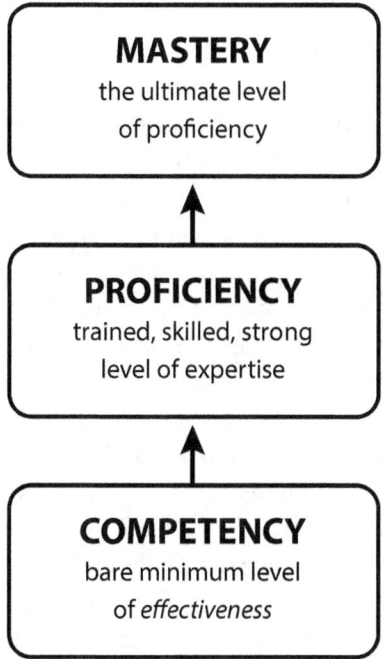

Figure 13: The Three Degrees of Effectiveness

As you go through the Application phase and undergo a process of iterative execution, tracking, learning and refinement in terms of how you are relating and applying what you now have a solid level of *awareness* of, you will end up causing a level of *effectiveness* in that matter (Aspect of Being in this context). This is not just about how you convey and project yourself through your Aspects of Being, it applies to almost anything in life, including your skills. The higher the level of your overall *effectiveness*, the greater the probability that you will achieve your objectives and hence fulfilment. Remember, as Meta Factors, *awareness*, *integrity* and *effectiveness* are to be applied to each and every Aspect of Being in a similar manner. In other words, you first become aware of a particular Aspect of Being, then you gradually cause a level of *effectiveness* in how to **be with** that Aspect of Being, and finally you integrate that into your life so you can execute on it, which is what **Being, in action** is all about. When we do this with **all** Aspects of Being, we achieve wholeness or *integrity*, leading to overall *effectiveness* in life.

Now, let's zoom in to each degree of *effectiveness*, beginning with step one: competency, the bare minimum of *effectiveness*. The word 'competent' is defined by the *Oxford English Dictionary* as 'having the necessary ability, knowledge or skill to do something successfully; acceptable and satisfactory, though not outstanding.' When you are not competent in something you are either a novice, meaning you don't know how much you don't know and how incomplete you are (unconsciously ineffective), or you are an amateur, meaning you are aware of how much you don't know but you know how incompetent you are at the moment (consciously ineffective). Once you determine how a lack of *effectiveness* in a particular Aspect of Being – for example, having a relatively unhealthy relationship with *responsibility* – is suppressing your desired outcome and then **address** and **rectify** it, you will develop a healthier relationship with *responsibility* to the point where you would be considered competent (consciously effective). To give that a measurable context, you could say that when you can rely on yourself handling a lack of *responsibility* almost 70%[173] of the time, you may be considered competent. Referring back to the Application phase, this is when you can catch yourself not being responsible and turn it around on the spot around seven out of every ten times.

Proficiency is one level higher than competency. When you are proficient you would have the ability to identify whenever the shadow is starting to creep in and interrupt and address it relatively quickly, or at least more easily than when you are only competent. The *Merriam-Webster Dictionary* defines the word 'proficient' as 'being well advanced in an art, occupation or branch of knowledge' and the *Cambridge Dictionary* defines it as 'very skilled and experienced at something'. In the context of the Being Framework, to be proficient is the second degree of *effectiveness*, particularly in how you relate to and act upon your Aspects of Being. To give this a measurable context, proficiency is where you are in charge around 85% of the time, meaning you are able to consistently and reliably pre-empt and address a shadow part of yourself, for example when you lack *responsibility* or *authenticity*.

If you are striving to become a high achiever, your ultimate goal would be to gain mastery. The *Oxford English Dictionary* defines mastery as

---

[173] Any percentages referred to in this chapter are mainly to make the explanations as tangible as possible and are not to be taken literally.

'comprehensive knowledge or skill in a particular subject or activity'. In terms of the Being Framework, it means you could be considered to have extraordinary *effectiveness*. This doesn't mean you are perfect, but that you strive for perfection as much as possible. With mastery more than 95% of the time, *reliability*, consistency and *effectiveness* are present.

There are some who portray themselves to be masters, however, they are the polar opposite of those with authentic true mastery. These 'imposters' generally have low *vulnerability*, a bloated self-image and an exaggerated and arrogant persona. When you authentically have mastery over your Aspects of Being, you know yourself to be reliable and are consistent in catching yourself and interrupting the shadow right at the time – or preferably before – an incident occurs as a result of applying vision and discernment, through ontological responsiveness, in a practical manner.

Effectiveness (to any degree) is not specific to certain behaviours, although behaviours – more specifically behavioural patterns – may be the apparent evidence of a degree of *effectiveness*. A measure of one's *effectiveness* is the extent to which he or she can produce accomplishments that are of value to their life, an organisation, a society or even the whole of humanity without incurring more costs than the accomplishment is worth. In other words, the value it delivers should always be more than the cost (time, care, energy and resources) incurred to deliver it.

Consider *effectiveness* as a worthwhile performance. *Effectiveness* is the ratio of valuable accomplishments to costly and ineffective efforts. These ineffective efforts are the result of one's troubled relationship (shadow) with particular Aspects of Being and the resulting dysfunctional behavioural patterns. Note that a high performer does not necessarily always have a high degree of *effectiveness*. *Effectiveness*, in this context, is meeting a desired outcome for a clear and well-defined objective at a value that is greater than the cost it incurs. Having said all of this, the higher your level of *effectiveness*, the higher the probability of success in achieving what you have set out to achieve with the lowest possible associated cost. That's because an individual who has the highest degree of *effectiveness* (mastery) around a matter would consume less time, energy and effort than a competent person would to produce the same outcome. Let's make it more tangible with an example. A competent junior computer programmer may take a week to come up with a desired algorithm while a senior computer programmer who has mastery in the field may come up with the same or a better quality outcome in a fraction of the time. This is why it may be wiser to choose to hire a person who has mastery in the field to avoid wastage.

Now let's zoom out. An individual who has a relatively higher degree of *effectiveness* in all Aspects of Being would participate in and contribute to the game of life (dealing with *Dasein* – being out there in the world) much more effectively than someone with a lower degree of *effectiveness*. This commonly results in wealth, financial wellbeing and a quality lifestyle, but these benefits are just the tip of the iceberg that others can see. Their *integrity* would bring about ease and flow in producing results in areas they care deeply about. Again, this is why, in part, some do considerably better in life than others. Wealth is just one of the by-products of their higher level of *awareness, integrity* and *effectiveness*. It is worth reiterating at this point that *integrity,* in this context, consists of the aggregation of your health or *effectiveness* in each and every Mood and Primary Way of Being while *effectiveness,* as a Meta Factor, consists of the aggregation of all Moods, Primary Ways of Being and Secondary Ways of Being. While the three stages of *awareness* result in **realisation** – making it real for yourself – the three degrees of *effectiveness* cause **actualisation** of that newfound *awareness* – transforming your *awareness* into reality – which is achieved through the iterative Application phase (continuous execution). So, **being effective** is having the power to produce a required effect (influence) and subsequently becoming fulfilled.

Ask yourself:

- How do I discover the areas in which I am ineffective, the matters I still do not know or have an authentic perception of? (unconscious ineffectiveness),
- What do I still need to work on to become effective at? (conscious ineffectiveness), and
- Which of my current qualities (e.g. Aspects of Being) do I still need to hone? (conscious *effectiveness*)

Leveraging the power of your polished Aspects of Being

It's quite common for our attention to be drawn to our shadow sides because we want to be 'perfect'. For instance, when reviewing your Being Profile report, you may have a tendency to zoom in on the lower scores, which are an indication of an ineffective relationship with an Aspect of Being, and your first instinct may be to jump in and address them right away without acknowledging your polished aspects, the Aspects of Being that you have a relatively healthier relationship with. For example, you may have a lower level of *courage* but a relatively healthier and more effective relationship with *fear* and *anxiety*. The higher levels highlight the Aspects of Being you have polished over time in your life. The point is, it is equally valuable to pay attention to your polished Aspects of Being as well as those which are less refined because they are assets you can leverage to transform and polish other Aspects of Being. For example, when your Being Profile report highlights that you have a high level of *vulnerability* and *care*, these Moods will support you when transforming your relationship with *responsibility* or *commitment*. As someone with a healthy relationship with *vulnerability*, you are far less likely to be in denial and will readily acknowledge problems, making you far more coachable than someone who is not vulnerable and open. A high level of *care* gives you the motivation you need to be willing to undergo transformation. Taking this example further, a healthy relationship with *freedom* will support you to be more self-expressive and a healthy relationship with *presence* and *authenticity* will support you to increase your *awareness* while a high level of *responsibility* can make it easier for you to polish your relationship with *commitment* and *forgiveness*, and so on. So, I encourage you to take your time to acknowledge and congratulate yourself for how you are being, particularly for the Aspects of Being you have a relatively healthy relationship with. This acknowledgement will pave your way and empower you to work on transforming and polishing the rest.

Contextualisation

Context is important when undergoing a process of transformation. By contextualising an Aspect of Being, you make it more tangible, concrete and relatable. For example, you may be more comfortable to start being vulnerable and authentic in the context of your intimate relationship before addressing your *vulnerability* and *authenticity* in the workplace. And when it comes to *self-expression*, you may be far more comfortable being self-expressive in one context than another. For example, some prefer to express themselves verbally, while others would prefer to express themselves through music or art. And then there are those who are more comfortable expressing themselves through the written word. Now, I am not suggesting you should always stay in your comfort zone, quite the contrary. It is more a matter of aiming low enough in the beginning to dare to take the first leaps necessary when undergoing transformation and then gradually taking yourself beyond your comfort zone. In fact, when you are ready, shifting context is a great exercise when working towards mastery. It's when you learn to fight in the cold despite shaking, and in the heat when covered in sweat and close to passing out through heat exhaustion. You learn to punch in water and also in sand. Changing context eventually brings ease and flow so that you can perform with grace under all circumstances. Beginning with a context that is familiar to you isn't the only way, but it's certainly the most tried and tested. Contextualisation leads to enlightenment and wisdom because it will teach you that you can learn about hunger without the need to die of hunger. You could even practise building 'muscles' around your Being in hypothetical scenarios and contexts.

By shifting contexts while polishing your relationship with your Aspects of Being, your *awareness* and *compassion* lead you to understand matters in life beyond your personal experiences. For instance, anyone with kids knows how challenging it is to raise them and manage a household, while working full time and maintaining a healthy relationship with your spouse, extended family and friends. And those who don't have kids could probably imagine what it would be like in comparison to living a single, relatively carefree lifestyle. Now, imagine the challenges facing the world's top CEOs who are responsible and accountable for the many people within their organisation as well as their end users, clients and shareholders. As a leader of an organisation, you couldn't possibly gain mastery around your Aspects of Being if you only ever focus on contexts directly relevant to you. For example, a high achiever must continually forgive their own mistakes as well as the mistakes made by their people, including those they don't have any direct influence over. This is why context is so important when it comes to transformation.

Conclusion

Part 3: Being, in Action focused on how to implement the Being Framework into your life. We began by examining the Being Profile assessment tool, explaining why and how it came to be, as well as a high-level explanation of how to introduce the tool and use it effectively. By measuring your Aspects of Being using the Being Profile, you become aware of how you, and/or the people and teams you work with, are BEING. We describe this as the 'as-is' model. The results allow you to predict future consequences and outcomes based on your relationship with each Aspect of Being and how this can be extended to others and teams to predict the likely future at an organisational level.

The next step is to use this newfound *awareness* to alter the course, which in turn changes the future, by moving towards the 'to-be' model. This is achieved by undergoing a process of transformation using the Transformation Methodology. We know transformation is possible because, as human beings, we are not static; we are not destined to be how we are now for the rest of our lives. We learnt that transformation is far more than just improving skills, increasing your knowledge or becoming a better version of you. Transformation demands changes in multiple layers of your Being to the point where you achieve a fundamental shift in your entire state of Being. We talked about the value of coaching when undergoing a process of transformation and how having an experienced Ontological Coach trained in the Being Framework will significantly amplify the *effectiveness* of your experience throughout the process of transformation and its outcome.

We then dived deeply into the Transformation Methodology itself, beginning with the Awareness phase – **Reception (information)** → **Perception (knowledge)** → **Conception (wisdom)** – before zooming into the iterative Application phase – **Execute** → **Track** → **Learn** → **Refine** → **Execute**. I walked you through each stage of the Application Phase, explaining what happens, what you need to do and what to expect in a step-by-step manner. Last but not least, we explored the degrees of *effectiveness* – **Competency (bare minimum of *effectiveness*)** → **Proficiency (strong level of expertise)** → **Mastery (the ultimate level of proficiency)**. You learnt that your degree of *effectiveness* is directly dependent on the health of your relationship with all Aspects of Being and that the goal, when transforming, is to climb the ladder of *effectiveness* over time to eventually attain mastery.

There are significant rewards with arriving at the top. But it comes at a cost unless you are willing to shine the light on your Being to reveal the shadow, and leverage your well-polished qualities to continually transform your relationship with your Aspects of Being to achieve a higher degree of *effectiveness* and *integrity*. Those costs may range from financial and legal to your own reputation. The more cogs in the machine that become polished and transformed, the easier it will be to support others in polishing and transforming themselves. Eventually, you will reach a point where you can undergo a continual series of transformations, which is how high achievers of the world continually adapt to new and ever-changing environments. And this is how you will manifest your Unique Being – the one-of-a-kind, one and only YOU – to the world for true fulfilment in all your endeavours and for the greater benefit of others and humanity, the ultimate objective of this paradigm.

WHERE TO FROM HERE?

Resources for further action

I believe that entrepreneurial ventures, businesses and not-for-profit organisations are amongst the best-suited vehicles in the world to solve key problems and pains for humanity.

However, when the shadow side of our Being takes control of our decisions and behaviours as leaders of these organisations, it leads to suffering for ourselves and causes suffering for others. Unpolished Being is the root of dysfunction in the world. At Engenesis, we use the vehicle of business as a springboard to bring about transformation in the world.

Those who are continuously polishing their Aspects of Being and attending to their *integrity* make decisions and take actions that reduce corruption and unnecessary suffering. If we carry out entrepreneurship and business effectively and foster a thriving economy led by integrous individuals, we will reduce poverty, suffering and related crime in the world. This is why I've spent years building – and am committed to continue to build – programs, products, services and a platform that serves people and supports them to attend to their Being.

Who would benefit from adopting the framework laid out in this book, and why?

Coach or Consultant – If you are in the business of developing and nurturing human to human relationships for the benefit of supporting your clients to effectively fulfil their goals, adopting the framework laid out in this book will significantly enhance what you do.

Leader – If you want to be coached yourself, for the sake of your own growth, or would like to incorporate coaching into your approach to leadership within your organisation to lift your people's ability to meet the organisation's goals, there are multiple resources here for you.

Professional – If you aspire to rise to leadership and authentically have your organisation fulfil its mission in the world, the pathways here will support you to address the areas where your Being is getting in the way.

Visit ashkantashvir.com/being for a complete list of resources and current information.

If you'd like to share this book with others, or if you would like more information about the book, you can visit beingbook.net

Connect with me

I am personally committed to supporting the leaders of the world to raise their *awareness* and shape a more accurate conception of reality. Connect with me at ashkan.engenesis.com to access my latest articles, videos and other content.

To learn more about my other projects and interests, visit ashkantashvir.com

Join our global community

Through the Engenesis Platform, you can get free access to the latest articles, videos, materials, workshops, courses and programs, many of which centre around the Being Framework, from our community of leaders, coaches, consultants and professionals. Create your free account at engenesis.com.

You can also join one of our many communities, which bring together those ready and willing to be with and attend to the shadow side of their Being and spur on effectiveness through a process of transformation to fulfil their objectives in life. Find a relevant community for you at engenesis.com/community

Key articles and resources related to this book's content

I'd like to make specific mention to the following articles that may be of interest and relevant to you now that you've finished reading this book.

- Article: Why Being matters
  engenesis.com/a/why-being-matters
- Article: How your Way of Being determines the results in your life – An introduction to the Being Framework
  engenesis.com/a/how-your-way-of-being-determines-the-results-in-your-life
- Article: How the integrity of our Being is critical to an organisation's performance – The application of the Being Framework in the workplace (includes 5 workplace case studies)
  engenesis.com/a/how-the-integrity-of-our-being-is-critical-to-an-organisations-performance-the-application-of-the-being-framework-in-the-workplace

More resources, including whitepapers, case studies and articles, are continually being added to support the community. You can keep up to date by visiting and registering an account on engenesis.com/c/being

Being Profile® Assessment and Debrief

Now that you've read this book, if you're interested in taking the next step towards *awareness*, *integrity* and *effectiveness*, the best place to start is by completing your own Being Profile® Assessment and Debrief. After completing the in-depth questionnaire – which takes around forty-five minutes – an Accredited Practitioner will walk you through your Being Profile® and map your Aspects of Being in relation to the results you are experiencing in your life. You can begin this process at beingprofile.com/assessment

Become a Being Profile® Accredited Practitioner

Are you a coach or a leader who wants to incorporate the Being Framework™ in your endeavours to support others to gain profound insights and access breakthrough performance?

Then apply to become a Being Profile® Accredited Practitioner here: beingprofile.com/accreditation

Thrive Coach Training Program

Would you like to take your coaching to the next level and coach others to produce even greater results? Coaches, those interested in coaching, directors, managers and leaders from around the world are participating in a unique thirteen-week program founded on the Being Framework™ that gives them the training and tools they need to thrive in a coaching capacity while being surrounded by a community of peers equally committed to deep personal growth and fulfilment. To learn more about how the program works, register your interest at beingprofile.com/thrive-coach-training

Engenesis Influence™ Leadership Program

Are you a manager or leader within an organisation that would like to implement positive change, address conflict constructively and grow your team and team culture successfully? The Engenesis Influence™ Leadership Program operates over twelve weeks and provides a transformational process where you will develop your leadership capabilities to the next level by adopting the Being Framework and leveraging the Being Profile in challenging business scenarios.

You can learn more at engenesis.com/program/engenesis-influence-leadership-program

Being Mastery® Program (invitation only)

If you want to change the entire trajectory of your life by tapping into your Unique Being and transforming yourself inside and out, right down to the very fabric of your Being, the Being Mastery™ Program will be an unforgettable experience for you.

As a participant in this unique program, you will completely transform your relationship with and conception of reality itself. Run over twelve months, the program takes you through a process of discovery, application and practice, including the Being Framework Transformation

Methodology™, alongside other changemakers, leaders and those committed to addressing the problems in the world starting with themselves and their community.

This program has a series of prerequisites and participation is by invitation only. You can learn more at beingprofile.com/being-mastery

The Being Profile® video case studies and stories

Access practical examples and stories of how you can apply the Being Framework™ in your life and/or business. Enjoy the ever-evolving library of videos available that showcase the extraordinary work achieved by our community by visiting youtube.com/engenesis

The Being Profile® for teams and organisations

Take your entire team or organisation through the Being Profile® and develop a common language and approach for accessing new levels of growth, performance, *effectiveness* and leadership. When combined with our private group workshops, you'll put your team through a shared discovery process of who and how they are being and how this can impact their collective performance. Speak to our team to learn more at beingprofile.com/get-in-touch

One-on-one ontological coaching

Working privately with an ontological coach who has been professionally trained by Engenesis is a radically effective way to build clarity on how you are being so that you can fulfil your objectives. Your coach will support you to cast a light on each of your Aspects of Being to ensure they shine bright and reveal their shadow, the key to effecting change. By working through the issues that typically sit behind your facades and go unaddressed, you'll be supported to shift issues that would otherwise remain unresolved and undergo a process of transformation. Our community of Thrive Coaches and Master Coaches span the entire globe, work across all industries and bring their unique experience and skills to serve you. To connect with a coach that is best suited to you, contact our team at beingprofile.com/enquiry

References

Please note, not all references provided here are directly referenced within the main content, however, all formed an important part of the background literature that laid the groundwork for this body of work.

Allen, S. (2018). *The Science of Gratitude* [White paper]. *Greater Good Science Center.* https://ggsc.berkeley.edu/images/uploads/GGSC-JTF_White_Paper-Gratitude-FINAL.pdf

Attār, F. Al-D., & Wolpé, S. (2017). *The conference of the birds.* W.W. Norton & Company.

Art Therapy. (n.d.) Psychology Today. Retrieved July 4, 2021, from https://www.psychologytoday.com/au/therapy-types/art-therapy

Ashford, S. J., & Stewart, B. J. (1996). Proactivity during organizational entry: the role of desire for control. *Journal of Applied Psychology, 81*(2), 199–214. https://doi.org/10.1037/0021-9010.81.2.199

Being assertive: Reduce stress, communicate better. (2020, May 29). *Mayo Clinic.* https://www.mayoclinic.org/healthy-lifestyle/stress-management/in-depth/assertive/art-20044644

Berne, E. (2016). *Games People Play: The Psychology of Human Relationships.* Penguin Life.

Berry, J. W., Worthington, E. L., Parrott, L., O'Connor, L. E., & Wade, N. G. (2001). Dispositional Forgivingness: Development and Construct Validity of the Transgression Narrative Test of Forgivingness (TNTF). *Personality and Social Psychology Bulletin, 27*(10), 1277–1290. https://doi.org/10.1177/01461672012710004

Brown, B. (2012). *Power of Vulnerability: Teachings on Authenticity, Connection, and Courage*. Sounds True.

Building Your Resilience. (2012). American Psychological Association. https://www.apa.org/topics/resilience

Burton, N. (2016, June 25). These Are the 7 Types of Love. *Psychology Today*. https://www.psychologytoday.com/au/blog/hide-and-seek/201606/these-are-the-7-types-love

Carver, R. (2003). *What we talk about when we talk about love: stories*. Random House.

Cohen, A. (2004, October 1). *Research on the Science of Forgiveness: An Annotated Bibliography*. Greater Good Magazine. https://greatergood.berkeley.edu/article/item/the_science_of_forgiveness_an_annotated_bibliography

Cohen, A. B., Malka, A., Rozin, P., & Cherfas, L. (2006). Religion and Unforgivable Offenses. *Journal of Personality, 74*(1), 85–118. https://doi.org/10.1111/j.1467-6494.2005.00370.x

Confidence. (n.d.). Psychology Today. https://www.psychologytoday.com/au/basics/confidence

Corbin, H., & Sadra, M. (2003). *Introduction to Sadr al-Muta'allihin Shirazi's al-Masha'ir* (K. Mojtahidi, Trans.). The Sadra Islamic Philosophy Research Institute.

Critchley, S. (2009, July 6). Being and Time, part 5: Anxiety. *The Guardian*. https://www.theguardian.com/commentisfree/belief/2009/jul/06/heidegger-philosophy-being

Crowther, P. (1988). Heidegger and the Question of Aesthetics. *Journal of the British Society for Phenomenology, 19*(1), 51–63. https://doi.org/10.1080/00071773.1988.11007841

Davis, T. (2019, March 11). What Is Self-Awareness, and How Do You Get It? *Psychology Today*. https://www.psychologytoday.com/au/blog/click-here-happiness/201903/what-is-self-awareness-and-how-do-you-get-it

REFERENCES

de la Huerta, C. (2014, April 21). The Power of Self-Expression. *HuffPost.* https://www.huffpost.com/entry/the-power-of-self-expression_b_5167635

Derrida, J. (1973). *Speech and Phenomena, and Other Essays on Husserl's Theory of Signs.* Northwestern University Press.

Derrida, J. (1986). *Margins of Philosophy* (A. Bass, Trans.). University of Chicago Press.

Doka, K. J. (2016). *Grief is a Journey: Finding Your Path Through Loss.* Simon and Schuster.

Domonkos, D., Gates, B., Myhrvold, N. & Rinearson, P. (1999). *The Road Ahead.* Pearson Education.

Downes, J. (2021, January 20). Transformational Leadership: Being Committed to Something. *Insigniam.* https://insigniam.com/transformational-leadership-being-committed-to-something-bigger-than-yourself-part-1/

Dreyfus, H. L. (1984). *What Computers Can't Do: The Limits of Artificial Intelligence.* (2nd ed.). Harper & Row.

Dreyfus, H. L. (1991). *Being-in-the-world: a Commentary on Heidegger's Being and Time, Division I.* MIT Press.

Dreyfus, H. L. (1992). *What Computers Still Can't Do: A Critique of Artificial Reason* (3rd ed.). MIT Press.

Dreyfus, H. L. (2000). *Heidegger, Coping, and Cognitive Science, Volume 2: Essays in Honor of Hubert L. Dreyfus* (M. Wrathall & J. Malpas Eds.). MIT Press.

Dreyfus, H. L. (2017). *Background Practices: Essays on the Understanding of Being* (M. A. Wrathall, Ed.). Oxford University Press.

Dreyfus, H. L., Dreyfus, S. E., & Athanasiou, T. (1986). *Mind over Machine: The Power of Human Intuition and Expertise in the Era of the Computer.* Free Press.

Dreyfus, H.L., Foucault, M., & Rabinow, P. (1983). *Michel Foucault*. University of Chicago Press.

Duffy, J. (2018, March 9). *The Singular Difference between Self-Expression and Seeking Acceptance*. Thrive Global. https://thriveglobal.com/stories/the-singular-difference-between-self-expression-and-seeking-acceptance/

Dutta, S. S. (2018, August 23). *Limbic System and Behavior*. News Medical. https://www.news-medical.net/health/Limbic-System-and-Behavior.aspx

Dutton, J. E., & Ashford, S. J. (1993). Selling Issues in Top Management. *Academy of Management Review, 18*(3), 397–428. https://doi.org/10.5465/amr.1993.9309035145

Enright, R. D. (1999). "Interpersonal forgiving in close relationships": Correction to McCullough et al. (1997). *Journal of Personality and Social Psychology, 77*(2), 218. https://doi.org/10.1037/0022-3514.77.2.218

Erhard, W., & Jensen, M. C. (2013). Four Ways of Being that Create the Foundations of a Great Personal Life, Great Leadership and a Great Organization -- PDF File of PowerPoint Slides. *Harvard Business School NOM Unit Working Paper No. 13-078*. https://doi.org/10.2139/ssrn.2207782

Erhard, W., Jensen, M. C., & Granger, K. L. (2013). Creating Leaders: An Ontological/Phenomenological Model. *The Handbook for Teaching Leadership: Knowing, Doing, and Being*. Sage Publications. https://ssrn.com/abstract=1681682

Erhard, W., Jensen, M. C., Zaffron, S., & Echeverria, J. (2018). Introductory Reading And 'Course Leadership Project' Part II For Being a Leader and The Effective Exercise of Leadership: An Ontological / Phenomenological Model. *Harvard Business School Negotiations, Organizations and Markets Unit Research Paper Series, 091*(10). https://papers.ssrn.com/sol3/papers.cfm?abstract_id=1585976

REFERENCES

Erhard, W., Jensen, M. C., Zaffron, S., & Granger, K. L. (2011). Course Materials for Being a Leader and the Effective Exercise of Leadership: An Ontological/Phenomenological Model. *Harvard Business School Negotiations, Organizations and Markets Unit Research Paper Series No. 10-091.* https://doi.org/10.2139/ssrn.1263835

Exline, J. J., & Baumeister, R. (2000). Expressing forgiveness and repentance: Benefits and barriers. In M. E. McCullough, K. I. Pargament, & C. E. Thoresen (Eds.), *Forgiveness: Theory, research and practice* (pp. 133–155). Guilford.

Farrell, J. B., & Strauss, K. (2013). The People Make the Place, and They Make Things Happen: Proactive Behavior and Relationships at Work. In R. L. Morrison & H. D. Cooper-Thomas (Eds.), *Relationships in Organizations* (pp. 107-136). Palgrave Macmillan.

Ferdowsi. (1010). *Shahnameh.* (n.p.)

Ferrier, L. (1982, September). Werner Erhard. *Scene.* Retrieved from Internet Archive, https://archive.org/details/WernerErhard-Scene-magazine

Forsyth, J. P. (2011, June 3). Cultivating Peace of Mind: Letting go of striving to be something other than we are. *Psychology Today.* https://www.psychologytoday.com/au/blog/peace-mind/201106/cultivating-peace-mind

Forsyth, J. P., & Eifert, G. H. (2016). *The Mindfulness and Acceptance Workbook for Anxiety: A Guide to Breaking Free from Anxiety, Phobias, and Worry Using Acceptance and Commitment Therapy* (2nd ed.). New Harbinger Publications.

Foucault, M. (1994). *The Order of Things: an Archaeology of the Human Sciences.* Random House.

Foucault, M. & Howard, R. (2001). *Madness and civilization : a history of insanity in the Age of Reason.* Routledge.

Fox, R. (1996). *Thrownness and Possibility* [Paper Presentation].

Fox, R. (2011). *Why Feelings Matter and How Feelings Work: Befindlichkeit* [Paper Presentation].

Fox, R. (2013). *The Language of Disclosiveness: Therapy and the Question of Being* [Paper Presentation].

Fox, R. (2014). *Spirituality in Existential Practice: Reconsidering Spirituality Through Phenomenology* [Paper Presentation].

Fox, R. (2015a). *Existential Paradox and Existential Intimacy* [Paper Presentation].

Fox, R. (2015b). *Is Dasein an Achievement? The Developmental Line of Existence* [Paper Presentation].

Fox, R. (2016a). *Existential Psychotherapy and Psychodynamic Psychotherapy: Essential Commonalities* [Paper Presentation].

Fox, R. (2016b). *Love is Strange: Illusions of Longing and Fulfillment* [Paper Presentation].

Frankfurt, H. G. (1969). Alternate Possibilities and Moral Responsibility. *The Journal of Philosophy, 66*(23), 829-839. https://doi.org/10.2307/2023833

Frankl, V. E. (1988). *Man's search for meaning* (Rev. ed.). Pocket Books.

Frings, M. S. (1988). Armenides: Heidegger's 1942–1943 Lecture held at Freiburg University. *Journal of the British Society for Phenomenology, 19*(1), 15–33. https://doi.org/10.1080/00071773.1988.11007839

Fromm, E. (1970). *The Crisis of Psychoanalysis*. Holt, Rinehart, Winston.

Fromm, E. (1976). *To have or to be?* Harper & Row.

Fromm, E. (1989). *The Art of loving*. Perennial Library.

Fromm, E. (1992). *The art of being*. Continuum.

Fromm, E. (2011). *Escape from freedom*. Ishi Press.

REFERENCES

George, B. (2003). *Authentic leadership: rediscovering the secrets to creating lasting value*. Jossey-Bass.

Girgždytė, V., & Sondaitė, J. (2010). *A phenomenological study of couple's partnership experiences*. Semantic Scholar. https://www.semanticscholar.org/paper/A-phenomenological-study-of-couple%E2%80%99s-partnership-Girg%C5%BEdyt%C4%97-Sondait%C4%97/48bf8d55b5cdea139927823058b2e47904daccaf

Glas, G. (2003). Anxiety – animal reactions and the embodiment of meaning. In B. Fulford, K. Morris, J. Z. Sadler, & G. Stanghellini (Eds.), *Nature and Narrative: An Introduction to the New Philosophy of Psychiatry* (pp. 231-260). Oxford University Press.

Glaser, J. E. (2016, February 15). Self-Expression: The Neuroscience of Co-Creation. *Psychology Today*. https://www.psychologytoday.com/us/blog/conversational-intelligence/201602/self-expression

Green, M. S. (2007). *Self-expression*. Clarendon Press.

Greenberg, M. (2012, August 23). The Six Attributes of Courage. *Psychology Today*. https://www.psychologytoday.com/intl/blog/the-mindful-self-express/201208/the-six-attributes-courage

Grieder, A. (1988). What did Heidegger Mean by 'Essence'? *Journal of the British Society for Phenomenology, 19*(1), 64–89. https://doi.org/10.1080/00071773.1988.11007842

Grinder, J., & DeLozier, J. (1987). *Turtles All the Way Down*. Grinder Delozier & Assoc.

Guise, S. (n.d.) The Psychology of Being Reliable. *Stephen Guise*. Retrieved February 27, 2018, from https://stephenguise.com/the-psychology-of-being-reliable/

Hafez, S. (2015). *The Complete Divan of Hafez: Including Ghazals Inspired by the Ghazals of Hafez by the Translator* (P. Smith, Ed., Trans.). CreateSpace Independent Publishing Platform. (Original work published ca. 1368 C.E.)

Hage, A. M., & Lorensen, M. (2005). A philosophical analysis of the concept empowerment; the fundament of an education-programme to the frail elderly. *Nursing Philosophy*, 6(4), 235–246. https://doi.org/10.1111/j.1466-769x.2005.00231.x

Hall, K. (2014, September 21). *Value Your Life Contributions*. Retrieved from Internet Archive, https://web.archive.org/web/20190212194428/https://blogs.psychcentral.com/emotionally-sensitive/2014/09/value-your-life-contributions/

Hall, K. D. (2016). *The Emotionally Sensitive Person: Finding Peace When Your Emotions Overwhelm You*. New Harbinger Publishing.

Harris, T. A. (2004). *I'm OK, you're OK*. Quill.

Harris, T. A., & Harris, A. B. (2011). *Staying O.K.: How to Maximize Good Feelings and Minimize Bad Ones*. Harper.

Hartog, D. N., & Belschak, F. D. (2007). Personal initiative, commitment and affect at work. *Journal of Occupational and Organizational Psychology*, 80(4), 601–622. https://doi.org/10.1348/096317906x171442

Heidegger, M. (2019). *Being and Time* (J. Macquarrie & E. S. Robinson, Trans.). Martino Fine Books. (Original work published 1962)

Herman, E. S., & Chomsky, N. (1988). *Manufacturing consent: the political economy of the mass media*. Pantheon Books.

Hollis, J. (2006). *Finding Meaning in the Second Half of Life: How to Finally, Really Grow Up*. Gotham Books.

Horgan, J. (2018, August 22). The Paradox of Karl Popper. *Scientific American*. https://blogs.scientificamerican.com/cross-check/the-paradox-of-karl-popper/

Hume, D. (2007). *A Treatise of Human Nature: Volume 2* (D. F. Norton & M. J. Norton, Eds.). Clarendon Press.

Isaac Newton. (1968). *The Mathematical Principles of Natural Philosophy: The Motions of Bodies v. 1*. Dawsons of Pall Mall.

Rumi, J. al-Din. (2004). *The Masnavi: Book One* (J. Mojaddedi, Trans.). Oxford University Press.

Rumi, J. al-Din. (2008). *The Masnavi: Book Two* (J. Mojaddedi, Trans.). Oxford University Press.

Jensen, M. C. (2014). Integrity: Without it Nothing Works. *Rotman Magazine: The Magazine of the Rotman School of Management, Fall Edition,* 16-20.
https://papers.ssrn.com/sol3/papers.cfm?abstract_id=1511274

Jung, C. G. (ca 1980). *Modern man in search of a soul.* Harcourt, Brace & World.

Jung, C. G. (1981). *Collected Works of C.G. Jung: Volume 9/1 Collected Works of C.G. Jung, Volume 9 (Part 1) ; Archetypes and the Collective Unconscious.* (G. Adler & R. F. C. Hull, Trans.). Princeton University Press.

Jung, C. G. (1983). *Memories, dreams, reflections* (A. Jaffé, R. Winston & C. Winston, Eds.). Fontana.

Jung, C. G. (1966). *Two essays on analytical psychology.* (R. F. C. Hull & G. Adler, Eds.). Princeton University Press.

Jung, C. G. (2012). *The Red Book: Liber novus: a reader's edition* (S. Shamdasani, Ed., S. Shamdasani, M. Kyburz, & J. Peck, Trans.). W.W. Norton.

Jung, C. G., Hinkle, B. M. (1921). *Psychology of the unconscious : a study of the transformations and symbolism of the libido, a contribution to the history of the evolution of thought.* Kegan Paul, Trench, Trubner.

Kane, R. (1985). *Free will and values.* State University of New York Press.

La Guardia, J. G., & Patrick, H. (2008). Self-determination theory as a fundamental theory of close relationships. *Canadian Psychology/ Psychologie Canadienne, 49*(3), 201–209.
https://doi.org/10.1037/a0012760

Lee, A. (2018, December 29). *Be Resourceful — One Of The Most Important Skills To Succeed In Data Science*. Towards Data Science. https://towardsdatascience.com/be-resourceful-one-of-the-most-important-skills-to-succeed-in-data-science-6ed5f33c2939

LePine, J. A., & Van Dyne, L. (1998). Predicting voice behavior in work groups. *Journal of Applied Psychology, 83*(6), 853–868. http://dx.doi.org/10.1037/0021-9010.83.6.853

Levin, S., & Greenfield, P. (2018, August 11). Monsanto ordered to pay $289m as jury rules weedkiller caused man's cancer. *The Guardian*. https://www.theguardian.com/business/2018/aug/10/monsanto-trial-cancer-dewayne-johnson-ruling

Lewis, T. E. (2017). Heidegger and Mood. In M. A. Peters (Ed.) *Encyclopedia of Educational Philosophy and Theory* (pp. 996–1000). Springer. https://doi.org/10.1007/978-981-287-588-4_133

Manchiraju, S. (2020, January 9). How to Find Inner Peace and Happiness. *Positive Psychology*. https://positivepsychology.com/inner-peace-happiness/

Margolies, L. (n.d.). *When Perseverance Costs You Success*. Dr Lynn Margolies. Retrieved July 4, 2021, from http://www.drlynnmargolies.com/when-perseverance-costs-you-success-a.htm

Marmer, M., Herrmann, B. L., Dogrultan, E. & Berman, R. (2012). *Startup Genome Report: A new framework for understanding why startups succeed*. Startup Genome. https://media.rbcdn.ru/media/reports/StartupGenomeReport1_Why_Startups_Succeed_v2.pdf

McCullough, M. E., Rachal, K. C., Sandage, S. J., Worthington, E. L., Brown, S. W., & Hight, T. L. (1998). Interpersonal forgiving in close relationships: II. Theoretical elaboration and measurement. *Journal of Personality and Social Psychology, 75*(6), 1586–1603. https://doi.org/10.1037/0022-3514.75.6.1586

Mechanic, D. (1991). Adolescents at risk: New directions. *Journal of Adolescent Health, 12*(8), 638–643. https://doi.org/10.1016/1054-139x(91)90012-m

REFERENCES

Miller, M. C. (2012, November 21). In praise of gratitude. *Harvard Health*. https://www.health.harvard.edu/blog/in-praise-of-gratitude-201211215561

Moore, R. L. & Gillette, D. (1990). *King, warrior, magician, lover*. Harper.

Morrison, E. W. (2002). Newcomers' Relationships: The Role of Social Network Ties During Socialization. *Academy of Management Journal, 45*(6), 1149–1160. https://doi.org/10.5465/3069430

Morrison, E. W., & Phelps, C. C. (1999). Taking Charge At Work: Extrarole Efforts To Initiate Workplace Change. *Academy of Management Journal, 42*(4), 403–419. https://doi.org/10.5465/257011

Munday, R. (2009, March). *Glossary of Terms in Heidegger's Being and Time*. http://www.visual-memory.co.uk/b_resources/b_and_t_glossary.html#a

Myss, C. (n.d.). The Second Mystical Law: Forgiveness is Essential. *Caroline Myss*. Retrieved July 4, 2021, from https://www.myss.com/the-second-mystical-law-forgiveness-is-essential/

OECD. (2015). OECD Science, Technology and Industry Scoreboard 2015. *OECD Science, Technology and Industry Scoreboard*. OECD Publishing. https://doi.org/10.1787/sti_scoreboard-2015-en

OECD. (2017). Chapter 2: Boosting R&D outcomes. https://www.oecd-ilibrary.org/sites/eco_surveys-aus-2017-7-en/index.html?itemId=/content/component/eco_surveys-aus-2017-7-en

Parker, S. K. (n.d.-a). *Importance of proactivity*. Sharon K. Parker. Retrieved July 4, 2021, from https://sites.google.com/site/profsharonparker/proactivity-research/why-proactivity-is-important

Parker, S. K. (n.d.-b). *Types of Proactivity*. Sharon K. Parker. Retrieved July 4, 2021, from https://sites.google.com/site/profsharonparker/proactivity-research/types-of-proactivity

Parker, S. K. (n.d.-c). *What is Proactivity*. Sharon K. Parker. Retrieved July 4, 2021, from https://sites.google.com/site/profsharonparker/proactivity-research/what-is-proactivity

Parker, S. K., Wall, T. D., & Jackson, P. R. (1997). That's Not My Job: Developing Flexible Employee Work. *Academy of Management Journal*, 40(4), 899–929. https://doi.org/10.5465/256952

Parker, S. K., Williams, H. M., & Turner, N. (2006). Modeling the antecedents of proactive behavior at work. *Journal of Applied Psychology*, 91(3), 636–652. https://doi.org/10.1037/0021-9010.91.3.636

Peterson, C., & Seligman, M. E. P. (2004). *Character strengths and virtues: a handbook and classification*. Oxford University Press.

Peterson, J. B. (1999). *Maps of meaning: The architecture of belief*. Taylor & Frances/Routledge.

Rank, J., Carsten, J. M., Unger, J. M., & Spector, P. E. (2007). Proactive customer service performance: Relationships with individual, task, and leadership variables. *Human Performance*, 20(4), 363–390.

Rappaport, J. (1984). Studies in Empowerment. *Prevention in Human Services*, 3(2-3), 1–7. https://doi.org/10.1300/j293v03n02_02

Rappaport, J. (1987). Terms of empowerment/exemplars of prevention: Toward a theory for community psychology. *American Journal of Community Psychology*, 15(2), 121–148. https://doi.org/10.1007/bf00919275

Rappaport, J., Swift, C. F., & Hess, R. (1984). *Studies in empowerment: steps toward understanding and action*. Haworth Press.

Resilience. (n.d.). Psychology Today. https://www.psychologytoday.com/au/basics/resilience

Rodrigo, P. (2011). The Dynamic of Hexis in Aristotle's Philosophy. *Journal of the British Society for Phenomenology*, 42(1), 6–17. https://doi.org/10.1080/00071773.2011.11006728

Royal Commissions. (2019). *Royal Commission into Misconduct in the Banking, Superannuation and Financial Services Industry.* Australian Government https://www.royalcommission.gov.au/banking/final-report

Rumi. See under Jalal Al-Din Rumi.

Rushd (Averroes), I. (1179). *Al-Kashf 'an Manahij al-Adillah (The Exposition of the Methods of Proof).* (n.p.).

Rushd (Averroes), I. (1981). *Ibn Rushd.* Islamic Information Services.

Ruspoli, T. (Director). (2010). *Being in the World* [Film]. Mangusta Productions.

Rye, M. S., Pargament, K. I., Ali, M. A., Beck, G. L., Dorff, E. N., Hallisey, C., Narayanan, V., & Williams, J. G. (2000). Religious perspectives on forgiveness. In M. E. McCullough, K. I. Pargament, & C. E. Thoresen (Eds.), *Forgiveness: Theory, research, and practice* (pp. 17–40). Guilford Press.

Sa'dī, & Edwards, A. H. (n.d.). *The Bostan of Saadi: One of the world's greatest masterpieces.* Iran Chamber Society. Retrieved from http://www.iranchamber.com/literature/saadi/books/bostan_saadi.pdf

Sa'dī & Thackston, W. M. (2017). *The Gulistan (Rose Garden) of Sa'di: Bilingual English and Persian Edition with Vocabulary.* Ibex Publishers.

Sadra, M. (2002). *Al-Mabda' wa'l-ma'ad fi al-hikmat al-muta'aliyah 2 vols.* The Sadra Islamic Philosophy Research Institute

Sadra, M. (2011). *A Collection of Philosophical Treatises, Vol. 3 (Iksir al-'arifin fi m'arifat tariq al-haq wal yaqin, al-Waridat al-qalbiyyah fi m'arifat al-rububiyyah)* (S. Y. Yathribi & A. Shafi'iha, Eds., Trans.). The Sadra Islamic Philosophy Research Institute

Sadra, M. (n.d.-a). *al-Masa'il al-qudsiyyah.* (n.p.).

Sadra, M. (n.d.-b). *al-Mazahir.* (n.p.).

Sadra, M. (n.d.-c). *al-Mizaj.* (n.p.).

Sadra, M. (n.d.-d). *al-Tanqih*. (n.p.).

Sadra, M. (n.d.-e). *al-Tashakhkhus*. (n.p.).

Sadra, M. (n.d.-f). *Hikmat Al Muta'alyahfi-l-asfar al-'aqliyya al-arba'a (The Transcendent Philosophy of the Four Journeys of the Intellect)*. (n.p.).

Sadra, M. (n.d.-g). *Iqad al-na'imin*. (n.p.).

Sadra, M. (n.d.-h). *Ittihad al-'aquil wa'l-ma'qul*. (n.p.).

Sadra, M. (n.d.-i). *Kasr al-asnam al-jahiliyyah*. (n.p.).

Sadra, M. (n.d.-j). *Limmi'yya ikhtisas al-mintaqah*. (n.p.).

Sadra, M. (n.d.-k). *Mutashabihat al-Qur'an*. (n.p.).

Sadra, M. (n.d.-l). *Sarayan nur wujud*. (n.p.).

Sadra, M. (n.d.-m). *Sharh-i Hikmat al-ishraq*. (n.p.).

Sadra, M. (n.d.-n). *Si Asl*. (n.p.).

Sapolsky, R. (2018). *Behave: the biology of humans at our best and worst*. Penguin Random House.

Self-Awareness. (n.d.). *iResearchNet*. https://psychology.iresearchnet.com/social-psychology/self/self-awareness/

Seltzer, L. F. (2015, October 21). The Complex Emotion of Courage: Do You Really Understand It? *Psychology Today*. https://www.psychologytoday.com/au/blog/evolution-the-self/201510/the-complex-emotion-courage-do-you-really-understand-it

Sharp, D. (1991). *C. G. Jung Lexicon: A Primer of Terms and Concepts*. Inner City Books.

Shoda, Y., Mischel, W., & Peake, P. K. (1990). Predicting adolescent cognitive and self-regulatory competencies from preschool delay of gratification: Identifying diagnostic conditions. *Developmental Psychology, 26*(6), 978–986. https://doi.org/10.1037/0012-1649.26.6.978

Smart, J. J. C. (1961). I.—Free-will, Praise and Blame. *Mind, LXX*(279), 291–306. https://doi.org/10.1093/mind/lxx.279.291

Smith, D. W. (2018). *Phenomenology*. In Edward N. Zalta (Ed.) The Stanford Encyclopedia of Philosophy (Summer 2018 Edition). Stanford Encyclopedia of Philosophy. https://plato.stanford.edu/archives/sum2018/entries/phenomenology/

Sonneborn, L. (2006). *Averroes (Ibn Rushd): Muslim scholar, philosopher, and physician of the twelfth century*. Rosen Central/Rosen Pub. Group.

Staub, E., & Pearlman, L. A. (2001). Healing, reconciliation, and forgiving after genocide and other collective violence. In *Forgiveness and reconciliation: Religion, public policy, and conflict transformation* (pp. 205–227). Templeton Foundation Press.

Strauss, C., Lever Taylor, B., Gu, J., Kuyken, W., Baer, R., Jones, F., & Cavanagh, K. (2016). What is compassion and how can we measure it? A review of definitions and measures. *Clinical Psychology Review, 47*, 15–27. https://doi.org/10.1016/j.cpr.2016.05.004

Taleb, N. N. (2012). *Antifragile: how to live in a world we don't understand*. Random House.

Taminiaux, J. (1988). The Interpretation of Greek Philosophy in Heidegger's Fundamental Ontology. *Journal of the British Society for Phenomenology, 19*(1), 3–14. https://doi.org/10.1080/00071773.1988.11007838

Tindale, C. W. (2007). *Fallacies and Argument Appraisal*. Cambridge University Press.

Trochim, W. M. K. (n.d.-a). *Theory of Reliability*. Conjointly. Retrieved from Internet Archive, https://web.archive.org/web/20210818174931/https://conjointly.com/kb/theory-of-reliability/

Trochim, W. M. K. (n.d.-b). *Types of Reliability*. Conjointly. Retrieved from Internet Archive, https://web.archive.org/web/20200509065551/https://conjointly.com/kb/types-of-reliability/

US Securities and Exchange Commission. (2010, July 15). *Goldman Sachs to Pay Record $550 Million to Settle SEC Charges Related to Subprime Mortgage CDO* [Press Release]. https://www.sec.gov/news/press/2010/2010-123.htm

What Is Compassion? (n.d.). Greater Good Magazine. https://greatergood.berkeley.edu/topic/compassion/definition

What Is Gratitude? (n.d.). Greater Good Magazine. https://greatergood.berkeley.edu/topic/gratitude/definition

What Is Neuroscience?. (n.d.). Psychology Today. Retrieved July 4, 2021, from https://www.psychologytoday.com/au/basics/neuroscience

White, C. J. (1988). Heidegger and the Beginning of Metaphysics. *Journal of the British Society for Phenomenology, 19*(1), 34–50. https://doi.org/10.1080/00071773.1988.11007840

Wihler, A., & Jachimowicz, J. M. (2016, October 17). *Proactivity Can Be a Double-Edged Sword*. Harvard Business Review. https://hbr.org/2016/10/proactivity-can-be-a-double-edged-sword

Wilber, K. (1999). *Integral psychology*. Shambhala Publications.

Wilson, C. (2006). Phenomenology as a Mystical Discipline. *Philosophy Now*. https://philosophynow.org/issues/56/Phenomenology_as_a_Mystical_Discipline

Wilson, J., & Foster, R. (2018). The Power, Structure, and Practice of Gratitude in Education: A Demonstration of Epistemology and Empirical Research Working Together. *International Christian Community of Teacher International Christian Community of Teacher Educators, 13*(1). https://digitalcommons.georgefox.edu/cgi/viewcontent.cgi?article=1159&context=icctej

Wittgenstein, L. (1972). *On certainty* (G. E. M. Anscombe & G. H. van Wright, Eds.). Harper & Row.

Wittgenstein, L. (1997). *Philosophical investigations* (G. E. M. Anscombe, Trans. 2nd ed.). Blackwell Publishers.

REFERENCES

Witvliet, C. van O., Ludwig, T. E., & Vander Laan, K. L. (2001). Granting Forgiveness or Harboring Grudges: Implications for Emotion, Physiology, and Health. *Psychological Science, 12*(2), 117–123. https://doi.org/10.1111/1467-9280.00320

Worthington, E. L. Jr. (2004, September 1). *The New Science of Forgiveness*. Greater Good Magazine. https://greatergood.berkeley.edu/article/item/the_new_science_of_forgiveness

Wrathall, M. A. (Ed.). (2013). *The Cambridge Companion to Heidegger's Being and Time*. Cambridge University Press.

Wrathall, M. A., & Malpas, J. (Eds.). (2000). *Heidegger, Authenticity, and Modernity: Essays in Honor of Hubert L. Dreyfus, Vol. 1.* MIT Press.

Zimmerman, A. (n.d.). *True Love Is Acceptance*. Dr Alan Zimmerman, CSP: The Positive Communication Pro. Retrieved June 19, 2012, from https://www.drzimmerman.com/tuesdaytip/relationship-management-is-the-key-to-healthy-relationships

Acknowledgements

Firstly, this book would not have been possible without the humble contribution of many of the world's greatest truth seekers, such as Martin Heidegger, Mulla Sadra, and numerous others. This content was built on the foundation they shaped, and I would like to acknowledge them.

This book would also not have been possible without the many corporate organisations, startups, small and large, and the individuals I have worked with who gave me the chance to understand and support them through their highs and lows, pain and suffering. Every leader I had the opportunity to work with expanded my awareness and understanding of the real problems out there and enabled me to develop and test insight-related discoveries through projects, workshops and coaching and consulting engagements. Furthermore, my work could not have turned into a valuable framework had I not had the opportunity to work side-by-side with professional and experienced coaches on a daily basis. I would like to acknowledge their generosity and the privileges I have been given to shape this body of work.

I would also like to express my gratitude and appreciation to all that the universe brought to me as part of my diverse and intense personal journey so far. While some of those messages were dark and hard to digest at the time, every experience, trigger and inspiration they sparked helped shape the person who was able to write this book. Today, I feel blessed for all my lack of accomplishments, expensive mistakes, adversities and catastrophes. So, I convey gratitude towards Existence and all its manifestations, as even the tiniest particle was a sign, taught me a lesson and contributed to my desire to polish my own Being.

I am compelled by the universe to acknowledge all four of my grandparents who instilled the courage in me to dare to BE out there in the world with kindness and care, and my parents who, in raising me, introduced me to what they knew to be virtuous.

There have been many other people who directly or indirectly contributed to this work and the person I am today. While it is impossible to name them all here, I would like to express my gratitude to each and every one of them and acknowledge their significant impact.

I owe an enormous debt of gratitude to those who gave me detailed and constructive comments and feedback throughout this journey, especially the first official cohort of coaches we worked with. In particular, my special thanks to John Lowe, who contributed by providing the intellectual insights as well as contributing to the tools layer of the framework and writing the Foreword.

Thank you to my beloved friend, John Smallwood. Without John's extensive industry knowledge and practical experience in coaching and coaching coaches, this content may have leaned slightly more towards being an intellectual and philosophical book rather than what it is today, a book that has genuine real world context and practical benefits.

A special thanks to my dear friend and business partner, Ariya Chittasy, whose support made it possible to run multiple businesses while simultaneously writing a book of this size and complexity. To my team at Engenesis, thank you for playing your role and supporting me on this front.

I would also like to acknowledge Phaedra Pym, the editor of this work, who went beyond her professional responsibilities and has been with me through the emotional burdens and anxieties. Her care and obsession with the content have made a significant difference to what is now available to you. An additional thanks to two other integral members of the production team, Eric and Thymen Hook, who have done a brilliant job to make the book easier to read in their design and production of the structure and layout.

ACKNOWLEDGEMENTS

Last but not least, I would like to thank my wife, Atefeh, for her exceptionally unique insights, feedback on the content and inspiration when the path of continuing this body of work was rocky, and for her understanding and patience over my incessant disappearances into my home office. Her constant contribution and partnership eased the suffering and served to restore my peace of mind and integrity when challenged. A lifelong partner makes both the journey and destination worthwhile.

Author Biography

Ashkan Tashvir built and launched the first of several businesses at the age of fifteen and subsequently led a series of businesses to become thriving and successful enterprises across various industries. With a master's degree in information systems management, he has worked on various technology projects. Over the years, his interest in business and entrepreneurship continued to evolve and he led or advised several startups and SMEs to become sustainable, scalable ventures before becoming an investor and venture builder himself.

In addition to his business and technological engineering qualifications and experience, Ashkan is a thinker, researcher, voracious reader and philosopher with a profound interest in and knowledge of metaphysics, ontology, epistemology, phenomenology and ethics. For more than a decade, he was driven by a quest to discover why there is so much dysfunction and suffering in the world and to find the answer to a burning question: 'Why are we human beings the way we are and what drives our decisions, behaviours and actions?' His quest led him to a crossroads between the realms of technology, business, leadership and philosophy. His interests extend beyond theory and abstracts of philosophy to their application in the economy, particularly in business and organisational leadership contexts.

Over the next ten years, he embarked on a journey of discovery, tapping into ontology, epistemology, phenomenology, philosophy, anthropology, literature, analysis and spiritual disciplines. Possessing a rare gift of being able to connect the dots between multiple domains, Ashkan applied a uniquely structured and holistic approach to the study of human consciousness, leadership, transformation and Being. This systemised, ontological approach, coupled with his broad and in-depth practical knowledge and experience in the field, led him to discover the answers he sought.

Observing a distinct lack of logical, ontological and systematic thinking in the areas of human consciousness, transformation and leadership, particularly in terms of how they empower people to generate opportunity and wealth for themselves and others, Ashkan set his mind to using his discovered knowledge to devise a series of practical frameworks, tools and methodologies, one of which is the Being Framework. This framework, which incorporates the Being Profile assessment tool and the Transformation Methodology, is now supporting people from all over the world to create significant economic and social benefits in their organisations and personally derive fulfilment from their contribution in life. He has since also designed and built the Genesis Framework™, a revolutionary business venture building paradigm.

Shifting his core focus to the human side of business, transformation and leadership, Ashkan and his team committed to serve millions. To date, they have supported thousands of startups, entrepreneurs and SMEs to amplify their effective exercise of leadership and build scalable, sustainable businesses from nothing more than their Being and the seed of an idea. He holds the belief that entrepreneurship is the greatest vehicle that exists to solve the most complex problems for humanity. His vision is for a new wave of the economy to develop and grow, where people are not only driving a healthy economy but are also minimising wastage and finding genuine meaning in their work.

Ashkan's extraordinary ability to see through human beings' false pretences arising from inauthenticity and a lack of vulnerability allows him to extract the hidden and unspoken truth and support people to confront what typically remains unaddressed. His personal commitment is to advocate for the truth seeker within by supporting human beings to raise their awareness and shape a more accurate conception of reality. His mission is to bring about transformation in the world, one story at a time, through individuals focused on who and how they are being in the world and leveraging their potential to tap into the power that lies within. Ultimately, this leads them to cast the light of their Unique Being out into the world and build a life of service, contribution, success, prosperity and fulfilment.

As founder and CEO of Engenesis, Ashkan heads a business movement of global venture builders, professional investors, business management consultants, advisors and coaches who adopt and apply his frameworks while also encouraging and facilitating their use by others for personal and organisational transformation. When not writing, studying, coaching or building his businesses, Ashkan spends his time close to nature with his wife, daughter and the family's beloved dogs. He enjoys cooking, singing and playing the oud and harmonica.

www.ingramcontent.com/pod-product-compliance
Lightning Source LLC
Chambersburg PA
CBHW071551080526
44588CB00010B/874